Article by Frank Cobling

BOOKS EDITED BY
FRANCIS COLEMAN ROSENBERGER

SIX VOLUMES OF
Records of the Columbia Historical Society of Washington, D. C.

"*Distinguished and useful series.*"
THOMAS C. PARRAMORE in *The North Carolina Historical Review*

Virginia Reader: A Treasury of Writings from the First Voyages to the Present

"*This readable anthology contains over eighty selections about Virginia or by Virginians, spanning some three and a half centuries of literary, intellectual, social and political history. A good many of the selections are all too little known, out of print, or difficult to obtain . . . a happy balance between the familiar and the unfamiliar, between the traditional and the uncommon . . . should appeal to specialist and layman alike, to non-Virginian as well as Virginian . . . admirable anthology.*"
WILLIAM PEDEN in *The New York Times Book Review*

Jefferson Reader: A Treasury of Writings About Thomas Jefferson

"*Francis Coleman Rosenberger, alumnus of 'Mr. Jefferson's University' and member of the Virginia bar, has steeped himself in Jeffersoniana and with keen discrimination has selected for his anthology the writings about the Master of Monticello which give not a composite biography but a likeness in three dimensions. . . .*"
THOMAS PERKINS ABERNETHY in *The New York Times Book Review*

American Sampler: A Selection of New Poetry

Selected for typography and design by the American Institute of Graphic Arts as one of the Fifty Books of the Year
"*A volume to be valued by lovers of fine books.*"
LAWRENCE FERLING in *The San Francisco Chronicle*

The Robinson-Rosenberger Journey to the Gold Fields of California, 1849–1850: The Diary of Zirkle D. Robinson

Selected for typography and design by the American Institute of Graphic Arts as one of the Fifty Books of the Year
"*Most interesting diary of a trip from the town of Virginia in Cass County, Illinois, overland to California.*"
JOHN FREDERICK DORMAN in *The Virginia Genealogist*

Records
of the Columbia Historical Society
of Washington, D.C.
1971-1972

Courtesy of the National Gallery of Ireland
Woodrow Wilson by John Singer Sargent. Painted in Washington, 1917.

Records
of the Columbia Historical Society of Washington, D.C.
1971-1972

Edited with an Introduction by
FRANCIS COLEMAN ROSENBERGER

ILLUSTRATED

Published by the Society

DISTRIBUTED BY THE UNIVERSITY PRESS
OF VIRGINIA

Copyright, 1973, by the
Columbia Historical Society
1307 New Hampshire Avenue, N.W.
Washington, D. C. 20036

The Records for 1971-1972
Whole Number Volume 48
(the 48th separately bound book)

Library of Congress Catalogue Card Number 1-17677
International Standard Book Number 0-8139-0501-x

PRINTED FOR THE SOCIETY AT THE WAVERLY PRESS, BALTIMORE, MARYLAND

Distributed by
The University Press of Virginia
Box 3608, University Station
Charlottesville, Virginia 22903

Contents

Introduction   xiii

Shipbuilding in Virginia, 1763–1774
WILLIAM M. KELSO   1

Theodore Roosevelt Island: A Broken Link to Early Washington, D. C. History
MARY E. CURRY   14

The Foxall-Columbia Foundry: An Early Defense Contractor in Georgetown
LOUIS F. GORR   34

Albert Gallatin in Washington, 1801–1813
RICHARD MANNIX   60

Gilbert Stuart in Washington: with a Catalogue of His Portraits Painted between December 1803 and July 1805
CHARLES MERRILL MOUNT   81

Benjamin Henry Latrobe and the Growth and Development of Washington, 1798–1818
EDWARD C. CARTER II   128

Columbian Academy, 1821–1897: The Preparatory Department of Columbian College in the District of Columbia
ELMER LOUIS KAYSER   150

*Kalorama: Country Estate
to Washington Mayfair*
 MARY MITCHELL   164

*The National Theatre in Washington:
Buildings and Audiences, 1835–1972*
 ROGER MEERSMAN and ROBERT BOYER   190

*Behind Prison Walls:
The Operation of the District Penitentiary, 1831–1862*
 DAVID K. SULLIVAN   243

*The Rise and Fall
of Washington's Inhabited Alleys, 1852–1972*
 JAMES BORCHERT   267

*A Toast to the Union:
Clark Mills' Equestrian Statue
of Andrew Jackson in Lafayette Square*
 ANDREW S. KECK   289

Defending Washington during the Civil War
 BENJAMIN FRANKLIN COOLING   314

*Adolph Cluss: An Architect in Washington
during Civil War and Reconstruction*
 TANYA EDWARDS BEAUCHAMP   338

*A Blueprint for Change: The Black Community
in Washington, D. C., 1860–1870*
 MELVIN R. WILLIAMS   359

Andrew R. Shepherd and the Board of Public Works
 WILLIAM M. MAURY   394

Contents

The Black Militia
in the District of Columbia, 1867–1898
  MARTIN K. GORDON ... 411

John Mercer Langston and the Rise of Howard Law School
  MAXWELL BLOOMFIELD ... 421

Gallaudet College: A High Victorian Campus
  FRANCIS R. KOWSKY ... 439

A National Monument for a National Library:
Ainsworth Rand Spofford
and the New Library of Congress, 1871–1897
  JOHN Y. COLE ... 468

November 24, 1873, The Precise Moment of Impressionism:
Claude Monet's "The Bridge at Argenteuil" at the
National Gallery of Art in Washington, D. C.
  CHARLES MERRILL MOUNT ... 508

Daniel Chester French:
His Statue of Lewis Cass in the United States Capitol
  MICHAEL RICHMAN ... 548

The Old Post Office Building in Washington, D. C.:
Its Past, Present and Future
  GAIL KARESH KASSAN ... 570

The East and West Wings of the White House
  ELLEN ROBINSON EPSTEIN ... 596

The Rabbit and the Boa Constrictor:
John Singer Sargent at the White House
  CHARLES MERRILL MOUNT ... 618

New Life in an Old Movement:
Alice Paul and the Great Suffrage Parade of 1913
in Washington, D. C.
    SIDNEY R. BLAND   657

The Relief of General Barnett
    BENIS M. FRANK   679

Flowers to Gladden the City:
The Takoma Horticultural Club, 1916–1971
    ARTHUR HECHT   694

A Portfolio of Washington Drawings
    PAUL BOSWELL   712

Revisiting Washington's Forty Boundary Stones, 1972
    EDWIN DARBY NYE   740

Baseball Reminiscences of Washington's Jesse "Nip" Winters:
"How I Struck Out Babe Ruth and Beat Lefty Grove"
    JESSE "NIP" WINTERS and JOHN HOLWAY   752

Washington's Jim Berryman, 1902–1971:
Cartoons of Senator Dirksen
    FRANCIS COLEMAN ROSENBERGER   758

A Member Reminisces:
Problems of a Professional Writer
    ALBERT W. ATWOOD   776

Georgetown: The Twentieth Century,
A Continuing Battle
    MATHILDE D. WILLIAMS   783

The Job of Editor
    FRANCIS COLEMAN ROSENBERGER   797

Members of the Society, 1972
    Compiled by R. J. MCCARTHY   801

In Memoriam: Deaths of Members   819

Presidents of the Society, 1894–1972   820

Officers and Managers of the Society, 1971, 1972   821

Index to Subjects   823

Index to Illustrations   841

Index to Authors   845

Introduction

One of the most satisfying rewards of the editor of the *Records*, as a measure of the usefulness of the volumes, is to see papers in the *Records* cited in the bibliographies of scholarly biographies and histories—as, for example, the paper by Herman R. Friis in the 1960–1962 volume of the *Records* on "Baron Alexander von Humboldt's Visit to Washington, D. C., June 1 through June 13, 1804" in the Select Bibliography of *Thomas Jefferson and the New Nation: A Biography* by Merrill D. Peterson (Oxford University Press, 1970). I use in my reading a yellow marking pen to note these citations and I find that I am using that pen with more and more frequency.

A more immediate evaluation of the worth of the *Records* is provided, in some measure, by the responses of our members and of other readers and by the appraisals of reviewers. The reception of the successive volumes continues to be gratifying. The 1969–1970 volume, covering a two-year period of the Society's activity, seemed generally regarded as equal or superior to the several preceding volumes which each covered a three-year period. As in the preceding volume, a few comments are quoted on the dust jacket of this volume and, more permanently, in the Advertisement pages at the end of the book following the indexes.

A cautionary note was sounded here and there. L. H. Butterfield, Editor in Chief of *The Adams Papers* at the Massachusetts Historical Society, wrote in a generous letter: "This is a very impressive showing, and I hope that the high standard can be maintained." With the 1971–1972 volume we have again undertaken a volume covering a two-year period of the Society's activity, rather than a three-year period, and I hope that the standard has been maintained—and perhaps, in some respects, improved upon.

As in preceding volumes, the editor's Introduction provides a convenient place for a word of biography about the authors of the papers.

WILLIAM M. KELSO (born 1941), author of *Shipbuilding in Virginia, 1763–1774*, is State Historical Archaeologist with the Virginia Historic Landmarks Commission. He received his B.A. from Baldwin-Wallace College at Berea, Ohio, in 1963, his M.A. from the College of William and Mary at Williamsburg, Virginia, in 1964, and his Ph.D.

from Emory University at Atlanta, Georgia, in 1971. He has served as Archaeologist of the Georgia Historical Commission and as a contract archaeologist with the Wormsloe Foundation, Savannah, Georgia, and with Carter's Grove Plantation, Colonial Williamsburg, Williamsburg, Virginia. He has written on historical archaeology in Georgia and Virginia. The editor suggests that his "Shipbuilding in Virginia, 1763–1774" will take on an added dimension of Washington area interest for the reader who will look up the paper "Georgetown and the Tobacco Trade, 1751–1783" by Richard K. MacMaster in the 1966–1968 volume of the *Records*.

MARY E. CURRY (born 1947), author of *Theodore Roosevelt Island: A Broken Link to Early Washington, D.C. History*, received her B.A. in history from Le Moyne College at Syracuse, New York, in 1969, and her M.A. in American history from American University at Washington, D.C., in 1970. She is a Catalogue Researcher at the National Portrait Gallery of the Smithsonian Institution and has done research for the Peabody Library Association of Georgetown on the Georgetown house survey, for Mrs. Mary Mitchell on Washington, D.C. history, and for Gunston Hall, Virginia. She is a member of the Columbia Historical Society, the National Trust for Historic Preservation, and the Archaeological Society of Maryland.

LOUIS F. GORR (born 1941), author of *The Foxall-Columbia Foundry: An Early Defense Contractor in Georgetown*, is Historian and Research Assistant to the Director of the National Museum of History and Technology of the Smithsonian Institution. He received his B.A. in 1963 and his M.A. in 1967 from the University of Nebraska at Omaha and will receive his Ph.D. in 1973 from the University of Maryland. He is a private consultant in programs for adult education. His fields of scholarly interest include the history of American technology, American material culture, and the history of printing. His articles and reviews have appeared in *The Progressive*, the *Bulletin of the Atomic Scientists*, and *Technology and Culture*.

RICHARD MANNIX (born 1943), author of *Albert Gallatin in Washington, 1801–1813*, teaches American history at Saint Peter's College in New Jersey. He worked for four years, first as Research Assistant and then as Associate Editor, on the microfilm edition of *The Papers of Albert Gallatin*, sponsored by New York University and the National Historical Publications Commission. He received his B.S. from Saint Peter's College and his M.A. from New York University and is completing his dissertation for his Ph.D. He has published articles in professional journals and has done free-lance writing.

CHARLES MERRILL MOUNT (born 1928) is, through a circumstance fortunate for the readers of this volume, the author of three papers here. Shortly after the editor first solicited from him a paper on Gilbert Stuart, Mr. Mount was called back to Europe, where he had previously lived for a number of years, and was not able to give his attention to the request until his return to the United States in 1972. Then in a productive summer of 1972 at Neponsit, New York, he prepared *Gilbert Stuart in Washington: with a Catalogue of His Portraits Painted between December 1803 and July 1805* for the *Records* and two additional papers, *November 24, 1873, The Precise Moment of Impressionism: Claude Monet's "The Bridge at Argenteuil" at the National Gallery of Art in Washington, D.C.* and *The Rabbit and the Boa Constrictor: John Singer Sargent at the White House*. Distinguished both as a painter and as a biographer, Mr. Mount has published a comprehensive volume on each of the three artists about whom he writes here. His *Gilbert Stuart: A Biography* was published by W. W. Norton and Company, New York, in 1964. His *Monet: A Biography* was published by Simon and Schuster, New York, in 1966. His *John Singer Sargent: A Biography* was first published by W. W. Norton and Company in 1955. A British edition was published in London in 1957. A third edition was published by the Kraus Reprint Company, New York, in 1969. He attended Columbia University in New York and studied painting under John Carroll at the Arts Students' League. He has worked as a portrait painter in France, Italy, England and Ireland. Beginning in 1954, he was a regular contributor to *The Art Quarterly* and has lectured at a number of American galleries and museums including the Corcoran Gallery of Art in Washington. In the early 1960's he represented the Corcoran to gather pictures in Europe for its Sargent exhibition. For the Pennsylvania Academy he wrote the catalogue for its Stuart exhibition. He has held a Guggenheim Fellowship in history and a research grant from the Archives of American Art. His portraits are displayed at the Grand Central Art Gallery and at Portraits Inc. in New York and at the Capricorn Gallery in Bethesda, Maryland. His paper here on Monet is afield of a narrow definition of the local history of Washington, D.C., but the editor has welcomed it as illuminating what is now a Washington resource, the collection of Monet's work at the National Gallery of Art.

EDWARD C. CARTER II (born 1928), author of *Benjamin Henry Latrobe and the Growth and Development of Washington, 1798–1818,* is Editor in Chief of *The Papers of Benjamin Henry Latrobe,* sponsored by the Maryland Historical Society with the assistance of a grant from the National Endowment for the Humanities. He received his A.B. in 1954 and his M.A. in 1956 from the University of Pennsylvania and his Ph.D. in 1962 from the Bryn Mawr College Graduate School. He has taught at St. Stephen's School in Rome and Phillips Academy and at the University of Delaware, the University of Pennsylvania, and the Catholic University in Washington. He has contributed to the *Pennsylvania Magazine of History and Biography, Pennsylvania History, Vermont History,* the *Maryland Historical Magazine* and other journals.

ELMER LOUIS KAYSER (born 1896), author of *Columbian Academy, 1821–1897: The Preparatory Department of Columbian College in the District of Columbia,* taught European history at George Washington University for fifty years and became Professor Emeritus in 1967. He contributed "The George Washington Universtiy" to the 1953–1956 volume of the *Records* and is the author of the comprehensive history of the University, *Bricks Without Straw: The Evolution of George Washington University,* published by Appleton-Century-Crofts, New York, in 1970. He received his B.A. from George Washington University in 1917, his M.A. in 1918, and his Ph.D. from Columbia University in New York in 1932. George Washington University conferred upon him its honorary LL.D. in 1948. In addition to a distinguished career as a teacher, he has been prominent in many Washington area community activities. He has served as First Vice President of the Columbia Historical Society and is a member of the Society's Advisory Committee on Historical Research.

MARY MITCHELL (born 1912), author of *Kalorama: Country Estate to Washington Mayfair,* is well known to all readers of Washington area history. She has contributed to three preceding volumes of the *Records* and is the author of *A Walk in Georgetown* (1966), *Divided Town* (1968), *Annapolis Visit* (1969), and *Washington: Portrait of the Capital* (1972), four volumes published by Barre Publishers, Barre, Massachusetts. A native of Minnesota and a graduate of Wellesley, she moved to Washington in 1953 when her husband, William Mitchell, became General Counsel of the Atomic Energy Commission in the administration of President Dwight D. Eisenhower.

ROGER MEERSMAN (born 1931), co-author of *The National Theatre in Washington: Buildings and Audiences, 1835–1972,* has been for nine years a member of the faculty of the University of Maryland, where he is Associate Professor and Director in the Department of Speech and Dramatic Art of the College Park Campus. Before coming to Maryland, he was active in theatre in Paris, California, Texas, and Pennsylvania. He received his B.A. from Saint Ambrose College at

Davenport, Iowa, and his M.A. and Ph.D. in theatre history and criticism from the University of Illinois. He has received a number of awards for research, teaching, and artistic endeavors. He has published scholarly articles on American theatre and French rhetorical theory of the Seventeenth Century in such journals as *Speech Monographs, The Speech Teacher, The Southern Speech Journal, The Educational Theatre Journal* and *Player's Magazine* and has served as a theatre and dance critic for various newspapers and journals. He is Editor in Chief and a contributing author of *The American Drama,* a projected eight-volume multi-media series on the development of the American drama and theatre which will be issued jointly by the Smithsonian Institution and Caedmon Records.

ROBERT BOYER (born 1939), co-author of *The National Theatre in Washington: Buildings and Audiences, 1835–1972,* is Assistant Professor of Comparative Literature at Ohio State University. A native of Washington, he received his B.A. and M.A. from the University of Maryland and his Ph.D. in theatre from Ohio State University. He has served as administrator of the Ohio State University Theatre Collection and of the Program of International Seminars in Theatre Research at the University. In 1970 he participated in a grant from the National Endowment for the Humanities to tour Shakespearean productions throughout the state of Ohio and in 1972 he participated in a National Endowment Artist-Teacher program. His special interests in theatre history include the Nineteenth Century British Theatre, early experiments in European realistic drama, and the literature of the Anglo-Irish conflict. As an actor, he has appeared in major roles in *The Cherry Orchard, My Fair Lady,* and *She Stoops to Conquer,* among many others, and his extensive directorial credits include the first European tour of *Jesus Christ Superstar.*

DAVID K. SULLIVAN (born 1934), author of *Behind Prison Walls: The Operation of the District Penitentiary, 1831–1862,* received his M.A. in American history from De Paul University in Chicago and is a Ph.D. candidate at Georgetown University. He became interested in the subject of the District prison system while he was a Fellow at the Smithsonian Institution. He is the author of "William Lloyd Garrison in Baltimore, 1829–1830" scheduled for 1973 publication in the *Maryland Historical Magazine.*

JAMES BORCHERT (born 1941), author of *The Rise and Fall of Washington's Inhabited Alleys, 1852–1972,* is a doctoral student in American Studies at the University of Maryland. He received his B.A. from Miami University in 1963 and holds master's degrees from

Indiana University and the University of Cincinnati. He has taught at Alabama A. and M. University in Normal, Alabama, and at the University of Maryland. His dissertation subject is "American 'Mini-Ghettoes': Alleys, Alley Dwellings, and Alley Dwellers in Washington, D.C." He is anxious to locate and interview former alley residents and others who have had contact with Washington's alleys.

ANDREW S. KECK (born 1902), author of *A Toast to the Union: Clark Mills' Equestrian State of Andrew Jackson in Lafayette Square,* taught History of Art at American University from 1946 to 1969. Upon his retirement in 1969, he became the first University Professor Emeritus from the College of Arts and Sciences. He received his B.A. from Williams College and his M.A. and M.F.A. in the Department of Art and Archaeology of Princeton University. Before coming to American University, he taught History of Art at Williams College and was a Junior Fellow at Dumbarton Oaks. During World War II, he served as an officer in the Naval Reserves. He was chosen to deliver the first annual Distinguished Faculty Lecture sponsored by the American University Chapter of Phi Kappa Phi.

BENJAMIN FRANKLIN COOLING (born 1938), author of *Defending Washington during the Civil War,* is Chief of the Research Studies Division of the United States Army Military History Research Collection at Carlisle Barracks, Pennsylvania. He was born in New Brunswick, New Jersey, and came to Washington, D.C. with his family the following year. He grew up in Washington and attended Washington public schools. He received his B.A. in 1961 from Rutgers University and his A.M. in 1962 and his Ph.D. in 1969 from the University of Pennsylvania. He has taught at the University of Pennsylvania and has served on the Editorial Board of *Military Affairs.* He is editor of *Soldiering in Sioux Country* (1971) and co-editor with Allan Millett of *Doctoral Dissertations in Military Affairs* (1972). His *Benjamin Franklin Tracy: Father of the American Fighting Navy* is scheduled for 1973 publication. He began contributing to scholarly journals when he was 24 with the publication of "The Battle of Dover" in the *Tennessee Historical Quarterly* and has contributed to the *Alabama Historical Quarterly, Arkansas Historical Quarterly, Civil War Times Illustrated, Delaware History, Journal of the Confederate Historical Society of Great Britain, Military Affairs, Naval War College Review, Nebraska History, Parameters: Journal of the U.S. Army War College, West Virginia Historical Quarterly* and other journals and to the *Encyclopedia Americana* and to such volumes as *American Military History* edited by Maurice Matloff.

TANYA EDWARDS BEAUCHAMP (born 1936), author of *Adolph Cluss:*

An Architect in Washington during Civil War and Reconstruction, received a bachelor's degree in philosophy from Vassar College in 1958 and a master's degree in history of architecture from the University of Virginia in 1972. Born in Takoma Park, she is the daughter of designer-inventor William R. Edwards and Bell Ward Edwards. Both her parents are Washingtonians with many memories of Cluss buildings and her mother and her aunt taught in the Franklin and Wallach schools. She has written for *Smithsonian* magazine and since May 1972 has been working with James M. Goode on his forthcoming book *The Outdoor Sculpture of Washington.* She is the wife of consulting engineer Ernesto Beauchamp and the mother of three daughters.

MELVIN R. WILLIAMS (born 1936), author of *A Blueprint for Change: The Black Community in Washington, D.C., 1860–1870,* has been Assistant Professor of History at Brooklyn College of the City University of New York since 1969. He received his B.A. in 1958 and his M.A. in 1960 at North Carolina Central University at Durham, North Carolina, and is a Ph.D. candidate in history at the Johns Hopkins University in Baltimore under the supervision of Professor David Donald. He was Assistant Professor of History at Knoxville College, Knoxville, Tennessee, from 1959 to 1965, Assistant Professor of History at South Carolina State College, Orangeburg, South Carolina, from 1965 to 1967, and Lecturer in History, Morgan State College, Baltimore, in 1968.

WILLIAM M. MAURY (born 1939), author of *Andrew R. Shepherd and the Board of Public Works,* is the Editor of *Capitol Studies,* the journal of the United States Capitol Historical Society. He received his B.A. from the University of Maryland and his M.A. from George Washington University. He is a Ph.D. candidate at George Washington University and is writing his dissertation, under the direction of Frederick Gutheim, on the territorial government of Washington, D.C.

MARTIN K. GORDON (born 1941), author of *The Black Militia in the District of Columbia, 1867–1898,* is a Ph.D. candidate in American Studies at George Washington University where he has been a University Teaching Fellow. He received his B.A. in 1963 from Notre Dame, his M.A. in 1965 from the University of Wisconsin, and a M.Phil. from George Washington University in 1970. He has contributed to *The American Archivist* and other publications.

MAXWELL BLOOMFIELD (born 1931), author of *John Mercer Langston and the Rise of Howard Law School,* is Associate Professor of American Social and Constitutional History at Catholic University in Washington. He holds degrees from Rice University, Harvard

Law School, and Tulane University. Before coming to Washington he taught in the History Department of Ohio State University and has been a member of the Texas Bar since 1957. He is the author of *Alarms and Diversions: The American Mind through American Magazines, 1900–1914* published in 1967 and has completed the final draft of a second book, *The Power Brokers: American Lawyers and Social Change,* a project sponsored in part by an American Bar Foundation Fellowship in Legal History. He has published a number of articles on legal and cultural subjects in such magazines as the *American Journal of Legal History, American Quarterly,* and *South Atlantic Quarterly.*

FRANCIS R. KOWSKY (born 1943), author of *Gallaudet College: A High Victorian Campus,* has been Assistant Professor of the History of Art at the State University of New York College at Buffalo, New York, since 1970. A native of Washington, he attended public and parochial schools of the District of Columbia and received his B.A. in the history of art from George Washington University in 1964. He attended the Institute of Fine Arts of New York University and received his Ph.D. in 1972 from the Johns Hopkins University in Baltimore. His dissertation subject is Frederick Clarke Withers.

JOHN Y. COLE (born 1940), author of *A National Monument for a National Library: Ainsworth Rand Spofford and the New Library of Congress, 1871–1897,* has been a member of the staff of the Library of Congress since 1967. He received a B.A. in 1962 and a M.L.S in 1963 from the University of Washington in Seattle and a M.Phil. in 1970 and a Ph.D. in 1971 from George Washington University. He has published articles in the *Journal of Library History* and the *Quarterly Journal of the Library of Congress.*

MICHAEL RICHMAN (born 1943), author of *Daniel Chester French: His Statue of Lewis Cass in the United States Capitol,* is Assistant to the Director of the National Portrait Gallery of the Smithsonian Institution. He attended St. Albans School in Washington, D.C., received an A.B. from Bowdoin College, Brunswick, Maine, in 1965, his M.A. from George Washington University in 1970, and is a Ph.D. candidate at the University of Delaware. The subject of his master's thesis is the sculptor Edward Kemeys and the subject of his doctoral dissertation is Daniel Chester French. He has lectured at the University of Delaware and has published in the *American Art Journal,* the *National Sculpture Review,* and other journals.

GAIL KARESH KASSAN (born 1947), author of *The Old Post Office Building in Washington, D.C.: Its Past, Present, and Future,* participated in the Smithsonian Institution's American Studies Program and did research into Washington, D.C. history and architecture while she was a student at the University of Maryland where she received her M.A. A native of South Carolina and an honor graduate in American History from the University of Cincinnati, she is now living in Atlanta, Georgia, where her husband is an intern in medicine.

ELLEN ROBINSON EPSTEIN (born 1947), author of *The East and West Wings of the White House,* is an Architectural Historian with the Office of Fine Arts in the General Services Administration. She is a native of Washington and attended Washington public schools. She received a B.A. in the history of art from Connecticut College for Women in 1969 and studied at the University of London. She has assisted in the research for a forthcoming volume by Paul D. Spreiregen. Her husband, David Epstein, is a Washington attorney who has a special interest in the history of the administration of President Franklin Pierce.

SIDNEY R. BLAND (born 1936), author of *New Life in an Old Movement: Alice Paul and the Great Suffrage Parade of 1913 in Washington, D.C.,* has been Associate Professor History at Madison College at Harrisonburg, Virginia, since 1965. He received his B.A. from Furman University at Greenville, South Carolina, in 1959, his M.A. from the University of Maryland in 1961, and his Ph.D. from George Washington University in 1972. He has taught at the University of Maryland and at George Washington University and has published "Aspects of Woman Suffrage Militancy in England, 1905–1914" in *Studies and Research,* Madison College, 1970.

BENIS M. FRANK (born 1925), author of *The Relief of General Barnett,* is head of the Oral History Unit, Historical Division, Headquarters, United States Marine Corps. An enlisted Marine in World War II, he was commissioned just before the outbreak of the Korean War and served with the First Marine Division in both. He is the author of *Okinawa: Capstone to Victory* (Ballatine Books, 1969) and of a number of articles in the field of military history. He is a Fellow of the Company of Military Historians and is managing editor of its quarterly publication *Military Collector and Historian.* He is a graduate of the University of Connecticut.

ARTHUR HECHT (born 1903), author of *Flowers to Gladden the City: The Takoma Horticulture Club, 1916–1971,* is an Archivist on the staff of the National Archives. He also serves as Archivist of the Takoma Park Historical Society. At the National Archives he has been concerned with postal records for twenty-five years and has served as a consultant on postal history for the Library of Congress and the Smithsonian Institution. He has written on historical and philatelic subjects and contributed to the 1966–1968 volume of the *Records*.

PAUL BOSWELL (born 1913), author and artist of *A Portfolio of Washington Drawings*, has written in response to a request for biographical information: "I am an artist neither by training nor by profession, but—if at all—by occasional bouts of patience. I am not even a Sunday painter: mostly just a November artist. I took degrees in English at Berea College and the University of Iowa and have worked at the Library of Congress (less four and a half years in the Army) for over thirty-six years. Most of the time at the Library I have served as Reference Librarian specializing first in state government publications and later in British Commonwealth government publications. The Boswells are a family of three English majors. My wife, Elizabeth, who took her degree from Duke, worked for seventeen years in the Library's Legislative Reference Service. Our son, Thomas, finished at Amherst and is now a sports writer for the Washington *Post*."

EDWIN DARBY NYE (born 1917), author of *Revisiting Washington's Forty Boundary Stones, 1972*, has for a number of years been the Washington representative of the First Financial Marketing Group of Boston. He is a third generation Washingtonian, attended the old Central High School, and went on to Johns Hopkins University. He served in the Pacific area in World War II, was captured by the Japanese, and spent nearly four years in a Japanese prison camp. His avocational interests are photography and local history.

JOHN HOLWAY (born 1929), who recorded the *Baseball Reminiscences of Washington's Jesse "Nip" Winters: "How I Struck Out Babe Ruth and Beat Lefty Grove"*, is an Economics Editor with the United States Information Agency. He has written in response to a request for biographical information: "The Winters piece is one of about fifty interviews I've conducted with old-time Black ball players. Others have been published in *Look* magazine, *American Heritage, Potomac, Baltimore Sun, Chicago Sun-Times, Washington Star, Detroit News, New York Folklore Quarterly, Journal of Popular Culture, The Sporting News*, etc. Of course I hope to put them all together into a book, as well as into a TV documentary tentatively scheduled for next spring. I've also published books on Japanese baseball and sumo wrestling."

ALBERT W. ATWOOD (born 1879), author of *A Member Reminisces: Problems of a Professional Writer*, has long been a valued member of the Columbia Historical Society and has served as a member of its

Board of Managers and as Vice President. He received his A.B. degree from Amherst in 1903 and has received honorary degrees from Amherst, Princeton, and Gallaudet. He served as financial editor of *McClure's Magazine* and of *Harper's Weekly* and was associated with other publications. Beginning in 1914, he wrote regularly for the *Saturday Evening Post* for twenty-five years and from 1941 to 1955 was a regular contributor to the *National Geographic Magazine*. He has taught at New York University and Columbia University and lectured at Princeton. Active in intellectual and cultural affairs in Washington, he has served as President of the Cosmos Club, President of The Literary Society, Chairman of the Board of Directors of Gallaudet College, and President of the Board of Trustees of the District of Columbia Public Library. He has contributed to the three preceding volumes of the *Records*.

MATHILDE D. WILLIAMS, author of *Georgetown: The Twentieth Century, A Continuing Battle,* has been Curator of the Peabody Library Association of Georgetown since 1950. A native of Washington, she received her A.B. and M.A. from George Washington University and has worked with the Public Library as a cataloguer, reference librarian, branch librarian, and editor. She is a member of the Board of Managers and of the Advisory Committee on Historical Research of the Columbia Historical Society and contributed "Old Georgetown as Chronicled in the Peabody Collection" to the 1960–1962 volume of the *Records* and "The Three Sisters Bridge: A Ghost Span Over the Potomac" to the 1969–1970 volume.

R. J. MCCARTHY (born 1896), who compiled the list of *Members of the Society, 1972,* has been Executive Director of the Columbia Historical Society since 1967. He attended the University of Pittsburgh and George Washington University and worked in Washington for thirty-six years with Government Services, Inc., where he was Director of Park Activities. He served overseas with the United States Army in both World War I and World War II and retired as Lieutenant Colonel.

I have continued, as for preceding volumes, actively to solicit papers in addition to those first delivered as addresses before the Society. Those which were first delivered as addresses before the Society are so identified, and the date of delivery indicated, in an unnumbered footnote at the bottom of the first page of the text of the paper.

The order of the papers here, as in preceding volumes, is roughly chronological by subject matter. The close reader will find, as in preceding volumes, some slight variations in the style of footnotes and citations and in other matters of form from paper to paper. I have continued, within what I consider permissible limits, to accommodate the individual preferences of the authors. I have been the more willing to do this because in a number of instances the authors wish to obtain individual offprints of their papers.

As in preceding volumes, I wish to express my gratitude to members of the Columbia Historical Society and to others who have extended kindnesses to me in the editing of the *Records*.

I am especially indebted to the nine members who have served with me on the Society's Advisory Committee on Historical Research: Henry P. Beers, Leonard Carmichael, Josephine Cobb, Herman R. Friis, Oliver W. Holmes, Elmer Louis Kayser, Wyndham D. Miles, Wilcomb E. Washburn, and Mathilde D. Williams. The retirement in 1972 of Miss Cobb from the National Archives and her return to her native Maine after thirty-six years in Washington is a loss which will be felt by the whole community. The retirement in 1972 of Dr. Holmes as Executive Director of the National Historical Publications Commission similarly will be keenly felt by friends of history everywhere. It is to be hoped that retirement from their rigorous professional duties will allow Miss Cobb and Dr. Holmes more time for the concerns of the Columbia Historical Society.

Homer T. Rosenberger, the President of the Columbia Historical Society since 1968, could not have been more helpful if he were the kin of the editor which many members assume that he is and which he is not.

Wilcomb E. Washburn, the First Vice President of the Society, has encouraged his students in the American Studies Program at the Smithsonian Institution to participate in the work of the Society which I hope has enriched their own studies as it has enriched the Society. I have welcomed them as contributors to the *Records* as I have other younger historians.

Robert A. Truax, the Librarian of the Society, has been consistently helpful and has generously shared his unique knowledge of Washington iconography.

All-too-brief acknowledgement is made in the italic line beneath each illustration to all those who have cooperated in the assembling and granting permission for the reproduction of the more than 300 illustrations in the volume.

In the printing of the *Records,* I have continued to benefit from the experienced and patient cooperation of Mrs. Constance B. Kiley of the Waverly Press. In a continuing effort to improve the physical book, this volume of the *Records* has been printed by offset to avoid the use of the coated paper, with its weight and gloss which some of our readers have found unpleasant, which was used in the immediately preceding volumes to accommodate halftone illustrations.

Lastly, I am deeply indebted to Walker Cowen, the able Director of the University Press of Virginia, through whose interest a formal agreement has been made between the Columbia Historical Society of Washington, D. C. and the University Press of Virginia for the distribution of the *Records* by the University Press of Virginia.

FRANCIS COLEMAN ROSENBERGER

Washington, D. C.
December 1972

Shipbuilding in Virginia, 1763–1774

WILLIAM M. KELSO

The purpose of the research reported here was to discover as much as possible about the nature and extent of shipbuilding in Virginia during a period of peacetime production, 1763–1774. Statistical information collected from the three available sources: the Naval Office lists, the *Liverpool* (England) *Plantation Register of Ships,* and the *Virginia Gazette*[1] showed that shipbuilding played an important part in the economy of Virginia during the twelve year period under study. During those years, the records showed that over 350 vessels were built in the numerous Virginia shipyards scattered along the Chesapeake Bay from Alexandria to Norfolk. The documents also revealed certain statistical data concerning vessel types and tonnage, annual fluctuation in production, general location and relative productivity of individual yards, and trend in ownership and registration of Virginia-built ships.

From the end of the French and Indian War until the troublesome years immediately preceding the American Revolution (1763–1774) Virginia shipwrights built at least 360 vessels totaling 25,627 tons, an average of thirty vessels and 2,156 tons each year. (See table 1.) But production varied drastically during the period. For example, in 1765 forty-seven ships were built in Virginia yards, while in 1774 production dwindled to seven. More specifically, vessel production increased sharply from thirty-one ships in 1763 to its peak in 1765, dropped gradually to twenty ships by 1770, but experienced a rush of activity in 1771 (thirty-seven ships) and 1773 (thirty ships) before production virtually ceased in 1774.

The total tonnage of Virginia-built ships also rose and fell sharply each year. Generally speaking, the tonnage varied in about the same proportion as the number of ships. However, during the years 1763, 1765, 1766, and 1768, tonnage was proportionately higher than the

---

The author wishes to express his appreciation to Dr. W. W. Abbott, Dr. John Selby, Dr. Edward Riley, Dr. Ira Gruber, and Harold B. Gill for guiding the research and reviewing the text of this paper.

[1] See "Note on Sources and Methodology" on page 10.

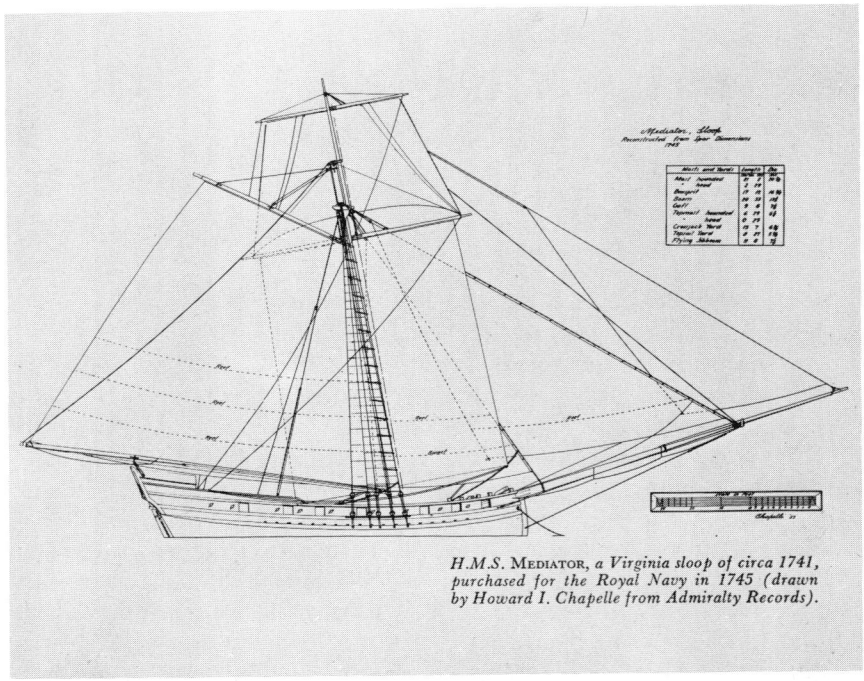

H.M.S. MEDIATOR, *a Virginia sloop of circa 1741, purchased for the Royal Navy in 1745 (drawn by Howard I. Chapelle from Admiralty Records).*

The Mariners Museum, Newport News, Virginia

A Virginia Sloop of about 1741

H.M.S. *Mediator,* purchased for the Royal Navy in 1745, drawn by Howard I. Chapelle from Admiralty Records.

total number of vessels built, indicating that during these four years there was a tendency to build larger ships.

Both the Naval Office lists and the *Virginia Gazette* mentioned five vessel types: snows, schooners, sloops, brigs, and ships. No other types appeared primarily because the Navigation Act of 1696 exempted all other ship types from registration and the Naval Office lists, the major source for ship types, included only registered vessels.

Of the 360 Virginia-built vessels listed, 308 had their type designated. Of these 308, 53 per cent (168) were sloops and schooners, 21 per cent (76) were brigs, 12 per cent (48) were ships, and 5 per cent (16) were snows. (See table 2.)

The production of sloops hit a peak in 1764, but by 1766 sloop construction had diminished to two. However, sloop-building thereafter gradually increased until it reached fifteen in 1773. Virginia shipyards produced schooners at a fairly even rate until 1771 after

TABLE 1

Year	1763		1764		1765		1766		1767		1768		1769		1770		1771		1772		1773		1774		Total	
	No.	Tons	No.	Tons	No.	Tons	No.	Tons	No.	Tons	No.	Tons	No.	Tons	No.	Tons	No.	Tons	No.	Tons	No.	Tons	No.	Tons	No.	Tons
	31	2785	39	2852	47	3880	37	3515	33	2474	27	2280	26	1480	20	1050	37	2454	26	1419	30	1797	7	475	360	25,627

A table showing the total number of vessels and the total tonnage of Virginia-built ships constructed in each of the twelve years in the period 1763–1774, compiled from the Virginia Naval Office lists (1763–1774), the Liverpool Registers (1763–1773), and the *Virginia Gazette* (1766–1774).

TABLE 2

Year	Snow No.	Snow Tons	Snow Aver.	Schooner No.	Schooner Tons	Schooner Aver.	Sloop No.	Sloop Tons	Sloop Aver.	Brig No.	Brig Tons	Brig Aver.	Ship No.	Ship Tons	Ship Aver.
1763	1	120	120	6	233	39	9	306	34	2	200	50	10	1590	159
1764	6	650	180	6	177	29	14	471	59	1	60	60	5	684	137
1765	3	310	103	8	263	33	6	220	36	12	850	70	9	1230	137
1766	1	100	100	7	266	38	2	100	50	10	880	88	6	1139	190
1767	2	170	85	6	194	32	5	185	37	7	530	76	2	340	113
1768	1	100	100	9	252	28	4	128	32	6	465	77	5	1155	231
1769	1	100	100	7	285	31	6	175	29	8	485	61	2	300	150
1770	—	—	—	8	443	55	6	217	36	5	270	54	—	—	—
1771	—	—	—	10	208	21	7	228	32	10	760	76	4	530	132
1772	—	—	—	6	229	38	12	330	29	6	550	92	2	310	155
1773	1	130	130	6	185	30	15	362	24	6	510	85	2	500	250
1774	—	—	—	1	25	25	2	40	40	3	244	81	1	160	160
Total	16	1680	105	80	2760	34	88	2762	31	76	5804	76	48	7928	165

A table showing the total number, total tonnage, and average tonnage of each type of Virginia-built vessel constructed in each of twelve years in the period 1763–1774 compiled from the Virginia Naval Office lists (1763–1774) and the *Virginia Gazette* (1766–1774).

which production rapidly fell off. Brigs apparently remained popular between their peak years, 1765 and 1771, but after the later year, brig construction decreased at almost the same rate as schooners. Production in Virginia of vessels designated as ships varied considerably from year to year, but the trend was toward a gradual decline in ship construction. Apparently there was little demand for snows during the period, for after 1764 production of snows virtually ceased.

Of the five types, ships and snows were the largest with the former averaging 165 tons and the latter 105 tons. Brigs averaged seventy-six tons while schooners and sloops, the smallest types, averaged thirty-four tons and thirty-one tons respectively. (See table 2.) The majority of Virginia-built schooners and sloops ranged from twelve to fifty tons, although occasionally schooners were as large as ninety-five tons and sloops as large as sixty-six tons. (See table 3.) Ships and snows were predominantly between 100 and 200 tons, but at times ships were built as small as 80 tons and as large as 305 tons. Brigs usually ranged from fifty to 100 tons; however, many brigs ranged in the 100–200 ton class. Listed largest to smallest as to the tonnage of the majority of each type, the vessels rank: (1) ships, (2) snows, (3) brigs, (4) schooners, and (5) sloops.

Of all the Virginia-built ships found, 122 ship entries specified

Shipbuilding in Virginia, 1763–1774

the Virginia county, city, or river of the ship's origin. In all, seventeen shipyard locations were named. (See table 4.) Of these, twelve were located within a thirty-five mile radius of Hampton Roads. Seven yards had immediate access to the James River while four were located close to the York River, one somewhere on the Rappahannock

TABLE 3

Range in Tons	10–50	50–100	100–200	200–	Lightest	Heaviest
Snow	—	3	12	—	70	130
Schooner	68	15	—	—	12	95
Sloop	80	7	—	—	12	66
Brig	6	52	17	—	25	170
Ship		1	36	11	80	305

A table showing the range in tons and the lightest and heaviest of the five types of Virginia-built vessels listed in the Virginia Naval Office lists (1763–1774) and the *Virginia Gazette* (1766–1774).

Library of Congress

A View of the Washington Area, showing shipping, about 1794

"Washington" by George I. Parkyns. From the District side of the Potomac above Georgetown. Probable date 1794. Date issued, September 1, 1795. An aquatint engraving in the Division of Prints and Photographs of the Library of Congress.

TABLE 4

Location of Shipyard	1763–1774													Total
	63	64	65	66	67	68	69	70	71	72	73	74	
Norfolk	6	3	13	17	10	9	9	3	9	2	3	1	83
Alexandria		3	3	1		1		1		2			11
Gloucester County	2			1	1	2		1					7
Elizabeth River			3										3
Suffolk					2				1				3
Northumberland Co.			1						1				2
Princess Anne Co.		1					1						2
Rappahannock River	2												2
Charles City Co.						1							1
Hampton								1					1
Nansemond Co.			1										1
New Kent Co.					1								1
Northampton Co.		1											1
Smithfield									1				1
Tanners Creek			1										1
York River											1		1
Yorktown					1								1
Total	10	9	21	19	15	13	10	6	12	5	3	1	122

A table showing the total number of ships built in every Virginia shipyard in each year of the period 1763–1774 compiled from the Virginia Naval Office lists (1763–1774), the *Liverpool Register* (1763–1773), and the *Virginia Gazette* (1766–1774).

River, two close to the Potomac River, and one on the Eastern Shore. Alexandria yards built at least eleven vessels during the period; shipwrights of Gloucester County, Elizabeth River, and Suffolk, at least three; the yards at Northumberland County, Princess Anne County and Rappahannock River, at least two; and at least one ship each was built in Charles City County, Hampton, Nansemond County, New Kent County, Northampton County, Smithfield, Tanners Creek, York River and Yorktown. (See table 4.)

But the yards at Norfolk vastly exceeded any other Virginia shipyard in quantity of production. For instance, of the 122 ships with the place of origin mentioned, eighty-three came from Norfolk while only eleven came from the second most productive yard, Alexandria. Further, Norfolk-built vessels comprised 23 per cent of the total 360 Virginia-built vessls. (See table 5.) Thus if all ship entries had shown the yard of origin, it seems reasonable to assume that no less than one-third (120 ships) and probably no less than one-half (180 ships) of the 360 Virginia-built ships would have been found to be products of Norfolk. Ships built at Norfolk tended to be larger than all other Virginia-built vessels. For example, Norfolk-built vessels averaged eighty-nine tons while the average size of ships built elsewhere

Shipbuilding in Virginia, 1763–1774 7

TABLE 5

Comparison of Norfolk Production with All Other Virginia Yards						Percentage: Norfolk and All Others	
Norfolk			All Others				
No.	Tons	Aver.	No.	Tons	Aver.	% No.	% Tons
83	7370	89	277	18,257	66	23	29

A table showing a comparison of the total number of vessels, the total tonnage, and the average tonnage of Norfolk-built ships with the total number of vessels, the total tonnage, and the average tonnage of ships built elsewhere in Virginia, 1763–1774, compiled from the Virginia Naval Office lists (1763–1774), the *Liverpool Register* (1763–1773), and the *Virginia Gazette* (1766–1774).

TABLE 6

Yard and % Built at Norfolk	Type									
	Snow		Schooner		Sloop		Brig		Ship	
	No.	Tons	No.	Tons	No.	Tons	No.	Tons	No.	Tons
Norfolk	4	350	11	339	9	293	9	670	9	1556
All Others	12	1330	69	2421	79	2469	67	5134	37	6372
% Norfolk and all Others	25%	21%	14%	12%	10%	11%	12%	12%	17%	19%

A table showing a comparison of the total number of vessels and the total tonnage by vessel types of vessels built at Norfolk, 1763–1774 with the total number of vessels and the total tonnage by vessel type of vessels built elsewhere in Virginia Naval Office lists, 1763–1774, and the *Virginia Gazette*, 1766–1774.

in Virginia were twenty-three tons lighter. (See table 5.) The yards at Norfolk equally manufactured schooners, sloops, brigs and ships, but built few snows. (See table 6.) However, when compared to the entire Virginia ship production, Norfolk built as much as 25 per cent of all snows, 23 per cent of all sloops and schooners, and 19 per cent of all ships.

The *Virginia Gazette* ship for sale advertisements disclosed various specific bits of information relating to shipbuilding in Virginia, among which were the types of wood used in Virginia construction, the kinds of shipcarpenters, the relationship of rigging to hulls, and the exact dimensions of two snows and a schooner. (See table 7.) Virginia shipbuilders used white oak timbers and planks in five of the vessels listed in the *Gazette*.[2] The brig *Industry*, however, contained

[2] *Virginia Gazette*, Purdie and Dixon, July 25, 1766; Purdie and Dixon, November 13, 1766; Purdie and Dixon, December 4, 1766; Purdie and Dixon, June 18, 1767; Rind, February 14, 1771.

TABLE 7

Type	Keel	Beam	Hold Clearance	Deck Clearance
Snow[a]	51'	21'	9'	3'1½"
Snow[b]	52'	21'	10'	—
Schooner[c]	36'	15'	8'	—

A table showing the dimensions of two Virginia-built snows and one Virginia-built schooner found in the *Virginia Gazette* ship for sale advertisements.

[a] *Virginia Gazette* (Rind), March 24, 1768.
[b] *Virginia Gazette* (Purdie & Dixon), September 3, 1770.
[c] *Virginia Gazette* (Purdie & Dixon), December 3, 1772.

a frame made of mulberry, cedar, and locust.[3] Since no other ship advertisements specified wood types, probably most Virginia builders used more inferior varieties. That is, if a given vessel contained the superior white oak, surely the salesman would have mentioned this fact as a selling point.

According to Benjamin Harrison, "prime hands" from Boston built his two ships advertised for sale in 1763[4] and 1772.[5] Because Harrison listed New England workmanship as one of the advantages of his vessels, apparently shipowners considered northern shipcarpenters superior to local workmen. Moreover, some of these local carpenters were Negro slaves. For example, advertised for sale with the ship *Polly* were eleven Negroes, some of them shipcarpenters, blacksmiths and sailors.[6]

The type of rig used in some Virginia-built vessels depended upon the choice of the owner. The new 176-ton vessel advertised by Alexander Moseley of Norfolk could "be made ship, snow, or brig as best suits the purchaser."[7] Moreover, the four-year-old snow, *Molly,* advertised for sale by John Herbert had recently been altered into a brig.[8]

The Naval Office lists also indicated the size of the crew for each ship. A total of 1,995 seamen sailed the 300 vessels listed. Ships generally sailed with a crew of thirteen, while sloops and schooners usually carried four to five sailors. (See table 8.)

Ordinarily, Virginia-built vessels were owned by individuals. However, as many as ninety-six companies owned single vessels while eleven companies and twenty-six private owners each possessed two

[3] *Ibid.*, Purdie and Dixon, June 14, 1770.
[4] *Ibid.*, Purdie and Dixon, August 11, 1768.
[5] *Ibid.*, Purdie and Dixon, November 19, 1772.
[6] *Ibid.*, Rind, September 22, 1768.
[7] *Ibid.*, Purdie and Dixon, September 29, 1768.
[8] *Ibid.*, Purdie and Dixon, September 7, 1769. The *Gazette* also gave the dimensions of two snows and a schooner. See table 8 for these figures.

TABLE 8

Crew	Type				
	Snow	Schooner	Sloop	Brig	Ship
Men	161	322	384	524	606
Average crew	11	5	4	7	13

A table showing the total number of men and the average size crew for each type of Virginia-built vessel which sailed in the period 1763–1774 compiled from the Virginia Naval Office lists (1763–1774).

or more craft. If the ownership by a single man of more than four vessels comprised a shipline, then four such lines existed in Virginia during the period 1763–1774. John Goodrich of Norfolk owned six vessels, John Thompson, probably of Surrey, and John Wilkins of Princess Anne County both owned five ships, and John Greenwood, also of Norfolk, owned four. Moreover, fifty-six vessels were both owned and operated by the same man, and in fourteen cases the owner and the captain of each ship had the same last name.

The Navigation Act of 1696 stipulated that all ships had to be registered at the owner's home port. The *Liverpool Register* and the Virginia Naval Office lists named the registration port of each vessel and showed that the Virginia-built ships owned in foreign ports had a tendency to be larger than Virginia-built ships that were owned by Virginians. (See table 9.) For example, foreign-registered ships averaged 112 tons while domestic-registered vessels were only half as large. Furthermore, 61 per cent of the Virginia-registered vessels were sloops, but ships comprised over 50 per cent of non-Virginia-registered craft. (See table 10.) Sloops and schooners accounted for only 17 per cent of the total foreign-owned, Virginia-built vessels.

During the years 1763, 1765, 1766, and 1771, both Virginia and non-Virginia-registered vessels were relatively large. (See table 9.) However, a trend for the whole period shows a definite tendency for the average size of foreign-registered ships to drop, whereas the size of vessels registered in Virginia tended to remain fairly constant.

CONCLUSION

Missing records make it impossible to know exactly how many more vessels were built in Virginia in 1763–1774 than the 360 vessels listed in the surviving Custom's Office statistics. However, a logical speculation can be made. The Custom's statistics found represent only a fraction of all the records kept by customs officials, probably no more than one-fourth. Therefore, the 360 vessels that I found in one-

TABLE 9

Year	Virginia-Registered Ships			Non-Virginia-Registered Ships		
	No.	Tons	Aver.	No.	Tons	Aver.
1763	21	1539	73	11	1415	129
1764	28	1598	57	10	1140	114
1765	31	2030	65	14	1605	115
1766	18	1161	64	18	2230	124
1767	17	879	52	15	1495	100
1768	21	1360	65	6	920	115
1769	21	1055	50	5	430	86
1170	17	812	48	2	170	85
1771	28	1568	56	8	756	94
1772	23	1114	49	2	185	92
1773	22	1094	50	8	703	88
1774	6	365	61	—	—	—
Total	253	14,835	55	99	11,049	112

A table showing a comparison of the total number of vessels, the total tonnage, and the average tonnage of Virginia-built vessels registered in Virginia constructed each year of the period 1763–1774 with the total number of vessels, the total tonnage, and the average tonnage of Virginia-built vessels registered in foreign ports compiled from the Virginia Naval Office lists (1763–1774) and the *Liverpool Registers* (1763–1773).

TABLE 10

Registration	Type				
	Snow	Schooner	Sloop	Brig	Ship
Virginia	10	72	83	68	23
Non-Virginia	5	4	3	6	25

A table showing a comparison of the total number of vessels by vessel type of Virginia-built vessels registered in Virginia with the total number of vessels by vessel type of Virginia-built vessels registered in foreign parts all constructed during the period 1763–1774 compiled from the Virginia Naval Office lists, 1763–1774.

fourth of all the possible sources may represent as little as one-half of the actual number of vessels constructed in Virginia. In that case, it could be safely concluded that shipbuilding indeed played a more vital role in the economic history of Eighteeneth Century Virginia than historians have realized.

NOTE ON SOURCES AND METHODOLOGY

The three sources used to compile the listing of ships built in Virginia between 1763–1774 (table 1) were the Virginia Naval Office lists, 1763–1774, the *Liverpool* (England) *Plantation Register of Ships*, 1763–1773, and the *Virginia Gazette*, 1766–1774.

Shipbuilding in Virginia, 1763–1774

Library of Congress

A View of the Washington Area, showing shipping, about 1800

"View of the Suburbs of the City of Washington" by George I. Parkyns. Apparently looking up the Potomac through Georgetown. An etching, 20 x 24 inches, in the Division of Prints and Photographs of the Library of Congress, circa 1800, and possibly unique.

Virginia Naval Office Lists

To assure that all ships trading with England's colonies were English-owned and English-manned as required by the Navigation Acts (1660–1663) the English Parliament established the Naval Office in 1676. The Naval Office, in turn, appointed a naval officer for each major ship clearance district in the American colonies with the instructions to check and report all ships entering or clearing his district.

By 1763, there were six Naval Office Districts in Virginia: Upper District of the James River, York River District, Accomac District, South Potomac District, Rappahannock River District, and Hampton District. Each Naval officer from the Virginia Districts submitted to the governor quarterly a list of ships which had entered or cleared his district. The governor sent all Naval Office lists either to the Board of Trade or to the Treasury Office. Hence, many of the Virginia Naval Office lists can be found in the Public Record Office of Great Britain.

The Public Record Office files include 246 Virginia Naval Office lists for the period 1763–1774: June 24, 1763–January 5, 1766 (98 lists), CO 5/1449; January 5, 1766–January 5, 1770 (96 lists), CO 5/1450; January 5, 1770–April 5, 1774 (52 lists), CO 5/1350–1352. The lists with P.R.O. numbers CO 5/1449 and CO 5/1450 were entitled: Shipping Returns. P.R.O. CO 5/1350–1352 were included in the Letters to the Secretary of State from the Governor, Lord Dunmore, with Enclosures and Replies.

Every list entry contains information grouped under the following headings: vessels entered and cleared, time of clearing, vessel's name, master's name, where and when built (name of colony or "plantation" built), kind of vessel, tonnage, number of guns and men, where and when registered, owner's name, character of cargo (often these accounts are elaborate and detailed), whither bound, and where and when bond was given. I collected only information under these headings: vessel's name, type of vessel, tonnage, where and when built, owner's name, master's name, men, and where and when registered.

The Naval Office lists for the period, 1763–1774, are incomplete. Each Naval Officer supposedly submitted a list of entrances and clearances four times a year except the officer in York District, who submitted his semi-annually. Therefore, for the twelve years, 1763–1774, there should have been as many as 528 entrance and clearance lists submitted. However, only 246 lists were found. Moreover, only 150 of these surviving lists specified the colony of origin of each vessel; none of the lists from the Rappahannock District did so but simply named "plantation" as the place where each ship was built.

The English government created a ship registration procedure to prevent foreign-built ships from trading in the British Empire. According to the Navigation Act of 1696, all shipowners had to register their vessels at the Customs Office of their home port.[9] The Customs Office, in turn, issued certificates of registration only to English owners of English-built ships. Because of this registration procedure all ports with Customs Offices had ship registration records. One such office was at Liverpool, England.

The *Liverpool (England) Plantation Register of Ships* title; H. M. Customs and Excise; Plantation Registers; Customs House, Liverpool can be found in the *Virginia Colonial Records Project* microfilm

---
[9] See Merrill Jensen, ed., *English Historical Documents* (New York, 1955), 359–364.

Shipbuilding in Virginia, 1763–1774

№511. Survey Reports LI №8–LI №10 of the *Virginia Colonial Records Project* list all the Virginia-built vessels appearing in the *Liverpool Registers* for the periods 1743–1773 and 1779–1784. Each registration entry included information under the following headings: vessel's name, type of vessel, where registered, tonnage, master's name, where and when built, and owner's name.

In the *Liverpool Register,* I found fifty-two Virginia-built vessels for the period 1763–1774. Forty-three of these fifty-two vessel entries specified the Virginia county, city, or river where each ship was built.

The Registers for other ports in the British Empire were not available and possibly do not exist. The number of Virginia-built vessels found in the *Liverpool Register* probably represent only a portion of Virginia-built vessels registered in Britain.

The Virginia Gazette

For the period 1766–1774, most issues of the *Virginia Gazette* are still available.[10] To find information concerning Virginia shipbuilding 1763–1774, I examined all the ship for sale advertisements in the *Gazette,* 1766–1774. In locating specific ship for sale advertisements, Lester J. Cappon's and Stella F. Duff's *Virginia Gazette Index* (Williamsburg, Virginia, 1950) proved helpful.

The *Gazette* included 119 ship for sale advertisements, 1766–1774, but only forty-six of these advertisements contained information relevant to shipbuilding in Virginia. This information included among other specific items the names of eight Virginia-built vessels not listed either in the Naval Office lists or the *Liverpool Register.*

---

[10] No issues of the *Gazette* are available for the period 1763–1766.

Theodore Roosevelt Island: A Broken Link to Early Washington, D.C. History

MARY E. CURRY

Theodore Roosevelt Island, located in the Potomac River between Rosslyn, Virginia, and the Rock Creek waterfront of Washington, D.C., gives the misleading appearance of being a vestige from the time the District of Columbia was a wilderness.[1] But where the statue of Theodore Roosevelt stands in the northern part of the Island was once a driveway leading to a late Eighteenth Century mansion house.[2] An orchard and a Civil War camp site were also on the Island. Today an observant visitor to the Island may see small pieces of glass and chinaware along the nature trails. This material is the last surface

---

Delivered before the Columbia Historical Society on January 18, 1972.

I wish to express my gratitude to Wilcomb E. Washburn, Director, American Studies Program, Smithsonian Institution; Harold K. Skramstad, Chief of Special Projects, Museum of History and Technology, Smithsonian Institution; Tim Rockwell; Robert H. McNulty; Richard J. Muzzrole and to my colleagues in the class: Mrs. Gail Kassan, Miss Antoinette Lee, David Schwulst, Robert A. Cotner, Louis Gorr, Charles A. Wood, Garth Sturdevan, Jack B. Hilliard, and Harry Foster.

I received valuable assistance from Miss Mathilde D. Williams, Curator of the Peabody Library Association of Georgetown; John T. Schlebecker, Curator of Agricultural History, Museum of History and Technology, Smithsonian Institution; Dr. Vivian Wiser, Historian, Department of Agriculture; Mrs. William Carl Bradshaw, Gunston Hall, Virginia; Miss Anne Fukua, Custis-Lee Mansion, Virginia; Lindsey Kay Thomas, National Park Service; Stuart M. Barnette, Cornell University, New York; Murray H. Nelligan, Historian, National Park Service, Philadelphia, Pa.; Wilford P. Cole, Keeper, Catalog of American Portraits, National Portrait Gallery, Smithsonian Institution.

[1] Figures 1, 2 and 3 show the Island in 1972, they were taken from Rosslyn Plaza, Rosslyn, Virginia, courtesy of Terry Dunnigan of Honeywell Inc.

[2] Figure 4 is the Robert King 1818 map of the Island, the driveway starts in the northern part of the Island closest to Georgetown.

A drawing with six contraband or Negro soldiers' quarters, two hospitals and other buildings on the Island is at the Cartographic Division, National Archives, RG 92 #24 Map 1 Seq. A, Records of the War Department, Office of the Quartermaster General, "Contraband Quarters Masons Island". The drawing is not dated and the camp's exact location on the Island is not specified.

evidence of more than a century of varied uses of the Island from the 1790's to about 1900. Additional evidence of the many uses of the land lies beneath the surface and can add to the written evidence

Author's photograph

Figure 1. May 1972 view of Theodore Roosevelt Island showing the visitor walkway in the middle of the island.

Author's photograph

Figure 2. May 1972 view of Theodore Roosevelt Island looking north to Georgetown. The old Causeway is not used for visitor access.

Author's photograph

Figure 3. May 1972 view of Theodore Roosevelt Island looking south. The Theodore Roosevelt Bridge crosses the southern tip of the Island.

about the Island's history. Because of the close connection with the social and cultural life of Georgetown and the District of Columbia after 1790, the Island's history deserves more attention than it has received.

In 1792 when John Mason inherited the Island it was a small part of a now lost Washington, a new city that for a long time was very rural with scattered mansion houses on large estates, and which had a shipping industry serving the needs of an agricultural area. The Island was a home for John Mason for about forty years until 1833.[3] It then became a recreation site, a commercial garden, a small Civil War camp site, and an athletic club and boating club site. The later uses could be more easily made of the Island because it had been highly cultivated and maintained by John Mason. Towards the end of the Nineteenth Century the Island became overgown with trees and brush and the buildings on the Island were deteriorated by weather, fire and neglect.[4]

In 1972 Theodore Roosevelt Island is a nature preserve of some eighty acres under the supervision of the National Capital Parks, National Park Service, Department of the Interior. It has planned nature trails and a memorial to President Theodore Roosevelt. In

---

[3] Robert A. Rutland, editor, *The Papers of George Mason 1725–1792*, three volumes (Chapel Hill, 1970), I, p. 153; George Mason gave his son John the island but it is not known exactly when John Mason began to live there.

[4] See Figure 8 for a 1906 view of Mason's home on the Island.

Theodore Roosevelt Island 17

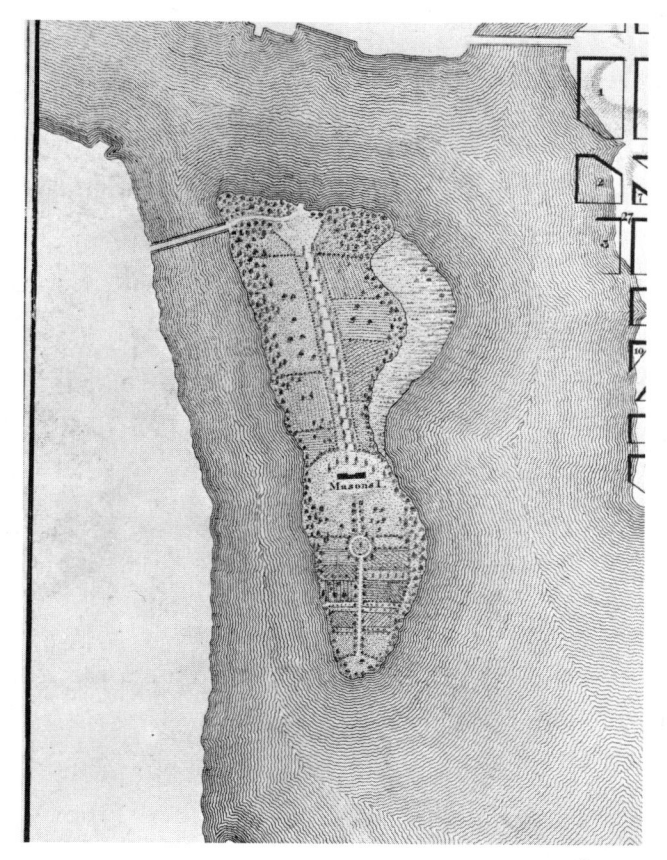

Library of Congress

Figure 4. Mason's Island from "A Map of the City of Washington in the District of Columbia" by Robert King, 1818. The causeway connects the northwestern part of the Island to the Virginia shore.

1967 the Roosevelt statue designed by Paul Manship and the memorial designed by Eric Gugler were officially dedicated and the Island was connected to the Virginia shore by a walkway from the middle of the Island.[5] The supervised planning of the Island's appearance had begun as early as the middle 1930's.[6]

The Theodore Roosevelt Memorial Association purchased the Island from the Washington Gas Light Company in 1931. The Island

---
[5] *Theodore Roosevelt Island, Washington, D.C.* (1969), one page brochure distributed by the National Park Service.
[6] Lindsey Kay Thomas, Jr., *Geomorphology and Vegetation of Theodore Roosevelt Island* (November, 1963), p. 2.

was then given to the Federal Government with the provision that it would be a memorial to Theodore Roosevelt.[7] In 1935 work was started to convert the Island into a nature preserve so that visitors could enjoy the type of outdoor beauty appreciated by Theodore Roosevelt.[8]

Despite the neglect and fire, John Mason's house's walls and several smaller buildings' walls survived until 1935. But to accomplish the Memorial Association's aims the ruins of his house were eradicated and all other signs of human habitation, including vegetation not native to the area, were removed.[9] Preserving the house site as a part of the District of Columbia's early cultural heritage was definitely not an aim of the Theodore Roosevelt Memorial Association, although Roosevelt's conservation interests could have justified preserving the ruins.[10]

Today, even with the documentation of John Mason's house it is impossible to be certain of the house site.[11] The excavation of his house ruins, thirty-five years of the wilderness preserve growing, and the crossing of Theodore Roosevelt Bridge effectively hide the house site. The ordinary visitor has no idea of where to look for Mason's home or how the Island appeared to early visitors to Washington, D.C.

The Island was first described by explorers who ventured up the Potomac River. One was Baron Christoph de Graffenried, a Swiss explorer and colonist who wrote a journal describing his travels in 1711. He depicted the future Roosevelt Island as "all cut out of rock, above it is a very fine and good soil, sufficient to support a whole family. Indians live there. One could make an impregnable fort of it." [12] The Island was of interest to early travelers for the same reason that Georgetown City developed as a trading center in the 1750's.

---

[7] *Theodore Roosevelt Island* (1969).

[8] "CCC Boys Transform Roosevelt Island From Jungle to Park" (*Washington Post* article, July 3, 1935), Roosevelt Memorial Folder, RG 66 Commission of Fine Arts 1910–1952 Project Files, Box 256, National Archives.

[9] Correspondence File on Roosevelt Island, RG 79 National Capital Parks, Box 608, National Archives.

[10] *Ibid.* August 14, 1936 letter to Canon Stokes from Hermann Hagedorn, Secretary of the Roosevelt Memorial Association. An attempt to preserve the house site was resolved by the Association's refusal to have Theodore Roosevelt share the Island with anyone. They believed to do so would detract from the visitors' impression of the wilderness preserve.

[11] Although the approximate site can be located by using the 1932 map (figure 10) both the 1970 American Studies class and later attempts in the winter of 1972 failed positively to locate the site.

[12] Quoted in *Georgetown Historic Waterfront, Washington, D.C.* (U.S. Commission of Fine Arts and the National Park Service, 1968), p. 8–9.

Its location below the Great Falls of the Potomac and near to Rock Creek made it a natural stopping point for exporting and importing goods. De Graffenried's mention of Indians living on the Island has been investigated recently in 1967 by Catholic University and in 1971 by American University.[13] Their archeological sites were in the northern part of the Island in the area closest to Georgetown, D.C.

Murray H. Nelligan, historian for the National Park Service, traced the early ownership of the Island through land records at the Maryland Hall of Records.[14] Captain Randolph Brandt owned the Island from 1682 until his death in 1698/99. Brandt was a soldier and an explorer who apparently knew of the Island from his military travels. In his will he left to his daughter Margaret, the wife of Francis Hammersley, the Island he had named "Barbadoes," near the falls of the Potomac River. In 1717 the Hammersley family deeded the Island to George Mason of Virginia.[15]

The Mason family owned the Island from 1717 to 1833. The Masons had been living in the colonies since the middle 1600's and had accumulated large land holdings in Virginia and in Maryland. They built mansion houses and were members of colonial upper class.[16] The Island presumably remained in its native state throughout the ownership of George Mason, statesman and builder of Gunston Hall. No mention of any improvements on the Island is made in his will, and his son John Mason who inherited it in 1792 appears to be the first to cultivate the land. After 1748 a ferry crossing the Potomac had been established on George Mason's property near the Island but it was not until more than fifty years later that a causeway was built from the Virginia shore to the Island and the ferry then crossed from the Island.[17]

By 1792 the city of Georgetown had been established across from the Island. The Island was considered even more valuable and interesting property because in 1790 it became part of the new Federal capital, the District of Columbia. It was in Washington County, District of Columbia.[18] The name of the Island was now Analostan or Mason's Island.

---

[13] Harvard G. Ayers, *Report of Archeological Testing of the Site TRI #1 on Theodore Roosevelt Island, Washington, D.C.* (1967).
Telephone conversation with Charles W. McNett, Jr. of The American University, Anthropology Department, January 1972.
[14] Murray H. Nelligan, *Analostan Island* (unpublished manuscript, 1950–51), pp. 5–15.
[15] Ibid., pp. 16–17.
[16] Kate Mason Rowland, *The Life of George Mason 1725–1792*, two volumes (New York, London, 1892), I, chapter I.
[17] Nelligan, p. 17.
[18] *The Agricultural Museum: Designed to be a Repository of Valuable Information to the Farmer and Manufacturer,* ... two volumes, (Georgetown, D.C., 1811/12), I, p. 12.

In 1792 John Mason was twenty-six years old. He had all the benefits of private schooling, contacts with the most prominent men of his time, and experience in the merchant business in France when he decided to buy property and settle in Georgetown.[19] He already owned the Island and land in what is now Rosslyn, Virginia from his father's estate. He was a businessman and a gentleman farmer. He owned a townhouse and a wharf in Georgetown, and he built and cultivated an estate and house on his Island close to Georgetown. The tax assessments for his property in Georgetown give a good idea of how wealthy he was. He was assessed an average of about $15,000.00 from the years 1800 to 1818 for his two story brick house, a warehouse and a wharf, furniture and some slaves.[20]

Several of John Mason's activities have been included in previous volumes of the *Records* of the Society.[21] He was a member of the social circle which included Dr. William Thornton, architect of the Capitol, and an associate of Presidents Jefferson, Madison and Monroe.[22] Appointed Brigadier-General of the Columbian Brigade of the Washington, D.C. Militia in 1802, he resigned in 1811. He became a Superintendent of Indian trade in 1811 and handled the furs that came into Georgetown from this trade. Later he was President of the Potomack Canal Company, and he was also the second President of the Bank of Columbia. In late 1815 he purchased Foxall Foundry from Henry Foxall. In the 1830's he was a vestryman of Christ Church in Alexandria, and he is buried with members of his family in the Christ Church burial ground off Wilkes Street in Alexandria. He and Anna Maria Murray of Annapolis were married in 1796 and had ten children, one of whom was U.S. Senator James Murray Mason.

John Mason's interest in the Columbian Agricultural Society of Washington, D.C. was closely related to his cultivation of the Island. In 1809 a letter was sent around the community promoting an agricultural society and the replies were sent to Mason.[23] The purpose

---

[19] Rowland, I, p. 97.

[20] City of Georgetown, Assessment of Real and Personal Property, Microcopy 605, rolls 7, 8, 9, 10, 11, National Archives.

[21] James F. Duhamel, "Analostan Island", *Records of the Columbia Historical Society*, 35/36 (1935); Frederick P. Todd, "The Militia and Volunteers of the District of Columbia 1783–1820", *Records of the Columbia Historical Society*, 50 (1948–1950); Mrs. Corra Bacon-Foster, "Early Chapters In the Development of the Potomac Route to The West", *Records*... 15 (1912). Louis Gorr's article in the 1971–1972 *Records*... has information about the foundry Mason purchased.

[22] "Diary of Mrs. William Thornton", *Records*... 10 (1907), p. 155, 169; *The Globe*, Washington, D.C. (newspaper) March 23, 1849, p. 4, obituary notice for General John Mason.

[23] Col. John F. Mercer to John Mason, Nov. 22, 1809, in Packet 6 "Clippings and Miscellaneous", Mason Family Papers, deposited by Philip Dawson, Manuscript Division, Library of Congress (on microfilm).

of agricultural societies was to improve agriculture and to encourage domestic manufactures. Mason was not only a member of the newly formed Columbian Agricultural Society but was a member of its standing committee in 1810 and in 1811, and a participant in the society's semi-annual exhibitions or fairs.

The Merino sheep "craze" of the first decade of the Nineteenth Century was one area that Mason specialized in. Merino sheep had much finer and longer wool than American sheep, and by breeding them farmers could produce fine woolens of their own and also encourage the increase of factories to weave the wool.[24] Evidence from family letters, from the Columbian Agricultural Society exhibitions, and from David Ballie Warden's chart of sheep fed on Analostan Island proves that Mason was raising Merino sheep on the Island at least during the years 1810 to 1812.

Warden's chart lists fifteen sheep of the Infantado, Paular, Viadillo, and Guadaloupe breeds.[25] Mason was breeding the sheep to sell as indicated in December 1810 when Henry Maynadier, a friend in Annapolis, wrote to report his progress in selling thirty ewes of Mason's.[26] Mason's participation in the agricultural exhibitions helped to establish his reputation as a successful sheep breeder. At the May 15, 1811 exhibition held at the property of Thomas Beall, he won first prize: "Premium 1—to the value of sixty dollars; for the best two tooth ram lamb of the fine wooled breed; adjudged to General John Mason, of Analostan Island, District of Columbia, for his seven-eighths blooded merino ram, Potomac Chief, of the breed of Col. Humphrey's flock." [27] At the May 1812 exhibition he maintained his reputation by winning first prize with another fine wooled lamb named Golden Fleece.[28]

During the life of the Columbian Agricultural Society, Mrs. John Mason also exhibited successfully at its fairs. In May 1810 she won two prizes, one was "Premium 6, for the best piece of cotton cloth suitable for pantalons or small clothes, not less than ten yards. Adjudged to Mrs. Anna M. Mason of Analostan Island, Washington county, District of Columbia" and the other was for the best piece of hempen or flaxen table linen.[29] At the November 1810 fair she again won

[24] P. W. Bidwell and J. I. Falconer, *History of Agriculture in the Northern United States 1620–1860* (Washington, D.C.?, 1925), pp. 217–220.

[25] David Ballie Warden, *A Chorographical and Statistical Description of the District of Columbia,* . . . (Paris, 1816), after p. 151.

[26] Col. Henry Maynadier to General John Mason, December 1, 1810, George Mason Family Papers, 1791–1850, 21 pieces mainly by or relating to John Mason, Manuscript Division, Library of Congress.

[27] *The Agricultural Museum,* I, p. 366.
[28] *The Agricultural Museum,* II, p. 325.
[29] *The Agricultural Museum,* I, p. 12.

for the "best pair of woven stockings of cotton or thread, full size."[30] The credit for winning does belong to her or to the Mason family since the constitution of the Columbian Agricultural Society specified that "no person shall be allowed to exhibit any article for premium unless it has been raised, grown, or made in some County of this District, or of the adjoining states, in which there shall reside at least one member of this Society, or any article for which a public premium shall have previously been given" and that "no premium shall be given for any articles of manufacture which have not been either spun or woven in the families from which they may be exhibited, and which have not been both spun and woven in this district or the adjoining states".[31]

The agricultural fairs were also social events which were enjoyed as such by the Masons as well as for the opportunities the fairs provided to display products of their Island farm.[32]

No doubt the Mason family's greatest agricultural success was the cultivation of Analostan Island into a showplace. In 1796, the year that John and Anna married, David Hepburn, a gardener, was employed. He worked on Analostan Island for six years and was given credit by Mason for all the improvements on the Island.[33] Hepburn was especially praised for his excellence in culinary and fruit growing.

The pleasing results of the Masons' interest and the gardener's work can be seen from comments made by travel journalists, from the descriptions by authors of guide books, from David Ballie Warden's chapter on the Island, from letters and from maps. The most famous map of the Island is the 1818 Robert King map. (See Figure 4.) The driveway, the fields, and the planned gardens are evidence of how cultivated the Island was. In the middle 1820's Anne Royall, a travel journalist, visited the Island and recorded her impressions. She pinpoints the flower and culinary gardens in the southern part of the Island and said that the northern part which contained the most land had an orchard and some tillable land.[34] About the gardens in the southern part she says, "that part adjacent to the house is appropriated to flowers, shrubs, grapes, and every rare plant, consisting

---

[30] *The Agricultural Museum,* I, p. 172.

[31] *The Agricultural Museum,* I, p. 10.

[32] *Report of the Commissioner of Agriculture for the Year 1866.* (Washington, D.C., 1867), pp. 518–522 describe the Columbian Agricultural Society meetings as reported in the *National Intelligencer.*

[33] John Gardiner and David Hepburn, *The American Gardener* (Washington, D.C., 1804), after p. 204, John Mason's testimony of the skill of the late David Hepburn.

[34] Mrs. Anne Royall, *The Black Book or A Continuation of Travels in the United States,* two volumes, (Washington, D.C., 1828), I, pp. 272–275.

of the various species of the four quarters of the globe. A great part of garden, some acres, consists of culinary vegetables. A row of trees leading down to the river divided the garden".[35] Her enthusiastic remarks about the flowers, shrubs, the broad straight walks, and the exact level squares of the southern gardens prove that the Island was as it appears in Robert King's map.

David Ballie Warden described the Island in the year 1811, a few years before the 1818 map and Anne Royall's visit. He observed that the blossoms of cherry, apple and peach trees, of hawthorn and aromatic shrubs, filled the air with fragrance; and that Virginia jessamine, poison-oak, several species of asclepias and sassafras trees grew well on the Island. An activity noted by Warden and one that probably tied in with Mason's interest in the agricultural exhibitions was that he cultivated a species of maize which was used as a purple dye, and that he also grew for the use of his family a species of cotton of the color of nankeen.[36]

Some of the plants on the Island came as gifts. J. W. Thomas of West River wrote to John Mason that he had heard "Mrs. Mason is desirous of some shrubs to plant on the island, and that the double blossoming almond would be acceptable." He sent some by a servant.[37]

Several early visitors to Georgetown and to Washington, D.C. wrote down their views of the Island estate. One of them, John Davis reported in July 1801 that "Mason's Island forms one continued garden." [38]

Descriptions of the Island in 1830 and 1835 guide books give some additional details about the buildings on the Island.[39] These sources together with the maps show that the house was at the end of long driveway, in the southern part of the Island, and at the highest point. An early watercolor picture of the mansion house gives an alluring view of the front of the house in its prime. (See Figure 5.)

The Island was lost by the Mason family in 1833. As early as 1826 the Island was used for security against a debt of $28,560.00. The

---

[35] Royall.
[36] Warden, pp. 134–151.
[37] J. W. Thomas to John Mason, March 23, 1803, "More or Less Official Papers Pertaining to Gen. John Mason", Mason Family Papers, Library of Congress (microfilm).
[38] John Davis, *Travels of Four Years and a Half in the U.S. of North America, 1798, 1799, 1801 and 1802*, included in *The District in the XVIIIth Century* . . . (1909), pp. 337–339.
[39] Jonathan Elliott, *Historical Sketches of the Ten Mile Square forming the District of Columbia* (1830), pp. 288–289, Mason's Island; Joseph Martin, *A New and Comprehensive Gazeteer of Virginia and the District of Columbia* (Charlottesville, Va., 1835), p. 494, "Annalostan Island."

Library of Congress

Figure 5. Early watercolor of John Mason's house. Original owned by descendants of the Mason family. Written evidence and archeological remains indicate that the house was built between 1792 and 1800.

terms of the Deed of Trust allowed the Masons to continue to live on the Island, but in 1833 it went to the Bank of the United States.[40] Losing the Island must have been a disappointment to the man who had cultivated it from the time he was in his late twenties to his sixty-seventh year, and who was well known as General John Mason of Analostan Island. But he continued to enjoy agricultural pursuits on his estate Clermont in Fairfax county, Virginia, until he died in 1849.[41]

When the Masons left the Island it was rented for recreational activities.[42] In 1838 the Bank of the United States put it in trust to Richard Smith who was holding the property for Clement Smith, William S. Nicholls, John Kurtz, John Carter, William Jewell, William W. Corcoran, Samuel Swartwont, Dudley Seldon, Elisha Riggs, Walter Mead, John S, and John Wheelright who were "tenants in

---

[40] Liber W.B. No. 16 (1825–1826) Deed of Trust recorded 31st March, 1826, John Mason to Richard Smith (Bank of the United States), p. 302 old, p. 233 new; Liber W.B. No. 46 (1833) Deed from John Mason and Wife to Bank of the United States, recorded June 18, 1833, p. 84. Recorder of Deeds, 6th and D Streets, N.W., Washington, D.C.

[41] Book W 1, April 1849, pp. 66–78, Inventory of the estate of General John Mason, Fairfax County Courthouse, Fairfax, Virginia.

[42] *National Intelligencer*, July 22, 24, 25, 30th, 1834, notice of a balloon ascension from "Analostin Gardens" (Mason's Island) on Wednesday, July 30th.

common".[43] One of the tenants, John Carter, purchased the Island in 1842 for $8,600.00.[44] Before buying the Island Carter made an agreement with Alexander Garden "to cultivate jointly Analostan Island." [45] It was a commercial venture which was still in existence in 1850 when Carter died. According to the December 1841 agreement, Garden lived on the Island and contributed provisions for the workers employed to cultivate the land. This commercial gardening consisted of four hundred peach trees, one hundred and fifty rose bushes, and asparagus, parsnips, carrots, cabbages, and rhubarb.[46]

After Carter's death, William A. Bradley bought the Island in 1852 for $2,571.50.[47] Bradley apparently added a building to the west shore of the Island as maps of this time have his name beside the structure.[48] He rented the Island for commercial gardening according to Jacob W. Powers, one of his tenants from 1859 to 1863. Powers reported that the Island usually rented for $900 to $1,000 a year since it was used for agricultural purposes. His arrangements with Bradley allowed lower rent because he was to spend his money for improvements to make the Island into a resort place. The Island under Powers contained "about eighty acres of land susceptible of cultivation and most of it under cultivation. The buildings consist of the 'Mansion House', out houses, cellars, ice house, barn and stables".[49] His money was spent making repairs to the mansion house and several other buildings, building a dancing saloon, and two wharves, one on the north end and one on the east side of the Island. He also trimmed the fruit and ornamental trees and the shrubbery and put the grounds in order.[50]

Unfortunately for Powers, in May 1861 the Island was occupied by the United States Army. They left in May 1862 but returned a few months later in September 1862 and were there at least through the Summer of 1863.[51] The Commissary department and a camp of Negro

[43] Liber W.B. No. 67 (1838), p. 42–62, Bank of the U.S. to Richard Smith, Trustee, Recorder of Deeds, D.C.
[44] Liber W.B. No. 95 (1842), p. 145 old, p. 107 new, Richard Smith and Wm. S. Nicholls to John Carter, Deed recorded Sept. 17, 1842, Recorder of Deeds, D.C.
[45] Estate of John Carter. No. 3084 Old Series. Suitland Records Center, Md., contains the 1841 agreement between Garden and Carter, an 1852 appraisal of improvements on the Island, and the 1852 sale of Analostan to W. A. Bradley.
[46] *Ibid.*
[47] *Ibid.* and see Maud Burr Morris, "William A. Bradley...", *Records of the Columbia Historical Society*, 25 (1923).
[48] A. Boschke map, p. 19, Figure 11 in Thomas, op. cit.
[49] March 5, 1863 affidavit by Jacob W. Powers, Analostan Island, D.C., Quartermaster Consolidated File, Office of the Quartermaster General, RG 92, National Archives.
[50] *Ibid.* September 26, 1863 affidavit of Jacob W. Powers.
[51] *Ibid.* June 18, 1863 letter.

soldiers were the second occupants. Damage was done to the Island by a number of cattle which fed on Powers' crops or otherwise destroyed them. The stone walls serving as enclosures around the Island were torn down by the Army to construct landing places.[52] In the spring of 1863 Powers lost his lease to the Island because he could not pay the rent. He was depending upon money from the Island's use as a resort area and as a commercial garden.

Bradley bought back the unusued portion of Powers' five-year lease, but he tried to rent the Island again while arguing with the Government for back rent payments and damages. When Bradley died in 1867 he still owned the Island and his estate included some bills to be paid for lumber and shingles which had been sent to the Island.[53]

An 1871 map of the Island (see Figure 6) shows both the driveway and Mason's house still existing. Small buildings to the left of the house may have been the out houses, gardener's house, stables, and barn mentioned by Powers. Another shorter driveway leads to Bradley's building. The Island is cleared in the northern section but the planned gardens seen south of the Mason house in 1818 have disappeared.

Sometime after Bradley's death the Columbian Athletic Club leased the Island to use as a practice area.[54] It had ball fields, tennis courts, a running track and a grandstand on the Island but left in 1892.[55] In the 1880's or early 1890's a photograph was made of the Mason house (see Figure 7). The portico seen in the much earlier watercolor was by now destroyed although its platform remained. The windows and chimney appear very similar to the early picture.

After 1892 the Analostan Boat Club used the Island but the house was suffering from age and neglect. Burned trees around the house indicate that a fire extensively damaged the mansion about 1906. (See Figure 8.)

From 1913 to 1931 the Washington Gas Light Company owned the Island. It was no longer cultivated and trees and plants grew wild. By the 1930's the remaining house walls were in a tangle of trees and underbrush. (See Figure 9.)

---

[52] *Ibid.* March 24, 1862 letter.

[53] Estate of William A. Bradley, No. 5530 Old Series. Suitland Records Center, Maryland; Wills NO. 10, Nov. 3, 1864 to Sept. 7, 1867, p. 475 for will of W. A. Bradley, written August 7, 1866, recorded September 3, 1867, Suitland Records Center, Md.

[54] Edith M. Sprouse, *A History of Theodore Roosevelt Island* (unpublished manuscript, Catholic University of America, 1967), p. 12, reports that the athletic club did not lease the Island until 1889.

[55] James Franklin Hood, "The Cottage of David Burnes and Its Dining-Room Mantel", *Records of the Columbia Historical Society*, 23 (1920), p. 5.

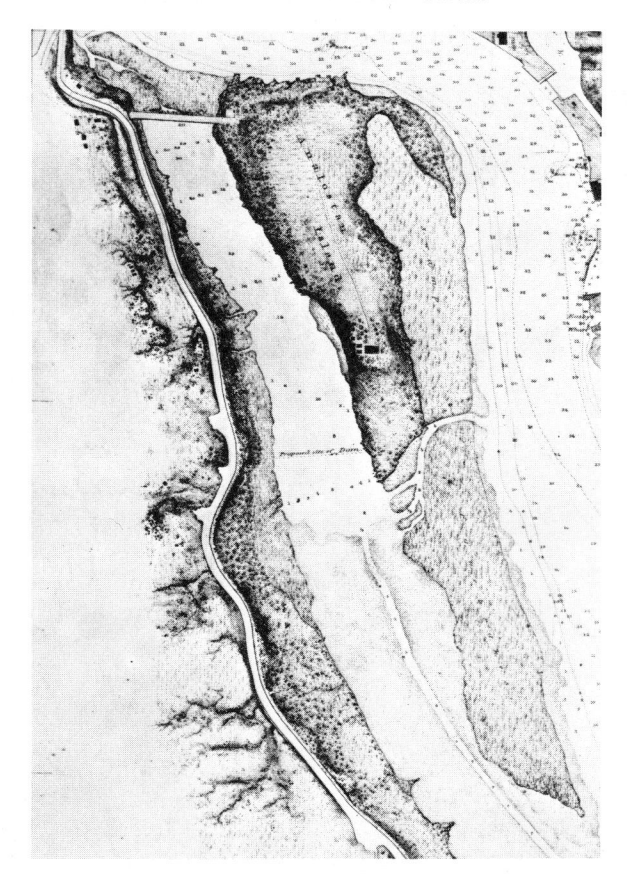

Library of Congress

Figure 6. Analostan Island from "Hydrographic Map of the Potomac River from Aqueduct Bridge, Georgetown to Long Bridge, Washington, D. C." by Major William P. Craighill, Corps of Engineers, United States Army, 1871.

In spite of the uncontrolled growth of vegetation, the walls and foundations of both the mansion house and several smaller buildings to the west or Virginia side survived as is shown in an interesting 1932 map. (See Figure 10). This map gives the land elevations and trees on the Island and locates the ruins of the mansion.

In March 1935 a camp of Civilian Conservation Corps youths who were staying nearby in Virginia started clearing the Island. It was described then as an "almost impenetrable jungle".[56] Their activi-

---
[56] "CCC Boys Transform Roosevelt Island...", RG 66, National Archives.

Library of Congress

Figure 7. Photograph of John Mason's house from the north, about 1880–1890.

National Archives

Figure 8. Photograph of John Mason's house from the north, about 1906.

ties revealed a hermit who had been quietly living there for six years.[57] Dead trees and underbrush were removed by the C.C.C. and also vegetation that was not suitable for the aim of a "climax forest".[58]

[57] *Ibid.*
[58] *Ibid.*; Thomas, p. 2.

Theodore Roosevelt Island 29

Library of Congress

Figure 9. Photograph of west wing of John Mason's house from the north, about 1936.

A climax forest would be the result of centuries of undisturbed growth. The human additions to the Island interfered with this plan and so orchard trees, box elders, and building remains were eliminated.[59]

In the spring of 1936 it was decided that work on the Mason house ruins must be finished by the end of August. This decision allowed only twelve weeks for Stuart M. Barnette, an architect in the National Park Service, and the C.C.C. to explore, excavate, and record General Mason's house.[60] Numerous photographs were taken of the walls, basements, house trim, and of special features such as a dutch oven, windows, steps and artifacts found with their excavations. Brick walkways, a well and out buildings were also revealed, all of which today exist only in photographs.[61] The pictures show an interesting early Washington, D.C. architecture, and give a brief glimpse of a wealthy early Washingtonian's style of living.

The artifacts found that summer included eyeglasses, chinaware, and house materials such as nails, locks, hinges, and tie bars. (See Figure 11.) No doubt due to the time allowed, shovels were used on

---
[59] Thomas, p. 2.
[60] May 22, 1936 Memorandum to Mr. Chatelain, Central Classified File 1933–1949, Box 608, RG 79 National Capital Parks, National Archives.
[61] *Historic American Buildings Survey, Washington, D.C. 131,* Prints and Photographs Division, Library of Congress.

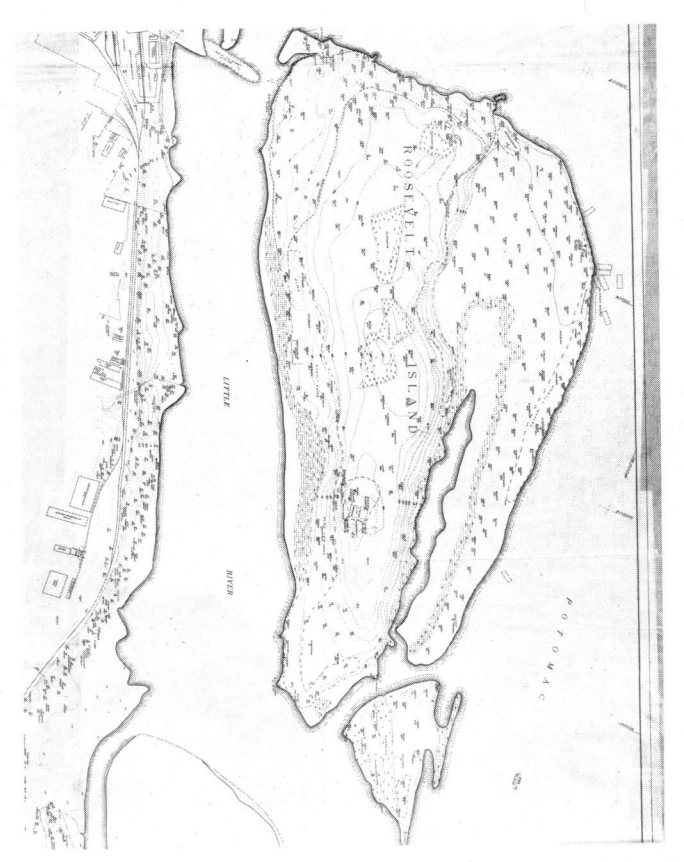

National Archives

Figure 10. "Roosevelt Island and Virginia Shore Topographical Survey," 1932, showing elevations, trees and remains of buildings.

the site and then wheelbarrows of dirt were screened to find artifacts.[62] Their relationship to other artifacts was not determined. But the final resting place for the artifacts in Figure 11 is not on a museum shelf but burial close to the now vanished house site.[63]

Despite the loss to comparative historical archeology these artifacts assure that a trace of John Mason's home will be on the Island he once cultivated into a charming environment.

When the excavation of the house ruins was finished and more clearing done, about 25,000 to 33,000 trees were planted on the Is-

---
[62] *Ibid.*
[63] May 1972 letter from Stuart M. Barnette to the author, to the best of his knowledge the artifacts were buried but he was not present to witness it.

Figure 11. Artifacts found in ruins of John Mason's house, 1936.

land.[64] With the climax forest planted the only other major changes to the Island have been the crossing over the southern tip by the Theodore Roosevelt Bridge which was started in 1959, and the addition of a formal memorial to Theodore Roosevelt in the northern part. Work started on the memorial in 1963 and was completed in 1967.

New evidence of John Mason's home on the Island was found in the spring of 1970 by a graduate class in the American Studies Program of the Smithsonian Institution. The students worked under the general guidance of Wilcomb E. Washburn and under the direct supervision of Harold K. Skramstad. Permission was received from the National Park Service to do an archeological project in the vicinity of the Mason house. Class members each did historical research on some aspect of the Island's history or on John Mason's life to complement written and physical evidence.

The site chosen was on the Virginia side of the Island and down a hillside from the approximate site of the smaller buildings seen in the 1932 and 1871 maps. A ten foot square area was carefully excavated with trowels. The artifacts were placed in bags giving the level where they were found and were later washed and labeled by Mrs. Gail Kassan, a class member who also put many pottery fragments together. The artifacts are the property of the National Park

---

[64] Thomas, p. 2.

32   Records of the Columbia Historical Society

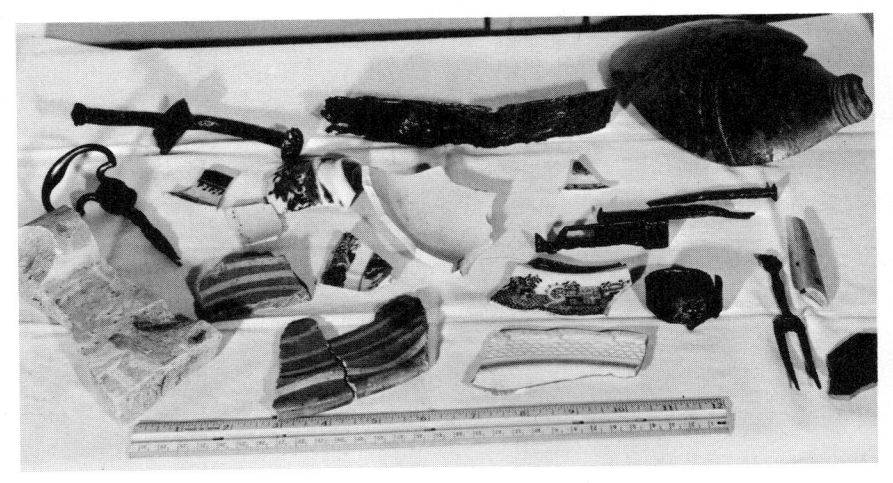

Author's Photograph

Figure 12. Artifacts found on Theodore Roosevelt Island, 1970, by the American Studies Class, Smithsonian Institution.

Service but are being studied by Robert H. McNulty, one of the archeological consultants for the class.

A great variety of objects was discovered. (See Figure 12.) Fragments of an earthenware plate made in Alexandria by Henry Piercy between 1790 and 1800 were found.[65] A Mediterranean import of earthenware with a yellowish-green glaze,[66] a two pronged fork and one half of its bone handle, and many fragments of pearlware, creamware, porcelain, nails, glass, and stoneware were uncovered. One stoneware fragment had what may be an "M" on it. The artifacts date from the late Eighteenth Century to the middle Nineteenth Century.

Since the objects were found with many pieces of pig and cow bones[67] and with kitchenware fragments, it is possible that the hillside examined was a dumping ground for one of the smaller buildings and thus the 1970 site contained an original trash pit from Mason's time.

The 1970 artifacts are valuable for comparative historical archeology. Comparisons can be made with artifacts found in port towns such as Alexandria and Annapolis to establish more precise trade

---

[65] Identified by Richard Muzzrole of the Alexandria Archeological Project.

[66] Identified by Ivor Noël Hume of Colonial Williamsburg, information courtesy of Harold K. Skramstad.

[67] Identified by John Paradiso, Museum of Natural History, Smithsonian Institution.

patterns, and for information about early local craftsmen such as Henry Piercy of Alexandria.

More significant for Washington, D.C. history, the artifacts are tangible proof of John Mason's vanished early American home on Analostan and add to the fascinating record of the Island as it has journeyed in time from wilderness to cultivation and back to wilderness.

The Foxall-Columbia Foundry: An Early Defense Contractor in Georgetown

LOUIS F. GORR

The Foxall-Columbia Foundry in Georgetown was once one of the most important industries in the District of Columbia and was among the earliest members of young America's infant "military-industrial complex." The foundry was active from 1800 to 1854, a time punctuated by two major wars, a multitude of frontier Indian battles, and the establishment of a modern military bureaucracy. It began by supplying the Federal government with high-quality ordnance. From 1800 to 1809 it was the sole supplier of outstanding government guns. In 1809 it was joined by the Richmond Foundry, and later by the Bellona Foundry of Powhatan County, Virginia, the West Point Foundry of Cold Spring, New York, the Fort Pitt Foundry of Pittsburgh, Pennsylvania, and the Alger Foundry of Boston, Massachusetts.[1] It ended as an enterprise gone sour.

Nothing remains of the foundry. Its site on the bank of the Potomac River near the Three Sisters is a densely wooded arbor concealing scattered slag deposits and several ruined foundations. The

---

Delivered before the Columbia Historical Society on April 18, 1972.

Thanks are due to my colleagues at the Smithsonian Institution who offered assistance during the course of research. Mathilda D. Williams, Curator of the Peabody Library Association of Georgetown, helped to find material on the site of the foundry. The staff of the National Archives cannot be praised enough for their customary extraordinary assistance.

[1] But there were several other, smaller foundries already casting when Foxall began operations in Georgetown. One of the most well-known was the Principio Iron Company of Cecil County, Maryland. Another was Samuel Hughes' Mont Alto foundry and furnace in Pennsylvania. The Principio was inadequate for the government's purposes. John Clarke, returning from a visit to Foxall's Eagle Iron Works in 1798, visited the Principio and reported that the foundry was "...so badly planned, so temporarily built, and the guns so badly made." *Calendar of Virginia State Papers*, VIII, 456, quoted in Kathleen Bruce, *Virginia Iron Manufacture in the Slave Era* (New York: The Century Co., 1931), p. 114. The story seems to have been the same for the other foundries left over from the Revolutionary era.

The Foxall-Columbia Foundry

records of the foundry have suffered the same fate, having been destroyed or dispersed, and comparatively few government documents survive. Most of the history of the foundry remains unfortunately obscure.[2] But it played such a unique role in early American military history that its own history needs to be written. Just enough survives today to piece together a profile of the Foxall-Columbia Foundry. The profile, while necessarily incomplete, reveals an enterprise based on military contracts begun as a noble and patriotic endeavor, continued as a profitable business, and terminated as a failure.

The foundry passed through three periods in its life. From 1800 to 1815 it was variously known as the Foxall Foundry after its owner and operator, Henry Foxall, and as the Columbia Foundry after its proximity to the District of Columbia. John Mason purchased the foundry in 1815 and operated it until his death in 1849; from 1816 it was known exclusively as the Columbia Foundry.[3] The final period was an ignominious one of five years from 1849 to 1854; during that time it was operated by Mason's son and executor, James Maynadier Mason. The foundry flourished from 1800 to about 1840 and began to die during the early 1840's. The first half of its life was one of progress and ingenuity. The second half was one of misjudgement and technological lag.

When the United States government moved in 1800 from Philadelphia to Washington, Henry Foxall was asked to move with it. Foxall, a prominent English iron-founder and entrepreneur, was owner of the Eagle Iron Works on the Sckuylkill River in Philadelphia. There he cast a few cannon for the Federal government but devoted most of his work to the casting of stoves, agricultural im-

---

[2] The early years of the foundry were treated by Madison Davis in "The Old Cannon Foundry Above Georgetown, D.C., and its First Owner, Henry Foxall," *Records of the Columbia Historical Society*, XI (1908), 16–70, but his emphasis was on the life of Foxall and the building of Foundry Church in Washington. Otherwise, information about the foundry is sparse. The conclusions made in this article have been based largely on data uncovered in the collections of the National Archives. Material relevant to the Foxall-Columbia Foundry has been found in the following records groups: RG45, Naval Records Collection of the Office of Naval Records and Library; RG46, Records of the House of Representatives; RG79, Records of the National Park Service; RG92, Records of the Office of the Quartermaster General; RG98, Records of the United States Army Commands, 1784–1821; RG156, Records of the Office of the Chief of Ordnance; RG217, Records of the United States General Accounting Office; RG393, Records of the United States Army Continental Commands, 1821–1920.

[3] It was occasionally called the "Columbia Foundry" prior to 1816, but beginning in that year the name is used exclusively. From 1800 to 1815 the name "Foxall Foundry" was the most frequently used. Occasionally it was known by its corporate name, "Henry Foxall & Co., Georgetown."

plements, and other iron objects. Foxall had earned a reputation for superior workmanship, and in 1800 he moved to Georgetown at the personal request of Thomas Jefferson. The new foundry was to be devoted exclusively to the casting of cannon, shot, and carriages for the War and Navy Departments. The new foundry was one of the largest in the nation and for several years received nearly every government contract for ordnance. Undoubtedly Foxall kept abreast of the latest European improvements in iron working. His foundry likely exhibited great modernity and used the best equipment available. Foxall himself designed and supervised the construction of the entire facility. Other founders, including those with an eye to sharing the lucrative government business, visited Foxall on a regular basis; he hosted several potential competitors at the foundry. John Clarke of Virginia visited him in 1801 and asked for assistance in establishing a similar foundry in Richmond. Foxall accommodated the request by designing the buildings for Clarke and suggesting the machines that should be installed. Clarke's enterprise became the Richmond Foundry and for a few years shared the military contracts with his consultant.[4]

In its simplest form a cannon foundry consisted of the following operations: First the pig iron from the ore field was blasted into molten form in a special furnace. The liquid metal ran from the blast furnace into molds in a sand floor. After hardening the molds were then smoothed and polished. During the Revolution cannon were cast around a core in the mold so that a hollow tube would result. Henry Foxall, however, followed the latest European practice of casting into a solid mold and boring the cannon with a special machine. Peter Verbrugger in Holland and John Wilkinson in England had devised machines to bore cannon in the 1770's and 1780's, and Foxall was one of the earliest founders in America to use them. (See figures 1, 2.) Cannon made in that fashion were much more accurate than the hollow-cast pieces. Foxall was a pioneer in using boring machines to make cannon, and when other foundries were begun they also used boring machines. Boring remained the chief means of making cannon until Thomas Rodman invented a new way of casting in the 1840's.

The Foxall Foundry cast all kinds of ordnance. Ordnance in the period from 1800 to 1815 was made exclusively of iron[5] and was

---

[4] *Calendar of Virginia State Papers*, IX, 237, 241-3. Quoted in Bruce, *Virginia Iron Manufacture in the Slave Era*, p. 116.

[5] Bronze, an alloy of copper and tin, was generally used for the very best cannon until about 1801 when the Secretary of War, Henry Dearborn, ordered all cannon to be

Reproduction from the Smithsonian Institution

Figure 1. Boring machine made by John Wilkinson in 1774.

Henry Foxall most likely used boring machines similar to this one made by John Wilkinson in 1774. Wilkinson was the leading English iron worker of the Eighteenth Century and applied for a patent covering a "New Method of Casting and Boring Iron Guns or Cannon" shown here. It was based on a similar design by Peter Verbruggen in 1772. From L. T. C. Rolt, *A Short History of Machine Tools* (Cambridge, Mass.: The MIT Press, 1965).

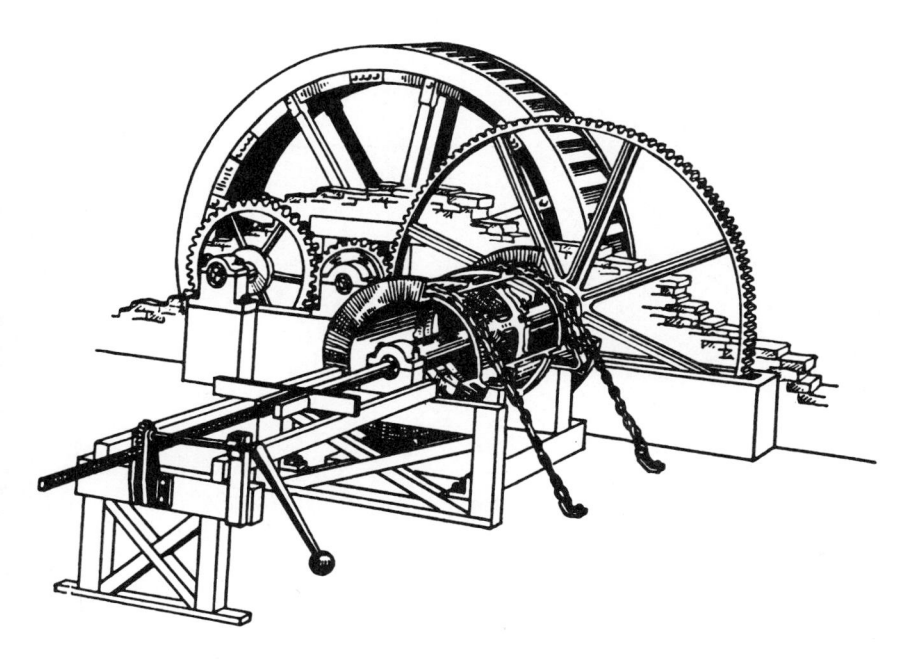

Reproduction from the Smithsonian Institution

Figure 2. Water power operated boring machine.

John Wilkinson designed a cylinder-boring machine which could be adapted to cannon boring. Like the Foxall machinery, this machine operated by water power. From L. T. C. Rolt, *A Short History of Machine Tools* (Cambridge, Mass.: The MIT Press, 1965).

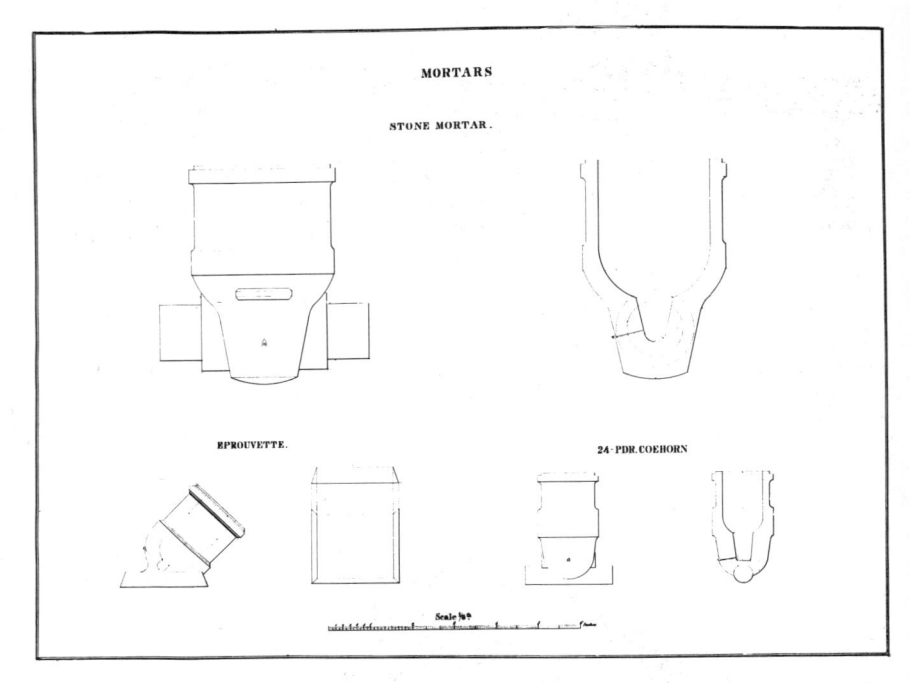

Reproduction from the Smithsonian Institution

Figure 3. Mortars.

Figures 3, 4, 5, 6, 7 and 8 are examples of ordnance and ammunition cast at the Foxall-Columbia Foundry. These scale drawings were made by Louis de Tousard in his *American Artillerists' Companion, or Elements of Artillery: Treating of All Kinds of Firearms in Detail, and of the Formation, Object, and Service of the Flying or Horse, Artillery, Preceded by an Introductory Dissertation on Cannon*, 3 volumes (Philadelphia: Bradford and Inskeep, 1813).

of two major categories—field artillery and seacoast artillery. The old nomenclature of seige-guns and garrison-guns was abandoned for several years.[6] The first category consisted of light cannon with portability and maneuvreability: 6- and 12-pounder cannon, 8- and 10-inch light mortars on carriages, 24-pounder Coehorn assault mor-

cast in iron. Bronze had to be imported from Europe and was expensive. Iron was an abundant native material and could be obtained in both quantity and quality. It is likely that Foxall relied on the best iron available nearby, which would have been from the Virginia sources of Rockbridge and Botecourt Counties and the Cowpasture River Valley. He may also have obtained iron from the Catoctin region in Maryland. Ironmakers in those regions had a reputation for producing the "toughest dark grey pig iron" obtainable anywhere. Pig iron from the Virginia iron fields was used as far away as New York state. According to a contemporary account in the *Richmond Courier* and carried in *Niles' Register*, XLVIII, 364.

[6] Harold L. Peterson, *Round Shot and Rammers* (Harrisburg, Pa.: Stackpole Books, 1969), p. 74.

The Foxall-Columbia Foundry

SEA COAST 42-POUNDER GUN.

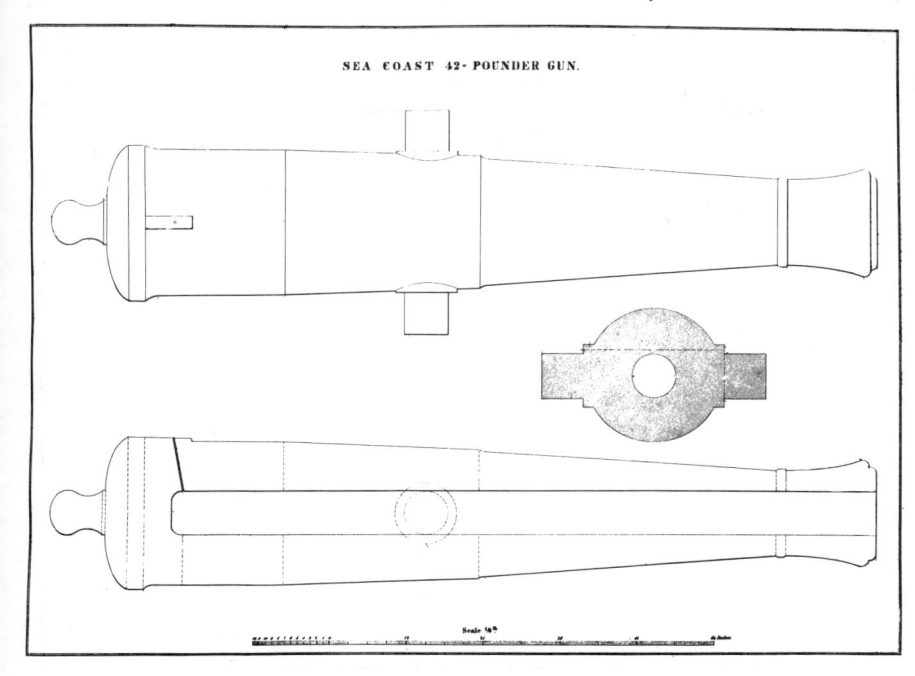

Reproduction from the Smithsonian Institution

Figure 4. Sea Coast 42-Pounder Gun.

tars, and occasionally 18- and 24-pounder battering howitzers. Seacoast artillery was heavy and designed for permanence. It included 18-, 24-, 32-, and 42-pounder cannon and the same weight howitzers, 10- and 13-inch heavy mortars, and 50- and 100-pounder Columbiads.[7]

---

[7] "Pounder" refers to the weight of its cannonball. Cannon and other ordnance fired either solid balls or hollow shells; balls were used for breaking walls of forts or hulls of ships while shells exploded spreading incendiary or fragmentation pieces. Cannon were intended for long-range firing, howitzers for short-range, and mortars for lofting. Columbiads were the most powerful of all and could fire a ball or shell as far as three miles. For convenience I have used the generic terms "cannon" and "ordnance" to include the various kinds of howitzers, mortars, and cannon. For students of the period's artillery there is the continuing enigma of the "Columbiad," a cannon cast in 50- and 100-pounder (and occasionally larger) sizes. The Columbiad was the first heavy shell-firing gun employed by the United States Army. It was invented by George Bomford, who later became Chief of Ordnance, about 1812, according to Wingate Reed, "Decius Wadsworth, First Chief of Ordnance, 1812–1821," *Army Ordnance*, XXV, (1943), 114–16. Some say that the cannon took its name from Joel Barlow's 1807 epic poem, *The Columbiad*. Others suggest that it derived from the foundry at which it was cast, Henry Foxall's. One such view is that of the British observer, William James, in his *Full and Correct Account of the Chief Naval Occurrences of the Late War Between Great Britain and the United States of America* ... (London: Printed for T. Edgerton, 1817), p. 5. A good survey of the Columbiad question is in Emanuel Raymond Lewis, "The Ambiguous Columbiads," *Military Affairs*, XXVIII (1964), 111–22.

SEA COAST 8-INCH HOWITZER.

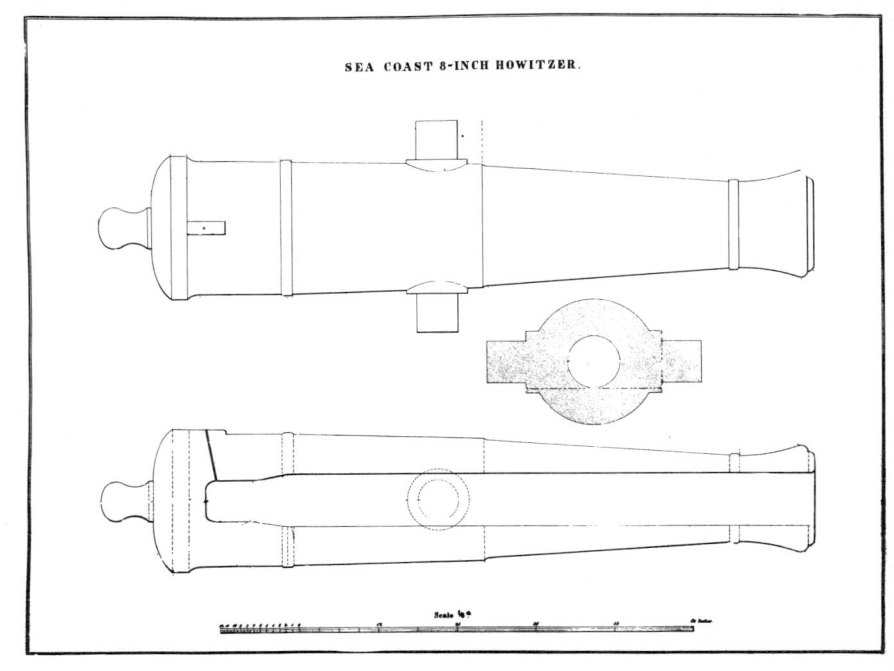

Reproduction from the Smithsonian Institution

Figure 5. Sea Coast 8-Inch Howitzer.

(See figures 3–8 for examples.) The classification of ordnance between 1800 and 1840 was noted for its disorder and confusion. In 1818 the Secretary of War, John C. Calhoun, initiated a new classification consisting of field, siege-and-garrison, and seacoast artillery.[8] But it was not until 1841 that a fully detailed and organized system of classification of American artillery was undertaken.[9] Henry Foxall, and later John Mason, apparently was not affected by the confusion in artillery nomenclature—he cast every description of weapon for both the War and the Navy Departments.

---

[8] Maurice Matloff (ed.), *American Military History* (Washington, D.C.: Government Printing Office for the Office of the Chief of Military History, 1969), p. 156.

[9] In 1840–41 Captain Alfred Mordecai of the Ordnance Department began to work on his official guide ordered by the Ordnance Department, *Artillery for the Land Service of the United States, as Devised and Arranged by the Ordnance Board* (Philadelphia: J. B. Gideon, 1849). This guide fully classified the ordnance of the United States Army and was used as the official ordnance manual. Earlier guides, such as the Army's *American Artillerist's Companion* ... (Philadelphia: Bradford and Inskeep, 1813), by Louis de Tousard, and the Navy's *Marshall's Practical Marine Gunnery* ... (Norfolk, Va.: C. Hall, 1822), by George Marshall, were not nearly so detailed and comprehensive.

The Foxall-Columbia Foundry

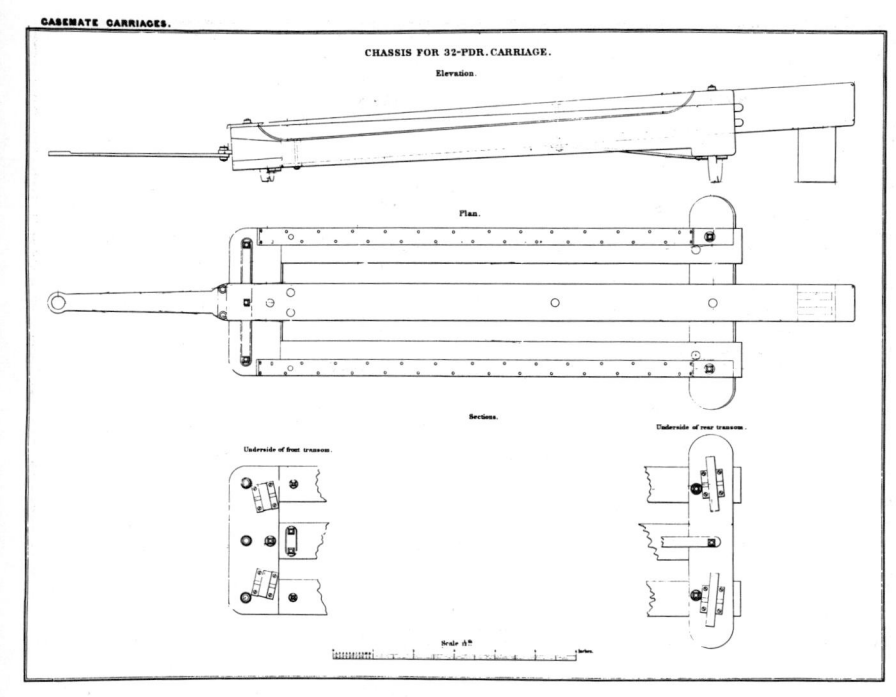

Reproduction from the Smithsonian Institution

Figure 6. Chassis for 32-Pounder Carriage.

In the beginning the Foxall Foundry was not large, but it was efficient and modern. An 1803 map of the Potomac River includes a cross-section of the foundry site and shows it as consisting of a blast furnace, a boring mill, and three unidentified buildings.[10] (See figure 9.) The boring mill made the foundry modern. The location made it efficient. The Potomac River afforded a waterway by which to obtain iron ore and to ship the finished weapons. The nearby town of Georgetown provided labor. A small stream emptying into the river was used to fill a large reservoir from which the boring mill was operated by water wheel. At some time after 1803 Foxall seems to have enlarged the foundry, for his successor mentioned no improvements on the site made after its purchase in 1815. Yet an account furnished by John Mason in 1836 described a facility several

---

[10] Map drawn by Benjamin Henry Latrobe, "No. II of Plans, and Sections of the Proposed Continuation of the Canal at the Little Falls of the Potomak to the Navy Yard in the City of Washington." Library of Congress, Geography and Map Division.

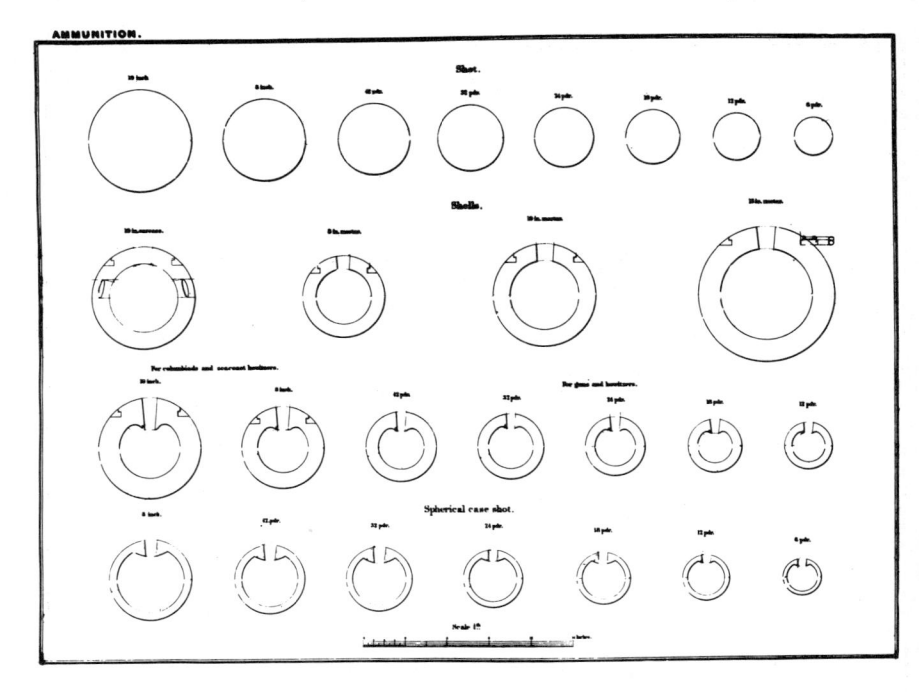

Reproduction from the Smithsonian Institution

Figure 7. Ammunition.

times larger than that shown in the map of 1803. Mason's description is worth printing in its entirety for it is the only concrete description of the foundry that survives. Mason first described the general appearance of the foundry:

> It is situated on the northern margin of the River Potomac about one mile above the western limit of the City of Washington. There is good navigation for vessels of two or three hundred tons to the spot. On it are erected a number of substantial and capacious buildings of stone and brick, conveniently arranged and furnished with the requisite water wheels, machinery, implements, and tools for carrying on actively the different branches of the work in which the establishment is engaged. It binds on the river and has deep water touching it for upwards of seven hundred feet. The [Chesapeake and Ohio] Canal pervades it for a distance of about eight hundred feet. An extensive wharf on the river side gives the facility of loading and taking off from large vessels everything from or to the tidewaters of the Chesapeake or seaward. And the banks of the Canal in the interior of the site afford the same advantages

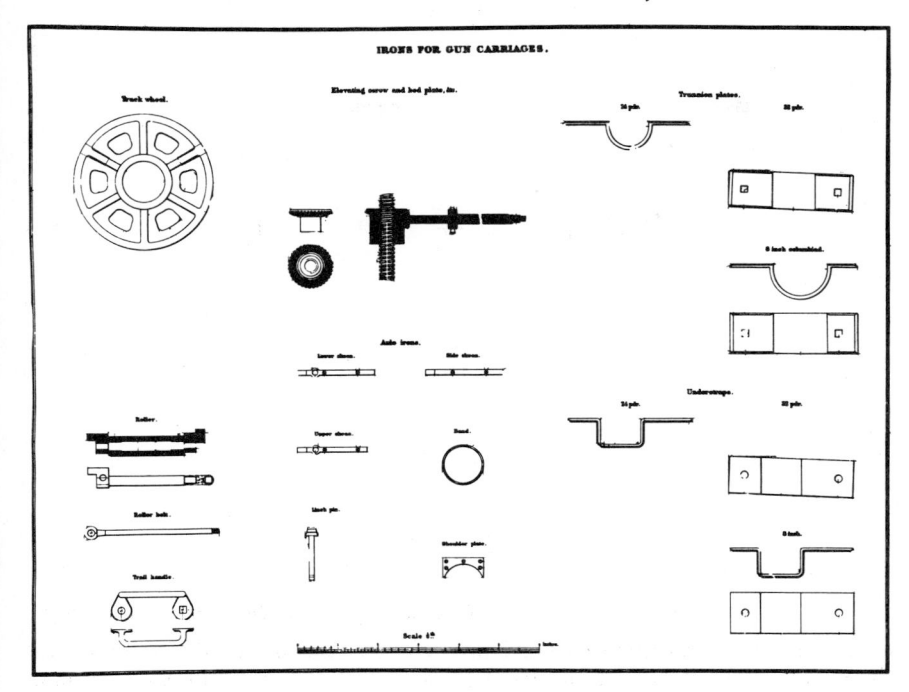

Reproduction from the Smithsonian Institution

Figure 8. Irons for Gun Carriages.

on both sides of it for what may come from or be sent to the upper country.[11]

He then described in detail the buildings, their functions, and their equipment:

> A capacious and lofty casting house of stone, containing four large air furnaces, with double stacks; an extensive moulding floor; deep pit for casting cannon; drying room, with iron doors, for baking gun-moulds; three powerful cranes, fitted with the requisite iron pinnions, sleeves, and chains; a room for preparing moulding materials; iron railway and carriage for moving guns in and out of the drying room; railway and carriage for transporting same from the casting house to the boring mill.
>
> A stone building adjoining the [casting house], containing a cupola

---

[11] Letter from George Mason to George Bomford, January 22, 1836. Accompanies House of Representatives Bill 106 and Report 669, "National Foundry," 24th Congress, 1st Session. In National Archives (hereafter abbreviated as NA) Records Group 46, Records of the House of Representatives. Hereafter cited as "National Foundry Report."

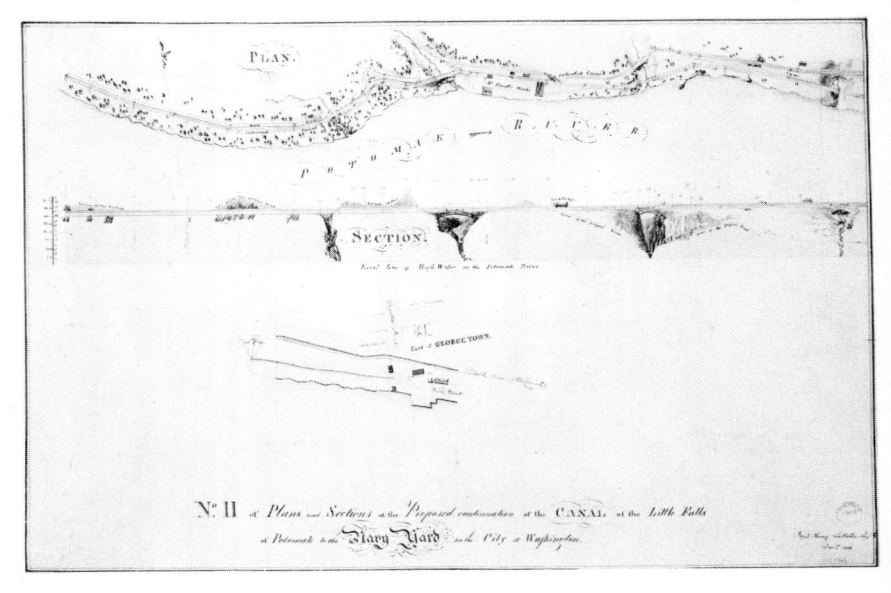

Reproduction from the Library of Congress

Figure 9. Map drawn by Benjamin Henry Latrobe in 1803 showing the location of the Foxall Foundry near the Three Sisters of the Potomac River.

furnace, bellows, with horizontal wheel and machinery for working it, and casting floor.

Two large stone mill houses for boring cannon, both having four floors, including the basement stories, fitted with large water wheels, enclosed in tight water chambers to secure their running in times of frost, geered throughout with iron; one mill containing four frames, and the other five, for boring cannon, provided with all the requisite railways, advancing carriages, racks, levers, rods, bits, and other tools for boring and turning cannon of all dimensions. Attached to the shaft of one of the water wheels is a complete set of machinery for cutting the heavy screws and nuts of the transoms for iron gun-carriages; and in the interior is a set of machinery for cutting large flat-threaded screws. In the same millhouse is geered and worked by water power, machinery for turning the trunnions of guns; and three large lathes for turning gun patterns; iron-shot moulds, and other work of iron and wood, besides a foot-lathe. On the exterior, against one of the walls, is fitted a machine with iron sleeve and chains for breaking up, by means of heavy drops, old cannon and other massive castings so as to accommodate the fragments for reception and fusion in the furnace. In both boring mills are laid, on heavy horizontal timbers, extending through the houses, on the second story and thence into the yard, iron railways and truck carriages for moving and hoisting cannon in and out of the boring frame; and in both are, in the second stories, extensive carpenters' shops for preparing patterns, flasks, &c., and garret stories for storing and preserving patterns and utensils; and basement stories for receiving, as they fall from the guns, and storing, the gun borings.

It is significant that there were two boring mills and that they were so large. They were capable of producing as many as nine cannon at one time. The water wheels were of the latest design and the lathes were well-used.[12] The system of railways suggests that the foundry utilized an early form of production line, perhaps similar to those used by such men as Simeon North and Eli Whitney, who made small arms for the government. Mason described the foundry in still more detail:

> Adjoining the upper mill-house is a frame building used in connection with it for the purposes before mentioned.
> There are two capacious blacksmiths', or forges', shops, one of stone and the other of brick; and a third of wood, and smaller, all provided with the necessary apparatus and tools.
> There is a row of convenient sheds divided into rooms, some closed, and some open on one side, for cleaning and storing castings; and for receiving and preparing clay and sand for the furnaces, moulding, &c., and other sheds for laying away cannon and storing materials.
> There are two office rooms with fireplaces, one near the lower and one at the upper mill, for superintendent and clerks.
> Two brick dwelling houses for workmen, one with four, and the other with three rooms.
> Among the quantity and variety of implements, tools, and etc., are:
> A swing-cart, with high and substantial wheels, with lever rachet and chains for taking up and moving heavy cannon;
> A carriage with four iron wheels for moving light cannon;
> A gin and deerboon steelyards for weighing cannon, &c., &c.;
> Machine, geered with iron sleeve and clasp tongs for dropping and proving shot;
> A number of cast-iron flasks, their part secured with wrought iron bands, pins, clasps, &c. for moulding and casting cannon, carronades, gunnades, howitzers, mortars, mortar-beds, &c. of every description, from the largest to the smallest calibre; a quantity of iron-shot moulds of all sizes; a great collection of patterns for guns of every sort; shells,

---

[12] Good descriptions of the machinery of the period can be found in Joseph W. Roe, *English and American Tool Builders* (New Haven: Yale University Press, 1916) and L. T. C. Rolt, *A Short History of Machine Tools* (Cambridge, Mass.: MIT Press, 1965).

grape, and cannister shot, &c., &c., and for wheels and machinery of every kind.[13]

While Mason might have made the extensive additions it is unlikely that he did so. The description above is of a sophisticated cannon foundry operated under the watchful eye of a master founder such as Foxall.[14] Mason was not a founder; to him the foundry was an investment property. Also, Mason frequently mentioned his achievements; his letters constantly refer to some new contract, idea, or speculation. Yet there is no mention of a massive overhauling of the foundry itself. The rapid arming undertaken by the government to meet the emergencies of the War of 1812 could have been the stimulus to expansion. It is known, for example, that cannon from the foundry were widely deployed in both land and naval engagements between 1812 and 1814. Foxall's cannon were also used in the many frontier expeditions against Indians such as the early battles in Georgia and Florida in what was to be the Seminole War. Only a large foundry, such as that described above, would have been able to provide large numbers of many types of cannon for varied uses.

The superiority of the Foxall Foundry and its products is attested to by the story (perhaps partially apocryphal) of the British assault on the District of Columbia in 1814. The excellent location of the foundry almost proved to be fatal. When General Ross and his troops marched on the capital city he was reported to have been intent on destroying the famous foundry as well as the Capitol, White House, and departmental buildings. Not only were Henry Foxall's weapons being used against British forces, but the founder himself, a former Englishman, was thought a traitor to England. A severe windstorm prevented British soldiers from reaching beyond Washington into Georgetown and they retreated to their ships anchored in the nearby Patuxent River. It is curious that while the Secretary of the Navy ordered the Washington Navy Yard destroyed, no one ordered the destruction of the Foxall Foundry—a place as crucial as the Navy Yard to the war effort.

It is difficult to generalize further about the output of the foundry; none of the foundry's records survive and many government contracts have been lost to time. However, all the indications are that there was a large output of cannon. Foxall had no competitors to speak

---

[13] Letter from John Mason to George Bomford, January 22, 1836, in "National Foundry Report."

[14] According to Tousard's ordnance manual of 1813 (see footnote 9) and Andrew Ure's Dictionary of *Arts, Manufactures, and Mines; Containing a Clear Exposition of Their Principles and Practice* (New York: D. Appleton and Co., 1842).

of. The Richmond Foundry produced a small number of cannon, less than two dozen annually between 1810 and 1814.[15] They were reported to have been of inferior quality. Until Joseph McClurg built the Fort Pitt Foundry in 1814, Foxall's was the only source of quality cannon for the service. McClurg had started in business with his Pittsburgh Foundry in 1804 and had produced a few government cannon, but the number was inconsequential until he built the Fort Pitt Foundry ten years later.[16] The government also bought cannon for the British War from a number of small private founders who were equipped to cast firebacks and stoves and plows rather than cannon and ammunition. Their cannon were similarly weak in quality and small in number. There were no other competitors worthy of the name until after the foundry's sale to Mason.

The first government contract Foxall is known to have signed is dated January 4, 1799. At that time he was still at his Eagle Iron Works in Philadelphia. The contract, a personal and informal one between Secretary of the Navy Benjamin Stoddert and Foxall, called for $23,000 worth of cannon of all sizes to be "cast solid and bored truly." No specific number of cannon was mentioned, but Foxall was to deliver weapons from "such models as may from time to time be determined by the Secretary of the Navy." He was required to deliver an average of four finished guns each week until the contract was fulfilled.[17] It is unknown whether Foxall signed additional contracts while in Philadelphia. The next surviving one bears a date of October 17, 1800, and was made between the Department of the Navy and "Henry Foxall & Co., Georgetown." It stipulated that Foxall could deliver 148 cannon of various sizes in either Pennsylvania or Maryland. He would receive $18,000 for the order.[18] It is likely that he was in the process of dissolving his partnership with Robert Morris in the Eagle Iron Works and moving to Georgetown to oversee construction of the new foundry. On December 20, 1800, four days before the purchase of the land for the foundry was completed, he signed a contract for additional cannon.[19] He was apparently in full production and making about a hundred cannon per

---

[15] *Calendar of Virginia State Papers*, X, 422; quoted in Bruce, *Virginia Iron Manufacture in the Slave Era*, p. 116.

[16] According to the still authoritative work of J. Leander Bishop, *A History of American Manufacture from 1608 to 1860 . . .* , 3rd edition, 3 volumes (Philadelphia: Edward Young and Co., 1868), II, 204.

[17] NA, RG45, Naval Records Collection of the Office of Naval Records and Library.

[18] NA, RG45, Naval Records Collection of the Office of Naval Records and Library.

[19] NA, RG45, Naval Records Collection of the Office of Naval Records and Library. John Clagett Proctor, *Washington: Past and Present*, 2 volumes (New York: Lewis Publishing Co., 1930), II, 693, notes that Foxall bought the land from Francis Deakins on Christmas eve, 1800.

year by some time late in 1801 or early in 1802. For by January, 1802, he had signed another four contracts. Four contracts per year was the usual number for the Foxall Foundry between 1801 and its sale in 1815. From January, 1801, to December, 1802, Foxall made about two hundred cannon of various sizes and the necessary shot to accompany them.[20] A few years later Albert Gallatin mentioned in his well-known report on American manufactures that the foundry had a capacity of some three hundred cannon per annum, in addition to carriages and ammunition for them.[21] Foxall did not have to worry about his income during his ownership of the foundry. Not only did he have a guaranteed buyer for his product—more than could be said for many merchants at the time—but he also enjoyed a virtual monopoly.[22]

Henry Foxall sold the foundry to John Mason in December, 1815.[23] The price Mason paid for the facility is unknown, but he assumed control of the entire operation and all properties associated with it. Mason continued the name of Columbia Foundry which Foxall had given it some time about 1806 or 1807.[24] Mason also continued the near monopoly of the foundry in casting government ordnance. It was not until 1816 that John Clarke built the Bellona Foundry in Powhatan County near Richmond; and Gouverneur Kemble built the West Point Foundry at Cold Spring, New York, in 1817.[25] Mason and the other founders, as Foxall before them, received approximately $150.00 per ton of iron. An 1809 Ordnance required open bidding for government contracts by all prospective contractors—whether makers of boots, clothing or ordnance. But the law seems to have been of little hindrance to the founders, including Mason. In 1824 when John Quincy Adams became President, Mason and Clarke sought an audience with him to try to prevent the issuing of a competitive bidding regulation in the War and

---

[20] NA, RG45, Naval Records Collection of the Office of Naval Records and Library. NA, RG96, Records of the United States Army Commands, 1784–1821.

[21] Report by Albert Gallatin, 1810, *American State Papers, Finance,* (Washington: Gales and Seaton, 1832-61), VI, 429. Gallatin's estimate suggests that the enlargements to the foundry were made some time between 1803 and 1810.

[22] For a contemporary overview of the financial and economic conditions see Tench Coxe's *A Statement of the Arts and Manufactures of the United States for the Year 1810* (Philadelphia: A. Cornman, 1814) and his *Supplementary Observations* (1814).

[23] According to Davis ,"The Old Cannon Foundry Above Georgetown . . . ," 29.

[24] The name "Columbia Foundry" appears on a few contracts for those years, but "Foxall Foundry" appears with more frequency. It is possible that Foxall changed the name officially when he enlarged the foundry.

[25] Bruce, *Virginia Iron Manufacture in the Slave Era,* p. 116, and Bishop, *A History of American Manufacture from 1608 to 1860,* III, 485.

Navy Departments.[26] Young dissident officers in the military departments demanded more careful control over the founders, who apparently were given great latitude in both their work and fees. The demands reached a climax in the movement for a national foundry in the 1830's and 1840's. The government's position, however, was agreeable with Mason and Clarke and, presumably, the other founders, each of whom enjoyed the privileged status of membership in the infant military-industrial complex. In that time of "good feelings" when things military were discouraged the official position was that the existing foundries were adequate for the needs of the service and that they even saved the government money. Government-owned foundries would be too expensive and too difficult to maintain. As the annual report of the Ordnance Department put it in 1825:

> As the existing cannon founderies, as well as the manufactories of small arms, had been established under assurances of continued support from the Government, if their terms and the quality of their work should prove satisfactory. These founderies have accordingly continued to furnish all the ordnance required for public service, both for the War and the Navy Departments.[27]

The department's reasons were clear and expressed as a palliative to those who may have objected:

> The experience required in a practice of many years enables [the existing founders and foundries] to furnish ordnance of a more safe and durable description, and of a better quality generally, than could be expected from new establishments.[28]

Interestingly, the government already maintained national arsenals at Washington, Pittsburgh and Watervliet, where carriages and ordnance accessories were made. The founders made the same equipment, so there is no reason to doubt that the arsenals could not have been equipped to cast cannon just as the foundries had been equipped to build carriages.

In 1826 accusations of monopoly were made again and the Ordnance Department took care to ensure that its largesse was divided

---

[26] John Quincy Adams, *Memoirs of John Quincy Adams, Comprising Portions of His Diary from 1795 to 1848*, Charles Francis Adams, ed., 12 volumes (Philadelphia: J. B. Lippincott and Co., 1874–77), VI, 543.

[27] Annual Report of the Ordnance Department, November 29, 1825, in *A Collection of Annual Reports and Other Important Papers Relating to the Ordnance Department, Taken from the Office of the Chief of Ordnance, from Public Documents, and from Other Sources*, 4 volumes, Stephen V. Benet, ed. (Washington, D.C.: Government Printing Office, 1878–80), I, 130. Hereafter cited as *Annual Reports*.

[28] *Annual Reports*, I, 130.

evenly among the foundries. In 1807 the government had begun the practice of regular stockpiling and building forts. And between 1807 and 1812 some three million dollars were appropriated for the purpose of building new fortresses and supplying them with ordnance.[29] After the Treaty of Ghent stockpiling and construction continued and was expanded.[30] Moreover, Secretary of War John C. Calhoun and President James Monroe were busy establishing military outposts throughout the Louisiana Purchase, all of which needed large numbers of light cannon and ammunition. According to the biographer of Monroe, the President's favorite project was the building of fortresses and in 1820 saw that an appropriation of $800,000 was made especially for building.[31] The year before the Chief of Ordnance, Decius Wadsworth, had written in a letter to his superior in the War Department that the monopoly system was sufficient for the public need.[32] It may have been an American distrust of the military. But it also may have been letters such as Wadsworth's to Calhoun that sanctioned the existing system. At any rate, such reports were likely popular with John Mason and his fellow founders.

The Ordnance Department was generous to its weapons contractors. In 1817 Chief of Ordnance Wadsworth complained that the annual appropriation for weapons—$30,000—was too low and should be substantially increased. The reason he offered was that Mason had recently purchased the Foxall Foundry and was awaiting a payment of some $25,000 for cannon cast to complete Foxall's outstanding contracts. In addition, Wadsworth said, the Ordnance Department had already contracted for an additional $20,000 worth of cannon from the Columbia Foundry, bringing the total owed to Mason to $45,000 for the year. The least amount the department needed to continue efficiently was $100,000.[33] In 1824, however, the sum of $100,000 was not a sufficient appropriation to meet "existing obligations." Chief of Ordnance George Bomford expressed concern that the founders, including John Mason, would withdraw from government casting were they not provided with the usual number of con-

---

[29] *American State Papers, Military Affairs,* edited by authority of Congress by Walter Lowrie and Mathew St. Clair Clark, 7 volumes (Washington, D.C.: Government Printing Office, 1832–61), I, 219–22.

[30] Emanuel Raymond Lewis, *Seacoast Fortifications of the United States* (Washington, D.C.: Smithsonian Institution Press, 1970), offers a careful discussion of fortresses of the period.

[31] Harry Ammon, *James Monroe: The Quest for National Identity* (New York: McGraw-Hill, 1971), p. 471.

[32] Letter from Decius Wadsworth to John C. Calhoun, December 6, 1819, *Annual Reports,* I, 57.

[33] Letter from Decius Wadsworth to the Secretary of War, February 25, 1817, *Annual Reports,* I, 78.

tracts. Accordingly, he recommended that the "requisite supply" of cannon should be contracted for immediately.[34] Mason's income from the foundry in the 1820's was about $25,000 from each the War and Navy Departments. According to Ordnance Department records each of the other foundries received a like amount.

The years of the 1820's were probably the best ones of the Columbia Foundry under Mason's control. Continued fortress construction, military expeditions in the frontiers, a growing sailing navy—all those activities required ordnance, and Mason supplied at least a fourth of it. Planned obsolescence also seems to have played a role in the fortunes of the Columbia Foundry. Between 1812 and 1820 a new way of carrying cannon on carriages had been devised and the merits of bronze cannon as opposed to iron were once again debated. The French "Gribeauval" carriage system was in vogue in the American Army during the War of 1812; shortly after, Decius Wadsworth found a better way of trailing guns on a carriage and recommended it to the Secretary of War. However, the Gribeauval system was retained until 1827–1828 when an inspection team reported that the French had adopted the stock-trail system recommended by Wadsworth. The new system was not implemented on a full scale until 1836, but the founders were kept busy casting cannon to fit on them before adoption as well as the new carriages themselves. The War Department's report for 1831 declared that at least 9,128 cannon of all sizes would be needed as soon as possible.[35] The Columbia Foundry would thus be able to provide a considerable number of cannon for several years. Cast iron cannon had performed well during the War of 1812, and they made adequate field artillery. But improvements in powder by such men as the Duponts in Wilmington led to the iron cannon's bursting in use. Cast iron was not able to stand up under increased powder charges. For successful use the cannon had to be limited to a small powder charge. Stronger guns were needed. Several Boards of Ordnance met through the 1830's and recommended bronze to replace iron.[36] The Columbia Foundry was reported to have cast a few bronze cannon at the higher rate paid for experimental work in the late 1820's.[37]

By about 1835 the fortunes of the Columbia Foundry began to

---

[34] Letter from George Bomford to John C. Calhoun, February 14, 1824, *Annual Reports*, I, 119.

[35] Annual Report of the Secretary of War, 1831, *Annual Reports*, I, 231.

[36] See the annual reports of the Ordnance Department for 1831, 1835, 1837, 1838, and 1839. *Annual Reports*.

[37] According to allusions in official communications from the Ordnance Department to the War Department in 1828–1831. *Annual Reports, passim.*

decline. There were two chief reasons for the change. First, the campaign for a national foundry was renewed with vigor greater than ever before. Second, cannon were being discovered to be weak and poorly made. The concern for the poor cannon gave fuel to the arguments for a national foundry. Also, John Mason was nearly seventy years old by that time and had reportedly put the day-to-day operation of the foundry into the hands of a manager. Mason himself was not a founder; he was an entrepreneur who happened to own a foundry. By 1835 Mason's personal fortunes declined as well. Two years earlier the Bank of the United States through the Bank of Columbia of W. W. Corcoran foreclosed on a mortgage Mason had taken out on his Analostan Island estate in 1826.[38] In that year he had lost a great sum of money on a poor land speculation and was deeply in debt. His 1836 offer to sell the foundry to the Federal government suggests that he tried to obtain some ready cash.

In 1835 Mason's good friend and benefactor, Chief of Ordnance Bomford, told the aging businessman of the growing desire to build a national foundry to be of the same scale as the national arsenals. Bomford was a practical man who believed that it would be more efficient for the government to assume control of an existing foundry than to build an entirely new one. In the same vein, Bomford believed that the Columbia Foundry would be the best choice for such an endeavor. It was, after all, a large facility, had cast quality weapons for many years, and was close to the seat of government. Accordingly, he drafted an official letter to Mason requesting him to submit to the Ordnance Department "... a statement showing the area of the site [of the foundry], with the buildings, improvements, and machinery therein, the magnitude of power, and the quantity of work the establishment is now capable of performing per annum." He asked Mason to include in the statement the "... maximum power, and greatest extent of manufacture to which the [foundry] may be increased." [39] Bomford more than likely knew very well the answers to the questions he asked of Mason since they conversed and visited each other frequently. The letter to Mason was probably the result of an official procedure.

---

[38] According to deeds of trust in 1826 and 1833 made by John Mason. Mason speculated a great deal. He owned mills in Virginia, was a shareholder and officer of the old Potomack Canal Company, was an officer of the Bank of Columbia, and was always looking for profit-making opportunities. Thanks to Mary Curry who so kindly let me examine her notes on Mason. Mason's letters to David Baillie Warden also allude to speculations of various kinds. David Baillie Warden Collection, Maryland Historical Society.

[39] Letter from George Bomford to John Mason, October 17, 1835. Accompanies "National Foundry Report."

Mason's reply to Bomford was mentioned above and included a lengthy description of the Columbia Foundry. It revealed that the foundry would be an ideal site for a national foundry and that few improvements had been made since its transfer from Foxall to Mason in 1815. The only substantial change in the facility Mason is known to have made was the addition of an access road under the new Chesapeake and Ohio Canal in 1831 and overflow pipes to increase the flow of water to the boring mills' water wheels.[40] Mason's reply also revealed that the annual output of cannon had not changed since 1810; it was still estimated to be about three hundred cannon each year. While the needs of the War and Navy Departments increased, the output of the Columbia Foundry remained static. There is a suggestion that Mason let the foundry fall into a state of disrepair. The House Committee on Military Affairs located a millwright at the Columbia Foundry, George Starbuck, who was willing to testify as to the condition of the place based on his own work there. Whether Starbuck's comments were the result of an objective opinion or of a dislike for John Mason we shall probably never know—there remains only Mason's indignant reply to the committee. In it he quotes his employee as having said that the machinery was "old and dilapidated," that it was ". . . inconvenient, and almost entirely useless." [41] Mason argued that ". . . the buildings (exclusive of some sheds for minor purposes) are all of either brick or stone—principally of the latter—constructed of the most durable manner, and several of them of modern erection. The machinery is of the best in workmanship; and the best adapted to the work it was intended to perform. Being everywhere iron-geared, it is made susceptible of long use and is in fact so used because it has not required renewal." [42] The committee recommended against the construction or the purchase of a government foundry and recommended that the matter be given more thought.

Mason's indignation at Starbuck's testimony may have been prompted by an honest desire to uphold the good name of his business, or it may have been an earnest attempt to sell the foundry. The affair occurred only three years after Mason's loss of his Analostan Island estate. In 1835, however, Mason was opposed to the idea of a national foundry, maintaining that such an institution would

---

[40] Contracts dated March 26, 1831, April 30, 1830, and March 31, 1831. NA RG79, Records of the National Park Service.

[41] Quoted in a letter from John Mason to Col. Richard M. Johnson of the House of Representatives Military Affairs Committee, March 19, 1836. Accompanies "National Foundry Report."

[42] Letter from John Mason to Col. Richard M. Johnson, March 19, 1836. "National Foundry Report."

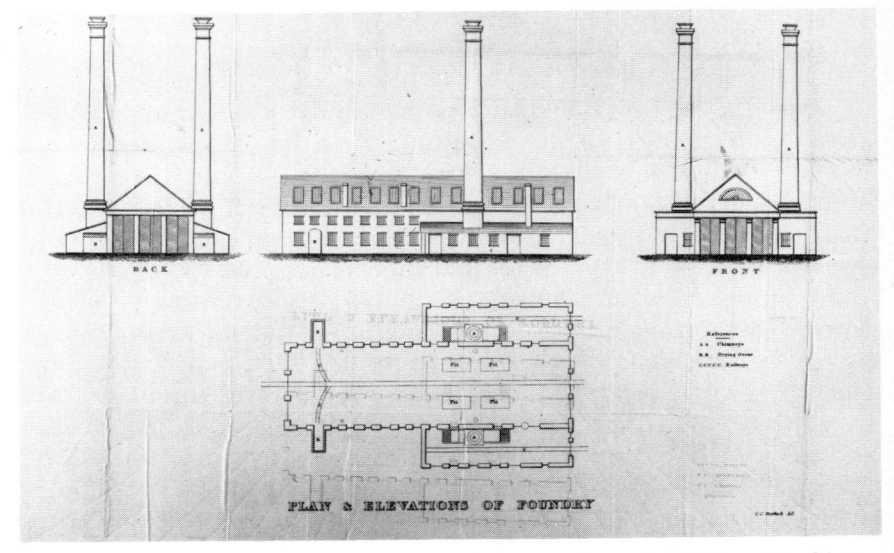

Reproduction from the National Archives

Figure 10. Plan and Elevation of Foundry by George Starbuck.

Figures 10, 11 and 12 are plans and elevations drawn by George Starbuck in 1836 for a Congressional committee investigating the feasibility of building a national foundry. They show how Starbuck envisioned the proposed foundry. Since Starbuck was a millwright at the Columbia Foundry these drawings could have been based on the buildings already standing. The boring mill is similar to the description furnished by John Mason, and cursory archeological investigation of the site of the Columbia Foundry reveals ruined foundations arranged in a manner similar to that shown in Figure 12.

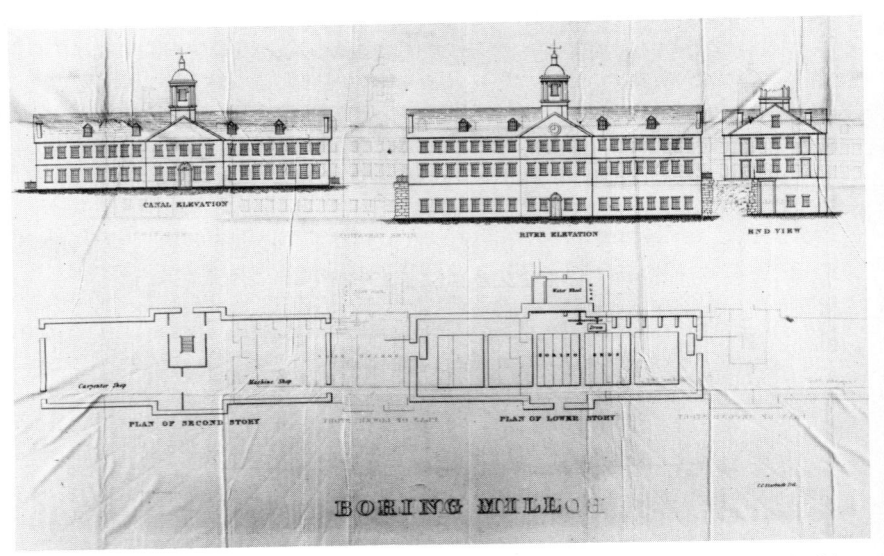

Reproduction from the National Archives

Figure 11. Plan and Elevation of Boring Mill by George Starbuck.

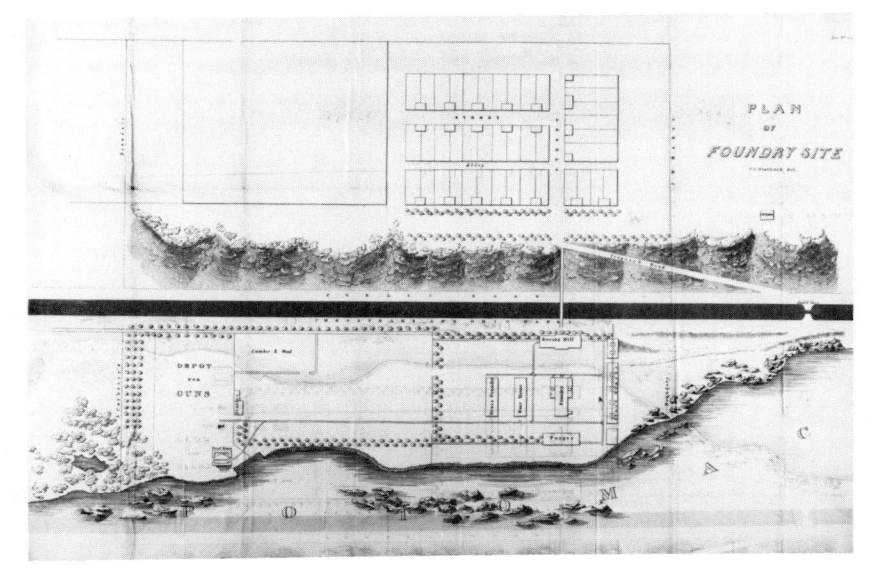

Reproduction from the National Archives

Figure 12. Plan of Foundry Site by George Starbuck.

destroy the initiative of private businessmen. He set a high price, obviously intended to repel the interest shown by some in the foundry: $100,000. That price would have eliminated it from serious consideration as a potential national facility. But less than a year later Mason lowered the figure to $75,000, a sum that would have been more attractive to the military. In 1836 Mason argued strenuously that his foundry should be purchased immediately and that since the government was going into the casting business it should have the privilege of starting with his foundry.[43]

Mason's motives behind the refusal, then the urgency, to sell are not clear. On the one hand his personal fortune was apparently low, as he had lost a great sum of money and had not been able to recoup his losses. On the other hand the foundry was making a steady gross income of about $50,000 per year. A report in 1834, for example, stated that Mason was paid $94,288.72 by the Ordnance Department for deliveries of cannon and accessories from April 15, 1830, to May 23, 1834.[44] Such a sum would have generated an annual gross income from the Ordnance Department alone of about $23,000 per year. He received a similar sum from the Navy Department. Reports from

[43] "National Foundry Report."
[44] NA, RG156, Records of the Office of the Chief of Ordnance.

the late 1830's show that he continued to receive about $23,000 each year from each department. For deliveries of cannon and ammunition made from March 30, 1836, through December 4, 1838, he received $41,353.12.[45] And from a report made in 1839 it is learned that he received a payment of $22,512.80 from the Ordnance Department for deliveries in the year period from October, 1838, to October, 1839.[46]

However rosy the financial picture appears it must be sullied by the fact that most of the deliveries made in the 1830's were delinquent and were for old contracts. More serious, Mason appears to have been negotiating for new contracts without the means of completely honoring the old ones. Overdue delivery lists in the Ordnance and Navy Departments regularly referred to the lateness of Mason's production. Frequently they suggested that steps be taken to stimulate the Columbia Foundry to greater output, but that it was likely difficult to do, considering the extreme lateness of many of the contracted-for deliveries.[47]

Things were made even more difficult for the Columbia Foundry when the Ordnance Department continued the extensive reorganization and modernization begun in the early 1830's. In 1832 the Ordnance Department was reorganized, and in 1834 Army regulations gave the department full responsibility for the design of artillery. The renewed insistence on a national foundry was probably an outgrowth of the newly-achieved independence of the department. Another result—one more far-reaching for the Columbia Foundry—was the initiation of a rigid inspection system. Growing out of the contest throughout the 1830's between iron and bronze as materials for cannon the inspection system brought the military into the future and left the Columbia Foundry in the past. George Talcott, a young Captain of Ordnance in 1836 and a leader of the national foundry movement, became Chief of Ordnance in 1839. In that year he began to redefine the minimum standards for ordnance.[48] By 1840 Talcott saw to it that samples were collected from the cannon made at each foundry and had them subjected to tests for specific gravity and tensile strength. The tests proved that the old guns were not of uniform quality and were not fit weapons for a "modern

---

[45] NA, RG156, Records of the Office of the Chief of Ordnance.
[46] NA, RG156, Records of the Office of the Chief of Ordnance.
[47] NA, RG156, Records of the Office of the Chief of Ordnance.
[48] There is a good discussion of the changes in Constance McLaughlin Green, Harry C. Thompson, and Peter C. Roots, *The Ordnance Department: Planning Munitions for War*, Office of the Chief of Military History (Washington, D.C.: Government Printing Office, 1955), p. 17, and Bruce, *Virginia Iron Manufacture in the Slave Era*, pp. 118–19.

army." Most of the guns were found to be of inferior workmanship.[49] Talcott himself wrote of the bad guns:

> Reasons existed for the belief that the iron cannon furnished by contractors for the use of the United States were not of such quality as the wants of the service demanded, nor as good as they might be made by the exercise of the proper degree of skill. It was known that the founders were able to graduate the strength of the guns, so as to meet the powder-proof required by the Department, but it was thought not advisable to put the cannon to very severe proofs by gunpowder, because although a gun might sustain all that was required, and, therefore, be received into service, it was found that the gun was sometimes injured by the powder-proof and failed afterward with only service charges.[50]

Such drastic problems led the Board of Ordnance, a group of experts first convened in 1831 to consider the change to bronze cannon, to recommend the appointment of an inspector to oversee the manufacture of cannon at the foundries. In 1841 the Secretary of War, Joel Poinsett, approved of the recommendation and appointed Major William Wade as "attending agent." The position was confirmed by law in 1842.[51] The new position came none too soon, for in 1841 cannon cast at the Columbia Foundry exploded in use killing several soldiers; the report of the Ordnance Department for 1842 recommended that casting be suspended indefinitely at the Columbia Foundry.[52] Soon thereafter a resident inspector was stationed at each of the four foundries with the express purpose of looking after the government's interests. Once again there was a debate as to whether there should be a national foundry, but the military continued to rely upon the private founders. Nevertheless, the law of 1842 creating the position of inspector also provided a way for the Ordnance Department to prescribe specific rules for the selection and casting of metals as well as for the steps in the process of manufacturing artillery. By 1845 there was established the policy of requiring each founder to cast a single trial gun before proceeding to complete the ordered weapons.[53] A national foundry was the only other alterna-

---

[49] *Reports of Experiments on the Strength and Other Properties of Metals for Cannon, with a Description of the Machines for Testing Metals and of the Classification of Cannon in Service. By Officers of the Ordnance Department of the United States Army. By Authority of the Secretary of War* (Philadelphia: H. C. Baird, 1856), pp. 325 ff.

[50] Letter from George Talcott to J. C. Spencer, May 31, 1842, *Annual Reports*, I, 444.

[51] James A. Huston, *The Sinews of War: Army Logistics, 1775–1953* (Washington, D.C.: Government Printing Office for the Office of the Chief of Military History, 1966), p. 119.

[52] NA RG156, Records of the Office of the Chief of Ordnance.

[53] Letter from George Talcott to Commander C. Morris, March 29, 1845, *Annual Reports*, II, 35.

tive and the government was not yet ready to take that step, although it was only a matter of time. By about 1845 the Columbia Foundry was reduced to making little other than shells and cannon balls to be fired from the guns made at other foundries.[54]

By late in the 1840's the other foundries were undertaking retooling and modernization. The Mexican adventure in 1846-1848 gave them plenty of work and an ideal opportunity to devise new weapons and new ways of making them. R. P. Parrott, who joined the West Point Foundry in 1836, was designing the famous Parrott Gun, soon to be used in the Civil War. He was also expanding the West Point's facilities and preparing it for advancing weapons technology. By 1848 the West Point Foundry was making cannon for the government as well as making hydraulic presses, engines, general castings, wrought-iron pieces, and steam engines, among other items. Parrott, as Kemble had done before him, steadily introduced the latest processes for work in cast and wrought iron. The story was similar at the Fort Pitt Foundry and Cyrus Alger's South Boston Iron Works. While Alger, a distinguished and inventive iron master, is not listed as having cast cannon for the government before 1841, he seems to have made up for lost time. By 1848 he was making large numbers of experimental cannon, time fuses, and forms of rifled cannon, the latter being ordinary cannon with their bores rifled for increased fire-power.

Men such as John Dahlgren and Thomas Rodman were also busy finding new ways of designing and building cannon. Dahlgren, a naval officer trained in artillery, redesigned cannon altogether. He determined that a thick breech with a thin muzzle would take fullest advantage of the principle of the "curve of pressures" and withstand an extremely powerful charge. Rodman, an army officer, devised a way of casting cannon similar to that of the Eighteenth Century and before. He cast the gun around a hollow core, thus making a tube directly from the mold. Each layer of cast metal was cooled successively by circulating water, thereby making a superbly strong gun capable of any degree of powder charge. "Rodman Guns" and "Dahlgren Guns" were famous long after 1900. The Columbia Foundry advanced in no way. Advancing technology left the Columbia Foundry struggling to fulfill old contracts with outdated weapons.[55]

---

[54] An examination of the available contracts for the period shows that the Columbia Foundry was largely engaged in casting shells and shot, and that few pieces of ordnance were cast there.

[55] The Columbia has occasionally been unfairly accused of having cast the cannon that exploded on the USS *Princeton* in 1844, killing the Secretary of the Navy, the Secre-

John Mason died in 1849 at the age of 83; his son and executor, James Maynadier Mason, continued to operate the foundry until 1854. In that year it was sold to Spencer B. Root. The output of the foundry after Mason's death was almost non-existent. Shortly thereafter it became the site of a beer garden.

The Foxall-Columbia Foundry was one of the earliest of American "defense contractors." In its half-century history such enterprises progressed from informal shops based on gentlemen's agreements to sophisticated industries. Technology progressed from the handcraft of skilled artisans to the carefully engineered products of production lines. The military, too, made advances in what is now called scientific management, quality control, and research and development. The Foxall-Columbia Foundry began as a pioneer and died as a laggard.

---

tary of State, and other notables. In reality, one Captain Robert Stockton made a poor but deceptively similar replica of a Columbiad designed by the Swedish inventor, John Ericsson, for his ship, the *Princeton*. Ericsson's cannon was of high quality metal, the product of a trained metallurgist and inventor. Stockton's was too weak even to be fired.

Albert Gallatin in Washington, 1801–1813

RICHARD MANNIX

The weather was intensely cold in that first week of January, 1801, when Albert Gallatin left his home at New Geneva, Pennsylvania and crossed the Allegheny Mountains. His destination on this annual journey had, for five years past, been Congress Hall in Philadelphia. But now, at the beginning of his sixth year as United States Congressman from western Pennsylvania, his journey would end in a new federal capital at Washington.

In fulfillment of the bargain struck between Hamilton and Jefferson back in 1790, the federal government had, through the summer and autumn of 1800, gradually and somewhat reluctantly removed itself from the comfort of Philadelphia to the raw wilderness on the Potomac. The executive departments had been the first to make the change, late in June, 1800; and, on November 1, President Adams had taken up residence in the bare frame of a presidential house. Congress sat for the first time in the new federal city on November 22, by which date all functions of federal authority, and their unfortunate civil servants, had been relocated.*

Gallatin was late in arriving. Delayed by personal business, and then detained en route by rain and snow, he finally entered the new capital on January 12, 1801, a very cold and weary traveller. "I took good care of myself," he assured his wife, "and arrived without accident and in good health. I have not even got a cold." [1]

But if he had survived the hazards and discomforts of the journey, he had his doubts about how long he could survive as a resident of the City of Washington. He was lonely and depressed, and Washington was a "hateful place." [2] There was some comfort in dreaming of the

---
* The United States Mint and the Bank of the United States remained in Philadelphia.

[1] Albert Gallatin to Hannah Nicholson Gallatin, January 15, 1801, New-York Historical Society.

[2] Albert Gallatin to Hannah Nicholson Gallatin, August 17, 1802, New-York Historical Society.

day, about seven weeks away, when Congress would adjourn and he could return to his wife and two sons; or in resolving, again and again, never to separate himself from them for so long a period. Being unable to muster many truly comforting thoughts, he found himself continually working these over in his head. But the loneliness remained. "I am distressed beyond what I can express," he wrote to his wife, "and nothing reconciles me to our separation but its short duration." [3]

The city itself certainly offered no diversion or distraction. After living there only three days he described it as "on the whole dull," a place that affords neither news nor entertainment. "It is not a town, it is inconvenient, we cannot legislate as well nor as cheap as if we were in a city. The distance from the public offices is an immense objection. Everyone is sick of the place. Instead of being called Washington City, it ought to bear another name." [4]

As soon as he arrived in Washington, Gallatin took up residence at Conrad and McMunn's boarding house on the southeast corner of New Jersey Avenue and C Street S. W., where he shared a room with Congressman Joseph B. Varnum of Massachusetts. The rate, "including attendance, wood, candles, and liquors," was $15 a week, which was, he thought, "somewhat dearer than either in Philadelphia or New York." [5]

The company was good enough, "but it is always the same, and unless in my own family, I had rather now and then see some other persons." There were from twenty-four to thirty boarders at Conrad and McMunn's in those early months of 1801. Jefferson was there, still awaiting some resolution of the deadlock between himself and Aaron Burr in the presidential election. Others included John Langdon of New Hampshire, Samuel Smith of Maryland, John and Wilson Cary Nicholas of Virginia, and Abraham Baldwin of Georgia. At table, said Gallatin, were it not for the presence of the wives of Congressmen Theodorus Bailey of New York and John Brown of Rhode Island, we "would look like a refectory of monks." [6]

As for the city itself, he carefully described it in his first letters to his wife. "Our local situation," he wrote, "is far from being pleas-

[3] Albert Gallatin to Hannah Nicholson Gallatin, January 29, 1801, New-York Historical Society.
[4] Albert Gallatin to Hannah Nicholson Gallatin, January 15, 1801, New-York Historical Society.
[5] Ibid.
[6] Albert Gallatin to Hannah Nicholson Gallatin, January 15, 1801, New-York Historical Society.

The Metropolitan Museum of Art
Gift of Frederic W. Stevens, 1908

Albert Gallatin by Gilbert Stuart. Oil on canvas. 29⅜ in. x 23⅞ in. Painted in Washington.

Gallatin's wife, Hannah Nicholson Gallatin, complained that Stuart had "softened" her husband's features.

ant or even convenient." In addition to Conrad and McMunn's, there were, around the Capitol, about seven other boarding houses, "one taylor, one shoemaker, one printer, a washing woman, a grocery shop, a pamphlets and stationary shop, a small dry goods shop, and

- First Gallatin residence, May, 1801
- Gallatin residence, August, 1801 to April, 1813

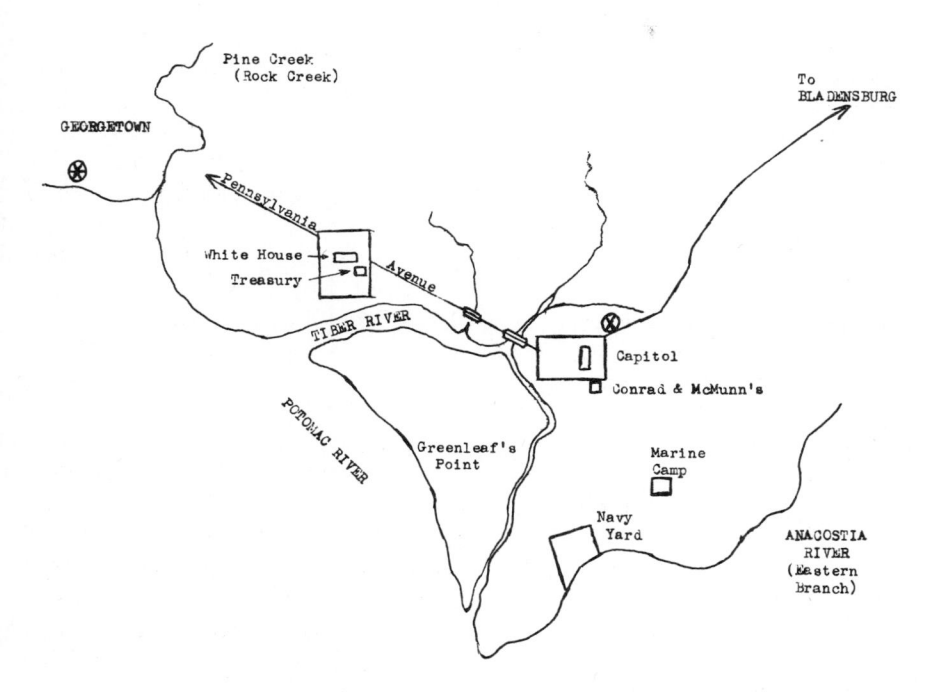

Sketch by Richard Mannix

Sketch showing the locations of Gallatin's first and second residences in Washington and Conrad and McMunn's boarding house where (with Thomas Jefferson and others) he first stayed.

an oyster house. This makes the whole of the federal city as connected with the Capitol." [7]

But there were two other distinct sections of the city somewhat separated from the Capitol area. What was intended to be "the commercial part of the city," about three-quarters of a mile from the Capitol, "on or near the Eastern Branch," was nothing more than "half a dozen houses, a very large but perfectly empty warehouse and a wharf graced not by a single vessel." The whole of this

---
[7] Albert Gallatin to Hannah Nicholson Gallatin, January 15, 1801, New-York Historical Society.

section was separated from "the Capitol Hill and the little village connected with it" by a large swamp.[8]

There were, in the same area, about twenty empty buildings erected by a speculator named Greenleaf, said Gallatin; as well as twenty unfinished two-story houses which had been started back in 1796 by Robert Morris and John Nicholson. When, in 1797, their speculative empire collapsed, and both Morris and Nicholson were thrown into debtors' prison, the buildings were abandoned. In 1801 they were still unfinished, and would remain so for many years, eventually falling into ruin before being removed.[9]

In the other direction, to the north and west of the Capitol, lay the President's house, with the same swamp intervening. "A small stream ... decorated with the pompous appellation of 'Tyber' feeds without draining the swamp." The only means of communication between the Capitol and the President's house was by a narrow causeway "which measures one mile and a half and seventeen perches" and which they call "the Pennsylvania Avenue." There were no houses along that causeway, nor could there be "without devoting their wretched tenants to perpetual fevers." [10]

But beyond the President's house the city showed some promise. The ground between the executive mansion and Georgetown, which lay at a distance of about a mile and a half farther along Pennsylvania Avenue, was high and level and dry, and was already being occupied by "the public offices and from fifty to one hundred good finished houses, the most elegant being the President's house." The section seemed certain to prosper. It communicated with Georgetown by means of two bridges over the Rock Creek. And because the "public offices" had chosen the site, people who have business with the government would naturally be drawn there. Gallatin was confident that this part of the city "will improve considerably and may within a short time form a town equal in size and population to Lancaster or Annapolis." [11]

"But *we* are not there," he lamented. "The distance is too great for convenience from thence to the Capitol." Six or seven members of Congress were living in Georgetown, and three others lived near the President's house. But everyone else was crowded into those eight

---

[8] *Ibid.*

[9] Albert Gallatin to Hannah Nicholson Gallatin, January 15, 1801, New-York Historical Society; see also Bryan, W. B., *A History of the National Capital*, I, (New York, 1914–16), 175, 181.

[10] Albert Gallatin to Hannah Nicholson Gallatin, January 15, 1801, New-York Historical Society.

[11] Albert Gallatin to Hannah Nicholson Gallatin, January 15, 1801, New-York Historical Society.

boarding houses near the Capitol.¹² "You may suppose," he wrote on another occasion, "that being all thrown together in a few boarding houses without hardly any other society then ourselves, we are not likely to be either very moderate politicians or to think of anything but politics. A few indeed drink and some gamble, but the majority drink nought but politics, and by not mixing with men of different or more moderate sentiments, they inflame one another." ¹³

The greatest inconvenience, he felt, was not being able to have a room to himself. "As to our fare, we have hardly any vegetables, the people being obliged to resort to Alexandria for supplies; our beef is not very good; mutton and poultry good; the price of provisions and wood about the same as in Philadelphia." But worst of all was the loneliness he felt. "Lonesome as you are now situated, believe me, my dear girl, I feel not less so in this place parted from you and from our dear children. But you know that my absence is not intended to be long and that it is *intended* to be the last." ¹⁴

Because of the disordered state of the mails in the new capital, Hannah Nicholson Gallatin did not hear of her husband's safe arrival for almost a month after he wrote that description—a very long, anxious month. Could Washington be that far away? It took less than a week for a letter to reach New Geneva from New York City. She had naturally imagined the worst before his first letter arrived on February 5.

"What a dismal place the federal city must be," she wrote in reply. "I hope Congress does not mean to continue there. I think Baltimore would suit them much better, and they would still remain in the state of Maryland too." She was, of course, concerned that he was so "uncomfortably fixed", with not even a room to himself. But she could not let the opportunity pass to scoff at his determination never to let public life separate him from his family. "Remember," she wrote, "that it is *intended* to be the last time that you will have anybody but your own family for roommates, and this delightful thought must and will console you. Ah! Albert! how often have you expressed this to your poor wife, but no matter, I feel myself more determined this time than ever I did before, and I think this will have some influence on future arrangements." ¹⁵

Unfortunately, "future arrangements" were being determined else-

---
¹² *Ibid.*
¹³ Albert Gallatin to Hannah Nicholson Gallatin, January 22, 1801, New-York Historical Society.
¹⁴ Albert Gallatin to Hannah Nicholson Gallatin, January 15, 1801, New-York Historical Society.
¹⁵ Hannah Nicholson Gallatin to Albert Gallatin, February 5, 1801, New-York Historical Society.

where. Exactly one week before Hannah expressed her own determination in this regard, Gallatin had made a significant discovery: "the newspapers have made me Secretary of the Treasury, hereafter, . . . I may tell you that I have received no hint of that kind from Mr. J." [16] But then Jefferson would not be chosen President until February 17, when, after thirty-six ballots, the House of Representatives finally broke the electoral tie; and then all doubts would be eliminated.

In his letter of February 19, Gallatin confirmed his wife's suspicions that public life was still very much in his future:

> Amongst those nominations which, as communicated yesterday to me by Mr. Jefferson, are intended to be made, the most obnoxious to the other party, and the only one which I think will be rejected, is that of a certain friend of yours. That *he* should be fixed at the seat of government and should hold one of the great offices is pressed on *him* in such manner and considered as so extremely important by several of our friends, that *he* will do whatever is ordered.[17]

Because Mr. Adams had "improperly" called the Senate to meet on March 4, "when three of the newly elected Republican Senators cannot attend, and the expected Republican Senator from Maryland is not yet elected," it seemed likely that the Senate would be hostile to Mr. Jefferson's nominations.[18] No problem was anticipated in getting approval of Madison to the State Department, Henry Dearborn to the War Department, or Levi Lincoln as Attorney General. But Gallatin had been, and would continue to be, the particular target of Federalist ire; and because it was felt that his nomination would not be approved, the administration determined, at Gallatin's suggestion, to delay submission until the new Senate convened the following December, at which time confirmation seemed more likely.[19]

Though there was, said Gallatin, "a chance that we may have to leave (Washington) next fall if the senate shall then refuse to confirm," he nevertheless instructed his wife to prepare to remove to Washington on or about May 1. "But I must state one thing," he continued:

> Remember that whatever may be our station this side of the moun-

---

[16] Albert Gallatin to Hannah Nicholson Gallatin, January 29, 1801, New-York Historical Society.
[17] Albert Gallatin to Hannah Nicholson Gallatin, February 19, 1801, New-York Historical Society.
[18] *Ibid*.
[19] Albert Gallatin to Hannah Nicholson Gallatin, February 26, 1801, New-York Historical Society; Albert Gallatin to Hannah Nicholson Gallatin, March 5, 1801, in Henry Adams, *Life of Albert Gallatin*, (New York, 1943), 265.

tains, it will be essentially necessary that we should be extremely humble in our expenses. This I know will be found by you a little harder than you expect, for the style of living here is Maryland-like, and it requires more fortitude to live here in a humble way than it did in Philadelphia; but I repeat it, it will be strictly necessary, and on that you must resolve before you conclude to leave our present home.[20]

You might, when you see this city, hope that the Senate does refuse the nomination, he said. "Mrs. Smith is here and hates the place." [21] The mud is so thick on some days, and the "houses are so scattered here that without a carriage you cannot move except along one direction where we have a footway." As for himself, he was already finding some compensation for the inconvenience. "The ladies in this vicinity begin to appear quite handsome; so that it is time that I should go home." [22]

Before being designated as Secretary of the Treasury, Gallatin had actually planned to make this his last term in the House, and to devote himself thereafter to the study of law and to establishing a legal practice in New York, where his wife could be close to her family.

> Were my wishes alone to be consulted, I would have preferred my former plan with all its difficulties.... The place of Secretary of the Treasury is doubtless more eligible and congenial to my habits; but it is more laborious and responsible than any other, and the same industry which will be necessary to fulfill its duties, applied to another object, would, at the end of two years, have left me in possession of a profession which I might have exercised either in Philadelphia or New York.[23]

But it was, of course, not to be.

On March 4, 1801 Thomas Jefferson was inaugurated, and on the following day all of the members of the new President's cabinet, with the exception of the Secretary of the Treasury, were approved by the Senate. "Mr. Adams left the city at 4 o'clock in the morning. You can have no idea of the meanness, indecency, almost insanity of

---

[20] Albert Gallatin to Hannah Nicholson Gallatin, February 23, 1801, in Adams, *Life of Albert Gallatin*, 263–64.

[21] Albert Gallatin to Hannah Nicholson Gallatin, March 5, 1801, in Adams, *Life* ..., 265. "Mrs. Smith" refers to Margaret Bayard Smith, wife of Samuel H. Smith, editor of the *National Intelligencer*. Mrs. Smith would become Hannah Gallatin's closest friend and companion in Washington.

[22] Albert Gallatin to Hannah Nicholson Gallatin, February 26, 1801, New-York Historical Society.

[23] Albert Gallatin to Maria Nicholson, March 12, 1801, New-York Historical Society.

his conduct, specially of late. But he is fallen and not dangerous. Let him be forgotten." [24]

Gallatin remained in Washington three more days to confer with Madison in order that they might agree on the general outlines, "the leading principles," which the new administration would follow.[25] And then it was home to New Geneva—the day he had so anxiously awaited since January 12 when he first arrived in the federal city. But how different things were now, how drastically his future had been altered in a few short weeks. Instead of retiring from the House to a comfortable law practice in New York, he would spend the next twelve years of his life as Secretary of the Treasury for two Presidents—twelve years as a resident of that "hateful" city, and much of the time without the company of his wife and sons.

But in March, 1801 his chief concern was in finding a home for his family in Washington.

> This place is so little like anything else that I hesitate where to fix myself. I do not know whether it will be better to take a house in Georgetown where I shall have the advantages of a market, and of a school for James, or whether I should select a place in some elevated and countrylike part of the city, or whether I should take a house close by the public offices. I think, upon the whole, that it will be better to let Hannah chose for herself.[26]

He invited Hannah's sister, Maria Nicholson, to join them in Washington. Since the Gallatins were expecting their third child in August, Maria would be a great comfort to her sister in the new environment. But then, too, he had a special place in his heart for this sister-in-law. Both he and Hannah were, for instance, concerned that, though a girl in her twenties, Maria was as yet unmarried. And so his invitation included a description of the local prospects: "As to beaux, except in winter, there are but few here of my acquaintance.... As to the manners of the people here, you know this is Maryland and although there is a mixture in the city, the gentlemen in the vicinity are generally Marylanders or Virginians." [27] Maria would spend many winters with the Gallatins, and, on one of her visits to their home, meet Congressman John Montgomery of Maryland whom she would marry in 1809.

On May 13, 1801 Albert Gallatin once again entered the federal

---

[24] Albert Gallatin to Hannah Nicholson Gallatin, March 5, 1801, in Adams, *Life* ..., 265.
[25] *Ibid.*
[26] Albert Gallatin to Maria Nicholson, March 12, 1801, New-York Historical Society.
[27] *Ibid.*

city, this time accompanied by his pregnant wife and his two sons: James, who was four years old, and Albert Rolaz, who had just celebrated his first birthday. The decision having been left to her, Hannah determined initially that they would live in that part of the city which her husband had described with such optimism. Accordingly, their first house was in Georgetown. And after a brief stay there they moved to a house closer to the presidential mansion.

But this first summer in Washington was a bad one, and Hannah, disputing her husband's contention that this was the healthiest location, and concerned lest the heat and "miasmic vapors" of the city affect the health of the children as well as her own delicate condition, insisted upon another move. In mid-August they rented a mansion on the Capitol hill, northeast of the Capitol, on the road to Bladensburg—a healthier location in her estimation. Ironically, Gallatin found himself back in that part of the city he had originally thought to be so uncongenial. But "I think it will be necessary to indulge (my family). I do not foresee any inconvenience from it. It is substituting precisely twenty minutes ride to ten." And he had to agree with his wife: "It may be prejudice; but I think, and this summer's experience confirms it, that it is a more healthy situation." [28]

The house on Capitol hill would be Gallatin's residence for his entire tenure as Secretary of the Treasury, and his family's residence during the winter months. After experiencing one summer in Washington, it became his practice, thereafter, to send Hannah and the children to live with his father-in-law in New York City for the summer months, while he toiled on in the heat, and joined them, if he could, for a week or two before bringing them back to Washington.

Because Gallatin was the only member of the Cabinet living near the Capitol, this house naturally became, in the evenings, a center of entertainment and discussion, one of the chief links between the White House and the administration supporters in Congress. And from it, every morning, the Secretary could be seen setting out for his day at the office, either by carriage, or as he often did, on foot, carrying an umbrella to protect himself from the sun.[29]

By the time Gallatin had gotten his family settled in Washington, the face of the city was already beginning to change. William Cranch, the assistant judge in the United States Circuit Court who administered the oath of office to Gallatin, described "considerable altera-

---

[28] Albert Gallatin to Thomas Jefferson, August 18, August 24, 1801, Jefferson Papers, Library of Congress.
[29] Albert Gallatin to Hannah Nicholson Gallatin, June 6, 1804; Hannah Nicholson Gallatin to Albert Gallatin, July 5, 1807, New-York Historical Society.

tions" which had been made in the President's house:

> Instead of entering at the back door through the salloon, the entrance is at the front door on the North side of the house, through the great hall; the steps have been carried round and only a circular balcony and balustrade left on the south side. The bank on the East, North, and West sides of the House, has been cut slanting into a (glacis?) and covered with sods, and a light fence run round on the top of the bank. The levee room is the President's office, and the large room at the East end of the House is divided into two rooms for the secretary. The bells are all hung. If these household improvements are the prototype of his political improvements, we shall have no cause of complaint.[30]

The summer and autumn of 1801 were, for the new Secretary of the Treasury, taken up with mastering the details of his department's business and with filling appointments. "I find there is not much mystery in the mere routine of official duties, and that I will be able to go on well enough with that part of the business without as much labor as I apprehended." But learning the routine took considerable application, and when his work day was finished he found he had no time to himself.[31] As he wrote later in his life, when the Treasury post was again offered to him by President John Quincy Adams: "To fill that office in the manner I did, and as it ought to be filled is a most laborious task and labour of the most tedious kind. To fit myself for it, to be able to understand thoroughly, to embrace and to controul all its details, took from me, during the two first years I held it, every hour of the day and many of the night and had nearly brought a pulmonery complaint. I filled the office 12 years and was fairly worn out." [32]

On such a tedious schedule, the weather naturally affected his health. "Whenever it is intensely hot, application to business affects me very much: when the weather is cool or moderate, I can go on very well. . . . I cannot write after dark at all." [33]

But this did not concern him nearly as much as the way in which the weather affected his family. His children were very sick in that first summer of 1801—indeed, the whole "city is sickly".[34] And this

---
[30] William Cranch to John Adams, May 13, 1801, Massachusetts Historical Society.
[31] Albert Gallatin to James Witter Nicholson, July 17, 1801, New-York Historical Society.
[32] Albert Gallatin to James Gallatin, February 19, 1825, New-York Historical Society.
[33] Albert Gallatin to James Witter Nicholson, July 17, 1801, New-York Historical Society.
[34] Albert Gallatin to Thomas Jefferson, August 18, 1801, Jefferson Papers, Library of Congress.

hastened their removal to the house on Capitol hill, where, on August 22, Hannah gave birth to a daughter, Catherine. Excited as he was over the new arrival, Gallatin was, nevertheless, much distressed at the unhealthiness of their situation, and seeing to Albert's innoculation, sent the boy to live with his aunt at Montgomery Court House, about sixteen miles from the city. "Perhaps I will take him still farther in the country." [35]

It was a confirmation of his worst fears when, in the following year, in April, 1802, with the children sick once again, the infant Catherine died after only two days of illness. It threw a dark shadow over life in Washington, and made society distasteful to Gallatin. As to the "acuteness of Hannah's feelings, I need not say how she has felt under the stroke." [36] And the misfortune would be followed by the loss of another infant daughter in 1805, and a third in 1808, all under similar circumstances. One other daughter, Frances, who was born in February, 1803, would survive.

As for his own safety and comfort, Gallatin seemed less concerned. He applied himself to the business of the Treasury all year round, "as long as Mr. Jefferson and public opinion in some degree requires it." [37] During most of the summers between 1801 and 1813 he would be the only member of the administration, sometimes the only important public official, who dared stay in Washington. Jefferson, for instance, having had long experience with the climate of the area, made a point of being away during August and September, and wondered at Gallatin's willingness to remain:

> I consider it as a trying experiment for a person from the mountains to pass the two bilious months on the tidewater. I have not done it these forty years, and nothing should induce me to do it. As it is not possible but that the administration must take some portion of time for their own affairs, I think it best they should select that season for absence. Gen'l Washington set the example of those two months. Mr. Adams extended it to eight months. I should not suppose our bringing it back to two months a ground for grumbling. But grumble who will, I will never pass those months on the tidewater.[38]

During the months of August and September, then, the business

---

[35] Albert Gallatin to Thomas Jefferson, August 24, 28, 1801, Jefferson Papers, Library of Congress.
[36] Albert Gallatin to James Witter Nicholson, April 30, 1802, New-York Historical Society.
[37] Albert Gallatin to Hannah Nicholson Gallatin, July 4, 1807, New-York Historical Society.
[38] Thomas Jefferson to Albert Gallatin, September 18, 1801, New-York Historical Society.

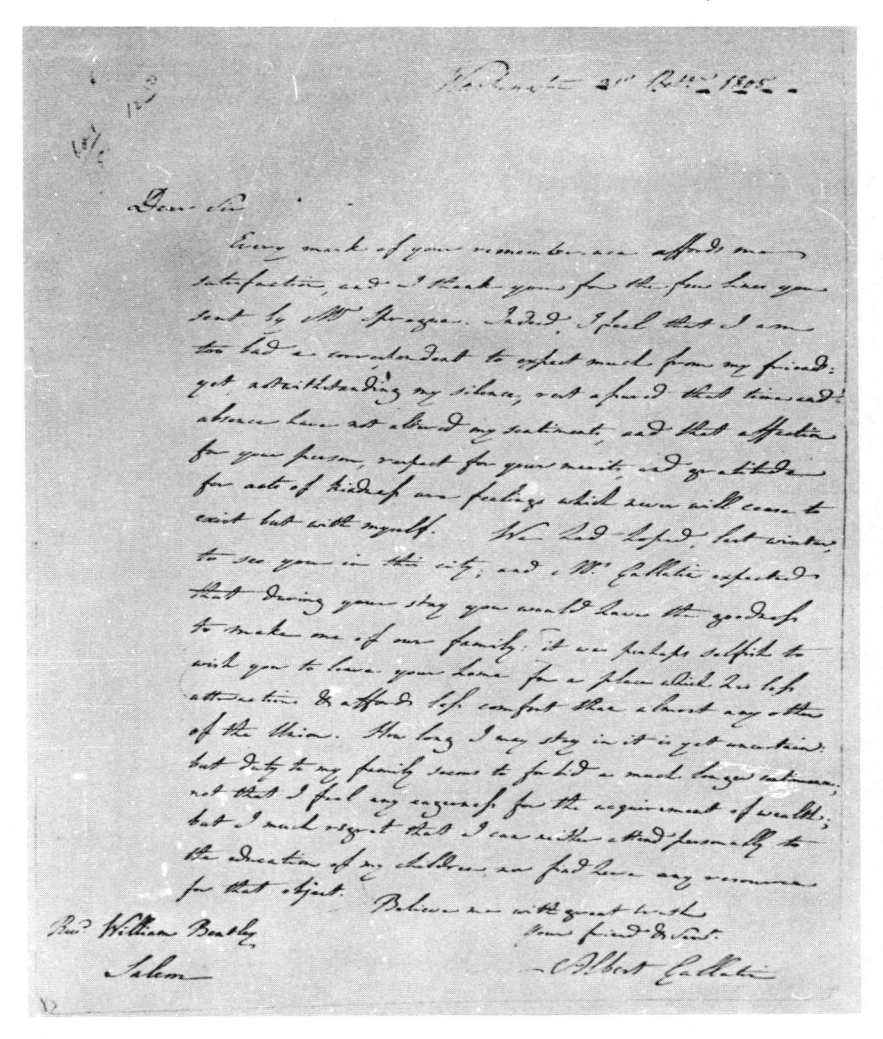

*From the Microfilm Edition of
The Papers of Albert Gallatin*

Holograph letter from Albert Gallatin in Washington in 1805.

of governing the nation was conducted by mail between Gallatin and Jefferson, and after 1809 between Gallatin and Madison. Gallatin sent on more important matters for the President's decision, while handling routine matters on his own, and in every other way acting as the head of the government. But even this was not always possible. In August, 1802, for instance, all business in the capital had to be suspended, for "although I am yet well," wrote the Secretary, "the weather is intensely hot and bilious complaints begin to appear. General Dearborn left the city this morning, he had been unwell for several days; my first clerk is expected daily, the next is sick and unable to attend, and so is Miller, the Commissioner of the Revenue; the Auditor was complaining and is gone." [39]

When, in June, 1807, the United States Frigate *Chesapeake* was attacked by the British ship *Leopard,* and war with Britain seemed likely, panic gripped the nation. Everyone agreed that Congress had to be quickly called into session. But when Gallatin recommended that it be called into session immediately, his proposal was rejected. It would be well into July before enough Congressmen could reach Washington, and "the principal objection will not be openly avowed, but it is the unhealthiness of this city." [40] Instead, Jefferson called Congress to meet on the fourth Monday in October—the 26th of that month—exactly four months after the *Chesapeake* incident.

Unfortunately, if protecting his family from the "bilious climate" required that they be separated from him during the summer, then once again those feelings of loneliness would return. On August 17, 1802, everyone else having fled the city or fallen ill, Gallatin wrote to Hannah:

> I am as low-spirited as before; it will never do for me to keep house apart from you and in this hateful place. . . . I am good for nothing during your absence; the servants do what they please; everything goes as it pleases. I smoke and sleep; mind nothing—neither chairs, bedstead, or house. . . . I grow more indolent and unsociable every day. If I have not you and the children, . . . I cannot tell what will become of me. . . .[41]

He actually embarrassed himself when he wrote again, with much emotion, a few days later:

> Nothing but the hope of seeing you has kept in any degree my spirits from sinking. Whether in the plains or over the hills, whether in city or in retreat, I cannot live without you. It is trifling with that share of happiness which Providence permits us to enjoy to be forever again and again parted. I am now good for nothing but for you, and good for

---

[39] Albert Gallatin to Thomas Jefferson, August 24, 1802, Jefferson Papers, Library of Congress.
[40] Albert Gallatin to Hannah Nicholson Gallatin, July 10, 1807, New-York Historical Society.
[41] Albert Gallatin to Hannah Nicholson Gallatin, August 17, 1802, New-York Historical Society.

nothing without you; you will say that anyhow I am not good for much; that may be, but such as I am, you are mine, and you are my comfort, my joy, and the darling of my soul.[42]

And summer after summer Hannah would write from New York to assure him that she and the children were well, though she would be much better if she had him "to plague a little"; and that they missed him very much and anxiously awaited the time at the end of each summer when he could get away from Washington to join them and all the Nicholsons for a great family reunion. Until then, "there is not an evening passes but I accompany you in imagination in your solitary walks with your segar, on the pavement before the door, or backwards and forwards in one of the rooms." [43]

Though he was, at the time, complaining about his own discomforts, John Randolph of Roanoke, nevertheless, struck a sympathetic chord when he wrote to Gallatin in June, 1805: "Public life, with all its drawbacks, has its pleasures and advantages everywhere but in Washington. I believe we are pretty well united in opinion on the merits of this capital of the nation, where the wretched exile is cut off from all information, society, or amusement, and where the common necessaries of life can be procured not without difficulty, and the most enormous expense." [44]

When, early in 1804, Secretary of War Dearborn decided to build his own home in the federal city, it came as a surprise to many, including Hannah Gallatin, who reflected a lingering disbelief that the government really meant to remain there permanently. "I am indeed surprised and sorry," she wrote to her husband, "that General Dearborn has determined to build in Washington. I am sure he will regret it, it is a place that never will be of any consequence even if the national government should remain there." [45]

Certainly as the time approached when Gallatin had to consider how to provide for the education of his children, his position in Washington became even more untenable, as the city had little to offer in that direction. In October, 1805, he wrote to Reverend William Bentley of Salem, expressing disappointment that Bentley had been unable to visit them in Washington the previous winter, but then offering an immediate apology: "It was perhaps selfish to wish you to

---

[42] Albert Gallatin to Hannah Nicholson Gallatin, August 24, 1802, New-York Historical Society.

[43] Hannah Nicholson Gallatin to Albert Gallatin, June 5, 1804, New-York Historical Society.

[44] John Randolph to Albert Gallatin, June 28, 1805, New-York Historical Society.

[45] Hannah Nicholson Gallatin to Albert Gallatin, June 5, 1804, New-York Historical Society.

leave your home for a place which has less attraction and affords less comfort than almost any other of the Union. How long I may stay in it is yet uncertain." James was of school age, "and duty to my family seems to forbid a much longer continuance; not that I feel any eagerness for the acquirement of wealth; but I much regret that I can neither attend personally to the education of my children, nor find here any resource for that object." [46]

One of the things that seemed to concern Gallatin about the City of Washington was the very noticeable military presence in the city. Much as it went against the philosophy of the Jefferson administration, a marine barracks had been established near the wharfs on the Eastern Branch in 1801. And on one occasion in 1802, Gallatin attended a diner party to which all the socially eligible ladies and gentlemen of the city, about one hundred and fifty in number, had been invited. The party was held near the Navy Yard in a tent, an enclosure formed with sails stretched about six feet high. Most of the guests were delighted with the whole affair, but "to me it looked very sober and dull," wrote Gallatin.

In any case, marines had been placed as sentries around the tent to prevent intrusion by the rest of the populace. "The very sight of a bayonet to preserve order amongst citizens arouses my indignation," he continued. "And you may judge of my feelings when I tell you that one of the sentries actually stabbed a mechanic who abused him because he had been ordered away. The bayonet went six inches in the body and close to the heart. He is not dead but still in great danger and the marine in jail. Such are the effects of what is called discipline in times of peace."

If we have to have an army, thought Gallatin, why can it not be a little one, and why can it not be distributed among distant garrisons where there are no other inhabitants? The expense would make this intolerable enough. "But I never want to see the face of one in our cities and intermixed with the people." [47]

If the summers in Washington were to be avoided, the winters were not to be missed. The "rounds of dinners, fishing, club feasts for ladies, turtle feasts, plays, routs, and drawing rooms," were without end, especially, as Mrs. Samuel Smith said, when all the Secretaries were in town.[48] Gallatin tried, as much as possible, to avoid

---

[46] Albert Gallatin to William Bentley, October 31, 1805, New-York Historical Society.
[47] Albert Gallatin to Hannah Nicholson Gallatin, July 7, 1802, New-York Historical Society.
[48] Albert Gallatin to John Montgomery, July 12, 1809, New-York Historical Society; Margaret Bayard Smith, *First Forty Years of Washington Society*, ed., Gaillard Hunt, (New York: 1965), 27.

formal entertaining. The location of his house near the Capitol made it, on many a winter evening, a meeting place and a center for discussion among Congressmen and Senators and members of the administration; and Gallatin enjoyed the pleasant conversation, unadorned with liquors and cakes. But whenever Hannah gave a party he felt out of place and somewhat annoyed.

Many seem to have noted the fact and attributed his aversion to parties to the fact that he was as diligent in managing his domestic budget as he was in managing the finances of the United States. The Federalist Senator from New Hampshire, William Plumer, thought Gallatin did little entertaining because he was "frugal and parsimonious", so frugal that he was even "very inattentive and negligent of his person and dress. His linen is frequently soiled and his clothes tattered." As for Mrs. Gallatin, said Plumer, her husband's frugality had made of her "a domestic wife averse to company." [49]

William Duane, editor of the Philadelphia *Aurora,* and by no means an admirer of Gallatin, seems to have gotten much mileage and many laughs out of a story he often told of an experience on the Baltimore stagecoach. As the coach passed Gallatin's house, one of Duane's fellow passengers asked the driver who lived there. "Lives?" replied the driver, "Why nobody lives there." But it was evening and there were lights burning inside the house. Surely someone was there. "Oh yes," said the driver, "the Secretary of the Treasury *breathes* there." The driver had apparently, somehow, tasted of Gallatin's parsimoniousness.[50]

But even sympathetic observers had stories of Gallatin's strenuous efforts not to exceed the $5,000 he got as a Cabinet member. Hannah, for instance, complained constantly that he barely gave her enough money to care for the horses. And Gallatin, himself, regreted the fact that he would often take his budgetary frustrations out on his wife or the household slaves and servants.[51]

A family friend, Senator Jonathan Roberts of Pennsylvania, who, like Marie Nicholson, courted and married through the agency of the Gallatin home, preserved his favorite bit of legend. Since the Secretary loved cigars, Hannah, who Roberts described as "by no means a pretty woman, but she was a reading woman and a politician,"

---

[49] William Plumer, *Memorandum of the Proceedings in the U.S. Senate, 1803–1807,* ed., Everett S. Brown, (New York: 1923), 634.
[50] William Duane to Henry Dearborn, July 3, 1810, Duane "Letters", ed., Worthington C. Ford, Massachusetts Historical Society *Proceedings,* Second Series, XX, 337.
[51] Hannah Nicholson Gallatin to Albert Gallatin, June 5, 1804; Albert Gallatin to Hannah Nicholson Gallatin, June 6, 1804, New-York Historical Society.

offered a suggestion. Noticing that he bought cigars a quarter's worth at a time, she pointed out that he would save if he purchased a box at a time. He tried it and discovered that while the cigars were less expensive, the habit became more expensive because he smoked more than he formerly had. His rate of consumption actually doubled, and he determined then and there to make all of his purchases on a retail rather than a wholesale basis. "More was used when it could be dropped from the barrel, while less was used from frequent scarcity." [52]

When Madison became President in 1809, and the pace of entertaining was stepped up under the influence of his wife, Dolley, the Gallatins became more involved in the rounds of parties. Duane complained now that Gallatin "feasts sumptuously every day, and what is more, invites large companies to dine with him." [53] And visitors began to describe the Gallatins as hosts. Mrs. William W. Seaton, whose husband succeeded Samuel H. Smith as editor of the *National Intelligencer,* attended a ball given by Hannah in January, 1813. It was, she said, "more select, more elegant than I have yet seen in the city." She marveled at the amount and variety of refreshments, as well as the "antiquated dames... decked with lace and ribbons... rouged excessively"—Mrs. Gallatin no less than anyone else. But at least the hostess did not deceive herself that it hid her age, reported Mrs. Seaton. She rather defended it "as indispensible to a *decent* appearance." [54]

Author Washington Irving thought that Hannah was the "most stylish woman in the drawing room.... She dresses with more splendor than any of the other of the noblesse. I could not help fancying that I saw two or three of my bonds trailing in her train." [55]

To the Secretary of the Treasury, it was all still a big headache. He confessed that he would probably never be very comfortable in Washington society, or any fashionable circle, and longed for his New Geneva home. "My wife is quite dissipated and takes me along. But I am nevertheless very dull, and sigh for the cottage." [56] He still preferred an evening of simple conversation, and would, for that

---

[52] Jonathan Roberts, "Memoirs of a Senator from Pennsylvania: Jonathan Roberts, 1771–1854", ed. Philip S. Klein, *Pennsylvania Magazine of History and Biography*, LXI, 446–52; LXII, 64–97; 213–48, 361–409, 502–51.

[53] Duane, "Letters", 337.

[54] Josephine Seaton, *William Seaton of the "National Intelligencer"*, (Boston: 1871), 90, 91.

[55] Washington Irving to James Renwick, November 24, 1812, in Irving, *Letters to Mrs. William Renwick and Her Son James Renwick*, no date, 16, 17.

[56] Albert Gallatin to John Montgomery, July 12, 1809, New-York Historical Society.

> TREASURY DEPARTMENT,
> JUNE 18TH, 1812.
>
> SIR,
>
> I hasten to inform you that War was this day declared against Great Britain.
>
> I am respectfully,
> Sir,
> Your obedient servant.
>
> *Albert Gallatin*
>
> *The Collector of customs for the district of New Haven*

*From the Microfilm Edition of
The Papers of Albert Gallatin*

Notification from Albert Gallatin of the declaration of war on June 18, 1812.

reason, always remember the visit of Thomas Paine to his home in 1802, or that of the Prussian naturalist, Alexander von Humboldt, in June, 1804. John Melish, passing through Washington in 1809, visited Gallatin to ask for help in composing his book of travels through the United States. And in February, 1806, Gallatin entertained the New York painter, William Dunlap.

Dunlap reported being impressed by Gallatin's "black, intelligent, and piercing eye." Though it had been twenty-six years since Gallatin had emigrated from Geneva to the United States, his French accent was still pronounced. "But he speaks English with great correctness." He was a thin man, about 5'9" or 10", weighed about 150 pounds, and had "dark hair, coarse and bushy, yellow complexion, long nose, hideous mouth and teeth." [57]

To the very end of his twelve years as Secretary of the Treasury, Gallatin thought Washington a miserable place and longed to retire to New Geneva. But in all those twelve years he had returned to western Pennsylvania for very brief visits only in 1803, 1806, and 1810. He had gotten out of touch with local politics there, and even more importantly, with his personal financial investments. A gun factory which he had started at New Geneva had to be abandoned in 1801 for lack of state arms contracts;[58] and the New Geneva Glass Works, of which he was half-owner, and which would continue to operate, nevertheless, showed no profit. He always felt that his absence from New Geneva, the fact that he could not personally supervise the operation of the Glass Works, was the chief reason for its poor showing. By 1806, $20,000 had been invested in the factory, but still no profit. The workers advised him that unless the plant were moved to a different location, the enterprise would never prosper. Since public life prevented him from attending to the removal of the plant, Gallatin was forced to accept a one-seventh share in the new firm of Repert and Company, which moved the operation across the Monongahela River into Greene County and made it profitable.[59]

Gallatin's land holdings were also jeopardized by his preoccupation with public business. He had once had great plans for New Geneva, a town which he, in partnership with four other men, had planned and promoted. But it was difficult to find buyers for the town lots, especially after the Glass Works was removed, and Gallatin, himself, had not been able to personally supervise the sale of lots since 1795 when he first left for Congress. By the time he left the Treasury in 1813 he still held 100 of the 167 lots in the original plan of the town.

In Virginia, Ohio, and Kentucky he held lands valued at $12,000, on which he continued to pay taxes, but which he had consistently refused to sell or improve because he thought it improper for a federal official, who administered the land office, to profit in any way on land holdings. For twelve years he simply did what he could to protect his

---

[57] William Dunlap, *Diary*, (New York, 1930), II, 384.
[58] Clement Biddle to Albert Gallatin, November 24, 1801, New-York Historical Society.
[59] Albert Gallatin to James Witter Nicholson, January 11, 1808, August 20, 1806, New-York Historical Society; Albert Gallatin to Matthew Lyon, May 7, 1816, New-York Historical Society.

land against squatters and rival claimants, but not always with much success.[60]

It was not with great sorrow, then, that Albert Gallatin gathered up his family and, on April 21, 1813, finally left the City of Washington. The United States was then at war with Great Britain, and Gallatin had been chosen to join the American commissioners appointed to negotiate a peace. On May 9, with his son James as his personal secretary, he sailed for St. Petersburg in Russia.

His twelve years in Washington had both begun and ended, it seems, somewhat dramatically. Back in January, 1801, while he was crossing the mountains on his way to Washington for the first time, Hannah had reported seeing a comet, a "large ball of fire in the sky." It made "such a luminous appearance that the girls in the kitchen came screaming into the house, thinking the world was at an end. It was accompanied with the most tremendous noise resembling the firing of the heaviest canon I ever heard and appeared to shake the house to its very foundation." It was a strange coincidence, occurring as it did just as the new capital was being established; perhaps it was an omen.[61]

About a year after the Gallatins left Washington, in August, 1814, while Albert Gallatin was in Ghent working for peace, the British army entered the City of Washington. When someone fired at them from one of the windows of the Gallatin house, they turned their guns upon the building, and once again a "luminous appearance" was made against the sky.

---

[60] Albert Gallatin to Matthew Lyon, May 7, 1816; Albert Gallatin to James Witter Nicholson, May 5, 1813; Savary de Valcoulon to Albert Gallatin January 11, 1810; Thomas Worthington to Albert Gallatin, March 21, 1803, New-York Historical Society.

[61] Hannah Nicholson Gallatin to Albert Gallatin, January 8, 1801, New-York Historical Society.

Gilbert Stuart in Washington: with a Catalogue of His Portraits Painted between December 1803 and July 1805

CHARLES MERRILL MOUNT

For twenty months in the new city of Washington Gilbert Stuart made his last cryptic strut across the world's stage. Fate, circumstances, and his own remarkable gifts, had made him laureate of the young Republic. By becoming fixed in Stuart's immensely vital and life-like portraits George Washington, his Generals, Adams, Jefferson, their wives, Cabinet members, and friends, already had been given the unique historic vitality which has never left them. Now, following the government from Philadelphia, Stuart functioned again to record personalities who were forming the nation's new capital. Unaccountably, this enigmatic personality then suddenly waltzed himself off to what ultimately became an obscure pauper's grave in Boston.

Washington represented Stuart's last brief bask in the limelight he loved so well. He displayed all the blazing genius of his artistry coupled with the exceptional weakness of character which destroyed both career and man. Charles Willson Peale, the artist who knew Stuart in Philadelphia and Washington, considered him "an indolent, thoughtless being." A superficial judgement, it is instructive that a comparison of letters written by the two men immediately establish Stuart's greater literacy. An added paradox is that whereas Peale was a compulsive letter-writer, Stuart rarely could be forced to touch ink to paper, for Gilbert Stuart was an immensely complicated human being. The strange artistic phenomenon who flashed for twenty months through Washington in fact was a very superior and accomplished man, untidy in dress it is true, frequently rude, yet at the same time polished in manner, urbane, distinguished in speech and bearing, knowledgeable in many fields, and above all a supreme

*The Pennsylvania Academy of the Fine Arts
Harrison Earl Fund Purchase, 1899*

Dolley Madison by Gilbert Stuart. Painted in Washington.

The central work of the most important "set" which Stuart painted in Washington, this represents Dolley Madison when she was official White House hostess for President Thomas Jefferson and was employing her position to send Stuart sitters. The head only was finished before June 3, 1804, when Stuart was six months in Washington and "all the rage."

master of his craft. That he was acutely aware of his own abilities helped no one.

To him Washington was only one more in a long acquaintance with capital cities. In London he learned his craft from Benjamin West. Rising into eminence he was bested in polite in-fighting by Sir Joshua Reynolds. That was only natural, for Reynolds' cold professional wrath had been perfected while keeping his two principle rivals, Gainsborough and Romney, from exhibiting at the Royal Academy. Stuart threw Reynolds the unexpected afront of actually taking away male patronage. Towards him Reynolds showed no mercy. Plunged into debt, Stuart fled to another capital, Dublin, where for six years he exerted a monopolistic control over patronage which set the pattern for America.

War with France, the shortness of the Dublin portrait season, and a desire to seek greener pastures than those of the Emerald Isle, all conspired to bring Stuart to his native American shores in 1793. Born at Rhode Island in 1755, at thirty-eight he was so much a Londoner to recognize anything native in his manners or speech was impossible. Furthermore, he returned as an established institution. With him he brought a royal suite that included not only engravings of his portraits painted for the ruling classes of England and Ireland, but letters of introduction, an English wife, numerous children, and the miniature painter Walter Robertson to produce the smaller versions of his portraits which were an adjunct of his trade. It was with such an entourage that Van Dyck had travelled, and never for a moment did Stuart doubt that he would repeat his own clamorous successes in London and Dublin. Quickly he skimmed the cream off New York society, painting not only John Jay, but the principal merchants, their families, and Hudson Valley landed proprietors like Renselaer and Roosevelt.

This was just to get the taste of their money, for Stuart knew very well that European painters established fortunes by creating large display pieces from state portraits. These could profitably be multiplied by corps of assistants. And though he had failed to bring competent European assistants with him it was George Washington, President of the United States, at that moment the most famous man in the world, who was the real game Stuart sought. The presence of this most important subject in Philadelphia, where Stuart soon followed him, brought the artist back to his own central orbit in a national capital. He entered upon the main stream of American patronage, wrestled single-handed with enormous display portraits of Washington, and for half a dozen years until the capital removed itself to

Photograph from the author

Portrait by Gilbert Stuart probably of Mrs. Robert Smith. Painted in Washington.

Closely related to the portrait of Dolley Madison painted in the summer of 1804, this may demonstrate the first and less felicitous employment of the same elements.

the new city of Washington, experienced the greatest prosperity of his lifetime. It was his busiest period, and curiously, a devoted artist, he responded with the most accomplished and elegant portraits of his career. So great was their delicacy, grace, and dexterity, these Philadelphia portraits would have fitted naturally into the panelled chambers of Versailles.

At the removal of the government from Philadelphia Stuart's career faltered, and it was observable to those about the artist that he did so himself. For the first time his innate tradesman's shrewdness had abandoned him. He stayed on in Philadelphia, where afternoon tipsiness, the result of his habitual lunch-time indulgence in wine, became more notable, as was the unevenness of his temper. This was the period of legendary color in his career, when he was seen kicking a side of beef across the street to his butcher's because it was too bad to be touched. Less notice has been given the fact that out of compassion he bought a slave he discovered being beaten by his master. Possessed of no ready money, a trait common to him in good times and bad, he hastily signed a promissory note for five hundred dollars. The note was not met, and May 12, 1801, the sherriff seized Stuart's entire property. Mrs. Stuart and nine children were taken to live with friends. Only the intercession of President Thomas Jefferson himself preventing an advertized sale from taking place. Stuart then was struck by another execution, this one brought about in behalf of an older creditor left behind in the British Isles.

What money he had saved from his exertions was safely invested in the purchase of a farm, which, in reversion to the values of his Rhode Island childhood, he dreamed would bring him peace. But the documents were not properly made over to him and on the death of the seller Stuart discovered that the whole of the funds put into this transaction, $3,442, were lost. Filled with an inner turmoil that neither wine, adulation, nor his wife could quiet, Stuart deteriorated. His uncle, the Philadelphia banker Joseph Anthony, wrote that he was "in very indigent circumstances; never works but when compelled to by necessity. . . ." and if this was an unsympathetic verdict it was common in an age that neither recognized nor understood the mechanics of hypertension and nervous breakdown. It was shared by all Philadelphia with the exception of America's leading poet, Sarah Wentworth Apthorp, Mrs. Perez Morton, to whom the baffled artist turned for a comfort he failed to receive from his irate and impoverished wife.

Whatever the full nature of that relationship, at this moment Mrs. Stuart packed for herself and her children and left the artist. In these intensely complicated personal, domestic, and professional circum-

Photograph from Peter A. Juley & Son, New York

Anne Allston by Gilbert Stuart. Painted in Washington.

This is a picture which demonstrates how successfully Stuart expressed youth. As in all his portraits, only the head was painted from the model. The hand is from Van Dyck, the column and drape from Rigaud. The Empire style chair appears to be unique in Stuart's work though several Empire furnishings make their appearance in his Washington portraits.

stances, Gilbert Stuart whose portraits were unequalled by anyone then alive unless Thomas Lawrence, galvanized himself into following the departed government to the new city of Washington.

At Christmas 1803 Stuart found Washington a hapazard conglomeration of half-constructed government buildings, accentuated in its disorder by an immense Capitol building and a barnlike Presidential palace. Despite its newness to Stuart a sense of familiarity must have been everywhere, for to this center from the far corners of the nation came much the same collection of country worthies and their dusty henchmen that each year had flocked to Philadelphia and, before that, to Dublin. In preparation for his arrival Benjamin Henry Latrobe, the distinguished architect, had erected a specially designed studio on a lot that Latrobe himself owned. Stuart was to rent this, thus permitting the architect to pay taxes on the land as well as the costs of construction. But that was calculating without Stuart. The room itself, for it appears to have been little more than that, with no living accommodation, was not completed. Latrobe wrote from Philadelphia, December thirteenth:

> I have understood that Mr. Stuart has departed for Washington. If so, you will see one of the greatest, if not the most pleasant, originals in the United States. His presence, and probably his conduct, leaves me nothing certain to say respecting his painting room, but... I shall come prepared to make good all deficiencies on my arrival. ...

Like any man long practicing a profession Stuart correctly calculated the effect of his arrival in Washington. He brought a number of unfinished canvases begun at Philadelphia, among them Joseph Priestley, and the already famous unfinished second life portrait of George Washington. These exerted their natural attraction, as did his acquaintance with all the leaders of the government, met and dined with and often painted at Philadelphia.

His rapid penetration to the very center of society was no new phenomenon. He had accomplished nothing less in Dublin, New York, and Philadelphia. To Washington he brought his international reputation coupled with the capacity to recount his adventures with charm and a hilarious wit. Because he had no wife, hostesses now found him an advantageous guest and a useful one, and no one realized this sooner than Dolley Madison, wife of the Secretary of State. President Thomas Jefferson was a widower. In the President's mansion the functions of hostess were being performed by the effervescent, stylish, and plainly enchanted Mrs. Madison. Stuart's entrance into this

Collection of Carolina Art Association
Gibbes Art Gallery, Charleston, South Carolina

Thomas Lowndes by Gilbert Stuart. Painted in Washington.

This is one of the first portraits to be done in the new ultra-high collar and cravat, a smothering French style which reached America while Stuart worked in Washington. The head illustrates the wonderful economy of modelling and simplicity of form which Stuart could employ when at his best. Unaccustomed to painting ears, which throughout his lifetime had been covered by wigs or long hair, Stuart was not yet so able with them as he later became in Boston.

Collection of Carolina Art Association
Gibbes Art Gallery, Charleston, South Carolina

Mrs. Thomas Lowndes by Gilbert Stuart. Painted in Washington.

Painted without the accessories that were more typical of Stuart's Washington period, this is one of his best characterized and most sympathetic efforts. Note that he has made a special effort with the highly successful ear.

world coincided with an event of special happiness, the planned marriage of Anna Payne, Mrs. Madison's younger sister, to Richard Cutts, in April 1804.

Dolley Madison brought a gaiety to Washington the young American capital had not known under the brief guidance of Abigail Adams. And as best she was able Mrs. Madison deliberately followed the fashions of London and Paris. The era of wigs ended abruptly for ladies as well as gentlemen. Dolley Madison took the lead in washing all traces of powder from her lustrous black hair and wearing it well pomaded. In further defiance of previous convention she discarded the lace cap and appeared bare-headed. A collection of these shining and unadorned heads quickly sprouted near the center of otherwise blank white canvases in Gilbert Stuart's painting room. To each lady he promised the completion of a body and necessary accessories at his first convenience. Mrs. Cutts, who following her marriage departed for her husband's native state of Maine, would prove infallibly that out of sight was surely out of mind, for her portrait begun among the first group Stuart undertook in Washington would be among the last completed.

Dolley Madison's habit of treating small things large and large things small was exactly appropriate to the function she now served of attracting other important, famous, or conspicuous persons to Stuart's painting room. Brilliant in the things she did not say or do, Dolley Madison was catalyst of the success sparkling about the battered Stuart. Alone except for the occasional presence of his eldest son Charles, and the useless slave he had purchased on such calamitous terms, he relaxed in the warm glow of renewed fashionability. Portraits in a heightened and perfected sumptuousness derived from the French master Rigaud grew on his easel, and that satisfaction, against the stimulating background of a new city replete with gay camping-out atmosphere, brought him a renewed vigor in his profession.

Unfortunately new stimulus now, in his forty-ninth year, had the further effect of fatiguing him. He grew more irascible and careless in dress. Able to forget himself only in the absolute concentration of his work any interruption infuriated him. More than in the past he showed himself to be ill-tempered, angry, and impatient. Yet a succession of incidents such as would ruin a lesser man left unaffected the steady flow of sitters to his studio during the first six months.

Not that every portrait did not show some mark of his state. Secretary of the Treasury Albert Gallatin, Swiss by birth and speaking with a colorful trace of his native tongue, became a success only because his bald dome induced the artist to try for its luster. James

Madison, Secretary of State, seemed strangely vacuous when Stuart had done with him. But an ebullient Dolley Madison shook the roguish artist to responsive performance. Eyes narrowed with suppressed mirth, her mouth mutely grinning, though she did not inspire his greatest brillance the opaque expression and flacid surfaces of some recent efforts were overcome.

Chattering as sweetly by letter as in person, Dolley Madison noted, June 3, 1804: "Stuart has taken an admirable likeness of Mr. Madison; both his and mine are finished." Two days later she added: "... Dr. & Mrs. Thornton sat yesterday for the last time to Stuart," but these pictures, when he came to finish them suffered from lack of interest. Examination of the four pictures that occupied Dolley Madison suggests that her statement that her portrait and Mr. Madison's were "finished" in fact meant only that the heads were completed. For it always had been Stuart's habit to complete heads from the living model, then put aside the canvases until under pressure from anxious subjects he worked on figures, draperies, and backgrounds in batches of five and six. The existence of these "sets" of pictures, where technical, stylistic, and material components are closely related, is the final method of following Stuart's production.

That the two Thornton portraits and the two Madison portraits are from the same mould, fashioned by a juggling of the same accessories, suggests that they were completed side by side after the Thorntons' last sittings, June fourth. Stuart donned the same coat when he himself modelled before a mirror for the bodies of the two gentlemen. His cravat remained unchanged while he copied it for both. Studio hands, the same employed since the dawn of his career in London, were given both portraits. The same chair was added. The same curtain, following identical patterns, was brushed onto each canvas with identical carressing touches. The addition of a library shelf indicated Madison's legal training. Dr. Thornton, whose hand derives from Raphael's *Alba Madonna* (as had scores of Stuart's hands since first employed for his London portrait of Sir Joshua Reynolds) had to be contented with the same breviary held by the Madonna.

Mrs. Thornton, considered a figure of considerable charm in Washington, fared less well. The elements of the Dolley Madison portrait were duly repeated, though the attachment of the body to the lady's rigid jaw remained a trifle uncertain. A vignette with organ pipes was inserted, indicating the musicianship with which she entralled Washington's supper parties. Nonetheless Stuart's brush acted in a decidedly perfunctory way. Clearly the artist drove him-

National Gallery of Art, Washington, D.C.
Mellon Collection, 1942

William Thornton by Gilbert Stuart. Painted in Washington.

This portrait of the architect William Thornton was completed at the same time as that of James Madison. When personality failed to interest Stuart his portraits become bland or empty, like this one made up of spare parts familiar from other pictures being completed in the summer of 1804.

National Gallery of Art, Washington, D.C.
Mellon Collection, 1942

Mrs. William Thornton by Gilbert Stuart. Painted in Washington.

Painting Mrs. Thornton, a French woman who sang at her own suppers in Washington, Stuart included a set of organ pipes, an instrument on which he was himself a virtuoso performer. But the portrait is completed so perfunctorily as almost to suggest disdain of the subject. Stuart had a horror of elbows, lopping them off whenever they appeared in his pictures.

self to do work for which he had no feeling, and at least part of the cause was purely physical.

Though he had experienced heat in the New York summers, then suffered it more in the decade passed at Philadelphia, the marshland on which Washington was being built brought him down with hot and cold flashes, shivering fits, and a violent quaking. That his attacks were of the malarial character which hit Washington residents was certain. The effect was devastating upon a man who daily was required to perform a task demanding attention, delicacy, and craftsmanship. He immediately proclaimed to all who would listen an ardent desire to leave Washington.

At Dr. Thornton's home Stuart found the Secretary of State and Mrs. Madison in attendance for dinner, and there too was Charles Willson Peale. Mrs. Thornton sang to the assembled company in her native French, then English and Italian. Peale, when he called at Stuart's painting room in the following days, was treated with a slyness he did not relish. Stuart enquired whether Peale had a good room for painting in Philadelphia, intimating he might return to paint a picture improving on Peale's self-portraits:

> I told him I had not a good room, nor was it worth while for him to take it. He replied that he believed he would paint a better portrait of me than yet was done—that we do not know our own faces, alluding, I suppose that altho' ... [I] had often essayed to take my own likeness, yet that done by another artist would give a more faithful expression.
> I thanked him for [the] intention, and passed it by....

To sitters it was quite clear Stuart was ill. Dolley Madison heard from a friend; "I can tell you nothing new. Stuart is all the rage. He is almost worked to death and everyone is afraid they will be the last to be finished. He says: 'The ladies come to me and say, *Dear* Mr. Stuart, I'm afraid you must be very tired. You really must rest when *my* picture is done.'" And Peale noted the obvious variations in quality:

> This morning in viewing Mr. Gabriel Stuwarts paintings, amongst them was a very excellent portrait of the Marquis Case d'Yrujo and his lady. The latter was a very handsome picture but not so strikingly like as that of the Marquis.

Elegant as the Marquis' portrait undoubtedly is, neither it nor that of his wife has any of the finer qualities for which Stuart is venerated.

For all its bland pleasantness the portrait of the Marchioness Casa D'Yrugo is once more a recasting of the elements that had been so successfully employed in the picture of Dolley Madison. And these

Georgetown University

Archbishop John Carroll by Gilbert Stuart. Painted in Washington.

This portrait of Archbishop Carroll of Baltimore was commissioned by Robert Barry who later had his own two daughters painted by Stuart. The book shelves suggest that the portrait was finished at the same time as the portrait of James Madison in 1804. Another clue is that the curtain takes the same shape as in the Dolley Madison portrait.

appear still again in another picture obviously on his easel that feverish summer of 1804, Mrs. John Thomson Mason. The comparison of these two ladies, wearing almost identical dresses invented by Stuart from some current French source (possibly Madame Hamelin by Jacques Louis David), equipped with the same round shoulders and plump bosom, seated in the same chair against the same curtain, is instructive of the erratic nature of Stuart's work that summer. For Mrs. Mason, whose upper hand is derived from the famous self portrait with her daughter by Vigée-Lebrun, is certainly one of Stuart's finest most transparent efforts at flesh painting. It is as lovely as any female portrait ever painted. For the Marchioness the very same elements dealt out at the same moment fail. Somewhere in the alchemy of an inconstant human nature lies the answer, which defies both historian and critic.

More closely related to Mrs. Madison's portrait is another recently sold in London at Sotheby's (March 25, 1962, lot 104) and which for want of better evidence probably represents Mrs. Robert Smith, whom in her letter of May 7, 1804, Mrs. Cutts records was sitting to Stuart. If the portraits of the Dolley Madison "set" were to be arranged by chronology one would believe this canvas to come first, simultaneous with or preceding Dolley herself. Here all the elements are just being fitted into place, a trifle awkwardly and without the assurance that followed in Mrs. Madison's picture. The arm and chair arrive on his canvas too low for attractive design; the square architectural block on which a column sits is an architecturally correct feature which lacks artistic grace. The curtain falls in precisely the shape that was transferred to Mrs. Madison's canvas, whose sky is painted with the same impasto touches. All the infelicities of Mrs. Smith's portrait are corrected when he reaches Dolley Madison: chair and arms are raised, architectural block is eliminated, a too insistent shadow falling on the lady's neck is replaced by suave halftone.

The summer of 1804, weighing refinements only an artist of his caliber could deal with, feverish and ill, frequently bedridden, Stuart seemed a resentful tyrant, ever prepared to hurl studied insults at those who troubled him. A lady who broke into his concentration by rising from her seat to look over his shoulder was given a text from St.-James: "A man beholdeth his natural face in a glass and goeth his way, and straightway forgetteth what manner of man he was;" but voluble amiability soon vanished. "Excuse me, madam, I cannot paint by direction," he announced. He strode across the room, rang for his servant, and ordered the picture taken away. Floods of tears

National Gallery of Art, Washington, D.C.
Gift of Jean McGinley Draper, 1954

Mary Barry by Gilbert Stuart. Painted in Washington.

Stuart responded to Miss Barry's typically Irish face. He had lived six years in Ireland and now gave great attention to the round bland surfaces and complex lip forms. This is almost his last effort to do the landscape background so favored in English portraits but which he found American sitters did not welcome. Below the chin the body is insecurely constructed and the dog (from a Reynolds portrait) amorphous.

The Cleveland Museum of Art
Gift from J. H. Wade

Mrs. John Thomson Mason by Gilbert Stuart. Painted in Washington.

Perhaps the most lovely of Stuart's Washington portraits, Mrs. Mason is shown wearing the special dress with V-cut sleeves which Stuart developed. Like the hand, copied from a portrait by Vigée-Lebrun, probably the dress never existed.

could not save it. He painted a rich but unlovely wife twice (possibly Mrs. Peter Van Ness) without pleasing her husband. The request that he try a third time was dodged with a hint of Elizabethan bawdiness, Stuart observing wives seldom were pleased with pictures of their husbands unless they were living ones. The cause he advanced for husbands being as seldom pleased was considered too colorful for preservation. Its rudeness found the men bawling at each other, until Stuart jumped from his chair, laid down his pallette, and took a large pinch of snuff: "What damned business is this of a portrait painter," he exclaimed. "You bring him a potato and expect he will paint you a peach!"

Despite fevers Stuart labored on through the summer because of continuing personal and domestic problems. Banished to Bordentown, New Jersey, a censorious wife was heard loud and clear. Her needs, and those of nine children, made it difficult for him to meet demands for old debts left behind in Philadelphia. The income from current portraits, for each of which he was now receiving two hundred dollars, was augmented by a continuous production of his famous "Athenaeum" heads of George Washington. After waiting three years the American Philosophical Society had received its replica shortly before he left Philadelphia. Another completed version had been brought with him to Washington where it was quickly sold to Colonel John Tayloe for the famous Octagon House, designed by Dr. Thornton. Portraits of Colonel Tayloe and his wife were a part of the "set" completed with the Madisons.

It was an insalubrious but prolific period, yet money melted away and his wife's angry attacks followed him. Nor can it be claimed that Stuart was living with any extravagance. To cut his expenditure he slept in his studio, evidently with his son Charles and his manservant. To eliminate even this expenditure he failed to pay rent. What value his man-servant was to him is debatable, for he appears to have caused some of the domestic anguish Stuart knew, especially when Mrs. Stuart suddenly claimed that Edward Stow, a Philadelphia friend charged with transmitting funds to her, had kept the money for himself. "A being so base and impudent" Stuart called the woman who made this charge, and he answered with towering indignation in one of his few preserved letters:

> Nothing could give me more surprise and concern than to find that any censure should reach so sincere and disinterested a friend as I have on all occasions found you [Stow] ... Truth, my dear friend, is

National Gallery of Art, Washington, D.C.

Mrs. Lawrence Lewis by Gilbert Stuart. Painted in Washington.

This portrait of Mrs. Lewis sets a new romantic mood never seen previously in Stuart's work. The hand is from Reynolds' portrait of the actress Mrs. Abingdon and appears again in the portrait of John Randolph completed at the same time.

National Gallery of Art, Washington, D.C.
Mellon Collection, 1942

John Randolph by Gilbert Stuart. Painted in Washington.

The flat area of background, a classic device probably derived from the French pictures of David that were arriving in engravings, is a new feature shared with the portrait of Mrs. Lawrence Lewis.

simple but powerful, and I know no way to repel so infamous an attack as by stating it.

First then—I never did until the present moment direct to you or to your care any letters containing money for the use of my family nor for any other purpose.... That there were three letters, of which I obtained no account, containing money—forty dollars each. They were directed to Mrs. Stuart at Bordentown, but they never reached the Post Office, which is about two miles from my lodging. The weather being severe, the idle rascal who I had entrusted them to had concealed them in his own box. Thus, sir, I hope I have removed entirely anything that could give either of us uneasiness.

One hundred dollars were enclosed, and Stuart promised to send another hundred the following day. It is significant that this figure was the sum he demanded at the commencement of each portrait. One can judge the frequency with which he was starting new heads during these first months at Washington, for he promised that a third hundred would be sent the day after that for the purpose of returning a loan from Isaac Franks in Philadelphia and to meet a grocery bill long overdue. A point of contention existed, as always with this extraordinary man:

... I must insist on the deducting one hundred dollars, which is the price of the head of Washington which has been spoiled by Franks making a hole through it.

That so much industry on the part of a man in shattered health should have generated more debts was symptomatic of Stuart's larger faults and his consistent failure to organize himself into an efficient picture-producing instrument. Except for some few that had been under-painted by John Vandelyn in Philadelphia, the production of Washington replicas remained entirely in Stuart's own hands. Well trained in a London where the most sophisticated studio practices had been employed since Van Dyck introduced them, Stuart's failure to organize an effective studio is striking. He himself had assisted Benjamin West, then later Reynolds, for whom he occasionally filled in areas of drapery and foliage in the huge portraits on which Reynolds' considerable fortune rested. Were he unable to train competent assistants in America then Stuart was obliged to send for them to London.

After Washington's death in 1799 Stuart's imposing full-length portrait of that world famous hero, not to mention the more easily proliferated bust portriats—for Stuart had done two of these from life—became the most sought-after images in the world. The de-

Mrs. Susan Lowndes-Marques
Monte Estoril, Portugal

Joseph Priestley by Gilbert Stuart. Begun in Philadelphia.

The head was done in Philadelphia and left unfinished. In Washington contention raged about the portrait as the Philosophical Society attempted to make Stuart complete it. After promises, and a bond given by William Thornton, Stuart sold it to another buyer, T. B. Barclay of Liverpool.

mand was greater than there had been for Riguad's regal image of Louis XIV or Reynolds' George III. Those artists, like every official painter with a patent upon an image, had seen that these profitable images were produced by a group of highly competent assistants. This was the steady income on which the economics of a functioning studio could be based. Yet this was a necessity to which Stuart never responded and America already was being flooded by forged Stuart portraits of Washington created by Winstanley or painted on glass in China.

From the moment he arrived in the nation's new third capital Gilbert Stuart had become once more what he had been during his first six years at Philadelphia, official portraitist to a government and a nation. His was the indelible distinction of having patented the only persuasive image of this young country's reigning deity, George Washington. Possessed of the most complete competence in his craft America ever had seen, Stuart at the same time possessed areas of excruciating blindness in his character. For either he did not understand his position and what it required of him, or he was incapable of rising to that eminence his own genius with the brush gave him. In the city of Washington, for the last time, circumstances thrust upon him a position that Titian, Van Dyck, Rigaud, or Sir Joshua Reynolds, would have savoured to the full. He had pre-eminence without competitors, ample demand for his work, adulation both personal and artistic, and an opportunity to reap the greatest rewards possible to an artist. His only response was to sink deeper into the mire of pettiness, tipsiness, and debt, that previously had destroyed his Philadelphia career.

In fact it would appear that while he should have been wrestling with the organization of a functioning portrait studio Stuart's mind was elsewhere entirely. For Sarah Morton's loyalty to her husband, her habit of puritanical self-examination, and her decided religious views, had induced in her an acute sense of guilt over her relations with Stuart. She herself described "the early morning and late evening, given to the question of her own faults, many mistakes, and continued affliction." These uncertainties made their relations less of a comfort and more of a strain. Now, after two years, Perez Morton had wound up his business in Washington. Accompanied by his wife he returned to Boston. Filled with anxieties, love of family, and pride in her husband, Mrs. Morton departed, not without asking Stuart to follow. And he, poor benighted fool, decided immediately he would do so. In that same June, 1804, while canvases related to the portrait of Dolley Madison increased in number,

Colonial Williamsburg

James Madison by Gilbert Stuart. Painted in Washington.

Stuart's first portrait of Madison. A letter from Dolley Madison of June 3, 1804, indicates that it was completed by that date. The portrait is slighted, suggesting that in spite of Madison's important position in the government he did not interest Stuart.

Mrs. Madison wrote to her sister: "[Stuart] has now nearly finished all his portraits and says he means to go directly to Boston. . . ."

Unexpectedly, departure of America's greatest poet to Boston lessened the strain on Stuart. As personal torments perceptibly eased, his landlord failed to request unpaid rent, and a tide of affluence slowly accumulated about his untidy figure, Stuart's natural resilience again became conspicuous. He remained ill, but caught hold of himself, and soon was inventing new compositions to replace the threadbare Dolley Madison formula. New angles and, strange for him, even new effects of light were seen. A more romantic atmosphere made its tentative appearance as Anne Allston was dressed up in a sumptuous well-knit example of his high-Rigaud manner. A picture of Congressman John Randolph, built around a hand from Reynolds' Mrs. Abingdon, was enlivened by a new spirit. Much the same Byronic mood found its way into a similar composition surrounding the distinctly romantic head of Mrs. Lawrence Lewis, who before her marriage was Nelly Parke Custis, Martha Washington's granddaughter. His art had begun to move ahead once more, and the returned sympathy of these works marks the start of a healthier phase.

To go to Boston remained always in his mind, and events conspired to give him added inducements. On Christmas Day, 1804, former Senator Jonathan Mason of Massachusetts, a man of considerable wealth and prominence and a member of Sarah Morton's Boston circle, arrived in Washington with his family. Though his visit would be for a fortnight only the Senator had the temerity to ask the dilatory Stuart for portraits of both his daughters Anna and Miriam. To paint off heads, and pocket the one hundred dollars first fee, was no new tactic in Stuart's life. By this practice he had amassed sufficient funds to slip quietly out of Dublin eleven years before.

Stuart's willingness to practice a certain sly trickery upon the demanding Senator was therefore quite natural, and his success was enhanced by an exceptionally lovely likeness of Miriam Mason. Her pure complexion, soft coiffure, and heaven-bent eyes exerted that special charm Stuart frequently found in young girls. Though incomplete this delicate study, so unlike anything within the competence of any purely native painter at that period, highly gratified the Senator. He invited Stuart to Boston to complete these portraits and paint himself and his wife. To Latrobe Stuart announced a plan that is a carbon copy of his earlier strategem in Ireland, though set forth with a new politeness in its terms. Were he to finish all the portraits he had begun, and begin no new ones, he explained, he

*Bowdoin College Museum of Art
Bequest of James Bowdoin III*

James Madison by Gilbert Stuart. Painted in Washington.

This portrait of the Secretary of State is an example of the dignity with which Stuart could endow an official portrait. Begun from the first life portrait, the altered lighting in this head indicates that Stuart got renewed sittings from Madison in June–July 1805. The canvas was taken unfinished to Boston when Stuart left Washington.

Colonial Williamsburg

Thomas Jefferson by Gilbert Stuart. Painted in Washington.

Jefferson sat in June 1805 for his second life portrait by Stuart. An original and four replicas of it by Stuart are known. Stuart induced the President to give him the 1805 sittings by saying that he was unhappy with the portrait which he had painted in 1800 (which is known today only through engravings and which Stuart may have sent to England without Jefferson's knowledge). As was the case with the 1800 portrait, Stuart did not deliver this one (painted on his usual 25 x 30 inch canvas and so unrecognizable by Jefferson as intended for the larger portrait ordered from Stuart by James Bowdoin) to Jefferson either.

In 1821, sixteen years after the sittings, Stuart finally sent to Jefferson, in response to repeated prodding, a portrait which he represented to be the original life portrait. It is not credible that he was telling the truth. This portrait shows the manner of painting typical of Stuart in 1821. It also employs Stuart's materials of that late date, a wood panel 26½ x 21¾ inches. I judge this to be a very late replica painted by Stuart on a visit to Bowdoin College in Maine where his larger portrait of Jefferson painted for James Bowdoin in 1805 then hung.

My reason for selecting the Williamsburg portrait, reproduced above, which was in the possession of James Madison in 1814, as the original is that of those remaining it is the most consistent with Stuart's other 1805 work from a living model.

could wind up his affairs in Washington within six weeks. Freed of these commitments he would move on to Boston, though at the same time he admitted fear of travelling the great distance by coach. "I could do nothing with him, not even get him to paint my own portrait, which, if he ever paints it, will cost me 1000 dollars & more," commented Latrobe, for better than a year's rent was unpaid.

Whether Stuart undertook to act upon this plan must remain open to speculation. Knowledge of his habit patterns suggests that when outlining it to Latrobe, an action parallel to outlining his Irish flight in advance to James Dowling his Dublin studio assistant, his real intention was to decamp in the night without notice. Whatever the reality of what rattled within his mind, Stuart's fevers returned. "... He cannot paint at present," Latrobe noted March 12th. Nor could he flee, so life in Washington continued.

Latrobe entertained legitimate fears for his chances at this juncture:

> I fear indeed that he will lay his bones in Washington, and it seems of the highest importance that some of his family should attend him. He is miserably off, though his life and his residence ... are of his own choice. He has one man servant, who does exactly what he pleases, & is seldom with him. He has shut himself up in a little building never intended for a habitation but only for a painting room; where he boards himself, *after a fashion,* with the assistance of his man servant when he can get him to the place, and where he sleeps. The house is remarkably comfortable & warm, but in the present state of the drainage of the city the situation must be unhealthy in warm weather.... But should he continue sick there will be an end to all his exertions, & I think he runs the risk of dying for want of good nursing where he is.—I shall write to him,—but he is a man who answers no letters....

The following day Latrobe did write, urging Stuart to abandon Washington. "Let me in the meantime intreat you to leave that sink of your health, your Genius, & your interests, Washington. I am often angry with you for having staid so long. Get into the packet [boat] at Georgetown if you cannot bear a carriage,—get away, any where, but get away." Only illness and his natural inertia held Stuart in a situation that, had they any hold on reality, his friends should have urged him to guard with all his might. The great figures of the young Republic had passed before his easel. Already he had painted three Presidents, and a fourth (Madison) whose elevation was still hidden in the recesses of time. He was creating a unique visual record of United States history, and living in the only place

Bowdoin College Museum of Art
Bequest of James Bowdoin III

Thomas Jefferson by Gilbert Stuart. Painted in Washington.

Jefferson did not sit for this, one of Stuart's finest works. It was begun in June 1805 from Stuart's second life portrait of Jefferson and is distinguished by the remarkable dignity which Stuart gave his portraits intended for official purposes.

where he could indefinitely serve this function, with all its profitable attributes.

For could he not multiply images of *all* the Presidents just as he had done with Washington? Ought he not to have had a functioning studio turning out *groups* of Presidents: Washington, Adams, Jefferson, Madison, to be hung in the public buildings and great houses everywhere being erected. Not since Rubens had established himself in Antwerp at a moment of parallel church-building had there been such an opportunity for an artist to produce numbers of canvases in the largest scale. With friends like these Stuart had no need of enemies, though it must be admitted the greatest of his enemies remained his unalterable and ill-coordinated self.

Not alone replicas of Presidents could have been supplied by a well organized studio. The Spanish Minister, Marquis D'Yrugo, ultimately ordered an estimated two replicas each of his own portrait and his wife's, creating a total of six portraits. The sheer repetition was an abuse to a nervous system in the state of Stuart's. The D'Yrugo portraits are notable for a certain wooliness and lack of solidity, a feature that increasingly crept into Stuart's work. The wonderfully controlled facture of his pictures, so perfectly creating an illusion of weight and three dimensions, was possible only because flesh areas were underpainted in black and white monochrome. To this doggedly correct work the early sittings on each portrait were given over.

Later, the head carefully "colored" not always from the living model, for Stuart's clearest examples of flesh painting betray the existence of a formula, the artist had the less agreeable task of doing the same monochrome underpainting for arms and hands. The tedium of such an exact preparation while alone in a studio was an incessant struggle. Increasingly this preparation was skimped, until the hands, which in Mrs. Mason or Dolley Madison are a part of the picture's charm, in Mary Barry became distinctly bad. In certain works everything but the head became amorphous. Yet such freely painted portions are touched in with dexterity and grace, for once he was at work with color the delight in his own facility obviously gave him new heart and he worked with the old application.

To social Washington little of this was visible. Its enthusiasm remained unbounded, and probably at the urging of D'Yrugo the adenoidal Prince Jerome Bonaparte, youngest brother of the newly crowned Emperor of the French, arrived at the studio with his eighteen year old Baltimore bride, Elizabeth Patterson. Himself only nineteen, young Bonaparte required the sponsorship of Spain, for vast sums melted at an alarming rate as this couple paraded America

*Museum of Fine Arts, Boston
Bequest of Minna Bartlett Hall*

Mrs. Thomas Bartlett by Gilbert Stuart. Painted in Washington.

Closely related to Stuart's portrait of Mrs. Richard Cutts, this is among the last group which Stuart finished in Washington. The cap, which does not appear in Stuart's other Washington pictures, may have been added later in Boston where Mrs. Bartlett lived. The hand is the same as that in the portrait of Mrs. Thomas Lowndes.

Gilbert Stuart in Washington

on an extended honeymoon. Society was scandalized by the brevity of the modes Prince Jerome imported from Paris for his wife. "All that Madame Bonaparte wore I could put in my pocket," wrote one who saw her at a ball, and her animal pleasure in herself is equally attested by the bare-breasted portrait later painted of her in England by Vigée-Lebrun.

Like Philadelphia and Baltimore before, Washington derived a season's diversion from adoring this child couple, while Thomas Jefferson in his role of philosopher-President penned avuncular recommendations of the Patterson family to Napoleon. Well he might, for the princely darling of social America remained among them contrary to his brother's imperious wish, and had married without the Emperor's consent. The recipient of Jefferson's epistolary effort was too preoccupied to reply. After his coronation at Notre-Dame, Napoleon had turned his back on a glowering England to defeat the combined armies of Russia and Austria at Austerlitz. When he had rested Napoleon declared his brother's marriage invalid, and informed an unhappy Pope it had been performed not by the Bishop of Maryland (another of Stuart's Washington subjects) but an ignorant Spanish priest.

Young women in their early ripeness often before had evoked responsive performance from Gilbert Stuart, but the effect of Elizabeth Patterson was instantaneous. He had stated to Latrobe that he would complete the canvases already begun but begin no new ones before departing for Boston. Illness had prevented him from carrying out this scheme immediately. Now, roused from his fevers, he painted three heads of Elizabeth Patterson on one canvas, an idealized frontface, deep-cut Grecian profile, and tip-tilted three-quarter face. Each conveyed the clear girlish skin, pink lips, white neck, and curiously elfin eyes of his radiant subject. His sketches delighted him, *and were finished,* not as portraits with the addition of three separate draperies, but to represent angelic heads floating in cloudy heavens. The very last Royal Academy exhibition Stuart had seen in London in 1787 had included a canvas of five such little childish heads by Reynolds.

After this most eloquent of compliments, and a silken show of courtesy, Stuart found the arrogant French Prince delighted him less. Soon Jerome suggested his wife might have been provided with clothing, convulsing the artist's delicate emotional balance. "That you can buy at any milliner's shop in the city," he barked. And having revealed himself for the captious cross-grained fellow he was, he refused to touch Bonaparte's picture further, or deliver *either.*

Collection of Carolina Art Association
Gibbes Art Gallery, Charleston, South Carolina

General John R. Fenwick by Gilbert Stuart. Painted in Washington.

This is a portrait of the same group as the unfinished Jerome Bonaparte. Note the identical placement of darks surrounding the head. The uniform is executed with great delicacy and Stuart's special "loaded touch" in the flashes of gold.

Photograph from the author

Jerome Bonaparte by Gilbert Stuart. Painted in Washington.

This portrait, painted about February 1805, of the youngest brother of the French Emperor is one which Stuart scarcely intended to finish. Stuart's departure from Washington was already planned. The portrait of General John R. Fenwick, of the same "set", suggests how this would have looked completed. Despite its brevity nothing could improve on its incisiveness.

Witt Library
Courtauld Institute of Art

Elizabeth Patterson, Madame Jerome Bonaparte by Gilbert Stuart. Painted in Washington.

Painted about February 1805, Stuart refused to deliver this or the companion portrait of her husband. The poor ear is typical of Stuart up to this point in his career but in none of the three heads did he miss her special charm.

Stuart's display of temperament with the Bonapartes would be the more convincing were we unaware that before they arrived in his studio he had determined to finish no more portraits at Washington. An act of the simplest expediency, permitting the artist to pocket half-fees for the two portraits without the labor of completing them, his attitude towards the Bonapartes reflects a deeper deterioration apparent in his character. He had never recovered from the nervous condition that seized him in Philadelphia. How far he was relieved from it at any subsequent moment in his history requires a fine point of judgement, for as a human being he was never again really normal.

All subsequent behavior must be judged with this in mind, for his existence had settled down to a course of lies and hypocrisies each of which inevitably would lead him to some act of outright dishonesty. No longer sure of the difference between right and wrong and impatient of such awkward distinctions, he reeled about, dazed but smiling, taking quantities of snuff, and playing on the sympathies of those who recognized his artistic stature. "Being a man of genius of course [he] does things differently from other people," opined Dolley Madison. She might have added that sober he was an alliance of anxieties and nervous compulsions, drunk he lacked all judgement or self-control. He was the instant victim of his own frailties, and a bully, a liar, and a cheat. Florid of face, a little careworn and dusty looking, a bit thin on top, his nose packed with quantities of brown snuff from the ever-present box, Gilbert Stuart followed a devious path that was leading him to oblivion.

From an artist of genius, the greatest head-painter of his day, he had degenerated into an unscrupulous adventurer, whose most devious side was reserved for the Presidents of his native land. George Washington never had received anything but a replica of the second portrait painted, and question now arises whether in fact he received that. Far away in Massachusetts where he was retired in defeat John Adams mused in letters: "Stuart has taken a portrait of me, and intends, I suppose, to have it engraved. In that case—but nothing can be depended on. His health and motives are so precarious." News of Stuart's latest triumph in Washington caused Adams to repeat himself sulkily: "I know nothing of Stuart's success. I sat to him, at the request of our Massachusetts Legislature; but have never seen anything but the first skech." Adams had not mentioned, as he might, that Stuart had failed equally to deliver the portrait of his wife. But then, the second President had lost no money, which kept him ahead of his successor.

To Thomas Jefferson the artist was obliged for what he found most offensive of all, a great favor, done him in 1801 when Jefferson had prevented the sale of his household furnishings. As Vice-President in the Adams administration, Jefferson earlier had sat to Stuart in Philadelphia and payment was recorded in his account book: one hundred dollars paid on May 12, 1800. No picture was received by Jefferson. The fact that an engraving of this portrait appeared in London the following August (1801) leads to speculation that Stuart had sent the picture to England without the owner's knowledge.

The answer to that question of propriety is dwarfed by the further revelation that when he moved to Washington, Stuart sold this picture, already paid for by Jefferson, to Senator Samuel Smith of Maryland. The receipt in Stuart's own script has been preserved:

> Received 22 Dec. 1803 from S. Smith fifty dollars in part payment of a Portrait of Mr. Thomas Jefferson to be delivered in six weeks.
>
> Gilbert Stuart

In legal terms Stuart was guilty of fraudulent conversion. He had sold property that belonged to President Jefferson, and the ignoble fact to be faced is that it had become an habitual practice.

A considerable documentation exists surrounding the full-length portrait of George Washington ordered by General Charles Cotesworth Pinckney at Philadelphia in 1797. On July 22 of that year Stuart received $500 as payment in full. Though Stuart failed to complete a large canvas begun of Pinckney at the same time, the pic-

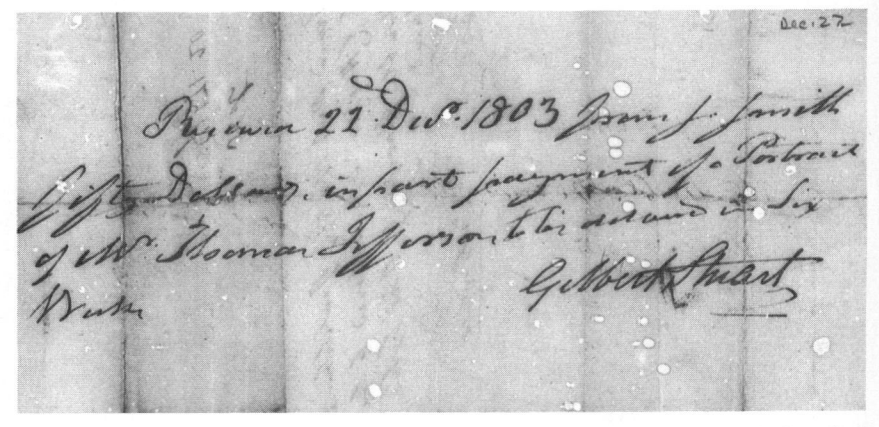

Massachusetts Historical Society

Holograph receipt from Gilbert Stuart to Senator Samuel Smith of Maryland for part payment for a portrait of Thomas Jefferson.

ture of Washington was left in his studio where Washington himself saw it on New Year's day. This large canvas was to have been sent to France where General Pinckney had been appointed Ambassador. In the confusion surrounding the French government's refusal to receive Pinckney, Stuart profited by selling the picture of Washington a second time, to Gardiner Baker, proprietor of a museum in New York. Now in 1804 General Pinckney, who had Stuart's receipt for full payment on the Washington and had never received it or his own portrait, was writing repeatedly to Stuart for explanations. Needless to say he received no reply.

Such persons fared better at Stuart's hands than those who still were willing to believe in the feverish man they found, for they were the objects of his tricks of confidence. He had grown fond of his treacheries and dazzled everyone as he deceived them by telling his own story with persuasive intensity. An extraordinary instance developed around the portrait of Joseph Priestley, abandoned in Philadelphia seven years before. Priestley died, and the Philosophical Society, for whom the picture was destined, became more anxious to possess this image done from life. At first Dr. Thornton was asked to assist: "with a view to get the portrait, [I] . . . have offered even to take it unfinished. . . ."

Other parties became involved too. When he recorded his own mission Charles Willson Peale did not suspect he had been duped:

> His picture of Dr. Priestley for the Philosophical Society very like, though quite an unfinished picture. . . . I was desired by several of the members of the society to urge Mr. Stewart to finish this picture, and he promised me he would have it done it about 3 weeks. . . .

Another year passed. Eventually Dr. Thornton gave bond for the artist's performance. This benevolent interest suffered extinction when Stuart blithely defaulted. He *preferred* to sell his picture twice, and the portrait, very hastily completed, was carried away by T. B. Barclay of Liverpool, an English relative of the subject.

Living by his wits, no longer interested in a steady flow of work which his failure to organize a functioning studio left him incapable of dealing with, in his fiftieth year Gilbert Stuart was content to proceed from one deceit to another. The intensity of his personality and the force of each lie, backed by his international reputation as an artist, made him a confidence trickster of remarkable gifts. By the spring of 1805 his sheer love of tricks had wound him into the depths of a hundred dishonorable circumstances. Exulting in them as though they were triumphs of ingenuity, he felt also an overwhelming terror of being found out. For were he prosecuted criminally the recital of his collected deeds in a court inevitably would send him to prison. As in London and Dublin he was so awkwardly involved he had lost his way and the only relief he could envision was flight.

Such a solution had the merit of familiarity and appealed to him. As he ruminated certain facts stood out to form a pattern. Senator Mason undoubtedly had invited him to Boston, the city where Sarah Morton lived with her husband. Her earlier liaison with the artist had escaped notice. Her gentle hand, deftly suggesting, arranging, and informing, can be detected behind the succession of events that now preceded Stuart's flight. President Jefferson had just appointed her friend, James Bowdoin, Ambassador to Spain. Bowdoin suddenly desired to carry with him to Madrid portraits of the President and Secretary of State. On March 25, 1805, he contacted Henry Dearborn, the Secretary of War:

> I shall be much obliged to you to procure me the portraits of Mr. Jefferson and Mr. Madison if a good painter can be found in Washington, and they should be willing to take the trouble of sittings therefore. I should like to have them done by Stuart. . . . Please to let ye pictures be half length and of a size to match each other. . . .

To Stuart this order came as both an embarrassment and a facility to further treachery. Though vacuous, his head of James Madison painted the previous year would provide the basis for a half-length. Presumably Madison would loan him the picture, but of President Jefferson neither the President nor Stuart now possessed a likeness. That would require delicate handling lest Jefferson wanted an explanation concerning the portrait he paid for in 1800. An experienced and persuasive liar, Stuart informed the President he was dissatisfied with the first picture: "and [he] therefore begged me to sit again, and he drew another which he was to deliver to me instead of the first, but begged permission to keep it until he could get an engraving from it."

Jefferson therefore was not informed Stuart's real motivation was the Bowdoin order, though it was being executed for the man he had just appointed Ambassador to Spain. And to top this chicanery, after proposing a new portrait to the President, to replace that done earlier, Stuart did not deliver this picture either, on the same hoary ground of desiring an engraving. President Jefferson appears to have been more than ordinarily obtuse. At these same sittings, in June 1805, he asked Stuart to do a medallion head, simulating low relief, of the sort he had seen decorating French salons. A rare effort in profile, done in a manner he had never before essayed and in an aqueous medium on paper, Stuart achieved the desired result to perfection. Jefferson therefore paid him again:

June 18, 1805

> Mr. Jefferson presents his compliments to Mr. Stewart, and begs leave to send him the enclosed for the trouble he gave him in taking the head á la antique....

"So! You have come to take off a few heads of the members of Congress, and give them a brushing, which is much wanting," he bantered when, with his son Rembrandt, Charles Willson Peale appeared again. "We spent the greater part of this morning in Mr. Stuart's painting room; Rembrandt is not discouraged by what he saw there," Peale categorically noted. Earnest, bumbling old Peale, with his clutter of ideas and projects and his enormous seriousness, never failed to strike Stuart as faintly ridiculous. Cheerfully, and with an unfaltering joviality, Stuart explained technical procedures to the young Rembrandt Peale, nor could he miss sight of the grave-demeanored father, who, hovering about, bore the air of an apostle observing the mysteries.

The patronizing offer made the previous year of a portrait by which posterity could remember Peale had acted like a challenge, not on the father who in Philadelphia already had painted small scale oil portraits of Stuart and his wife (Metropolitan Museum) but his son Rembrandt who aspired to be a portraitist. Vain Stuart pulled his few black hairs forward over his brow where they hung in disorder, while he volubly entertained his painters. His pleasure at being "peeled" was diminished by the shock of Rembrandt's portrait, for when he looked he found an ogre upon the canvas. The handsome youth who in London had suggested the swagger of King Charles had become a hard-faced, bulbous, red extrovert, time-ravaged and replete with uncouth, leering expression. Accustomed to this less scrubbed side of his father, young Charles Stuart volunteered it was the best likeness he had seen. But the sitter pretended no pleasure he did not feel, laughing at the image of "an awkward clown."

All the careful preparations that had preceded earlier flights from London and Dublin were now in an advanced state. Secrecy was essential, and not a word was leaked to the Peales, for they were in touch with the Philosophical Society to whom he still owed the portrait of Priestley. No one in Washington was told either. His plan

The New-York Historical Society, New York City

Gilbert Stuart by Rembrandt Peale. Painted in Washington.

Calling it "an awkward clown," Stuart did not appreciate this devastating portrait painted of him in his Washington studio by Rembrandt Peale. It demonstrates, too truthfully, how the handsome young man who first made his mark in London had become uncouth and dishevelled. It was painted in July 1805, a few days before Stuart disappeared from Washington forever.

was to bring with him to Boston the two unfinished half-lengths of President Jefferson and James Madison, for the latter of which he had persuaded the Secretary of State to give him at least one fresh sitting. When completed after his arrival in Boston these two pictures of the heads of the government would be his showpieces, and would provide necessary coin. Matters were accordingly arranged with the agents of Mr. Bowdoin. June 27, 1805, a letter therefore was dispatched from the Washington to the Boston agent: "Mr. Stuart... will take [the two uncompleted portraits] ... with his other effects to Boston, and when completed there will deliver them to you, to be forwarded to Mr. Bowdoin...."

The last canvases he completed in the sultry heat of his last days at Washington suffered from lack of interest. Among them, Mrs. Anthony Merry, wife of the British envoy, held a heterogeneous dog whose obscene grin mocked its mistress. Awkward and ill considered the arrival of this portrait elicited gracious notice from the Ambassador:

> Mr. Merry presents his compliments to Mr. Stuart, and begs leave to accompany the enclosed notes with his acknowledgements, for the valuable portrait of Mrs. Merry, on which Mr. Stuart has had the goodness to exert his talents with so much success.
> Washington, July 3d, 1805

This, the last design to leave his easel in Washington, belonged to a "set" with Mrs. Van Ness. They superceded the more felicitous compositional invention employed for portraits of Mrs. Bartlett and, at last, Dolley Madison's sister, Mrs. Cutts, who had waited longest of all. Perhaps the only courtesy recorded at the moment of his sudden disappearance from Washington was a note to Mrs. Cutts, which refered to the snapping baroque curtain in her portrait, one of his finest inventions, whose outline he suggested was his own profile. His jest was not flattery, for suggestive of a purse-lipped satyr, the curtain resembled Stuart's warped psyche more closely than his crumbling Georgian exterior.

The dominating darker side of his nature was about to defeat him utterly as leaving behind twenty months unpaid rent to Latrobe he removed himself from Washington and the center of the world's stage. A rash, improvident act, an astonishing error of judgement, it served to demonstrate that Gilbert Stuart had grown so enamored of running his head against walls at last he was building them expressly for the purpose.

GILBERT STUART'S PORTRAITS PAINTED AT WASHINGTON, DECEMBER 1803–JULY 1805

This catalogue lists only the canvases Gilbert Stuart worked on while resident in Washington. To be historically valid the list includes every canvas it can be established he set brush to in the city. Thus a picture he only completed in Washington, like Joseph Priestley, or began, like the half-lengths of Jefferson and Madison, is included. The purpose is to make a definite listing of the actual labors he performed within a given framework of time and place. It is to be seriously lamented that there is no way to determine now which of his George Washington replicas also were executed in Washington, for they might add substantially to the mass of work he did.

Some few pictures can definitely be established as painted in Washington from primary documentary materials. From these basic examples Stuart's manner during those twenty months has been determined. The further works have been recognized by their technical features, or by relating them to "sets" of pictures one or more of which is known to have been executed in Washington. Asterisks (*) mark those pictures I have been unable to see or examine in photographic form. While in each case the inclusion has seemed warranted I am unable to verify the authenticity of these works from personal knowledge. Unless otherwise specified the medium is oil on canvas and the size 25 x 30 inches.

An effort has been made to bring the ownership of each picture up to date and it will be seen that a number of alterations have been made since the appearance of my complete Gilbert Stuart catalogue raisonné in 1964 (W. W. Norton & Co., New York). When it has proved impossible to bring the ownership down to the present a date indicates when the picture last was located.

ALLSTON, ANNE
    Miss Elizabeth W. Ball (1927)
BARRY, MISS ANN
    National Gallery of Art, Washington.
BARRY, MISS MARY
    National Gallery of Art, Washington.
BARTLETT, THOMAS, M.D.
    Panel, 28½ x 23½ inches. Museum of Fine Arts, Boston.
BARTLETT, MRS. THOMAS
    Panel, 27⅝ x 23⅛ inches. Museum of Fine Arts, Boston. The cap is an unusual feature for a Washington work, and may have been added later in Boston.

BONAPARTE, PRINCE JEROME
   Mrs. W. A. Harriman.
BONAPARTE, MADAME JEROME (ELIZABETH PATTERSON)
   Count Adam Moltke-Huitfeldt.
BOWDOIN, JAMES
   (1) Present location unknown.
   (2) Replica*, said to have been in possession of Princess di Pandolfino (1875)
BOWDOIN, MRS. JAMES
   On loan to Bowdoin College Museum of Art.
BULLUS, DR. JOHN
   Robert L. Fowler, Jr. (1926)
BULLUS, MRS. JOHN
   Robert L. Fowler, Jr. (1926)
CALVERT, GEORGE
   Dr. T. Morris Murray (1926)
CALVERT, MRS. GEORGE AND HER DAUGHTER CAROLINE
   Dr. T. Morris Murray (1926)
CARROLL, ARCHBISHOP JOHN
   Georgetown University
CUTTS, RICHARD
   Mrs. Walter Farwell (1926)
CUTTS, MRS. RICHARD
   George B. Cutts (1926)
D'YRUGO, MARQUIS
   Thomas R. McKean. In 1926 two replicas were said to be in possession of Spanish descendants.
D'YRUGO, MARCHIONESS
   Thomas R. McKean. In 1926 two replicas were said to be in possession of Spanish descendants.
FENWICK, GENERAL JOHN R.
   Carolina Art Association, Gibbes Art Gallery, Charleston, S.C.
GALLATIN, ALBERT
   Metropolitan Museum
JEFFERSON, THOMAS
   (1) The second life portrait. Williamsburg Collection, Williamsburg, Virginia.
   (2) Enlarged replica of second life portrait, 46½ x 38¾ inches. Bowdoin College Museum of Art.
   (3) The third life portrait, as a classic medallion; aqueous medium on paper. Fogg Museum.
LEWIS, MRS. LAWRENCE
   National Gallery, Washington, on loan from Mrs. Edwin A. S. Lewis.
LOWNDES, THOMAS
   Carolina Art Association, Gibbes Art Gallery, Charleston, S.C.

LOWNDES, MRS. THOMAS
　　Carolina Art Association, Gibbes Art Gallery, Charleston, S.C.
MADISON, JAMES
　　(1) First life portrait. Williamsburg Collection, Williamsburg, Virginia.
　　(2) Second life portrait. Begun as a replica of earlier picture the different lighting establishes that Madison gave at least one sitting for this, making it into a life portrait. 46 x 38 inches. Bowdoin College Museum of Art.
MADISON, MRS. JAMES (DOLLEY PAYNE)
　　On indefinite loan to the White House (red room) from Pennsylvania Academy of Fine Arts, Philadelphia.
MASON, MISS ANNA POWELL*
　　33 x 27 inches. Mrs. Courtlandt Parker. Said to have been painted at Christmas 1804 together with her sister Miriam. The picture is unknown to me and I cannot verify where or when it was done. However another portrait of the same subject (Collection Francis C. Gray) is distinctly a Boston period work and casts doubt on this one having been done in Washington.
MASON, MRS. JOHN THOMSON
　　Cleveland Museum.
MASON, MISS MIRIAM
　　Panel, 22 x 16 inches. Mrs. Charles W. Amory.
MEEKER, WILLIAM
　　28 x 23 inches. Mr. & Mrs. Robert I. Gale, Jr.
MERRY, MRS. ANTHONY
　　Panel. Don Jose de Lazaro, Madrid (1926). Stuart is stated by various sources to have painted a companion portrait of her husband. However there appears to be no evidence of this.
PORTRAIT OF A MAN
　　Sold at Sotheby's, March 25, 1962, No. 105.
PORTRAIT OF A MAN
　　Sold at Sotheby's, March 25, 1962, No. 106.
PRIESTLEY, JOSEPH
　　Mrs. Susan Lowndes-Marques.
RANDOLPH, JOHN
　　National Gallery of Art, Washington.
ROBERTS, WILLIAM
　　David Stockwell, Inc., Wilmington, Delaware.
SMITH, MRS. ROBERT
　　Sold Sotheby's, March 25, 1962, No. 104.
TAYLOE, COLONEL JOHN
　　Edward D. Tayloe (1926)
TAYLOE, MRS. JOHN
　　Edward D. Tayloe (1926)

THORNTON, SIR EDWARD
    Not Located.
THORNTON, DR. WILLIAM
    National Gallery of Art, Washington.
THORNTON, MRS. WILLIAM
    National Gallery of Art, Washington.
VAN NESS, JOHN PETER
    John Van Ness Philip (1926)
VAN NESS, MRS. JOHN P.
    Carroll Van Ness, Jr.

Benjamin Henry Latrobe and the Growth and Development of Washington, 1798–1818

EDWARD C. CARTER II

By the summer of 1806, Benjamin Henry Latrobe (1764–1820), the great American architect and engineer, had been Surveyor of the Public Buildings of the United States for over three years and Engineer of the United States Navy since 1804. Latrobe's chief responsibility, the U.S. Capitol, was progressing brilliantly despite the attacks of Dr. William Thornton whose original plan for the building Latrobe was required generally to follow, the criticism of tight-fisted Congressional committees, and the difficulty of securing proper building materials and skilled workers. The architect would not move his family to Washington until the following summer. His numerous projects in Baltimore, Delaware, and Philadelphia required his constant attention, although Robert Mills, his invaluable assistant, watched over his Philadelphia commissions, and the faithful but emotional John Lenthall served as Latrobe's clerk of the works in Washington. As Talbot Hamlin writes in his superb study of the architect, "In all this period Latrobe was busy—frantically, almost maniacally so." [1] His lucrative position as Engineer of the Chesapeake and Delaware Canal evaporated as the project ran out of funds. In April he had asked President Jefferson to raise his federal salary to $3,500 per year, an increase that would justify a permanent move to Washington.

Latrobe's anxiety over his professional future and the separation from his family may in part explain the gloomy quality of the following journal entry for August 12, 1806:[2]

Bishop Carol, (*one of the best Men in the world*) being here, I

---

[1] Talbot Hamlin, *Benjamin Henry Latrobe* (New York: Oxford University Press, 1955), p. 209.

[2] August 12, 1806, The Journals of Benjamin Henry Latrobe, The Papers of Benjamin Henry Latrobe, Maryland Historical Society (hereafter cited as Latrobe Journals).

Collection of Mrs. Gamble Latrobe, Wilmington, Delaware
Photograph by Jack E. Boucher

Benjamin Henry Latrobe. Portrait by Rembrandt Peale, about 1816.

walked a little before Sunset to Mr. Brent's to see him.[3] As I passed over the uninhabited part of the town between the Capitol and his house, which is a low swampy piece of ground covered with Bushes, a tall middle aged woman popped out upon me from a crossroad with a Gun in her hand. As I was then thinking, certainly not upon a *Gun* in the hand of a woman, I started a little back. Sir, says she, pray for God's sake buy this piece of me. There was a wildness in her look, which induced me to think her crazy. I therefore took the Gun from her, and putting the Ramrod into it, found it was loaded. I asked how she came to carry a loaded Gun, and laughing said, that she would get more by *presenting it*, than asked money for it. She said she did not know it was loaded, and seemed frightened at the circumstances. To account for her offering it for sale she said she was a widow with several small children, that her husband had had money when he came hither, but had on his death left her in great distress; that the present drought had prevented her getting any meal, that all her children were sick, her money gone, and that she was now beginning to live upon her furniture and cloaths. The thing she could best spare was the fowling piece and etc. Her distress seemed unfeigned and extreme. While I was talking to her one of my people came up who knew her. I gave her some trifling relief and he bought the Gun. But what is to become of a widow with sick children in this wretched and desolate place, when the present temporary relief is expended! The City abounds in similar cases. The families of Workmen whom the unhealthiness of the city and idleness arising from the capricious manner in which the appropriations for the erection of the public buildings have been granted, giving to them for a short time high wages, and again perhaps for a whole season not affording them a weeks work have ruined in circumstances and health, are to be found in extreme indigence scattered in wretched huts over the Waste which *the law* calls the American Metropolis, or inhabiting the half finished houses, now tumbling to ruins which the madness of speculation has erected. Besides these wretched remnants of industrious and happy families, enticed hither by their own, golden dreams, or the golden promises of swindling or deceived speculators, there are higher orders of beings, quite as wretched and almost as poor, tho' as yet not quite so ragged. These are Master Tradesmen, chiefly building artisans, who have purchased lots, and perhaps built houses in which they have invested their all. Many of them brought hither, and have sunk, the earnings of a laborious life, which in any other spot would have given to them ease, and to their children education. Distress and want of employ has made many of them sots; few have saved their characters,

---

[3] John Carroll (1735–1815), first Roman Catholic Bishop in the United States, first archbishop of Baltimore (1808) for whom Latrobe was building the Baltimore Cathedral. Latrobe probably refers to Mayor Robert Brent—one of Washington's wealthiest citizens—for whom he designed the magnificent house "Brentwood," built in 1818. Both men became close friends of the architect.

most of them hate, envy, and calumniate each other, for they are all fighting for the scanty means of support which the city affords. Above these again are others who brought large fortunes to this grand vortex that swallowed every thing irrecoverably that was thrown into it. Law, Duncanson, Stoddert,[4] and many others from afluent circumstances, are involved by their sanguine hopes in embarrassments from which nothing but the grave will set them free. Of the adventurers and the swindlers whom the establishment of the city brought hither few remain. S. Blodget is confined in the bounds of the prison, and collects $5 subscriptions for the establishment of the University.[5] Greenleaf pays an annual visit to the courts of justice, for the purpose of *testing titles* to lots, and also as agent for his creditors who hold Assignments on his city property.[6] The rest have disappeared or are dead.

Daily thro' the city stalk the picture of famine L'enfant and his dog.[7] The plan of the city is probably his, though others claim it. It is not worth disputing about. This singular Man, of whom it is not known whether he was ever educated to the profession, and who indubitably has neither good taste, nor the slightest practical knowledge, had the courage to undertake any public work whatever that was offered to him. He has not succeeded in any, but was always honest, and is now miserably poor. He is too proud to receive any assistance, and it is very doubtful in what manner he subsists.

Geo. Hadfield, once a promising young artist was sent hither by the English Society of Dilettanti at the request of Genl. Washington and employed to direct the public buildings.[8] Too young to possess experience, and educated more in the room of design, than in the practical execution of great works, he was no match for the rogues then employed in the construction of the public buildings, or for the charlatans in architecture who had designed them.[9] All that he proposed however proved him a man of correct taste, of perfect theoretic knowledge, and

---

[4] Thomas Law (1756–1834) later a friend and associate of Latrobe, William Mayne Duncanson (?–1812), and Benjamin Stoddert (1751–1831). All three men were active in real estate promotion and speculation. Law may well be considered one of the founders of Washington and one of the city's greatest supporters. Stoddert served with great ability as Secretary of the Navy from 1798 to 1801.

[5] Samuel Blodget (1757–1814), after making a fortune in the East India trade, designed the first Bank of the United States in Philadelphia, first purchased Washington real estate in 1792, and like Law, became active in promoting the city's development.

[6] James Greenleaf (1765–1843) another famed speculator.

[7] Pierre Charles L'Enfant (1754–1825) selected by Washington to make the plan for the new Federal City.

[8] George Hadfield (1764–1826) the talented architect who served as the second superintendent of the construction of the U. S. Capitol. Dr. Thornton's harassment and lack of cooperation caused Hadfield to resign in 1798.

[9] This is a slap at Latrobe's *bête noire*, Dr. William Thornton (1759–1828), the successful competitor for the design of the U. S. Capitol. If he knew little of structural problems, his designs for the Tayloe mansion, the beautiful Octogon House, and Tudor Place demonstrate his brilliance in this area of architecture.

of bold integrity. He waged a long war against the ignorance, and the dishonesty of the Commissioners and of the workmen. But the latter prevailed, for General Washington, led by his feelings, and possessing no knowledge of this subject sided against him. Thus has Hatfield [sic] lost the most precious period of his life, that of the practical study of his profession in the first Works he might have executed, and loiters here, ruined in fortune, in temper, and in reputation. Nor will his irritable pride, and neglected studies ever permit him to take the station in the Art, which his elegant taste, and excellent talents ought to have obtained.

To go thro' the List of injured fortunes or ruined characters which this establishment has caused, would fill a Volume. The conduct of the original proprietors, who have killed the goose that would have laid the golden eggs, is another very copious subject or remark.

At present the expenditure of money under my direction on the public buildings relieves in some measure the general distress. I employ scarce any Master Workmen, but do the work by the day under proper Superintendants, of whom the chief, and he would be the chief any where, is John Lenthall, great Grandson of the cidevant president of the Rump parliament under Richd. Cromwell. I found him here nearly as badly off as any of the rest, who had sunk their property in buildings. I wish I could reward his merit as it deserves. . . .

This fascinating description which was intended for no other eyes than its author's reflects more than Latrobe's narrative talents; it reveals his antipathy for the planning of the Federal City and for the execution of its public buildings. Our purpose is to consider briefly Latrobe's attitudes toward the growth and development of Washington, the reasons for his judgments, and his theoretical and material contributions to the city's expansion.[10]

Latrobe's work in Washington may be divided into three periods. From late in 1802 when he produced a plan for a covered drydock to house Adams' 74's, the great frigates, until June 1807, the architect was travelling between the Capital and his various homes and commissions to the North. The next four and a half years saw Latrobe a resident of Washington. Although carrying forward important work

---

[10] The author will not touch on the technical aspects of Latrobe's architectural and engineering work in Washington. For enlightenment in these matters, the reader should turn to the excellent scholarship of Talbot Hamlin and Paul F. Norton, most particularly: Hamlin, *Benjamin Henry Latrobe*, Chaps. 13, 14, 15, 18, and 19 and "Federal Architecture in Washington: The First Fifty Years," *Magazine of Art*, 43 (Oct. 1950): 223–229; Norton, "Latrobe, Jefferson, and the National Capitol" (Ph.D. diss., Princeton University, 1952). For a full survey of Latrobe scholarship see Norton, comp., "Benjamin Henry Latrobe," in *Papers, Vol. 9*, of the American Association of Architectural Bibliographers, William B. O'Neal, ed. (Charlottesville, Va.: University Press of Virginia, 1972), pp. 53–84.

in Philadelphia, he concentrated on the U.S. Capitol which progressed steadily from 1808 to the War of 1812 with a minimum of difficulties, and numerous other federal projects including work in the Navy Yard and the repairs and completion of the President's House. He was busy with private commissions such as improvements to Joel Barlow's "Kalorama" and his post as Engineer of the Washington Canal.

The outbreak of war brought federal work to a halt, and from 1813 to March 1815 Latrobe and his family were in Pittsburgh where he was engaged in an ill-fated scheme to build steamboats. Then President Madison appointed Latrobe Architect of the Capitol and charged him with the rebuilding of the blackened shell. From April 1815 until November 20, 1817 when he resigned the post, the great architect enjoyed a period which "professionally, ... , was the most brilliant Latrobe had ever known." [11] There can be no doubt that throughout those years he was the architectural and engineering force of the Capital. He was responsible for the two great structures then rising and the line of communication joining them. He worked for the Navy and other government departments, and designed churches, banks, and various beautiful private residences such as the Van Ness and Decatur houses. Not only did he shape the nature of government architecture, but, "Perhaps more than any other single individual, Latrobe was responsible for the creativeness, restraint and elegance of detail that characterized this early Washington [private] architecture." [12] In addition, he built bridges and directed the most important engineering project of the period, the Washington Canal. He was also appointed Surveyor of the City of Washington in 1815.

Surely no man was better acquainted with the physical environment of Washington. Yet, one reads through Latrobe's journals, letters, public reports, and other published works and is struck with the almost total lack of attention paid to the topography of the city. This is a departure from Latrobe's usual habit of recording the configuration of any area he visited. He was vitally interested in geology, water supply, ground cover, animal life, and the weather. His journals and letters abound with such information. Why then this apparent indifference to the topography of Washington and even seeming hostility to its plan and the nature of the city's growth?

Benjamin Henry Latrobe had traveled widely in Europe and visited and studied the topography and urban design of its major cities. Thus he was acquainted with the great buildings and open spaces of Sixtus V and his successors' Rome, the dramatic Seventeenth and Eighteenth

---

[11] Hamlin, *Benjamin Henry Latrobe,* p. 460.
[12] Hamlin, "Federal Architecture in Washington," pp. 226–227.

Century development of Paris, and, of course, the important changes that took place in London during his eleven year residence (1784–1795). He probably knew of the contemporary work of Paul Nash. Two American cities, however, gave him his practical education in the problems of urban planning: Richmond and Philadelphia. In both of these communities, Latrobe was forced to deal with geological matters such as rock stratification and the nature of sand, clay, and other soils. This in turn required that he make a precise survey of each city's topography and its adjacent river system.

Latrobe was particularly impressed in 1796 by Richmond's location and its amazing similarity to its mother city in England. He noted, "the windings of the James river have so much the same *cast* with those of the Thames, the amphitheatre of hills covered partly with wood partly with buildings, and the opposite shore with the town of Manchester in front, and the fields and woods in the rear, are so like the range of hills on the South bank of the Thames, and the situation of Twickenham on the north backed by the neighbouring woody parks, that if a man could be imperceptibly and in an instant conveyed from the one side of the Atlantic to the other he might hesitate for some minutes before he could discover the difference." [13] A decade and a half later he would refer to Washington as "this desolate city" when comparing its land values to those of Richmond, "which possesses advantages of fuel, water for mills and manufactures, and navigation superior to any other in the Union. . . ." [14] He constructed his first great public building in America in Richmond, the Penitentiary. Latrobe also drew a brilliant set of plans for a great cultural center, a single structure containing a theater, hotel, and assembly rooms. Although Richmond's resources could not sustain such a project and it was never erected, the design demonstrates Latrobe's dedication to urban cultural unity on a grand scale.

Philadelphia provided other intellectual exposures. Here was a city situated between two rivers whose Vitruvian checkerboard design was punctuated and tied together by five great public squares. Here Latrobe built his superb Bank of Pennsylvania and numerous private residences. More important in terms of urban design, in 1801 he constructed the nation's first waterworks, the most important engineering achievement of the period. In so doing, he came to consider the health and sanitation requirements of the entire community. Latrobe there-

---

[13] Latrobe wrote a full and lyrical comparison of the two sites. April 7, 1796, Latrobe Journals.

[14] Latrobe to Richard Micher, August 11, 1809, The Letterbooks of Benjamin Henry Latrobe, The Papers of Benjamin Henry Latrobe, Maryland Historical Society (hereafter cited as Latrobe Letterbooks).

fore thought of Philadelphia and its people as an organic unity that was dependent on its regional environment for vital support.

Throughout his European and American experiences Latrobe must have been formulating his criteria for successful urban design and development. One can find evidence of his ideas in continual literary and artistic descriptions of the topography and placement of buildings in towns he visited such as Norfolk, Williamsburg, and Richmond. By 1804, he had settled on certain theoretical precepts governing the design of American cities. These are embodied in his survey of the town of Newcastle and his "design of an entire new city on the banks of the Susquehanna, an enlargement of the village called Nescopek." The Newcastle survey also included specific plans for the future development of the town. As Hamlin points out, "the report containing Latrobe's criticism and suggestions is another evidence of its author's interest in the hygiene of the cities and the enormous importance of correct orientation in street and house design." The plan for Nescopek allowed the architect to detail "all he knew about American needs and all he dreamed of for the American town of the future. He planned ample promenades along the river bank and a large town square, around which he would group the important public buildings. The streets were oriented so as to take the best advantage of the sun and of prevailing winds. Vistas were considered; most of the major streets, he says, have either public buildings or the water as climaxes. And, asking the owner—or the trustees—to retain an ample area for public uses, such as the support of an academy, he remarks that such a scheme is so cheap in America and its results so beneficial to a town that even selfish interests rather than public spirit should endorse it." [15]

Both reports contained recommendations for the location of towns, the orientation of streets, and the placement of houses thereon in light of American climatic conditions.[16] Latrobe was convinced that because of the prevailing winds and the transit of the sun "that we have in America only *one* good aspect—the *South*—next to the South is the North aspect...." [17] For purposes of health, comfort, and the

---

[15] Hamlin, *Benjamin Henry Latrobe*, pp. 212-213.
[16] "Plan of the Town of Newcastle," Division of Historical and Cultural Affairs, Hall of Records, Dover, Del., and Latrobe to Samuel Mifflin, March 30, 1805, Latrobe Letterbooks.
[17] "Plan of the Town of Newcastle." Earlier Latrobe had developed his concepts for the proper placement of dwellings and the interior arrangement of rooms in his design for "Old West" at Dickinson College. Latrobe to Hugh Henry Brackenridge, May 18, 1803, Dickinson College. See also Hamlin, *Benjamin Henry Latrobe*, p. 193 for a partial quotation from this interesting letter.

preservation of buildings the streets of cities should be laid out on a north-south and east-west axis, and when possible the majority of the houses should be oriented in a southerly direction. Thus Latrobe's city blocks would be rather thin rectangles with the long sides running east-west. He also firmly believed that the eastern shores of rivers were unhealthy and that every effort should be made to establish cities and towns on the western shores or at points to the windward of rivers.

Thus Latrobe advocated certain principles in the location and design of urban areas:

1. A city should be established only in an area which promised support for commercial or industrial growth.

2. If a river or a body of water was present, a city should be placed on the western shore.

3. Streets were to be laid out carefully on a north-south and east-west axis. The majority of the dwellings should face in a southerly direction.

4. A good potential water supply was a necessity.

5. Great care was to be exercised in matters of public health and hygiene when laying out streets and locating houses and their privies.

6. The city plan was to be compact but with ample internal space for recreation and for the support of education. The physical nature of the city hopefully would foster a sense of community.

7. Every effort was to be made to develop good lines of internal and external communication.

8. A Classical or Vitruvian design was preferable to a Baroque one.

Latrobe's earliest contact with Washington city planning came during his visit to Mount Vernon in July 1796. At that time, the General discussed at some length his efforts to foster the "establishment of the University at the federal city." [18] Evidently the architect did not actually visit the city until April 13, 1798, during his first trip to Philadelphia. He noted this event twice in his journals:

> Breakfasted the morning of the 13th at Spurriers; dined at Bladensburg. Bladensburg is a little village on the Eastern branch of the Potowmac, and has a very picturesque situation in a deep valley, surrounded by woody eminences. We stopped a few minutes in the Federal City, during which time I rambled over the *Capitol*.[19]
>
> The Capitol in the foederal City, though (as I mentioned in my journal to Philadelphia,) it is faulty in external detail, is one of the first designs of modern times. As I shall receive a plan of it from either Dr.

---

[18] July 19, 1796, Latrobe Journals. Latrobe visited Mount Vernon on July 17–18.
[19] April 20, 1798, Latrobe Journals.

Thornton, or Mr. Volney,[20] I mean to devote a particular discussion to it at my leisure.[21]

Latrobe passed through Washington a second time on November 30 or December 1, 1798, and later noted that he spent the day there, "and confirmed the opinion formed of the buildings going forward there in my first visit. . . ." [22] Perhaps he also surveyed the present site of the Octogon House, now the home of the American Institute of Architects, at the corner of New York Avenue and Seventeenth Street, N.W. About that time, he executed his first Washington architectural design. It was a mansion for Colonel John Tayloe. Talbot Hamlin felt the design was "one of great originality." [23] However, it was Dr. Thornton who was chosen to build Tayloe's residence. This may have had an unsettling effect on the two men's early relationship.

It cannot be said that Benjamin Henry Latrobe took on the post of Surveyor of the Public Buildings of the United States with a burst of enthusiasm and a sense of total commitment. In November 1803, he wrote to John Lenthall that, "I have great reason to be dissatisfied with my Canal Directors [of the Chesapeake and Delaware Canal]. But I have put my hand to the plough and dare not look back. Their next meeting will make me a Delaware man or a Washingtonian." [24] A year later, in an attempt to calm his easily offended clerk of the work's feelings, Latrobe observed, "that I care not a straw about the public, and very little about the public buildings, but I care a great deal about *you,* and as you say, the conduct of the Blockheads in the Senate, will certainly ruin all the individuals who were not original proprietors of the Soil of the City." [25] Regardless of his ambivalence when he wrote these words, Latrobe was already well launched on a journey that would bring him both renown and despair.

It is instructive to read Benjamin Henry Latrobe's observations on the growth and development of the Federal City for they reveal how the architect slowly came to accept the possibility that, in time, the vision of Washington and Jefferson might be realized, and that indeed there was some merit in that vision. The fullest statement of the archi-

---

[20] Constantin F. C. Volney (1757–1820), the French radical who apparently included many of Latrobe's observations in his *Tableau du climat et du sol des États-unis d'Amérique.*

[21] April 27, 1798, Latrobe Journals.

[22] September 17, 1799, Latrobe Journals.

[23] Hamlin, *Benjamin Henry Latrobe,* p. 102.

[24] Latrobe to John Lenthall, November 27, 1803, Latrobe Letterbooks.

[25] Latrobe to John Lenthall, March 28, 1804, Latrobe Letterbooks. Congress was threatening to stop further appropriations for construction of the U. S. Capitol because it judged Latrobe's progress to be unduly slow and overly expensive.

tect's judgment is found in a letter of May 29, 1806, to Jefferson's friend Philip Mazzei (1730–1816), the Italian scientist, who had discovered and dispatched to America the two young scultors, Giuseppe Franzoni and Giovanni Andrei whose extraordinary work on the Capitol Latrobe so valued. After thanking Mazzei for securing the services of those men and commenting on their talents, and outlining the work he had planned for them, Latrobe continued:[26]

> The establishment of the federal city was one of the offsprings of that revolutionary enthusiasm, which elevated the american mind far above the *Aera* in the life of our nation, then present. It has been said that the idea of creating a new city—better arranged in its local distribution of houses and streets—more magnificent in its public buildings, and superior in the advantages of its site to any other in the World, was the favorite folly of General Washington. Its existence at last was due to a compromise of interests between the Eastern and Southern States. After the law had established, that there should be a city, General Washington seems to have thought that everything had been done towards *making* it. He himself built two indifferent houses in it. Everything else was badly planned and conducted. L'Enfant's plan has in its contrivance everything that could prevent the growth of the city. The distribution of the public buildings over a space five miles in length and three in breadth prevents the possibility of concentration. The proprietors of the soil, on which the town is to be spread are rivals and enemies, and each opposes every project, which appears more advantageous to his neighbor than himself. Speculators of all degrees of honesty, and of desperation made a game of hazard of the scheme. The site itself is upon a river noble in its extent and depth of water below the city, but above of difficult navigation, and running thro' a country comparatively barren in the materials of commerce—agricultural produce. On the map the Potowmac appears a mighty river, but in fact it is, with the exception of the Shenandoah and a few other branches, the drain of Mountains and barren country. But the principal disadvantage under which this establishment labors is the preoccupation of its commerce by the cities of Baltimore and Alexandria and the town of Georgetown. The two latter cities are in truth the factories of Philadelphia Baltimore and Norfolk. The principal part of near a Million of dollars disbursed in the federal city passes thro' Alexandria and Georgetown to our large seaports. These two towns have accordingly prospered and increased, and may be compared to a pair of fat twins who are suckled by a consumptive mother. The plans of the public buildings were obtained by public advertisement offering a reward for that most approved by Genl. Washington. General Washington knew how to give liberty to his country, but was wholly ignorant of art. It is therefore not

---

[26] Latrobe to Philip Mazzei, May 29, 1806, Latrobe Letterbooks.

to be wondered, that the design of a physician,[27] who was very ignorant of architecture was adopted for the Capitol, and of a carpenter for the president's house.[28] The latter is not even original, but a mutilated copy of a badly designed building near Dublin. If these buildings are badly designed, they are still more indifferently executed. One wing of the Capitol was finished in 1800 when Congress removed hither. The french proverb, "The shortest follies are the best," ought then to have been remembered by the National Legislature; and indeed the Legislature never would have been removed to Washington had not a hope of gaining Southern votes for the reelection of Mr. Adams prevailed over the aversion of the federal party generally to remove the seat of Government from a large and convenient town to an anomalous kind of settlement, neither village, town nor city.

The present president, whose talents, virtues, and great patriotism you know too well to render it necessary for me to say anything to you on his character, has been the only real patron of the city. He has caused excellent roads to be made between the public buildings, and has lent his influence and example to every measure that could promote its growth and prosperity. But it is, I fear, beyond the power and influence of his or any other Administration to *force* a city on a spot all the advantages of which have been rendered of no avail, by the prior establishments which, with capital already accumulated, wharves and warehouses already built, markets already established, and commercial connexions, domestic and foreign already made, are its rivals.

Latrobe's various Reports of the Surveyor of the Public Buildings addressed to the President are correct and formal and in no way reflect his dissatisfaction with the city's growth. However, there are strong hints of the architect's displeasure in his *Private Letter to the Individual Members of Congress* of 1806.[29]

Four years later when Latrobe was engaged in the planning of the Washington Canal for which he had made drawings as early as 1804, his comments regarding the city's progress were far more favorable. Early in 1810, he confided to Colonel Tatem of Norfolk:

We are going this Summer to cut a Canal from the Potowmac thro' the heart of our city to the Harbor or Eastern branch. Upon the whole the city *"looks up"* considerably. It must necessarily become one day or other a great place. A few hundred Years hence some historians may notice the labors of Yourself and perhaps mine; with a *skim* of praise

---

[27] Dr. Thornton.
[28] James Hoban (1762–1831) the Irish-born architect of the White House.
[29] B. Henry Latrobe, *A Private Letter to the Individual Members of Congress on the Subject of the Public Buildings of the United States at Washington from B. Henry Latrobe, Surveyor of the Public Buildings* (Washington City: Printed by Samuel H. Smith, 1806), pp. 5–6 and 16–19.

qualified by an apology for us, in these words, "considering the infancy of the arts and of the empire." This is all we have to hope or expect.[30]

Latrobe was enthusiastic about the canal for it held out the promise of solving some of the city's communication and transportation problems and drawing Capitol Hill and the western portion of the city more closely together. Unfortunately, the Directors of the Company rejected Latrobe's demand for stone locks and wooden ones were constructed instead. A heavy storm in the summer of 1811 destroyed one of the locks and after that the canal deteriorated so rapidly that it never fulfilled its projected purpose. During its construction, Latrobe was amazed to learn that no official survey of the city existed;[31] with the cooperation of his friend Nicholas King, the city surveyor, he made a new survey for his own use.[32]

The summer of 1810 witnessed an explosion of building which the architect reported to his correspondents, many of whom owned property in the city and eagerly awaited news of such activity. He wrote to his friend Thomas Law, then probably summering in Vermont, that:

> Between the Capitol and President's house, there is a great bustle in building. Huddleston, the stonecutter fills up with good brick houses the space between Lindsay's and Charles Jones's so that that square will be compleat.... The Bank of Washington are [sic] also going to build next door to your house occupied by Poydras.... As commissioners of the new Turnpikes we have already laid out the Bladensburg road over excellent ground and the Directors will I believe be able to get to work in 10 days more. We are now exploring the others.
>
> Thus you see we are active enough, and if the city does not improve and ultimately become worthy of its name it is not our fault.[33]

In much the same vein, he informed James Martin of Jamaica, Long Island, "it is in contemplation to carry a turnpike road direct from the Capitol towards Frederic, the part of the country which must make the city commercial, if ever it is to become so; and in order to effect this the New Jersey Avenue has been opened, and the Workmen are now busy upon it, so that before the end of the summer there will be an excellent road thro' the neighborhood of your lots...." [34] A few months later, Latrobe was assisting the British chargé d'Affaires, John Morier, in selecting a site upon which a residence

---

[30] Latrobe to Col. Tatem, February 5, 1810, Latrobe Letterbooks.
[31] Latrobe to Elias Caldwell, July 31, 1810, Latrobe Letterbooks.
[32] Hamlin, *Benjamin Henry Latrobe*, p. 353.
[33] Latrobe to Thomas Law, July 17, 1810, Latrobe Letterbooks.
[34] Latrobe to James Martin, July 21, 1810, Latrobe Letterbooks.

might be built.[35] For the moment, the doubter had been transformed into the booster.[36]

By the end of 1812 the bubble had burst. The failure of Congress to recharter the first Bank of the United States, the endless war rumors, the actual outbreak of hostilities in June, all combined to shake public confidence. Then all federal construction came to a halt and financial stagnation set in. He cautioned Augustus Uz who wished to establish a business for "coloring and ornamenting Walls" to stay clear of the city.[37] Latrobe explained although "There are not many cities in the U. States, which in proportion to their size are more rapidly increasing in inhabitants and buildings than Georgetown; and Washington is not much less improving. . . . But you know well that the present state of the Treasury puts an end to all public expenditures, excepting those of a military nature, and that therefore, probably for several Years, the public buildings will not afford you any business. . . . As to private buildings, . . . only two good houses which are now building in the city will not be ready before next Summer. . . . Were I in your situation, I would not quit a large and populous and wealthy city to look for business in the infant and scattered establishment of Columbia." Prophetic advice, for the following year Latrobe was on his way to Pittsburgh in an attempt to bolster his sagging fortunes.

The British visitation of 1814 returned Latrobe to Washington a year later as Architect of the U.S. Capitol. He informed his father-in-law, Isaac Hazlehurst:[38]

> A great[er] benefit could not have accrued to this city than the destruction of its principal buildings by the British. It has now acquired the confidence of its own inhabitants in its permanence, and every body who could save a little money, is now employing it in building himself a house. This year more substantial brick buildings have risen up, than in any 5 Years before, and the straggling houses are now uniting into something like streets. Several very considerable dwelling houses are under my direction, and one especially for General Van Ness is the largest private house I have designed. . . .[39]

---

[35] Latrobe to John Morier, October 27, 1810, Latrobe Letterbooks.
[36] Latrobe also engaged in real estate speculation. He leased a lot at Sixth and C Streets N.W. in 1803, where he built a small building for Gilbert Stuart to use as a painting room. Stuart was to pay rent to help Latrobe carry the lot. Unfortunately, by 1805 the artist was ill and impoverished. Latrobe, genuinely disturbed by Stuart's unhappy plight, did his best to help the noted painter. In the end, however, Stuart departed, never having paid a cent of rent. Later, Latrobe enlarged the building to serve as a small steam engine factory. This effort also proved profitless.
[37] Latrobe to Augustus Uz, June 18, 1812, Latrobe Letterbooks.
[38] Latrobe to Isaac Hazlehurst, July 27, 1816, Latrobe Letterbooks.
[39] Hamlin claims it was "in many ways its author's domestic masterpiece" and points

As to the Capitol it goes on but slowly, and while the system under which the public buildings are *by Law* conducted is a very bad one, dispatch and oeconomy are out of the question.

Latrobe was struggling by then with the hostile Commissioner, Colonel Samuel Lane, but a year later his artistic frustration manifested itself in a letter to Thomas Jefferson, "The Capitol is growing into a more intelligible form and arrangement, than it had since its destruction by the British. If the permanence of the seat of the Government at Washington would not have been endangered by it, it would have been better in every point of view that the wish of Adm. Cockburn had prevailed over the humanity of Genl. Ross, and the whole building had been destroyed by Gun powder. At less expense to the U. States, a much more convenient, and magnificent building could have been errected, than will be made of the ruins of the former." [40] But the architect rushed the work forward and brought it to near completion, an incredible achievement in so few months, before his temper snapped in front of President Monroe as a result of Lane's continual, malignant attacks.

Latrobe resigned his post on November 20, 1817. He completed "the drawings for the entire building and they were in Monroe's hands before the new year came in." [41] With the loss of this great commission, Latrobe was forced into bankruptcy, and his Washington career was ended. By mid-January, Latrobe, depressed and shaken, had departed for the promise of Baltimore, a promise that would prove illusionary. He left the Federal City a financially ruined and bitter man. In the end, he had judged Washington to be an "overgrown village, tortured as it is by the calumniating spirit of a village without its innocence and afflicted by all the diseases of a city, without one of its advantages." [42]

One must not confuse Latrobe's final spate of bitterness with his earlier disapproval of the general plan of Washington and its pattern of growth and development. Here he was consistent. He objected to the monumental size of the city's design, which he thought was dehumanizing. He judged its execution to be far beyond the financial and technical resources of both government and private interests. Given the design, he correctly believed that government and private building was fitfully carried out and often haphazardly located.

out "that in its heyday it was accepted as perhaps the greatest of the Washington private homes." *Benjamin Henry Latrobe,* p. 457.
[40] Latrobe to Thomas Jefferson, June 28, 1817, Latrobe Letterbooks.
[41] Hamlin, *Benjamin Henry Latrobe,* p. 452.
[42] Latrobe to George Boyd, September 30, 1816, Latrobe Letterbooks.

Finally, better than anyone else, he knew too many of these structures were ill-conceived and badly built.

What then would Latrobe have done, given the restrictions imposed by L'Enfant's plan, to help Washington function more efficiently, provide for intelligent growth, and create a sense of community among its inhabitants? What, in fact, did he accomplish besides creating private dwellings of great beauty and utility and establishing "a standard for governmental building that was to persist for generations?" [43]

Latrobe was convinced that Washington would never function efficiently until the problems posed by its vast interior distances were resolved. Only then could a rational pattern of growth be established. Latrobe believed that the Washington Canal, properly designed and constructed, would help to resolve this basic problem and to engender the city's commercial and industrial development. In the architect's original "plan the canal led from the Eastern Branch, crossed the axis of the Mall a little to the west of the Capitol at the foot of Capitol Hill, and then turned west, following Pennsylvania Avenue and the north edge of the Mall to the Potomac," [44] entering that river at the mouth of the Tiber River south of the President's House. The canal would facilitate construction of both federal and private buildings along its route, allow supplies to pour into the city from both the eastern and western hinterlands, make Washington a major *entrepôt* for both Virginia and Maryland flour, and provide the inhabitants with rapid transit between the Navy Yard and the western end of the city.[45] Had the canal been constructed exactly as its engineer desired, these expectations might have been realized. Despite its failure, the Washington Canal must be counted as one of Latrobe's major efforts to actualize L'Enfant's plan.

Latrobe also attempted to promote the city's communication with the outside world in other ways. In December of 1802, he had prepared detailed "Plans and Sections of the Proposed Continuation of the Canal at the Little Falls of Potomak to the Navy Yard in the City of Washington." [46] In 1808, he offered General John Mason of Georgetown a design for a bridge over Rock Creek, and three years

---

[43] Hamlin, *Benjamin Henry Latrobe*, p. 456.

[44] Hamlin, *Benjamin Henry Latrobe*, p. 352.

[45] For a detailed statement of the promoters' plan and expectations see [Thomas Law], *Observations on the Intended Canal in Washington City* (City of Washington, 1804).

[46] These plans are in the Map Division of The Library of Congress. They are signed, "Benj. Henry Latrobe Engineer," but it has been suggested that they were drawn, in part, by Nicholas King.

later he served as consultant to the Washington Bridge Company which owned a span over the Potomac.[47] He was also chairman of the commissioners of the Baltimore-Washington turnpike in 1810.

As the city acquired adequate internal and external systems of communication, its development could proceed in a more orderly fashion. The problem of how to fill those vast empty spaces remained. Latrobe's answer was to plan a series of highly integrated buildings and monumental structures. Two were to serve as focal points at either end of the Mall. Others were intended as bases of future governmental or private construction. All attempted to humanize the empty void by creating a sense of community. Only two of the following five projects were undertaken, but both collectively and individually they attest to Latrobe's genius in the field of urban design.

Latrobe's first major work was the rebuilding and expansion of the Washington Navy Yard, which he undertook late in 1804. Formerly the yard had been a collection of sheds and slipways laid out in a random fashion on the northern shore of the Eastern Branch from Seventh to Ninth Streets, S.E. Latrobe regularized the existing structures, cleared the remaining ground, and submitted a plan for a series of "new buildings [that] would form an efficiently related group." [48] In his letter of May 18, 1805, to the Commandant of the Navy Yard, the architect stressed the Yard's poor location;[49] he suggested that his plans were open to review and comment by the professional naval officers who worked there. It was an ambitious scheme that proceeded with the blessing of Secretary Robert Smith. A modern yard emerged: new stone-faced wharves, rebuilt slipways, a canal that allowed ships to be refitted deep in the yard itself, and storage and shop buildings located along the canal. New timber and mast sheds, and residences for the commandant and the skilled workmen were constructed. According to Hamlin, "The whole plan was a study in providing the most efficient relationship for a large group of essentially industrial buildings. The structures themselves were of the simplest types. Architectural display was limited to the main gate." [50] The final result was an impressive example of large scale integrated planning.

Latrobe's two Mall projects, although never undertaken, must be considered in conjunction here. In 1810, when designing the Washington Canal, Latrobe attempted to tie it definitely "with the Wash-

---

[47] Latrobe to John Mason, June 22 and 24, 1808, Latrobe Letterbooks. Hamlin, *Benjamin Henry Latrobe*, pp. 350–351.

[48] *Ibid.*, p. 296.

[49] Latrobe to the Captain Commandant, Thomas Tingey, May 18, 1805, Latrobe Letterbooks.

[50] Hamlin, *Benjamin Henry Latrobe*, p. 297.

ington plan and the Capitol" by creating "a formal settling basin on the Capitol axis. Here, . . . , was to be erected the Tripoli Monument, as the chief element in a compact, integrated monumental center just beneath Capitol Hill. If this had been carried out and the Greek Doric propylaea which Latrobe designed for the Capitol had been built, together they would have formed one of America's first serious attempts at site composition in the grand manner." [51]

Six years later, the architect turned his attention to the western end of the Mall, "that intended great unifying element for the city" which still "lay virtually unoccupied." In 1816, Latrobe was designing a national university that was to be placed directly on the Capitol axis and due south of the President's House. John Reps describes the plan as follows:[52]

> The University was to occupy a walled enclosure extending from 13th to 15th Streets and from B Street southwest (now Independence Avenue) to the Tiber Canal on the north. At the eastern entrance Latrobe proposed a university church standing in the center of a circular space marking the intersection of 13th Street and a boulevard down the center of the Mall. Beyond a gate this boulevard was to continue to the central building, an observatory, with the library and refectory occupying its north and south wings. Colonnaded passageways led beyond to corner structures to be used for professors' houses. Extending at right angles to the east were ranges of connected buildings at either end of the main building. In the center of each, Latrobe showed additional residences for professors flanked on either side by student lodgings. At the end of the projecting wings were to be the medical hall and lecture rooms.

Had these two projects been completed, the city would have taken on a grander aspect, the Mall would have begun to play its assigned role, and, perhaps, the university would have moderated Washington's parochial intellectual atmosphere.

Latrobe was always perplexed and disturbed by the divisive effect of L'Enfant's plan on the function of the government itself. The officers of the executive branch lived at some distance from each other. The members of Congress were lodged in boarding houses on and near Capitol Hill, far from the President. The result was a breakdown of communication between the two branches and a virtual legislative paralysis during Madison's administrations. Strong cliques formed around each cabinet officer and dominated both houses of Congress.

---

[51] *Ibid.*, p. 352.
[52] John W. Reps, *Monumental Washington: The Planning and Development of the Capital Center* (Princeton, N. J.: Princeton University Press, 1967), p. 36.

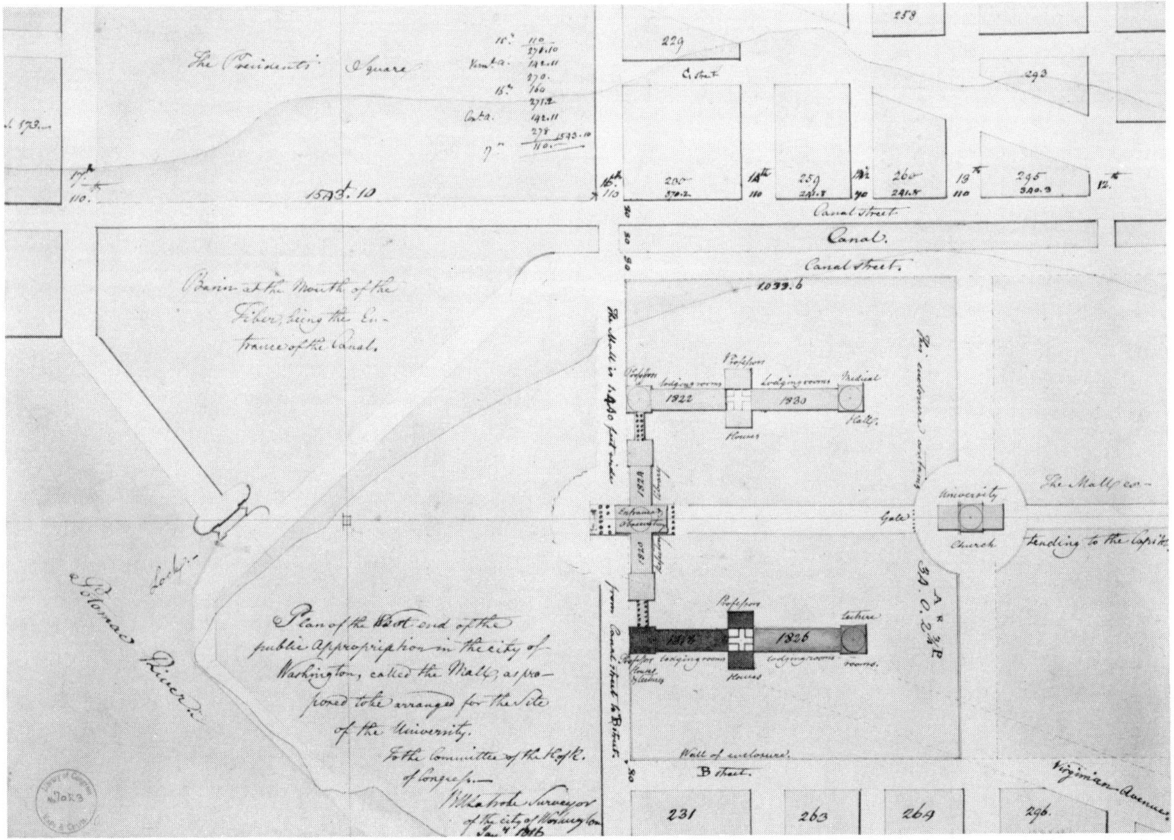

Latrobe's plan of the west end of the Washington Mall, including the site of the proposed National University, Jan-

There was little administration leadership in either Senate or House.[53]

In 1812, Latrobe proposed an idea to Thomas Law, the real estate promoter, that was intended to remedy the executive situation. He began by observing:[54]

> There can be no doubt, but that the local inconveniences attending the establishment of the seat of Government in this city, not only harrass personally the members of the Executive and Legislative branches of government, and those whose affairs bring them to Washington, but that they have a very considerable effect upon the course of public measures. It is now too late to complain of the plan of the city. Many of its objectionable points are incurable altogether and will be felt as long as this remains a city. Others can be remedied, but the present period is unfavorable, rather because the courage to attempt them is wanting and the local prejudices and interests too powerful to admit any successful opposition, than from the great difficulty in the measures that could be adopted, or from the actual injury which private individuals might suffer. One of the greatest of these inconveniences is certainly that which you point out. The officers of government are inaccessible to each other, and to the Members of congress with great inconvenience and expense of hack hire because there are no where in the vicinity of each other, and at a moderate average distance from the public buildings, such houses as would afford them commodious residences.

The architect then demonstrated how far the various cabinet officers lived from each other and from the President. The solution to the problem was to build a series of residences in close proximity. Latrobe suggested the site of the Bank of the United States whose recharter had been recently defeated. He wrote that the location "is exceptionable as being much nearer to the Capitol than to the presidents house, but in every other respect is admirably situated. It lies East of square 491, and extends from the top of the hill down to the Avenue. On the South side of the Pennsylvania Avenue, the public ground extends beyond the Maryland Avenue and the View is uninterrupted down the Potowmac. It is perhaps the handsomest situation in the whole city, excepting that of the President's house."

The architect went on to describe the project and his potential financial interest in it:

---

[53] For a full examination of the impact of distance and the division of the three branches caused by the L'Enfant plan see, James Sterling Young, *The Washington Community, 1800–1828* (New York and London: Columbia University Press, 1966).

[54] Latrobe to Thomas Law, March 20, 1812, Latrobe Letterbooks.

Were I employed to design houses on this square for the residence of the Secretaries, I would place them on the North line of the square. They should be 27'6" front each in one Block, the entrance should be on the North side, and the slope of the hill to the South would furnish a handsome Garden of any extent as far as the line of the Avenue. The houses should have a basement story of about 8'6" or 9 feet. The principal story would then be elevated about 10'6" above the natural surface, and command a very magnificent prospect, a bed chamber story of four rooms would be over the principal story. The stables would be built on the East and West flanks of the square at a small distance from the houses.

I have made a design and estimate for such a block of houses, and altho' I am not much inclined generally to meddle with the execution of public works, I do not hesitate to say that I would willingly enter into a contract to erect and compleat the *houses and stables* in a very sound and handsome manner, and to enclose the ground for $60,000, or $12,000 each. By this contract, I should certainly not make my fortune, but I should not be a loser, and should Government issue Treasury notes, as has been proposed I would willingly take them in payment, or receive in lieu of payment an annual rent of 6000 per Annum, or 10 percent on the expenditure, till the principal should be redeemed, which it would be the interest of Government to do as soon as possible.

The houses would be of a handsomer character and more convenient than any at present in the city, but they would still be *no palaces*.

With the conflict with Great Britain fast approaching, Law was unable to gather sufficient political and financial support to bring Latrobe's scheme to fruition. Both Washington and the political process were the losers.

Following the Treaty of Ghent, Latrobe was able to bring his talents to bear on the development of an even more famous square, the President's (now called Lafayette) Square. With the central portion of the Capitol, his three structural masterpieces on the square comprise the city's existing Latrobe heritage. "It is remarkable that the atmosphere of perhaps the country's most important public square comes, at least in part, from three works linked with Latrobe—St. John's Church, the Decatur house, and the front colonnade of the White House which was carried out by Hoban in 1824 on the basis of the design projected by Latrobe as early as 1808." [55]

When the canal and these five projects are laid out on a map of Washington, the scope and sophistication of Latrobe's work, although only partially realized, is impressive. Individually and as a unit, these architectural and engineering undertakings represented advanced

---

[55] Hamlin, *Benjamin Henry Latrobe*, p. 468.

integrated planning unique in the United States. True, Latrobe was working within L'Enfant's city design; he was not adjusting it. But Latrobe exercised thoughtful judgment in determining what sequence of development would best rectify L'Enfant's shortcomings and create a true city. These works all illuminate to some degree Latrobe's taste and skill in urban design.

Despite the architectural and engineering achievements that so benefited Washington and enhanced its grandeur, Latrobe never appears to have accepted either the city's design or its prevailing pattern of development. His initial judgment was continually reinforced throughout his Washington career. He objected to the site and L'Enfant's plan on aesthetic and theoretical grounds, for both violated a number of his urban design precepts. Washington was badly situated in an economic sense; it was located on the eastern shore of the Potomac; it was not compact; it was a Baroque city. His professional exiences in Washington had never been satisfactory. He suffered at the hands of Congress, Commissioner Lane, and President Monroe; which caused him to denigrate, often unjustly, the government's halting attempts to advance federal construction and thereby stimulate private development as well. Certainly, Latrobe was never totally committed to Washington. He preferred Philadelphia, whose intellectual, artistic, social, and economic life rendered it a true city in his eyes. From the start, Latrobe had to make economic sacrifices to work in Washington.[56] Finally, perhaps Latrobe, forced to conform to Thornton's design for the U.S. Capitol, transferred a major portion of his hostility towards this predetermined plan to another, that of Pierre Charles L'Enfant.

Did the great professional Latrobe fail to comprehend completely the vision of the gifted amateur Jefferson of a monumental city serving as the focal point of national pride and unity? Regardless of the answer, Washington is the richer for the years Latrobe lived and worked there. The U.S. Capitol and Lafayette Square proclaim his great powers of mind and spirit. His taste, skill, and devotion to his profession fashioned a standard for governmental building which has endured to modern times. He created the profession of architecture in America. In the Twentieth Century, Latrobe's heirs—architects, engineers, and urban planners—have worked toward a contemporary realization of L'Enfant's plan for the Federal City. In the end, Washington has also become the city of Benjamin Henry Latrobe.

[56] The Directors of the Chesapeake and Delaware Canal Company docked his salary on every occasion he travelled to Washington. His government salary fell short of those reductions. Latrobe to Isaac Hazlehurst, July 19, 1806, Latrobe Letterbooks.

Columbian Academy, 1821–1897: The Preparatory Department of Columbian College in the District of Columbia

ELMER LOUIS KAYSER

In its century and a half of existence, what is now known as George Washington University has had three names: Columbian College in the District of Columbia (1821–1873), Columbian University (1873–1904), and George Washington University (1904–   ). It has had three major locations, each roughly coinciding in time with the use of the three names: College Hill in Mount Pleasant (1821–1884), H Street between 13th and 15th Streets (1884–1910), and the area south and east of Washington Circle (1912–   ).

During the first seventy-six years of Columbian College's life, its Preparatory Department played a significant role. Such accounts of a historical nature concerning George Washington University as were written before *Bricks Without Straw*[1] practically ignored it. The minutes of the Board of Trustees give it but little attention and that is limited to appropriations for building from time to time, infrequent mention of the appointment of members of the staff, and enrollment figures included from time to time, in reports to the Board. The reasons for this paucity of special mention of the Preparatory Department are not hard to find.

The Preparatory Department was an integral part of the College. The College faculty supervised its work and its members frequently gave instruction in the Prep. So close was the tie that enrollment figures of the College and the Prep are frequently not separated but listed simply under "classical". It was anticipated that Prep students with special qualifications might take single College subjects while still in Prep, and allowance for this was made in the schedule of tuition charges. Although when later a terminal course was estab-

---

Delivered before the Columbia Historical Society on February 16, 1971.

[1] Elmer Louis Kayser, *Bricks Without Straw: The Evolution of George Washington University,* New York, 1970.

Columbian Academy, 1821–1897

lished in Prep and those who completed it were given a High School Certificate, the only formal evidence of the completion of the classical prep course that was given was a certificate of admission to the College.

The opening of a preparatory department was recommended to the Board on May 16, 1821, and the first group of students assembled in the newly completed college building[2] included among its 30 students 10 preparatory students. The enrollment built up steadily during the first five years from ten to twenty-four students.

The Board minutes leave us relatively in the dark during the period when deepening financial difficulties and attendant internal dislocations, followed by herculean and successful efforts to regain solvency, absorbed much of the attention of the Board and the President of the Faculty. The effect of the stresses of the time is seen in the rapid rotation of principals of the Preparatory School. Seventeen men held that office between 1822 and 1849.

A turn in the tide occurred in that latter year. On March 17, 1848, John Withers, the most generous of the College's early benefactors, made a sizable gift, a portion of which was earmarked for the building of a preparatory school on a lot belonging to the College in the city. That building, located at 14th and N Streets, on Square 242, was completed in the fall of 1849. It was a brick structure of two stories, 25 by 38 feet. A temporary principal, Jonathan Tilson, was appointed pending completion of the arrangements with Zalmon Richards as permanent principal.[3]

Richards was a graduate of Williams in the class of 1836. His ability as a schoolman was evidenced by his later selection as Superintendent of Schools of the District and his election as first president of the National Education Association.[4] Appointed principal in 1849, as such he was to collect all bills and, out of the gross receipts, employ necessary assistants and pay costs of advertising, cleaning, fuel and ordinary repairs. He was to settle with the Treasurer semi-annually, retaining three fourths of the net as his compensation and paying the remaining fourth to the Treasurer as the college's share.[5] Hopes that a degree of permanence had been attained proved groundless. Richards resigned in the summer of 1851, and the school building which cost $1,700 to construct and the lot it occupied were sold for the sum

---

[2] *Minutes of the Board of Trustees,* January 15, 1822.
[3] *Ibid.,* June 9, 1848; September 3, 1848.
[4] Howard Lincoln Hodgkins, compiler, *Historical Catalogue of the Officers and Graduates of the Columbian University,* Washington, 1891, p. 47.
[5] *Minutes of the Board of Trustees,* March 30, 1849.

George Washington University Collection

John Withers (1776–1861), Trustee of Columbian College, 1832–1861, principal benefactor of the early Preparatory School.

of $2,500 in the following fall. The school was moved back to College Hill.[6]

In the early 1850's registration began to increase. President Joel Smith Bacon reported to the Board in June 1852 that the combined registration of College and Prep amounted to 100.[7] That meant that

---
[6] *Ibid.*, July 5, 1851; November 15, 1851.
[7] *Ibid.*, July 15, 1852.

the capacity of the College building had been reached and more space was required. Accordingly the Trustees in 1853 had the building housing the philosophical apparatus remodeled, at a cost of $730, by raising the roof for a second floor so as to provide room for the Preparatory School. George S. Bacon, who was appointed principal at this time for three years, was directed to pay the interest on the cost of remodeling out of the income of the school from tuition.[8]

The growth of the public secondary school movement elsewhere had, by this time, made glaringly obvious the limited opportunities offered in the District which had yet no public high school. A committee of the College Trustees conferred with the Trustees of the Public Schools of Washington to urge them partially to atone for the lack by sending a few of their advanced students to the Prep to pursue their studies at the expense of the Public School Fund.[9] The Prep School itself was in no financial condition to grant any more free tuition. Some generous people did come forward and agree to underwrite the expenses of individual students. The Board held strictly to the policy that the school be maintained by student fees and a formal instruction was spelled out in 1855 that the Board was not to be involved in any pecuniary liability.[10] It was only three months later that the Board involved itself in pecuniary liability and the continued growth of the Prep was one of the reasons.

The Reverend Mr. (later President) George Whitefield Samson made the recommendation and the Board approved. On a site north of the Faculty houses and west of the College building there was erected for the steward a house of three stories with a back building of two stories. The main house was 40 feet deep and 28 feet wide; the back building 30 feet deep and 16 feet wide. The lower floor was supported by pillars and used as a refectory, the second floor contained the living quarters of the steward's family, and five rooms on the third floor were used by boarders from Prep. The structure cost $3,850. Cash was required because the wary builder demanded a $1,000 installment paid when the roof was on, another when the walls were plastered, and a third installment when the building was completed, with the rest within six months. Uninvested endowment funds (to be paid back!) were used for the purpose. The sum of $450 was added to the cost when it was decided to build a third floor on the back building to give additional rooms for prep boarders.[11]

In the years just preceding the War of 1861–1865, the Prep School

---

[8] *Ibid.*, August 9, 1853.
[9] *Ibid.*, February 2, 1855.
[10] *Ibid.*, April 15, 1855.
[11] *Ibid.*, October 10, 1855.

enjoyed a brief period of prosperity with an enrollment reaching into the seventies. To the College, it had become a marked finanical asset. In 1859–1860, Prep brought in $2,000 of which $500 went to the Principal, $200 to extra teachers, and a surplus of $1,100 to the college treasury. It was felt expedient to change the tuition fee to $50 per year.[12] At the time of the outbreak of hostilities between the states, the student body came entirely from the District, Maryland, and the south. Soon it was restricted to youth from the District. The early years of war were a period of great disquiet and uncertainty for the local population. The future of the Capital itself was questioned. Many people left Washington for other areas where the chances of actual combat were small. Transportation was all but halted, construction ceased, and many business enterprises ceased to function. Unemployment was high, the economy shaky, and life increasingly difficult. But when the government began to meet its problems in a positive way with the organized defense of the Capital, the formation here of the Army of the Potomac, the application of industry to war needs, and the formation of a vast civil, as well as military, administrative personnel, the picture changed and the city experienced a war boom. Student registration during the period expressed the mood and the state of mind and pocketbook of citizens of the District. After reaching a record low in registration for the time in the beginning of 1862, two years later the registration reached a record high in 1864–1865 and continued to increase, though in not as spectacular a fashion, in the years that immediately followed. The District and its institutions alike were moving up to a new plane. While the College had shown no phenomenal growth, the Prep did with a registration regularly of more than 100 students.

The expansion of physical facilities, even though there had been increased room made available as recently as 1855, was mandatory. In 1866–1867, along with improvements on the grounds, a new school was built at a cost of $8,450 with an additional $1,000 for heating. An appropriation of $500 was made for furniture, apparatus, and maps for the Preparatory Department. Quite legitimately, tuition was increased to $60 per year, room rent was at $40 for one in a room, $20 each for two, and $15 for more than two.[13]

As the 1870's went on, as the Prep quarters and the equipment began to show wear and tear, and as College Hill seemed more and more distant from the thriving city that had taken form adjacent to it, the student body began to decrease in size and fell well below the

---

[12] *Ibid.*, June 26, 1860; October 10, 1860.
[13] *Ibid.*, June 25, 1866; June 25, 1867; January 13, 1869; June 8, 1869.

previous registrations of a hundred or more. The Board again appealed to its friends to endow scholarships for the support of pupils from the public schools.[14] It began to consider actively the removal of both College and Prep to the city. (Being north of the Boundary, College Hill was in the County and not in the City of Washington.) It was confidently stated that the removal of the Prep to the city would double the size of its student body. This was music to the ears of the hard-pressed Board. The College was generally accumulating an annual deficit. Because of the nature of its set-up the Preparatory School could not incur a deficit and was turning over an annual surplus to a depleted treasury.

The Treasurer's Report for 1882 shows the purchase of lots 5 and 6, Square 250, at a total cost of $7,000. The school building on the site was ready for occupancy in December 1882, the cost of construction being met by a loan. The total expenditure for the building equipped was $27,039.25.[15] With the sale of College Hill completed, the College was without a home and temporarily was the guest of the Prep in its new quarters until a new university building could be completed.

On September 17, 1884, Otis Tufton Mason (1839–1908), the most distinguished principal of the school, resigned and was succeeded by Andrew P. Montague who was to receive a salary of $1,500 per year with an additional $25 a month for house rent.[16]

Mason began his twenty-three years as principal immediately after his graduation from Columbian College in 1861. While serving as principal he carried on those studies and research in ethnology that were in time to make him an outstanding authority in the field. He gave up his principalship in 1884 to become curator of the Department of Ethnology in the National Museum.[17] Mason's years as the head of Prep were fruitful ones. His connection with the school ended just as it moved from its location on College Hill to the new building constructed for it at 1339 H Street.

The high ideal that Mason set for the school is eloquently set forth in the 1883–1884 catalogue:[18]

> The government of the school in all its details is so administered as to banish ignoble incentives and to make its pupils self-reliant gentlemen. The motives which actuate honorable business men are inculcated, and

[14] *Ibid.*, June 25, 1867.
[15] *Ibid.*, June 14, 1882; June 18, 1883.
[16] *Ibid.*, September 17, 1884.
[17] George Crossette, *Founders of The Cosmos Club of Washington, 1878*, Washington, 1966, pp. 115–117.
[18] *Catalogue of the Columbian College Preparatory School*, Washington 1884, p. 4.

the greatest freedom allowed to individual action which is consistent with healthy discipline and self-respect. The fact is never lost sight of, that habits of accuracy, industry, and perserverance, acquired in youth,

Photograph from "Founders of the Cosmos Club" by George Crossette, 1966

Otis Tufton Mason (1838–1908), Principal of the Preparatory School, 1861–1884.

are the best security for success in manhood. Even in the award of premiums the reward of diligence and energy, which any one may acquire who will make the effort, is the motive, and not the excitement of envy through personal contest.

The Preparatory Department was designed primarily to afford thorough training for admission to college. This was done by three or later four classes. In addition, the department offered a high school course, "occuping two years, for pupils who have completed their studies in the common English branches, either in public school or elsewhere." A student in either branch had to pursue the study of Latin during his entire residence in the school except in the second year of high school. Vocal music and elementary drawing were taught to all pupils and attention to declamation and composition was required throughout. Penmanship was a required subject in all courses, except the second year of the high school course.

The college preparatory curriculum required reading, spelling, arithmetic and Latin throughout, one year of geography, three years of grammar, one term each of botany and physical geography, two years of history, three years of Greek, two years of bookkeeping, three terms of algebra and one of geometry, and a year of French.

The shorter high school course did not require Greek, but it did require two years of French and one of English and two years of botany.[19]

Boarding students were lodged in the house of the Principal and, as the catalogue pointed out, were "treated as members of the family". Charges were substantially the same as for college students. To stimulate achievement, prizes galore were available; a first and second prize for scholarship were offered in each of the four classes and a large number of gold and silver medals for punctuality and deportment were awarded. Monthly reports were sent to parents who were requested to communicate with the President of the College or the Principal of the School on their receipt.[20]

A student paper, *The Spectator,* was published for a time, but unfortunately no copies have been preserved in the University Collection. There has been preserved, however, an amazing run of the minutes of the Hermesian Literary Society.[21] Hermesian was active during the great part of the School's existence. The Society had its own library with the volumes bearing the Hermesian bookplate. The

---
[19] *Annual and Historical Catalogue of the Officers and Students of the Columbian College, D.C. 1868,* Washington, 1868, pp. 31, 32.
[20] *Catalogue of the Officers and Students of the Columbian University,* Washington, 1881, pp. 56–58.
[21] *Minutes of the Hermesian Society,* 1861–1869. University Archives.

design of the plate is a drawing of a turtle, on the underside of which are other figures and signs and two sets of initials, the meaning of all of which is today far too arcane for the comprehension of the uninitiated. The neatness and orderliness of the minutes of the weekly meetings assiduously recorded decade after decade by these youths bear eloquent testimony to the sound training that they had received. Absence, excused or unexcused, failure to perform an assigned duty, or overdue retention of library books, led to the assessment of fines, duly recorded. The amount most often levied was five cents, but sometimes the fine was as heavy as a quarter of a dollar.

At every regular session, following the fixed order of business, there was discussion followed by a formal debate on a subject by a team announced at the preceding meeting. A vote was taken to determine which team had proved its contention, and a critic proceeded to discuss the debating skill of the participants as shown in their presentation of facts and argument. The type of subject chosen will occasion no surprise. For example, in the spring of 1863 we find these subjects debated: Which leads the more hazardous life, the sailor or the soldier? Which is the more useful to the world, the farmer or the mechanic? Which rendered the greater service to the world, Sir Isaac Newton or Benjamin Franklin? Can there be any single form of government adopted to provide for the necessities of all men? Which is the greater blessing to mankind, sight or hearing? Which is more detrimental to the community, credulity or suspicion? When they debated the question: Which exerts the greater influence over man, women or money?, these adolescent philosophers, out of the vastness of their experience, decided emphatically that women did.[22] On April 18, 1865, the Hermesians were assembled in a special session of sorrow. They passed a resolution which demonstrated their knowledge of what was proper and appropriate, along with youth's urge to say, what a good boy am I! The resolution was in three parts. The first recorded the sorrow of the Society at the nation's loss of its leader by assassination. The second decreed that all members and honorary members "wear crepe for the customary time on the left arm". But the third directed the appointment of a committee to have "the resolutions printed in the newspaper that has the largest circulation"![23]

The student grade books for the period 1865 to the closing of the school have been preserved.[24] They record academic standing month

---

[22] *Ibid.*, March 27, 1863; April 12, 1863; April 17, 1863; April 24, 1863; May 8, 1863; May 15, 1863; May 27, 1863.
[23] *Ibid.*, April 18, 1865.
[24] *Grade Books of the Preparatory Department*, 1865–1896. University Archives.

by month for each subject, attendance at class and at chapel, and demerits, exactly what was put on the reports sent to parents.

The splendid new building to which the school moved following the sale of College Hill still stands at 1339 H Street and has been in regular use longer than any other building which the University occupies today. At the time it was considered quite a showplace. Henry Bacon's large historical painting *The Boston Boys* was presented to the school by William Wilson Corcoran to grace the Reception Room in the new building and this room was designated as the regular meeting place for the Board of Trustees.[25] The removal of the school to the city did not bring about the hoped-for doubling of the enrollment. The Prep did hold and even slightly increased its numbers. This in itself was an achievement for the public school system had now gone into secondary education, presenting a form of competition that the school had not previously had to face. When in 1886–1887 the College reached its nadir with a pitiful enrollment of 30, there were 94 preparatory students. Professor Montague's tenure as principal was interrupted by periods of illness.

On June 17, 1895, the name of the Preparatory Department was changed to Columbian Academy, and William Allen Wilbur made dean at a salary of $1,800.[26] It was already evident that the days of the Academy were numbered. The public school system was now well developed and the need for a private academy seemed no longer apparent. Under Wilbur's leadership the faculty continued to function, and its minutes record no indication of an end in sight. They have all of the customary drabness of pedagogic routine. The roll of students regularly was read and characteristic observations on individuals who were found wanting were made. For example, at the meeting of December 19, 1895, we can see the nature of the comments as the names of students were called:[27]

Student A: He is failing in Latin
Student B: Very poor in French, should have more English grammar
Student C: Reported by Prof. Wilbur as talking too much; very poor in reading
Student D: Unsteady in his work, improved in mathematics, deportment very bad from association with P_____.

On April 29, 1897, the Trustees ordained the discontinuance of the Academy. The building, adapted for use as a hospital, was de-

---
[25] *Minutes of the Board of Trustees,* June 6, 1883.
[26] *Ibid.,* June 17, 1895; March 11, 1896.
[27] *Faculty Minutes of the Preparatory Department, December 19, 1895–February 8, 1897.* Meeting of December 19, 1895. University Archives.

Photograph from "The National Cyclopedia of American Biography," Volume 33, 1947

William Allen Wilbur (1864–1945), Dean of Columbian Academy, 1895–1897.

Photograph from Elmer Louis Kayser

The Preparatory School, 1939 H Street, N. W., 1882–1897.

voted henceforth to the healing of men's bodies, rather than the cultivation of youthful minds. William Allen Wilbur became Professor of English in the College.[28] The second oldest branch of the University had passed into oblivion.

The Preparatory School, which in its last hours had adopted "the Columbian Academy" as the name for its epitaph, had completed its mission. As it came to the end of its career, it had adapted its courses to what had become the fairly standard requirements for college admission. The public high schools, now located in residential areas throughout the city, had done the same thing. The need that existed in 1821 had now been met fully by the public high school. But beyond that, growing sensitivity as to the maintenance of college standards, sharply marked off from secondary school ones, made it desirable to dispense with preparatory departments and any effect they might have in blurring the distinction between the two. Time and educational fashions change: today would probably think differently.

In numbers the student body of the Preparatory School always exceeded and frequently doubled that of the College. The names of most of the families important in the financial, professional, and social life of the community appeared on the student lists of the Prep. Its influence might have been even greater had not the Trustees been anxious that the school be insulated from any possibility of involving them in liability for any losses that might be incurred. When the school was very small its income yielded only a meagre salary to its teachers. Rotation was rapid, because there was little financial inducement to stay. There was much free tuition, because youths of limited means were frequently extended full or partial scholarships. On the surface this looked like generosity on the part of the school. In fact, however, because it meant reduced salaries, it was really benevolence extended by the teachers. The school suffered long from a lack of having its own school building, by being quartered, as it were, on the College in any available space.

A consciousness of all of these difficulties seemed to dawn on the Trustees when in 1848 they decided to build a school away from College Hill, and in the heart of the city, and called Zalmon Richards, an able schoolman, to be "permanent" principal. The change in attitude was reflected in a marked growth of the school. In fact, the Prep might have been easily developed into a very welcome source of income for the under-financed College.

The Prep School did not die prematurely. For three-quarters of a century it was an important unit in the total educational resources of

---

[28] *Minutes of the Board of Trustees,* April 29, 1897.

the District. A secondary school system, maintained by public funds, took over in a more comprehensive way what the Prep had tried to do. Adorned by the more elegant name of the Columbian Academy, Prep, at the mature age of seventy-six, bowed out, its mission completed.

Kalorama: Country Estate to Washington Mayfair

MARY MITCHELL

In 1890 the Commissioners of the District of Columbia extended the limits of Washington City out into the county beyond Boundary Street, or Florida Avenue as we know it today. Before that for almost a century Kalorama was a large estate of great natural beauty rising through wooded terrain to a height of two hundred feet above Rock Creek. With a perimeter of almost two miles it lay in the curve of the Creek, included a locally famous mill site, that of Evan Lyons, reached its southern extremity at the corner of 22nd and P Streets, and then, encompassing Sheridan Circle, continued up 23rd Street to the long wooded parcel high above the Creek near Taft Bridge.

Told from generation to generation as part of the local legend, its romantic story up to 1909 was the subject of a fine paper read before this Society on April 3 of that year by Mrs. Corra Bacon-Foster.[1] But since then much has happened to justify a review of its history, the circumstances leading up to its subdivision, and the development of its status today as a first-class residential area.

James Woodress has written in *A Yankee's Odyssey* an excellent account of the life of Joel Barlow, the poet, statesman, and friend of Thomas Jefferson, who first named it "Kalorama" and established its reputation.[2] The present Joel Barlow, a descendant of the original Joel's brother Aaron, and a Life Member of this Society, has collected Barlow's publications and memorabilia for historians to study. Also a rearrangement of maps and archives at the Library of Congress, combined with easy access to widely expanded resources of the Washingtoniana Division of the Martin Luther King Memorial Li-

---

Mary Mitchell spoke on a related subject before the Columbia Historical Society on May 16, 1972.

[1] Corra Bacon-Foster, "The Story of Kalorama," *Records of the Columbia Historical Society*, 13 (1910), pp. 98–118.

[2] James Woodress, *A Yankee's Odyssey: The Life of Joel Barlow* (Philadelphia, 1958).

*From a photograph in the
Columbia Historical Society Collection*

Kalorama. Oil painting by Baron Alexander Bodisco (1786–1854), the Russian envoy to the United States from 1837 until his death in 1854.

Bodisco, described by Constance McLaughlin Green as "wealthy and worldly-wise," married Harriet Brooke Williams and lived during his later years in Georgetown at 3322 O Street, N.W. His painting of Kalorama was made about 1840.

brary, and those of the Columbia Historical Society itself,[3] now permit a much fuller account of this unique section of historic Washington.

Looking at its history overall, the single outstanding fact is the homogeneous quality of its residents who have always been educated people of taste and sufficient means to live anywhere in America they chose and who have selected this part of the capital to settle in.

Kalorama was originally part of a 600-acre tract called The Widow's Mite, patented by Charles II to John Langworth who emigrated to America and settled in St. Mary's County, Maryland. His brother James arrived in 1668, and since there were no sons to either of these men, and the childless colonial settler was subject to special taxes, John sold the tract to Anthony Holmead, another English settler. Holmead also proved childless and persuaded his nephew, named for him, to emigrate in 1750 and inherit the estate.

The tract of land fell within the bounds of the District and thus the second Anthony Holmead's name appears in the agreement made between the Commissioners of the City and the original proprietors. He married and sired a large family of daughters and sons.

Calling it Rock Hill, Holmead built his seat 150 feet above Rock Creek on what is now S Street, precisely between the houses now numbered 2300 and 2301. A simple three-story brick house, it had a pleasing facade, mansard-type roof, and a surpassing view on a clear day over the Creek and Georgetown to Alexandria.

After the District was laid out in 1791, Holmead, feeling the tax-pinch of excessive landholdings, in 1795 sold a piece of The Widow's Mite, about thirty acres, and the part eventually named Kalorama, to Gustavus Scott, a native of Maryland and a District Commissioner. Then staking out a long narrow parcel of fifty-six acres for himself a short distance east on a higher knoll, with access to Boundary Street, he erected another, less pretentious, brick house and ran a substantial fence between the two properties.

Wanting to live in a manner similar to the other two commissioners, Scott, who called his estate Belair, added gardens and landscaping to the seat, but over-extended himself. Trying to stave off a disaster, he sold two small parcels on Rock Creek as mill-seats to Edgar Patterson and Evan Lyons. Just below what is now the P Street Bridge, Patterson built a paper mill, and soon the bridge of

---

[3] A profile medallion portrait of Joel Barlow by Gilles-Louis Chrétien in the collection of the Columbia Historical Society is reproduced as the frontispiece, and an enlargement of it is reproduced on page 327, of the *Records of the Columbia Historical Society of Washington, D.C., 1960–1962*.

sorts spanning the Creek at this point came to be known as the Paper-Mill Bridge. A vital link between the North and the South, it led to the Georgetown-Bladensburgh turnpike along Boundary Street which then took travelers like George Washington and Thomas Jefferson on up past the entrance portals of both Belair and the Holmead estate en route to Philadelphia. Lyons turned his long narrow piece bordering the Creek into a grist mill with a millpond and a race, opposite what is now Montrose Park and Dumbarton Oaks.

In 1802, Thomas Jefferson, then in the White House, hearing of Scott's financial difficulties and that the property might be for sale, wrote Joel Barlow in Paris. While he knew Barlow mostly by reputation as a liberal pamphleteer and poet, he hoped to draw this compatible Republican back to Washington. "There is a most lovely seat joining the City," he wrote Barlow, "on a high hill commanding the Potomac River, with superb house and gardens." But Barlow and his lovely wife Ruth were enjoying the excitement of the early Napoleonic era and at this time ignored Jefferson's suggestion.

In 1803 Scott died, bankrupted, and the widow sold Belair for $16,000 to William Augustine Washington, the first President's nephew, former aide-de-camp, and an executor of his will. Although he remodeled the old house, adding an east wing and ballroom, after five years for some compelling reason he decided to sell the seat at a loss and move to Charleston, S.C. where he died a short time later.

The buyer was Joel Barlow. By 1807, after seventeen years abroad, he had returned to America, published his widely acclaimed book *The Columbiad*, a labor of many years, and was ready for a pleasant retirement. He paid $14,000 for the estate.

This talented, resourceful and energetic liberal lived a singularly rich and productive life. Born in Redding, Connecticut, in 1754, son of a landholder and farmer, he attended Yale University in the same class as Noah Webster, became the "fighting chaplain" of the Third Massachusetts Brigade, and after 1782 returned home to marry Ruth Baldwin. This however did not deter him from joining a group of Revolutionary veterans who were organizing the Ohio Company to open up a vast tract of southeast Ohio along the Scioto River. Knowing him to be articulate and persuasive, the Company sent him abroad in May 1788 to interest European investors. Although this ambitious enterprise failed, he managed to bring to London his "dear Wifey" and from there supported them both with such ardor as a pamphleteer and exponent of the French Revolution's liberal principles that he was made a Citizen of France. This unusual honor was

*On display in the Diplomatic Reception Rooms,
Department of State, Washington, D. C., 1972*

Joel Barlow (1754–1812). Portrait in oil by Charles Willson Peale (1741–1827).

Barlow and his friend Robert Fulton (1765–1815) often visited Peale's museum and Peale painted them both for his museum gallery. The painting of Barlow, still in its original Peale museum frame, once hung in Independence Hall and was recently presented by Joel Barlow of Washington, D.C. to the Department of State.

Kalorama: Country Estate to Washington Mayfair

shared in his generation with only George Washington, Alexander Hamilton, James Madison, and Thomas Paine.

By now he and Ruth had a wide circle of friends and considerable linguistic proficiency. Utilizing these resources to capitalize on the British blockade of France, he made a fortune as a shipping agent and broker by slipping American cargoes into France. He even spent a year in Hamburg, Germany to work with Scandinavian traders selling potash to the French. The Barbary pirates were harassing American shipping in the Mediterranean, impressing our seamen and seizing the ships' cargoes. Made American Minister to these unscrupulous tryants from Tunis, Tripoli, and Morocco, he proved himself able and stubborn and after three years of negotiations concluded his mission with a peace and honor. In a letter to Ruth, he attributed his victory to growing "large mustaches, long, long, beautiful and black (a little gray, however). Feeling a lamb at heart, my mustaches give me very nearly the air of the tiger."

During his life in Paris, he had become an intimate friend and supporter of the inventor Robert Fulton who was experimenting with a steamboat model. The Barlows, having no children, invited their "dear Toots" to live with them which he did throughout the next ten years.

Barlow was long occupied with his epic poem, *The Columbiad*, begun as the nine-part *The Vision of Columbus* (1787), and published in 1807 as a magnificent quarto volume of 450 pages with twelve illustrations by Robert Fulton and a London artist, Robert Smirke. Produced by a Philadelphia publisher for $10,000, it was the most beautiful book yet manufactured in America and one which Charles Willson Peale found worthy of a place in his museum, called The Temple of Wisdom, in Philadelphia.

After the Barlows arrived in Washington, Joel wrote to a nephew: "I have here a most delightful situation. It only wants the improvements we contemplate to make it a little paradise... I find the name Belair has been already given many places in Virginia and Maryland; so on the advice of friends we have changed it to one that is quite new, Kalorama, from the Greek signifying 'fine view'."

From another part of the letter we learn that Kalorama contained thirty acres, that he was buying an additional acre to provide frontage on Boundary Street, and a twenty-acre parcel to the north, for a barn and orchard, to be called the Upper Field. He cut roads, fitted up stables, and added two wings. Fulton, who joined them in 1808, helped design a summerhouse on the highest knoll. Leaving the natural woodland in its simple beauty, Barlow worked contentedly,

Frick Art Reference Library, New York

Mrs. Joel Barlow (Ruth Baldwin). Pencil drawing by Charles de Villette (born 1792) made in Paris in 1811 or 1812.

Beneath the oval portrait is an inscription in French by Villette which is in translation: "A very like portrait of Mrs. Barlow, wife of Mr. Barlow, ambassador of the United States of America in France after Gerry and Marshall, done by me while she was here. It has been damaged I know not how during an absence in the fall of 1850. Mr. Barlow is the author of the English poem, The Columbiad. He died in 1810 (sic), I believe in

Kalorama: Country Estate to Washington Mayfair

On display in the Diplomatic Reception Rooms, Department of State, Washington, D. C., 1972

Kalorama. Oil painting on panel by Charles Codman (1800–1842). 13¼ x 23½ inches.

In the background is the mansion with the portico about whose design Barlow and Benjamin Henry Latrobe corresponded. The relationship between the mansion and the pond seems incorrect, since the pond was west of the mansion.

furnishing the house with rare paintings, bric-a-brac and curios from seventeen years' wanderings abroad. Jefferson often rode out to consult on foreign policy matters and exchange ideas on seeds and agricultural tools. Congressmen, foreign visitors of note, authors, artists, men of ideas in every calling, frequented his parlors. When Fulton finally finished his experimental model of the steamboat, the *Cler-*

Poland, going or coming back from seeing the Emperor in the winter. He is the author of the verses in English which are on the back of the portrait of my sister painted by Fulton, the famous inventor of steam ships, and whom I saw come back to my mother greatly disappointed and crying in despair. He had just left the 1st Consul for whom he had offered to build ships. He was saying to my mother: Would you believe that he has not understood me!" The Villette family were neighbors of the Barlows in Paris. The Fulton portrait of Villette's sister Charlotte, whose mother, Countess Charlotte de Villette, was an adopted daughter of Voltaire, is in the Fulton collection of Randall J. LeBoeuf of Old Westbury, Long Island, New York.

The portrait of Mrs. Barlow measures 16 x 12½ inches and is drawn on paper, cut out, and affixed to a paper backing on which Villette's inscription is written. Owned by Samuel L. M. Barlow of New York and exhibited at the Detroit Institute of Fine Arts, it was purchased by Maury A. Bromsen Associates, Inc. of Boston. Dr. Bromsen had it cleaned in 1956 by Frank W. Dolloff, Chief Conservator of Prints, Watercolors and Drawings of the Boston Museum of Fine Arts. It was purchased in May 1971 by the Connecticut Historical Society.

THE POND WHERE ROBERT FULTON TRIED HIS FIRST BOAT.
Columbia Historical Society Collection

"The Pond Where Robert Fulton Tried His First Boat," an illustration in W. A. Croffut's "Queer Corners at the Capital," *Frank Leslie's Popular Magazine,* September 1888.

mont, using local joiners and blacksmiths for his labor, Barlow is said to have dammed up Rock Creek below Lyons millpond to provide a place large enough for the successful experiment.

Inspecting this area today, between the steep rocky banks of Montrose Park and the high elevation of Massachusetts Avenue just before the Bridge, you can readily imagine this event. Barlow and Fulton would have had the model hauled down S Street to the banks back of the Japanese Embassy and launched the model there. Three two-lane branches of Rock Creek Parkway run parallel here, and space abounds in which the millpond could have been made into a small lake.

All too soon, in a dramatic manner, the end came to this idyll at Kalorama. James Madison persuaded Barlow that as a Citizen of France he was the only American who could arrange a badly needed commercial treaty with the Napoleonic government. Leasing Kalorama to the French Minister, M. Serurier, Joel left for Paris with Ruth and his nephew Thomas, in August 1811. He remained there for more than a year while the French delayed. Finally when Napoleon was closing in on Moscow, the Emperor invited him to meet in Vilna, Poland, to conclude a treaty. Barlow and his nephew traveled in his own coach through Alsace-Lorraine, Frankfurt-am-Main, and Konigsberg, "riding all day along the Baltic coast," passing roads cut up from the passage of Napoleon's armies the day before and beginning to freeze into ruts. Napoleon was shortly defeated by the Russians in the Battle of Berezina. With the treaty manifestly lost, the Barlows left the ancient Lithuanian city of Vilna to arrive in a snowstorm, just ahead of Napoleon, at Zarnoviec, a village near Cracow. In a state of advanced pneumonia, Barlow died on Christmas Eve, 1812. His body still lies there, in a local churchyard, and the present-day Joel Barlow hopes to return it when possible to the poet and statesman's birthplace at Redding, Connecticut.

Ruth returned, a lonely widow, to her estate. With her sister and brother-in-law, Clara and George Bomford, she lived there until her death in 1818. Then her brother Henry Baldwin, Associate Justice of the United States Supreme Court, took possession of "Kaloramer" (as it was spelled out by the recorder of the deed).

During the period 1818–1822 several unusual tenants were sheltered there. The first was Mrs. Theobald Wolfe Tone, wife of the Irish patriot whom the Barlows had known in Paris and for whom they built the west wing. The second was the body of Commodore Stephen Decatur who was mortally wounded in a duel with James Barron on March 20, 1820. Mrs. Susan Decatur, a friend of Clara's, begged to settle her husband's remains in the Barlow-Bomford mausoleum in a grove at what is now the intersection of Massachusetts and Florida Avenues where the Luxembourg Embassy stands. This was done, and Mrs. Decatur herself spent some time recovering her spirits at Kalorama. A third tenant was Henry Middleton, Representative from South Carolina, who became Minister to Russia. A fourth was Baron von Greuhn, the German Minister, who had fallen in love with and married the Middleton family's governess.

Buying Kalorama in 1822, Colonel George Bomford gradually assembled the estate into the property of ninety acres which became the subdivision of 1887. Chief of Ordnance of the United States Army in the War of 1812, Bomford invented a gun called "The Columbiad" which was used until after the Civil War. A promoter involved in Washington real estate, Bomford, like Gustavus Scott, started out on a grand scale. Finding the fence which Holmead had erected in 1795 an eyesore, he bought this five-acre stretch and tore it down. Mrs. Bomford, an enthusiastic florist, developed the gardens with a conservatory for orchids, rare plants and trees, planting the first sugar beets in her vegetable garden.

In the 1830's, Congress allowed water from the Chesapeake and Ohio Canal to be diverted for producing waterpower at millsites. Mortgaging Kalorama, Bomford built a large gristmill with a giant 34-foot millwheel where the Washington Flour Mill stands today. In 1841 he bought the beautiful high wooded section of twenty acres north of Belmont Road and running east to where the Taft Bridge crosses Rock Creek ravine on Connecticut Avenue. Part of the historic patent called "Pretty Prospect," it includes today the French Embassy. In 1844, the gristmill burned and, mortgaging Kalorama still further, Bomford built on the same spot a cotton mill which had three thousand spindles and one hundred operatives. Although the city of Georgetown remitted all taxes to aid him, he found himself financially seriously embarrassed. Kalorama had to be sacrificed in 1846. It is said that Bomford never recovered from these reverses, dying of a broken heart in a modest house on I Street in 1848.

Fortunately a buyer, who paid only $25,000 for the estate, turned up immediately and a new era in Kalorama's history began. The new purchaser was Thomas R. Lovett, aged twenty-eight, of Philadelphia, as trustee for his mother, Mrs. Charles Fletcher.

After shipping the remains of Stephen Decatur from the Barlow-Bomford mausoleum to St. Peter's Church Yard, Philadelphia, the Lovetts boarded up the brick mausoleum, let the woods grow around it, and settled down to enjoy their unusually lovely new home in its park-like setting and the animated social life of the small but growing capital.

Who were the Lovetts, why did they come to Washington, and who was Charles Fletcher, are unanswered questions. The answers may perhaps be found in family research in Philadelphia and New York, research not germane to the central Kalorama story, although any such unanswered questions present a challenge to the historian.

Some information can be drawn from archival sources in Washington. When she arrived at Kalorama, the English-born Mrs. Fletcher was in her forty-seventh year, her children had all been born in New York, and they were with her at Kalorama. Her children were Louise Lovett Lansing, aged 28, whose husband was Captain Arthur Lansing of the United States Army; Charlotte Lovett Bostwick, al-

Kalorama: Country Estate to Washington Mayfair

ready a widow at 26; Thomas, 24; George, 22; Emma, 20; and Anna, 18. The 1850 census listed Mrs. Fletcher's assets as $50,000. Fletcher had nothing, and gave his occupation as farmer.

Tax assessments and the 1860 census reveal more. The land was assessed at $21,500, the mansion at $10,000, and it was equipped with $2,000 worth of furnishings. A carriage worth $150 was drawn by horses of equal value. Up the hill, the Holmeads used a more expensive carriage and had two cows worth $50, while the Lovetts had a $15 cow. Yet it appears that they did like their comforts. While the Holmeads had no domestics beyond one fifteen-year old girl, the Lovetts had a cook, a chambermaid, and a German coachman. Since there was no gardener listed on an estate famous for its gardens and horticulture, it can be assumed that Charles Fletcher took over the work of gardener and, being a Massachusetts Yankee, enjoyed this daily contact with a rocky soil and wooded terrain not unlike that of his native state.

Around 1850, Thomas, the oldest son, entered the diplomatic service and was sent to the American Legation in Constantinople as attaché to the American Minister. Later, George, the next son, was listed in the census as a lawyer. These facts suggest that Mr. and Mrs. Fletcher had not put down family roots in Philadelphia, that they liked country living combined with proximity to public life and a cosmopolitan atmosphere which could give the sons an opportunity to enter the professions they preferred and the daughters exposure to suitable unmarried men. By 1860 Emma had married Commodore (later Rear Admiral) Samuel Livingston Breese, who commanded the Brooklyn Navy Yard in the Civil War. Anna married George Maulsby, Medical Director of the Navy. George married Miss Caroline de Belen, granddaughter and ward of Baron de Belen of Belgium, who was educated at the Georgetown Visitation Convent, and whom he met at a ball at the Belgian Legation. The composite is strongly reminiscent of Jane Austen, and by reading any of her novels you could reconstruct the general tenor of the Lovetts' life at Kalorama in rural Washington society.

During the Civil War, because of its isolation, the mansion was confiscated by a regiment from Illinois as a Union Army smallpox hospital. The family spent the duration in Philadelphia. The Army did not leave until after a gala ball on Christmas Eve in 1865 to celebrate their departure. The east wing caught fire and was badly gutted. Thomas Lovett, somehow hearing of the event, arrived in time to rescue an Aztec idol which was being dragged down the hill. Captain Lansing had brought the idol from Mexico some eighteen years before, as he had the great iron cannon balls adorning the gateposts of the entrance driveway and gatehouse.

It is doubtful that Thomas Lovett ever returned to live permanently at Kalorama, or that his sister Charlotte, with whom he seems to have had a special relationship, ever did. In 1855 he purchased a large piece of property in Mount Airy, a Philadelphia suburb, but never recorded it. After his death, still a bachelor, in 1875, his sisters did record it, and in 1887 erected there in his memory the Lovett Memorial Library, now a branch of the Philadelphia Free Library system. Mrs. Charlotte Bostwick endowed it with $25,000 in cash for maintenance.

Mrs. Caroline Heilmann, librarian at the Lovett Library, 6945 Germantown Avenue, ascertained these facts for me, and wrote that: "In our auditorium (the original building) there is a portrait of Thomas R. Lovett, and the following engraved plaque:

> Thomas R. Lovett
> 1821–1875
> A resident of Mount Airy for 13 years. His interest in books and the lack of reading facilities in the neighborhood at that time led his sister Charlotte Lovett Bostwick to found this library and endow it in his memory on February 17, 1888.

Mrs. Fletcher evidently considered Kalorama her home, for after the Civil War, now a widow, she returned, and died there in 1868. The 1870 census does not list any residents at Kalorama. But from an interesting document at the Land Deeds Office, dated November 2, 1871, we find that George S. Lovett had decided to return to the family mansion and run the property. On that date he leased to Austin P. Brown the right to open and work a stone quarry, at Brown's expense, on the steep bank of Rock Creek somewhere below the present-day Islamic Mosque. The agreement provided that Brown's books must be open to Lovett at all times. The load of one horse would count as one-half cubic yard of stone; the load of two horses as one yard; of three horses as one and a half; and of four horses as two cubic yards of stone. Brown could take sand at the rate of ten cents per load, could erect buildings and stables, and for soapstone he must pay fifty cents per cubic yard. He was not to cut any more trees than necessary for the quarry.

While George Lovett was certainly not impoverished, he did need funds if he was to return the mansion to its former state and live as befitted a gentleman in the opulent Grant administration. Selling the western parcel of the estate of forty acres to the Freedmen's Sav-

Kalorama: Country Estate to Washington Mayfair 177

ings and Trust Company, he refurbished the mansion with $6,000 of the proceeds and brought the mansion back to its former assessed value of $10,000. (In 1872 it had been assessed at $6,000, and four years later the taxes reflected the improvement.)

In 1880 a census return lists daughters eighteen and twenty years of age; and a document relating to the sale of the estate in 1887 was signed by a son living in Conejo County, Colorado. George's first wife, Caroline de Belen, died in the 1870's, for by 1880 he had married again to Emmeline Boggs, a woman of character as was shown in the events preceding the final dispersion of the estate.

For a decade Kalorama had been living on borrowed time. Beginning on the northeast side of Washington, beyond Boundary Street, large estates had been sold to Catholic University and other Catholic organizations and to Howard University which developed LeDroit Park. Columbian College on Meridian Hill had moved downtown and the Hill was being subdivided and settled with houses.

With the death of George in 1882, Emmeline Lovett became head of the family. One year later the District Commissioners confiscated an east-west strip fifteen feet wide for a subterranean tunnel for an aqueduct through the heart of the Upper Field. Urban living was pushing against Kalorama and rapidly appreciating land values must have appeared to Mrs. Lovett like the handwriting on the wall.

In 1883 a real estate operator purchased the western parcel, which had been sold to the Freedman's Bank for $15,000, for twice that amount. Then in 1885 came a wealthy Bostonian, Gardiner Greene Hubbard, father-in-law of Alexander Graham Bell and established in Washington since 1879, who bought this parcel for $60,000. He had it surveyed and platted by Herman Viele to meet District regulations for widths of streets and dimensions of squares. Calling it Belair Heights, after the former name of Kalorama, he sold it on January 11, 1887, to a New York syndicate for $300,000.

Projecting designs for the extension of Massachusetts Avenue beyond Boundary Street and then across a bridge into the county, the Commissioners held a hearing in November 1886 for those whose land was affected—the Lovetts. A circle, to be called Decatur Circle, was planned for the lower portion of the estate. Citing even the Barlow-Bomford tomb, and declaring this had been sacrosanct in the Lovetts' title to the property, the embattled Mrs. Lovett told reporters of the *Evening Star* that the plan to deflect the line of Massachusetts was offensive, that the District authorities had no right to use land in this arbitrary fashion, and that it was an invasion of personal rights.

National Geographic Society

Gardiner Greene Hubbard. A photograph published in the *National Geographic Magazine,* May 1896.

Hubbard purchased the western parcel of Kalorama in 1885 and had it plotted for subdivision.

In 1890 Congress made the District Commissioners legal successors to the Levy Court which had governed the county since 1791. The Commissioners extended the city limits and their jurisdiction in-

Kalorama: Country Estate to Washington Mayfair 179

definitely beyond Rock Creek, changed the name of Boundary to Florida Avenue, and demolished the mausoleum in 1892. (This controversial acre became city property, and as such could be made available to a foreign country for an embassy.)

At length the Lovett heirs could no longer fight these pressures or refuse the price offered for Kalorama's sixty acres. On November 11, 1887, a Philadelphia syndicate composed of John C. Bullett, James D. Cameron, and Anthony J. Drexel, paid $5,900 an acre for the sixty acres, and all three widows, Charlotte Bostwick, Anna Maulsby, and Emma Breese, arrived to sign the deed. "This transaction," said the *Star* on January 15, 1888, " was the highest ever made in this area for land beyond the Boundary. . . . The contrast is striking between the unimproved Kalorama property enclosed by its rough stone wall, and the handsome houses along the end of Massachusetts Avenue near Rock Creek." H. B. Looker had platted the property, including the circle at the north end of 24th Street, calling the subdivision Kalorama Heights, and the syndicate put its sale into the hands of Thomas J. Fisher and Co., a real estate firm still in business in Washington today. In 1888, the mansion was torn down, and later Mrs. Emmeline Lovett and her daughter Annie, the only Lovetts left in Washington, were living at 2203 Massachusetts in one of a new row of brick houses.

If the northern parcels of Kalorama were inactive, the southern part was marked by the opposite atmosphere. In 1890 for the first time one finds in the plat-books the Circle named for Sheridan. Congress granted the officers of the Army of the Cumberland the right to commission John Quincy Adams Ward, the sculptor, to carve an appropriate statue for this Circle. After spending thirteen years designing a statue, Ward was not able to satisfy either the officers or Mrs. Sheridan (who often remarked that she would rather be the widow of Sheridan than the wife of any man alive). Gutzon Borglum was given the commission and his model was accepted in January 1908.

Recalling that Sheridan was only thirty-three years old when he won fame, and saying that he wanted to portray the general not only as a warrior but also as a young man, Borglum requested President Theodore Roosevelt that Lieutenant Philip H. Sheridan, Jr. be given leave from the Army to pose in his father's uniform—with sabre and hat and sitting on his Mexican saddle with authentic trappings. Roosevelt granted the young Sheridan leave for the purpose.

Sheridan's horse, called "Winchester," almost equally famous, also served as a model. Although the horse had died in 1878, his fame in military annals was such that the Army of the Cumberland had him

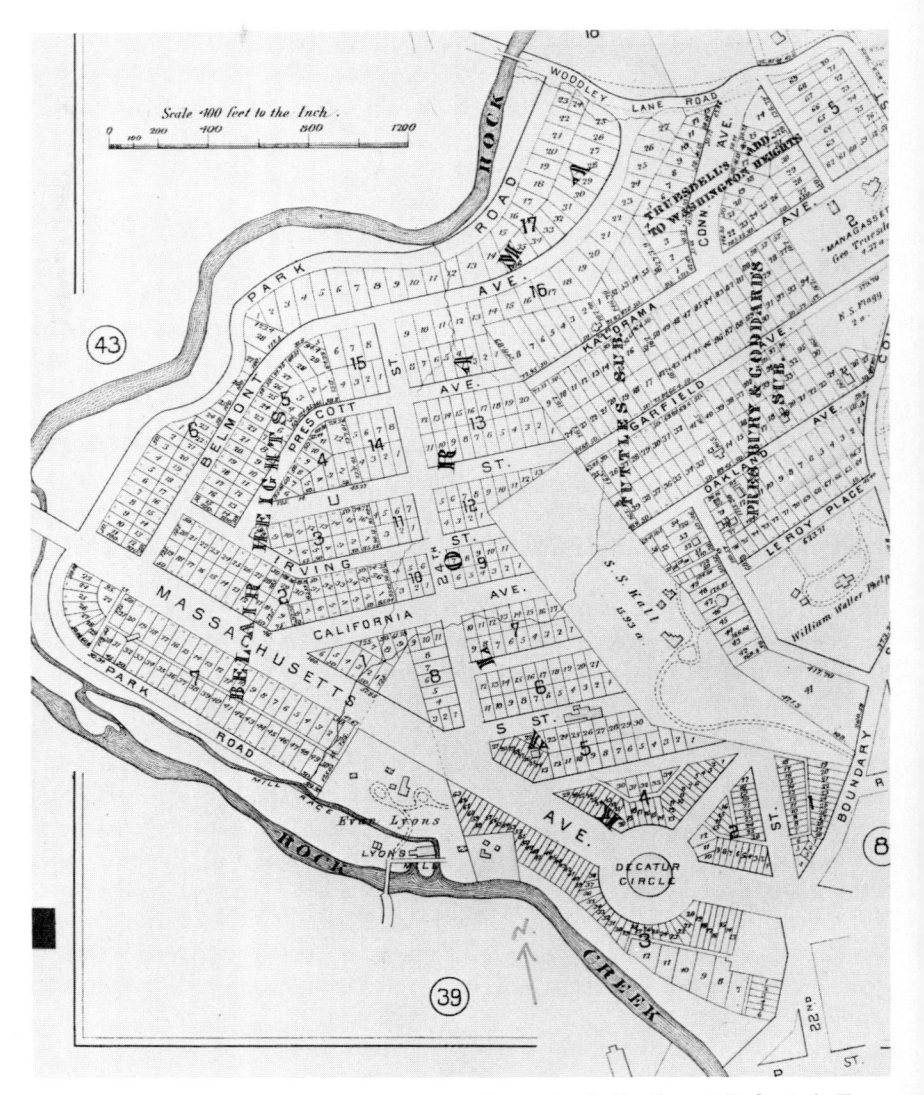

From the Collection of Robert A. Truax

Map of Kalorama in 1887. Section from Plate 40, *Surveys and Plats and Properties in the City of Washington, D.C.*, compiled and published by G. M. Hopkins, C. E. Philadelphia, 1887.

stuffed and mounted on Governor's Island in the Hudson River and Borglum could easily see him there. (The horse is still preserved and is on the third floor of the Smithsonian's Museum of History and Technology.)

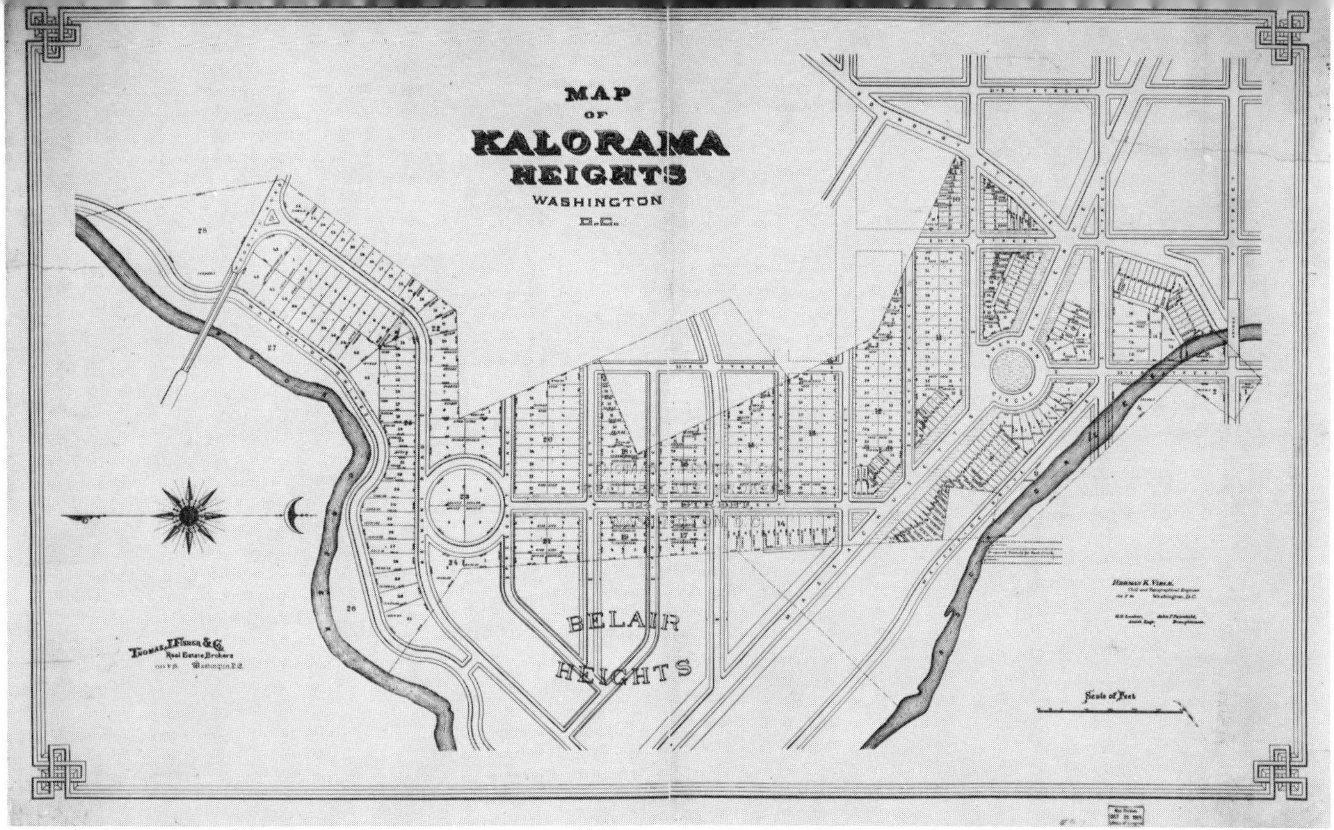

Reproduction from Mary Mitchell

Map of Kalorama Heights prepared by Thomas J. Fisher and Co.

Kalorama Heights is the sixty acre tract which the Lovett family sold in 1887 to the Philadelphia Syndicate. Belair Heights is the thirty acre tract which George Lovett sold in 1872 to the Freedman's Saving and Trust Co.

The result of Borglum's imagination and skill was a unique equestrian monument. It was not placed on a high pedestal but only three feet off the ground. The pose was a "snapshot" of one stirring moment. Shown one and three-quarters his actual size in the monument, the horse was of Black Hawk blood and was presented at the age of three to Sheridan in 1862 by officers of the Second Michigan Cavalry in Rienzi, Mississippi. Ridden by Sheridan in forty-eight engagements and battles until the peace at Appomattox, the horse became legendary because of his stamina, cool head under fire, and intelligence.

The moment Borglum chose to immortalize was that on October 19, 1864, when Sheridan, warned that General Jubal Early's Confederates were unexpectedly about to defeat his troops encamped at Cedar Creek, near Winchester, Virginia, galloped back the twenty miles through the night from Winchester to cheer on his men at dawn. He checks his horse suddenly so that "Rienzi" (he was later renamed "Winchester") falls back on his haunches and stiffens his forelegs to retain balance, while "Little Phil" whips off his hat in response to his cheering and later victorious regiment. The poet Thomas Buchanan Reed commemorated the event in his poem "Sheridan's Ride."

The reaction to this monument was varied. Some critics said the horse looked stuck in Cedar Creek mud. Another said: "After years of waiting, it seems we are to have a freakish statue of Sheridan, for surely if Jackson is mounted on a hobby-horse in front of the White House, Sheridan is mounted on a jumping-jack with its legs pulled together." Still another accused Borglum of representing Sheridan as a traffic-control officer—the year was 1908 and the horseless carriage was just coming into use.

Reconstructing the development of Sheridan Circle first as a fashionable residential area and later as part of Embassy Row has been fascinating research. May I acknowledge here the sustained help of Mary E. Curry who sought out for me the data on Sheridan and his horse and building permits for the elaborate mansions which soon adorned the Circle.

When the statue was unveiled on November 26, 1908, the widow, Mrs. Sheridan, and her daughters, Mary and Louise, had already (in 1905) built and moved into her house, which now belongs to the Greek Embassy, at 2211 Massachusetts Avenue. Here they paid $200 extra for a fourth floor balcony onto which they could step and look toward "Papa's Circle." By 1903, scattered houses along that first stretch of Massachusetts Avenue between Florida Avenue and the

Kalorama: Country Estate to Washington Mayfair 183

Circle were occupied. Beyond the Circle only two houses in a row of four were built, 2338, where Wilcomb E. Washburn, our Society's Vice President, now lives, and 2332.

On the Circle itself, and on R Street, separated by only a small triangular boulevard, four houses had appeared. In 1903 Mrs. Alice Barney had a studio house at 2306 R Street, and in 1904 she built a formal home at 2223 R Street, after moving from Rhode Island Avenue where her husband had died. Chief Justice Charles Evans Hughes bought this mansion in 1931 after Mrs. Barney moved to Hollywood, and he occupied it until his death in 1948. It is now the Burmese Embassy. By October 1908, 2221 Massachusetts Avenue, now the Greek Embassy, had been finished by Henning Jennings; and 2253 R Street was completed for Mrs. Emma Fitzhugh and is now the Philippines Embassy.

Half completed and then finished the next year were 2249 Massachusets Avenue for Mrs. C. Peyton Russell, now the Embassy of Sweden; 2234 Massachusetts Avenue for Mrs. Joseph Beale, once the Egyptian Embassy; and 2241 R Street for Frederick A. Keep, now the Embassy of the State of Viet Nam. With exception of the Korean Embassy at 2320 Massachusetts Avenue, built in 1920 by Harry Wardman, the English builder, the remaining residences, continuing as far as Decatur Place and including the Turkish Embassy, were completed by 1913.

Due to the intelligent real estate promotion of Thomas J. Fisher, Kalorama Heights became a fruitful field for the work of leading contemporay domestic architects, all showing in their designs the influence of the Ecole des Beaux Arts in Paris. These were George Oakley Totten, Nathan Wyeth, and Waddy Wood. Resembling French chateaux, the style of these stately townhouses was as desirable then as the amalgam of plate glass, plain surfaces, and flat or domed rooflines seems to architects and clients today. Costing anywhere from fifty to more than one hundred thousand dollars (the Turkish Embassy built by Edward Everett, inventor of the bottlecap, cost $225,000), they were well built, elaborately designed, and owned by socially prominent people, many of whom had houses in Bar Harbor or Newport and had chosen Washington for the same reasons Joel Barlow did a century before.

Let us consider a typical house, 2315 Massachusetts Avenue, now the Embassy of Pakistan, whose architect was George Oakley Totten, and whose first owner was Mrs. Francois Berger Moran. Around 1910 land was valued at between $2 and $4 a square foot. Costing originally $62,000, an average for the Circle, it has four stories, an attic and a basement, is made of stone and brick, is heated by steam, has an elevator, and was wired for electricity. This last innovation was common to all the residences. The option of an "automobile-house" was not in the building permit, although you find an occasional one listed in permits for Georgetown owners as early as 1904. Presumably these people still used carriages, and kept their horses and vehicles in a nearby livery complex. The reception rooms of 2315 Massachusetts Avenue have imported ceilings made of canvas and hand-painted in oil, made to fit the rooms and shipped to this country in sealed tubes. Like her contemporaries and neighbors, Mrs. Moran was active in patriotic and philanthropic organizations and she raised money for Democratic campaigns.

With their spacious rooms, elegant appearance, convenient location, and solid construction, it is no wonder that eventually when the fashionable trend moved further west and into Georgetown, all but one of these townhouses eventually became embassies. In 1932 the trend-setting British Embassy moved from Connecticut Avenue and N Street across Rock Creek to its present site. Afterwards many other embassies and legations moved from east of Dupont Circle and the Sixteenth Street area to Kalorama, and by the mid-1930's this wooded, rolling and pleasant area became noted for its diplomatic flavor and personalities.

An exception was 2306 Massachusetts Avenue where Mrs. Alice Barney built her studio house in 1903. Given by her two daughters in 1960 to the Smithsonian Institution, it is today an office for the Institution's circulating exhibitions. A picturesque and non-conforming personality, who boasted she was once engaged to the explorer Henry Stanley, Alice Pike was the daughter of a theatre and distillery proprietor in Cincinnati. At seventeen she married Albert Clifford Barney, a railroad car manufacturer, and moved to Washington. When he died in 1904, she was forty and left with five million dollars.

Behind a facade reminiscent of a Spanish mission, she performed her own plays, painted portraits of prominent socialites,[4] and wrote poetry, in an atmosphere heavy with ornate Seventeenth Century Spanish furniture. Even today the house looks surprisingly personal. A balcony overhangs the studio-salon where she must have played an impassioned Juliet to an equally ardent Romeo. A dining room on a half-level with highback oak chairs and red velvet cushions offers

---

[4] A reproduction of Alice Barney's "Portrait of Miss C" from the Catalogue of the Eighth Annual Exhibition of the Society of Washington Artists, 1898, appears on page 285 of the *Records of the Columbia Historical Society of Washington, D.C., 1960–1962*.

Kalorama: Country Estate to Washington Mayfair

another setting for her entertainments. Scorpions decorate hallway posts, and doors open from odd parts of the house, showing her personal direction about how she wanted things done regardless of architecture. Her garden facing onto Rock Creek ravine was ornamented with statues and vases. One of these statues was that of a nude girl, delivered to the house uncrated, and left on the sidewalk. Such a crowd gathered that the police were called to control it and dispense the queues of curious, ordering Mrs. Barney to remove her possession to the bushes in the rear.

Yet this apparently egocentric, showy personality had her serious, civic-minded side. She built the Sylvan Theatre on the Washington Monument grounds, much used in summer today, and she established Neighborhood House on N Street, S.W. in an area noted at the time for its poverty and needy children.

In her fifties she found Washington too confining and moved to Hollywood where she died in 1931. At her own direction her tombstone carried the legend: "The Talented One." This may well have been true, and the phrase could also describe many another Kalorama resident before her time and afterwards.

Between 1890 and the end of the first World War, the streets and blocks around the periphery of Kalorama Heights had seen an almost frantic engineering activity. Water and sewer mains were laid, streets levelled, gaslamps and later electric and telephone lines were installed, drinking fountains for animals were built, and pumps, hydrants, wells, and traps were constructed to make the area liveable. Lots in these peripheral areas sold quickly, and it soon was solidly built up along Leroy Place, Phelps Place, the east end of California Street and Bancroft Place.

The District engineers, on February 17, 1892, removed fourteen bodies from the mausoleum to Rock Creek Church Cemetery for burial in a lot which George Bomford had bought. Among them were the bodies of Ruth Barlow, Abraham Baldwin (her brother and Senator from Georgia), Clara and George Bomford, and several Bomford descendants named French. The mausoleum was then demolished and the last trace of the Barlows at Kalorama was gone.

S Street developed early and to this day retains it prestige. Graded but still lacking water-mains in 1907, it boasted two handsome brick dwellings erected opposite each other, both undoubtedly using the ample 30-foot wells of the old mansion because the street did not have water-mains until later. The house at 2300 S Street was built in 1901

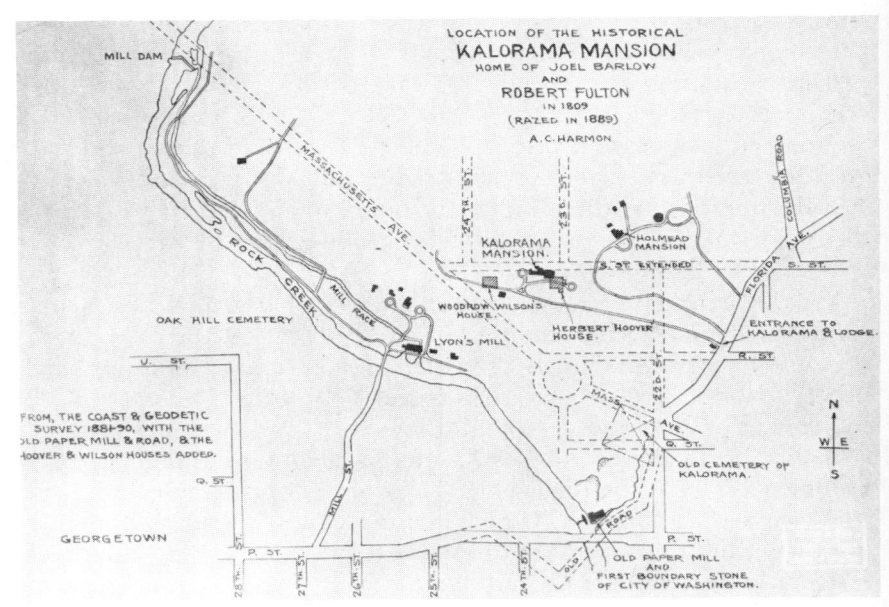

Map Division, Library of Congress

Map by A. C. Harmon showing places of historical interest in the Kalorama area.

by Thomas S. Gale, salesman for Thomas J. Fisher and Co., and that at 2301 S Street in 1907 by William A. Mearns, a banker.

By 1914, with all other utilities installed, George Hewitt Myers had two splendid architectural gems, 2310 and 2330 S Street, designed by John Russell Pope, and adorned with shutters, pillars, pediments and all the other trappings of Georgian Revival grandeur typical of Pope's eclectic Beaux Arts style. Myers, a financier and investment banker, had become interested in Oriental rugs while he was a college student at Yale. As his interest and that of his wife expanded, so did his real estate. By 1925 his three houses, 2310, 2320, and 2330 S Street included a gallery and museum for their collection. At his death in 1957 he left $1,485,000 to maintain the Textile Museum which today attracts many scholars and tourists.

Another famous house on this street is 2340, built in 1916 by Henry Parker Fairbanks who sold it to Woodrow Wilson after Wilson left the White House. Wilson died there on February 3, 1924, and the property now belongs to the National Trust for Historic Preservation.

The rest of Joel Barlow's Kalorama remained unimproved until

Kalorama: Country Estate to Washington Mayfair 187

well after World War I. Two circumstances account for this unusual situation. The first was the difficulties engineers encountered in the uneven, steeply rising topography of Kalorama and Belair Heights, left behind in the District appropriations for development in the headlong rush to cross Rock Creek and urbanize what became Cleveland Park and its environs.

The other reason takes us back to 1795 when Anthony Holmead moved from Rock Hill to his 56-acre parcel and built the brick house which stood there for 134 years. You will note on the map of the entire area, taken from G. M. Hopkins Plat-book for 1886, the funnel-shaped property belonging to S. S. Kall and running down to Boundary Street where its entrance was. S. S. Kall was not a man but a widow, Sophia Speake Kall, the great-granddaughter of Anthony Holmead himself. His descendants had lived in his family seat since then, and as developers bought property in the 1870's and 1880's between what became Phelps Place and Florida Avenue, and then subdivided it, the District engineers kept pace and installed sewers and water and other improvements, but always had to stop when they reached the long Holmead property line. It was not until 1894 when Mrs. Kall died at the age of 62 that any of the fifty-six acres was sold. This piece had become literally "The Widow's Mite."

Within ten years the remaining property passed into other hands in a singular disposition of ownership. The first to go was a northern running piece from Bancroft Place roughly to Wyoming Avenue, bought by James Lowndes, a developer who soon built it up solidly. The second was the most southern triangle formed by 22nd Street and Decatur Place which the French government bought around 1900 as an embassy site. The fourth, a seven-acre square bordered by 23rd and S Streets, was purchased by Mr. and Mrs. E. N. Mitchell who never built the house they wanted. But after her husband's death, and before departing from Washington, Mrs. Mitchell in 1918 left the land and several thousand dollars to the District to be used as a park, but first and foremost as a suitable plot in which to bury her pet poodle Bosque who had travelled around the world with her. His grave enclosed by white chains is in the middle of a charming little playground and a plaque on the wall of a playhouse tells the story.

The remaining fifteen-acre plot on which the last of the homes of the original proprietors stood has a more colorful history. In 1905, through the efforts of Count von Bernsdorff, the German ambassador, his government decided to build a magnificent white marble embassy to cost more than a half million dollars. But due to the presence on the opposite side of 22nd Street of the French Embassy, and the onset of hostilities between the two nations, this plot stood vacant until Private Jeremiah Sullivan of the District Police Force, industriously pounding the beat, suggested that he move into the house and "watch" the property for the Germans. During the War the Swiss government administered the territory. In the city's crowded condition, with no parking anywhere except on Sully's beat, an Army officer suggested he put up some parking sheds for transients along the edges. The Swiss agreed. Sully left the Police Force and lived in the house as caretaker and rental agent, making a good thing of the deal. The District complained that the sheds were a fire hazard. Sully's response was in effect: "They're on foreign territory." The war ended, the parking sheds remained, Sully died, and his son Eugene replaced him. At length in 1929 the German Embassy gave him thirty days to vacate before taking over the property and then demolished the house and the sheds. During World War II it became alien property, and on February 1, 1947, a court decree gave title to it to the United States government. Today it is an empty bleak stretch with an abandoned school building, once belonging to the Holton-Arms School, on the corner at 22nd Street, and along the edges, craggy tall oaks, relics of the Holmead ownership.

This is why today the area has such a unusual character. Some streets follow the familiar Washington grid, others zig and zag, twist and curve following the topographical lines of the former wooded knoll. If you walk along R Street and S Street and Decatur Place, you can see the massive high retaining walls, which owners had to erect to hold their levels. Built in the 1920's and 1930's and some as late as the 1950's, the houses are similar in appearance, characterized by the Georgian Revival style and almost all well-maintained. Numerous embassies and legations lend the section an attractive foreign look. The most beautiful of these is that of the French at 2221 Kalorama Road. The French government bought in 1936 the mansion built in 1911 by John Hays Hammond, a multi-millionaire mining engineer. It occupies most of the "Pretty Prospect" parcel added to Kalorama by George Bomford in 1841.

Many well-known people have lived and do live here. The first house erected was that of Samuel Kauffman, Chairman of the Board of the *Evening Star,* in 1924 at 2330 Tracy Place. Kalorama Circle, divided into quadrants and each quadrant into three lots, was given, instead of the usual equestrian statue, twelve handsome houses. The last two, No. 20 and No. 26 were erected as late as 1956 and 1958. Five Presidents have lived in Kalorama. William Howard Taft lived at 2215 Wyoming Avenue and Warren Harding at 2314. Franklin D.

Roosevelt, as Assistant Secretary of the Navy, lived at 2131 R. Street. Herbert Hoover owned 2300 S Street and Woodrow Wilson 2340. To sum up, in fewer than two hundred houses, ranging in assessed value, as of 1970, from $35,000 to $160,000, artists, writers, senators, cabinet officers, Supreme Court Justices and others prominent in government have made their homes in this cohesive residential area which a columnist recently compared to "Mayfair in London, Parioli in Rome, El Viso in Madrid, and St. Cloud in Paris."

The $14,000 with which Joel Barlow bought Kalorama would today scarcely buy a sideyard or a garden. But the "most delightful situation" of which he wrote continues in Kalorama in the ambience of culture and elegance of its design for living.

The National Theatre in Washington: Buildings and Audiences, 1835-1972

ROGER MEERSMAN AND ROBERT BOYER

The National Theatre in Washington, D. C. is one of the oldest business enterprises in the nation's capital and one of the senior playhouses in the United States. First opened in 1835, six different structures on the same site have provided a continuity of entertainment rare in most American cities. Over the years, Presidents, members of Congress, diplomats, and countless ordinary citizens have comprised the National's patronage.

To list the great variety of performers—actors, actresses, musicians, dancers, and entertainers—who have appeared at the National Theatre would be to catalogue nearly every important theatrical personality, both native and foreign-born, to appear on the American stage since 1835. Similarly, the types of entertainment presented, from minstrel shows and sensational melodramas to grand operas and classics of serious drama, span the entire range of American theatrical taste during these many decades. Of particular concern in this paper are the development of the physical theatre building and the composition and behaviour of the different audiences which have populated the theatre.

Before the government of the United States moved from Philadelphia to Washington in 1800, many towns near Washington had been visited by troupes of professional players. As early as 1790, *The Beggar's Opera* was performed in the area by McGrath's Company of Comedians. In 1799, a troupe of strolling players headed by Archibald Marlborough and Hamilton Sterling gave candlelight performances in Georgetown taverns, employing meager costumes but no scenery. A tax of six dollars for each performance was levied by the city, but the tax was remitted after petition to the authorities.[1]

---

[1] Alexander Hunter and J. H. Polkinhorn, *The New National Theatre, Washington, D.C.* (Washington, D.C.: R. O. Polkinhorn and Sons, 1885), p. 6. For further information see *Washington City and Capital* (Federal Writers' Project, Works Administration. Washington, D.C.: U.S. Government Printing Office, 1937).

The National Theatre in Washington, D.C. 191

By July 1800, the six Executive Departments of the national government had completed their transfer to Washington and following closely upon their heels was the New Theatre of Philadelphia, managed by Wignell and Reinagle. The company had closed in Philadelphia on May 14, 1800, and moved to Washington to perform in August in the United States Theatre, built into Samuel Blodgett's Great Hotel on the north side of E Street, N.W. between 7th and 8th Streets. Just before the theatre opened a great storm destroyed most of the scenery of the company and after a season lasting only one month the company ceased operations about the 15th of September.

This early period saw heroic but futile managerial struggles for both financial and artistic success. In 1803 a number of prominent citizens started plans for the construction of a new theatre which, after many problems of financing and constructing, finally opened on November 16, 1804, under the name of the Washington Theatre. The opening bill was a "Grand Medley Entertainment" by a Mr. Maginnis from London. A. I. Mudd describes the entertainment as a collection of "songs, magic, dancing and acting automatons, mechanical pictures, and spectacular effects." [2] The entertainment must have proven successful, for he performed nightly, varying the arrangement of the different acts, until the theatre closed for the season on December 17, 1804. For sixteen years, the theatre presented a variety of fare ranging from light comedy to Shakespeare and other classics. The Washington Theatre survived the burning of the city by the British in June of 1815, only to succumb to fire on April 19, 1820.

A year later, in August of 1821, a new theatre, also calling itself the Washington Theatre, was opened on Louisiana Avenue between 4½ and 6th Streets. The new Washington Theatre was an improvement over the old one: the auditorium seated approximately 700; the acoustics were good; liquor was excluded from the box lobbies; and smoking was absolutely prohibited. From 1821 to 1836 the theatre underwent numerous modifications and changes of name and was the showcase for a number of the notable performers of the day. However, the theatre could not withstand the competition of the new and modern National Theatre which had opened on December 7, 1835, and the old Washington Theatre, then called the American Theatre, closed on February 8, 1836.

Washington was a rough city exhibiting little refinement at the

---

[2] A. I. Mudd, "Early Theatres in Washington City," *Records of the Columbia Historical Society* (Washington, D.C.: Columbia Historical Society, 1902), V, 71. Mudd's collection of materials concerning the early Washington theatre is deposited in the New York Public Library Theatre Collection, catalogued under the symbols MEEZ nc.

time of the opening of the first National Theatre. On either side of Pennsylvania Avenue, the main thoroughfare, there were houses of every kind, many badly in need of repair. It was reported that "Washington was a dead city with no business; the only money in circulation came from government employees." [3] The unpaved streets made theatre-going a difficult task. Pennsylvania Avenue was a mudhole in bad weather and it cost as much as ten dollars to hire a carriage from the residential areas to the theatre. Despite these hardships, a group of far-sighted citizens saw a potential audience for a new center of entertainment and from their negotiations came the first National Theatre.

THE FIRST NATIONAL THEATRE BUILDING, 1835–1845

Two playhouses existed in Washington at the time of the building of the first National, but they were "crude affairs without proper ventilation, lighting and comfort." [4] In 1834 a group of civic leaders, consisting of Henry Randall, Richard Smith, Cornelius McLean, J. George Gibson, and William Brent, instituted a business enterprise to provide Washington with a new place of entertainment. Although several of the original partners failed to subscribe their portions of the funds, William W. Corcoran ultimately supplied the necessary amount. Lots three and four on square 234, located just west of 13th and E Streets, N.W., were purchased from John Mason on October 16, 1834, for the purpose of erecting a theatre building.

The original plan had been to locate the theatre in the triangular park in front of the present National, but this idea was abandoned. Instead, it was built on the site of an earlier place of amusement called the Rotunda,[5] which was located only a few hundred yards from Pennsylvania Avenue—the only street in Washington that was lighted at night by oil lamps. Beneath the site, in a large sewer-like enclosure, runs Tiber Creek.[6] Originally, the planners had chosen a site closer to the Capitol but, realizing that commerce was moving westerly in the city, they decided upon an area closer to the White House.

Begun early in 1835, the theatre was finished in November. Mudd describes the building as follows:

> It was of Roman Doric, resting on a basement 13 feet 6 inches in height with a portico 41 feet 6 inches long by 12 feet 9 inches in

---

[3] George Atkinson and Victor Kiraly, *A Great Curtain Falls* (New York: Strand Press, 1950), p. 37.

[4] *Washington Post,* November 22, 1922.

[5] *Washington Post,* December 6, 1927.

[6] Access to Tiber Creek was possible through a trap door in the basement under the stage until it was sealed off in the early 1950's to eliminate danger.

breadth, consisting of four brick Roman Doric columns 29 feet 6 inches in height with antae, entablature, and ballustrade. The front was 76 feet 6 inches wide, the building running back 150 feet and 50 feet in height. It was stuccoed in imitation of granite and had five large doors and a like number of windows in front.

The parquette was arranged so that the floor could be removed in order that the building might be used as an amphitheatre. The stage was 68 x 71 feet.

The dome was painted a pale cerulean blue and was divided into four allegorical designs. The first represented the Genius of the Institutions of the country, designated by Power and Wisdom repelling Tyranny and Superstition. The second represented Truth at the altar from which the Spirits of War and Peace had taken the sword and torch. The third represented the Goddess of Wisdom presenting a medallion of Washington to the Goddess of Liberty, who returned a wreath to crown her favorite son—Fame proclaiming Victory and Peace. The last represented Justice protecting and guiding the commerce and manufactures of America. All the ornaments of the interior were of a national character representing, either by allegorical design or historical illustrations, important events in the history of the country. What had in the earlier theatres been known as the pit was done away with and in its place a parquette was substituted and connected with the lower boxes. Then there was the first gallery or first tier, second tier and the gallery. A part of this gallery was set apart for persons of color.[7]

The opening of the new theatre was anticipated with some excitement as is evident from the following notice published in the *National Intelligencer:*

> The lovers of drama will be pleased to learn that this new and beautiful theatre will certainly open on Monday next. The construction of the theatre is notable both for its commodiousness and for seeing and hearing. The arrangement of the seats are [sic] very convenient, and the decorations will be elegant in every respect. The dome of the theatre is finished and is a most beautiful thing of its kind, and when the house is lighted up, the effect will be exceedingly brilliant....
>
> The artist is a Mr. White from New York. The painting of the principal scenery is entrusted to Mr. Kerr. In consequence of fitting up the theatre, it is advisable to observe that the pit is done away with and the space is occupied by what is termed a "parquet" which is connected with the lower boxes and is fitted up so that it will be equally desirable for the ladies to frequent as the lower boxes. The entrance and

---

[7] A. I. Mudd, "The Theatres of Washington from 1835 to 1850," *Records of the Columbia Historical Society* (Washington, D.C.: Columbia Historical Society, 1930), VI, 223–224.

price of the parquet will be the same, and the convenience and gratification of the ladies have been consulted on this occasion.

The second tier of boxes will be fitted up quite as handsomely as the lower tier, and will be equally commodious; but to meet the wishes of the citizens generally, and the constant playgoers, the price of admission will be considerably less. This tier of boxes will have the advantage of a handsome saloon being attached to it, where coffee, fruit and confectionery will be served. The gods will be pleased to see that their comforts have been duly attended to, and they will find very excellent and convenient quarters in the usual place at the usual price.[8]

On the first night, December 7, 1835, the full house was treated to a reading by Mrs. Hughes of the prize opening address written by Mr. Vose of Baltimore. This was followed by the comedy, *The Man of the World,* and the afterpiece, a musical farce called *Turn Out.* According to the *National Intelligencer,* a good class of Washington citizenry attended the opening night:

> The parquet and boxes were filled with ladies and gentlemen, and the 'tout ensemble' must have formed a highly gratifying 'coup de'oeil' to the spirited manager, precursor, it is hoped, of what he may expect throughout the season, providing he realizes the assurance and promises which he has made.

The gallery "gods" were sent aloft, and the pit, which had previously been the gathering place for the more boisterous and rowdy patrons of the theatre, became the "parquet" and seated the highest class of citizens. The lower classes were removed to the upper gallery. There were other innovations and points of interest in the new National Theatre as is evident from the reporter's description:

> The form of the first tier of boxes is embellished with slight sketches in imitation of bas-relief, and surrounded by correspondent ornaments representing brilliant events in maritime history, discovery, and naval achievements. The second tier of boxes is ornamented in similar style, referring to victories, treaties, agriculture, etc. The proscenium shows the same colors and style of ornaments. In the arch thereof is a representation of the Declaration of Independence, supported on the wings of Time. The curtain displays an equestrian statue of Washington in front of rich drapery, which is partly drawn aside and displays the tomb of Washington, Mount Vernon, etc. It is intended as a substitute for the green curtain, and the change will doubtless be approved of. The machinery and stage arrangements, all excellent of their kind,

---

[8] From the *National Intelligencer* as quoted in Hunter and Polkinhorn, *The New National Theatre,* p. 13.

are by Mr. Varden; and the whole was lighted by new and splendid lamps made expressly for this establishment.[9]

On the ground floor was the parquet and above this two tiers of boxes on the sides near the proscenium opening flanked by balconies with benches extending along the sides and encircling the rear of the auditorium. The number of boxes on each level is now not definitely known, but it seems clear that there were at least six—three on each side. It is probable that these levels were duplicated and that there were six on each tier making a total of twelve boxes. On the second level there was also a saloon dispensing refreshments. Above the second level was a third, consisting solely of an open gallery encircling the auditorium. Here the "gallery gods" sat and a portion of this area was designated for Negroes.

Using the designs of the Chestnut Street Theatre in Philadelphia and the Park Theatre in New York as a guide,[10] it can be assumed that there was an apron, possibly six to eight feet in depth, before the proscenium opening. The two tiers of boxes probably began at the downstage edge of the apron and between the ends of the boxes and the proscenium aperture there was, on each side, a proscenium door. It is logical to assume also that there was a small pit for musicians at the front of the apron.[10]

The first National prospered from 1835 until January of 1844 when the stockholders began growing anxious about the financial status of the theatre. Receipts had not been covering expenses, and several of the investors divested themselves of their stock at quite low prices. The theatre, which cost $45,000 to build, was sold for $13,500 to General Van Ness, Benjamin Ogle Taylor, and Richard Smith, all prominent citizens of Washington. The theatre was temporarily transformed into a circus—the pit becoming an amphitheatre for clowns, trained horses and educated dogs. The new owners reopened the National as a theatre again on February 11; the building having been thoroughly scrubbed, the front of the theatre painted, more stoves placed in the house, and more lamps hung to eliminate gloom.

The highlight of 1844–1845 at the National Theatre was not a

---

[9] Mudd, "Early Theatres in Washington City,", V, 85.

[10] This reconstruction is based upon the well known engraving of the Chestnut Street Theatre (1794), Philadelphia, and the water color of the Park Theatre (1821), New York. The former is reproduced in Oral Sumner Coad and Edwin Mims, Jr., *The American Stage*. Volume XIV of the *Pageant of America* (New Haven: Yale University Press, 1929) XIV, 37. The interior of the Park is found in Barnard Hewitt, *Theatre U.S.A. 1665 to 1957* (New York: McGraw-Hill, 1959), p. 104. The exterior of the Park can be found in Brooks McNamara, *The American Playhouse in the Eighteenth Century* (Cambridge: Harvard University Press, 1969), p. 134.

theatrical event, but the Inauguration ball of President Polk on March 4, 1845. The following night, between eight and nine o'clock, during a performance of *Beauty and the Beast,* a fire broke out in the oil room located near the rear of the building. The edifice was soon in flames, but the audience, although panic-stricken, all reached safety, for the alarm had been given in time.[11] The *National Intelligencer* reported that seven or eight dwelling houses adjoining the theatre were also destroyed by the flames that were fanned by west winds. Two companies of firemen from Alexandria dragged their equipment eight miles across the Potomac River and were wildly cheered as they reached the theatre, but because of a lack of water the firemen were unable to save the building.[12] This was a tragic blow for there was reportedly no insurance whatever on the building.[13]

THE SECOND NATIONAL THEATRE BUILDING, 1850–1857

Two Washington businessmen, Messrs. Willard and Reeside, purchased the burned-out National Theatre in 1850 and had the theatre hastily rebuilt and enlarged to seat 3,400 persons. Using the old walls and what could be salvaged of the former building's bricks, Washington workmen erected what was to be called the National Hall. An architect, Robert Mills, checked the structure, along with builders Joel Downer and James King, and after the examination called it sound, certifying that every part of it was strong enough to hold with safety the largest group that could be accommodated there.

The new theatre was packed for the two Jenny Lind concerts on the 16th and 17th of December 1850; and on January 21, 1851, the National Hall was leased to a circus troupe. Many tiers of temporary seats were erected and, during an exciting part of the performance, the pressure of the large crowd caused the west wall of the building to fall outward. A great confusion followed but, as no one was hurt, the performers continued to the scheduled finish of the entertainment. Immediately after the circus departed, the owners had the hall torn down and began to plan a grander theatre building which was to replace it.

On December 15, 1852, the second playhouse, as such, on the site—but actually the third structure—opened with the President and his Cabinet in attendance. It is safe to speculate that this second playhouse was somewhat similar in design and arrangement to the first.

---

[11] William Tindell, *Standard History of Washington* (Knoxville, Tenn.: H. W. Crew and Company, 1914), p. 501.
[12] *National Intelligencer,* March 7, 1845.
[13] *National Intelligencer,* March 6, 1845.

The National Theatre in Washington, D.C. 197

On the ground floor was the parquet with comfortable, individual seats. Within a few years, the custom developed of designating the front rows of seats next to the orchestra pit as the "orchestra" while those at the rear were called the "parquet" and sold at half the price of the former. There were six boxes on the first tier only—three on each side—beginning at the downstage end of the apron. These came to be called "private boxes." Flanking these was the first or dress circle, an open balcony with benches encompassing the sides and rear of the auditorium. Above this was a second circle, called a gallery, and later the family circle (for whites only); still above this was another gallery (for blacks).

Although stage aprons did not begin to vanish until 1863 and 1869[14] the proscenium doors were vanishing in the new theatres of 1855 and 1858.[15] In their places proscenium boxes were embedded in a deep proscenium archway, usually two or three on each side. It is unlikely that these boxes were three levels high. The two top ones—one on each side—being on the level of the black gallery were designated "colored boxes."

This building lasted only four years, for on January 12, 1857, fire began in the property room in an upstairs area as stagehands prepared the scenery for the *Olympic Rivals,* a production by a New York repertory company. Fortunately no one was injured in the blaze and the troupe gave a performance in the Odd Fellows' Hall the next evening without the company's scenery and costumes which had been destroyed in the fire. Washingtonians responded generously to the troupe's plight and later a ball was given to benefit the players. A resolution was passed by the planning committee for the event that high government personages, including ex-President and Mrs. Tyler and Mrs. Madison, be asked to attend as patrons.

The burning of the National Theatre caused the owners of Carusi's Saloon to remodel their building into a theatre. This same location had also been The Theatre and the City Assembly Rooms. The new house of entertainment took the name The Washington Theatre and provided the city with dramatic productions while the National was in ruins.

---

[14] For example, see the reproduction of Brougham's Lyceum, 1863, in Coad and Mims, *Pageant of America,* XIV, 114; and the reproduction of Edwin Booth's Theatre, 1869, in Hewitt, *Theatre U.S.A.,* p. 215. Both of these new houses had no forestages nor aprons.

[15] For example, see the reproduction of Niblo's Theatre, 1855, in Coad and Mims, *Pageant of America,* XIV, 221; and Laura Keene's new theatre, 1858, in Coad and Mims, XIV, 204. Both of these new theatres had aprons but not proscenium doors and the proscenium boxes overhung the apron.

No structure was built on the site of the National during the following six years; little construction of any kind was being done in Washington because the city was considered too near the slave states to be safe from the war that seemed inevitable. There was near real estate panic in the city at one point; and during the early months of the Civil War, with battles in nearby areas, no investor could take the risk of building on Washington property.[16] The economic climate was to change, however, and the 13th and E Street site would again house a theatre.

THE THIRD NATIONAL THEATRE BUILDING, 1862–1873

The burned-out shell of the National had remained since the fire of 1857 and the property had passed through many hands, when, after a series of complications as to who owned the property, Davidge and Ennis were established as trustees by a ruling of the Equity Court on June 13, 1858. These men proceeded to sell the property to W. E. Spaulding and William W. Rapley for $35,000.

Toward the end of 1861, confidence had been restored in the potential of the District of Columbia and there was a new wave of prosperity in the city with real estate becoming excessively valuable. This, coupled with the need for amusement in the tense war-time city, prompted the rebuilding of the National. At first, a rather crude structure called King's Amphitheatre was erected on the site for the purpose of holding circus performances. On November 7, 1861, the Washington public was informed through an advertisement in the *Washington Star* that the new place of amusement would open its doors for the first time. However, within seven months another structure arose on the same site, and Grover's National received much praise upon its opening on the anniversary of Shakespeare's birthday in 1862:

> Mr. W. E. Spaulding has erected the New National without regard to cost, upon the site of the old building.... This building as completed has the capacity for about two thousand persons. The ceiling and walls are elegantly frescoed and the boxes neatly and tastefully painted and panelled. To sum it up, Mr. Spaulding has erected the largest, most comfortable and most elegantly located theatre in the city.[17]

However, within seven years, the physical condition of the building had deteriorated to such an extent that it received public notice

---

[16] Hunter and Polkinhorn, *The New National Theatre,* p. 41.
[17] *Washington Star,* April 24, 1862.

The National Theatre in Washington, D.C.

From the Collection of Robert A. Truax

The Third National Theatre Building, 1862–1873.

A note on the reverse of the original indicates that this photograph was made on January 10, 1868, five years before the building was burned on January 28, 1873.

by John B. Ellis who wrote in his guide book to Washington that both the National Theatre and Wall's Opera House were

> ... old fashioned and dirty. They would rank as second-class establishments in other cities and contrast strangely with the audiences which they sometimes contain. Performances are given during the winter only, and the establishments are managed on the 'star' system. Generally, a very fair business is done during the season, for the city is full of strangers and others with plenty of time, who would gladly avail themselves of the amusement thus offered them.
>
> The acting is scarcely above the average except when some travelling company visits the city. Actors who could not earn a decent living in our larger cities flourish in Washington and furnish food for the dramatic criticisms of the 'grave and reverend signeurs of the Government.' [18]

---

[18] John B. Ellis, *The Sights and Sounds of the Nation's Capital* (New York: United States Publishing Co., 1869), p. 451.

Further evidence of the decay in the physical plant may be seen in a piece of correspondence sent to the Mayor and City Council of Washington by John M. Gordon. His letter sheds light on several of the inadequacies in the National at the time:

> I beg to call your attention to what I deem a great evil and dangerous nuisance. I mean the custom at the Theatres [Wall's and the National] of placing chairs in the gangway on crowded nights. In case of panic from any cause, as from fire, when an actress sets her dress in flame from the footlights (which ought to be protected by wire coverings,) and then setting fire to the inflammable scenery, which happened in Baltimore, or from the burning of a playbill falling from the gallery upon the lamp below, as I saw occur at the National Theatre, or from the breaking of a bench or chair, a thing not uncommon, that part of the audience not trampled under foot, would be suffocated with smoke or burnt up with fire.

Gordon went on to request a law forbidding the placing of chairs in the aisles at public assemblies, and then continued:

> In your National Theatre, the spectators from the orchestra, parquette and dress circles, containing a thousand or more persons, men, women and children, debouch from one narrow entrance where there is a flight of stairs placed as a kind of man mash trap. It requires from ten to fifteen minutes, as I have observed by my watch, for an audience to retire in good order.
>
> The people in the third tier have to descend a steep, narrow, corkscrew staircase, about four feet wide. It would of course be crammed and choked in an instant, and no one behind the obstruction would escape the flames.[19]

There is no evidence that the management took any steps to remedy the conditions which Gordon described, if indeed they were even aware of them.

Considering the unsafe condition of the National, fortunately there was no audience in the house when the theatre again burned, this time at eleven o'clock in the morning of January 28, 1873. There was no death or injury even though the Alice Oates Opera Company was in the process of departing when the conflagration began. Only the rear and north part of the building burned. William Rapley, the co-owner, had arrived a few minutes before the fire began and watched the $138,000 building burn. Mr. Saville, the lessee at the time, and the Alice Oates Company lost considerable property in the fire. Mr.

---

[19] John Montgomery Gordon, "Several Letters to the Mayor and City Council of Washington on the Subject of the Public Theatres, Pennsylvania Avenue and the Canal" (Pamphlet) (Norfolk: Virginia Printers, 1870), p. 5.

Rapley subsequently bought out Mr. Spaulding and began to rebuild the theatre immediately. The owners had only $98,000 in insurance on the structure at the time it was destroyed.

THE FOURTH NATIONAL THEATRE BUILDING, 1873–1885

President Grant attended the opening of the fourth building on December 1, 1873. In all likelihood, it was very similar to the previous structure. Those portions of the earlier building which had not burned remained as they were. On December 2, *The Washington Star* briefly reported that the opening "was a very brilliant spectacle. The decorations of the house are exceedingly neat and tasteful, the colors harmonize well, the light is good, and when the seats are filled with a fashionable audience such as that of last night, the effect is quite fine."

The inauguration of the new building received little attention in the press and its exact design is now unknown. It may be assumed that it resembled the third building in interior arrangement except that the apron or forestage had now finally disappeared. It is probable that the proscenium boxes continued on several levels and it is apparent that there was an inclined orchestra, parquet with two levels of balconies, the dress and family circles.

For twelve years the National survived but once again, for the fourth time in fifty years, fire destroyed the theatre building. On February 27, 1885, only three hours after Wallack's New York Company completed its performance of *Victor Durand*, the building was again engulfed in flames, and by 2:30 a.m. the rear wall collapsed, to be followed by the front wall one-half hour later.[20] The loss was estimated at $150,000; the owners had less than a quarter of that amount in insurance on the building. The Miller and Jones Billiard Parlor over the lobby was destroyed as were the sample rooms for the firm located on the west side of the lobby.

THE FIFTH NATIONAL THEATRE BUILDING, 1885–1922

By the latter part of April, 1885, construction had begun on a new building and it was ready for occupancy in October of the same year. The New National Theatre, as it was called, seated 1,900 people. Although the structure was completed in early September, almost five weeks were needed to finish the ornate interior decorations. Among the new features were an asbestos fire-proof curtain for the stage; spacious seating (twenty-one inch wide seats with a wide space between rows); a heavily-carpeted orchestra; a beautifully carpeted

---

[20] *Washington Star*, February 28, 1885.

green room (14' × 14'); twenty-four dressing rooms; and a hundred-burner chandelier hanging in the house which was convertible to electricity. According to one source, the entire new theatre was lighted by electricity.[21] The new building was heated by steam. The entrance to the dress circle was twenty-eight feet wide. The cost of the entire structure was in excess of $200,000. The architect for the front was A. B. Mullett, and for the theatre proper J. B. McElfatrick and Sons, who had designed some of New York's finest theatres. The McElfatrick design was so successful that, structurally, the present building is essentially the same.[22]

The orchestra and parquet seats were reached by climbing a short series of steps from the lobby and entering into the raked auditorium. There were twelve enclosed boxes, six on either side of the stage, and the boxes were in three pairs at the levels of the orchestra, the balcony and the gallery. The latter were, doubtless, occasionally still referred to as the dress and family circles. According to a review in the *Washington Star* of October 6, 1885, the new theatre was well received on opening night:

> The decoration of the lobby was particularly remarked. Hoyt's beautiful curtain was applauded as the asbestos curtain was drawn up disclosing it to view. At the end of the second act there was loud and long continued calls for Mr. Rapley, but the gentleman did not appear. Finally, Dr. Frank T. Howe came before the curtain, and in the name of Mr. Rapley, who was too modest to appear himself, made a happy little speech of thanks.

The front curtain, so well received on opening night, lasted only five years; and in 1890 the theatre owners commissioned the artist E. A. Morange to design and execute a new decorative main curtain. Morange created a work depicting an allegory of spring, consisting of two classical women in a chariot drawn by a team of birds in flight amid voluminous drapes. As the chariot crosses the sky, the two women strew petals to the earth.

Between 1885 and 1922 the National Theatre prospered, even though it met with increasing competition from motion pictures. It became apparent to Mr. Rapley, however, that the 1885 theatre was

---

[21] *Washington Post,* December 6, 1927.

[22] In a letter sent by Scott Kirkpatrick, the manager of the National Theatre, to the *Washington Post-Times Herald* on July 14, 1958, the acoustics of the theatre are praised: "The acoustics of the National are excellent. Kept essentially the same as the design of McElfatrick and Sons of New York who designed the 1880 [1885] building, departments of architecture from many universities send students to study the acoustics of the National."

no longer suitable for the productions being booked in from New York and that among the audiences of the 1920's the theatre had the reputation of being dated. It was true that the stage facilities and auditorium, despite some minor alterations that had occurred during the 37 years, were still best suited to Nineteenth Century drama. It was decided completely to renovate the building, tearing down and rebuilding major portions of the 1885 structure.

In the late spring of 1922, the final production was given in the thirty-seven year old playhouse. Rachel Crother's *Nice People,* which a year earlier had opened New York's Klaw Theatre, was the closing play. After the final curtain fell the orchestra played "Auld Lang Syne"; then the curtain rose once more and the audience remained silently in their seats while stagehands removed all the scenery. It was, as the *Washington Post,* reported on November 27, 1922, a "unique ceremony in the history of the theatre."

THE SIXTH NATIONAL THEATRE BUILDING, 1922 TO THE PRESENT

The sixth building, which opened for the first time in the fall of 1922, and is little modified today, is structurally very similar to the McElfatrick design of 1885. The adherence to the earlier design was deliberate, for the 1885 building had proven so successful from an acoustical standpoint that the owner wished no major structural modification. On January 28, 1922, an immense accumulation of snow caused the roof of the Knickerbocker Theatre to fall in upon the audience, killing and injuring a number of persons, and the Commissioners of the City of Washington ordered all theatre roofs to be reinforced with steel beams. Mr. Rapley, the owner, had the reinforcement of the National which was then being rebuilt made through exterior addition rather than interior change which might have altered the acoustical properties of the theatre.

The word "New" was dropped from the name and when the theatre opened on November 27, 1922, it was called simply The National Theatre. The renovation was so extensive that only the walls remained the same as the 1885 structure. The columns which had supported the two balconies in the old building and had caused some viewing problems were replaced by a thirty-ton steel girder supporting the weight of the tiers. At the first balcony level there were twelve boxes, six on each side; at the gallery level there were two, one on either side. The boxes were not covered or framed in any way, as was the earlier fashion, but were suspended from the side walls. The orchestra pit was enlarged by placing three feet of it under the stage. It was three feet wide at each end and graduated to seven feet at the center. The lighting booth, which had jutted out into the gallery of the 1885 building, was set into the rear wall.

At the time of the opening, the remodeling had not been completed. The walls were painted white and much of the old stage drapery had been hastily installed. The management announced that in the summer of 1923 new decorations and curtains would be added. This plan was carried out and before the 1923 fall season the front was reconstructed with the addition of a smoking room and lounge, now called the mezzanine lobby. The seating capacity of the new building was only fifteen persons fewer than that of the old theatre. Just as his father had been thirty-seven years before, W. H. Rapley was on hand to receive the praise for his new National Theatre:

> Any report of the proceedings at the National Theatre last night should begin at the beginning and recount the cordial "congratulations" with which some 1400 play-goers greeted W. H. Rapley at the threshold of his new playhouse. Judging from the handshaking, the smiles, the bows from row to row, the veritable screen of chrysanthemums in the foyer, the sheaf of telegrams which kept pouring in . . . it was a sort of homecoming spirit which pervaded the audience.[23]

The theatre remained under the complete control of the Rapley family until April 26, 1928, when W. H. Rapley sold a half interest to A. L. Erlanger, who had been the National's booking agent in New York for thirty years.

After eighty-four years of interest in the National, the Rapley Company of New York sold the theatre to the Munsey Realty Company of Washington on May 6, 1942.

EARLY WASHINGTON AUDIENCES

When the first National Theatre building opened in 1835, its two rivals, as has been noted, were such as to be described as "crude affairs without proper ventilation, lighting and comfort." The audiences which customarily attended the theatre in Washington at the time have been described in terms to suggest that they fit such standards. Frances Trollope, mother of the novelist Anthony Trollope, visited the theatre during her stay in the Washington area in 1830–1831 and commented:

> The theatre was not open while we were in Washington but we afterwards took advantage of our vicinity to the city, to visit. The house is very small, and most astonishingly dirty and void of decoration, considering that it is the only place of amusement that the city affords.

---

[23] *Washington Post*, November 28, 1922.

The National Theatre in Washington, D.C.

I have before mentioned the want of decorum at the Cincinnati theatre, but certainly that of the capital at least rivalled it in the freedom of action and attitude; a freedom which seems to disdain the restraints of civilized manners. One man in the pit was seized with a violent fit of vomiting, which appeared not in the least to annoy or surprise his neighbours; and the happy coincidence of a physician being at that moment personated on the stage, was hailed by many of the audience as an excellent joke, of which the actor took advantage, and elicited shouts of applause by saying, "I expect my services are wanted elsewhere."

The spitting was incessant; and not one in ten of the male part of the illustrious legislative audience sat according to the usual custom of human beings; the legs were thrown sometimes over the front of the box, sometimes over the side of it; here and there a senator stretched his entire length along a bench, and in many instances the front rail was preferred as a seat.

I remarked one young man, whose handsome person, and most elaborate toilet, led me to conclude he was a first-rate personage, and so I doubt not he was; nevertheless, I saw him take from the pocket of his silk waistcoat a lump of tobacco, and daintily deposit it within his cheek.[24]

The situation had apparently not greatly improved by 1852, for when the second National opened on December 15, 1852, a program note read: "Gentlemen are earnestly requested to use the spittoons and spare the floor."

That the owners of the first National anticipated the behavior of the audiences is suggested by their new arrangement of the interior of the auditorium which as has been noted sent the more rowdy element to the upper tiers and reserved the orchestra area for the more cultivated element. Even though the *National Intelligencer* noted the number of ladies and gentlemen who attended the opening of the theatre, they did not continue to patronize the theatre and often it was attended only by the rowdier theatre-goers. In 1836, a year after the opening of the theatre, six private boxes in the second tier were arranged and appointed quite elegantly for the accommodation of families. The price was set at ten dollars, but even after this was reduced the boxes were never well patronized and they were finally eliminated.[25] In an effort to improve both the quantity and quality of the audience, the next year the manager, Henry Ward, set aside one night a week for juveniles, hoping to encourage family attend-

---

[24] Frances Trollope, *Domestic Manners of the Americans*. Edited by Donald Smalley (New York: Alfred A. Knopf, 1949), pp. 233–234.
[25] See Mudd, "The Theatres of Washington From 1835 to 1850," VI, 231.

*National Portrait Gallery, Smithsonian Institution
Gift of the Kathryn and Gilbert Miller Fund
in memory of Alexander Ince*

Edwin Forrest as Metamora. Painted by Frederick S. Agate, about 1830.

Edwin Forrest was America's first native-born star and became the epitome of the American Heroic School of Acting. A big, muscular man who prided himself on his physique and vocal powers, Forrest was always more popular with the masses than with the sophisticated. Forrest's supporters were responsible for the Astor Place riot on May 10, 1849, during the performance of the English actor William Charles Macready as Macbeth. A public feud had broken out between Macready and Forrest during the latter's tour of England in 1845. For more than thirty years Forrest was a favorite of Washington audiences.

National Portrait Gallery, Smithsonian Institution

Charlotte Cushman. Painted by William Page, 1853.

Charlotte Cushman was America's first great actress and was considered to be the finest interpreter of Lady Macbeth in her time in the United States or England. Her style of acting "had sweep and power and majesty. She painted with bold strokes and unmixed colors. Her characters emerged in heroic outline." She made her first Washington appearance at the National Theatre on April 1, 1853, and continued to return to the theatre in a variety of Shakespearean and non-Shakespearean roles for the entire length of her career.

National Portrait Gallery, Smithsonian Institution
Transfer from the Cooper-Hewitt Museum of
Decorative Arts and Design
Gift of Miss Charlotte Arnold, 1920

Edwin Booth as Iago in Shakespeare's *Othello*. Painted by Thomas Hicks, 1868.

From 1856 when Booth made his eastern debut until his death in 1893, he was a star of the first magnitude. He felt that art should interpret, exalt, and ennoble. Wilson describes Booth as a "man of average height, endowed with agility and excellent coordination. He was always praised for the eloquence of his movements. When it came to intellectual and spiritual grasp, Booth was never equalled." Booth first appeared at the National Theatre in 1859.

National Portrait Gallery, Smithsonian Institution
Gift of Mr. and Mrs. Walter Schnormeier, 1967

Minnie Maddern Fiske. Painted by M. Colin, 1893.

    Minnie Maddern Fiske was a pioneer in the development of the American theatre. Her career marked a break with the romantic traditions of the Nineteenth Century and heralded the introduction of modern realism into the American theatre. From 1870 to 1930 she was a dominant force in the development of greater truthfulness in American acting and during those sixty years she was a frequent visitor to the National stage.

National Portrait Gallery, Smithsonian Institution
Transfer from the National Collection of Fine Arts
Gift of Henry Harkness Flagler, 1932

Richard Mansfield as Beau Brummel. Painted by Orlando Rouland, 1907.

Richard Mansfield, the British-born actor, first appeared in the United States in 1883 and quickly rose to stardom. Although a noted Shakespearean actor, one of his roles most popular with audiences was that of Beau Brummel in the play of that name written for him by Clyde Fitch in 1890. Mansfield's most significant contribution to Washington theatre was his introduction of Ibsen to Washington when Mansfield produced *A Doll's House* during two special matinees on November 27 and 30, 1889.

ance. Plays suitable to this type of audience were selected and booked for those evenings and persons under fourteen years of age were admitted to the first and second tier at half the regular price.

Mr. Ward tried valiantly to improve business at the National, but he wrote a letter at midnight on Monday, December 10, 1838, the first day of the meeting of Congress, addressed "To the Theatrical Population of Washington and the District of Columbia" in which he complained of the poor attendance that evening on the opening night of the season. He explained that it cost him $1,300 a week to maintain the stock company and an additional $1,300 a week for the "stars" the audience demanded. He claimed that for three years he had been losing money in his efforts to bring the best theatre in the whole world to Washington and he pleaded for better support for his theatre:

> For three seasons this has been borne patiently and silently, but continued losses compel me to make known my position, and to solicit your exertions and interest in my behalf. If the fine arts, as we are instructed to believe, are effective instruments for promoting the best interests of man—if the pleasure of the virtuous is their aim and the test of their success, it is the duty of every good citizen to encourage their cultivation, and this appeal will not be made in vain: but, if on the contrary, public opinion is opposed to those professors who are become the commentators on the works of the poet, and living illustrations of his ideas, to public opinion I shall bow, and in justice to my Company and myself, speedily remove from a scene of continued mortification and neglect.

Mr. Ward did not receive much encouragement; in fact, writing in the *Gentleman's Magazine,* Asmodeus advised Ward to quit:

> If he will pardon an old "looker on here in Vienna" or his plainness of speech in offering advice, where it has not been asked, I would seriously advise him to relinquish the attempt of establishing a theatre in Washington, entirely; and will freely give him a few reasons for such advice.
> People come to Washington, either to advance their own political party, or personal ends, and they have neither time nor inclination—neither freedom of mind, nor freedom from occupation, sufficient to enable them to spend their evenings at the theatre. At least, they think so, which comes to the same thing.
> Again, a very numerous class, even of members of Congress, come to Washington simply and solely for the money they make while there. This is a truth, which I can illustrate by a curious fact, that accidentally came to my knowledge. A member of Congress, from a

northern State, during the six or seven months of the last long session, paid his travelling expenses, and his board and contingent expenses, out of his salary for that time, and carried home, (for a clear profit) eighteen hundred dollars, last July. His whole spending money, for casual outlays for that long period, was exactly *twenty-three dollars!* What care such people for the theatre, Master Ward![26]

Mr. Ward, however, did not quit and he continued to present such internationally known stars as Junius Brutus Booth, James Hackett, Fanny Davenport, Edwin Forrest, John Vanderhoff, and Edwin Booth. The Washington society which Ward had hoped to attract to his theatre showed up *in toto* for the 1840 appearance of the internationally known ballerina Fanny Elssler.

Fanny Elssler's appearance was a sensation. One critic has written that "her Gisselle was concrete, passionate and down to earth. She displayed a richness of mimicry and gesture." [27] The most noted danseuse of her day, she enchanted her audiences with the "grace and loveliness of her undraped limbs." [28] Patrons vied with each other in cheering her; men threw their watch chains and rings to the stage and women their bracelets. Miss Elssler became the toast of Washington. When she visited the Capitol, the Senate "rose as she entered, and the House insisted that she sit in the Speaker's chair." [29] President Van Buren received her in official audience and Congress "adjourned every evening she danced in Washington because most members attended her performance and there was no quorum anyway...." [30]

Mr. Ward appealed again to Washington audiences on the occasion of his benefit farewell in January, 1844:

> Mr. Ward presents his compliments to the Washington public, and, in announcing his farewell benefit, trusts the efforts he has made to entertain them will be remembered in his favor. He hopes that the stockholders will buy tickets and not enter upon their passes, ditto the press, in fact the free list will positively be suspended. In conclusion, Mr. Ward respectfully solicits 'one and all' to flock to the theatre and give him a 'bumper at parting.' [31]

Neither the financial situation nor the class of audiences improved after Mr. Ward's departure. The poor receipts were partially due to

---

[26] Asmodeus, "Asmodeus at the Capital", *Gentleman's Magazine and American Monthly Review,* IV, 1, (January, 1839), p. 50.

[27] Marc Slonim, *Russian Theatre* (New York: Collier Books, 1962), p. 95.

[28] Hunter and Polkinhorn, *The New National Theatre,* p. 19.

[29] Coad and Mims, *The American Stage,* XIV, 111.

[30] Anatole ChuJoy, *The Dance Encyclopedia* (New York: A. S. Barnes and Company, 1949), p. 169.

[31] Hunter and Polkinhorn, *The New National Theatre,* p. 20.

LAWRENCE BARRETT

THE
Distinguished Tragedian,
AT
NATIONAL THEATRE,
JNO. T. FORD, Lessee and Manager.

MASTERLY INTERPRETATIONS OF SHAKSPEARE, LYTTON BULWER, and ROBERTSON,

Beginning Monday, February 10th, 1879.

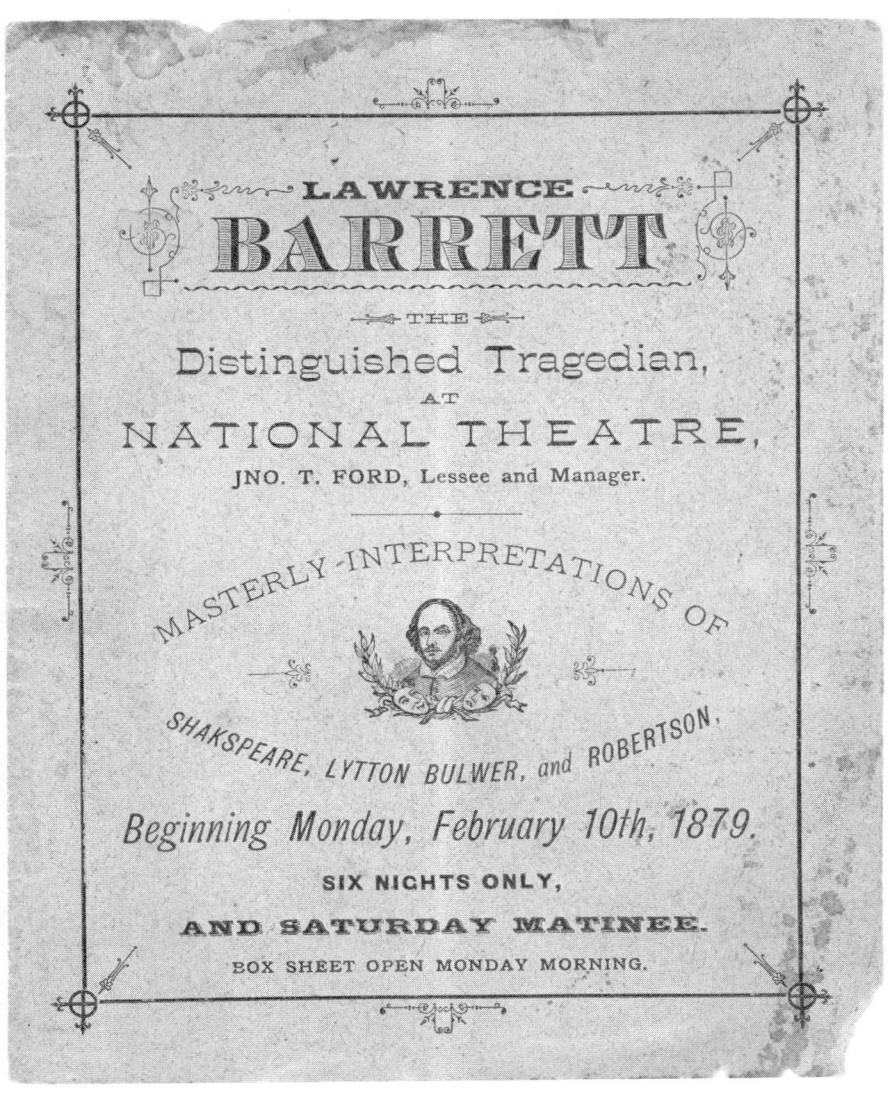

SIX NIGHTS ONLY,

AND SATURDAY MATINEE.

BOX SHEET OPEN MONDAY MORNING.

Martin Luther King Memorial Library
Washingtoniana Collection

Four-page advertising folder for the National Theatre performances of Lawrence Barrett for the week of Monday, February 10 through Saturday, February 15, 1879.

CONCLUSIONS OF THE CRITICS.

"RICHELIEU."

"The character of *Richelieu* as interpreted by Mr. Barrett, stands forth alone, it has no match, and almost no rival among the works of dramatic inspiration, Mr. Barrett moves and speaks as did the Cardinal Richelieu.—*Boston Journal*

"HAMLET."

Mr. Barrett's *Hamlet* is a classical and very thoughtful impersonation, its numberless beauties, its deeply introspective atmosphere, and the scholarship which the artist shows, makes it a Hamlet of heart and brain. —*Detroit Free Press.*

"OTHELLO."

"The *Iago* of Mr. Barrett is a wonderfully artistic and skilful piece of acting. To those who have ever seen Mr. Barrett, nothing more can be said to advantage, all praise being but repetition.—*Cleveland Herald.*

"THE MARBLE HEART."

"Mr. Barrett's rendition of *Raphael* in this beautiful play was finished and masterly; his mad scenes and pictures of passion were grand; the climax culminating in his death, while at work, all marked the acting of a master.—*Cincinnati Enquirer.*

CONCLUSIONS OF THE CRITICS.

"RICHELIEU."

"Mr. Barrett's *Richelieu* is an impersonation of high artistic merit. Elaborate, and studied to a fault; instinct with passionate fervor and life. His finished elocution is in this play brought into requisition with admirable effect."—*Chicago Tribune.*

"MERCHANT OF VENICE."

"*Shylock*, the Jew and usurer, as seen upon the stage portrayed by Mr. Barrett, is not so repulsive; he is still avaricious, harsh, and revengeful, but the intense passion he displays are felt to have some just and reasonable cause. It should be seen by all lovers of great acting.—*Nashville Inquirer.*

"DAVID GARRICK."

"Mr. Barrett as *Garrick*, achieved an undeniable success, the man of honor, and the earnest impassioned lover, (as the great actor Garrick has been developed by the dramatist) were presented with consummate grace, delicacy and fervor; in fact the character as portrayed seemed the reflex of Mr. Barrett's own personality."—*Detroit Post.*

"RICHARD III."

"Mr. Barrett as *Richard*; the crafty nature and villanous ambition of the character of the Duke of Gloster, (as drawn by the author,) Mr. Barrett assumes, but he does not give it all the hideousness that is too often associated with its representations; in fact, his conception and conclusion may be regarded as in the main correct, and his rendition is an intelligent and artistic performance throughout."—*Cleveland Leader.*

LAWRENCE BARRETT.

the type of audiences frequenting the National, for the theatre seemed to appeal primarily to rowdy types and "street arabs;" it was still not drawing fashionable patronage. A letter sent to Washington newspapers and the National management suggests the situation. The writer of this tongue-in-cheek letter, dated Washington, Friday, January 17, 1845, signed himself "The Old Sitter," and wrote to the *National Intelligencer* as follows:

> I beg leave to submit through the columns of your paper the subjoined rules for the better management of the theatre.
> Vive la politesse!
> 1. That no spectator be expected to sit if he chooses to stand, it being a gross infringement of the rights of an American citizen to attempt to restrict or otherwise regulate the free use of his limbs.
> 2. That for like reason, he elevates his legs, or sticks them out at any angle, oblique or acute, most condusive to comfort.
> 3. That the good old national divertisement of chewing and spitting tobacco, *ad libitum,* is an inalienable right of the American citizen.
> 4. That on a benefit night any individual may use three seats for the accommodation of his feet, cudgel, dog, or any other indispensable appurtenance.
> 5. That no spectator either sitting or standing be subjected to that impertinent cry of 'hats off in front.'
> 6. That any attempt to supress loud talking, whooping, hee-hawing, swearing or the like, will not be tolerated as it is a most flagrant violation of that great safeguard of the Republic, the liberty of free speech.
> 7. That in the event of a set-to between two belligerents, that they be allowed to have it out, undisturbed to those minions of the law, called policemen.
> 8. That for the encouragement of native musical talent, the standing overture shall be some approved chef-d'oeuvre of the great Ethiopean masters, as "Possum Up the Gum Tree," "Sally Come Up," "That Yellow Gal Smiled at Me."
> 9. That a copy of these regulations be affixed to the playbill.
> Salve Republica!

The wave of mass hysteria which had started in New York on the arrival of Jenny Lind, the Swedish Nightingale, in January of 1850 reached Washington in December. The National had burned in 1845 and had remained in ruins until 1850 when the theatre was hastily rebuilt and enlarged to hold 3,400 people for her concert. The box office was to open at nine a.m. on December 12, 1850, for ticket sales to the first concert, but a crowd began to form in front of the theatre as early as midnight of the previous evening. The entire Washington police force was called out to keep order as the line grew longer and the customers became more anxious. Tickets cost $7.00, $5.00 and $4.00, a considerable advance over the standard prices of which the top was $1.00. Soon after her arrival in Washington, President Fillmore called on her at her quarters; but she was not in. She later returned the call at the White House.

Once again the highest class of audience turned out to see a foreign star. On December 16, 1850, the date of the first performance, the audience began to assemble at six o'clock. Within a few minutes there was not even standing room available in the theatre. Among those assembled were President Fillmore and his family, Daniel Webster, Henry Clay and General Scott. On December 17, the date of her second concert, the overflow crowd again included the President, his Cabinet and the members of the Supreme Court.

Rowdy audiences, however, and the appearance of the police at the theatre, seemed to be normally expected as a note on the program for the April 3, 1853, performance of *The School for Scandal* and *Roland for an Oliver,* suggests; it warned the audience, or reassured it, whichever the intention may have been, that "An EFFICIENT POLICE will be in constant attendance to preserve strict order."

Strict order could never be maintained when Edwin Forrest, the greatest American tragedian of his time and the epitome of the American Heroic School of Acting, played in Washington. Every one of his appearances at the National filled the theatre to overflowing with cheering, boisterous, and at times unruly audiences. Although he had a few detractors, Forrest's "style of acting was immensely appealing to the majority of playgoers. They idolized this handsome powerful man who handled his body like an athlete. They enjoyed watching his naturalistic movements and gestures, and especially the explosions of physical action in his portrayals." [32] The explosions on the stage were matched by equal explosions of approval from the members of the audience. B. A. Jamison recounts that during the middle of a performance of *Richelieu* at the National in the early 1850's, "as if animated by an electrick spark, the entire audience rose and voiced its unbounded enthusiasm." [33] Audience support for Forrest actually increased after he lost a notorious divorce case in 1852. As Richard Moody points out, Forrest was thoroughly American and "unconsciously embodied and represented in himself 'the vital, burly aggressive Americanism of his age.'" [34]

---

[32] Garff B. Wilson, *A History of American Acting* (Bloomington, Indiana, 1966), p. 29.
[33] B. A. Jamison, *Memories of Great Men and Events 1840–1861* (c. 1917), p. 242.
[34] Richard Moody, *Edwin Forrest First Star of the American Stage,* (New York Alfred A. Knopf, 1960), p. 396. The behavior of Washington audiences of the time doe

NATIONAL THEATRE.

Lawrence Barrett

Monday Evening, February 10th, 1879,

BULWER'S Great Play in Five Acts, entitled:

RICHELIEU;

OR,

The Conspiracy.

Cardinal Richelieu,	**Lawrence Barrett**
DE MAUPRAT,	Mr. Thos. W. Keene
KING LOUIS,	Mr. Wm. Burton
GASTON,	Mr. Jas. Galloway
DE BERINGHEN,	Mr. Harry Rainforth
BARADAS,	Mr. Chas. Waverly
JOSEPH,	Mr. M. Lanagan
HUGUET,	Mr. Carl Ahrendt
FRANCOIS,	Mr. Geo. Hoey
DE CLERMONT,	Mr. Walter Collier
CAPTAIN OF GUARDS,	Mr. W. H. Burton
FIRST SECRETARY,	Mr. Sutherland
SECOND SECRETARY,	Mr. Archer
THIRD SECRETARY,	Mr. Sheild
JULIE,	Miss Henrietta Vaders
MARIAN,	Miss Bella Mackenzie

Courtiers, Pages, Conspirators, Etc.

TUESDAY, LAWRENCE BARRETT AS HAMLET.

Martin Luther King Memorial Library
Washingtoniana Collection

Eight-page advertising folder for the National Theatre performances of Lawrence Barrett for the week of Monday, February 10 through Saturday, February 15, 1879.

LAWRENCE BARRETT

Tuesday Evening, February 11th, 1879,

SHAKSPEARE'S MASTER PIECE

HAMLET.

HAMLET,	**Lawrence Barrett**
GHOST of Hamlet's father,	Mr. Thos. W. Keene
KING,	Mr. Carl Ahrendt
POLONIUS,	Mr. M. Lanagan
LAERTES,	Mr. Geo. Hoey
HORATIO,	Mr. W. H. Burton
OSRIC,	Mr. H. Rainforth
ROSENCRANZ,	Mr. Jas. Galloway
GUILDENSTERN,	Mr. Walter Allen
MARCESSAS,	Mr. J. Sutherland
BERNARDO,	Mr. Walter Collier
FIRST ACTOR,	Mr. Robt. Downing
SECOND ACTOR,	Mr. J. Moroso
FIRST GRAVEDIGGER,	Mr. Chas. Waverly
SECOND GRAVEDIGGER	Mr. Jno. Mincher
FRANCISCO,	Mr. W Archer
PRIEST,	Mr. Chas. Sheild
OPHELIA,	Miss Henrietta Vaders
QUEEN,	Mrs. Octavia Allen
ACTRESS,	Miss Marion Booth

Pages, Gentlemen, Guards, Etc.

WEDNESDAY, LAWRENCE BARRETT as **KING LEAR.**

LAWRENCE BARRETT

Wednesday Evening, February 12th, 1879,

Will be presented for the first time in this city, a translation from a Spanish Drama, expressly for Lawrence Barrett, by Wm. D. Howells, Esq., entitled:

A

NEW PLAY!

Yorick, a Comedian in Shakspeare's Theatre, **Lawrence Barrett**
MASTER JOHN HEYWOOD, Manager Globe Theatre with Master Shakspeare—1603 . . . . Mr. T. W. Keene
MASTER EDMUND, actor of Young Heroes at the Globe Theatre . . . . Mr. Geo. Hoey
MASTER WALTON, leading actor at the Globe Theatre,
Mr. Chas. Waverly
MASTER WOODFORD, author of the "New Play," Mr. M. Lanagan
THOMAS, Prompter of the Globe Theatre, ... Mr. Jas. Galloway
ADAM, an old servant of Yorick, ... Mr. W. H. Burton
ALICE, wife of Yorick, and actress at the Globe Theatre,
Miss Henrietta Vaders

THURSDAY, RICHELIEU.

LAWRENCE BARRETT

Thursday Evening, February 13th, 1879,

Second and last time of BULWER'S Great Play in Five Acts, entitled:

RICHELIEU,
OR;
The Conspiracy.

Cardinal Richelieu, ... **Lawrence Barrett**
DE MAUPRAT, ... Mr. Thos. W. Keene
KING LOUIS, ... Mr. W. H. Burton
GASTON, ... Mr. Jas. Galloway
DE BERINGHEN, ... Mr. Harry Rainforth
BARADAS, ... Mr. Chas. Waverly
JOSEPH, ... Mr M. Lanagan
HUGUET, ... Mr. Carl Ahrendt
FRANCOIS, ... Mr. Geo. Hoey
DE CLERMONT, ... Mr. Walter Collier
CAPTAIN OF GUARDS, ... Mr. W. H. Burton
FIRST SECRETARY, ... Mr. Sutherland
SECOND SECRETARY, ... Mr. Archer
THIRD SECRETARY, ... Mr. Sheild
JULIE, ... Miss Henrietta Vaders
MARIAN, ... Miss Bella Mackenzie
Courtiers, Pages, Conspirators, Etc.

Friday, Benefit of Lawrence Barrett,
Great Double Bill, "Merchant of Venice" and "David Garrick,"
MR. BARRETT,   -   as **SHYLOCK and DAVID GARRICK**

LAWRENCE BARRETT

BENEFIT,

Friday Evening, February 14th, 1879.

A Double Bill, commencing with Shakspeare's

Merchant of Venice.

Shylock, ... **Lawrence Barrett**
GRATIANO, ... Mr. Thos. W. Keene
DUKE, ... Mr. Chas. Waverly
ANTONIO, ... Mr. Carl Ahrendt
LORENZO, ... Mr. Jas. Galloway
BASSANIO, ... Mr Geo. Hoey
TUBAL, ... Mr. M. Lanagan
SALANIO, ... Mr. Walter Collier
SALERINO, ... Mr. W. H. Burton
SALERIO, ... Mr. Walter Allen
LAUNCELOT, ... Mr. Harry Rainforth
OLD GOBBO, ... Mr. Robt. Downing
BALTHAZAR, ... Mr Jno. Mincher
PORTIA, ... Mrs. Octavia Allen
NERISSA, ... Miss Emma Vaders
JESSICA, ... Miss Marion Booth

To be followed by the Beautiful Play of

DAVID GARRICK.

David Garrick, ... **Lawrence Barrett**
INGOT, ... Mr. M. Lanagan
CHIVY, ... Mr. Harry Rainforth
SMITH, ... Mr. W. H. Burton
BROWN, ... Mr. Robt. Downing
JONES, ... Mr. Walter Collier
GARRICK'S SERVANT, ... Mr. Jas. Galloway
INGOT'S SERVANT, ... Mr. Sutherland
ADA, ... Miss Henrietta Vaders
MRS. BROWN, ... Mrs. Germon
MRS. SMITH, ... Mrs. Thorpe

Lawrence Barrett

MATINEE

Saturday, February 15th, 1879, at 2 o'clock,

The Beautiful and Thrilling Play, entitled The

MARBLE HEART, OR THE SCULPTOR'S DREAM

THE DREAM.

PHIDIAS (the Sculptor), ... **Lawrence Barrett**
DIOGENES, ... Mr. Thos. W. Keene
GORGIAS, ... Mr. Geo. Hoey
ALCIBIADES, ... Mr. Carl Ahrendt
STRABON, ... Mr. Walter Dennis
THEA, ... Mrs. Henrietta Vaders
ASPASIA, ... Miss Burney
LAIS, ... Miss Henry
PHRYNE, ... Miss Reed

Athenians, Citizens, Slaves, Etc.,

THE DRAMA.

Raphael Duchelet, a Sculptor, ... **Lawrence Barrett**
VOLAGE, ... Mr. Thos. W. Keene
VEANDORE, ... Mr. Geo. Hoey
VISCOUNT, ... Mr. Harry Rainforth
LORD MERTON, ... Mr. Wm. Burton
DE COURSEY, ... Mr. Jas. Galloway
JOHN, ... Mr. Walter Allen
BAPTISTE, ... Mr. W. Collier
MARCO, ... Miss Henrietta Vaders
MARIE, ... Miss Octavia Allen
MADAME DUCHAELET, ... Mrs. Germon
CLEMENTINE, ... Miss Booth
FEDORA, ... Miss Stuart
MARIETTA, ... Miss Henry
JULIA, ... Miss Reed

SATURDAY NIGHT, RICHARD III.

NATIONAL THEATRE.

Positively Last Night of the Engagement of

LAWRENCE BARRETT

Saturday Evening, February 15th, 1879,

SHAKSPEARE'S HISTORICAL PLAY

Richard the III.

RICHARD,	**Lawrence Barrett**
RICHMOND,	Mr. Thos. W. Keene
KING HENRY,	Mr. M. Lanagan
BUCKINGHAM,	Mr. Geo. Hoey
PRINCE OF WALES,	Miss E. Vaders
DUKE OF YORK,	Miss Florence Lecroix
STANLEY,	Mr. Chas. Waverly
NORFOLK,	Mr. Wm. Burton
RATCLIFE,	Mr. Jno. Reibert
CATESBY,	Mr. Jas. Galloway
TRESSELL,	Mr. Walter Collier
OXFORD,	Mr. Walter Allen
BLUNT,	Mr. J. Sutherland
LORD MAYOR,	Mr. H. Rainforth
TYRRELL,	Mr. R. Downing
LIEUTENANT OF TOWER,	Mr. J. Atwell
LADY ANNE,	Miss Marian Booth
QUEEN,	Mrs. Octavia Allen
DUCHESS,	Mrs. Germon
PAGES,	Misses Henry and Reed

Press of HALLOWELL & CO.,
125 South Third Street, Philadelphia.

The foreign visiting stars, whether they were in drama, dance or opera, seemed always to draw the better Washington audiences to the National. Sarah Bernhardt's first Washington appearance was no exception. The *Washington Post* of April 9, 1881, reported following her opening performance as Gilbert in *Frou Frou:*

> The audience last night at the National Theatre, despite the treble prices, was not only immense, but of the highest quality, almost everyone of prominence in society, of public and professional life, was there. Many were there who had not been in a theatre for years. Madame Bernhardt won more and more upon her audience, and she was called out by the wildly enthusiastic audience again and again.

Besides the foreign visting stars, the opening nights of each of the new National Theatres drew the fashionable and important. Frank Carpenter reminisced about the opening of the fifth National on Monday, October 5, 1885:

> On the last day of last February [1885] the old National Theater, lying within three blocks of the White House, was a mass of smoking ruins. This week, only seven months later, a magnificent new structure stands in its place, and on Monday night the new National was thrown open to the public. Rhea was the star and *Lady Ashley* the play. All fashionable Washington was there. The beaux appeared in their claw-hammer coats, the belles were attired in evening dress. President Cleveland, however, was absent and the only member of the Cabinet present was Secretary Lamar, who occupied a box at the left of the stage.[35]

In the years since it was open in 1835, every President of the United States, except Eisenhower, has visited the National Theatre, but no other President has shown an interest in theatre to the degree that Lincoln did. He was a devoted patron of Grover's Theatre (the National Theatre) during the years of his presidency and he became a

---

not seem different from that of the San Franciscan audiences who attended the Jenny Lind Theatre, the American and the Adelphi: "I must mention here the Americans' strange manner of applauding a favorite actor of a good scene. In France, and everywhere else in Europe that I know anything about, we clap and sometimes shout bravo, and whistle only when we are disgusted. Actors at home are terrified and paralyzed if an audience whistles; Nourrit, once so well-known in Paris, is even supposed to have died from it. But with Americans, whistling is an expression of enthusiasm; the more they like a play, the louder they whistle, and when a San Francisco audience bursts into shrill whistles and savage yells, you may be sure they are in raptures of joy." From the Journal of Albert Benard de Russailh, translated and edited by Clarkson Crane as *Last Adventure: San Francisco in 1851* (San Francisco: The Westgate Press, 1931), as quoted in Hewitt, *Theatre U.S.A.*, p. 166.

[35] Frank G. Carpenter, *Carp's Washington* (New York: McGraw-Hill Book Company, 1960), pp. 253-254.

close friend of the manager. An early indication of the President's association with the theatre is in a letter, dated August 29, 1862, from John Hay to J. G. Nicolay, both secretaries to Lincoln. Hay wrote that "Grover's reopens next Saturday." [36] It appears that he referred to a reopening after a summer respite, for the management had been presenting plays for more than four months at the time of the letter.

On Saturday, April 11, 1863, John Wilkes Booth, the handsome younger brother of Edwin Booth, appeared at the National as Richard III. It was the younger Booth's first performance in Washington. The audience was large and the President sat in a private box with his host Senator Oliver Morton. In this year John Wilkes Booth headed Mr. Grover's stock company.[37] He seldom played the theatre and it appears that he was for the most part on the road.

Hay's diary, in an entry for November 9, 1863, records another Lincoln visit to a Booth performance: "Spent the evening with President, Mrs. L., Mr. Hunter, Cameron, and Nicolay. J. Wilkes Booth doing 'The Marble Hart'. Rather tame otherwise." [38] According to Leonard Grover, the National's manager, the theatre was Lincoln's favorite pastime, not merely a way for the President to be seen in public.[39] Carl Sandburg verifies this opinion in his famous Lincoln biography:

> Alone often, yet again with varied companions, Tad and Mrs. Lincoln, Brooks, Hays, Sumner and others, the President went to the drama, visiting Grover's theatre perhaps a hundred times since coming to Washington. When there was an opera at Grover's Mr. Lincoln invariably attended with the President. "Mr. Grover, I really enjoy a minstrel show," Lincoln suggested once. And when Grover ... announced Hooley's Minstrels soon to come, Lincoln laughed, "Well, that was thoughtful of you." [40]

Tad Lincoln, the President's youngest son, was much taken with the theatre and often attended Grover's with his father. The boy set up a miniature playhouse in one of the rooms of the White House and properties and costumes from the National often found their way there on loan from Mr. Grover. The manager recounted the story of the evening in 1864 when Tad

---

[36] John Hay, *Lincoln and the Civil War in the Diaries and Letters of John Hay* (New York: Dodd, Mead and Company, 1959), p. 44.

[37] Frances Wilson, *John Wilkes Booth* (Boston: Houghton Mifflin Company, 1929), p. 14.

[38] Hay, *Lincoln and the Civil War*, p. 118.

[39] Leonard Grover, *Lincoln's Interest in the Theatre* (Limited Edition, n.p., n.d.), p. 1.

[40] Carl Sandburg, *Abraham Lincoln* (New York: Harcourt Brace Co., 1954), p. 600.

The National Theatre in Washington, D.C.   229

left his father's box and went backstage and got a costume too large for him and during the number "Rally Round the Flag", appeared on stage in "The Seven Sisters".... The President had a bad quarter of a minute of shock at the sight, but the humor of the situation quickly restored him, and he laughed immoderately.[41]

On June 8, 1864, Lincoln went to the National in hopes of escaping the tension of the Republican convention being held in Baltimore. Grover showed him to his seat and, the manager related, at about nine o'clock, "a messenger came from the White House with a telegram, instructed to deliver it to me. It was addressed to Mr. Lincoln, I took it to him and it was found to contain the first news for him of his nomination." [42]

On one occasion upon leaving a performance at Grover's the Lincoln party encountered a jeering mob that was abusing the drunken coachman who was to drive the Lincolns and their guest Mr. Colfax to their respective homes. Mr. Grover took the reins and drove the notables to their residences. Grover wrote, "I knew that I had extricated him [Lincoln] from a very annoying situation." [43]

President Lincoln had planned to take his son Tad to Grover's on April 14, 1865, the night of Lincoln's assassination. The production billed for that evening was *Mazeppa, or the Wild Horse of Tartary*, featuring Kate Vance and her trained horse Don Juan. Lincoln was offered a box by the management for the occasion but on the prompting of his wife decided to go to Ford's Tenth Street Theatre where he was shot by John Wilkes Booth. Booth had obtained a box at Grover's next to the one intended for the Lincoln party, having talked his friend John Deery into buying it for him. The details have been recounted by Grover from a conversation with Deery, then the billiards champion of the United States who kept a saloon over the entrance to the National. Booth had often used the saloon as a loafing place. Grover has written:

> Booth came to his [Deery's] office, and pleading that he did not want to put himself under obligation to Mr. Hess, who was my associate in the management, by accepting a complimentary box, which of course would have been tendered him should he offer to pay at the box office, asked Deery to go down and buy a box as though for himself and handed him the money to pay for it. Deery said that he did as he was requested and if Mr. Lincoln had visited my theatre that night, Booth would have had the adjoining box.[44]

---

[41] Grover, *Lincoln's Interest in the Theatre*, p. 4.
[42] Grover, p. 6.
[43] Grover, p. 9.
[44] *Ibid.*

NEW NATIONAL THEATRE.
WASHINGTON, D. C.
W. H. RAPLEY, Manager.

SATURDAY EVENING, — — — — — — — — — MAY 5th, 1888,

Grand Production for the Benefit of

✳ The ✠ Statue ✠ of ✠ Washington, ✳

TO BE PRESENTED BY

The United States to the Republic of France,

OF THE LATEST AND GREATEST NEW YORK SUCCESS,

PAUL KAUVAR

— BY —

STEELE MACKAYE.

THIS PERFORMANCE IS GIVEN UNDER THE AUSPICES OF

The President and Mrs. Cleveland,

THE FOLLOWING DISTINGUISHED COMMITTEE OF LADIES:

MRS. NATHAN APPLETON,
MISS FLORENCE BAYARD,
MRS. SECRETARY FAIRCHILD,
MRS. DON M. DICKINSON,
MRS. SENATOR SHERMAN,
MRS. SENATOR HEARST,
MRS. SENATOR MANDERSON,
MRS. F. M. B. SWEAT,

MRS. SENATOR J. P. JONES,
MRS. SENATOR PALMER,
MRS. SECRETARY ENDICOTT,
MRS. JUSTICE FIELD,
MRS. SENATOR STANFORD,
MRS. SENATOR STOCKBRIDGE,
MRS. SENATOR WALTHALL,
MRS. S. V. WHITE,

AND MRS. WASHINGTON MCLEAN;

And the Following Executive Committee of Ladies and Gentlemen:

MRS. SENATOR JOHN P. JONES,
MRS. SENATOR THOMAS W. PALMER,
MISS FLORENCE BAYARD,
SENATOR W. B. ALLISON,
SENATOR J. D. CAMERON,
SENATOR JOHN T. MORGAN,
REPRESENTATIVE J. J. HEMPHILL,

REPRESENTATIVE H. H. BINGHAM,
MR. M. P. HANDY,
MR. F. A. RICHARDSON,
MR. W. STILSON HUTCHINS,
MR. D. R. McKEE,
MR. JAMES R. YOUNG,
MR. W. F. O'BRIEN,

AND COL. THOMAS P. OCHILTREE.

THIS PRODUCTION IS A TRIBUTE TO THE CAUSE FREELY OFFERED BY

MR. HENRY C. MINER, — — — — — —
— — — — — — STEELE MACKAYE,

And the Following Volunteer Cast:

GENTLEMEN:

PAUL KAUVAR	STEELE MACKAYE
HONORE ALBERT MAXIME, Duc de Beaumont	FREDERIC DE BELLEVILLE
MARQUIS DE VAUX, alias GOUROC, one of the public accusers of the Revolutionary Tribunal	WILTON LACKAYE
GENERAL DELAROCHE, Commander of the Royalist Forces in La Vendée	NESTOR LENNOX
GENERAL KLETERRE, Commander of the Republican Forces in La Vendée	M. B. SNYDER
COL. LA HOGUE, on the staff of General Delaroche	LESLIE ALLEN
DODOLPHE POTIN, an usher of the Revolutionary Tribunal; afterwards sergeant in the Battalion of the Bonnets Rouges	SIDNEY DREW
CARROL C., a typical Anarchist and a Republican Representative in La Vendée	GEO. FAWCETT
BOURROTTE, a "Sans-Culottes"	EDWARD COLEMAN
GOUJON, a Corporal in the Battalion of the Bonnets Rouges	E. M. HURD
TABOOSE, an ... d'Armes	J. F. WENTWORTH
FIRST O...	E. P...
SECO...	

Martin Luther King Memorial Library
Washingtoniana Collection

Silk Souvenir Program for the National Theatre performance of *Paul Kauvar* by Steele Mackaye, May 5, 1888, "under the auspices of The President and Mrs. Cleveland."

..., an usher .... DREW
...on of the Bonnets Rouges .... tribunal, after .... GEO. FAWCETT
... a typical Anarchist and a Republican Representative in La Vendée
BOURIOTTE, a "Sans Culottes" .... EDWARD COLEMAN
GOUJON, a Corporal in the Battalion of the Bonnets Rouges .... E. M. HURD
TABOGSE, an officer of Gens d'Armes .... J. F. WENTWORTH
FIRST ORDERLY .... E. R. SPENCER
SECOND ORDERLY .... A. S. PALMER
FIRST SANS CULOTTES .... RUFUS WILLIAM
SECOND SANS CULOTTES .... R. S. McBRIDE

LADIES:

DIANE DE BEAUMONT, daughter of the Duke .... Miss CARRIE TURNER
NANETTE POTIN .... Miss HELEN MAR
SCARLOTTE .... Miss LIZZIE RECHELLE

AND THE FOLLOWING TRAINED AUXILIARIES:

LADIES.

Miss Bunes.	Miss Moore.	Miss Becks.	Miss Marshall.
Miss Pierson.	Miss Maguire.	Miss Forster.	Miss Gianetti.
Miss Frozar.	Miss Hughes.	Miss Wellars.	Mrs. Hughes.
Miss Weeks.	Miss Naylor.	Miss Lavard.	Miss Hearn.
Miss Smith.	Mrs. Bowars.	Miss Arnold.	Mrs. Lack.

GENTLEMEN.

Mart Townsend.	Wm. Sharkey.	Chas. Belmont.	T. Mitchell.
Henry Schaffer.	Wm. Brown.	H. Marks.	B. Fisher.
W. W. Waters.	Geo. Masten.	C. M. Mackay.	Chas. Nuger.
Geo. Turner.	Frank Comstock.	T. Jarvis.	H. Frees.
F. Duley.	Wm. Chambers.	S. Sullivan.	J. Smith.
P. King.	E. Reynolds.	E. Russell.	Daniel Charles.
R. Ryan.	S. H. Caruth.	J. Godfrey.	S. Rosenthal.
J. Sheehan.	J. Sawyer.	G. B. Merton.	A. Goldsmith.
R. Mansfield.	G. Shaffer.	P. Berger.	Jas. O'Brien.
Rufus Williams.	C. Bird.	J. J. Blake.	Wm. Mack.
Benj. Binns.	H. Hamill.	Chas. Marshall.	C. Brady.
John Kenny.	W. Sullivan.	H. Gordon.	G. Harvey.
Ben. Sharwood.	F. Medina.	M. Brickner.	C. King.
Al. Young.	Ed. Ryerson.	L. T. McDermott.	J. Macarthy.
Chas. Norman.	E. Morrison.	F. Allen.	
Geo. Hopper.	F. Blake.	J. Harris.	

Charles Haslam .... Business Manager of "Paul Kauvar" Company
Jere. Stevens .... Stage Manager
Ralph Welles .... Assistant Stage Manager
John Ginsinger .... Master Mechanic of Miner's Newark Theatre
Charles W. Heinert .... Assistant Master Mechanic of Miner's Newark Theatre
Joseph Logan .... Master Mechanic "Paul Kauvar" Company
Harry Cashon .... Chief Flyman of H. C. Miner's Newark Theatre
Charles Dunlap .... Master of Properties of Miner's Newark Theatre
Ed. Lawrence .... Master of Properties of "Paul Kauvar" Company
A. C. E. Sturgis .... Chief Electrician of Miner's Newark Theatre
William Maston .... Assistant Electrician of Miner's Newark Theatre
Charles L'Orange .... Musical Director of Miner's Newark Theater

The Tableau of the "Dream" in the First Act represents

"THE TYRANNY OF TERROR."

SCENE—FRANCE. TIME, 1794.

ACT I.—THE TERROR. Scene—The interior of the study of Paul Kauvar.
ACT II.—THE INHUMANITY OF MAN.—Scene—Prison of the Conciergerie adjoining the Revolutionary Tribunal in Paris.
ACT III.—THE CONFESSION. Scene—The Grand Hall of the Chateau of Delaroche in La Vendée.
ACT IV.—ON PAROLE. Scene—Same as Act III.
Three minutes will elapse between Acts IV. and V.
ACT V.—"'TWIXT LOVE AND HONOR." Scene—Same as Act IV.

The Tableau which concludes this performance, and rivals in power and beauty the famous dream scene of the first act, represents allegorically

"THE CONQUEST OF EVIL."

It is a poetic picture, full of deep thought and careful study. The central figure is that of the Angel of Conquest, with one foot upon the prostrate fiend Anarchy, holding high that irresistible weapon of progress, the Sword of Light. The fiend carries in his hands the Torch and Flag of Anarchy, and with these is about to sink into the Abyss of Darkness.

RUFUS H. DARBY, PRINTER, WASHINGTON.

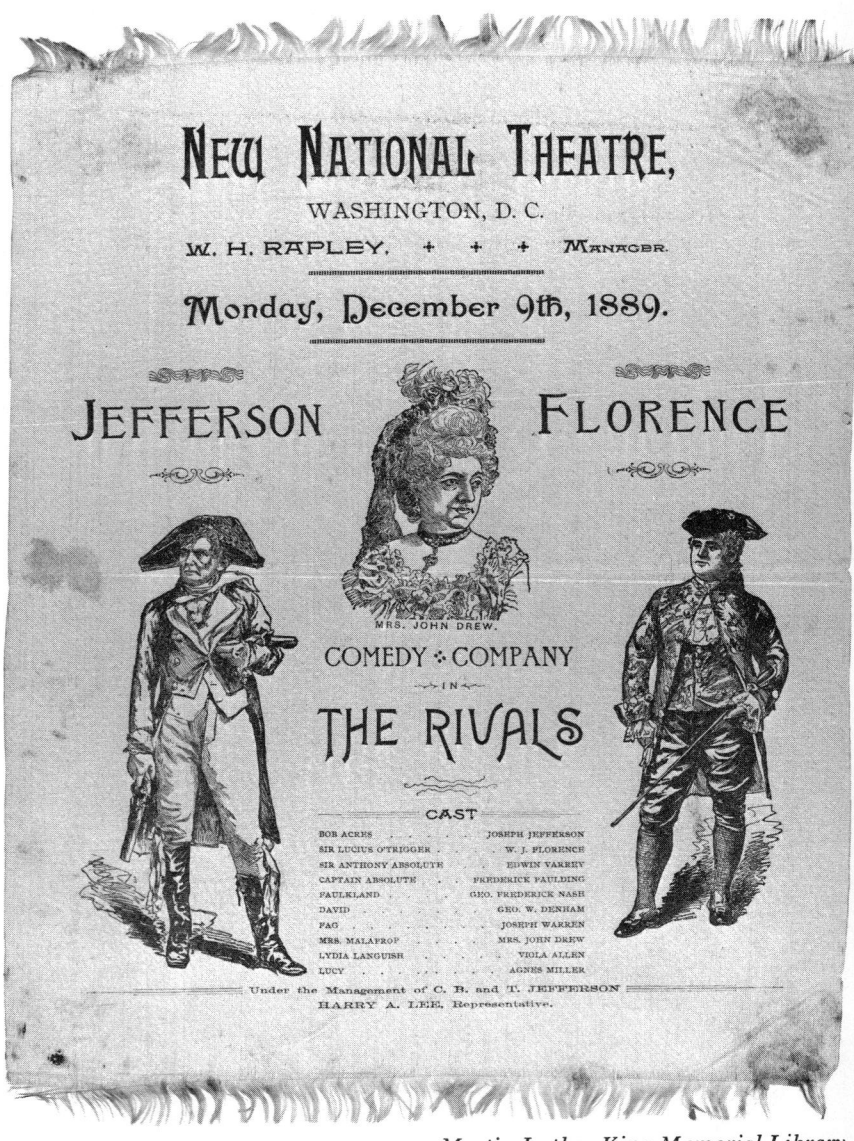

*Martin Luther King Memorial Library
Washingtoniana Collection*

Silk Souvenir Program for Joseph Jefferson's production of *The Rivals* at the National Theatre on December 9, 1889, one of the most popular productions ever presented at the National Theatre.

PALAIS ROYAL

THE following clippings from the newspapers make it very apparent that The Palais Royal, situated the corner of Penna. avenue and Twelfth street, is headquarters for Gloves.

The Evening Star,
Nov. 29, 1889.

"It is a fact that the stock of Gloves carried by The Palais Royal is as large as any other two glove stocks in town. The result of so large a variety is a perfect fit can be guaranteed any hand not positively deformed."

The Evening Star,
Nov. 15, 1889.

"There are reasons why The Palais Royal can afford less profit than those who sell Gloves on credit. No better illustration than the 98-cent Undressed or Suede Kid Gloves."

The Washington Post,
Nov. 23, 1889.

"Another consideration: The 'Palais Royal' Gloves are certain to fit correctly, because styles are shown for those with long or short fingers, thin or plump hands."

JOHN H. MAGRUDER

The Largest Importer and Dealer in Groceries and Wines

1417 New York Avenue.   Uptown Store: 1122 Connecticut Avenue.

F. A. KENNEDY CO'S Celebrated New England FRUIT CAKE

EVERY CAKE GUARANTEED   IN DECORATED PACKAGES.

Wash'n Danenhower
[Successor to Danenhower & Son]

1115 F STREET N. W.,
Washington, D. C.

CORRESPONDENCE SOLICITED.

Real Estate,
Rents, Loans,
AND
Fire Insurance.

RAMSEY & BISBEE, PRINTERS

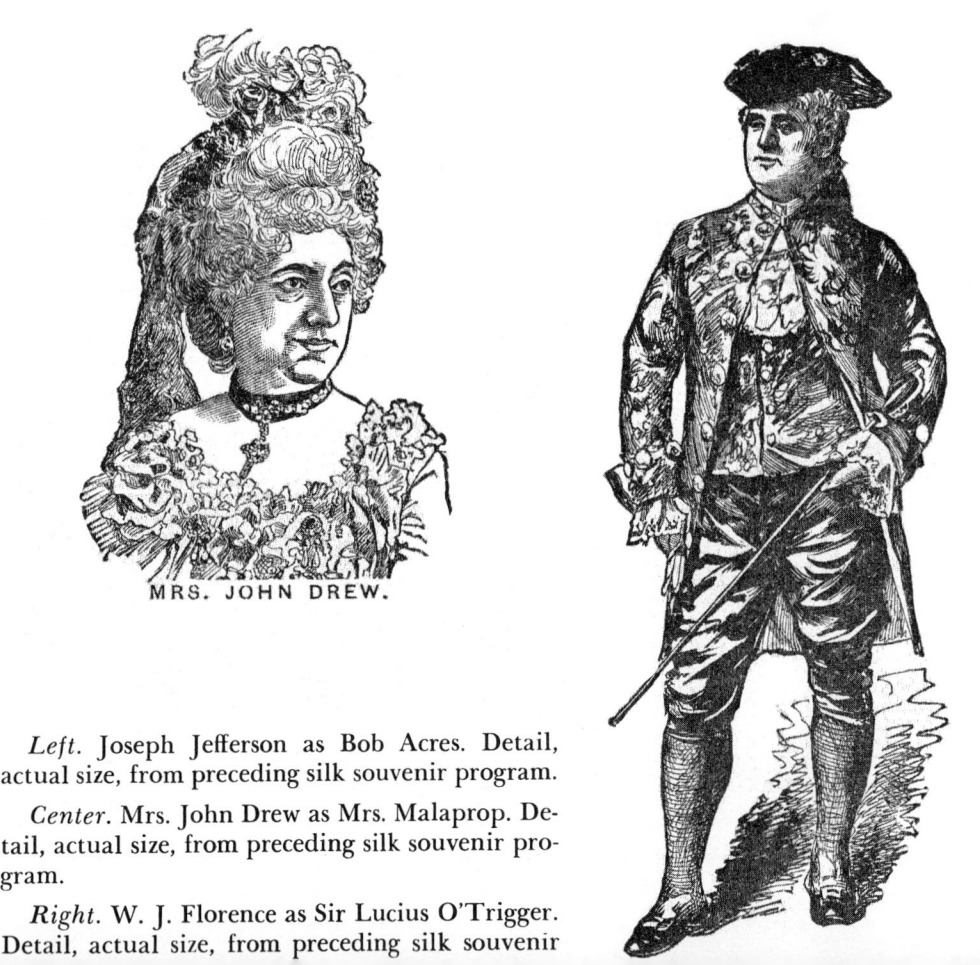

MRS. JOHN DREW.

Left. Joseph Jefferson as Bob Acres. Detail, actual size, from preceding silk souvenir program.
Center. Mrs. John Drew as Mrs. Malaprop. Detail, actual size, from preceding silk souvenir program.
Right. W. J. Florence as Sir Lucius O'Trigger. Detail, actual size, from preceding silk souvenir

New National Theatre
W. H. RAPLEY, Manager.
WASHINGTON, - - - D. C.

Wednesday Evening, Oct. 1st, 1890.

SOUVENIR PROGRAMME
TO THE
Wholesale Druggists' Association
OF AMERICA.

The De Wolf Hopper Opera Bouffe Company
Under the direction of
Messrs. Chas. E. Locke and J. Chas. Davis,
—IN—

"Castles in the Air."
Libretto by Chas. Alfred Byrne. Music by Gustave Kerker.
Produced under Stage Direction of Max Freeman.

CAST OF CHARACTERS.

Pilacoudre, the Judge	Mr. De Wolf Hopper
Repetito, his clerk	Mr. Alfred Klein
Cabolastro, a wealthy citizen	Mr. Thomas Q. Seabrooke
Jocrisse, a young officer	Mr. Edmund Stanley
Chief of Police	Mr. Lindsay Morison
Pierre, a barber	Mr. George Wade
Bul-Bul, a young nobleman out at elbows	Miss Anna O'Keefe
Blanche, daughter of Cabolastro	Miss Della Fox
Angelique, his wife	Miss Sylvester Cornish
Louise, his niece, betrothed to Jocrisse	Miss Elvia Crox
Victorine, a glover	Miss Lilly Fox
Stephanie, a perfume vender	Miss May Levinge
Desiree, a jeweler	Miss Louise Edgar

Glovers, Perfumers, Barbers, Cobblers, Police, Boys, Venders, Idlers and Attendants.

The tender, heart-touching ballad of childhood's days which Mr. Hopper sings in the last act of "Castles in the Air," about the little pig that went to market, is the joint effort of Mr. Cheever Goodwin and G. A. Kerker. Mr. Goodwin wrote the words and Mr. Kerker the music.

SCENE—The Island of Martinique, W. I.
TIME—Any the audience may choose to imagine.

SYNOPSIS.
ACT I.—Public Square at St. Pierre, Martinique.
ACT II.—House of Cabolastro.
ACT III.—Gardens of House.

Executive DeWolf Hopper Opera Bouffe Company.
Proprietors and Managers............Messrs. Chas. E. Locke and J. Chas. Davis
(Also Managers, Emma Juch Grand English Opera Company.)
Director..Mr. B. D. Stevens
Business Manager..Mr. Ben Tuthill
Musical Director..Mr. Adolph Nowak
Stage Manager...Mr. Herbert Cripps
Press Department...Mr. Frank Dupree

Martin Luther King Memorial Library
Washingtoniana Collection

Silk Souvenir Program for the performance of the De Wolf Hopper Opera Bouffe Company at the National Theatre on October 1, 1890.

Booth wrote a letter in which he attempted to justify to the public the contemplated assassination—a letter which he sent to all Washington newspapers—in the manager's office of the National when neither Mr. Hess nor Mr. Grover was present. Booth signed it: "Men who love their country more than gold or life. J. W. Booth—Paine—Atzerodt—Herold." [45]

Tad Lincoln attended the National that evening despite the fact that his parents went to Ford's. It was in the lobby of the National, as he awaited his parents' carriage to take him back to the White House, that he learned of his father's assassination. Grover, who was in New York at the time of the tragedy, received a telegram from his associate manager: "President shot tonight at Ford's Theatre. Thank God it wasn't ours. C. D. Hess." [46]

Following the assassination, with all of the theatres of Washington closing, Grover issued the following announcement:

> The manager deems it proper to announce that in view of the terrible calamity which has befallen our country in the untimely death of our beloved President, he considers it meet and proper that the National shall remain closed until the general grief that overshadows our community shall have subsided. Therefore we close the theatre indefinitely.[47]

The theatre reopened in the fall for one more season under Grover's management. On June 1, 1866, John Ford, whose ill-starred Tenth Street Theatre would remain closed for more than 100 years, temporarily took charge of the National. Mr. Ford had been imprisoned with his brother for thirty-nine days after the Lincoln assassination until their innocence was established.

THE NATIONAL THEATRE'S SEGREGATIONIST POLICIES

The segregation of black spectators into the upper regions of theatres in the United States had been an accepted practice long before the National Theatre first opened in 1835. A playbill for a New York performance, dated January 19, 1768, has the following: "Ladies and gentlemen will please send their servants to keep their places at four o'clock." Blacks went to keep seats for their masters and when the latter arrived the blacks were marshalled up into the gallery to await their "honours" at the close of the performance.[48]

---

[45] Philip Van Doren Stern, *The Man Who Killed Lincoln* (New York: Random House, 1939), p. 65.
[46] Grover, *Lincoln's Interest in the Theatre*, p. 9.
[47] Hunter and Polkinhorn, *The New National Theatre*, p. 50.
[48] Richard Davey, "The Beginnings of the Drama in America," *National and English Review* (London) XIX (August, 1892), 807.

The policy of segregating blacks in the National began when the first National opened in 1835 with a portion of the gallery set apart for "persons of color." It is not now known how many blacks were in attendance at the theatre on March 5, 1845, to see *Beauty and the Beast,* a farce entitled *Stage Struck Nigger,* and the Congo Melodists, but the *National Intelligencer* of March 7 reported that the cause of the fire which had demolished the theatre on the 5th was "a candle without a stick left burning on a table by a negro. . . ."

When the second National opened in 1850, the policy had not changed and again blacks were relegated to the top-most gallery, and the two boxes flanking the gallery were designated the "colored boxes."

The third National also had its "colored parterre" although the theatre's chief competitor, Ford's Theatre, excluded blacks entirely from its performances. This tendency in the nation's capital fully to exclude blacks from public places helped to secure the passing of the Civil Rights Act of 1875 which, in 1883, the Supreme Court held unconstitutional. The lack of a "colored parterre" in Ford's Theatre seems to account for its 100 fewer seats than the National.

Apparently by the time the fourth National opened in 1873, it too was following the accepted custom of excluding blacks entirely from its auditorium.

In the 1920's an attempt to bring D. W. Griffith's *Birth of a Nation* to the National threatened to provoke racial disorder. Controversy kept Washington the last major city in the country to see the silent film masterpiece. The motion picture was touring the country with a baggage car of effects to be used backstage in lieu of a sound tract. A black group complained about the theme of the motion picture and the management of the theatre decided to make as much of the controversy as possible. They proceeded to emphasize the film's black-white conflict in all advertising. According to Atkinson and Kiraly, the management prepared for a riotous reception when the film arrived in the city but at the premier the black was "conspicuous by his absence" and the work played for six weeks to capacity audiences.[49]

In February 1933, the National Association for the Advancement of Colored People requested that the author Marc Connelly and the producer Rowland Stebbens withdraw their play *The Green Pastures* from the National before the completion of its run. The grounds for the request were that the playhouse was segregated and that actor Richard B. Harrison who played De Lawd was receiving threats. Mr. Stebbans stated that it was the theatre's business if it wished to ex-

---

[49] Atkinson and Kiraly, *A Great Curtain Falls,* p. 31.

clude blacks, and his agent in Washington claimed that Mr. Harrison and the rest of the company were most anxious to continue the run for the rest of the Washington engagement. Blacks were admitted to a special performance of the play on February 26, 1933, which was a benefit for the Improved Benevolent Order of Elks.[50]

After an announcement that the National would exclude blacks during the playing of George Gershwin's *Porgy and Bess* in March 1936, manager Steve Cochran, under pressure from a group of Howard University professors, changed his ruling. Also interested in altering the ban was the American Federation of Labor through the American Federation of Teachers' Unions. In addition the Theatre Guild had written the management urging the change of policy and the leading actor, Todd Duncan, former professor of music at Howard University, who sang the role of Porgy, was influential in the reversal of the racial policy for the production. Other than for this production, segregation was lifted for *This is the Army* and *Winged Victory* and for one performance of *Pins and Needles*. Blacks were admitted on a limited basis also to *As Thousands Cheer* in the mid-1930's and to Paul Robson's production of *Othello*.

Black resentment toward the segregation policy reached a crucial stage on January 13, 1947, when pickets protesting racial discrimination at the theatre began marching in front of the playhouse. President Truman passed their lines to attend *Blossom Time,* but he later told reporters that he was not aware of the pickets at the time of his attendance at the theatre.[51]

The National management posted a sign in the lobby stating that if tickets were presented by any persons not conforming to the theatre's policy admission would be denied and no refund made. This was to prevent blacks from trying to gain entry on tickets purchased by whites and then, when refused admission, turning them in for refund after resale was impossible. Miss Ida Fox, executive secretary of the Committee for Racial Democracy, warned on December 7, 1946, that legal action would be taken if refunds were refused.

On January 23, 1947, it was announced that more than twenty New York theatre personalities, including Helen Hayes, Oscar Hammerstein II, Frederic March, and Corneia Otis Skinner, had signed a boycott pledge against the National and the Lisner Auditorium of George Washington University for their policy of segregation. The pledge read:

I condemn and decry the practice of discrimination in the theatre

---

[50] *New York Times,* February 16, 1933.
[51] *Washington Post,* January 23, 1947.

as an action completely in disagreement with all basic principles of the profession.

As a first step to combat this evil, I will not knowingly contract to perform in any play in any theatre in the city of Washington which practices such discrimination toward either audience or performer.

Thirty-six playwrights signed a petition several days later in which they stated that they would never permit their plays to be performed at the National until blacks were admitted. The distinguished Robert E. Sherwood, one of the leaders, suggested to Marcus Heiman, an owner of the theatre, that he try out a non-discriminatory policy to test whether in fact Washington theatre-goers would refuse to attend the playhouse under desegregated conditions as Mr. Heiman had claimed. Mr. Heiman replied that moves against racial discrimination should be made on a broader basis than an attack on his theatre alone.[52]

On January 31, 1947, a suit was filed in the Municipal Court for the District of Columbia by Edward B. Henderson against the National management stating that Henderson, a black, was not admitted to the theatre solely because of his race. This was one of several suits filed in the District as a test of the Civil Rights Act of 1875 which outlawed segregation in public places. On June 3, 1948, Judge Frank H. Meyers dismissed the suit on the basis that the Supreme Court had in 1883 held the 1875 Civil Rights law unconstitutional as an attempt by Congress to create a code of municipal law for the regulation of private rights.[53] Henderson appealed the case.

In January 1947, five persons associated with the Committee for Racial Democracy filed suit against the National Theatre for refunds for tickets. The *Star* reported that the theatre was counter-charging that the tickets were bought fraudulently and "in furtherance of a deliberate scheme to cause the theatre financial loss." [54] The Municipal Court, however, has no record of the counter-charge. Edward Plohn, the theatre manager at the time, told Judge Nadine Galligher during the trial that the exclusion of blacks was based on the management's belief that their admission would be distasteful to the regular clientele and would be financially harmful to the theatre. He stated that after a discussion with Police Superintendent Harvey B. Callahan of "the risks of mixed audiences" the theatre owners decided to uphold their policy of segregation.[55] Mr. Plohn also stated that the pur-

---

[52] *New York Times,* January 26, 1947.
[53] *Washington Post,* June 3, 1948.
[54] *Washington Star,* March 15, 1948.
[55] *Washington Star,* April 8, 1947.

chasers concealed the fact that the tickets were bought for blacks contrary to business policy. On April 28, 1947, a judgement in favor of the plaintiffs with the assent of the National's attorneys was entered in the court records. The judgements were noted as fully paid and satisfied on July 29, 1947.

Actors' Equity Association announced in April 1947 that the National would have to discontinue its discriminatory racial policy or forfeit the services of all actors belonging to the Association. The theatre was given until June 1, 1948, to comply in order to provide a period in which to "gradually and unobtrusively drop its bars against its Negro patrons." [56] On August 12, 1947, the management of the National announced that it would not alter its racial policy regardless of the position of Actors' Equity unless the segregation policy in Washington generally was changed either by legal action or by mutual consent of business and civic groups.

The Municipal Court of Appeals at this time upheld the decision of the Municipal Court in the case of Edward B. Henderson on two legal grounds: (1) that the Municipal Court's jurisdiction was not sufficiently broad for it to be a proper forum for the action, and (2) that the Supreme Court had found the Civil Rights Act of 1875 unconstitutional.[57]

In June 1948, an announcement was made that the National would become a motion picture theatre. This was in answer to the Equity ruling that its actors could not perform in it as a segregated house after a deadline extended to August 1, 1948. Marcus Heiman, president of the theatre corporation, stated that change in Washington's racial situation should be brought about in a lawful and orderly way, not in a single theatre. Heiman said that the management had received offers as early as 1941 to convert the theatre to the showing of motion pictures. The Washington Arts Center Association tried to rent the theatre in May of 1948, but manager Edmund Plohn declined the offer.

The renovation to films cost $50,000 and on October 16, 1948, the converted National opened as a cinema house with the British film *The Red Shoes*. Brightly colored decor in a Chinese motif was adopted and the entire house was repainted and pastel stage hangings were added. Picketing began again under the direction of Miss Fox who represented at this time the Council for Civil Rights.[58]

On March 30, 1951, Howard S. Cullman of New York attempted to buy the National to convert it back into a playhouse on a non-

---

[56] *Washington Post*, April 24, 1947.
[57] *Washington Star*, November 3, 1948.
[58] *Washington Capital Times*, October 23, 1948.

The National Theatre in Washington, D.C. 241

segregated basis but was unsuccessful. In November 8, 1951, the firm of Aldrich and Mayers announced that it had leased the theatre effective May 4, 1952, and would open it as an integrated theatre.

The fall season of 1952 saw the return of live drama to the National. Again the theatre was refurbished, with new paint, curtains, seats and carpets, predominately yellow and white, and an impressive white eagle mounted above the proscenium. This time, $75,000 was spent.[59]

In 1958, a syndicate headed by Frank B. Luchs purchased the theatre and the adjacent Munsey Trust Building. A year later, the J. H. Tenney Company of New York secured both for $4,250,000.

The National Theatre changed hands again on May 1, 1972, when the Nederlander Family of Detroit assumed control of the theatre operations. They instituted their own subscription series, called the Playgoer's Series, to replace the Theatre Guild Subscription Series which had for many years been presented at the National.

Whether or not the National Theatre will be able to meet the competition of the recently opened John F. Kennedy Center for the Performing Arts and today's six other professional theatres in the Washington area to remain a primary source of professional theatrical entertainment is yet to be determined. Whatever the future, the National Theatre of Washington, D. C. has had a long and proud history.

BIBLIOGRAPHY

BOOKS AND PERIODICALS

American Theatre, Washington, D.C. Playbills, December 25, 1835 to February 7, 1836. Washington, D.C.: J. Elliot, printer, 1836.

ASMODEUS. "Asmodeus at the Capital," *Gentleman's Magazine and American Monthly Review*. IV, 1, (January, 1839).

ATKINSON, GEORGE AND VICTOR KIRALY. *A Great Curtain Falls*. New York: Strand Press, 1950.

CARPENTER, FRANK, G. *Carp's Washington*. New York: McGraw-Hill, 1960.

CHUJOY, ANATOLE. *The Dance Encyclopedia*. New York: A S. Barnes and Co., 1949.

COAD, ORAL, SUMNER AND EDWIN MIMS, JR. *The American Stage*. Volume XIV of the *Pageant of America Series*. New Haven: Yale University Press, 1929.

COLLES, H. C. (ed.). *Grove's Dictionary of Music and Musicians*. Volumes II, III, IV. New York: The Macmillan Co., 1952.

ELLIS, John B. *The Sights and Secrets of the National Capital*. New York: The United States Publishing Co., 1869.

DAVEY, RICHARD. "The Beginnings of the Drama in American," *National and English Review* (London), XIX (August, 1892).

FORCE, WILLIAM Q. *Picture of Washington and Its Vicinity for 1848*. Washington, D. C. William Force, 1848.

GATCHEL, THEODORA, DODGE. *Rambling Through Washington*. Washington, D.C. *The Washington Journal*, 1932.

GORDON, JOHN MONTGOMERY. "Several Letters to the Mayor and City Council of Washington on the Subject of the Public Theatres, Pennsylvania Avenue and the Canal." Norfolk, Va.: Virginia Printers, 1870.

---

[59] *Washington Post*, September 1, 1956.

GROVER, LEONARD. *Lincoln's Interest in the Theatre.* Limited edition. n. p., n. d.
HAY, JOHN. *Lincoln and the Civil War in the Diaries and Letters of John Hay.* New York: Dodd, Mead and Co., 1939.
HEWITT, BARNARD. *Theatre U.S.A. 1668–1957.* New York: McGraw-Hill, 1958.
HUNTER, ALEXANDER AND J. H. POLKINHORN. *The New National Theatre, Washington, D.C.* Washington, D.C.: R. O. Polkinhorn and Sons, 1885.
JAMISON, B. A. *Memories of Great Men and Events 1840–1861.* (c. 1917).
JEFFERSON, JOSEPH, III. *The Autobiography of Joseph Jefferson.* New York: Century Co., 1889.
KELLY, EDWARD, J. *The Crime at Ford's Theatre.* Alexandria, Va.: Action Publications, 1944.
"Lincoln Museum and the House Where Lincoln Died, Washington, D.C." National Park Service Historical Handbook Series Number 3, 1953.
MCNAMARA, BROOKS. *The American Playhouse in the Eighteenth Century.* Cambridge: Harvard University Press, 1969.
MOODY, RICHARD. *Edwin Forrest: First Star of the American Stage.* New York: Alfred A. Knopf, 1960.
MUDD, A. I. "Early Theatres in Washington City," *Records of the Columbia Historical Society.* Washington, D.C. 1902, Vol. V.
MUDD, A. I. "The Theatres of Washington from 1835 to 1850," *Records of the Columbia Historical Society.* Washington, D.C. 1903, Vol. VI.
ODELL, GEORGE, C. *Annals of the New York Stage.* Volumes VII, VIII, X, XII, XIV. New York: Columbia University Press, 1937.
RIDER, FREEMONT. *Rider's Washington: A Guidebook for Travelers.* New York: The Macmillan Co., 1924.
SANDBURG, CARL. *Abraham Lincoln.* New York: Harcourt Brace and Co., 1954.
SHERMAN, ROBERT L. *Drama Cyclopedia, A Bibliography of Plays and Players.* Chicago: the author, 1944.
SMILEY, ROBERT, WAGNER. *The Night Side of Washington.* Washington, D.C.: n. p. 1894.
STAPLES, O. G. *A Descriptive Sketch and Guidebook to All Points of Interest in Washington.* New York: Photo Engraving Co. n.d.
STERN, PHILIP VAN DOREN. *The Man Who Killed Lincoln.* New York: Random House, 1939.
TINDALL, WILLIAM. *Standard History of Washington.* Knoxville, Tenn: H. W. Crew and Co., 1914.
TROLLOPE, FRANCES. *Domestic Manners of the Americans.* Edited by Donald Smalley. New York: Alfred A. Knopf, 1949.
Washington, City and Capital. Federal Writers' Project, Works Progress Administration. Washington, D. C.: U. S. Government Printing Office, 1937.
WILSON, FRANCIS. *John Wilkes Booth.* Boston: Houghton Mifflin Co., 1929.
WILSON, GARFF, B. *A History of American Acting.* Bloomington, Indiana, 1966.

NEWSPAPERS

Capital Times. Washington, D.C. October 23, 1948.
Washington Intelligencer. January 19, 1845. March 6, 1845. March 7, 1845. January 13, 1853. December 21, 1866.
Washington Daily News. October 31, 1935. December 17, 1935. January 23, 1947.
Washington Post. November 22, 1922. November 28, 1922. November 2, 1927. December 6, 1927. April 24, 1932. May 16, 1932. April 18, 1935. February 2, 1937. October 13, 1945. January 23, 1947. April 24, 1947. June 4, 1948. September 1, 1956.
Washington Star. November 6, 1861. April 24, 1862. December 2, 1873. April 9, 1881. February 28, 1885. October 6, 1885. October 3, 1898. January 2, 1902. August 30, 1915. November 26, 1922. November 27, 1922. April 26, 1928. Febraury 21, 1929. June 23, 1929. April 22, 1932. June 19, 1934. April 6, 1936. May 6, 1942. October 9, 1942. April 8, 1947. March 15, 1948. November 5, 1948. September 7, 1960.
Washington Times-Herald. February 15, 1934. January 9, 1938. January 8, 1942.

Behind Prison Walls: The Operation of the District Penitentiary, 1831–1862

DAVID K. SULLIVAN

In April, 1831, Thomas Williams, recently convicted of stealing one barrel of flour valued at six dollars, took up residency in the newly constructed District penitentiary. As Williams passed through the gates of the fortress-like structure on the banks of the Potomac to serve his one year sentence, a new era began in the treatment of District criminals.

At the beginning of the Nineteenth Century, the criminal codes of most jurisdictions, including the District of Columbia, prescribed death for a wide variety of crimes, and corporal punishment, such as whipping and branding, for other, less serious offenses. In the first decades of the new century increasing opposition arose to these laws, primarily because of the supposed ineffectiveness of the punishments in deterring crime. Many judges and juries, motivated in part by the humanitarianism of the period, were reluctant to impose sentences which seemed excessively harsh and brutal. Or, if corporal punishment was inflicted, the recipients often became more embittered toward and alienated from society. In either case, justice was not properly served.

These concerns led to the enactment of new statutes which were designed to be more humane and, at the same time, it was fervently hoped, would enable criminals to reform. The new approach provided for the imprisonment of offenders at hard labor and under rigidly controlled conditions conducive to transforming convicts into model citizens. Since existing prison facilities, intended only for short term confinement, were deemed inadequate to fulfill the rehabilitative functions and goals envisioned by the penal reformers, new prisons—penitentiaries—were constructed in many parts of the country.

Propelled by this national movement, Congress appropriated funds

---

Delivered before the Columbia Historical Society on February 15, 1972.

in the latter half of the 1820's for a penitentiary in the District. Until then the only prisons were two jails, one in Washington, the other in Alexandria. Both were used primarily for pretrial detention and the confinement of debtors and runaway slaves. Neither was suitable for long term imprisonment and the requirements of the penitentiary system. In 1831, when the new prison, designed by Charles Bulfinch, was ready for occupancy, Congress rewrote the District criminal codes inherited from colonial Maryland and Virginia. The new statutes, which applied only to free persons, abolished corporal punishment entirely and limited the death penalty to murder, treason, and piracy. Other offenses, except the most minor, carried peni-

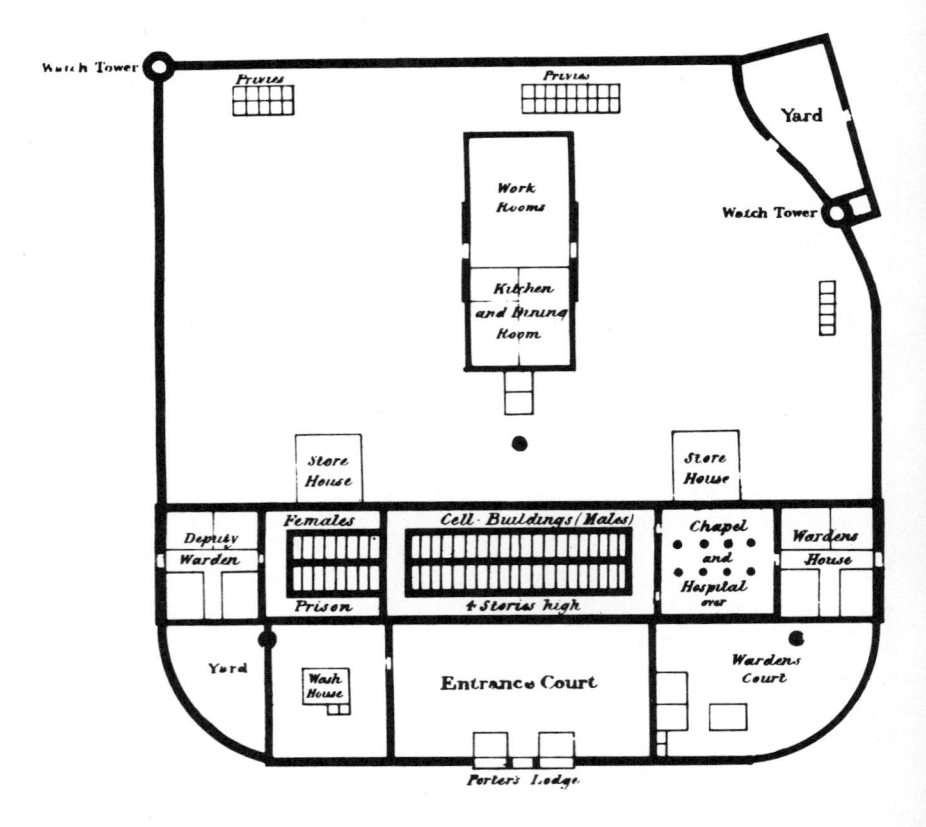

Library of Congress

"Plan of the Penitentiary at Washington for the District of Columbia." From William Crawford, *Report . . . on the Penitentiaries of the United States,* London, 1835, "Ordered by The House of Commons to be Printed, 11th Augt. 1834."

Library of Congress

Charles Bulfinch, architect of the District penitentiary.

A drawing by an unidentified artist from a portrait by George B. Matthews.

tentiary sentences ranging from ten to thirty years for rape to one to three years for stealing goods or money valued at five dollars or more.[1] It was shortly after the passage of this act that Thomas Williams, the first of hundreds of persons who in the next three decades were to inhabit the penitentiary, crossed the threshold of the new institution.

---
[1] U.S., *Congressional Debates*, 21st Cong., 2nd Sess., 1831, appendix, pp. 20–23.

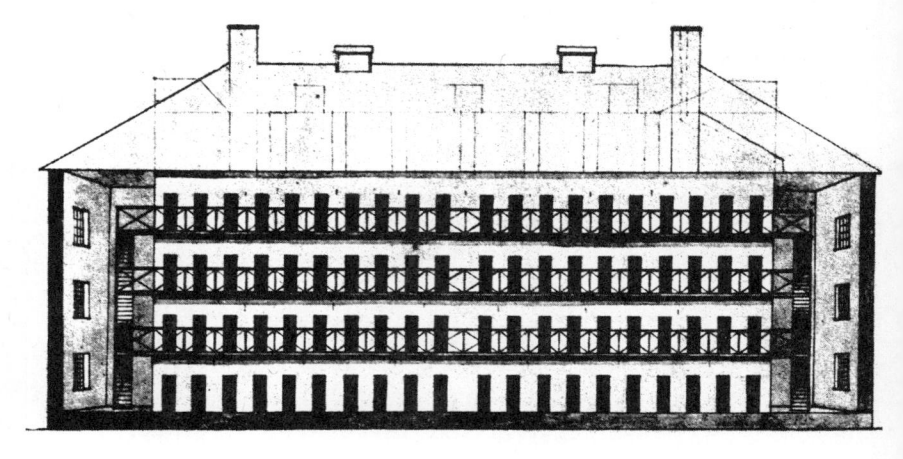

Library of Congress

Charles Bulfinch's drawing of the main building of the District penitentiary.

The District penitentiary, like similar prison facilities built during this period, sought to create an environment in which prisoners would be inculcated with attributes which were highly valued by society—a useful occupation, respect for authority, industriousness, personal discipline, and temperance. The formidable, quasi-military appearance of the exterior of the prison and its orderly and spartan interior provided a visual representation of many of the goals of confinement. The operation of the penitentiary and the daily life of the convicts completed the picture.

The rule that "every convict shall be industrious" provided the cornerstone of the penitentiary system.[2] Hard and long labor, principally shoemaking at the District prison, had several redeeming features other than its direct impact on the character of the inmates. It helped to defray operating expenses, reminded prisoners of the punitive aspects of their confinement, and, according to some observers, so occupied and exhausted the workers that they had no time or energy to concoct escape plans.

The regulations for the District penitentiary drawn up by Congress in 1829 and the supplementary rules of the inspectors of the prison also reflected the desire that convicts be infused with proper traits.

---

[2] "Rules and Regulations Adopted by the Board of Inspectors for the Government of the Penitentiary," Jan., 1830, U.S., Congress, House, *Annual Report of the Inspectors of the District Penitentiary*, 1842, 27th Cong., 3rd Sess., Doc. 67, Ser. 420, p. 25.

Each convict had a separate cell (seven by three and one half by seven feet), enabling him to meditate on his past misdeeds and at the same time avoid debilitating associations with others. The requirement that absolute silence be maintained was established for the same purposes. Food and clothing were "coarse" and uniform. Additional regimentation was achieved through strict scheduling of the time and activities of the convicts.[3]

To assist prisoners in reshaping not only their behavior but their attitudes as well, moral and religious training was an important part of penitentiary existence. Officials placed great value on instruction given by the chaplain. One warden asserted that there was "no point in the system more necessary and useful." While the officials may not have been concerned about moral reformation in the same way that the chaplain was, they nevertheless had other good reasons for encouraging it. In 1834 the chaplain was praised for his aid in "enforcing obedience, good order, and industry." Another time, the inspectors noted with satisfaction that religious instruction and services were important elements in "producing [the] subordination" that they found during their periodic visits to the prison. "Lessons of moral character" read at mealtimes were, according to one warden, also beneficial in subduing the restless convicts.[4]

An important adjunct to the work of the chaplain was secular education. Chaplains were especially eager that convicts learn to read so that they could make use of the Bibles placed in every cell. Also, a prison library, well stocked with religious tracts, was available for interested inmates. Some of the volumes, which at times numbered 700, had been selected for the District penitentiary by Dorothea Dix, the famous reformer, who visited the prison in the late 1840's.[5]

Because prison officials saw a close relationship between discipline and reformation, the infliction of punishment posed no dilemma. When other efforts failed, the officers believed they had no other alternative. "We have endeavored to impress upon . . . the prisoners that we are their friends, laboring for their good," said one warden, and, he added, "we are much grieved whenever their conduct calls for exemplary punishment." The only issue which caused concern was whether corporal punishment should be permitted. The 1829 congressional act which set down the general rules for the District prison stated, rather vaguely, that the inspectors were to prevent "all tyrannical or violent behavior." For over twenty years, until 1854,

[3] *Ibid.*, pp. 20–26; and U.S., *Statutes at Large,* IV, 1829, pp. 365–69.
[4] *Penitentiary Report,* 1842, p. 5; 1834, p. 3; 1844, p. 7; and 1849, p. 8.
[5] *Ibid.*, 1853, p. 22; 1848, p. 6.

the inspectors prohibited corporal punishment, decreeing that the maximum penalty for infractions should be bread and water in solitary for twenty days.[6]

Even this seemed rather harsh for the majority of offenses, which usually involved abusive language, insolence, disobedience, fighting, talking, refusing to work, or spoiling materials. These and others generally indicated the frustrations of prison life and, often times, simply the need to express normal emotions. Samuel Peoples, for example, was given five days in solitary for whistling and singing in the workshop. Mary Batteman was punished for talking to men through a keyhole, and John Kelly for mimicking a cat.[7]

Some were not entirely satisfied with these penalties. Warden Isaac Clarke, who served from 1832 to 1841, continually objected to the prohibition against physical punishment. "No prison can be perfect unless corporal punishment is used," he declared in his first year as warden, because the "depraved and corrupt" prisoners were not deterred by "established punishments." Clarke traced the high recidivism recorded in 1835 to the "good" food and the "mild" rules of the District penitentiary.[8] A few years later the warden was charged by a former convict of countenancing, if not participating in, the whipping of prisoners.[9] And many decades later, a long-time resident of the District related that her brother had described to her the beating of inmates with wooden paddles during Clark's administration.[10]

Many prison officials, on the other hand, expressed reluctance to resort to corporal punishment. In 1849, Warden Thomas Fitnam stated, with unusual candor, that the "ill nature and domineering spirit too often manifested by those clothed with a 'little brief authority'" tended to result in the "worst possible effects." Fitnam did not define what he meant by the "worst possible effects," but statements by others who objected to physical punishment suggested that their concern was primarily over the supposed inefficacy of such penalties rather than their inhumanity. Warden Thomas Thornley

---

[6] *Ibid.*, 1840, p. 5; U.S., *Statutes at Large*, IV, p. 369; and "Rules and Regulations of the Inspectors," *Penitentiary Report*, 1842, p. 26.

[7] Penitentiary Punishment Book, 1831–1847, National Archives, Department of the Interior, Record Group 48, District Penitentiary, Book 36, n.p.

[8] *Penitentiary Report*, 1832, p. 6; 1835, pp. 4–5.

[9] William Nash to Martin Van Buren, Dec. 8, 1837, U.S., Congress, House, *Charges Against Officers of the Penitentiary*..., 27th Cong., 2nd Sess., 1842, Doc. 174, Ser. 404, pp. 43–45; and Nash to Henry Wise, chairman of the House District Committee, Dec. 8, 1837 and Mar. 14 and 16, 1838, National Archives, Record Group 233, House, District Committee, Petitions and Memorials, 25A–G4.1.

[10] Jeannie T. Rives, "Old Families and Houses—Greenleaf's Point," *Records of the Columbia Historical Society*, V (1902), p. 56.

stated that his experience had taught him that "kind but positive admonitions" were "more successful in subduing the stubborn heart than a resort to the lash." Another warden, who reported discovering that illegal corporal punishment had been inflicted on convicts in the previous administration, asserted that his use of "reason" rather than the "whip" had been more effective in bringing refractory prisoners to submission. With considerable pride, he stated that this approach had led a particularly incorrigible inmate to become "one of the most docile and respectful" of his charges.[11]

In 1854, in tandem with a national trend to tighten prison discipline, the inspectors of the District penitentiary modified the regulations of 1830 by authorizing corporal punishment.[12] Initially, perhaps because of the personal views of the warden, this new power was used sparingly, but beginning in early 1859, following a sharp rise in the prison population and the arrival of a new warden, whipping and tricing became regular occurrences, constituting about twenty per cent of all punishments.[13]

The use of positive incentives to secure discipline and reformation among convicts was rare, though some prison officials sought authorization to adopt them. In the 1850's particularly, a succession of wardens requested that the federal government permit the penitentiary officers to initiate a "task" system in which prisoners would be awarded monetary renumeration for work done over a specified quota. The task system, one of these wardens wrote, would increase the interest of the convicts in their labor and give them concrete evidence of the value of diligence and industry. Further, upon release, the former convicts, with money in their pockets, could "travel beyond the sphere of the prison circle" and go, without advanced prejudice, to faraway places to pursue honest careers.[14] In spite of these advantages, the task system was not adopted until the 1860's.[15] And it was not until then that another incentive program—time off for good behavior (one month per year)—was approved by Congress.[16]

---

[11] *Penitentiary Report*, 1849, p. 8; 1857, p. 9; and 1848, p. 4.
[12] Minutes of the Inspectors of the District Penitentiary, National Archives, Record Group 48, Department of the Interior, District Penitentiary, Book 39, Jan. 16, 1854, pp. 319–20.
[13] Penitentiary Punishment Book, 1854–1860, Book 38, n.p.
[14] *Penitentiary Report*, 1855, pp. 2–3. Similar statements can be found in almost every annual report of the 1850's.
[15] *Ibid.*, 1862, p. 4; and Penitentiary Day Book, 1858–1861, National Archives, Record Group 48, Department of the Interior, District Penitentiary, Book 29, n.p. In the late 1850's the prisoners were awarded tobacco for extra work. See *Penitentiary Report*, 1857, p. 3.
[16] U.S., *Congressional Globe*, 37th Cong., 2nd Sess., 1862, appendix, p. 423.

While prison authorities may have been successful in maintaining good order and submission, they were less adept in fulfilling the penitentiary's major goal of the permanent reformation of the prisoners. A table in the 1846 annual report showed that sixty of the 410 convicts received since the opening of the prison in 1831 were repeaters, many three or four times.[17] During the 1850's the number of commitments to the penitentiary averaged about fifty per year, almost double the rate in previous years and, adjusted for the retrocession of Alexandria in 1846, a much sharper rise than the increase in the population of the District.

Prison officials refused to recognize or acknowledge that the penitentiary system might have weaknesses. The blame for recommitments was almost always placed on the convicts. In 1836, for example, the warden said that some criminals were "so habitually disposed to evil, that no moral impressions can be made upon them." In 1839, the large number of recommitments was explained by the statement that these persons were "entirely without the pale of improvement." Again, in 1851, the inspectors, in accounting for the high recidivism, noted that nearly all recommitted prisoners were "incorrigible" and "constitutional thieves," unable to resist temptation and unaffected by religion or work. Another board of inspectors suggested that the "unreformable class . . . be congregated upon one of the islands in the Pacific." [18]

The single most important concern of prison authorities, as measured by the space alloted to the subject in annual reports, was the financial results of the penitentiary's operations. The congressional act of 1829 which laid down the broad rules for the administration of the District penitentiary required an explanation each year if the prison failed to be self supporting. Since this was almost always the case, nearly every annual report contained references, often of great length, to the financial problem. The time and effort devoted to this phase of the District penitentiary no doubt had an adverse impact on the inmates' reformation, supposedly the principal interest of prison officers.

Most penitentiaries also were hard pressed to cover operating costs, but the District penitentiary was burdened by a particular handicap. Because it had been built for a much larger number of convicts than were actually imprisoned there during most years, the per inmate fixed operating expenses, especially for the staff, were accordingly

---

[17] *Penitentiary Report,* 1846, p. 19.
[18] *Ibid.,* 1836, p. 2; 1839, p. 2; and 1851, pp. 2–3.

higher than normal. The inspectors pointed out in 1839 that the average inmate population for the preceding five years had been eighty, as compared to a capacity, including the women's quarters, of about 220.[19] This was a major factor in the prison's losses, which, without adjustment for capital costs, averaged more than $11,000 annually between 1838 and 1842.[20]

Prison officials had many other reasons to explain the poor financial results. The character of the convicts was a favorite theme. Age, infirmities, stupidity, and insanity were mentioned by one warden. Frequent reference was made to the prisoners' lack of skills, their unproductivity, and their inability or unwillingness to learn and cooperate. Repeated recommendations that inmates be allowed to earn money for overwork were partially aimed at surmounting these attributes. Also, prison authorities complained that by the time convicts were trained properly their sentences had terminated, though this argument seemed spurious. In 1857, for instance, over two-thirds of the prisoners had been confined two years or more.[21]

Black prisoners were especially subjected to official censure. When it was recommended in the 1840's and 1850's that convicts from other parts of the country be sent to the District penitentiary to better utilize the partially empty facility, one reason given was that this would lower the proportion (which averaged nearly fifty per cent) of blacks and thereby increase productivity per inmate.[22] The warden appointed by the new Republican administration in 1861, H. I. King, expressed his opinion that the black convicts were the major source of the poor financial condition of the prison. The "colored" prisoners, he said in his annual report, were "notoriously unprincipled" and often "stupid and inapt." Furthermore, he claimed, these "perverse and intractable apprentices" compounded the difficulties by entering prison "with a predetermination to do as little as possible." [23]

One legitimate obstacle to a better financial performance of the District penitentiary was the need to consider competition with free labor. Prison authorities were continually faced with demands by the laboring classes of the community that the penitentiary refrain from employing convicts in skilled trades. The workers' concern was undoubtedly not only with competitive products but also with the ex-

---

[19] *Ibid.*, 1839, pp. 2–3.
[20] *Ibid.*, 1842, pp. 11–12.
[21] See, for example, *ibid.*, 1837, p. 5; 1839, p. 2; 1853, p. 3; and 1857, pp. 6 and 8.
[22] Robert Coltman, warden, to House District Committee, Apr. 10, 1846, National Archives, Record Group 233, House, District Committee, Papers and Reports, 29A-D4.3.
[23] *Penitentiary Report*, 1861, p. 1.

pectation that released convicts would swell the ranks of skilled workers in the area. Not long after the penitentiary opened, several hundred citizens of Washington informed Congress that convict labor was destroying "all fair competition" and rendering free labor "unproductive." If not checked, the memorial warned, honest mechanics might become paupers or criminals themselves. The petitioners concluded by asking that labor be abolished at the prison and that the inmates be placed in solitary confinement.[24]

Presentments at other times offered different solutions. One suggested that prisoners be employed in deepening the District harbor, filling marshes, or building and repairing roads. Another petition to Congress, from approximately 100 local cordwainers, recommended that the government purchase the prison's output. In 1846, Andrew Johnson, reflecting his working class background, introduced in the House of Representatives a resolution which would have required that the District Committee determine how inmate labor might be redirected to avoid all competition with District workers. Should the Committee find that impossible, the Johnson resolution proposed that the District penitentiary system be abolished altogether. A partial solution was also advanced by the *National Intelligencer,* which suggested deporting all black convicts.[25]

By 1849, Congress had become so concerned about the penitentiary's finances that the House organized a select committee to investigate the situation. The committee, chaired by Horace Mann, who had taken an active interest in prison reform in his home state of Massachusetts, concluded that the cost of supporting convicts at the District prison was "sufficient to maintain them very respectably at many of the genteel watering places in the country." The committee recommended that the Army, which had an arsenal adjacent to the prison, take over the facility and that District convicts be sent to the Maryland and Virginia penitentiaries.[26] This recommendation was not adopted at the time, but the continuing threat of its revival prob-

---

[24] Petition of several hundred citizens of Washington to Congress, n.d., National Archives, Record Group 233, House, District Committee, Petitions and Memorials, 23A-G4.4.

[25] Petition of thirty journeyman cordwainers to Congress, Mar. 7, 1844, National Archives, Record Group 46, Senate, District Committee, Petitions and Memorials, 28A-G3; petition of about 100 journeyman cordwainers to Congress, Feb. 1839, *ibid.,* 25A-G5; U.S., *Congressional Globe,* 29th Cong., 1st Sess., 1846, p. 755; and *National Intelligencer,* June 6, 1837, p. 3.

[26] U.S., Congress, House, Select Committee on the District Penitentiary, *Penitentiary in the District of Columbia,* 30th Cong., 2nd Sess., 1849, Rpt. 140, Ser. 545; and National Archives, Record Group 233, House, District Committee, Papers and Reports, 30A-D26.5 and D26.6.

Library of Congress

Horace Mann (1796-1859), elected as a Representative in Congress from Massachusetts to fill the vacancy caused by the death of John Quincy Adams, was chairman of the select committee of the House which investigated the financial condition of the District penitentiary.

ably led prison authorities to concentrate even more on financial matters.

The prison officials also recommended many solutions, one of which was that the District penitentiary, as originally intended, receive convicts from other jurisdictions in order to achieve full capacity and the consequent financial benefits.[27] It was not until the late 1850's that this course was adopted, but then the lack of sufficient work space and facilities to keep all the convicts employed presented a new problem. In the meantime, the authorities tried various techniques to cut costs, increase productivity, and insure good prices and a certain market for the prison's output. The most persistently pursued objective was the task or quota system which was viewed as an ideal method of improving productivity and achieving more satisfactory discipline. But by the time it was put into practice in the early 1860's, the officials had virtually given up on ever making a profit. In 1860, the inspectors and warden related that several attempts to contract for the sale of prison products had failed; that not a single bid had been received for a proposal to hire out fifty or sixty convicts; that the prejudice against the competition of "cheap convict labor with honest mechanic ingenuity and enterprise" continued to be "deep seated and radical"; that the building was too small and inadequately equipped; that many new inmates were so inept that they hampered production; and that, in any event, the goods which were produced were difficult to sell in the marketplace at reasonable prices.[28]

One factor that contributed to a less than fully effective administration of the District penitentiary, as of many others in the country, was the political nature of appointments. Wardens, appointed by the President, were generally replaced when new national administrations came into power: 1841, 1845, 1847 (due to the death of the previous warden), 1849, 1850, 1853, 1859, and 1861. None were professional prison administrators. Jonas Ellis (warden from 1850 to 1853) was a "mechanic" and Charles Sengstack (1847–1849) and Thomas Fitnam (1849–1850), chosen during the years of the penitentiary's most serious financial crisis, were businessmen.[29] The inspectors, also appointed by the President, were changed with almost the same regularity as the wardens and normally were members of the local legal profession.

Two wardens were charged with incompetence. The penitentiary's first warden, Benjamin Williams, was accused of "abuse of trust, . . . neglect of duty, and . . . want of capacity" for misappropriation of funds and other delinquencies. Williams fled the District soon after the charges were presented to President Andrew Jackson, who, after

---

[27] See, for example, *Penitentiary Report,* 1841, p. 4. This recommendation can be found in virtually every annual report of the 1840's and 1850's.

[28] *Ibid.,* 1860, pp. 1–4.

[29] *Washington News,* May 25, 1850, p. 3; Sengstack to Horace Mann, Feb. 28, 1849, National Archives, Record Group 233, House, District Committee, Papers and Reports, 30A-D26.5; and *Penitentiary Report,* 1849, p. 6.

the inspectors noted that they did not anticipate Williams' return, appointed a new warden.[30] A charge of incompetence and malfeasance was also leveled in the late 1830's against Warden Isaac Clarke, who had replaced Williams in 1832. The warden's use of convict labor for private purposes and the physical abuse of prisoners were among the allegations. While Clarke was apparently not entirely innocent, the accusations were probably exaggerated for political purposes. President Martin Van Buren reviewed the case and found "insufficient evidence" to establish a "corrupt design," but at the same time he suggested that the warden had not displayed the "caution and precision" which were "requisite to prevent all danger of imputation." [31]

The purpose of the penitentiary was not only to confine and reform convicted criminals but also to remind citizens of the District of the consequences of criminal activity. Yet the overt relationship between the prison and the community was rather limited. Exceptions occurred whenever citizens believed that the penitentiary or its inmates were a threat to the community's security or well being. Protests over the competitiveness of prison labor were the best examples. Another instance occurred when prison officials, in the hope of improving financial results, suggested that non-District criminals be incarcerated in the prison. One warden felt compelled to reassure District residents that this would not lead to an increase in the area's crime rate. Given sufficient funds, he said rather unconvincingly, released convicts would quickly return to their home states or territories.[32]

Community interest in the penitentiary was principally manifested in newspapers and in inspection tours by local authorities. Reports of the prison from these sources, however, were generally uncritical, measuring the caliber of the institution and the success of its operation primarily in terms of cleanliness, neatness, discipline, and order. One newspaper editor, who visited the prison frequently, spoke mainly of the "clean and wholesome" cells, the "good nutritious soup and wholesome bread," the orderliness of the convicts as they marched through the prison, and the presence of Bibles and other religious works. A report by the grand jury of the criminal court following an inspection of the prison read much the same.[33]

[30] Penitentiary Minute Book, National Archives, Record Group 48, Department of the Interior, District Penitentiary, Book 39, 1832, pp. 59-75.
[31] House, *Charges Against Officers of the District Penitentiary,* 1842, Doc. 174. For Van Buren's comments, see p. 62.
[32] *Penitentiary Report,* 1848, p. 9.
[33] *Washington News,* Nov. 18, 1854, p. 2; and grand jury of the District criminal court to the inspectors of the penitentiary, n.d., Penitentiary Minute Book, National

Particularly in the early years of the penitentiary's operation, persons from outside the District showed considerable interest in the prison. Foreign visitors came to the United States in the 1830's to investigate the new penitentiary system and frequently included the District prison on their itinerary. The most famous, the Frenchmen Gustave Beaumont de la Bonniniere and Alexis de Tocqueville, limited their comments to the penitentiary's high cost, which they ascribed to the natural extravagance of the central government.[34] William Crawford, who had been commissioned by the British government to inspect the new American system of criminal punishment and reformation, criticized the poor arrangement of the cells and the lax discipline, though he seemed impressed with the quality of the goods produced by the inmates in the workshop.[35] A French penologist, Frederick de Metz, also reported that discipline was poor but praised the religious and secular instruction offered to the prisoners.[36]

Among well-known Americans who wrote of their reaction to the District penitentiary, Dorothea Dix was the most prominent. She, like many others, stressed the efficiency rather than the efficacy of the prison, commenting chiefly on its cleanliness, good ventilation and "close" discipline. Miss Dix noted approvingly that there was an officially appointed chaplain but she was critical of his practice of allowing certain convicts to teach others.[37] Her concern about the insufficient library which, according to the warden, created a "sensation in her mind," led Miss Dix to spend $100 of her own funds to restock the bookshelves.[38] Ethan Andrews, an abolitionist who came to the capital in the 1830's to report on the District slave trade, considered the management of the penitentiary to be "preeminently excellent." [39]

Archives, Record Group 48, Department of the Interior, District Penitentiary, Book 39, Mar 28, 1851, pp. 294–95. For additional examples of reports by visitors from the District to the prison, see *Washington News,* Aug. 16, 1851, p. 3 and Feb. 19, 1853, p. 2; and *Washington Weekly Star,* Jul. 31, 1858, p. 3 and May 14, 1859, p. 2.

[34] Gustave A. Beaumont de la Bonniniere and Alexis de Tocqueville, *On the Penitentiary System in the United States* . . . , trans., Francis Leiber (abridged ed.; Carbondale, Ill.: Southern Illinois University Press, 1964), p. 104.

[35] William Crawford, *Report . . . on the Penitentiaries of the United States* (Montclair, N.J.: Patterson Smith, 1969; originally published, 1835), appendix, pp. 102–03.

[36] Orlando F. Lewis, *The Development of American Prisons and Prison Customs, 1776–1845* (Montclair, N.J.: Patterson Smith, 1967; originally published, 1922), pp. 264–65, citing De Metz.

[37] Dorothea Dix, *Remarks on Prisons and Prison Discipline in the United States* (2nd ed.; Philadelphia: Joseph Kite & Co., 1845), pp. 34, 47–48, and 58–59.

[38] *Penitentiary Report,* 1848, p. 6; and 1851, p. 20.

[39] Ethan A. Andrews, *Slavery and the Domestic Slave Trade in the United States* (Boston: Light & Stearns, 1836), p. 127.

Library of Congress

Dorothea Lynde Dix (1802–1887), pioneer in American prison reform and in the care of the poor and the insane, donated one hundred dollars for the purchase of books for the library of the District penitentiary.

The perspective of the inmates of the District penitentiary can only be surmised since few left any record of their view of incarceration. Many convicts must have felt somewhat victimized immediately by the severity of the penalty, especially if they were aware that one of the principles of the penitentiary system was to apportion the punishment to the crime. Stealing was the most frequent offense for which persons were sentenced and imprisonment for one or two years for the theft of goods valued at as little as twenty dollars, and often less, was not uncommon. John Martin, for example, was sentenced to one year in the penitentiary for stealing "miscellaneous items" worth eight dollars. William Adams received three years in 1851 for taking a five dollar robe and James Shorter spent three years in the prison for the theft of boots worth less than eleven dollars.[40]

Once in prison, inmates worked from sunup to sundown, six days a week. Two meals, generally consisting of pork or beef, bread and potatoes, were served each day. Besides having to maintain silence, the prisoners were forbidden to have visitors or even send or receive mail without special permission. And they were, of course, required to act with complete deference to the entire prison staff.

The counselling and instruction offered by the chaplain must have been a welcome interlude for many convicts, though not necessarily for the reasons intended by prison officials. Sessions with the chaplain provided a release from the imposed silence, as did secular education, especially for those few inmates who were selected as teachers. Chaplains often noted the willingness of convicts to discuss religious topics, apparently unaware that many were probably anxious to talk no matter what the subject. This, too, may have partially accounted for the "affection" which prisoners were reported to have had for the chaplain.[41]

On rare occasions, convicts were permitted to deviate from the usual routine. In 1859 the prisoners were granted their request to stage a Fourth of July celebration, to which "quite a number" of District citizens were invited. The affair was held in the prison chapel, which was adorned with a large banner that proclaimed: WE STILL LOVE OUR COUNTRY. On the program were hymns, prayers, and songs including "Do They Miss Me at Home?", "The Flag of the Free" and "The Star Spangled Banner." One of the readings, no doubt performed with considerable feeling, was the Declaration of Independence. Another all-too-infrequent instance of self expression occurred in 1860 when several inmates displayed their ingenuity by constructing, at "trifling cost," an "entire stock of machinery of the most improved style of workmanship." [42]

---

[40] Penitentiary Commitments, 1831–1862, National Archives, Record Group 48, Department of the Interior, District Penitentiary, Box 22, commitment 325, and Box 23 commitments 430 and 520.

[41] See, for example, *Penitentiary Report,* 1834, p. 3; 1837, p. 6; and 1857, p. 22.

[42] *Washington Star,* Jul. 9, 1859, p. 3; and *Penitentiary Report,* 1860, p. 5.

Library of Congress

"Scene of the Washington Riot," illustration from *Frank Leslie's Illusrated Newspaper,* June 20, 1857.

Normally, however, such opportunities were lacking, and the prisoners' activities sometimes took destructive turns. Escapes and prison revolts occurred, but even these were rare due to the tight security and discipline. Large scale confrontations between prisoners and their keepers brought swift retaliation. In 1856, for example, about fifty convicts refused to work. All were promptly put on bread and water for seven to ten days.[43] The futility of a mass rebellion no doubt curtailed more frequent uprisings. The lack of communication with the outside kept public awareness of what was happening inside the penitentiary at a minimum. And even if wide public knowledge of prison conditions and of the legitimate grievances of the inmates had existed, it probably would not have elicited much sympathy in an essentially deferential society which did not understand, much less countenance, challenges to authority by convicted criminals.

Prisoners were therefore left to protest or express themselves in smaller ways. They devised ingenious methods to communicate with one another.[44] Louisa Rowan must have had at least a few moments of glee when the warden's wife took the first sips of the tea which Louisa had laced with pepper. But such acts of defiance rarely succeeded and generally brought harsh retribution on the perpetrators. Miss Rowan,

[43] Penitentiary Punishment Book, 1854–1860, National Archives, Record Group 48, Department of the Interior, District Penitentiary, Apr. 1856, n.p.
[44] *Washington Star,* Apr. 10, 1858, p. 3.

described as the "most depraved" in the prison after the incident, was whipped and placed in solitary confinement.[45]

Prison officials seldom provided assessments of the reactions of the prisoners to their incarceration in the District penitentiary and when they did there seemed to be a lack of objectivity. In the 1850 annual report the inspectors observed that few convicts made complaints to them even though they were privileged to do so.[46] These officers, in concluding that the inmates were therefore contended, gave no hint that they had considered the possibility that convicts might not complain simply because they were fearful of retaliation by those against whom they had made accusations.

The prison officials occasionally referred to the "contentment" and "high degree of cheerfulness" of the convicts,[47] but at the same time the staff was apprehensive that such displays of apparent cooperation were made from ulterior motives. Prisoners' claims that they had been "saved" were received with caution since authorities believed that these professions might have been made to "serve some temporal interest." One warden avowed not to give special treatment to "reformed" convicts lest others succumb to the "temptation of hypocrisy."[48] Thus inmates had no incentive, other than fear, to conduct themselves in the manner sought by the officers of the prison.

Naivete or self service seemed to have led some prison authorities to a distorted view of the reactions of prisoners to confinement. Chaplain William Ferguson affirmed that many convicts would "bless the day" that they were sent to the District penitentiary. And Warden Robert Coltman claimed that prisoners had left "with the warmest expression of thanks . . . and best wishes for our well being."[49] Such comments are hard to accept at face value. The assessment of prison life by more detached observers, a Sioux Indian delegation which was in Washington and visited the District prison, may have been more valid. It was, said a spokesman for the group, "the most frightful punishment conceivable."[50]

For all its shortcomings, the District penitentiary was probably, until the late 1850's, a less intolerable prison than similar institutions in the country. Up to that time, the number of inmates was

---

[45] Penitentiary Punishment Book, 1860–1862, National Archives, Record Group 48, Department of the Interior, District Penitentiary, Sept., 1862, n.p.
[46] *Penitentiary Report,* 1850, p. 2.
[47] *Ibid.,* 1844, p. 9; and 1848, p. 2.
[48] *Ibid.,* 1834, p. 7; 1835, p. 10; 1840, p. 5; and 1855, pp. 14–15.
[49] *Ibid.,* 1842, p. 10; and 1846, p. 4.
[50] *Washington Weekly Star,* Mar. 27, 1858, p. 3.

relatively small, never exceeding 100 in any year, well below the prison's maximum capacity of more than 200. This insured that there would not be undue pressure on the prison facilities or its staff and that the prison could be something more than a mere custodial institution. The convict's identity was not totally destroyed and prison officials, especially the chaplain, could establish some rapport with individual prisoners.

This situation came to a halt in the late 1850's, when the prison population began to rise sharply and strain the capacities of the facilities and staff. In 1857, 103 prisoners were confined in the District penitentiary during the year. This increased to 139 in 1858, 163 in 1859, and 226 in 1860. There was a brief plateau in 1861, when 236 prisoners were incarcerated, but in 1862, with the addition of over 100 soldiers, the number escalated faster than ever before to an all time high of 332.[51] The rise itself, its rapidity, and the increase in the percentage of convicts who had committed more serious crimes, caused a noticeable deterioration not only in the administration of the District penitentiary but also in the attitudes of convicts and the staff.

The central feature of the penitentiary system, convict labor, was undermined because there were insufficient facilities to keep all inmates fully employed.[52] In 1858 the prison hospital was closed and converted into a workshop. Seriously ill convicts were placed on cots in the main passage and were subjected, the warden admitted, "to all the inconveniences and noise necessarily occurring by persons passing by." The death of four inmates during the year was unprecedented. Despite this costly attempt to salvage the labor system, Warden King stated that when he assumed his duties in 1861 about one-half of the prisoners were idle.[53]

Discipline, too, began to break down. A new warden in 1859 told of finding an "almost entire want" of order when he took over. The inmates, he said, displayed an alarming degree of "recklessness" and "insolence." In addition, escapes and escape attempts took a sharp upturn during this period. In 1861, there were four successful escapes, which the warden attributed to the time and opportunity which unoccupied and inadequately supervised inmates had to devise

---

[51] *Penitentiary Report*, 1857, p. 20; 1858, p. 13; 1859, p. 15; 1860, p. 21; 1861, p. 16; and 1862, p. 28.

[52] See, for example, *ibid.*, 1857, p. 6; 1859, p. 1; 1860, p. 4; and 1861, p. 2. At the same time, however, outside laborers were hired for several days to clear clogged sewers since "it was not deemed expedient or humane to compel the convicts to perform this repulsive duty." *Ibid.*, 1859, pp. 16–17.

[53] *Ibid.*, 1858, pp. 2–3; and 1861, p. 2.

plans.[54] While factors other than the rising number of prisoners may have contributed to these general conditions, and though some corrective action was able to be taken, the operation of the penitentiary had clearly deteriorated.

The optimism and buoyancy that had characterized most of the reports of the prison officials diminished measurably and were replaced by increasing pessimism and despondency. In 1858, the chaplain noted uncharacteristically that some convicts were "suffering great mental depression." Later he portrayed the life in prison in previously unheard of terms. It was, he declared, "enough . . . to degrade, depress, and discourage the poor convicts from leading a life of honesty and virture." By 1861, even the warden was describing the penitentiary as "at best, a dreary, lonesome habitation." [55] These statements contrasted strikingly with those which earlier had enthusiastically, if not accurately, portrayed the "contentment" and "cheerfulness" of the convicts.

At the time this deterioration was reaching advanced stages, the demands of the war effort intervened. President Abraham Lincoln reported to Secretary of the Interior Caleb Smith, who had jurisdiction over the District penitentiary, that the prison was "absolutely necessary" for military purposes. Lincoln, in his capacity as commander-in-chief, ordered Smith to turn the penitentiary over to the War Department and transfer the convicts to other prisons. These directives were carried out in September, 1862.[56] Thereafter, criminals from the District were sent to the Albany, New York State prison,[57] and the District penitentiary became part of the Army Arsenal. With the exception of its use a few years later for the confinement, trial, and execution of those charged with conspiracy to assassinate Lincoln, the District penitentiary never again served the purposes for which it had been originally constructed.

The worsening of the operation of the prison may have contributed to the ease with which Congress accepted its closing, and the displeasure of many congressmen over the confinement of soldiers there was probably an additional factor. In the summer of 1862, it

---

[54] *Ibid.*, 1858, p. 3; 1859, pp. 2–3; 1860, p. 22; and 1861, pp. 2 and 17. See also, *Washington* Star, Apr. 10, 1858, p. 3; and *Washington Weekly Star,* Dec. 3, 1859, p. 2 and Oct. 27, 1860, p. 2.

[55] *Ibid.*, 1858, p. 16; 1860, p. 1859, p. 19; and 1861, p. 3.

[56] Roy P. Basler (ed.), *The Collected Works of Abraham Lincoln* (New Brunswick, N.J.: Rutgers University Press, 1953–1955), Vol. V, pp. 429–30.

[57] Amos Pilsbury, warden of the Albany prison, to Caleb Smith, Sep. 25, 1862, National Archives, Record Group 48, Department of the Interior, District Penitentiary, Box 131.

Library of Congress

Photograph of the District penitentiary, about 1865, after it had been taken over by the United States Army for use as an arsenal.

Columbia Historical Society Collection

"Penitentiary Building at Washington, in which the Conspirators are Confined and Undergoing Trial." Published sketch by Joseph Hanshew.

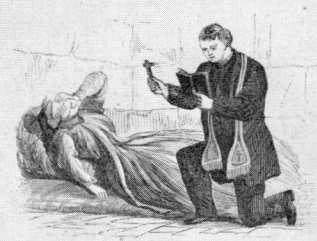

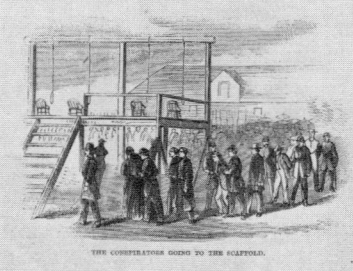

"Scenes in and around the Old Penitentiary, Washington, D. C., on the day of the Execution of the Conspirators," illustration from *Frank Leslie's Illustrated Newspaper,* July 22, 1865.

The District Penitentiary, 1831–1862

Columbia Historical Society Collection
Sketch of a portion of the District penitentiary by M. Morgan.

was revealed that over ninety court-martailed servicemen were in the prison. Most had been committed for minor, non-penitentiary offenses. Yet, said Senator Henry Wilson of Massachusetts, these men were being "degraded as felons." After much discussion in both houses of Congress over how to deal with those few incarcerated for more serious crimes, the Congress passed an act which provided that no military personnel were to be confined in the penitentiary unless they were convicted of offenses for which District laws authorized confinement in that prison. All servicemen then in the penitentiary who were not in that category were discharged.[58] The debates over this issue certainly did not enhance the reputation of the District penitentiary among congressmen.

In their last annual report in 1862, the inspectors of the penitentiary confidently expressed their hope that Congress would provide

---

[58] U.S., *Congressional Globe,* 37th Cong., 2nd Sess., 1862, pp. 2597, 2615–17, 2668–70, 2717–18, 3129, 3278–79, 3301, 3310, 3312, 3323, 3352, 3378–79, 3394, 3397, and appendix, p. 412; U.S., Congress, Senate, *Imprisoning Soldiers and Volunteers in the District Penitentiary,* 37th Cong., 2nd Sess., 1862, Doc. 55, Ser. 1122; and U.S., Congress, House, *Prisoners in the District Penitentiary by Sentence of Courts-Martial,* 37th Cong., 2nd Sess., 1862, Doc. 127, Ser. 1138.

funds for a new penitentiary "with all the modern improvements." The newly created metropolitan police also urged the establishment of a new penitentiary. "No community in this country," the 1862 police report asserted, was "so inadequately supplied with prison accomodations." [59] In April, 1864, the House District Committee reported a bill appropriating $250,000 for the construction of a penitentiary and for a much needed new jail and a house of refuge for juvenile offenders.[60] James Blaine of Maine and others vigorously opposed the measure, principally because of the financial failure of the previous penitentiary. As a consequence, the bill was recommitted to the District Committee.[61] That action proved to be momentous, for Congress would not again seriously consider a penitentiary for the District for many years.

The operation of the District penitentiary in the three decades of its existence had demonstrated that the eagerness and optimism of the penal reformers who had introduced the penitentiary system in the United States in the early Nineteenth Century had been exaggerated. When the District prison was taken over by the War Department in 1862, the comment was made that the closing was "not much to be regretted." [62] This sentiment was apparently shared by much of the community and a majority in Congress. A well intentioned endeavor had come to a troubled end.

---

[59] *Penitentiary Report*, 1862, p. 3; and *Annual Report of the Metropolitan Police*, 1862, p. 3. See also the 1863 *Police Report*, pp. 13–14.

[60] In June, 1862, before the penitentiary was closed, the House District Committee had proposed a similar bill with a $200,000 appropriation, but this was rejected by a seventy-three to thirty-three vote. See U.S., *Congressional Globe*, 37th Cong. 2nd Sess., 1862, pp. 2687–90.

[61] U.S., Congress, House, District Committee, *Penitentiary in the District of Columbia*, 38th Cong., 1st Sess., 1864, Rpt. 41 (to accompany H.R. bill 169), Ser. 1206; and U.S., *Congressional Globe*, 38th Cong., 1st Sess., 1864, pp. 331, 494, 1396, 1470, 1473–75, and 1491–94.

[62] *Penitentiary Report*, 1862, p. 3.

The Rise and Fall of Washington's Inhabited Alleys: 1852–1972

JAMES BORCHERT

Late in the evening of August 5, 1914, and again on the morning of the following day, during her few brief moments of consciousness, Ellen Axson Wilson told her husband: "I should be happier if I knew the Alley Bill had passed." In her last hours of life, the First Lady sought Congressional approval for a bill abolishing alley housing in Washington, a goal for which she had worked during much of the time of her residence in the White House.[1]

Ellen Wilson was not alone in her interest in Washington's inhabited alleys. A later First Lady, Eleanor Roosevelt, also was actively involved in the fight to rid the city of this "menace". The alleys were the subject of an extensive body of writing during the first half of the Twentieth Century. The topic of countless newspaper articles, alley housing was also the subject of a multi-volume governmental study, "The President's Homes Commission" (1908), and numerous individual studies including one book-length work, Charles Weller's *Neglected Neighbors* (1909), and one play, Ernest Culbertson's *Goat Alley: A Tragedy of Negro Life* (1922).

Despite the number of studies, articles, and books about the subject, however, little is known about the origins of such housing.[2] Nor has its rise over time been traced spatially and demographically. While much has been written on the efforts to abolish alley dwellings, there has been no discussion of their eventual near demise. It is the purpose here to offer some tentative answers to these problems.[3]

---

[1] "Mrs. Wilson's Death and Washington's Alleys," *Survey*, 32 (August 15, 1914), 515; and Mrs. Ernest P. Bicknell, "The Home-Maker of the White House," *Survey*, 33 (October 3, 1914), 22.

[2] Constance McLaughlin Green observed that the city historian should discover if the "rise of the alley dwelling" was chiefly a development of the Reconstruction era or after, or of an earlier period. Constance McLaughlin Green, "Problems of Writing the History of the District of Columbia," Columbia Historical Society *Records*, 51–52 (1955), 132.

[3] The major emphasis is on the inhabited alleys of the Federal City. Although such alleys in Georgetown predated those of the Federal City, and alleys were later inhabited just north of Florida Avenue, the largest and most significant concentrations were in the Federal City.

Like other American cities of the mid-Nineteenth Century, Washington was a pedestrian city. Most Washingtonians walked on their various journeys to work and to shop. As a result, the 40,000 inhabitants of the Federal City clustered around the major places of work.[4]

Washington's population growth in the 1850's, as other, larger American cities had experienced earlier, began to strain at the spatial limits imposed by the pedestrian city. Although the city continued to expand slowly outward during the decade, this physical growth was insufficient to house the new population. Consequently, more intensive land use became necessary.

One form of this more intensive land use was the subdivision of lots within the built-up parts of the city. Since most lots were covered with buildings on the front or street side of the lot, this subdivision occurred at the rear of the lots, on that part facing the service alley. As early as 1852, plat books indicate the beginnings of this movement in five blocks within the established part of the city.[5] In each case, the alley cut straight through the block with the rear subdivided lots being smaller than those on the street. The 1856 plat book shows a continuation of this trend with four more squares having such subdivisions.[6] While two of these blocks were laid out essentially like those of 1852, two had subdivisions on interior alleys that were connected to the outside of the block only by another alley. This latter layout, often called a "blind" or "hidden" alley, was to become the most common form. Unlike the former alleys that were easily accessible and visible from the streets, these blind alleys were virtually hidden away inside the block. It was this feature that most disturbed reformers and police alike.[7] An example of this "hidden community"

---

[4] Albert Boschke, "Map of Washington City ..." (1857). (Geography and Map Division, Library of Congress). The map shows all buildings in the city of that year, and the clustering effect is strongly evident.

[5] Squares 387 and 465 in Southwest and 568, 569 and 624 in Northwest all show subdivisions of land fronting on 20 to 30 foot alleys. *Maps of the District of Columbia and City of Washington and Plats of the Squares and Lots of the City of Washington* (Washington, 1852), 61, 71, 86, 94.

[6] Squares 367, 378, 448 and Reservation 10 in Northwest. William Forsyth, *Plats of Subdivisions of the City of Washington, D.C.* (Washington, 1856), 15, 17, 21, 60.

[7] A typical blind alley was an alley 30 to 40 feet wide in the shape of an "H", located in the interior of a block. The houses were constructed on this interior alley with the only connection to the street being by another alley, 10 to 15 feet wide. An example of this type of alley can be seen in Block Maps 1 and 2 for Square 368. There were, however, other alley layouts that were more problematic. Many of these were really minor streets rather than alleys and were usually 45 feet wide running straight through the block. Some of these were referred to as alleys at one time and as streets at others. Thus, Organ Alley of 1858 became Madison Street in 1871, although no physical change occurred. Police census takers and housing reformers often included some of these

Photograph 1. Alley Dwellings in Logan Court, Northwest, November 1935, photograph by Carl Mydans.

*Library of Congress
Farm Security Administration Collection*

is suggested by the 1935 photograph of Logan Court, Northwest. (See Photograph 1.)

Although it is impossible to determine from these sources whether or not dwellings were built on these subdivisions as early as 1852 or even earlier, it seems safe to assume that if they were not as yet built, the "developers" of these various areas had certainly conceived of building dwellings that would face on narrow alleys. The size of the lots virtually precluded their use for anything other than dwellings.

The *Report of the Board of Health* in 1854 does suggest that some alleys were inhabited. Seeking to account for the higher death rate for children under fifteen years of age, the Health Officer observed that "much the larger proportion of these deaths are from among the children of negro [sic.], of foreign, and of destitute native parents, who usually reside in alleys, and in the suburbs." [8]

Albert Boschke's "Map of Washington City" (1857), gives a clue to the spatial locations of the alleys. Although in many squares it is difficult to determine whether the buildings indicated are sheds,

"minor streets" in with their alley enumeration, while many other "minor streets" were not so included, so that the definition of an inhabited alley had both a social and physical dimension.

[8] *Report of the Board of Health of the City of Washington—1854* (Washington, 1854), 1.

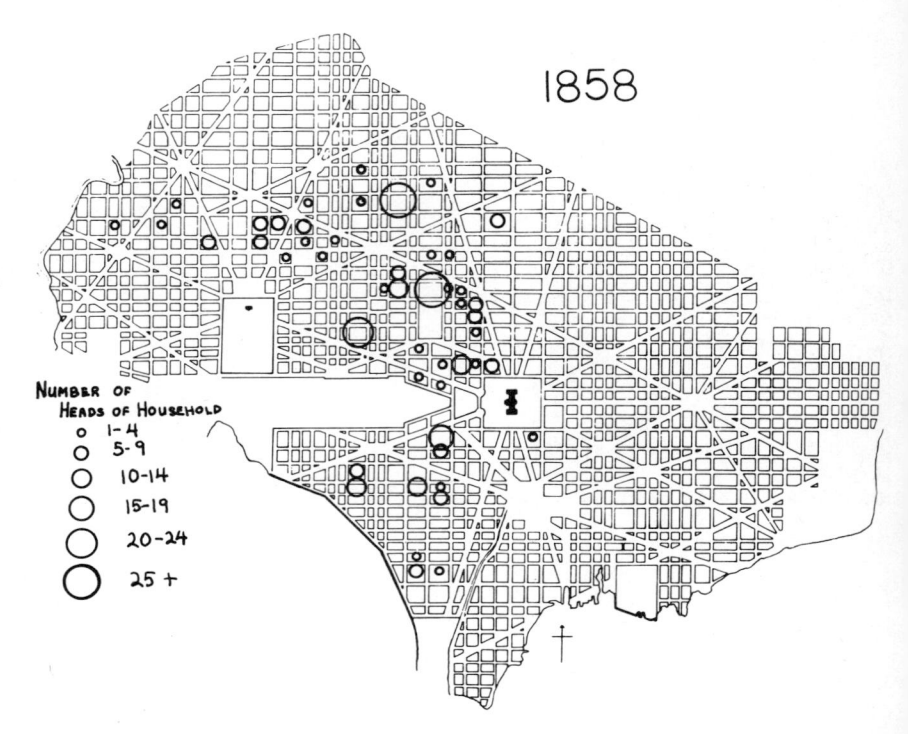

*By the author from William Boyd, "Boyd's
Washington and Georgetown Directory-1858"*

Map 1. Inhabited Alleys by Heads of Household, 1858.

stables or houses, in at least thirteen blocks in Northwest and six in Southwest, there are, fronting on the alleys, distinguishable row houses with small but demarcated back yards. These inhabited alleys all fall within the most densely settled part of the city, that between First and Fifteenth Streets West, F Street South and N Street North.

The most concrete evidence of the existence and extent of pre-Civil War alley housing, however, comes from the 1858 city directory. The directory, which sought to list the names, addresses, occupations and race of all heads of household, had at least 348 names with alley addresses. It is possible to locate 49 inhabited alleys from these addresses.[9] (See Map 1.) In light of the fact that many census and city

[9] William Boyd, comp., *Boyd's Washington and Georgetown Directory 1858* (Washington, 1858). Unfortunately, many of the addresses listed in the directory are impossible to locate, e.g. "Alley between G and H". Addresses which list three streets do indicate an approximate location, but it is impossible exactly to pinpoint many such alley locations. Thus, alleys indicated on Maps 1 and 2 are in many cases merely approximate locations.

The Rise and Fall of Washington's Inhabited Alleys

directory enumerators notoriously miss many people, and especially those in "hidden" alleys, as well as the fact that only the head of household was reported, the names in the city directory probably represented a proportion of the alley population comparable to the visible part of an iceberg.[10] By 1860, the Commissioner of Health warned that "of late years alleys are being closely built up with tenements in which many people are crowded together." These alleys were "narrow and a large proportion of them" had "only a single outlet." [11]

There are several theories as to who built these alley houses. One explanation suggests that the "space in the back of the houses was used for slave quarters, thus they became a gathering place for slaves." [12] In southern and border cities with sizable slave populations, however, slave quarters faced the rear of houses on the street and were separated from other lots and the alley by a wall.[13] Alley houses, on the other hand, faced directly onto the alley and were separated from houses on the outside of the block by a narrow alley and fences. A more plausible explanation was offered by a long-time resident of "Foggy Bottom". He remembered that C. A. Snow, publisher of *The National Daily Intelligencer*, had owned property in Square 28 (Snow's Court between Twenty-fourth and Twenty-fifth Streets, New Hampshire and K Streets, Northwest). "Prior to the Civil War," Snow "constructed a greenhouse and four frame houses in the interior of the block, and it was called Snow's Alley. The four houses were occupied by Irishmen, one of whom Mr. Snow employed in the greenhouse." [14] Boschke's map tends to confirm this story although there is no listing in the city directory for 1858. During the Civil War, however, the government used the houses for barracks for disabled soldiers.

Other inhabited alleys must have started in a similar fashion, probably by one or several land owners in a block subdividing the property at the rear of their houses, constructing tiny wooden row

---

[10] Peter Knights' research on city directories of ante-bellum Boston suggests that directories report about 75 per cent of the heads of households listed in the census, but that strong variations occur with regard to race and class. Not surprisingly, blacks and the poor tend to be under reported. Peter Knights, "City Directories as Aids to Ante-Bellum Urban Studies: A Research Note," *Historical Methods Newsletter*, II (September, 1969), 1–10.

[11] *Report of the Commissioner of Health—1860* (Washington, 1860), 4.

[12] Marion M. Ratigan, "A Sociological Survey of Disease in Four Alleys in the National Capital," (Unpublished Ph.D. dissertation, Catholic University of America, 1946), 76.

[13] Richard Wade, *Slavery in the Cities* (New York, 1964), 59–60.

[14] Daniel D. Swinney, "Alley Dwellings and Housing Reform in the District of Columbia," (Unpublished M. A. thesis, University of Chicago, 1938), 70–71.

Lewis Wickes Hine Collection
George Eastman House, Rochester, New York

Photograph 2. Purdy's Court, near the Capitol, 1908, photograph by Lewis Wickes Hine.

houses and then renting them to the unskilled workers of the city who could not afford the new houses being constructed on the "fringe" of the city. The occupations of alley dwellers in 1858 confirm this latter contention with nearly sixty per cent falling into the unskilled category. Further, most alleys had fewer than ten names listed as living in them, suggesting that initially alley construction was on a small and limited scale. And as in the case of "Snow's Alley", whites made up the majority of alley dwellers.[15] In 1858, sixty-five per cent of alley residents were white. Despite the sizable minority of black alley dwellers, the alleys were highly segregated. Of the forty-nine alleys, twenty-one were all white, seventeen all black and only nine had less than a two-thirds majority of one race.

Although alley dwellings were a fairly well established institution prior to the Civil War, it was, nevertheless, the substantial growth

---

[15] Most studies, however, contended that "Negroes were the original inhabitants of alleys and are destined to be the final occupants of the dwellings." William Henry Jones, *The Housing of Negroes in Washington, D.C.* (Washington, 1929), 31.

The Rise and Fall of Washington's Inhabited Alleys 273

of the city's population and especially the black population, that speeded the building of alley houses. In the decade following the start of the war, the city grew by more than 48,000, of whom over half were black. The new population was thrust on a city that was hardly ready for such growth. There were neither sufficient numbers of buildings to house the newcomers nor was there an efficient means of moving them daily from one part of the city to another. For those with enough money and leisure time, horse drawn cars did offer the beginnings of a transportation system. But for most, the various journeys about the city remained pedestrian ones. Thus, there was a substantial impetus for the continuation and expansion of alley dwelling construction.

The result is strongly reflected in the city directory of 1871, which listed nearly 1,500 heads of households and approximately 118 identifiable alleys. As in 1858, the alleys were concentrated in the older sections of the city, between First and Fifteenth Streets West with the beginnings of a new focal point in "Foggy Bottom".[16] (See Map 2.) These figures are undoubtedly very conservative for only two years later the Board of Health reported 500 inhabited alleys.[17] Nevertheless, the directory figures do reflect a substantial growth in the numbers of inhabited alleys and the population of each alley. By 1871, six alleys had forty or more names of heads of household, and another five alleys had from thirty to thirty-nine.

The question of who was responsible for alley house construction is equally problematic for the post-Civil War period. Some of the freedmen who came to the city were housed in barracks "in and around Washington." Many others set up living quarters in shantytowns like "Murder's Bay", a "vile place, both physically and morally," located where the Federal Triangle is today.[18] Similarly, some freedmen must have erected their own houses on alley property with much of the material for such housing being "obtained from abandoned army camps and hospitals."[19] In contrast, an elderly woman stated that "the first alley dwellings, exclusive of servants and slave quarters, were constructed prior to the Emancipation Proclama-

---

[16] William Boyd, comp., *Boyd's Directory of Washington, Georgetown and Alexandria —1871* (Washington, 1871).

[17] Board of Health, *Second Annual Report* (Washington, 1873), 105.

[18] Commissioner of the United States Bureau of Refugees, Freedmen and Abandoned Lands, *Report* (Washington, November 1, 1866), 1; and Wilhelmus Bogart Bryan, *A History of the National Capital*, II (New York, 1916), 523.

[19] Ratigan, "Sociological Survey of Disease," 76; and George M. Kober, *The History and Development of the Housing Movement in the City of Washington, D.C.* (Washington, 1907), 5.

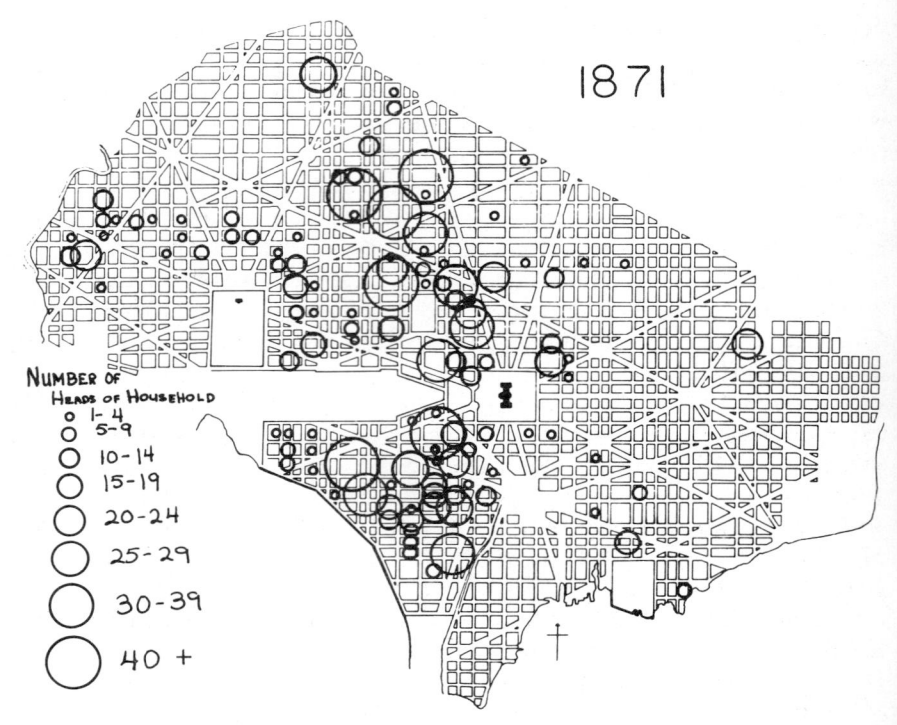

By the author from William Boyd, "Boyd's Directory of
Washington, Georgetown and Alexandria—1871"

Map 2. Inhabited Alleys by Heads of Household, 1871.

tion by philanthropic individuals who were interested in providing shelter for the run-away slaves from the South." The informant was the daughter of a former member of the Friends' Society which "during and after the Civil War . . . built a number of alley dwellings for philanthropic and not economic reasons." [20] The 1871 directory does carry a listing for "Quaker's Buildings" in Square 276, but no names

---

[20] Swinney, "Alley Dwellings and Housing Reform," 16–17. It should be pointed out here that virtually all sources, including those who considered slave houses as the forerunner of alley dwellings, agreed essentially that "The first of the ill-fated alleys, as present day Washington knows them were laid out in 1867." Federal Writers Project, *Washington: City and Capital* (Washington, 1937), 75. The tremendous increase in alley housing following the war as well as the change in the race of residents undoubtedly led many observers to conclude that alley dwellings were the product of that period without looking for evidence in earlier years. Thus, Swinney, who suggests pre-Civil War origins for Snow's Court, concluded that "The philanthropic motives of a few individuals and the Friends' Society probably started the movement to inhabit the alleys." Swinney, "Alley Dwellings and Housing Reform," 18.

had that address. Later alley censuses do, however, indicate alley residents in "Quaker Alley".[21]

Undoubtedly many property owners continued to subdivide their rear lots and construct houses for rent. But the phenomenal increase in the numbers of alley residents suggests that alley property development must have also been carried out by "developers" who were concerned with such construction on a somewhat larger scale, and who did not necessarily own any land in the block save the alley property.

Thus, the older spatial relationship between the owner's residence and his alley property probably began to be broken in the period following the war. By 1913, few alley property owners lived in the same block as their property, while only fifteen alley houses were owned by their occupants. Although alley property in a given block might have a different owner for nearly every house, another block might have only a few owners controlling a large number of houses.[22] In either case, the alley houses appear to have been a good investment. Reform groups after the turn of the century often complained that alley house owners received "about twice what is considered a fair return in street property." [23]

As the extent and number of alley residents increased as a result of the considerable population growth of the 1860's, so too did the large influx of freedmen change substantially the complexion of alley residents. By 1871, 81 per cent of the heads of household reported were black, only 19 per cent white. While white heads of household increased by only 64 in the 13 years since 1858, Negro heads of household increased by 1,083. Nevertheless, the occupational structure remained basically the same, with the majority of alley residents falling into the unskilled and menial service occupations. As Table 1 indicates, however, white alley residents appear to have gained some occupational mobility, moving into higher occupational "levels". Black alley residents, excluded by racial antagonism from many economic activities, maintained the same occupational distribution in 1871 as in 1858.

The level of segregation increased in the 1871 alleys. Only twelve per cent of the alleys, as opposed to eighteen per cent in 1858, had less than a two-thirds majority of any one race, and only three of these had

---
[21] Alleys often had uncommon names. One of the ways they got these was by "the Directory men while canvassing, generally from some local cause." Boyd, *Boyd's Directory...1871,* M.

[22] 63rd Congress. 1st Session. Senate. Committee on the District of Columbia, *Persons Owning or Renting Houses or Rooms in the So-Called "Inhabited Alleys" in the District of Columbia* (Washington, 1913).

[23] Edith Elmer Wood, "Four Washington Alleys," *Survey,* 31 (December 6, 1913), 251.

TABLE I
Occupations of Alley Dwellers by Race—1858–1871

	1858			1871		
Occupation	Black N (%)	White N (%)	Total N (%)	Black N (%)	White N (%)	Total N (%)
1. Unskilled and Menial Service	68 (56)	137 (61)	205 (59)	646 (54)	130 (45)	776 (52)
2. Semi-Skilled and Service	30 (25)	12 (5)	42 (12)	318 (26)	29 (10)	347 (23)
3. Petty Proprietors, Managers and Officials	1 (1)	6 (3)	7 (2)	39 (3)	22 (8)	61 (4)
4. Skilled	8 (7)	41 (18)	49 (14)	85 (7)	50 (17)	135 (9)
5. Clerical and Sales	0	1	1	8 (1)	5 (2)	13 (1)
6. Semi-Professional	0	2 (1)	2 (1)	6 (1)	3 (1)	9 (1)
7. Proprietors, Managers and Officials	0	0	0	0	3 (1)	3
8. Professionals	0	1	1	1	0	1
9. Miscellaneous	14 (11)	27 (12)	41 (12)	101 (8)	49 (16)	150 (10)
Total N =	121	227	348	1204	291	1495

Source: William Boyd, comp., *Boyd's Washington and Georgetown Directory—1858*. William Boyd, comp., *Boyd's Directory of Washington, Georgetown and Alexandria—1871*. Occupational categories based on those used by Peter Knights, *The Plain People of Boston: 1830–1860* (New York, 1971), 148–152.

twenty or more heads of household listed. Similarly, two studies utilizing sample area data from the 1880 census found that the "alleys were much more strongly segregated" than the population on the outside of the blocks.[24]

Alley house construction, however, was not able to keep pace with the demand for inexpensive housing. This increased demand made it possible for alley house owners to charge higher rents resulting in severe over-crowding in many alleys. It also affected the conversion into "dwellings" of many alley buildings originally intended for other uses. Health officials reported many alleys were "lined on both sides with miserable dilapidated shanties, patched and filthy", while many frame dwellings had "leaky roofs, broken and filthy ceilings, dilapidated floors." They were "unfit for human habitation," but most property owners were "mean enough to charge rent for them." [25] In fact, virtually any building bordering on an alley could be con-

[24] John P. Radford, "Patterns of White-Nonwhite Residential Segregation in Washington, D.C. in the Late Nineteenth Century," (unpublished M.A. thesis, University of Maryland, 1967), 60; and James Borchert, "Race and Place: An Attempt at a Community Study," (unpublished manuscript, 1972), 9.

[25] Board of Health, *Second Annual Report*, 105; *Third Annual Report* (Washington, 1874), 186; and *Annual Report, 1877* (Washington, 1878), 46.

The Rise and Fall of Washington's Inhabited Alleys

verted for dwelling purposes, as in the case of William Walker, who in 1877 converted two brick stables in Carlin's Alley, Southwest, into "dwelling houses".[26] Fortunately, much of the new building in the 1870's and 1880's was of more substantial frame and increasingly brick construction. Normally these houses were two-story row houses of four or more units each, as illustrated by the accompanying photographs.[27] Though each set of houses varied, an average house was about twelve feet wide and twenty-four feet deep with one or two rooms on each floor. A small back yard contained a water hydrant, privy, and shed. The extent of crowding is evident in the fact that often two different families shared one house. This crowding along with unsanitary outhouses, dilapidated construction, and limited economic opportunity were largely responsible for a high death rate among alley dwellers.

Alley house construction continued throughout the 1880's and into the 1890's, until a Congressional ban in 1892 halted further construction. It was not until 1897, however, that the city learned of the full extent of alley habitation. In that year, the Police Department was commissioned to make a special census of the alleys. The census reported 237 blocks with one or more inhabited alleys in the Federal City section exclusive of Georgetown and the "suburban" areas. The total alley population of the Federal City was 17,244 (11 per cent of the city population), of which 16,046 were black and 1,198 were white. Blacks made up 93 per cent of alley residents, and black alley dwellers accounted for nearly one-fourth of the city's non-white population.[28] And as the proportion of Negro alley residents continued to rise, so too did the levels of segregation with 152 alleys all black and 13 all white.

The spatial locations of alleys continued to follow the earlier patterns. (See Map 3.) The greatest concentration occurred in Southwest, with the Northwest concentration between First and Fifteenth Streets spreading north and west (into the Shaw area) reflecting the construction on both street and alley that had occurred in that area since 1880. As well, the concentration in "Foggy Bottom" began to expand east and north meeting the northwest concentration four blocks north of the White House. Northeast and Southeast also witnessed some alley

---

[26] Washington *Post*. December 27, 1877, 3.

[27] These photographs not only show the basic facade of alley houses but also suggest the communal nature of many of these "hidden" alley neighborhoods. Many of Lewis Hine's alley photographs, of which the "1908—Purdy's Court" is only one example, revealed high levels of personal interaction among alley residents. Gordon Park's photographs of Washington alleys also documents this neighboring for a later period.

[28] Commissioners of the District of Columbia, *Annual Report—1897* (Washington, 1897), 195–202.

development, but most alleys here had smaller populations and were more widely dispersed.

The police census of 1897, however, is not entirely satisfactory. Undoubtedly its estimate was conservative. Many police, according to folklore, were afraid to enter the alleys alone and even when accompanied by reinforcements they generally kept their "pistols at the ready". Secondly, many alley dwellers had little love or affection for the police, or reputedly, for any stranger in their alley, so that gaining accurate information could not have been very easy, if in some cases it was even possible. For example, a special agent for the Department of Labor concluded after an intensive study of 13 alleys in the preceding year: "I have no doubt that lodgers are harbored in these alleys whose presence . . . is always concealed." [29] Similarly, Charles Weller, Secretary of the Associated Charities, concluded that the census did "not inspire him with confidence as to its accuracy." [30]

Another approach to alley enumeration was made by the Monday Evening Club in 1912, when it compiled a "Directory of Alleys" in an effort to publicize the "hidden" communities "menacing" the city. They found 240 blocks with inhabited alleys in the Federal City, and 3,102 alley houses.[31] Since alley dwelling construction had ceased in 1892, there was little change in the general spatial organization of the alleys. (See Map 4.) There were, however, three more alleys reported in 1912 than in 1897, and some change in location among smaller alleys.[32]

These latter two maps (3 and 4) probably represent the high water mark for alley dwellings in Washington. The 1897 police census reported the total alley population to be just over 19,000, while the Monday Evening Club estimated it at about 16,000 in 1912. But a number of forces were at work that began slowly to diminish the size and extent of inhabited alleys.

The most obvious force seeking to remove alley housing came from government officials and reformers. The conditions in alleys had not gone unheeded by health officials. From 1873 until its abolition in 1877, the Board of Health condemned 958 alley shanties of which nearly 300 were demolished.[33] Governmental reorganization in 1878

---

[29] Clare de Graffenried, "Typical Alley Houses in Washington," *The Woman's Anthropological Society Bulletin*, 7 (November 14, 1896), 12.

[30] Charles Weller, *Neglected Neighbors* (Philadelphia, 1909), 11–12.

[31] The entire District of Columbia had 270 alleys with 3,337 houses. Monday Evening Club, *Directory of Inhabited Alleys of Washington, D.C.* (Washington, 1912).

[32] This movement reflected one of the continuous problems of alley enumeration: the tendency for alleys with smaller populations to disappear or appear as the result of a move by one or two families from one alley to another.

[33] Board of Health, *Annual Report—1877*, 47.

1897

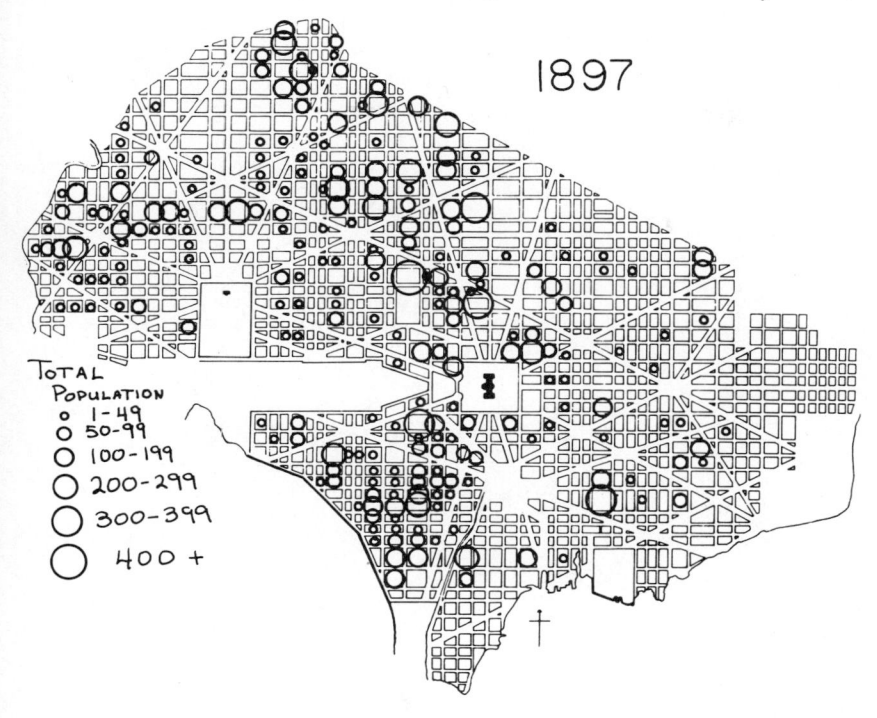

TOTAL POPULATION
o 1-49
o 50-99
O 100-199
O 200-299
O 300-399
O 400+

By the author from the 1897 Annual Report
of the Commissioners of the District of Columbia

Map 3. Inhabited Alleys by Total Population, 1897.

and 1879, however, failed to give the health officer the power of condemnation held earlier by the Board. Without such power, little could be done about unsound and unsanitary alley houses.

In 1892, Congress did prohibit further housing construction on alleys less than thirty feet wide and not provided with sewers, water mains, and light. No construction was to be permitted on the interior "blind" alleys. Although the Commissioners were given the power to convert such blind alleys into minor streets, insufficient funds and complicated legal actions made implementation virtually impossible.[34]

Beginning in 1894, a number of reform-minded citizen groups began actively propagandizing for the abolition of all alley housing either by destruction or by the opening up of blind alleys. Reformers argued that alleys were dangerous not only for health reasons, but because the alleys were "hidden communities" which bred conditions of vice, crime and immorality.

---
[34] Swinney, "Alley Dwellings and Housing Reform," 23–27.

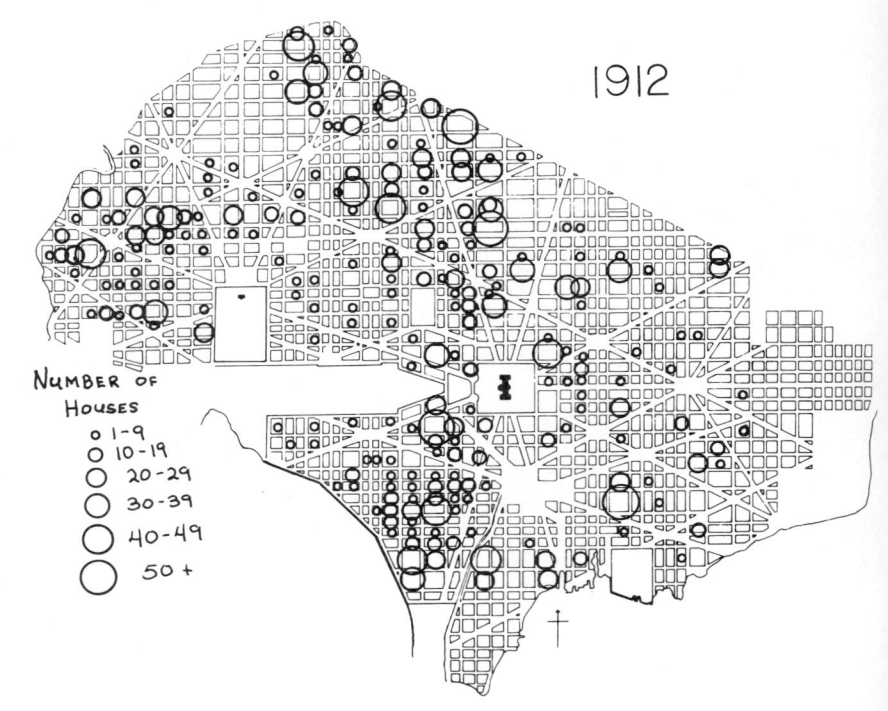

By the author from the Monday Evening Club, "Directory of Inhabited Alleys of Washington, D.C."

Map 4. Inhabited Alleys by Number of Houses, 1912.

In 1904, reformers brought Jacob Riis to Washington to visit the alleys and report his findings to Congress. Riis's report, coupled with a major publicity campaign to expose the alley evils, won over President Theodore Roosevelt. Addressing Congress in 1904, Roosevelt urged a systematic study of the alleys and concluded that the "hidden residential alleys are breeding grounds of vice and disease and should be opened into minor streets." [35]

Few alleys were converted, but the reformers' agitation was rewarded two-fold with the restoration of condemnation powers and the appointment of the President's Homes Commission. With these successes, the reform movement dissipated temporarily and even the publication of the Commission's reports in 1908 failed to revive any interest. The Board for Condemnation of Insanitary Buildings did, however, have an impact on the alleys. From the time of its creation

---

[35] Theodore Roosevelt, *State Papers as Governor and President* (New York, 1926), 229.

The Rise and Fall of Washington's Inhabited Alleys 281

in 1906 to 1911, the Board reported 375 houses destroyed and 315 repaired.[36]

By 1911, the housing reform movement was again active with publicity campaigns that surpassed even those of 1900 to 1906. This time reformers were able to gain conversion of one major alley. Congress appropriated $78,000 to clear and reclaim Willow Tree Alley, Southwest (Square 534). This alley, one of the largest and most "notorious" in the city, was converted into an interior playground. By 1914, the movement reached its peak having enlisted the "best" of Washington society to make a "grand tour" of the alleys. Ellen Wilson led some of these "tours" and actively sought passage of legislation ending alley dwelling. Her deathbed request was in great part responsible for the passage of such legislation, which was to go into effect on July 1, 1918. World War I and the housing shortage brought on by it, however, led to the postponing of the provision. After the war, Congress passed further extensions on the deadline and the legislation was finally emasculated in 1927 by an adverse court ruling.

Thus, despite more than twenty years of vigorous reform efforts to abolish alley housing, little had been accomplished. Although police census statistics showed a one-third decline in alley population between 1897 and 1913, few considered this to be an accurate reporting of alley dwellers.[37] In spite of the relative ineffectiveness of the reform movement, a survey of alleys in Northwest and Southwest in 1927 did show a substantial decrease in the number of alley buildings used for residential purposes. (See Map 5.) While only 26 new houses had been added in the 15 years, 868 were no longer used as dwellings. Nearly 40 per cent of the houses, then, had been removed from the housing market largely due to forces other than those related to the reform movement.[38]

One of these forces was challenging alley houses long before 1912. A sample study of changing land use in six northwest alleys from 1888 to 1904 suggests that alley housing was barely holding its own against other land uses. While houses increased 7 per cent, stables increased by 16 per cent and warehouses, shops and businesses by 314 per cent.[39] Business demands on alley property, of course, varied greatly depending on an alley's proximity and accessibility to business needs. Al-

---

[36] Thomas Jesse Jones, "The Alley Homes of Washington," *Survey*, 28 (October 19, 1912), 68.
[37] Commissioners of the District of Columbia, *Annual Report—1913*, III (Washington, 1914), 8.
[38] Jones, *The Housing of Negroes*, 161–165.
[39] Borchert, "Race and Place," 19–20.

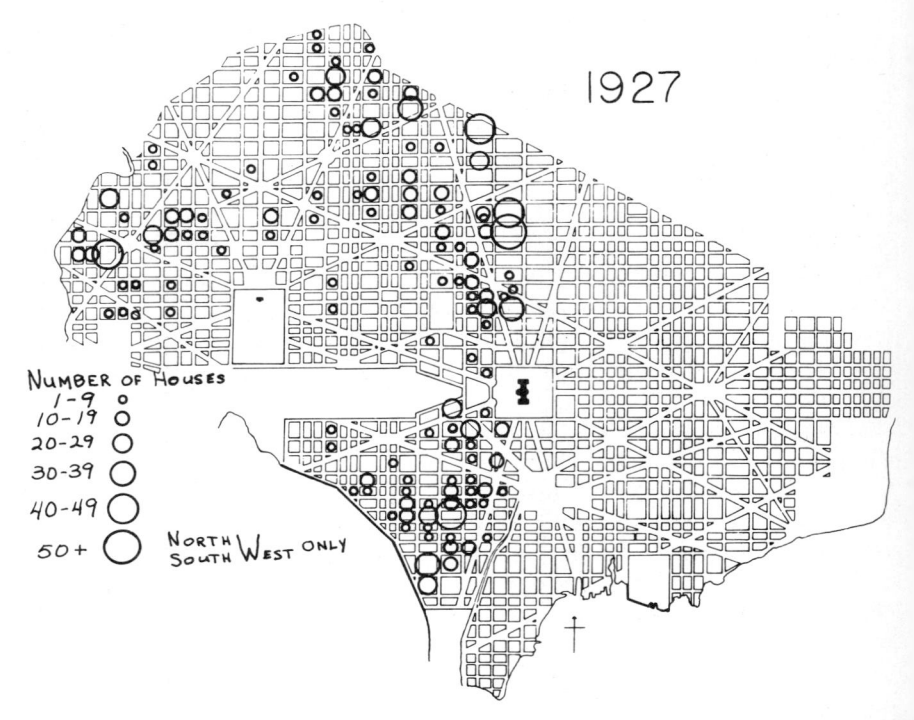

By the author from William Henry Jones, "The Housing of Negroes in Washington, D.C."

Map 5. Inhabited Alleys of Northwest and Southwest Washington by Number of Houses, 1927.

though business demands on alley property were as yet relatively small, they were steadily increasing.

A comparison of land use between 1904 and 1928 for 9 sample alley blocks confirms this increasing intrusion of business uses on alley dwellings. It also reveals another incursion of even more importance. Inconsequential in 1904, automobile garages in 1928 were a major factor in the alleys. While dwellings in the 9 sample blocks decreased 50 per cent and stables all but disappeared, garages increased from 0 to 244. Certainly not all the former residences became garages but a substantial number did. In the case of Blagdon Alley, for example, business use took over 15 houses and garages 27. Only 15 houses of the 57 dwellings of 1904 were inhabited in 1928.[40] (See Block Maps 1 and 2.)

[40] Five of the sample blocks were from Northwest, two from Southwest, and one each from Northeast and Southeast. Sanborn Map Publishing Company, *Insurance Maps of*

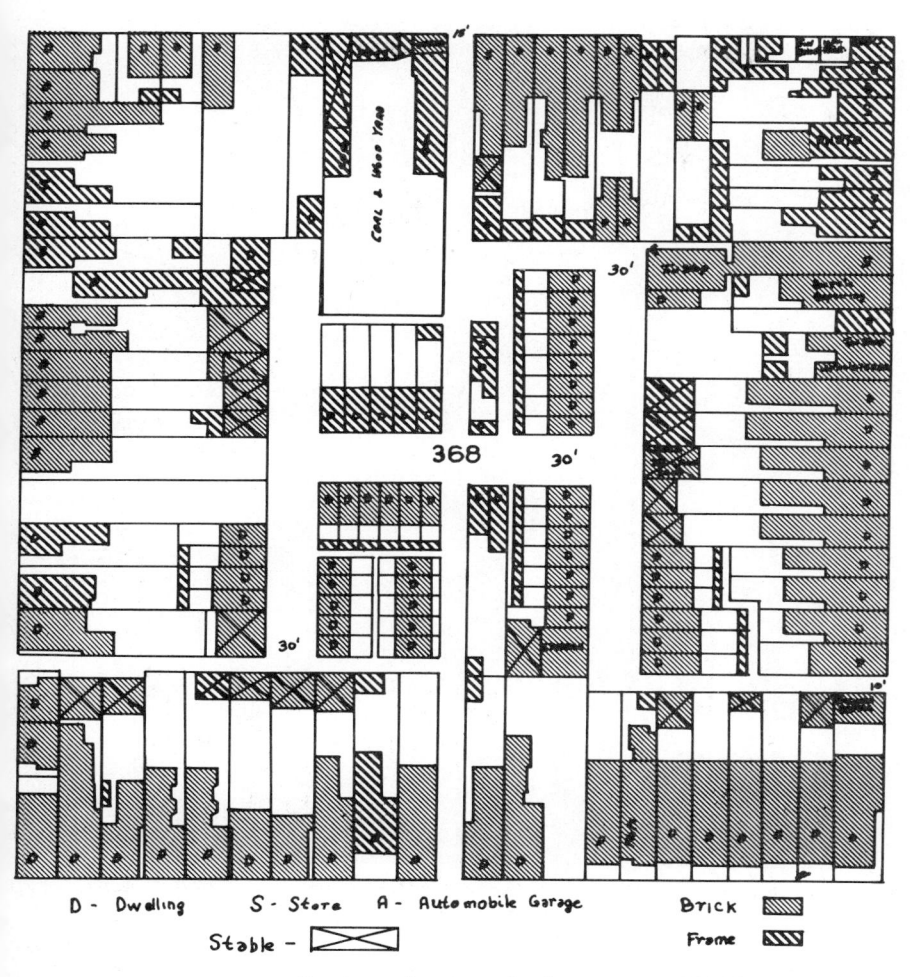

D - Dwelling   S - Store   A - Automobile Garage   Brick
Stable -   Frame

By the author from Sanborn Map Publishing Company, "Insurance Maps of Washington, D.C.," I.

Block Map 1. Square 368, Blagdon Alley, Northwest, 1904.

Where the progressive housing reformers largely failed, business and especially Henry Ford's inexpensive automobile were inadvertently successful in removing many, though far from all, alley houses. But there were other factors, less obtrusive and more difficult to document, that came into play to help sound retreat for the inhabited al-

---

Washington, D.C., I, II (New York, 1904); and *Insurance Maps of Washington, D.C.,* I, II, IV (Pelham, New York, 1928).

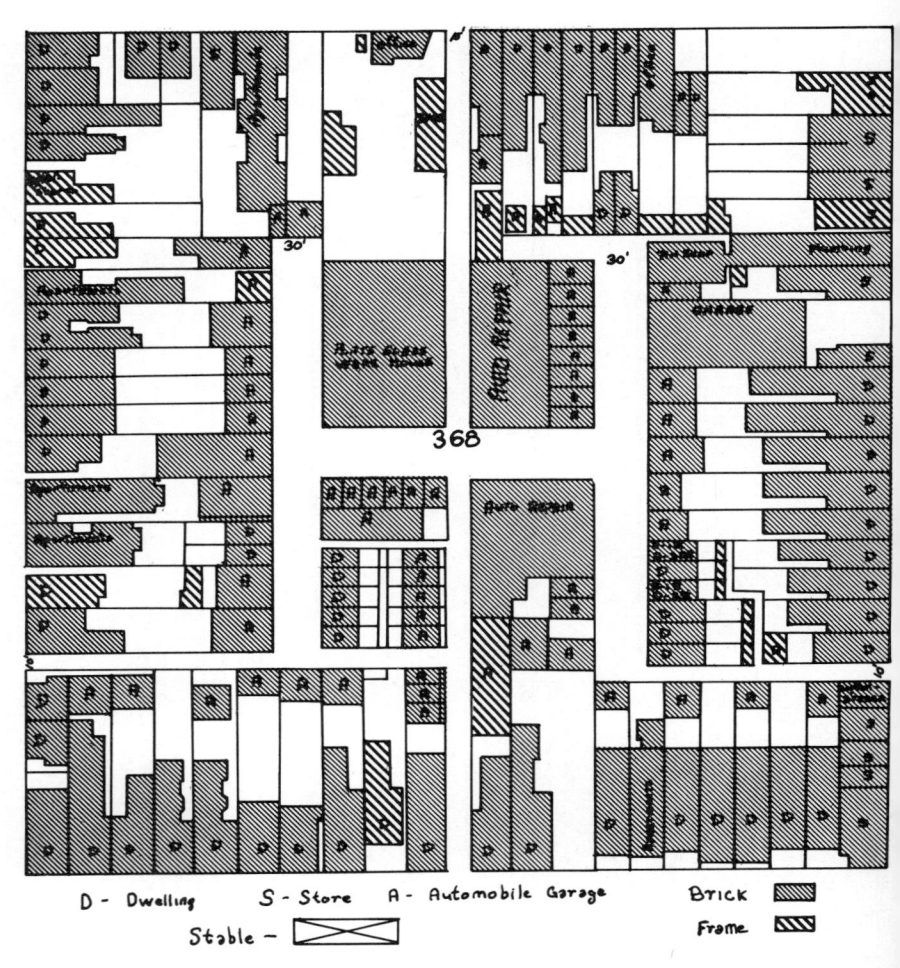

By the author from Sanborn Map Company, Inc.,
"Insurance Maps of Washington, D.C.-1928," I.

Block Map 2. Square 368, Blagdon Alley, Northwest, 1928.

leys. At the time Congress was banning further alley house construction in 1892, city trolley construction was already underway. Offering an inexpensive and efficient means of transportation, the trolley was the beginning of a release mechanism for the concentrated population of the pedestrian city.[41] As the trolley began to permit population

---

[41] Constance McLaughlin Green, *Washington: Capital City* (Princeton, N.J., 1963), 50.

dispersal, the pressure that helped create alley housing was released. At the same time housing was made available on the street as former city residents vacated their homes in the city for homes in the "suburbs". As the automobile came into wider use in the 1920's, the potential for an even greater exodus was established. Thus, the alley dwelling, a product of the pedestrian city, became an anachronism in the "trolley and automobile" city of the Twentieth Century.

The alley dwelling was an anachronism in other ways as well. While the compact, concentrated walking city of the Nineteenth Century "tolerated" the "mini-alley-ghettoes" within its blocks, the Twentieth Century "city beautiful" thrived on order, separation, and segregation

Library of Congress
Farm Security Administration Collection

Photograph 3. An Alley in Southwest Washington, November 1942, photograph by Gordon Parks.

Photograph by the author

Photograph 4. Terrace Court, Northeast, restored alley houses, July 1972.

of functions and people. The alley, then, became a threat to that new social consciousness and as a result "had" to be removed.[42]

Anachronisms, however, do not always disappear merely because they are anachronisms. And this was the case with alley dwellings. Although the number of houses had decreased by nearly 40 per cent by 1927, 1,346 alley houses remained occupied in Northwest and Southwest alone.[43]

With the depression, New Deal reform leaders again sought the removal of alley housing. In 1934, Congress created the Alley Dwelling Authority "to provide for the discontinuance of the use as dwellings of the buildings situated in alleys in the District of Columbia." [44]

---

[42] For an excellent discussion of the rise of "maxi-ghettoes" in Washington see Paul A. Groves and Edward K. Muller, "A Preliminary Enquiry into the Emergence of Negro Ghettoes: The Comparative Analysis of Washington, D.C. and Baltimore in the Late Nineteenth Century," (an unpublished paper presented at the Annual Meeting of the Association of American Geographers, Kansas City, April 24, 1972).

[43] Jones, *The Housing of Negroes*, 161–165.

[44] *U. S. Statutes at Large*, XLVIII, Part I (June 12, 1934), 930.

The Rise and Fall of Washington's Inhabited Alleys 287

Under the Alley Dwelling Authority, no alley houses were to be inhabited after July 1, 1944. Despite legal entanglements and limited funds, the Alley Dwelling Authority did make considerable progress in opening a number of alleys and "rejuvenating" the old dwellings. But as with the earlier reform movement, World War II and the resulting housing shortage postponed enforcement of the ban until 1955.

The changes in transportation that in great part made alley dwellings anachronistic conversely insured their survival, albeit on a small scale. As suburban tracts, based on automobile commuting, reached out farther and farther from the city during the late 1940's and early 1950's, a counter movement, small but distinguishable, began to flow back into the city. The movement to restore Georgetown began in the 1930's, and by the late 1940's and 1950's this small scale urban "restor-

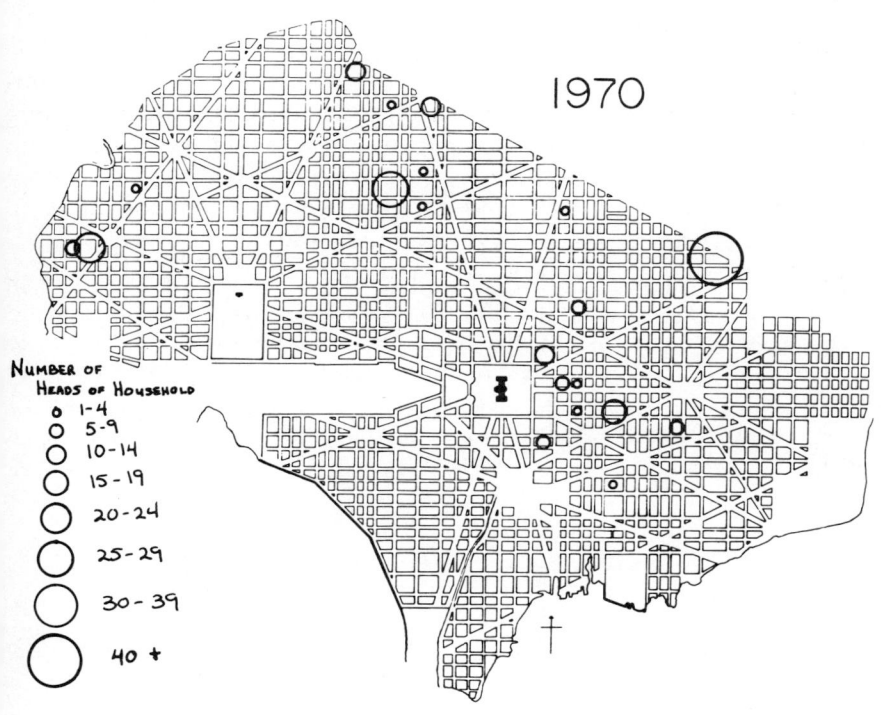

By the author from R. L. Polk, "Polk's Washington, D.C. Directory-1970"

Map 6. Inhabited Alleys by Heads of Household, 1970 (includes vacant houses).

ation" had begun on Capitol Hill and "Foggy Bottom". In 1954, citizens' groups involved in the restoration movement were successful in repealing the ban on alley dwelling that was to go into effect the following year, thus saving the former "slum" houses, which were renamed "coach-houses". (See photograph of "restored" Terrace Court, Northeast.)

By 1970, there remained at least 20 inhabited alleys, with 192 heads of household reported in the city directory. Forty-two houses were listed as vacant. (See Map 6.) Although some alleys in the Northwest and Northeast remained essentially the same as earlier alleys in socio-economic status, others in "Foggy Bottom" and on Capitol Hill have changed considerably. Unskilled workers, who once accounted for the majority of employed alley dwellers, made up only seven per cent in 1970, while professionals made up nine per cent.[45]

Thus, alley dwellings that began in Washington about 120 years ago as housing for laboring class whites, and which became "mini-ghettoes" for black residents for nearly a century following the Civil War, have become, for the most part, an expensive and highly sought-after residence for affluent Washingtonians. This is an ironic ending to the efforts of two First Ladies and countless reformers. Perhaps the greatest irony is that in 1970, two United States Senators and three members of the House of Representatives were residents of the same alleys Jacob Riis had warned Congress of in 1904:

> There is nothing good in that kind of alley. The people who live in there are as far off from the life that goes on outside as though they did not belong to you. . . . What ever standard you set up to live by and to live up to, they do not have. They can do almost as they please in there.[46]

[45] R. L. Polk, *Polk's Washington, D.C. City Directory, 1970* (Washington, 1970).
[46] Jacob Riis, "The Housing Problem Facing Congress," *Charities*, 12 (February 6, 1904), 163.

A Toast to the Union: Clark Mills' Equestrian Statue of Andrew Jackson in Lafayette Square

ANDREW S. KECK

Midway in the Nineteenth Century was a period of excited pride and daring promise in the United States of America. In 1850, California was admitted to the Union; two years later, Commodore Matthew C. Perry, by order of the Government of the United States, led a squadron of Navy ships through the China Seas to Japan in the hope, expressed by President Millard Fillmore, that the United States and Japan should live in friendship. The pioneer spirit had carried Democracy far and wide over land and sea. It remained for this same spirit to produce artists who would express the significance, even if only vaguely understood, of Democracy. Romanticism, then at its peak, was bound to affect these artists and make the task of finding explicit meanings in their products difficult for future critics. Such was the case, in general, along the eastern seaboard and, in particular, in the District of Columbia where daring schemes for expressing the American spirit in art were finding fulfillment. In 1850, Congress decided to enlarge the Capitol by the addition of two wings and to crown it with a lofty soaring dome. The architect, Thomas U. Walter, took several ideas for his dome from those of St. Paul's in London and of the Invalides in Paris; but he made no serious attempt to emulate the Baroque effects of unity and climax in his models. He had other ambitions for his dome: it was to rise above the old foundations as a great symbol of the Federal Union and Freedom. To this end it was to have thirty-six columns in its peristyle to signify the number of states in the Union when it was completed, and thirteen columns around its lantern in obvious reference to the original colonies. Above all was to stand a statue of

---

An essay read before a meeting of the Literary Society of Washington, D. C. on February 15, 1969; the host for the meeting, held at the National Geographic Society, was Melville Bell Grosvenor.

Freedom. Seen from the Mall, the dome would present an impressive silhouette and furnish an effective backdrop for romantic associations of national grandeur. While Walter was making these plans, a great obelisk was being erected as a memorial to George Washington. Few if any inquired into the reasons for associating an ancient Egyptian symbol of the Sun with the Father of Our Country. It was enough that the monument should attain a height more than five times that of the obelisks in London and Paris and that it should not be an imported monolith but of local construction. Pierre Charles L'Enfant had planned for an equestrian statue of Washington to stand where the obelisk was finally placed. The country had to wait for more than fifty years, from 1792 to 1853, before it could boast that it had an equestrian statue to rival those of the great cities of Europe. When the equestrian statue of Andrew Jackson, the subject of this essay, was erected in 1853, it filled a long-felt want. Although the statue in Lafayette Square was designed and cast by an untrained American who had never seen Jackson or an equestrian statue, it has proved to be a surprisingly successful artistic product of America.

The background of Clark Mills, the sculptor of this statue, his Yankee wit and ingenuity in devising a model for a horse balanced on its hind legs, and the pioneering spirit that led him to erect his own bronze foundry in Bladensburg, all make a fascinating story but would take too long for the telling here. This account will begin with the unveiling of the statue on January 8, 1853, exactly thirty-eight years after Jackson's victory at New Orleans. An American success story had been consummated; no one knew this better than the orator chosen for the inauguration ceremonies, the Honorable Stephen A. Douglas. In the opening paragraphs of his oration he said:[1]

> The statue before you is the work of a man exalted by his enthusiasm for the glorious deeds and wise acts of a hero and statesman. It is the work of a young, untaught American. I cannot call him an artist. He never studied or copied. He never saw an Equestrian Statue, nor even a model.... Proudly may we compare to the Equestrian Statues of Europe that noble Roman figure which preserves the form and features of our hero, and that colossal war-horse in bronze which will bear him in glory through future ages! I have seen delineations of the Equestrian Statues of Peter the Great, of Frederick the Great, and of

---

[1] "Oration of the Hon. Stephen A. Douglas on the Inauguration of the Jackson Statue (1/8/1853)," Washingtoniana Files (A. Jackson statue), Martin Luther King Memorial Library.

Library of Congress

Figure 1. Clark Mills. Equestrian statue of Andrew Jackson.

the Duke of Wellington, which are esteemed, I believe, the best specimens of that description of sculpture that modern Europe has been able to contribute to her collection of works of art. The horse of the great Czar is supported in its rampant position by resting on the hind feet with the aid of an unsightly contrivance of extending between its legs a serpent, which, by a bend in the body, connects with the tail of the steed and is fastened to the pedestal. That of the great Prussian monarch, designed to appear in motion, has one foot before and another behind fixed to the pedestal, a third lifted and supported by a prop to assist in sustaining the weight, and but one left free to give the semblance of life and movement. The rearing steed of the Duke of Wellington maintains its rampant position by the hind legs and tail being riveted to the massive pedestal. What a wonderful triumph has our untaught countryman achieved over these renowned trophies of European art in the hot and fiery charger before you, leaping "so proudly as if he distained the ground", self-poised and self-sustained on the single point whence he derives his motion. No props, no serpents, no unnatural contrivances are here. Nature, which has taught the impetuous steed to poise its weight and gather its strength to spring into the air, has given the genius who fashioned this group the power to impart grace and energy to the finely-balanced attitude, which makes the weight that others prop and hold by rivets furnish to the work its strength and stability.

From these comments it is clear that the accomplishment of balancing the rearing horse commanded the most attention and greatest praise. Yet, upon the unveiling, there were some, according to a newspaper account, who questioned the stability of the statue. To remove doubt on this score, Mills went to the front of the horse and threw his entire weight of 156 pounds on the forelegs. The statue stood securely. Mills had answered the sceptics. But he was not then, or later, called upon to defend his design, nor to state the message he was trying to convey with his rearing horse and its rider who lifts his hat high above his head. Evidently the country of Mills' day was content to accept the statue without questioning its artistic merits and without wondering about its expressive content. These matters became the concern of a later day, particularly of the 1920's, when art historians and critics of sculpture found the statue lacking in design and deficient in modelling. Lorado Taft, author of a standard history of American sculpture, and himself a sculptor, wrote of the work:[2]

> Who begrudges to-day to this brave pioneer his little meed of success? Let us hope that he never became conscious of his defects. No one of that first generation is more completely the machinist. His grasp of his subject is a purely mechanical one; his motif in the statue a problem in equilibrium. Having no notion, nor even suspicion, of dignified sculptural treatment of a theme, the clever carpenter felt nevertheless the need of a "feature". Perhaps he had heard of "action"! Possibly he had seen an engraving of Palconet's Peter the Great. At any rate, he built a colossal horse, adroitly balanced in the hind legs; and America gazed with bated breath. Nobody knows or cares whether the rider looks like Jackson or not; the extraordinary pose of the horse absorbs all attention, all admiration. There may be some subconscious feeling of respect for the rider who holds on so well, but in spite of his frank efforts to call attention to himself, the appeal is as meagre as his personal charm, as precarious as his seat.

A second criticism of the 1920's chosen for inclusion here is that of Charles Rufus Morey who dismissed Mills and the statue more bluntly in his book *The American Spirit in Art*:[3]

---
[2] Lorado Taft, *The History of American Sculpture*, New York, 1930, p. 127.
[3] Charles Rufus Morey, *The American Spirit in Art*, New Haven, 1927, p. 183.

He has at least the distinction of creating both our first and worst equestrian monument. The tour de force of balancing the defender of New Orleans so gallantly upon his rearing steed absorbed the craftsman's small creative ability; Mills was a caster rather than a modeler, giving the same metallic texture to Jackson's head, the horse's hide, and the holsters, hat and stirrups.

More than a full generation has passed since these critics of the Old Guard, if so they may be called, passed judgment on the statue in Lafayette Square. Perhaps the time has come to reevaluate it, this time by viewing it as a product of its own time and not that of Peter the Great. This will call for a brief historical survey of equestrian statues of more than life size standing in the round with the horse rearing on its hind legs. There are few examples. The motif of the rearing horse appears in ancient Greece and Rome, and continues into Byzantine art, but always in relief work and never, so far as I know, in the round. Also the motif in these early representations always features a cowering victim or a cringing supplicant under the raised forelegs of the horse. Not until the Seventeenth Century in Europe did the motif find its ways into sculpture. The Baroque period with its predilection for open forms and action released into space contributed the motif to art. As might have been expected, it was in Italy that the advance was made. It took the combination of a brilliant painter, a highly trained sculptor, and a world-famous scientist to bring it off.

Velazquez was the painter, Picetro Tacca the sculptor, and the scientist was Galileo; the subject, Philip IV, King of Spain. The commission called for a portrayal of the monarch in the act of accomplishing one of the exercises of the Spanish Riding School in which the horse's hind legs are almost straight in the instant before he leaps in the air. A Velazquez painting, such as that of Philip's son, Don Carlos, was the model for Tacca. The bronze equestrian statue in Madrid reveals the degree of success attained by the sculptor. The difficulties in casting a work of this design and of securing it to a foundation were, of course, immense. Here Tacca was fortunate to have help from the enormously inventive Galileo. Ludwig Heydenreich, from whom I take this point, has written:[4]

> It was Galileo who finally devised the technical construction by means of which the static difficulties in the erection of Tacca's Philip IV were overcome. This construction consisted of a metal base, built into the pedestal, and acting as a counterweight to the statue.

---

[4] Ludwig Heydenreich, *Leonardo da Vinci*, New York, 1954, p. 66.

The University Prints

Figure 2. Pietro Tacca. Equestrian statue of Philip IV. Plaza de Oriente, Madrid.

The statue is a tremendous tour de force. It met with undivided praise when it was unveiled in 1642. But it can be severely criticized as an interpretative portrait. Philip thrusts out his baton of command, throws back his head in triumph, but the effect is not convincing. For the Spanish king is not shown as a ruler of men but as a groom guiding his mount through an exercise. It is the disciplined, graceful horse which steals the show. It would take a far greater sculptor than Tacca to portray an individual astride a rearing horse and design a composition to bring out the character of the rider and his role in life.

The problems of designing and executing an equestrian statue in the round of monumental size with rearing horse were mastered by Gian Lorenzo Bernini, the outstanding artist of the Seventeenth Century in Europe. His statue of Louis XIV, carved in brittle marble, had a fateful history too long to be told here. When it reached Versailles in 1685, Louis took a deep aversion to it, had it transformed into the likeness of another man, and consigned it to a distant corner of the palace gardens. A model in terracotta, standing only thirty inches high, gives a good idea of the original statue seen at close range. Louis, symbolically linked by the artist with Hercules, has reached the summit of the steep hill of virtue and glory. The horse's forelegs are free in space, his hind legs drawn forward toward the middle of the body which rests on a moulded block of marble made to appear as a pillow, or, better still, as a spring to raise the horse even higher. One's attention does not remain with this feature, however, for Bernini so designed the work that the observer's eye is drawn to the head of Louis, the climax of the composition. Just as Louis was the climactic figure in an absolutist scheme of government with myriad parts, so Louis' head is the feature to which all the sculptured parts lead. The work is a marvel of naturalism with the bodies of horse and rider closely approximating natural forms. Bernini's stated aim was to make Louis appear as the embodiment of majesty and command. That he succeeds is due to the masterly way Louis subdues his spirited steed, and with an imperious gesture commands the invisible troops he is leading. His baton, grasped firmly in his right hand, describes an arc as it passes through the air from right to left. The recoil of the horse's head helps to establish this path of movement, effectively counterbalancing the forward movement of the horse. The energies displayed find release in Louis' head and in the Baroque surrounding space.

Only one equestrian statue patterned after that of Bernini achieved distinction in the Eighteenth Century. This is the statue of Peter

From "Gian Lorenzo Bernini, the Sculptor of the Roman Baroque" by Rudolf Wittkower, London, 1955

Figure 3. Bernini. Model for equestrian statue of Louis XIV.

the Great commissioned of Etienne Falconet by the Empress Catherine the Great and erected in St. Petersburg in 1782. Catherine had her illustrious predecessor portrayed not as a warrior but as the benefactor through whom European civilization was introduced into Russia. Rather than holding a baton, Peter's right hand is turned palm down as if blessing the ground and the city he founded. The results of two centuries of scientific study of physical anatomy came to fruition in the life-like quality of horse and rider and in the all-pervasive movement. Details are carefully controlled and surface textures are clearly differentiated. The Seventeenth Century Baroque insistence on a split moment of time is tempered to become a generalized time; movement flows gently and steadily through the entire composition. The flow of movement, probably suggested by a painting by Rubens, makes this one of the greatest equestrian statues of all time. Movement begins in the massive block of granite imported from Finland. There are no straight lines in the outline of this block, nor flat planes in its surface. From the pedestal, movement continues through the serpent into the horse and upward to the head of Peter. The horse seems to have mounted the block of granite with ease and to poise on its summit without strain. The huge frame of Peter is supported securely on the strong steed provided for him.

The Baroque effect of free action in space is achieved in the statues we have discussed through extraneous aids, such as Galileo's counterweight, Bernini's cushion, Falconet's serpent. Clark Mills, whose goal was a commanding silhouette, could do without these devices since he was not concerned with imparting a flow of easy movement to his statue. No one would claim that the statue of Andrew Jackson is a great work of art to be compared with the Peter the Great; but anyone can see that it would be helped, when observed at close range, by sharing some of the naturalistic properties stressed in the European statues. A better control of facts would substantially aid the representation artistically. Mills put too much emphasis, for instance, on the bridle reins and included two cinch belts where one would have sufficed to suggest the volume of the horse's fore-quarters. A better modelling of anatomy would have made the statue more acceptable. But if his Andrew Jackson was designed to be seen at a distance as an impressive silhouette, as I believe it was, then these assets would only indirectly improve it. It should also be kept in mind, in comparing the American statue with European statues, that Clark Mills was not called upon to evoke the spirit behind the representations of a Spanish king, a French absolute monarch, or an

The University Prints

Figure 4. Falconet. Equestrian statue of Peter the Great. Leningrad.

Figure 5. Clark Mills. Equestrian statue of Andrew Jackson.

Eighteenth Century Russian despot. His task was to present to an uncritical public a military hero who was a man of the people and their champion against aristocracy and privilege. Democracy and Equality were to be celebrated in this country in 1850 and not Autocracy and Hierarchy. It is to the great credit of Clark Mills that he was sensitive to the spirit of his country and found the means to express its ideals as well as he did. His statue must be judged not in terms of the Seventeenth Century but in those of his own day, the Nineteenth Century.

By 1850, the Romantic movement had been felt in this country for more than fifty years. It had dictated the style of our first Capitol with its low, squat dome like that of the Pantheon in ancient Rome; it suggested the octastyle doric temple fronts, like those of the Parthenon in ancient Greece, in the Patent Office building, now the home of the National Portrait Gallery. In Clark Mills' day, Romanticism affected the design of the Smithsonian Institution building with its north entrance patterned after the facade of the abbey church of St. Denis in Twelfth Century Paris. When one asks why the architect should have seen fit to associate medieval monasticism with the scientific building he was called upon to design, the answer can only be that he was swept along in the same romantic tide of vague idealization which I have already mentioned in connection with the Washington Monument. Clark Mills was caught in the same tide, but to what extent remains to be seen. Perhaps a brief examination of European representations of equestrian statues of the early Nineteenth Century will aid in this.

The Romantic movement, begun in England about the year 1760, soon spread to the continent. The visual arts in France had been sufficiently affected by the year 1800 to touch Jacques Louis David, painter of the Napoleonic period. When David told Napoleon that he wished to paint him sword in hand as he had appeared to his victorious Italian campaign, Napoleon is said to have replied:[5] "No, it is not with the sword that battles are won; paint me calm and serene on a fiery steed." David complied with a painting, measuring some 5 by 7 feet, to be seen today at Versailles. Napoleon is crossing the Alps through the little St. Bernard pass. Everything is done to dramatize the event and Napoleon's role in it. His name is traced in the snow, or rather carved imperishably in rock beneath the snow. With it are the names of Hannibal and Karolus Magnus, his two predecessors as transalpine conquerors. In the distance can be made out cannon left behind because of the difficulties of the crossing. But Napoleon goes on. For the moment, Nature aids him as a strong wind blowing from the rear propels him onto the summit. It sends the hero's cloak billowing around him; the tail and mane of his horse fly forward. This arresting silhouette dominates the painting. Napoleon's face is not the climax, for David has painted him calm and serene on a fiery steed, according to instructions, even though it is known that Napoleon made the crossing astride a surefooted mule. As Romanticism began, it was not truth that counted, but excitement.

Clark Mills was sensitive to the demands of Romanticism when he designed his bronze equestrian statue of George Washington, commissioned by Congress and unveiled in 1860. The wind blows fiercely through Washington Circle as it had on the Alps, sending the horse's tail and mane flying forward. Again Nature plays her

---

[5] William Fleming, *Arts and Ideas*, New York, 1955, p. 618.

Braun photograph No. 13533

Figure 6. Jacques Louis David. Napoleon crossing the Alps. Versailles Palace.

role, but only to send the horse trotting eastward on Pennsylvania Avenue at a clip too fast to suit the rider who reins in. Evidently the sculptor was trying valiantly to capture the effects so readily attained by David, the painter. It was of no avail that a wild horse

Library of Congress

Figure 7. Clark Mills. Equestrian statue of George Washington. Washington Circle, Washington, D. C. Lithograph by E. Sachse, Baltimore, about 1866.

captured on the plains near Fort Leavenworth, Kansas, served as model for Washington's steed. The excitement is lacking, and Clark Mills may be said to have failed in his attempt at Romanticism. The statue, nevertheless, shows Mills' propensities; these had been held in greater check when he designed his portrait of Andrew Jackson ten years previously.

Mills must have been guided in fashioning his equestrian statue of Jackson by reproductions of romantic paintings or by small romantic sketches imported from abroad. From these he probably got his idea of portraying Jackson on a rearing horse. For French romantic painters, Theodore Gericault in particular, were finding that they could work desired effects by reviving the Baroque motif of rearing horse and rider. In 1812, Gericault submitted to the Salon in Paris a large painting of an Officer of the Imperial Guard said to have been painted with characteristic romantic excess in twelve days. Critics sniped at its bad drawing. The primary concern of the artist, however, was not detailed surface treatment but a striking silhouette. This he achieved. The rider turns a full 180 degrees as he brandishes his sabre and brings into danger everything within the arc of its swing, including the horse's tail. The Rhode Island School of Design has a small oil sketch of this painting. It is superior, it seems to me, in its romantic qualities for everything is sacrificed to the silhouette: details of texture and surface are sloughed over, the face of the rider obscured. The gesture of the threatening sabre is the principal note struck in this bravura performance. Seeing it, one is made to realize that a work of art depicting a warrior mounted on a rearing horse is most truly romantic when the motif of a brandished sword is featured. The motif appealed so greatly to Francois Rude, the most romantic of sculptors, that he applied it even in a standing figure, as in his portrait of the commanding general of the Old Guard at Waterloo, Marshal Ney. It follows from this that the equestrian statue of Andrew Jackson is not a romantic work in full degree in spite of the rearing horse. How then is the statue to be regarded?

Instead of holding his sword on high, Jackson lifts his hat. The expressive content of the statue, its message, must be couched in this gesture of the raised hat. What did Mills intend to communicate with this novel motif? What facets of Jackson's character did he aim to interpret with it? The standard interpretation of the statue in Lafayette Square is that General Jackson is leading his troops to victory at New Orleans. It is difficult to accept the gesture as one Jackson would have made in order to incite his men to battle ardor. Did he have a presentiment that fewer than fourteen of his men would

Braun photograph No. 10340

Figure 8. Gericault. Officer of the Imperial Guard. Louvre, Paris.

*From "Gericault and His Works" by Klaus Berger,
University of Kansas Press, Lawrence, 1955*

Figure 9. Gericault. Oil sketch of Officer of the Imperial Guard. Rhode Island School of Design, Providence.

Library of Congress

Figure 10. Clark Mills. Equestrian statue of Andrew Jackson.

be killed that day? Certainly it is not a martial gesture and yet the view persists that the statue is a memorial to a man who was only a fighting man. The knowledge that the metal for the statue came from cannon Jackson captured from the British may account for the common misconception. The simulated spiked gunbarrel fence, imitating those at 28th and P Streets in Georgetown, is similarly misleading. When this ridiculous fence was added, I do not know, but it was not there in 1853. It was undoubtedly set up to discourage vandals; the scabbard has had to be replaced several times. The fence in combination with the baby-blue cannon carriages gives the whole enclosure the look of a play-pen with a rocking horse, the statue has been so dubbed, as the principal toy. No wonder that those who have seen Clark Mills' work in this light have clamored for its removal. In the 1920's such a strong rumor persisted that the statue was to be consigned to another site that President Warren Harding had to assure a Senator from Tennessee that no official action in that direction was contemplated. Opposition to the statue has continued; in the early years of World War II, a prominent official of the government's Metals Reserve Company proposed that if metal statues were to be melted down for armament materials the bronze statue of Andrew Jackson should be the first to be thrown into the furnace.

It must be granted that gunbarrel fence, blue cannon carriages and rearing horse create an aura in which the gesture of the raised hat is made to seem less than dignified. But no one at the time of the unveiling thought so. It will be remembered that Stephen Douglas spoke of the "noble Roman figure" whose horse "leaping so proudly" lent "grace and energy" to the statue. Douglas and his contemporaries realized that the statue was dedicated to both the Army and the People of the United States and that Andrew Jackson was being honored both as General and as President. The gesture of the raised hat can be documented as belonging to Jackson both as victor at New Orleans and as seventh President of the United States.[6] When Old Hickory was given a tumultuous reception by the city of New Orleans following the battle of January 8, 1815, he rode into the Cathedral Square, "his head uncovered," to pass like a Roman conqueror beneath a triumphal arch prepared for the occasion. After winning 56 per cent of the popular vote in the Presidential election of 1828, he responded to the huzzahs of the crowds "by tipping his hat to them." The gesture may also be connected with an event that took place much later in Jackson's career. This hypothesis is based on an inscription carved on the statue's pedestal, at first on its long side, facing south, but now on the western front. This inscription is: OUR FEDERAL UNION IT MUST BE PRESERVED, words spoken by Jackson at a famous dinner of the Democratic Party in 1830 at which John C. Calhoun and supporters of the nullification doctrine were present. Calhoun held that South Carolina had the right to nullify any tariff act passed by the Congress of the United States if the state considered the act to be unconstitutional. Jackson held that liberty and union were inseparable, phrasing his belief in the words that exploded in the face of Calhoun. The seven words of his toast took on the character of a political slogan as they resounded across the country. Their impact was still felt three years later when Jackson, after having been elected President for the second time, toured the eastern seaboard testing the people's response to his continued

[6] Robert Vincent Remini, *Andrew Jackson*, New York, 1966, pp. 73, 105, 120, 138.

Library of Congress

Figure 11. Clark Mills. Equestrian statue of Andrew Jackson. Lithograph by Wagner & McGuigan, Philadelphia, for Casimir Bohn of Washington.

stand against nullification. An eye witness has given a graphic account of his reception by the people, many of whom were seeing him at close range for the first time:[7]

> Those who witnessed any part of the grand tour will never forget the long processions; the crowed roofs and windows; the thundering salutes of artillery; steamboats gay with a thousand flags and streamers; the erect, gray-headed old man, sitting his horse like a centaur, and bowing to the wild hurrahs of the Unterrified with matchless grace.

Clark Mills, almost of voting age at this time, must have been impressed then and later by such descriptions. I think it not too far-fetched to hold that he was prompted somehow to incorporate this view of Andrew Jackson into his statue. In doing so he set himself a much more difficult task than the one Gutson Borglum met when he designed the statue of General Philip Henry Sheridan for Sheridan Circle. Here, if I see it correctly, the sculptor has commemorated only one event in the life of his subject and let it constitute the whole expressive content of the statue. General Sheridan is portrayed at the end of his famous ride from Winchester to Cedar Creek; he had ridden past the ranks of his retreating army and shouted:[8] "Face the other way, boys! We are going back!" With these words he wheeled his horse around as an example to his men. The statue, set low to the ground, is an embodiment of Sheridan's shouted command. The statue of Jackson, in like fashion, I submit, is in part an embodiment of a recited toast: the inscription on the pedestal linking the toast and the raised hat. When Clark Mills attempted to compound in one portrait the essence of military salutes, civilian huzzahs, and a presidential toast, he was giving expression to that vague idealism so characteristic of numerous artistic endeavors at the mid-point of the Nineteenth Century. There was daring promise in his résumé, but it was lost on later times.

Anyone who searches for more or less explicit meaning in a partly romantic statue such as that of Andrew Jackson must, perforce, become guilty himself of vagueness and idealization. I admit to both, particularly in the preceding paragraph and in the one now to come. In the year 1847, a bronze statue of Thomas Jefferson was placed in a circle on the White House lawn directly opposite the Jackson statue. The two Presidents then faced each other across Pennsylvania Avenue in direct confrontation. Jefferson, the author of the Declaration of Independence, and Jackson, the man of the people, were able

---
[7] Ibid.
[8] *Century Dictionary and Cyclopedia,* IX, 1911, p. 925.

The University Prints

Figure 12. Gutzon Borglum. Equestrian statue of General Sheridan. Sheridan Circle, Washington, D. C.

to carry on a dialogue for all to hear. The import of what was said between them, it may be thought, was not lost on spirits sensitive to the significance and meaning of Democracy. Certainly Walt Whitman, who spent the years immediately following the Civil War as a government clerk in Washington, must have listened to the discourse. In my opinion, he stated the real tenor of what was being said in the opening lines of the fourth part of his poem "Thou Mother With Thy Equal Brood":[9]

---
[9] Walt Whitman, *Leaves of Grass*, "Thou Mother With Thy Equal Brood," part 4.

Library of Congress

Figure 13. David d'Angers. Statue of Thomas Jefferson. Rotunda of the Capitol, Washington, D. C.

Library of Congress

Figure 14. Clark Mills. Equestrian statue of Andrew Jackson from the north side showing White House Circle with Jefferson statue. Lithograph by Sindairs for Casimir Bohn of Washington.

Library of Congress

Figure 15. Clark Mills. Equestrian statue of Andrew Jackson from the north side showing cannon carriages.

Sail, sail thy best, ship of Democracy,
Of value is thy freight, 'tis not the Present only,
The Past is also stored in thee,
Thou holdest not the venture of thyself alone, not of the Western continent alone,
Earth's *résumé* entire floats on thy keel . . .

This confrontation between Jefferson and Jackson, so apt and provocative, ended in 1874 when the statue of Jefferson was removed to the Rotunda of the Capitol. The statue of Jackson still stands in its original place in Lafayette Square, inviting passersby to ponder its message. Those who are best prepared to do this are those who see the gallant figure on horseback as his contemporaries saw him: a military hero, a man of the people, a toast to the Union.

Defending Washington during the Civil War

BENJAMIN FRANKLIN COOLING

Mention of defending Washington during the Civil War usually conjures visions of a bedraggled butternut host besieging the Federal City during hot days in July 1864, liberation of a wine cellar in Francis Preston Blair's Silver Spring mansion which somehow affected the Confederate's ability to puncture the Federal defense line, and a restless American President actually under enemy fire for the only time in our history (while in office) upon the parapets of Fort Stevens. Actually, the entire question of guarding the nation's premier city assumes added dimensions whether one treats the subject from today's concept of "deterrence" or in the overall context of continuing concern for Washington and national defense from 1789 to the present.[1]

A column in the Washington *Post* of July 30, 1972, posited the query: "Does Washington Need an ABM?" An accompanying cartoon showed sibling missiles clustered around that arch phallic symbol of our noble city, the Washington Monument, on its green launching pad slightly south of the White House. At the other end of the historical spectrum lies the phenomenon that our Founding Fathers expressed great concern as to the location of the national capital with reference to matters of naval defense. A quaint doggerel penned anonymously in 1789 highlighted such concern in an opening stanza:

O, What a charming thing and pretty,
To have a noble Federal City!
Surpassing in few years to come,
All that history says of Rome;
That ancient seat of arts and wars,
The mother of eternal jars!
Not near old oceans' margin built,

Delivered before the Columbia Historical Society on October 17, 1972.

[1] On the theme of deterrence and Washington's Civil War defenses as well as details of sources, see Benjamin Franklin Cooling, "Civil War Deterrent: Defenses of Washington," *Military Affairs*, XXIX (Winter 1965–66), 164–179.

Where blood by hogsheads may be spilt;
Where ships which vomit smoke and fire,
May force the people to retire;
May set a scampering our patricians,
Cursing all maritime positions.
Besides, all sea port towns, we know,
The floods of horrid vice o'erflow.

Thus this spectrum represents, perhaps, the continuing concern with defending the nation's capital—seat of power, government, the veritable nerve center of the land. We may be sure that the last phase of this saga has not been written even in our own time.[2]

Of course, the irony of the situation emerged in 1814 when the British completely circumvented the naval problem of attacking our capital and entered the District of Columbia by the back door via Bladensburg. Those Founding Fathers of the nation had fretted enough earlier to construct a small, inadequate position, variously called Fort Warburton or Fort Washington, across from Mount Vernon in 1809 and they had worried also about attack from the direction of the Blue Ridge (a threat which dissipated rapidly as the frontier moved westward). But none of this deterred the more sophisticated British who moved ingeniously on Washington by land.[3] Still, this remains another story in itself and somewhat extraneous to the present discussion.

The lessons of 1814 prompted Acting Secretary of War James Monroe and Major Pierre L'Enfant to reconstruct the masonry fort which may be seen today at Fort Washington—at a cost of $426,000. Until 1853 the fort was garrisoned; until 1861 it provided the sole defense of the Federal City (in a formalized sense) and it still pointed toward a nautical threat. But other clouds hovered on the national horizon in the 1850's and they grew steadily more stormy. Washington City slumbered on, naturally, with Congressional debates on the expansion of slavery producing more grist for the town's newspapermen than questions of national defense. Soirees occupied the minds of Washington's elite and oysters continued to titillate the palates of gourmets at Willard's and elsewhere. The rank and file of the city's hoi polloi braved the quagmires of Washington's streets in winter and the dust bowl, rambling cattle and pigs in the summer. An

---

[2] Henry R. Myers, "Does Washington Need an ABM?", Washington *Post,* July 30, 1972, D4; Marshall Smelser, "Naval Considerations in the Location of the National Capital," *Maryland Historical Magazine,* XLXI (1957), 74.

[3] Among the numerous accounts of the burning of Washington a useful work on the subject is Walter Lord, *The Dawn's Early Light* (New York, W. W. Norton, 1972).

abundance of flora as well as fauna caused one waggish Englishman to observe that never had he seen a forest adorned by a city.[4]

Then, suddenly, the secession winter of 1860–1861 was upon the nation. Washington, the city of magnificent distances, became a city on the edge of danger, treason, deceit, political maneuver, uncertainty and apprehension. During the five months between the secession of South Carolina in December 1860 and the arrival of the first volunteer regiments from the North in April 1861, Washington was a city in danger (from within as well as without). In this interval members of the incoming Republican administration—Abraham Lincoln and his close advisers—developed an intense concern about the safety of Washington. After all, it was the symbol of the Union which, in the eyes of at least some politicians, was capable of restoration at that point. Later it emerged as a supply center, staging area, and vast campsite for the collection of volunteers who went forth to restore that Union by force of arms in the guise of the Army of the Potomac. Thus this "symbol" or "sword" and its successful protection conditioned much of the conduct of the Civil War in the eastern theater.

Several factors emerge from the story of defending Washington from 1861 to 1865. On the one hand lies the fact that the Army of the Potomac itself was a protective force with a two-fold mission. It was charged both with the capture of the "rebel" capital at Richmond, or the defeat of Confederate forces defending that city, and with Acting as a covering force for Washington when combined with a series of field fortifications, heavy ordnance, and manpower garrisons. The role of the Army of the Potomac (or its equivalents) remains best understood in the first context from Bull Run to Appomattox. Yet it often found itself laboring under the second mandate. Similarly, the formal defensive system styled "the Defenses of Washington" has often been treated more from its technical aspects than as a viable part of a strategic concept. Washington's defenses can only be understood by a merger of these two institutions in the mind's eye of the reader.

It is always dangerous to separate history artificially into distinct phases. Yet, one phase of the story of defending the Federal City might be styled the "unprotected capital" for, prior to Fort Sumter's fall, Washington's military guard was more an illusion than a reality. Unlike many European capitals, the city never boasted sizeable complements of garrison or parade forces (the picture has since changed considerably). Available fighting forces in the view of Colonel Charles

---

[4] Cited in George T. Ness, "Under the Eagle's Wings: The Army on the Eve of Civil War," unpublished manuscript, 1971, 178.

P. Stone, newly appointed Inspector General for the District of Columbia, comprised 300 to 400 marines at the Marine Barracks, fifty-six officers and men of ordnance at the Washington Arsenal, and a somewhat nebulous militia system (abandoned although not legally abolished with Congress having passed no new law on the subject). Armed volunteers such as the Potomac Light Infantry in Georgetown, the National Rifles, the Washington Light Infantry, and something styled "the National Guard Battalion," were all well armed, yet of somewhat dubious loyalty in some cases (the National Rifles apparently being a hotbed of sedition) and more akin to the fashionable organizations of the 7th New York ilk than crack combat-ready units.[5]

Secretary of the Navy Isaac Toucey in January 1861 had ordered marines to both Fort Washington down the Potomac and Fort McHenry near Baltimore. Commander John A. Dahlgren had concentrated his heavy ordnance for defense of the Washington Navy Yard and even the army was on the move. General in Chief Winfield Scott (much less physically stable than his statue at Sixteenth Street and Massachusetts Avenue today) assigned Stone to organize and drill the District of Columbia militia, a feat which Stone reported accomplished by mid-February with a roster of thirty-three companies of infantry and two of cavalry—and devoid of the dissident elements of the National Rifles.[6] Scott, however, remained suspicious of the citizen soldiers (a mental block which continues to pervade the minds of many of our military professionals even today) and he drew in regular units from Kansas, Louisiana, and Georgia to stiffen the backbone of the militia. The tents of the regulars whitened Capitol Hill and elsewhere and their weather-beaten faces and the clouds of dust raised by their horses comforted the nervous residents, politicians, and administration-elect. Some of the worry was understandable since the New York *Times* and Richmond *Examiner* had carried stories since January that rebellious companies were drilling in Maryland and Virginia destined to prevent the inauguration of the new President in March. The rumor mills of the period worked overtime and the very real question existed whether or not any national government would reside on the banks of the Potomac on March 4, 1861.

Lincoln of course was inaugurated; Fort Sumter came under rebel-

---

[5] Margaret Leech, *Reveille in Washington* (New York, Harper, 1941), 4.

[6] Those elements of the National Rifles with Confederate interests were led across the Potomac and formed a company in the 1st Virginia, C.S.A. They enlisted at Alexandria with a number of other D.C. "volunteers" and were commanded by their prewar captain, F. B. Schaeffer; see Ralph Donnelly, "District of Columbia Confederates," *Military Affairs*, XXIII (Winter 1959–60), 207–208.

lious fire from South Carolina guns; and fears for the safety of Washington took on added significance as on the Potomac March winds gave way to the early daffodils of April. Lincoln's call for volunteers on April 15 fanned the flames of secession to the point that even Maryland entertained notions of associating more formally with her departing sister states to the south. The nation's capital became isolated for a time from the northern part of the old United States. Telegraph communications were severed and railroad bridges were burned north of Baltimore. Visible signs of panic became etched on the faces of the refugees who began to flee the District and business came to a virtual standstill in some quarters. The 6th Massachusetts clashed openly with secessionists in the streets of Baltimore and Lincoln ordered Dahlgren to hold the Anacostia bridge and guard the river approaches to Washington.

Scott and Stone tried to calm Lincoln and the cabinet as best they could and they did have a last ditch defense plan in mind. The subordinate officer proposed to defend three centers within the city; the city; the Capitol, City Hall hill, and the Executive Square.[7] Scott disagreed, claiming three centers to be excessive. He favored concentration at the Executive Square, where, with the Treasury building acting as a citadel, even the President and his cabinet could take refuge in the last extremity. The plan was never used for news cheered the city on April 24 that three volunteer regiments from the north had skirted Baltimore and landed at Annapolis with the help of the navy.[8] On the following day, the shouts of militiamen near the railroad announced the long awaited arrival of help—the 7th New York detrained in Washington to the martial strains of its regimental band. As flags fluttered in the spring breeze, the regiment precision-stepped up Pennsylvania Avenue to receive the personal thanks of President Lincoln. Arrival of the 8th Massachusetts and the 1st Rhode Island on April 26 set the pace for things to come as daily arrivals swelled the blue-clad host by mid-summer to seventy-nine units bivouacked in and around the capital.[9]

Still, across the Potomac lay Virginia, no longer part of the Federal Union after April 17, 1861. The possibility existed that enemy authorities might occupy Arlington Heights; and Alexandria, the seaport downriver, had already expressed strong secessionist sympathies. Hardly lacking aggressive tendencies, the Lincoln adminis-

---
[7] Marcus Benjamin, "The Military Situation in Washington, 1861," *Washington During Wartime* (Washington, Byron S. Adams Press, 1902), 19.
[8] Washington *Evening Star,* April 24, 25, 1861.
[9] Wilton B. Moore, "Union Army Provost Marshalls in the Eastern Theater," *Military Affairs,* XXVI (Fall 1962), 121.

tration organized a "Potomac Flotilla" to clear the Potomac and Chesapeake Bay areas of enemy shipping and also directed Scott to invade Virginia soil and establish bridgeheads for future operations. At 2 a.m. on the moonlit night of May 23–24, 1861, eight Federal regiments under commander of Colonel J. F. K. Mansfield crossed the river and took up positions in the Old Dominion. One column under Major W. H. Wood moved via the Georgetown Aqueduct; another column under Major Samuel P. Heintzelman crossed via the Long Bridge, and still a third contingent led by Colonel Elmer Ellsworth effected an amphibious movement to the Alexandria wharves.

Token Confederate forces, mainly at Alexandria, departed rapidly for Manassas Junction. Only Ellsworth proved to be a casualty as he was shot down while removing a Confederate flag at the Marshall House, a local hotel. As he descended to the street he was met by James T. Jackson, the proprietor. In the ensuing struggle Jackson killed the Union colonel, the Union gained one of its first martyrs, and in turn Jackson was dispatched by one of Ellsworth's escort soldiers.[10]

The morning of May 24 dawned mild and bright with youthful Union soldiers lounging in bivouacs on Arlington Heights and the high terrain west of Alexandria. But, as might have been expected, it was not long before their officers received orders to fortify their positions. Several isolated forts—bearing little resemblance to a defensive system—were constructed as footholds in Virginia. Among these earliest works were Fort Corcoran, with a perimeter of 576 yards; Fort Haggerty, (128 yards); and Fort Bennett (146 yards). Combined with block houses and rifle trenches, these three forts guarded the Aqueduct. Forts Runyon (1484 yards) and Albany (429 yards) were built to cover the Long Bridge. Fort Ellsworth (618 yards) guarded Alexandria.

The next seven weeks were devoted to completing this first formal defense of the southern land approach to Washington. There lay the apparent threat—in the sense of an organized Confederate army emerging from its staging area at Manassas. Little attention was given to reconnaissance or committee studies of any great circumferential defense system; army engineers and line officers alike were too busy drilling, organizing, and consolidating their positions. In traditional American fashion, it required a military disaster to awaken official Washington to the fact that it remained quite inadequately

---

[10] Washington *Evening Star*, May 25, 1861. Ellsworth, in making what now appears to be a grandstand play, became the first high ranking officer on either side to be killed in action during the war. This popular hero and friend of Lincoln received an elaborate funeral in the East Room of the White House.

protected. Thus, a second phase of defending Washington emerged in the wake of a July disaster on the hot, dry plains along Bull Run.

The chaos, the flotsam of battle—the remnants of a once formidable fighting force of 35,000 men which Brigadier General Irwin McDowell brought back from Bull Run—posed but one aspect of the post-battle problem for top Federal leaders. Military authorities discerned that in addition to rebuilding the field army they also needed a more elaborate system of formal protection for the capital. McDowell's successor, Major General George B. McClellan, while anxious to take to the field again, devoted much time and study to reorganizing his forces and constructing the defenses of Washington. The upshot was the assignment of a very capable engineer officer, Colonel (later Major General) John Gross Barnard, to supervise construction of what McClellan envisioned as a system of 48 forts, lunettes, redoubts and batteries, mounting 300 siege, field, and seacoast guns. Barnard became the veritable "father" of the defenses of Washington. Under his direction the few existing works were completed and new forts were surveyed, planned, and constructed to protect stream valleys, roads, and railroads which entered the Washington area. Little regard was given to the rights of local property owners as lines of rifle trenches, massive earthworks, and military roads cut across cultivated fields and orchards and often necessitated destruction of vast stretches of woodland and numerous buildings. In a perhaps apocryphal story, President Lincoln comforted a free Negro, Elizabeth Thomas, whose home had been leveled to make room for the magazine at Fort Massachusetts (later Fort Stevens). As she sat crying nearby with her six-months-old baby in her arms, Lincoln offered the solace: "It is hard but you shall reap a great reward." [11]

As summer turned to autumn the hardworking men in blue extended the line of fortifications to cover that burgeoning supply center at Alexandria. Fort Ellsworth and Fort Scott both became a reserve line of strongpoints. In addition, low water in the Potomac at that time of year caused the engineers to reevaluate the urgency of fortifying northern approaches to Washington. New fortifications were built, such as Pennsylvania (later Reno), Massachusetts (Stevens), Totten, Slocum, and Lincoln, which commanded road and rail arteries into the city. The wide gaps between these works were filled with smaller, supporting forts. Other strategic points such as the ridge east of the Anacostia River (or Eastern Branch) and the "receiv-

---

[11] Recounted in Wailliam Van Zandt Cox, "The Defenses of Washington—General Early's Advance on the Capital and the Battle of Fort Stevens, July 11 and 12, 1864," *Records of the Columbia Historical Society*, IV, (Washington, 1901), 138.

*National Archives
Brady Collection*

Major General John Gross Barnhard, "Father of the Defenses of Washington."

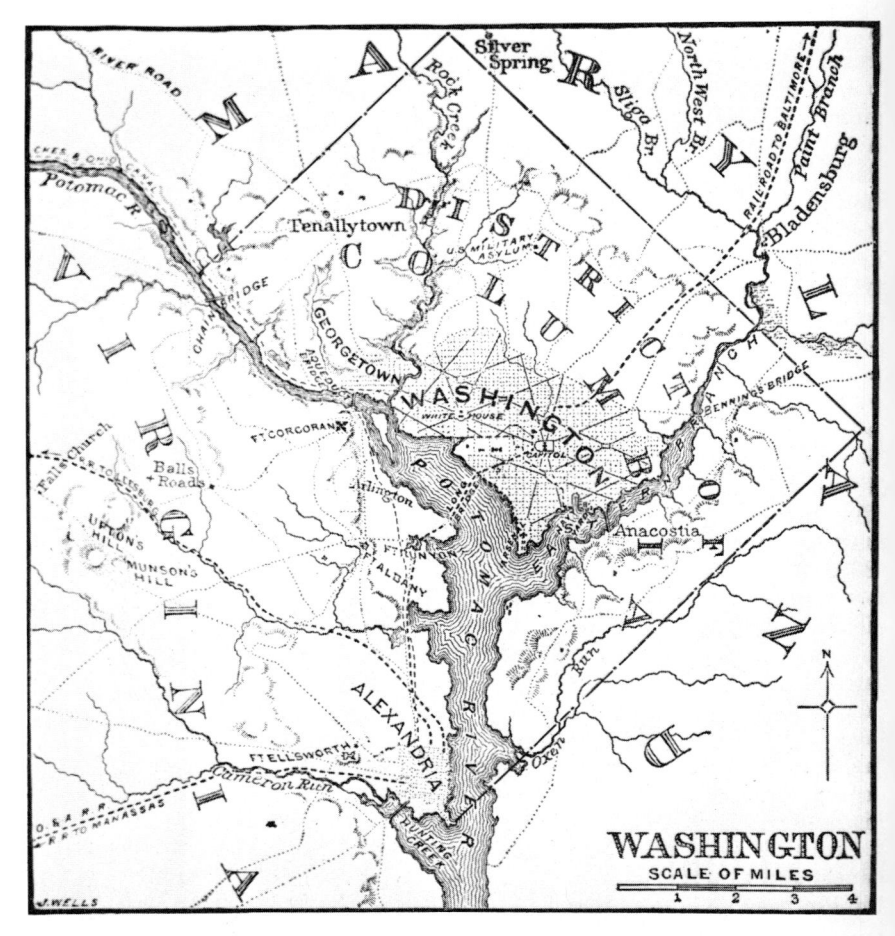

Battles and Leaders

Map of the Defenses of Washington, July 1861.

ing reservoir" (Washington's main water supply) received protection from field works and bristling cannon. By the end of the year Barnard and his colleagues could point proudly to an array of statistics concerning the formal defenses of Washington: 23 forts south of the Potomac, 14 forts and 3 batteries between the Potomac and Anacostia rivers, and 11 forts beyond the Anacostia; a total of 48 defensive works, greatly varying in size and shape, armed with 24 and 32-pounder seacoast cannon, 24-pounder siege guns, and some smaller field guns such as Parrotts and Napoleons, with magazines for one

Defending Washington during the Civil War 323

hundred rounds of artillery ammunition in each work—all designed to "shield" the Federal City.[12]

The fall and winter of 1861–1862 found Federal field forces around Washington essentially acting as a bulwark against the Confederate host on the Dumfries-Centerville-Leesburg line while the busy engineers developed Washington's formal networks of forts. But with the advent of the campaign season in the spring a third phase of defending Washington opened. McClellan sought to move his large army southward against Richmond. The stage was set for a major issue of command and control between the Chief Executive and his principal military commander, directly attributable to the question of defending the national capital.

Lincoln had specified as a condition for agreeing to McClellan's planned Peninsula campaign that Washington should be left secure against attack. By this stage of the war, both Lincoln and Secretary of War Edwin Stanton had developed something like paranoia about the city, undoubtedly traceable to the previous winter when the President had rather surreptitiously entered Washington prior to his inauguration under threat of assassination. Then, too, the early victories of the C.S.S. *Virginia* (Merrimac) in Hampton Roads had greatly agitated Washington authorities in early March 1862 when they feared that ironclad might dash up the Potomac and shell Washington. All in all, various notions were abroad in government circles as to just what comprised sufficient protection for the capital.

McClellan's corps commanders suggested a defensive force (entirely independent of the Army of the Potomac) ranging from 25,000 to 40,000 in number. McClellan, before his departure, reported statistics of 73,456 men and 109 guns available for Washington's protection but he included some 35,467 men in the Shenandoah Valley as part of this computation. This so-called numbers game, to which we have all become so accustomed in recent years of Vietnam body counts, withdrawal figures, and defense budget reports, became even more complex when on April 2, 1862, Brigadier General James Wadsworth, who commanded the defenses of Washington, reported that he really had only 19,022 "new and imperfectly disciplined men fit for duty." [13]

---

[12] John Gross Barnard, *Report on the Defenses of Washington to the Chief of Engineers, U.S. Army*, Professional Papers of the Corps of Engineers Number 20 (Washington, Government Printing Office, 1871), 12–15.

[13] United States War Department (compiler), *The War of the Rebellion: A Compilation of the Official Records of the Union and Confederate Armies* (Washington, Government Printing Office, 1880–1901), Series I, Volume XI, part 3, page 58; Emory Upton, *The Military Policy of the United States* (Washington, Government Printing Office, 1916 edition), 286–287.

The story of the administration's fear for the city with Stonewall Jackson on the prowl in the Shenandoah, their withholding of McDowell's corps from McClellan's army before Richmond, and the historiographical claims and counterclaims as to the effect of McClellan's misrepresentation, the breakdown in communications, and the Lincoln-Stanton part in the actual conduct of the war, are well known.[14] Less well known is the fact that Washington's formal defenses were not impregnable at this time; public exhileration over victories at Fort Henry and Fort Donelson in the west and McClellan's promises in Virginia had found reflection on Capitol Hill and Congress had appropriated $150,000 for completing the existing forts but nothing for any expansion of the network. There was no completely integrated line (especially north of the Potomac) and rather such detached works as then existed formed only strong points assisting a field force (the Army of the Potomac or some substitute) in defense of the city.

The danger to which Washington was subjected in August and September 1862 revealed the inadequacy of these existing defenses and the need for further improvement. Washington authorities reacted with customary fright as a second debacle at Bull Run and Lee's invasion of Maryland seemed to imperil the city. Withdrawal of garrisons led to the organization of government clerks and Barnard and his colleagues pressed urgently for replacements who might know how to work the heavy guns and equipment. But Lee remained wary of the combination of a rejuvenated Army of the Potomac and the fortification system and he turned away from a direct attack on Washington. When the gray tide receded back from Antietam, Washington authorities breathed a sigh of relief, for unmanageable artillery, wide gaps between forts, and the need for better river defenses were among the glaring deficiencies. Their immediate response was the time-honored device of establishing a commission to study the problem.

Stanton named this commission on October 25, 1862. Its members included Brigadier General Montgomery C. Meigs, the Quartermaster General; Brigadier General W. F. Barry, the Chief of Artillery; Brigadier General G. W. Cullum, Chief of Staff to the General in Chief; and, of course, Barnard. The group decided that 25,000 infantry, 9,000 artillerymen, and 3,000 cavalry were necessary for the

---

[14] Readers may wish to consult the following on this controversy: Bruce Catton, *Terrible Swift Sword* [The Centennial History of the Civil War] (Garden City, Doubleday, 1963); Allan Nevins, *The War for the Union: War Becomes Revolution 1862–1863* (New York, Charles Scribner's Sons, 1960); Kenneth P. Williams, *Lincoln Finds a General: A Military Study of the Civil War* (New York, Macmillan, 1950), Volume I; and T. Harry Williams, *Lincoln and His Generals* (New York, Alfred A. Knopf, 1952).

formal defense system. Only the artillerymen would be posted to the forts at all times with infantry encamped nearby and the cavalry patrolling outside the works. Naturally the whole force was expected to be professionally competent and well drilled. Commission members also suggested a 25,000-man maneuver force which could operate outside the defenses against any enemy attack column and "against more serious attacks from the main body of the enemy, the Capital must depend upon the concentration of its entire armies in Virginia or Maryland." [15]

The various suggestions of the commission were vigorously pursued during the early part of 1863. Many minor suggestions such as additions and alterations to existing forts, construction of five or six new works, and more adequate naval protection received attention. The Army of the Potomac at this point provided a convenient shield along the banks of the Rappahannock and while Chief Engineer Barnard complained about the dearth of labor for his projects—he was forced to hire civilian laborers on occasion—Congress appropriated $200,000 for improving the defenses. New forts, named generally for Federal officers killed in the war, were carved from the countryside surrounding Washington and several in the group protecting the reservoir above Chain Bridge were consolidated and renamed Fort Sumner.[16]

The engineers continued to worry about the Potomac gap in the defense perimeter so long as a threat existed of European recognition of the Confederacy. English and French warships allied with the Confederates could move up the Potomac past ancient Fort Washington and threaten the capital from the river side. The navy's unsung Potomac Flotilla was designed for river patrol, mine removal, and neutralization of shore batteries, but it would be no match for European ironclads. So, in 1863, Battery Rodgers at Alexandria and Fort Foote across the river were constructed and the experiences of two years of building forts enabled Barnard's officers and men to make these positions "model works." Both works were armed with 200-pounder Parrott rifles and 15-inch guns; their parapets of 20 to 25 feet in thickness were designed to absorb punishing blows from naval ordnance; and they were positioned to provide a deadly crossfire against vessels seeking passage. Ironically, neither fortification was ever subjected to the stern test of combat.[17]

The months of 1863 waned without serious threat to Washington and a degree of complacency prevailed among the citizens of the city

[15] *Official Records,* Series I, Volume XXI, 904–905.
[16] *Ibid.,* Series I, Volume XXVII, part 3, 596–597; and Volume XXVI, part 2, 154.
[17] *Ibid.,* Series I, Volume XXIX, part 2, 316.

and the garrisons of the forts. The young soldiers earned a reputation for unsullied white gloves and dress blue uniforms, their officers prospered in the social life which accompanied service near the capital, and Lee's invasion into Pennsylvania posed but a passing irritation. At that time, however, mechanics, laborers, and even one hundred army sutlers offered their services in defense of the city. But the threat subsided suddenly as the news of Gettysburg reached Washington.[18]

By the end of 1863, 60 forts, 93 batteries, and 837 guns encircled the city and 25,000 men were in position to man this complex. A connected system of fortifications now existed whereby every important point, at eight hundred to one thousand yard intervals, was occupied by an enclosed fort. Every important approach or depression, uncovered by a fort, was swept by a battery designed for field guns. The whole periphery was connected by rifle trenches which furnished emplacements for two ranks of infantrymen. Another phase in the history of the defenses had closed. As one bloody year dissolved into another, authorities in Washington finally felt their city capable of meeting any threat from a Confederate army. Then the most critical threat to Washington's safety shattered this confidence in the spring and summer of 1864.

The spring campaigns of Lieutenant General Ulysses S. Grant, with the staggering losses in the Wilderness, at Spotsylvania, and at Cold Harbor, swept experienced manpower from Washington's forts much to the consternation of the engineer officers. Skilled technicians were replaced by 100-day militia, scarcely the kind of personnel best suited for traversing heavy ordnance and maintaining coolness under enemy fire. Yet such soldiers garrisoned the works around the city in July when Confederate authorities ordered Lieutenant General Jubal Early's command on a diversionary raid to the gates of the capital to relieve pressure upon Lee's beleaguered forces in the Richmond-Petersburg lines and possibly free Confederate prisoners at Point Lookout, Maryland.

The story is well known with at least one full-length study of "Early's Raid" in print.[19] By July 11, 1864, Early's 14,000 men had crossed the Potomac, ransomed Frederick for $20,000, swept aside Major General Lew Wallace's totally inadequate blocking force at Monocacy (although in truth that action delayed the Confederates at

---

[18] Cooling, "Civil War Deterrent," 173–174.

[19] See Frank E. Vandiver, *Jubal's Raid: General Early's Famous Attack on Washington in 1864* (New York, McGraw-Hill, 1960); and Cox, "The Defenses of Washington," for examples of such treatment.

Defending Washington during the Civil War 327

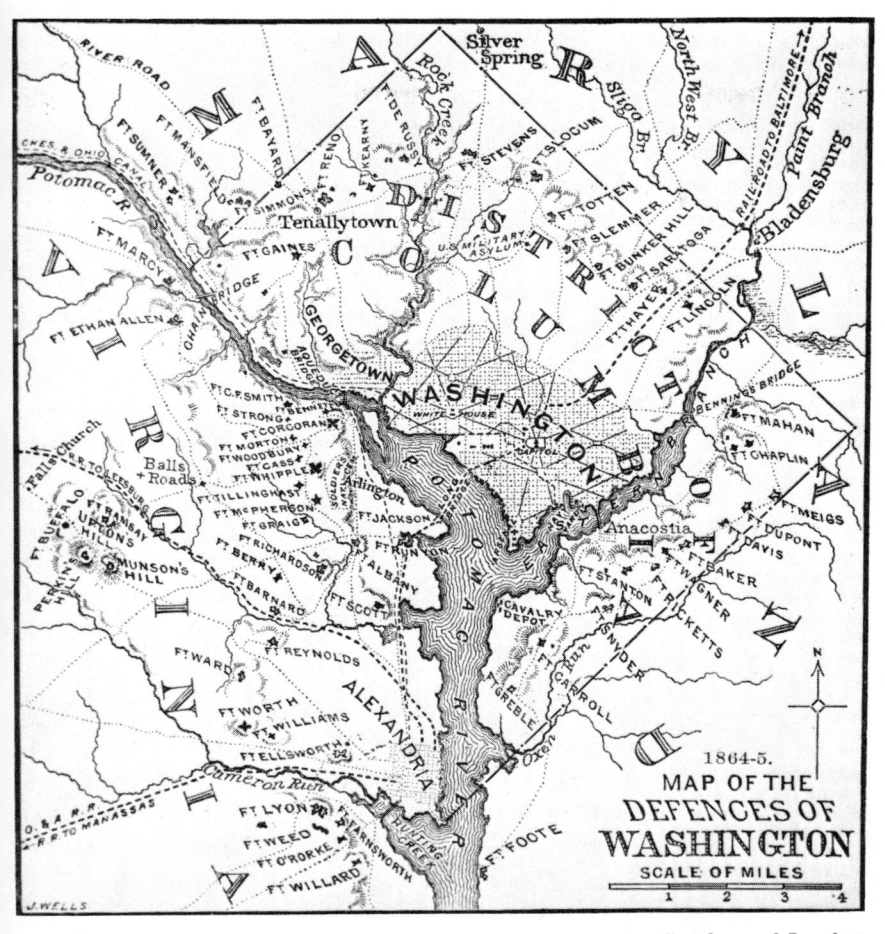

Battles and Leaders

Map of the Defenses of Washington, 1864–1865.

a strategic moment in their march on Washington), and appeared before the northern outskirts of Washington from Tennallytown eastward beyond the Seventh Street Road. On the Union side, Baltimore citizens manned the trenches of their city, convalescents from Washington were dispatched to guard the ferry and railroad at Havre de Grace, north of Baltimore, the Federal authorities in Washington made desperate attempts to collect a fighting force to throw against Early's main column as it moved the hot and dusty forty miles from Frederick. Barely 9,000 troops manned Washington's line of forts, most of them poorly trained, with even a "brigade" of Quartermaster Corps personnel pressed into the front lines. General officers were hardly lacking as indicated in Major General Henry Halleck's dispatch to one such hopeful: "We have five times as many generals as we want but we are greatly in need of privates. Anyone volunteering in that capacity will be thankfully received." [20]

Major General Christopher Augur commanded the department and ostensibly directed defense preparations. Other generals, however, were available and Quincy Gillmore, Alexander McCook, Martin Hardin, and E. O. C. Ord all found themselves commanding portions of the defenses and reserve camps.

The "Battle of the Suburbs" or "Battle of Fort Stevens" took place on July 11–12, 1864, stretching across a front from Fort Reno near Tennallytown to beyond Fort Totten with Fort Stevens and Fort DeRussy receiving the brunt of Early's attack. The fatigue of Early's men, the absence of decisiveness in the Confederate thrust on the first day, and the timely arrival of veterans of the VI and XXII Corps via water to Washington, all saved the Federal City. During the evening of July 11, the Confederate generals held a council of war in the comfortable home of Francis Preston Blair at Silver Spring, vacated at Early's approach. Present were division commanders Robert Rhodes, Stephen Ramseur, John B. Gordon, and John Breckenridge. As the wine from Blair's cellar flowed freely and Breckenridge received the butt of many jokes about sitting in the Vice Presidential chair at the Capitol on the morrow, the generals analyzed their position. As was the case with so many councils of war during that conflict, little was determined except to wait and see what the situation was in the morning.

The day dawned hot and sultry and Early found himself confronting the Union works now manned by Federals in faded blue. One brigade of these veteran troops mounted a small attack later in the afternoon which led to the filling of tiny Battleground National Cemetery on Georgia Avenue as well as the pushing back of the Confederate skirmish line. Civilian notables and generals watched the firefight from the parapets of Fort Stevens. Secretary of the Navy Gideon Welles and President Lincoln both expressed great curiosity from this vantage point and both soon came under a vicious sniper fire. The President remained oblivious until several officers were cut down nearby but even Major General Horatio Wright of the VI Corps was unable to pressure Lincoln into seeking a safer vantage point. Perhaps the insubordinate remark "Get down you fool!" at-

---

[20] Cox, "The Defenses of Washington," 140.

Plan of Fort Stevens as shown (Plate 22) in the Report of Major General Barnard on the Defenses of Washington, 1871.

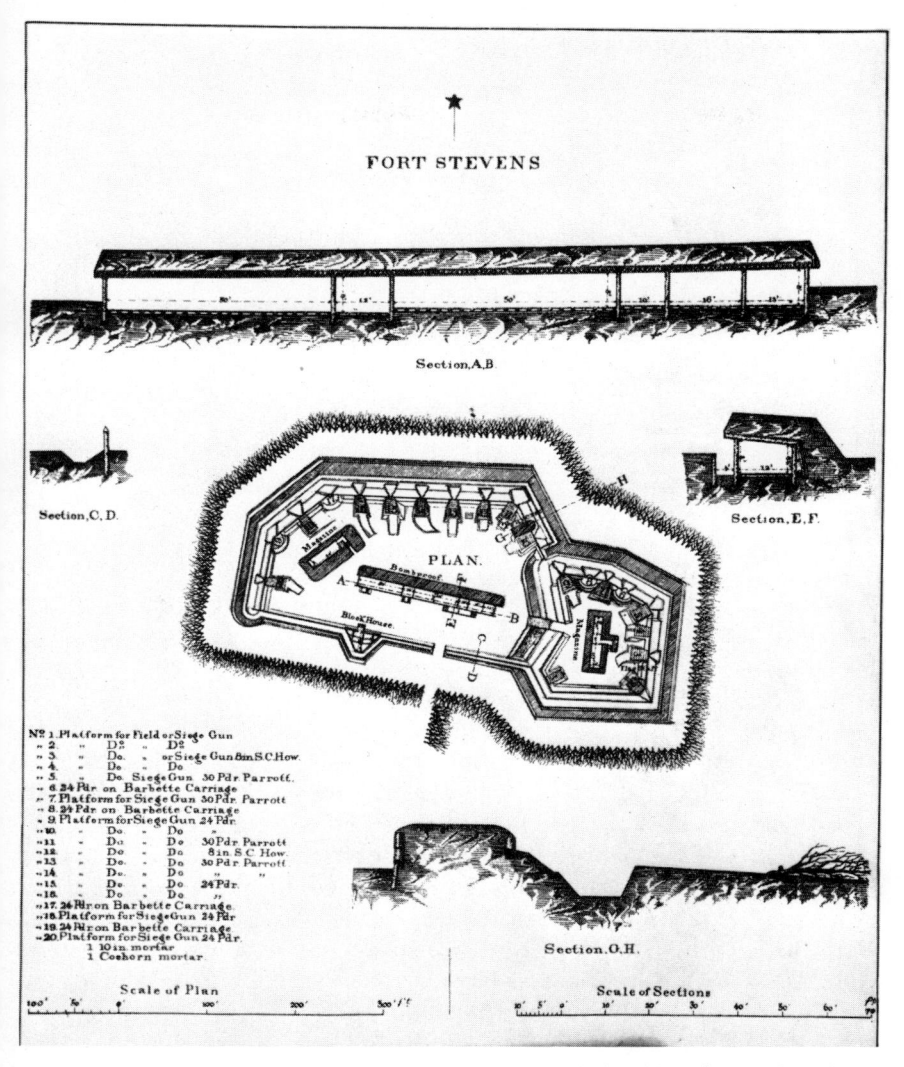

tributed to Wright's young aide, Captain Oliver Wendell Holmes, proved more effective.[21] In any case, Lincoln at last stepped down from the precarious observation platform.

---

[21] Leech, *Reveille in Washington,* 346; and Alexander Woollcott, "Get Down You Fool! Early's Raid and Meeting of Lincoln and Holmes," *Atlantic,* CLXI (1938), 169–173.

WINTER QUARTERS OF THE 36TH N.Y. VOL. BRIGHTWOOD.

Columbia Historical Society

Winter Quarters of the 36th New York Volunteers at Brightwood near Fort Stevens. Lithograph by J. Thoubboron.

Dusk ended the fighting and the Union skirmish lines were restored at heavy cost. Every regimental commander in the brigade fell killed or wounded. The brigade itself lost roughly one-fourth of its 1,000 men. But that night Early directed his tired force back to Virginia, passing through Rockville and Poolesville en route to Whites Ford and safety. Washington's defenders were overjoyed at merely saving the city and they mounted no immediate pursuit. The threat was gone and another phase of defending Washington had passed. Grant continued his relentless pressure at Petersburg. Nevertheless official Washington and the North were shaken by the audacity of Early's move. One may even speculate upon its effect on Republican political fortunes had the elections of that year been held in late July instead of several months later.[22]

The final phase of the Civil War defenses was anticlimactic. The threat to Washington decreased precipitously after Early's attack and the final elimination of a fighting force in the Shenandoah Valley in the fall of 1864. When Lee's army finally surrendered in April 1865, Washington's defense system was quite impressive: 68 enclosed forts and batteries were supported by 93 unarmed batteries for field guns.

---

[22] The London *Times* of July 25, 1864 concluded: "The Confederacy is more formidable an enemy than ever."

BATTERY RODGERS   ITS 15-INCH GUN

Miller's Photographic History of the Civil War

Battery Rodgers, Potomac River near Alexandria, Virginia. (Brady Collection B-95). A 15-inch Rodman gun is visible above the bomb-proofs.

National Archives
Brady Collection

Fort Carroll, showing Barracks. (Brady Collection B-476). Fort Carroll was close to Giesboro Point and housed the 67th New York Infantry.

Columbia Historical Society

Major General Horatio G. Wright (seated, fourth from right, with sash and sword) and Staff at or near Fort Stevens, 1864.

The aggregate perimeters of the forts themselves approached thirteen miles; 1421 gun emplacements had been constructed in the forts and batteries with 807 pieces of artillery and 98 mortars actually mounted. Three blockhouses, twenty miles of rifle trenches, and thirty miles of military roads (Military Road in northwest Washington being representative), were likewise built during the war.[23]

On June 23, 1865, Union authorities decided to retain selected forts for possible future defense of the city. North of the Potomac, Forts Foote, Carroll, Stanton, Baker, Mahan, Lincoln, Totten, Slocum, Stevens, Reno, and Sumner were retained. Battery Rodgers, Redoubts Weed, Farnsworth, and O'Rorke, and Forts Lyon, Ellsworth, Worth, Ward, Richardson, McPherson, Whipple, Morton, C. F. Smith, and Ethan Allen were to be maintained as a defensive line south of the Potomac. But the practicality of preserving obsolescent works in the absence of any definable threat soon led to complete abandonment of the defenses of Washington. Lieutenant Colonel

---

[23] Barnard, *Defenses of Washington*, 86.

Miller's Photographic History of the Civil War

Fort Lincoln. (Brady Collection BA-1910.) Fort Lincoln overlooked the Baltimore Turnpike and the tracks of the Baltimore and Ohio Railroad (and was on the site of the quondam National Training School for Boys).

B. S. Alexander, Barnard's successor as Chief Engineer of the defenses, closed out his account books on the forts on July 14, 1865. Even Fort Washington was abandoned in 1872.

Washington's Civil War forts crumbled before time and the elements as the years passed. Flurries of concern for the safety of the capital prompted new schemes, none of which encompassed the old Civil War forts.

In the period 1896–1921, river batteries, like Fort Hunt and Batteries Decatur, Many, and White, guarded the maritime approach to Washington with their concrete emplacements, 10-inch disappearing guns, and electrically triggered mines in the river.

The development of aerial bombardment brought a new threat and Army War College planners and students in the 1920's and 1930's grappled with the defense of the capital from a third dimension.

Anti-aircraft guns, NIKE batteries, and civil defense plans from the 1940's to the 1960's bring the discussion of defending Washington

*National Archives
Brady Collection*

A Fort near Washington. (Brady Collection B-479.) Almost certainly Fort Slemmer, showing Company I, 2nd Pennsylvania Artillery crossing the sally point and draw bridge, although the photograph has previously been identified both as Fort Massachusetts (later Fort Stevens) and as Fort Richardson.

full circle to the question of Sprint and Spartan missiles and the Sentinel and Safeguard ABM programs.[24]

The citizen will always wonder about the value of such expensive experiments in time, matériel, and humanity to guard the symbol of a nation. John Gross Barnard, the Civil War architect of the largest defense system ever possessed by Washington, thought the forts surpassed anything comparable in Europe at the time. Apparently

---

[24] On later defenses see, for example, Emanuel Raymond Lewis, *Seacoast Fortifications of the United States: An Introductory History* (Washington, Smithsonian Institution Press, 1970), 91; U.S. Army War College, Command Course 29, (1925–1926), Report of Committee 23, Defense of Washington, March 25, 1926, U.S. Army War College Curricular Files, U.S. Army Military History Research Collection, Carlisle Barracks, Pennsylvania; and William M. Bronk, "A History of the Eastern Defense Command" and William H. Cartwright, "History of Military District of Washington, 1942–1945," both unpublished monographs in General Reference Branch files, Office of the Chief of Military History, Department of the Army, Washington, D.C.

Columbia Historical Society

Fort Totten. (Brady Collection B-376.)

Columbia Historical Society

  A Fort near Washington. (Brady Collection B-627.) Almost certainly Fort Gains, although the photograph has previously been identified as Fort Totten.

others agreed with him as to their deterrent value, for $1.4 million and the 20,000 men generally held back from principal Federal operational forces in Virginia deterred Robert E. Lee from committing his own army in a headlong attack upon the city. Certainly today's military and civilian Department of Defense officials still give thought to the deterrent value of a defense system for the seat of government in the general scheme of national defense.

Today there are visible remains of the Civil War concept of defending Washington. The men and guns are gone and once proud parapets have diminished with age. Still some thirty-two remnants of the fortifications remain, representative of a lost grandeur and an important part of a great drama.

NORTH OF THE POTOMAC

Battery Martin Scott	Potomac Place N.W.
Battery Kemble	Chain Bridge Road, N.W.
Battery Vermont	Palisades Lane and Manning Place, N.W.
Fort Gaines	American University Campus
Fort Bayard	River Road and Western Avenue, N.W.
Fort Reno	Nebraska Avenue and Grant Place, N.W.
Fort DeRussy	Rock Creek Park near Oregon Avenue and Military Road, N.W.
Fort Stevens	Georgia Avenue and Quackenbos Street, N.W.
Fort Slocum	Oglethorpe Street and 3d Street, N.W.
Fort Totten	Fort Place, off North Capital Street, N.W.
Fort Bunker Hill	14th and Otis Streets, N.E.
Battery Jameson	Fort Lincoln Cemetery
Fort Mahan	Minnesota Avenue and Benning Road, N.E.
Fort Chapin	East Capitol Street and Benning Road, N.E.
Fort DuPont	Alabama Avenue, S.E.
Fort Davis	Pennsylvania and Alabama Avenues, S.E.
Battery Ricketts	Bruce Place and Fort Place, S.E.
Fort Stanton	Fort Place, S.E.
Fort Carroll	Nichols Avenue and South Capitol Street, S.E.
Fort Greble	Nichols Avenue, S.E.
Fort Foote	Fort Foote Road off Indianhead Highway (Maryland Route 210)
Fort Washington	Maryland Route 210 to Fort Washington Road

SOUTH OF THE POTOMAC

Fort Marcy	George Washington Memorial Parkway
Fort Ethan Allen	Glebe and Military Roads, Arlington
Fort C. F. Smith	2411 24th Street North, Arlington
Fort Strong	Spout Run Park, Arlington
Fort Whipple	present-day Fort Myer
Fort McPherson	Arlington National Cemetery
Fort Richardson	Grounds of Army-Navy Country Club
Fort Ward	City park on Braddock Road, Alexandria
Fort Scott	Aurora Hills section, Alexandria
Fort Willard	Belle Haven section, Alexandria

Preserved in most instances by the National Park Service (although the City of Alexandria has reconstructed a portion of Fort Ward and maintains the only museum devoted specifically to the defenses of Washington), these forts continue to serve an important function. In this era of recreation, parks, and concern for ecology, the remnants of the Civil War defenses of Washington provide a refuge for new generations of Americans against the urban blight which threatens all of us. They will remain as silent sentinels, monuments to that drama which shaped the destiny of a united nation. But they will also defend the needs of modern Americans for parkland and historic preservation and will prove useful servants of new plans and programs of the greater Washington of the future.

Adolph Cluss: An Architect in Washington during Civil War and Reconstruction

TANYA EDWARDS BEAUCHAMP

The years of Civil War and Reconstruction were critical in the development of the city of Washington. Disastrously rapid growth in population forced the implementation of long overdue public building programs. Municipal improvements were followed by large investments of private capital. At first development proceeded slowly. A vastly inflated economy and shortages of both labor and materials made all construction difficult and excessively expensive. During the Grant administration, however, financial conditions relaxed, an aura of prosperity and well-being prevailed, and construction boomed. The Panic of 1873, and the long depression which followed, curtailed building activities. The basic steps had been successfully taken, nonetheless, preparing the way for the great surge of construction which came in the 1880's and the attractive modern city which issued therefrom. In 1883 Joseph West Moore recorded the transformation:

> ... The streets were covered with an almost noiseless, smooth pavement. Fifty thousand shade-trees had been planted; the old rows of wooden, barrack-like houses had given place to dwellings of graceful, ornate architecture; blocks of fine business buildings lined Pennsylvania Avenue and the other prominent thoroughfares; blossoming gardens and luxuriant parks were to be seen on all sides; the squares and circles were adorned with the statues of heroes, and bordered with costly and palatial mansions; splendid school-houses, churches, market buildings, newspaper offices had been erected. The water-works and sewer system were unequalled in the country. Washington had risen fresh and beautiful, like the Uranian Venus, from stagnation and decay.[1]

During this period of radical and intense building activity the

---
[1] Joseph West Moore, *Picturesque Washington: Pen and Pencil Sketches* (New York: Hurst & Co., 1883), p. 52.

architect Adolph Cluss played a crucial role. Between 1862 and 1876 his office designed and superintended the construction of virtually all the public buildings erected by the Washington city government. A sewage disposal system recommended by Mayor Wallach to the

William S. Shacklette

Adolph Cluss

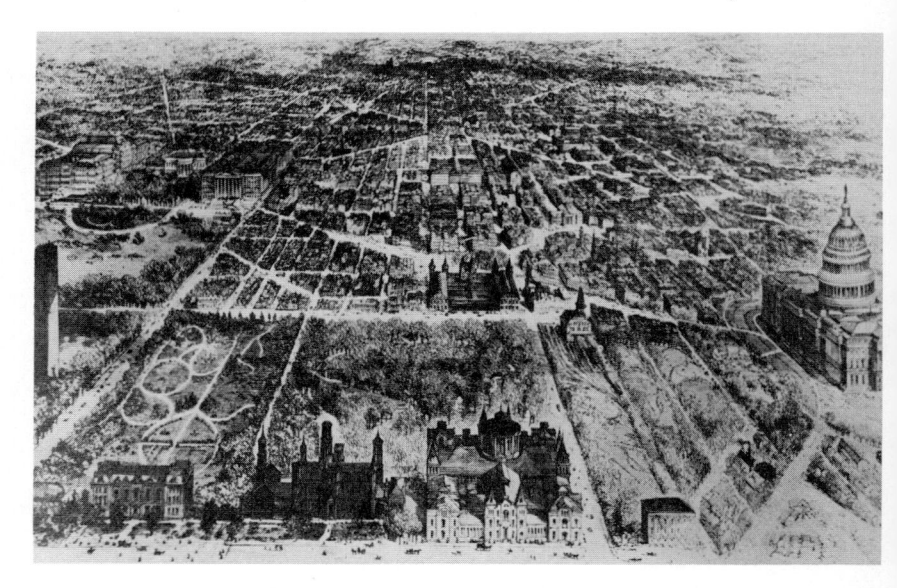

Harper's

View of Washington, 1882.

In the foreground, left to right, are the U.S. Department of Agriculture, the Smithsonian Institution, and the U.S. National Museum. Across the Mall is Center Market.

Secretary of the Interior in 1865 was of his design and later, as engineer member of the Board of Public Works, he was able to implement this and other important proposals. During the 1860's, the 1870's and the 1880's he was responsible for a substantial proportion of the booming private construction in the city. At this time also he was engaged in the design and construction of several buildings for the Federal government. A lithograph of Washington published in Harper's in 1882 shows the impact of Cluss on the city at that time. Of the buildings prominently drawn, almost half are of his design.

Adolph Cluss was born July 14, 1825, in Heilbronn, Würtemburg, Germany, the son of architect Heinrich Cluss.[2] He was trained as an architect and civil engineer, finishing his academic education in 1846. Germany was, at this time, in the midst of a railroad building boom and Cluss found his first employment as an assistant engineer on the construction of the railroad between Mayence and Mannheim on the

---

[2] According to William Shacklette, great grandson of Cluss, his grandfather as well as his father were architects.

Rhine. During the political upheavals of 1848 he emigrated to the United States, settling in Washington.[3]

Cluss served the United States government in various capacities for the next eighteen or twenty years, being first employed on field work of the Coast Survey.[4] In June of 1850 he went to work as a draughtsman in the ordnance laboratory of the Washington Navy Yard.[5] In November, 1855, he transferred to the office of the Supervising Architect in the Treasury Department.[6] Here he worked under the prolific Ammi B. Young, gaining experience in the design and construction of public buildings such as post offices and customs houses. While with Young, according to his own account, he had charge of one of the drafting rooms.[7]

In April, 1859, he returned to the ordnance laboratory of the Navy Yard where he remained for the next eight or ten years.[8] Though he is listed on the Navy Yard payrolls as a draughtsman, Cluss himself later referred to his position there as that of "... computer and constructor..." While in this capacity he designed and built the furnaces by which all the brass cannon of the Navy were cast during the Civil War.[9] In 1862, his good friend Admiral Dahlgren was appointed Commandant of the Navy Yard. Cluss accepted a confidential position under Dahlgren, testing new inventions, taking charge of the research and development operations of the laboratory. He was particularly concerned here with the ballistic pendulum.[10]

It was while thus employed in the Navy Yard that Cluss, in partnership with Joseph Wildrich von Kammerhueber, first ventured into private architectural practice. Kammerhueber had worked under Thomas U. Walter on the design and construction of the Patent

---

[3] *Report of the Joint Select Committee of Congress Appointed to Inquire into the Affairs of the Government of the District of Columbia* (Washington: Government Printing Office, 1874), p. 2049.

[4] *Ibid.*

[5] Payrolls 1844–1899 for the Washington Navy Yard, Records of the Bureau of Yards and Docks, National Archives Building, Record Group 71.

[6] A letter from Ammi B. Young to Captain A. H. Bowman, Engineer-in-Charge at New York, August 18, 1855, reveals that Young is considering hiring Cluss. Proofs of Office Letters, Office of Construction, January 3, 1855–November 15, 1856, Treasury Department, Records of the Public Building Service, National Archives Building, Record Group 121.

[7] *Report of the Joint Select Committee* ... p. 2049.

[8] Navy Yard Payrolls. These records are incomplete. The ordnance laboratory is not listed from August 1862 to August 1866 or after July 1867.

[9] *Report of the Joint Select Committee* ... p. 2049.

[10] *The National Cyclopedia of American Biography*, Vol IV (New York: James T. White & Co., 1897), p. 507.

George Washington University

Wallach School (now demolished) on Pennsylvania Avenue between 7th and 8th Streets, S.E.

Office and the Capitol dome.[11] Together they prepared the winning entry in a competition held in 1862 for the design of Wallach School. This school was to be the first in a series of aesthetically pleasing, modern, multi-classroom structures to be built throughout the city. The new buildings would replace the primitive and totally inadequate quarters formerly used as schoolhouses by the city. They would symbolize Washington's new commitment to provide "Schools for all; good enough for the richest; cheap enough for the poorest. . ." [12] and would be the initial step in the modernization of the city. The first school was to be named after Richard Wallach, the progressive mayor responsible for implementing the building program. Its site would

---

[11] August Gottlieb Schoenborn, "Sketch of My Education and Connection with the Extension of the United States Capitol, Washington D. C." This is published as Appendix A in Turpin C. Bannister's "The Genealogy of the Dome of the United States Capitol," *Journal of the Society of Architectural Historians,* Vol. 7, Nos. 1–2 (January–June 1948), p. 8 of the reminiscences, p. 19 of *JSAH.*

[12] J. Ormand Wilson, "Eighty Years of the Public Schools of Washington: 1805 to 1885," *Records of the Columbia Historical Society,* Vol. 1 (Washington: published by the Society, 1895), p. 136.

be an entire square on Pennsylvania Avenue between 7th and 8th Streets, S.E.

Cluss and Kammerhueber's design was based on studies they had made of the most innovative school architecture both here and in Europe. Superintendent J. O. Wilson later recalled: "In hygienic, pedagogic, and architectural arrangements the Wallach was in advance of its time and the promise of better things to come." [13] Upon completion of the school in 1864, the building committee commented:

> ... it gives us pleasure to state that much credit is due to the architects, Messrs. Cluss and Kammerhueber, for the general plan of the building, and more especially for the care with which the working plans and specifications were prepared, as well as for their unceasing vigilance in superintending the work, To them we are indebted in a great measure for the gratifying fact that the cost of the building when completed did not exceed, to any considerable extent, the amount of the original proposal for its construction. A plain, bald, unsightly structure is not necessarily an economical one. Comeliness and beauty in a building are more dependent upon the taste and skill of the architect than upon the amount of money expended.[14]

The following year Cluss and Kammerhueber began work on Franklin School. This building was constructed with almost incredible difficulty and expense due to wild inflation and severe shortages of materials and labor. Located on a lot facing fashionable Franklin Park at 13th and K Streets, N. W., Franklin School became the showplace of the Washington public school system and a prototype for advanced school construction both here and abroad. A model of it, together with plans and photographs of Wallach School and other subsequently constructed buildings, was sent to the World's Exposition at Vienna in 1873 as part of an American educational exhibit. The model, which was built to scale in one-story sections, cost $1,000 to construct and excited considerable interest. It was disassembled and carefully examined. Drawings of the exterior were made by educators from all over Europe. A "Medal for Progress" in education and school architecture was awarded.[15]

Similar prize-winning exhibitions were made at the international expositions in Philadelphia in 1876, in Paris in 1878, and in New

---

[13] *Ibid.*, p. 23.

[14] Board of Trustees of the Public Schools of the City of Washington, *Twentieth Annual Report of the Board, 1864* (Washington City: M'Gill & Witherow, 1865), p. 17.

[15] Board of Trustees ... Public Schools ... *1872–1873*, p. 13. Also J. O. Wilson, "Eighty Years ... ," p. 41.

Franklin School, at 13th and K Streets, N.W., about 1895.

Orleans in 1884. In Paris, Cluss won first honors. A model of Henry School was afterwards placed in the National Pedagogical Museum of France at the Palais Bourbon.[16] Seaton School (1871) on I between 2nd and 3rd Streets, N. W., Cranch School (1871) at 12th and G Streets, S. E., Sumner School (1871) at 17th and M Streets, N. W., Jefferson School (1872) at 6th Street and Virginia Avenue, S. W., Curtis School (1875) on O between 32nd and 33rd Streets, N. W., and Henry School (1878) on P between 6th and 7th Streets, N. W. were all designed and constructed by Adolph Cluss.

After their success in designing Wallach School, Cluss and Kammerhueber quickly developed a thriving architectural practice. They were known for their innovative approach to structure, form and function, their careful attention to the details of construction, and their ability to design imaginatively within a tight budget. They advertised themselves as architects and engineers and had their offices at the corner of 7th and F Streets, N. W. near the Patent Office. They designed a number of the churches built in response to the sudden in-

---

[16] Wilson, "Eighty Years...," p. 42. Also, Letter, Adolph Cluss and Paul Schulze to S. P. Langley, August 25, 1888, Smithsonian Institution, Archives, National Museum Building Commission, Plans and Contracts 1879–1882, Box 1.

crease in population. Notable among these was Calvary Baptist Church at the corner of 8th and H Streets, N. W. Financed by Amos Kendall, member of Andrew Jackson's Kitchen Cabinet and founder of Gallaudet College, construction was begun in 1864. The church was dedicated in June 1866, burned in December 1867, and rebuilt on its old foundations and according to the original plan by June 1869. Calvary was built with its main hall at second story level over a ground floor lecture room. The hall was designed auditorium-style with a circular platform and a pulpit which could be raised or lowered. Its handsome steeple was constructed of openwork iron.

In Baltimore in 1864, Cluss and Kammerhueber designed the Concordia Opera House for the newly formed Concordia German Society—an organization dedicated to "moral, scientific, literary, dramatic, agricultural and charitable purposes." [17] Located at the southwest corner of Eutlaw and German Streets, this structure contained a library, a gymnasium, dressing and exercising rooms, refreshment rooms, a large dining saloon, reception and drawing rooms in addition to its commodious concert hall. In its brochure the Society advertised it as the "best ventilated and most magnificently illuminated hall in the East." [18]

On January 24, 1865, the main building of the Smithsonian Institution was very seriously damaged by fire. The building committee for its reconstruction included Mayor Richard Wallach. On his warm recommendation Adolph Cluss was chosen as architect.[19] This was the beginning of an extended consulting relationship. The skill with which Cluss restructured the building, fireproofing and modernizing it while preserving the integrity of its Romanesque design, greatly impressed Joseph Henry, the Secretary of the Smithsonian. Until 1888 Cluss had charge of all the architectural problems of the Institution, including maintenance, remodellings and plans for future expansion.

Between 1867 and 1869 the firm designed and constructed the new Masonic Temple at the corner of 9th and F Streets, N. W. across from the Patent Office. This sumptuous building was constructed entirely of stone and elegantly detailed in the French Renaissance style now known as Second Empire. It contained shops on the street floor below the Masonic Hall. The over-extended budget did not permit construc-

---

[17] Isidor Blum, *The Jews of Baltimore* (Baltimore, Maryland: 1910), p. 27.
[18] Peale Museum, Baltimore, Md.
[19] Joseph Henry, "Report of the Secretary," *Annual Report of the Board of Regents of the Smithsonian Institution,...1865* (Washington: Government Printing Office, 1872), p. 19.

Calvary Baptist Church

Calvary Baptist Church, at 8th and H Streets, N.W. Photograph by Matthew Brady about 1866.

Supreme Council,
Scottish Rite of Freemasonry
Masonic Temple, at 9th and F Streets, N.W., about 1895.

tion of a projected mansard roof. For many years this building, located in the then-thriving downtown area was a source of great civic pride. At this time also Cluss and Kammerhueber designed the building and conservatories of the new Department of Agriculture for the Federal government. This structure was located on the Mall to the west of James Renwick's Smithsonian Institution building. Of press brick, brownstone and terracotta, in a restrained but picturesque style, it harmonized with the latter. During this period Kammerhueber's influence in the firm lessened. He resigned in 1868 and died in 1870.

Adolph Cluss was elected a Fellow of the American Institute of Architects on December 16, 1867. Throughout his life he played an active part in the affairs of the organization, reading several papers before its conventions and serving on committees. In 1890, when the A.I.A. was reorganized, he served a one year term on the Board of Directors. His papers include "Theory, Functions and Incidental Uses of Chimneys" (1869); "Architecture and Architects at the Capi-

William S. Shacklette

U.S. Department of Agriculture (now demolished) on the Mall, 1869.

tal of the United States from its Foundation Until 1875" (1876); and "Mortars and Concretes of Antiquity and Modern Times" (1888).

In the early 1870's Cluss built markets as well as schools for the city of Washington. Center Market was designed in 1870 and Eastern Market in 1873. Both replaced groups of unsanitary primitive sheds. Center Market, located on the site now occupied by the National Archives, was an especially fine structure. It was actually composed of four separate buildings grouped according to function and related through design to seem a single unit. The modern, spacious, thoughtfully designed multi-level structure included elevators, adequate parking for wagons and generous space for stands and stores. It was considered in many respects "the market *par excellance* of the country." [20]

At this time Cluss became involved in the real estate development operations of Alexander Robey Shepherd. Shepherd's Row, a block of residences at Connecticut Avenue and K Street, facing Farragut Square, was built for himself, Shepherd and Hallet Kilburn in 1872–

---

[20] Moore, *Picturesque Washington*, p. 260.

George Washington University

Stewart's Castle (now demolished) on Dupont Circle at Massachusetts Avenue and 20th Street, N.W.

1873. It was designed around a corner tower in a manner later much copied in the city. Another block of houses, the north side of K Street between 14th Street and Vermont Avenue, N. W., was cited by A. P. Clark in 1930 as one of the first examples of houses built under the 1870 parking legislation which allowed projections such as towers, bay windows and porches onto city property. Clark praised Cluss' restrained design as purely aesthetic in intention with bays "only an incident to the front and one story in height" with "no attempt to seize public space." [21] In 1873 Cluss built "Stewart's Castle" at the intersection of Connecticut and Massachusetts Avenues, N. W. for Senator William Stewart, the Nevada silver king. This elegant mansion, built on an irregular site, was more or less octagonal in plan. It had a curious entrance tower and central cupola and was richly detailed in the mansard-roofed Second Empire style.

---

[21] Appleton P. Clark, Jr., "History of Architecture in Washington," *Washington: Past and Present,* Vol. II (New York: Lewis Historical Publishing Company, Inc., 1930), p. 511.

In the spring of 1871 the Board of Public Works was created. Under the dynamic leadership of Shepherd a vast municipal improvement program was initiated. Streets were graded and paved, curbs and sidewalks installed, sewerage developed, and parks laid out and ornamented. Operations were begun in all parts of the city at once and urged forward at a rapid pace. In three years the city was transformed. The cost, however, was staggering. Estimated at $4,000,000, the actual cost was between $26,000,000 and $30,000,000.[22] Extravagance and corruption were charged and Congress—in 1872 and again in 1874—conducted two lengthy investigations. The Board expired by limitation in June 1874.

In October, 1872, President Grant appointed Adolph Cluss to the Board of Public Works following the resignation of architect Alfred B. Mullett. In December, 1872, he was appointed engineer member of the Board as well. During the investigation of the Board in 1874, he testified against Shepherd, comparing his organization to that of Boss Tweed in New York.[23] He sorely felt the lack of respect on the Board for the engineer and his staff. His testimony was intended to vindicate his "very able corps of assistants who have been trumpeted through the country as incompetents." [24] He commented to the amusement of the investigating committee and spectators that the Board "have so far murdered the reputation of able engineers as much as Blue Beard did his wives." [25]

Cluss moved his offices to Fifteenth and G Streets, N. W. in 1872, and in 1877 to the Corcoran Building at Fifteenth Street and Pennsylvania Avenue, N. W. In 1876 he entered into a partnership with Frederick Daniel. Daniel had apparently been a draughtsman in Cluss' office. *Boyd's Directory* indicates that Daniel was at the same business address as Cluss in 1871 and moved with him in 1872. The partnership was short-lived. By April, 1877, Daniel had been succeeded by Paul Schulze. Schulze had worked in Boston and New York, designing Boylston Hall and Appleton Chapel (1857) at Harvard, and being associated in the design of the New York Crystal Palace (1853).[26]

From 1877 until 1881, Cluss and Schulze were involved in the de-

---

[22] John W. Reps, *Monumental Washington: The Planning and Development of the Capital Center* (Princeton, New Jersey: Princeton University Press, 1967), p. 59.

[23] *Report of the Joint Select Committee* ... pp. 2153, 2172, 2173.

[24] *Ibid.*, p. 2105.

[25] *Ibid.*, p. 2153.

[26] Henry-Russell Hitchcock discusses Paul Schulze in *Architecture: Nineteenth and Twentieth Centuries* (Baltimore, Maryland: Penguin Books, 1958), p. 89. and in *The Architecture of H. H. Richardson and his Times* (Cambridge, Massachusetts: The M.I.T. Press, 1936), pp. 10, 22, 65, 184, 189.

sign and construction of the U. S. National Museum. Intended for the reception of exhibits donated to the Federal government at the close of the Centennial Exposition in Philadelphia in 1876, the Museum was placed under the supervision of the Smithsonian Institution and located on the Mall directly to the east of the Smithsonian's building. Its design was derived from exposition architecture and expressed Professor Henry's desire for a contemporary building perfectly adapted to its function as a museum. On its completion in 1881 it was commented:

> The new building ... has proved to be so well adapted for the reception of a great industrial Museum ... that there is every prospect that the Museum will develop into one of the most perfect and comprehensive of its class...[27]

> The new building more than meets all expectations. The illumination is perfect, the amount of space available for exhibition purposes is undoubtedly the maximum for its size, and the disposition of the exhibition-halls in a single level directly upon the surface of the earth, proves to be of great importance both to visitors and to those who arrange the collections.[28]

In 1883–1884 Cluss and Schulze reconstructed the east end of the Smithsonian building, expanding and fireproofing the structure. During the 1880's they also worked out designs for a second National Museum building to be placed west of the Smithsonian Institution. This structure was never built.

On September 24, 1877, a disastrous fire occurred at the Patent Office. A competition was held for its reconstruction in 1878 and the work awarded to Cluss and Schulze. This was carried on simultaneously with the building of the National Museum. Cluss and Schulze's work in the 1880's included the first notable apartment house in Washington, The Portland (1883), the Army Medical Museum and Library (1885), Catholic University (1887), The National Monument in Commemoration of the Independence of Mexico (1887), and the Soldiers and Sailors Monument in the State of Indiana (1888). A competition for the design of the Grant Memorial Tomb in 1888 was won by Cluss. Though he received the prize money, his design was not used. It was decided that the memorial should be executed by a New York State resident.

Cluss retired from active practice in 1890. In the years 1890–1895

---

[27] G. Brown Goode, "Report of the Assistant Secretary," *Annual Report of the Board of Regents of the Smithsonian Institution ... 1881* (Washington: Government Printing Office, 1882), p. 88.

[28] *Ibid.*, p. 94.

Smithsonian Institution

U.S. National Museum, main entrance, about 1895.

Smithsonian Institution

Design for the reconstruction of the interior of the U.S. Patent Office, Cluss and Schulze, 1879.

he served as inspector of public buildings of the United States throughout the country. His official reports while in this capacity are interesting for their insight into the technical problems of building construction. In his last years Cluss served as technical consultant to General J. M. Wilson, Chief of Engineers of the Army and to others.

Cluss was married to Rosa Schmidt, daughter of Jacob Schmidt of Baltimore, in February, 1859. The couple had seven children, four

Tanya Beauchamp

Portland Apartments (now demolished) on Thomas Circle at 14th Street and Vermont Avenue, N.W.

sons and three daughters. The sons died at tragically early ages—one as a child and the others as young men. The daughters lived lives of normal length. Anita, who strongly resembled her father, became noted as a harpist.[29] The Cluss residence was at 413 Second Street, N. W. in the pleasant middle class neighborhood surrounding Judiciary Square—within walking distance of Cluss' first office near the Patent Office. After the deaths of his wife and last son in 1894, Cluss went to live with one of his daughters, Lillian Cluss Daw, at 2301 H Street, N. W. He died there of heat prostration on July 24, 1905, shortly after his eightieth birthday. He is buried in Oak Hill Cemetery. Prominent architects of the city, including Gleen Brown, Snowden Ashford, W. M. Poindexter, C. A. Didden, James G. Hill and W. E. Donn served as pallbearers at his funeral. In its obituary notice *The Western Architect* noted: "To the older members of the

---

[29] John Clagett Proctor, *Proctor's Washington and Environs*, (written for the *Washington Sunday Star* 1928–1949), 1949, p. 299.

A.I.A. the name and familiar figure of Adolph Cluss is one of pleasant memories, for his place was that of a strong, conservative member and genial friend."[30]

At the end of the 1869 session of the American Institute of Architects at which Cluss read his paper on "Theory, Functions and Incidental Uses of Chimnies," Mr. F. H. Petersen, a visitor, commented:

> The two papers that have been read this morning, and the remarks of your Chairman, are, in my opinion, of the utmost importance. The first paper showed us how important science is in our profession. It was an absolute, technical, scientific essay, and it elicited discussion immediately. Every one saw how important it was to understand that thing completely, and therefore admitted silently that Science is an important element in Architecture. The second paper, very able and very interesting, started upon the point that scientific education is of no avail and no necessity for the student of Architecture; and that art and artistic views are exclusively necessary to the Architect....
>
> I think, sir, that both views have a certain degree of force. I think that we all will agree that without a perfect understanding of the laws of gravity, and of a great many other branches of applied science, we cannot expect to build anything that deserves the name of Architecture. When we remember that the briefest and best definition of Architecture is that of "beautifying utility," then we will all agree that to make a useful structure is the first thing and to beautify it and put it in accord with all the laws of art is the second thing....[31]

This conflict between beauty and utility marked American architecture in the 1860's and 1870's, reflecting the turbulence of the period. The Civil War had speeded up the industrialization of the country and had created unprecedented social and political situations. Architecture, under these conditions, was highly creative and open-ended on all levels. The many new inventions, such as the telephone, electricity, and the elevator, which were appearing so quickly; the multiplicity of new building types which accompanied the industrialization and reshaping of society; the development of totally new materials—such as iron, steel, and plate glass—whose technical capabilities were virtually unknown, continually redefined the role of architecture and the architect. A certain amount of aesthetic confusion was inevitable.

Cluss made his reputation as an architect of great technical skill able

---

[30] *The Western Architect*, Vol. 4 (December 1905), p. 11.

[31] *Proceedings of the Third Annual Convention of the American Institute of Architects: Held in New York November 16–17, 1869* (New York: published by the Institute, 1870), p. 44.

to design creatively in terms of function and the most up-to-date technology. A thorough professional, his values were entirely architectural. In his paper on the history of the architecture of Washington he criticized Dr. William Thornton as "an English amateur of versatile manners..." whose work on the U. S. Capitol Benjamin Latrobe had intimated was "... simply Pictorial..." and "... could not claim dignity and consideration as an architectural composition...."[32] Cluss obviously admired Latrobe and noted that he had been educated in Germany. Indeed, it is in Latrobe's tradition of the engineer-architect, the professional constructor, that Cluss stands.

In all his work Cluss' primary concern was that his buildings be impeccably constructed and function well. Problems of heating and ventilating, lighting, acoustics and fireproofing were carefully worked out. In his school designs, for example, he isolated classrooms from each other by strategically placed cloakrooms and circulation areas to minimize sound transmission. The teacher's desk was placed on a platform in a semi-circular niche, improving acoustics, saving space, and contributing an interesting design feature. Rectangularly shaped classrooms also improved acoustics while permitting floors of maximum strength at minimum expense. Larger areas of glass at the side and, when possible, the rear of the classrooms provided a favorable light. Low pressure steam-heating combined maximum safety with the most efficient service available.

The materials used by Cluss were invariably the most scientifically advanced, machine-made products available. His buildings were principally of brick with concrete footings, rolled iron beams and trusses, and cast iron columns. Roofs were metal or slate hung on iron purlins. Wood and other combustible materials were eliminated as completely as possible. Exteriors were of pressed brick with cast iron, sandstone and terracotta detail. Machine-made products were uniform and easily handled, contributing to efficiency and economy of construction. Often they possessed unique characteristics required by the new building types.

Cluss' aesthetic persuasion was picturesque and he worked toward intricacy and variety of massing, silhouette and surface texture and color. He abhorred what he considered meaningless ornament, however, and attempted to involve all design elements in the function of

---

[32] Adolph Cluss, "Architecture and Architects at the Capital of the United States from its Foundation until 1875," *Proceedings of the Tenth Annual Convention of the American Institute of Architects: Held in Philadelphia October 11-12, 1876* (Boston: published by the Institute, 1877), p. 39.

Adolph Cluss: An Architect in Washington

the structure. Of Franklin School it was observed, probably by Cluss:

> What forms the most notable feature in this school building is, that the huge ventilating flues, which generally form unseemly protuberances, have been grouped symmetrically on the four corners and shaped so as to form the most prominent part of the decoration; that the sub-strate of the characteristic bell-towers perform the most important parts in the combined system of heating and ventilation, and that, in short, architecture itself constitutes the decoration of the architecture; although there are also a few minute carvings, not discernable from a distance.[33]

His predilection for multi-functioning design elements can be seen also in the cast iron columns with foliated capitals at Calvary Church which contribute to the decor of the lecture room, support the structure of the upper hall, and function as part of the heating apparatus.

The dictum that architecture itself should constitute the decoration of architecture found expression also in structural ornamentation. Heavily corbelled cornices, integrated pilasters, bold belt courses and three-dimensional design devices characterized his brick work. Polychromatic effects were sought both by using bricks of different colors in geometric patterns and by contrasting brick with sandstone, cast iron or terracotta. Also of Franklin School it was remarked: "Monotony is avoided, and the general design is rendered more intelligible by the little interruptions of alternating the mass of red bricks by courses of stones of the warm, light complementary color."[34] Similarly, roofs combined red and green slates with the more common blue in geometrical patterns. Press bricks themselves, laid with a very fine joint, provided rich color.

Massing was often complicated but inevitably symmetrical. Advancing and receding planes, towers, bays, unusual roofs—all were used with an almost classical balance. Perhaps this was due to a basically rationalistic approach to design, perhaps to the greater economies possible with regular, repetitive forms. Cluss designed most commonly in the Second Empire style, sometimes in Romanesque or Mooresque. His use of styles was modernized, however, and bore little resemblance to the Romantic historicism of the ante-bellum years. It was decorative rather the evocative. Elements of different styles were often used together on the same building, and the buildings were aggressively contemporary.

---

[33] Board of Trustees of the Public Schools of the City of Washington, *Twenty-third Annual Report of the Board, 1866–1870* (Washington City: M'Gill & Witherow, 1870), p. 116.

[34] *Ibid.*

In his paper on the architecture of Washington Cluss made a revealing criticism of the then partially completed Washington monument. He called it "... an unpardonable anachronism...":

> An inscribed pillar detached from the palaces of the Pharaohs would be a most improper form for perpetuating the civil and military virtues of George Washington, one of the most humane of men. Architecture is defined as the material expression of the wants, faculties and sentiments of its age. Formal types and symbols, primarily the common property of groups of nations, have been gradually transformed and perfected in the onward march of civilization; and a return to the unarticulated mode of expression resorted to in the earliest stages of society would be a declaration of bankruptcy on the part of the taste of the age.[35]

Cluss goes on to criticize the fraud involved in constructing "... a huge unsightly pile of masonry faced with scaling cut stone, to palm it upon the public as an obelisk, simply because geometrical outlines have been copied off-hand, and finally to claim credit for surpassing the size of the original...." [36] He is also offended by triumphant comparisons of the height of the monument to the heights of various great European works of architecture such as St. Peter's in Rome or St. Paul's in London. He observes wryly: "This is probably the first time that any one to whom has been confided the shaping of a great national monument has undertaken to discard quality, and in earnest to compare by the surveyor's pole the work of genius with a pile of stone...." [37] This concern for modernity, for workmanship and for honesty of form and function leads away from the Romantic historicism of the ante-bellum years to more relevant contemporary concerns.

---

[35] Cluss, "Architecture and Architects," p. 44.
[36] *Ibid.*
[37] *Ibid.*

A Blueprint for Change: The Black Community in Washington, D.C., 1860–1870

MELVIN R. WILLIAMS

Reconstruction, said Melvin Drimmer, "was the boldest social experiment ever attempted in the United States up till the New Deal." Drimmer also said that "looking back at Reconstruction and considering American attitudes toward Negroes it must appear strange, not that it failed, but that it was tried at all." C. Vann Woodward accurately concluded that there is too much irony mixed with the tragedy of Reconstruction to call the period a Golden Age. Willie Lee Rose, perhaps more optimistic than Drimmer and Woodward, showed how Reconstruction in certain rural areas could have worked. She too, however, concluded that the social experiments on the Sea Islands of South Carolina and Georgia were examples of revolutions that went backward. Constance McLaughlin Green saw a social revolution beginning in Washington, D.C. in 1867 with black suffrage.[1] This study, too, raises some important questions: Were the changes that took place in the nation's capital during the 1860's bold social experiments? Did they constitute a social revolution? Were they merely social upheavals, or simply natural occurrences?

Blacks in Washington in the 1860's participated in a variety of activities. Some of the enterprises they performed with white allies: the drives for emancipation, black suffrage, and public primary education for blacks. Other activities Afro-Americans carried out basically alone. Many blacks married[2] and reared families. Some of them bought

---
[1] Melvin Drimmer, ed., *Black History: A Reappraisal* (Garden City, N. Y.: Doubleday and Co., 1968), 292; C. Vann Woodward, *The Burden of Southern History* (Baton Rouge: Louisiana State University Press, 1960), 107; Constance McLaughlin Green, *Washington: Village and Capital* (Princeton: Princeton University Press, 1962), 321.
[2] Washington's *Daily National Intelligencer*, Jan. 3, 1867, gave the following number of marriage licenses issued to black couples and to white couples: 1863—blacks, 444, whites 1,613; 1864—blacks, 447, whites 1,621; 1866—blacks 756, whites 1,359. Washing-

their freedom, or the freedom of their loved ones. They worked, acquired property, paid taxes, and through some of their taxes for a time aided public schools which barred black children. Blacks supported their own private schools. They maintained their churches and did charitable work through benevolent and social organizations. They read newspapers and sometimes contributed articles to black publications such as the *Baltimore Repository* and the *Philadelphia Christian Recorder*. Some black Washingtonians attended religious conferences and numerous lectures. Quite possibly some of them enjoyed dramatic productions and operas. There were times when some blacks, as well as a few whites, viewed the Liberian and other emigration movements as possible solutions to some of the problems of the 1860's. These campaigns suggest that a well organized black community existed in the Capital City at that time.

BLACK RESIDENCES

Before discussing where Afro-Americans lived, some facts about Washington in 1860 may be useful. The city's population in that year was 61,122. There were 1,774 slaves, 9,209 free blacks, and 50,139 whites. The city had seven wards. There were 1,170 blocks or squares bounded by twenty-one avenues and more than one hundred streets criss-crossing the city. Letters of the alphabet designated streets that ran east and west according to their location north or south of the Capitol, which was the dividing point. Thus A Street North and A Street South were the first streets north and south of the Capitol. Numerals designated the streets running north and south and distinguished them from each other by East and West according to their position in regard to the Capitol. Examples were First Street East and First Street West. A city ordinance required every building to display its street number. Lower numbers appeared at the city's boundaries and the nearer a building was to the Capitol, the higher was its number.[3]

---

ton's *Daily National Republican*, Nov. 29, 1862, said that Joseph Jackson and Letitia Simms married on Nov. 25 at the 15th Street Presbyterian Church; the pastor, Rev. W. B. Evans, officiated.

[3] Eighth U. S. Census, 1860: Statistics of Population (Washington: Government Printing Office, 1862), 588; William H. Boyd, compiler, *Boyd's Washington and Georgetown Directory* (Washington: Taylor and Maury, 1860), 7; Wilhelmus B. Bryan, *A History of the National Capital from its foundation through the period of the adoption of the Organic Act* (New York: The Macmillan Company, 1916), Vol. II, 491. The method I employed to determine the system of house numbering used in 1860 was to select from the city directory several names of black residents with low house numbers; then I checked census manuscript returns to learn the wards they resided in. For example, Jane Talbot lived at 95 K Street, North, in ward one; Isaac Fleetwood resided at 560 K Street, North, in ward three. Ward three was considerably closer to the Capitol than ward one.

A large number of free black families lived on streets distinguished by numerals West, and by alphabets North and South.[4] A sample of 236 names showed that eighty-nine black families lived on numeral streets West, sixty-one on alphabet streets North, and fifty-three on alphabet streets South. Only seven black families lived on numeral streets East. Sixteen black families had addresses on avenues and only six had alley addresses. Addresses on avenues did not distinguish North or South, East or West, and alley addresses usually did not have house numbers.[5]

Since large numbers of blacks lived on alphabet streets North and South, and on numeral streets West, there may be the temptation to conclude that a majority of Afro-Americans lived in the northwest and southwest sections of Washington. That was not the full picture, however. Free blacks lived in all wards although very few lived in ward six. Ward one had the largest free black population—2,116; 5,980 whites lived there also. Ward four, located mostly in northeast Washington, had 1,455 free blacks, and ward five, southeast of the Capitol, had 1,216. Ward four had the largest number of white residents, 10,068, and ward five ranked seventh with 4,953. Blacks, then, lived in all sections of the city. There were, however, clusters of black families in certain areas, especially in northwest and southwest Washington.[6]

Although there were no all-black or all-white wards, some degree of residential segregation probably existed. For example, one census-taker in 1860 visited fourteen families in succession—thirteen black and one white—and got information about seventy-two blacks and eight whites during the fourteen-family canvas. Similarly, another census-enumerator visited seven successive houses and nine families—all white—and recorded information about thirty-nine whites and one black female servant.[7] Due to the tedious nature of census-taking in

[4] *Boyd's Directory*, 1860, listed 1,139 names, occupations, and addresses of free blacks. It distinguished blacks by the abbreviation "col'd". With the use of information from manuscript returns I concluded that the blacks listed headed families. (See a description of the information found in returns in footnote 11.) From a sample of 236 names I located residences of blacks on specific streets and blocks. The sampling technique I used was to list all the information the directory gave for the first 115 blacks; then I included the information found on every additional ninth page. Initially I attempted to gather information about all blacks listed (this attempt accounts for the first 115 names), but when that proved too time-consuming, I used every ninth page. This method gave me slightly more than 20 per cent of the black names in the directory, systematically selected.

[5] *Boyd's Directory*, 1860, 36–162.

[6] *Ibid.*; Original Returns of the Assistant Marshals. Eighth Census of the United States for the Ditsrict of Columbia: 1860. National Archives Microfilm Publications, Rolls 102–105.

[7] *Ibid.*

1860 it is unlikely that an enumerator deliberately set out to canvas families of one racial group before surveying those of another if members of the two groups resided beside each other.

Just as there is evidence that some residential segregation existed in 1860, there is also evidence that some residential mixing occurred. William W. Corcoran, a white banker and southern sympathizer during the Civil War, who had real and personal estates valued at $1,500,000, resided at 310 H Street North in ward one. Sarah Bell, a black person who had real estated valued at $300.00, resided at 216 H Street North, one block west of Corcoran. Letha Turner, a black widow, resided in the same block as Corcoran, at 354 H Street North; and James Wormley, a black well-to-do restaurant owner, lived one street north of Corcoran at 314 I Street North. M. Brown, a black barber, resided with his family in close proximity to James G. Berrett, the Mayor of Washington in 1860; both lived in ward two.[8]

BLACK FAMILIES

Although there are difficulties in drawing a composite picture of Afro-American families in the 1860's, evidence suggests that black Washingtonians lived in conventional family units. There is also the possibility that some black families had boarders in their homes. A few examples illustrate the difficulty involved in drawing a clear picture of the family structure. William Brown, thirty-seven in 1860, was the head of a household of four persons. There was only one other person in the home with the surname Brown, a twenty-one-year-old female named Chrisan. The other members in the home were Harriet Gibbs, sixty years old, who washed clothes for a living, and Henry Hill, twenty-two, a fisherman. Conceivably no relationship existed between the four members of the household. It is possible, however, that Chrisan was the wife, or sister, or even daughter of William. Similarly, it is imaginable that Harriet was William's mother and that Henry was a boarder in William's home. The Winnie Painter family presents a parallel of similar uncertainty. Winnie Painter, seventy-seven, a mid-wife, had in her home Thomas Johnson, sixteen, and Adeline Johnson, seven. It is believed that Thomas and Adeline were brother and sister and that Mrs. Painter was their grandmother. It is equally possible that Mrs. Painter was simply a kind person who had compassion on two youngsters and received them into her home.[9]

---

[8] *Boyd's Directory*, 1860; Original Returns, 8th Census.

[9] *Ibid.;* Andrew Billingsley, *Black Families in White America* (Englewood Cliffs, N. J.: Prentice-Hall, Inc., 1968), 16–18; Daniel P. Moynihan, *The Negro Family: The Case for National Action* (Office of Policy Planning and Research, United States Department of Labor, 1965), especially page 5.

The following three examples demonstrate more convincingly that they were families in the conventional pattern. In each of them all members had the same surname as the head of the household. Also the age of each member indicated that the members could be either father, mother, or offspring, and in one case, grandmother. Lewis Hyson, a forty-year-old laborer, headed a house of four persons; others members were Harriet, thirty-five, and two boys, ages five and two. Very likely Harriet was Lewis's wife and the two boys their sons. In the James Barnes household, Barnes was thirty, Hannah was thirty-five, and five children ranged in ages from twelve to two. John Bridgely, thirty, headed a residence of five; the elder John, a five-year-old boy also named John, an eighty-year-old female and a seven-year-old girl, both named Minerva, and a thirty-five-year-old female named Isha made up the family. It is possible that the older John and Isha were husband and wife, that eighty-year-old Minerva Bridgely was John's mother, and that John and Isha had two children, the boy the namesake of his father, and the girl named in honor of her grandmother.[10]

Most black families were patrifocal: 5,356 black persons in 1,036 families resided in wards one, two, and seven, the wards with the largest black population. Of this number 663 black males headed families, and 373 females. The 1860 city directory listed 1,139 black heads of families; 784 were males and 355 were females. Thus both census manuscript returns and the city directory showed the ratio of male heads over female heads to be nearly two to one. As the black population increased, there was a corresponding increase in the number of black men who headed families. The 1862 directory listed 1,536 black family heads; 1,049 were males.[11]

Offhand it appears that the average size of black families in 1860 was between five and six persons. There are, however, several reasons for caution in affixing the size of Afro-American families. James Wormley and Alfred Jones were two of the wealthiest black men in the city. There were eleven persons in Wormley's family in 1860 and twelve in Jones's family, including his daughter, Matilda, a graduate of Oberlin College in Ohio. There is no reason to conclude that families with less wealth than these two had fewer members. No doubt

---

[10] Original Returns, 8th Census.

[11] *Ibid.; Boyd's Directory*, 1862. Manuscript returns for 1860 gave information for residents of each ward. Census takers listed the head of the household first, along with his age, sex, color, profession, trade or occupation, place of birth, and value of real and personal estates. They recorded similar information for each member over fifteen. Since census takers numbered families and houses in order of visitation, it is possible to determine if more than one family resided in the same house.

the average size of black families appeared to be between five and six because census-takers recorded one-member households as families.[12]

BLACK OCCUPATIONS

In 1860 Washington blacks earned their livelihoods in a variety of ways, although most of them worked in occupations categorized as unskilled by census enumerators and by the compiler of the city directory. Of the 784 black males listed in the directory, 313 were laborers, 77 waiters, and 51 hackmen. Among the 355 black females, 96 were washwomen. Some black Washingtonians were carpenters, plasterers, shoemakers, seamstresses, and barbers. Likewise some worked as gardeners, messengers, and cooks. Here and there one found a few teachers, businessmen, nurses, musicians and ministers.[13]

JOBS PERFORMED BY BLACKS IN WASHINGTON IN 1860

I tabulated some of the jobs held by certain blacks living in wards one, two, and three.

Laborers	84	Cooks	4
Washwomen	37	Businessmen	4
Hackmen	22	Whitewashers	3
Servants	22	Fishermen	2
Gardeners	12	Teachers	2
Carpenters	10	Sextons	2
Waiters	10	Tailors	2
Shoemakers	9	Nurses	2
Plasterers	7	Blacksmiths	2
Porters	7	Musician	1
Seamstresses	6	Midwife	1
Messengers	5	Minister	1
Barbers	4	No occupations listed	43
Total			319

Source: Population Schedules of the Eighth Census of the United States. City of Washington. National Archives Microfilm Publications, Roll 102.

There was little or no change between 1860 and 1862 in the types of jobs blacks held. A tabulation of all jobs held by blacks as listed in the 1862 city directory showed that 415 males worked as laborers,

---

[12] *Ibid.* 5,356 blacks in 1,036 families lived in wards one, two, and seven. I divided the number of blacks by the number of black families and got 5.1. There is a suggestion that black family heads were relatively young, even by 19th century standards. In studying blacks in wards one, two, and three with real estate valued at more than $300, I found that there were 143 family heads and their average age was 44.2. Admittedly that phase of the study omitted the vast majority of blacks who had property worth less than $300, or had no property at all.

[13] *Boyd's Directory*, 1860.

A Blueprint for Change 365

111 as waiters, and 88 as hackmen. 128 females worked as washwomen.[14]

Blacks in the District of Columbia owned $758,934 worth of real and personal property. The Census Office gave this analysis of property held by blacks in 1860.

THE VALUE OF BLACK-OWNED PROPERTY, 1860

Real estate	$612,040
Personal property	146,894
Total	758,934

9,956 blacks had no property
774 blacks had property valued less than $500
168 " " " " over 500 but less than 1000
153 " " " " " 1,000 " " " 2,000
40 " " " " " 2,000 " " " 3,000
18 " " " " " 3,000 " " " 4,000
10 " " " " " 4,000 " " " 5,000
5 " " " " " 5,000 " " " 6,000
6 " " " " " 6,000 " " " 7,000
1 black " " " " 7,000

Source: Letter from John G. Kennedy, Superintendent, Census Office, to Senator Lot M. Morrill. Published in the *Daily National Republican*, April 15, 1862.

Only 1,175 of the District's 11,131 black residents owned property in 1860, and most of those lived in the city of Washington.[15]

In terms of material possessions a few black families fared moderately well. The vast majority, however, had little in the way of wealth and barely eked out a day to day existence. An examination of black wealth in ward one shows clearly that only a few black families had much wealth. There were 2,135 blacks in 376 families. Eighty-eight heads of families had real estate valued at more than $100. Fifty of these persons' property appraised at $1,000 or more, twenty-two at $2,000 or more, and eleven at $3,000 or more. Of black family heads, 288, or seventy-seven per cent, had no real estate, or if they did, their property valued less than $100.[16]

Of 4,794 blacks living in wards one, two and three, 134 had real estate priced at more than $1,000, ninety had property worth between $300 and $900, and thirty-three had property appraised between $100 and $200; 4,537 Afro-Americans had no property, or if they did, it valued less than $100.[17]

---

[14] *Ibid.*, 1862.
[15] Letter from Kennedy to Senator Morrill.
[16] Original Returns, 8th Census, Roll 102.
[17] *Ibid.*, Rolls 102, 103.

RELIGIOUS, SOCIAL, AND BENEVOLENT ACTIVITIES

The black church played a central role in the lives of blacks. Constance Green, in writing about black religious activities in the 1830's and 1840's, said that Afro-Americans without any church affiliation had little standing in the black community.[18] No doubt the same situation existed in the 1860's. Washington had eleven black churches in 1862, and some traced their origins back a number of decades. These churches in 1862 had a total membership of 3,850. There were six black Methodist churches, four Baptist churches, and one Presbyterian church. The Asbury African Methodist Episcopal Church, on the corner of 11th and K Streets, had a membership of 600 and thus was the largest black congregation in Washington; John W. Lambert, a white man, was the minister. The second largest black church was the Israel Bethel Methodist Church with 500 members; Henry McNeal Turner, a black leader, was the pastor of this church located on South Capitol Street. Other black Methodist churches were the Zion Wesley on the Island with 400 members, Wesley Methodist on 17th Street with 450 members, Ebenezer Methodist at the Navy Yard with 250 members and the 200 member John Wesley Church on 24th Street. Of these last four churches, only Ebenezer had a white minister. The total number of Methodist worshippers in the city was 2,400.[19]

The four black Baptist churches in 1862 had a combined membership of 1,150; each had a black clergyman. Benjamin T. Tanner served the 400 members at the 19th Street Baptist Church, J. A. Handy the 400 members at Union Bethel on N Street, A. Bowman the 200 persons at Island Baptist, and Caleb Woodyard the 150 worshippers at Second Baptist on 3rd Street. W. B. Evans led the only black Presbyterian congregation in the city, the 300 member 15th Street Presbyterian Church.[20]

Washington's *Daily National Republican*, a chief spokesman for the radical Republicans, described black churches as large, well established, and well sustained. Worshippers numbered about 300 at each sermon. They dressed well, and had quiet, solemn services. One church had an impressive organ, and several had large, well instructed choirs. One or two of the churches paid its minister $1,000 a year. Of black clergymen the newspaper said that all were worthy men,

---
[18] Constance McLaughlin Green, *The Secret City: A History of Race Relations in the Nation's Capital* (Princeton: Princeton University Press, 1967), 40.

[19] The *Republican*, April 15, 1862. Much of this information on ministers of black churches came from the uncataloged vertical files on Black History in the Washingtoniana Room of the Washington Public Library (now the Martin Luther King Memorial Library).

[20] *Ibid.;* I do not know the race of W. B. Evans.

"and render the most efficient service. A more self-denying, persevering, laborious body of men cannot be found in any country. Their influence is deservedly great, and may be safely trusted by the friends of the Union and popular government." [21]

The churches served as cultural and intellectual centers, as well as houses of worship. The Lyceum of the Israel Bethel Church drew some of the most intellectually-minded Washingtonians of both races to listen to lectures, participate in discussions and to read papers on timely topics. On January 1, 1864, Charles Lenox Remond addressed the congregation at Israel Bethel. Samuel Chase, a black minister of Baltimore, spoke at the same church on the subject, "God's dealings with the children of Ham, and their future prospects" on May 19. The Reverend Daniel Payne, a black bishop, spoke at the Israel Church on November 24. Among the members of Congress who spoke at that church were Benjamin Wade, Thaddeus Stevens, and Henry Wilson.[22]

Israel Church was not the only one that sponsored noted speakers. Dr. John S. Rock, a Boston black physician and attorney, lectured at the 15th Street Presbyterian Church on May 22, 1862; Frederick Douglass addressed a gathering there on December 7. A Boston clergyman, Charles Spear, the white editor of the *Prisoner's Friend*, spoke at the 19th Street Baptist Church on May 24, 1862; Dr. J. B. Smith, of Haiti, lectured at the same church three days later on Haitian emigration; and on June 3, W. J. Watkins spoke on the same topic at the Zion Methodist Church.[23]

In addition to their religious and cultural roles, black churches also served as charitable agencies. On April 30, 1862 the Israel Church raised $61 to aid ex-slaves; the next day the Asbury A.M.E. Church collected $105.09 for the same purpose. Both of these churches gave "liberal" sums to support the dinner for ex-slaves on Thanksgiving Day in 1862. In 1864 the 15th Street Presbyterian Church sponsored Miss E. T. Greenfield, known professionally as the "Black Swan," in a series of concerts to aid a newly opened Freedmen's school. The churches provided clothing and food for the poor; they encouraged reading through their literary societies and libraries; they provided recreation through the use of their grounds and edifices; some housed private schools; and the churches maintained cemeteries for deceased members of the black community.[24]

---

[21] *Ibid.*

[22] The *Republican*, May 17, Nov. 25, 1862; Jan. 1, 1864.

[23] *Ibid.*, May 20, June 2, 1862; Jan. 5, Nov. 24, 1864. The newspaper referred to several black speakers as able men, well educated, and among the best orators in the country.

[24] *Ibid.*, May 5, Nov. 25, 1862, Jan. 28, 1864. The *Republican* did not define "liberal" sums.

Black churches served as hosts to a number of religious conferences. In February 1863, the Asbury Methodist Episcopal Church hosted the annual convention of that conference. Senator Waitman Willey of West Virginia and a Reverend Wyatt of the Wyoming Conference addressed the gathering. The convention collected $130 to aid missionary work. The Southern Annual Conference of the African Methodist Episcopal Zion Connection began its meeting on April 12 at the John Wesley Church. The annual conference of African Methodist Episcopal churches began its sessions on April 17, 1862 in the Israel Church; Bishop Daniel Payne presided. Other blacks who played prominent roles were R. H. Cain of Brooklyn, New York, Reverend Alexander Crummell, and John D. Johnson, the latter two commissioners of Liberia. The convention resolved that it would meet its obligations to Africa as soon as it received the necessary funds, and it praised the Senate for recognizing the independence of Haiti and Liberia. On December 31, 1862, a black convention, consisting of delegates from the black churches and organizations in the city, met at Zion Wesley Church. Among the several addresses delivered, John T. Costin's was the most eloquent. He called for the establishment of a hospital for the poor, and Thomas H. C. Hinton introduced a resolution calling for immediate action on the hospital proposal; another motion carried requiring each delegate to donate $10 toward a capital fund of $6,000. The Association of Impartial Progress met frequently and speakers gave advice to listeners on how to utilize their newly gained freedom.[25] A few black benevolent, business, social, and military organizations operated outside the influence of black churches, although at times churches provided meeting places for these organizations. On July 6, 1863, blacks met at the Ebenezer Church to draw up plans for a home guard. They sent a resolution to Congress saying that the black man wanted to show that he deserved "the citizenship which he now holds in common with the white man, by giving his blood freely for the preservation of the rights and immunities belonging to him." The black District of Columbia regiment, consisting of 770 soldiers in 1863, resulted from the Ebenezer meeting. In March of 1867 the National League of Black Soldiers and Sailors met at the 15th Street Presbyterian Church. M. T. J. Durant of Louisiana delivered the keynote address, entitled, "The Worth of the Colored Man to the Federal cause during the late rebellion." [26]

---

[25] The *Intelligencer*, Feb. 23, 1864; *Republican*, April 21, 1862, Dec. 31, 1862.
[26] The *Republican*, July 9, 1863; *Intelligencer*, March 1, 1867.

The Washington chapter of black Odd Fellows hosted that organization's nineteenth annual meeting held on October 7, 1863, at the Union Friendship Lodge on 15th Street. "A large number of delegates from northern and western states and the British provinces were present." The next day the convention sponsored a parade that went past the White House and City Hall, then proceeded up Pennsylvania Avenue to the Capitol. The black Collins band of Washington and the band of the black Seventh United States Troops of Baltimore led the parade. "When the parade passed City Hall, Mayor Wallach bowed his thanks. Not one unpleasant incident occurred." [27] The organization of black teachers and the Union Printing Joint Stock Association were business and professional organizations. The Union Printing Association, founded in 1867 with a capital investment of $2,000, wanted to establish a black daily newspaper in Washington. The organization of black teachers met monthly, usually at Soldier's Free Library on 5th Street. In 1867, John F. Cook and A. E. Newton were officers in the association. One of the projects of the association was the establishment of a program of studies for black schools that would parallel that of the city's white schools.[28]

PRIVATE EDUCATION FOR BLACKS

Private primary education for blacks had long been a tradition in Washington, and during the 1860's some black children still studied in private schools. In 1862 there were six such schools in the District of Columbia, five in Washington and one in Georgetown. The ones in Washington were: John F. Cook's school in the basement of the 15th Street Presbyterian Church located between I and K Streets, George F. T. Cook's school in the basement of the Israel Bethel Church on South Capitol Street, Matilda Jones's school in a hall over her father's store on K Street between 20th and 21st Streets, Enoch Ambush's Wesleyan Seminary on C Street, South, between 9th and 10th Streets, and C. Leonard's school on H Street near 14th Street. The one black school in Georgetown was Emma Brown's school in the basement of the Methodist Church on Beall Street. At one point the *National Republican* said that many students attended these schools, but later while giving the enrollments of each school, the paper showed that in fact only 270 children attended regularly. Each school had one teacher, who was black, and all except one had received his collegiate educa-

---

[27] The *Republican*, Oct. 8, 9, 1867.
[28] The *Intelligencer*, March 2, 9, 1867.

tion at Oberlin College in Ohio. The one exception, Ambush, had educated himself.[29]

Some of the subjects black youngsters studied were reading, arithmetic, recitation and geography. In most of the schools the "textbooks used were the same as those in Ohio," with the Bible serving as the principal reading blook. The *National Republican* wrote that black students "exhibited love for education and acquired the rudiments with marked success. In numerals and geography they soon become experts. In recitation, especially of descriptive poems, they were excellent." Tuition ranged from fifty cents to one dollar per month according to the subjects taught.[30] Constance Green said that by January, 1866, self-supporting schools taught by black teachers had increased to eight or ten and had a combined enrollment of nearly 500 students.[31]

It appears that the main way blacks could get a secondary education, if they remained in Washington, was in the normal department at Howard University. Congress chartered Howard in 1867, and established normal, collegiate, theological, law, medicine and agriculture departments. That assembly authorized the institution to grant diplomas and to confer degrees similar to those conferred by other universities. The dedication of the first three-story brick building took place on March 23, 1867. Initially forty students enrolled at Howard.[32]

FREEDOM

Basically Afro-Americans carried out the preceding activities alone. In several important drives, however, the major impetus for change came from radical Republicans in Congress and from those engaged in municipal politics in the District of Columbia. No doubt Reverend Henry Highland Garnet, the black clergyman of the 15th Street Presbyterian Church, recognized that blacks needed Congress's help when he exhorted the assembly to "emancipate, enfranchise, educate, and give the blessings of the Gospel to every American citizen."

Emancipation in Washington was one of the movements in which whites greatly aided blacks; it probably occurred for both political and humane reasons. In 1860 few whites overly concerned themselves

---

[29] The *Republican*, May 21, 1862. John and George Cook were brothers; their father, John, Sr., had been a teacher and minister. Matilda Jones's father was Alfred Jones. Emma Brown had attended school in Boston before going to Oberlin College. Enoch Ambush, the self-educated teacher, was moderatly wealthy and owned Wesleyan Seminary and the lot upon which it stood.
[30] *Ibid.*
[31] Green, *The Secret City*, 88.
[32] The *Intelligencer*, March 23, 1867.

with the number of blacks living in the city, and few thought that emancipation would occur soon. Several reasons accounted for this lack of concern. During the 1850's only 1,050 free blacks had settled in Washington compared with 3,350 in the 1840's. Whites believed that a declining rate of growth for the free black population would continue in the 1860's. Another reason for the lack of strong concern by whites was that most blacks who entered Washington in 1860 entered as slaves. In 1862, however, emancipation came and whites then expressed serious concern over the possibility of a large influx of blacks. The fears of whites multiplied as the black population of the city increased from 10,981 in 1860 to 35,455 in 1870. The white population also increased—from 50,139 in 1860 to 73,731 in 1870, but what alarmed whites most was the rate of increase. In the ten-year span the black population increased by 222 percent compared with 47 percent for whites. Emancipation was the chief catalyst for the increase in the number of blacks.[33]

Emancipation in Washington came on April 16, 1862, through congressional enactment. By this legislation Congress freed more than 1,700 slaves in the city of Washington and more than 1,300 in the remainder of the District of Columbia; the act provided compensation for slave owners.[34] Thus slavery ended in the nation's capital several months before President Abraham Lincoln's general Emancipation Proclamation went into effect on January 1, 1863. By freeing slaves in the capital, possibly Congress and the President sought a way to remove slavery as a basic issue in the Civil War. If compensated emancipation could be made to work in Washington, perhaps the neighboring states and eventually all slave-holding states would adopt this plan of emancipation. This action may be viewed as one political reason for abolishing slavery in Washington.

In spite of the importance of the political reason for emancipation, moral and humane considerations also played a role. On March 25, 1862, Senator Henry Wilson of Massachusetts delivered a speech on the Senate floor supporting the emancipation drive in the District of Columbia. After reviewing the "brutal laws" then in force against blacks, he said: "In spite of the degrading influences of oppressive statutes, the free colored population as it has increased in population, has increased also in property, in churches, schools, and all the means of social, intellectual and moral development." Wilson further reported that blacks had twelve churches valued at $75,000, and eight

---

[33] Green, *The Secret City*, 48; Ninth United States Census, 1870: Population (Washington: Government Printing Office, 1871), 97.
[34] *Congressional Globe*, 34 C., 2nd S., 1496.

schools solely supported by themselves. He emphasized that blacks were "compelled to pay for the support of public schools for whites from which their own children are excluded by law, custom, and public opinion." He concluded his speech by saying that some free black men had distinquished themselves by their intelligence and business capacity, and that free black men throughout the city would welcome persons freed through emancipation.[35]

Conceivably the *National Republican's* position on emancipation influenced the passage of Washington's edict abolishing slavery. Several months before emancipation the *National Republican* reported horror-filled, eyewitness accounts of slave-catching activities in the capital. In speaking of contrabands in the city the paper said that "a large majority of them are willing and anxious to be employed. These contrabands, in general, are not the indolent, vicious class of people which some interested parties would like to prove that all freedmen are." Later the newspaper stated that "a large number of contrabands heretofore subsisted at government expense are now being employed in the various government hospitals at wages ranging from $4 to $10 per month." [36]

A good example of radical sentiment favoring emancipation were the newsstories on March 24 and 29. On March 24, the paper pointed out that blacks held a considerable amount of property. "It appears, from careful examination, that this property amounts to at least five hundred thousand dollars." Individual blacks held property, consisting of houses, lots, and bank stocks, valued from $3,000 to $15,000, and hundreds of blacks owned property valued from $1,000 to $2,000. Emphasizing blacks' valuable contributions to society, the *National Republican* continued: "It is a fact proved by the record of the courts that no colored person who has had any opportunity for position has ever been convicted of crime in the District of Columbia. Considering the disability under which they all labor, this is an important fact." Even when the *National Republican* viewed the black prison population it was sympathetic. "The number of the more ignorant and neglected colored people in the penitentiary and jail is comparatively small. Anyone can prove this who will examine the official records of these institutions. The statement is substantiated by the records for thirty years past." The paper also lauded black benevolent organizations. "There has never been a free colored person buried in Washington at public expense. The people of color in the District have charitable societies among themselves—numbering some

---

[35] The *Republican*, March 27, 1862.
[36] *Ibid.*, Feb. 28, March 3, 13, 15, 28, April 8, 1862.

thirty in all—which take care of the sick and bury the dead. Neither the public nor the Government has ever been called on for a farthing for these objects." The article concluded by saying that in spite of blacks' activities and progress, "colored people encounter many oppressions." [37]

As the date for final congressional action on the bill for emancipation in the District approached, the *National Republican,* as if to make an even greater appeal for passage, pointed out that free blacks resided throughout the city. Large numbers of them lived in the vicinities of Capitol Hill, the Navy Yard, Meridian Hill, and in a section known as the Island. The Island, the paper reported, was the most densely populated black area. "Here many of them occupy small wooden tenements as they do in other places in the District, with garden patches attached. Nearly all of them have families, with the strongest natural attachments binding them to the soil and each other." [38]

In the concluding section of the newsstory the *National Republican* spoke highly of blacks' attachment to the United States and their readiness to take up arms in defense of the Union. Blacks, the paper reported, equated themselves with ancient Biblical peoples in their struggle for freedom. Blacks "think and speak of General Hannibal as one of their own immortal heroes. The brave deeds of [Toussaint] L'Ouverture abroad, and of [Crispus] Attucks and [Nat] Turner at home, are as familiar to these people as household words." [39] It is interesting that the newspaper cited L'Ouverture and even Nat Turner in a story directed to whites. Obviously conditions had changed to such a degree that fears of slave uprisings had greatly diminished.

The speech by Senator Wilson and the newsstories in the *National Republican* suggest the existence of a stable black society in Washington; radical Republicans used the presence of such a society with good effect in urging the passage of the emancipation act. Also, in 1862 the majority of Southern legislators had left Congress and there was less opposition to the emancipation bill than there would have been if more of these lawmakers had retained their seats.

Black Washington's response to emancipation was one of rejoicing, as well as calm rationalizing. "The colored churches of the District are to have a thanksgiving jubilee tomorrow, in view of the passage of the emancipation bill yesterday. Interesting services will be held in all their places of Worship." [40] On April 21, blacks held

---
[37] *Ibid.,* March 24, 1862.
[38] *Ibid.,* March 29, 1862.
[39] *Ibid.*
[40] *Ibid.,* April 12, 1862.

a meeting in the lecture room of the 15th Street Presbyterian Church with delegates from the different wards and churches in attendance. They unanimously adopted resolutions stating "that by our industry, energy, moral deportment and character, we will prove ourselves worthy of the confidence reposed in us—in making us free men." Blacks assured whites that "as in the past we have as a people been orderly and law-abiding, so in the future we shall strive with might and main to be in every way worthy of the glorious privilege which has been conferred upon us." [41]

PUBLIC EDUCATION FOR BLACKS

During the same month that blacks received their freedom, another stormy issue confronted the residents of Washington—the issue of establishing public primary schools for black youngsters between the ages of six and seventeen. This drive was another activity in which some whites, mostly Republicans, aided blacks.

A major avenue to education for blacks in Washington before public education was through schools established by Freedman's Aid societies and the Federal Freedmen's Bureau. While Congress debated emancipation in Washington, organizations such as the New York American Tract Society set up evening schools for blacks in the city. "We learn that Rev. Dr. H. W. Pierson has been organizing evening schools for blacks. This is a noble work. Nine schools are already open and are doing a good job." [42] Reading was the basic subject blacks studied in the evening schools and the principal textbook was a book of Biblical teachings published by the American Sunday School Union in Philadelphia. On April 17, the American Tract Society announced that George L. Sharer, a graduate of Princeton College, would assist Pierson in establishing additional schools for blacks. Another announcement in May said that the Society had sent additional teachers.[43]

The Freedmen's Bureau, after its creation in 1865, joined with Freedmen's Aid societies in providing education for blacks. In January, 1866, some 100 men and women taught about 5,600 blacks in fifty-four day schools, and twenty-five Sabbath schools taught more than 2,300 pupils. In June, 1866, a little more than a year after its establishment, the Freedmen's Bureau reported more than 10,000 blacks receiving some instruction.[44]

---

[41] *Ibid.*, April 28, 1862.
[42] The *Republican*, April 9, 1862.
[43] *Ibid.*, May 17, 1862.
[44] Green, *The Secret City*, 88.

Public education was another means of instruction for blacks in the 1860's; after 1868, it became the most important one. About that time philanthropists concluded that the black education program was so well established that it no longer needed their help and nearly all of them withdrew their aid.[45] Public education for Afro-Americans received a push forward on April 29, 1862 when Senator James Grimes of Iowa introduced in the Senate a bill that called for diverting ten per cent of black taxes into a separate fund to be used for educating black children. The bill instructed trustees of black schools "to provide suitable rooms and teachers for such a number of schools as in their opinion will best accommodate the colored children." The House passed the bill on May 15, less than a month after its introduction, "without a dissenting vote or a word of opposition"; the Senate passed it on May 21.[46]

Some suggestions why Congress speedily enacted the school law may be useful. The *National Republican,* in the forefront among Washington newspapers in the drive to end slavery, also led in expressing favorable opinion toward establishing black schools. In a lengthy newsstory on private black schools, the paper pointed out that from the white schools' position the only hint of the existence of black children in Washington was in the section of the *Directory of Public Schools* that listed the qualifications required for admission to public schools, and that qualification was the applicant must be white. The newspaper said that in order for black children to enjoy the same advantage as white children, there had to be more than 1,500 black pupils in public schools, whereas none then attended. Finally, the paper chided white Washingtonians for failing to concern themselves with black private schools. It said that

> no white citizen of the district has ever visited one of these schools; not an encouraging word has ever been spoken to either teacher or pupils, by the white teachers, by the trustees of the other schools, by the members of the Young Men's Christian Association, or by the pastors or members of the Christian Churches in this city or in Georgetown. The only notice taken of the black schools by the press was an attempt, a few years ago, by one of our contemporaries to get these schools destroyed by the mob.[47]

Senator Grimes' speech when he introduced the education bill in the Senate may have spurred Congress to act swiftly. Repeating

---

[45] *Ibid.,* 88, 89.

[46] The *Republican,* May 16, 21, 1862; *Congressional Globe,* 37th Cong., 2nd Sess., 1854 and Append., 356, 357.

[47] The *Republican,* May 21, 1862.

the statement that blacks helped support a school system that barred their children, the Senator pointed out that in 1861 blacks paid $36,000 in property taxes, and that $3,600 of those taxes went into the school fund. Congress found that it was not too difficult to establish a black school system that would receive funds only from black taxes and private contributions.[48]

Many white Washingtonians reacted harshly to the school law, nonetheless, and this reaction resulted in an ineffective school system for black children for several years. On the day the House passed the measure a group of Washington "Union Democrats and Union Whigs and other conservative voters" voiced their "uncompromising opposition to the effort which is now in progress to impose upon this city the odious task of schooling negro children." [49] White opposition seemed so strong that the *National Republican* cautioned silence on the entire question. The newspaper, however, could not resist reminding its readers that it had been less than six years since the *Daily National Intelligencer,* a chief spokesman of Democrats, published a communication from then Mayor Walter Lenox threatening mob action against anyone who opened a school for blacks. Nor did the *National Republican* avoid reminding its readers that in 1862 Lenox was in the Confederate army.[50]

The action of the mayor and the city council reflected white opposition to the school law. Although black schools legally came under Federal control, the money for their operation came from local taxes. Since Washington did not keep separate records of taxes paid by black and white residents, city officials merely allotted to the trustees of black schools what they thought to be appropriate. The council often delayed making any funds available, or when it did, it appropiated token amounts. In 1862 and 1863 allocations for black education were $265 and $410. For the same years the white schools received $29,000 and $36,000.[51]

The first black public school opened in the Ebenezer Church in March of 1864, nearly two years after enactment of the first black school law. Clearly Congress needed to pass additional measures. In the 1864 law, Congress removed taxes paid by Afro-Americans as the sole basis of black education. Instead Congress required Washing-

---

[48] *Ibid.*
[49] *Ibid.,* May 22, 1862.
[50] *Ibid.*
[51] *16th Annual Report of the Trustees of Public Schools,* 12, and *Register's Report of Receipts of Expenditures of the Corporation of the City of Washington for the year ending June 30, 1863.* Both are located in *Washington, D. C. City Documents,* 1852/53–1870/71 in the New York Public Library. (Hereafter cited as *Register's Report* with appropriate year).

ton to give to trustees of black schools the same proportion of the total school fund as the number of black children between the ages of six and seventeen bore to the number of white children. The act further provided for the Federal court of the District of Columbia to pay into the school fund one-half the money accruing from fines and forfeitures—a quarter to black schools and a quarter to white schools. City council, unfortunately, continued token payments; in 1864 black education received only $628 out of a total school fund of $25,000.[52]

Congress, in its continued efforts to secure educational opportunity for black children, authorized the use of empty army barracks for schoolrooms and gave three lots for black educational purposes. It also provided that funds due black schools be paid on October 1 of each year, if not, interest would accrue.[53]

Again on March 29, 1867, Congress, by Resolution Number 24, directed the Commissioner of Education to determine the number of children in the District of Columbia between the ages of six and seventeen and report whether Congress should enact additional legislation in order to secure equal educational advantages for black children with those of white children. The Commissioner reported that on November 11, 1867 the combined number of black and white children in the District entitled to school privileges was 27,624. Of that number 19,223 or 69.6 were white and 8,401 or 30.4 per cent black.[54] From the Commissioner's report, trustees of black schools determined that at least two-thirds of the black children had no opportunity to attend school, and the trustees requested city council to make available 30.4 per cent of the school fund for the 1868–1869 school year. The council responded with more money for Afro-American schools; total expenditures for the year ending June 30, 1869 were $258,042. White schools got $204,809 or 79.4 per cent and black schools received $53,233 or 20.6 per cent.[55] Black schools got considerably less than the sum requested but a good deal more than the $628 they had received in 1864–1865.

ENFRANCHISEMENT

Enfranchisement was Washington's third major drive in which whites, mostly radical Republicans, were the main participants. For

---

[52] Green, *The Secret City*, 69; *Congressional Globe*, 39th Cong., 2nd Sess., Append., 180.
[53] City council recorded the law in the *Journal of the Sixty-six Council of the City of Washington*, 1868–1869, Vol. II, 558, 559.
[54] *Ibid.; Congressional Globe*, 41st Cong., 2nd Sess., 4, 5. Resolution Number 24 authorized the special census of 1867.
[55] *Register's Report*, 1869, 164.

several years before enfranchisement, however, Afro-Americans in that city pressed for the right to vote by adopting resolutions and by signing petitions. The annual conference of African Methodist Episcopal Churches held in Washington in April of 1862 adopted one of these resolutions. In referring to the recent passage of the emancipation act and the Senate's recognition of the independence of Haiti and Liberia, the conference unanimously "resolved, that we will thank God and take courage, in view of all the events which are so rapidly transpiring, looking to our final enfranchisement." [56]

Petitions for local voting rights evoked more reactions from whites opposed to black suffrage than did resolutions. It is possible, too, that petitions had greater influence on members of Congress than did resolutions. In April of 1864 an appeal signed by 2,500 Washington blacks asked Congress for local voting rights. The request quoted from the Declaration of Independence; it pointed to Afro-Americans' military service; and it stated that "a large portion of the colored citizens of the District are property holders." [57] In the fall of 1865, John F. Cook and twenty-five other property owners signed and presented to Congress another petition stating their grievances and asking for the right to vote. On December 14, while Congress debated the suffrage bill, the Board of Common Council asked Mayor Richard Wallach to determine how many of the 2,500 signers of the April, 1864 petition were property holders, and that a copy of the petition be submitted to the council along with a list of all the signers. The Mayor immediately checked the names and reported only 573 taxpayers among the signers.[58]

In the winter of 1865 the Senate rejected the suffrage bill. The rejection resulted in part from the refusal in the same year of such northern states as Wisconsin, Minnesota, and Connecticut to extend the franchise to blacks. A stronger reason was that in a referendum in 1865 Washington and Georgetown whites voted against black suffrage. On December 13, 1866, however, the Senate reversed its earlier position and passed a voting bill. The next day the House concurred. President Andrew Johnson vetoed the bill on January 5, 1867. In his veto message he said that Congress had entirely disregarded the wishes of the people of the District of Columbia. "After full deliberation upon this measure, I cannot bring myself to approve

---

[56] The *Republican*, April 28, 1862.

[57] Petition S38A–J6, April, 1864. Petitions to the Senate are on microfilm in Record Group 46 in the National Archives.

[58] James H. Whyte, *The Uncivil War: Washington During the Reconstruction, 1865–1878* (New York: Twayne Publishers, 1958), 50; Green, *The Secret City*, 77; The *Intelligencer*, Dec. 14, 1865.

A Blueprint for Change

THE GEORGETOWN ELECTION—THE NEGRO AT THE BALLOT-BOX.

*Library of Congress
Microfilm Collection*

Thomas Nast cartoon in Harper's Weekly, March 16, 1867. "The Georgetown Election—The Negro at the Ballot Box." President Andrew Johnson is pictured on the left with a pocket full of vetoes and with "Ex CSA" (Confederate States of America) clutching his arm.

it, even upon local considerations, nor yet as the beginning of an experiment on a larger scale." Congress quickly overrode the veto.[59] The *Intelligencer*, in trying to explain why Congress passed the bill the second time after having rejected it the first time, said that members of that assembly had been deceived as to the views of the Washington community on the question of black suffrage. The newspaper alleged that congressmen had read one or two radical newspapers and had become convinced that Washingtonians' views had changed since the referendum of 1865. Charles Sumner gave another reason when he said that the issue of black suffrage involved more than just several thousand voters in the District of Columbia, but "it concerned the entire question of human rights everywhere throughout this land, involving the national character and its good name forever more." The real motive for the passage of the bill, however, was the practical necessity of radical Republicans to enfranchise blacks in

[59] The *Intelligencer,* Jan. 8, 1867; *Congressional Globe,* 39th Cong., 1st Sess., 3191, 3432; 2nd Sess., 304–314, Append., 9.

order to remain in power. Washington, then, was to serve the Republican party as a proving ground for black suffrage later to be applied to the country at large. Blacks got the ballot, not as a result of their resolutions and petitions, but because of the self-serving designs of a political party.[60]

Almost immediately following passage of the voting rights bill blacks began participating in Republican associations in their wards. The Washington *Evening Star* reported that on January 30 the Radical Republican Association of the seventh ward met at Turner Hall; about ninety persons attended, including fourteen whites. Several blacks supported a resolution, which was eventually withdrawn, condemning Mayor Wallach for his opposition to black suffrage. A news item in the *Intelligencer* said that "a meeting of the friends of the forward political movement was held last evening at the church at Fourth Street near L" and elected George Shanklin, white, chairman and George W. Hatton, a black citizen, secretary. "Speeches were made encouraging the colored people to come forward and unite their efforts in this movement, and to do all in their power to strengthen the work of the Republicans in the District."[61] Integrated Republican organizations existed in all wards and a number of blacks held positions, usually as vice-presidents, vice-chairmen or secretaries. In fact, the *Intelligencer* reported that the membership of all Republican associations consisted of a majority of Afro-Americans. At least one Afro-American called for all-black political organizations. O. S. Baker said that he opposed an affiliation between blacks and whites that tended to diminish blacks' proper representation. Sayles J. Bowen, a white Republican and a future mayor, opposed Baker's position. Bowen said that the purposes of Republican organizations were to harmonize the races, to give a fair share of the offices to each race, and for Republicans, black and white, to devote their energies to the best interest of the party. In a patronizing way he said that "if the white man offered colored men the right hand of fellowship, they should not refuse it."[62]

The suffrage act required the mayor of Washington to make

---

[60] The *Intelligencer*, Jan. 9, 1867; The Sumner quotation is in David Donald, *Charles Sumner and the Rights of Man* (New York: Alfred A. Knopf, 1970), 181: John Hope Franklin, *Reconstruction after the Civil War* (Chicago: University of Chicago Press, 1961), 196; Green, *Washington: Village and Capital*, 296.

[61] *Evening Star*, Jan. 30, 1867; The *Intelligencer*, March 2, 1867.

[62] *Ibid.*, March 2, 5, 6, 9, 15, 16, April 20, 1867. The officers were Ward I, John F. Cook, chairman, Solomon Johnson, secretary; Ward II, Enoch Ambush, secretary; Ward III, John T. Johnson, secretary; Ward IV, Benjamin McCoy, vice-president, George Hatton, secretary; Ward V, William H. Brown, secretary; Ward VI, George McReynolds, secretary; Ward VII, H. O. Johnson, vice-president.

available by March 1, of each year, a list of eligible voters. In carrying out that proviso, registrars appointed by the Federal court for the District began voter registration on March 18. It was perhaps symbolic of the recently gained right to vote that registration began in the black 19th Street Baptist Church. On the first day of registration 180 blacks and 152 whites registered. When the board of registrars finished its work in the first ward five days later 2,479 persons had registered, 1,457 blacks and 1,098 whites.[63]

Throughout the registration period the *Intelligencer* kept nearly a daily count of the number of black and white registrants. On April 11 the paper printed that 440 whites and 160 blacks had registered in ward four.

> This good result is attributed to the fact, that in this ward strenuous efforts were made to bring every man to the registration. If the Conservatives would but go to work earnestly in other wards and have every voter registered, the Radicals of this city would be put beyond resurrection on election day.

The newspaper, in stepping up its campaign to get whites registered, said after registration for ward four ended that the total number of voters registered for the ward was 2,679; whites numbered 1,666 and blacks 1,013, "giving the whites a majority in the registration of 653."

> Gentlemen well versed in our local politics and familiar with the opinions and views of the citizens of the ward, give the Radicals 200 white voters; and this is a large estimate. But admitting that they have that number, the Conservative, anti-Radical voters have a clear majority of 453, which at least secures the ward, and will go far toward routing the Radical candidates for city offices.

The paper bemoaned the fact that of the total number registered in wards one through four, blacks had a majority of 146.

> With such a showing as this, what supreme folly it is for the white voters to refuse to register! In the first, second, and third wards scarcely one-half of the names on the poll list one year ago will be upon the rolls under the new order of things, because the white voters held back and woud not be registered.[64]

The *Intelligencer* said that the reason many whites failed to register was due to their unwillingness to serve on juries along side black jurors.

---

[63] *Ibid.*, March 23, 1867.
[64] *Ibid.*, April 2, 12, 15, 1867.

At the close of registration for all wards, 8,240 whites and 7,271 blacks had registered. Blacks had the potential to be a viable force in local politics. They had majorities in wards one and two, and in the other wards white majorities ranged from 15 to 854.[65] A great concern for many whites was the undetermined number of white voters who might ally with black voters. If enough black and white coalesced, political control could rest with black and white coalitions.

The year blacks received the franchise, Washington's machinery of government consisted of a mayor, a board of aldermen and a board of common council. In even years voters elected the mayor for a two-year term through city-wide balloting. The board of aldermen consisted of fourteen members, two from each of the seven wards. Voters of the wards elected their aldermen for two-year terms also, but they usually elected one of the two in alternate years. Annual elections filled the twenty-one seats on the common council. All city officials could run for reelection. Congress had created that type of government in 1847, and at that time it had won popular approval of the majority of the white voters in the city.[66]

The municipal election held on June 3, 1867, was the first one since blacks had become enfranchised. George W. Hatton declined a councilmanic nomination from ward four, consequently no black candidate sought office in 1867. The lack of black candidates did not prevent the enthusiastic participation of black voters in the election. The *Evening Star* reported that on election day in one ward 451 blacks voted before 10:00 a.m., compared with only two whites in the same ward. In appraising the election the same newspaper said that "the election today is progressing quietly, putting to flight the fears of those who apprehended serious disturbances on the occasion of the first exercise of the right of franchise by the colored people."[67]

The *Intelligencer* had predicted correctly that if blacks received the franchise, Washington would soon see blacks elected to city offices.

[65] *Ibid.*, March 23, April 1, 5, 15, 20, May 7, 1867. The *Intelligencer* made these estimates; the Board of Registration did not identify black and white voters.

Ward I	blacks 1,457	whites 1,098	black majority 359
Ward II	" 1,419	" 856	" " 563
Ward III	" 708	" 723	white majority 15
Ward IV	" 1,013	" 1,666	" " 653
Ward V	" 717	" 964	" " 247
Ward VI	" 1,723	" 1,577	" " 854
Ward VII	" 1,234	" 1,356	" " 122

[66] Constance McLaughlin Green, *Washington: Village and Capital* (Princeton: Princeton University Press, 1962), 163.

[67] *Evening Star,* June 3, 1867.

In the election of 1868, John F. Cook, a teacher, won a seat on the board of alderman, and Carter A. Stewart, a barber, out-polled his opponent in a race for the common council; both represented ward one.[68] The election of Republicans Cook and Stewart, however, was just one phase of the bitterly fought campaign of 1868. The mayoral race between Republican Sayles J. Bowen, reportedly a staunch believer in equal rights for blacks and one of the first trustees of black public schools, and the Democratic challenger John T. Given was the most hotly contested one the city had seen. The outcome of the election was in doubt until June 17, when District Circuit Judge George P. Fisher ruled that Bowen had won the election with 9,170 votes to Given's 9,087, a majority of only eighty-three. The court also validated the election of Cook and Stewart, but not until it had voided the election of two white soldiers. The decision gave Republicans control of both boards; unfortunately, it also generated intense bitterness among many white residents.[69]

Bowen's administration began under serious difficulties. His majority on the two boards was only a nominal one, and it was hard for him to get an increase in the funded debt. Yet his administration made some progress, especially in the form of street improvements. The quieting of rumors that the capital would be removed to St. Louis, Missouri aided Bowen's administration, so did the election of Ulysses S. Grant to the Presidency of the United States. The employment of a sizable number of blacks, mostly as day laborers on city improvement projects, kept a large bloc of these voters allied with Bowen. The employment of blacks also led to the charge that Bowen squandered city funds—a charge that later harmed his bid for re-election.[70]

The 1869 election of councilmen and aldermen was another stormy one. Some blacks had become sufficiently disenchanted with Bowen's administration that they formed an opposition movement called the "Colored Citizens Movement." On election day open clashes occurred between dissident blacks and those backing Bowen. The election, however, resulted in an almost clean sweep for the Republicans. Only three Democrats remained on the board of aldermen and none on the council. Blacks won more races in that election than at any other time between 1868 and 1871, the year municipal elections ended. A black man won a seat on the council from each of the seven

---

[68] Washington's *Daily Morning Chronicle,* June 4, 1868; *Evening Star,* June 3, 1867.
[69] Whyte, *The Uncivil War,* 67, 69, 70.
[70] Green, *Washington: Village and Capital,* 318.

TABLE I
Washington D.C.'s Black Councilmen, 1869–1870
Daily Morning Chronicle, Evening Star, June, 1869

Name	Ward	Total No. of Votes
Robert Thompson[c]	I	1,846
Henry H. Piper[a]	II	1,687
John T. Johnson[b]	III	1,255
George W. Ratton[c]	IV	1,428
Andrew B. Tinney[b]	V	1,124
Frank B. Gaines[a]	VI	873
Sampson Netter[c]	VII	1,897

[a] Reelected in 1870 along with four other black councilmen.
[b] Defeated in 1870.
[c] Did not seek reelection in 1870.

wards. Steward won in a race for the board of aldermen, and Cook became city registrar with a winning margin of more than 5,000 votes over his white Democratic rival.[71] The *Evening Star* and the *Republican* said that the black candidates had the ability to perform well. Of the winning black candidates, Robert Thompson and Frank B. Gaines had been slaves; John T. Johnson had been the reading clerk for the council; Andrew B. Tinney was a brick-layer at the Navy Yard; Sampson Netter was a minister; Henry Piper, "a man of some education", was a watchman at the Treasury Department. The seventh councilman was George W. Hatton, a former sergeant-major of a black regiment; Hatton, a foe of Bowen, had emerged as an effective black leader.[72]

As the June 5, 1870 municipal election approached, "the social revolution" that had taken place for the past several years, and the rise in the city debt loomed large as campaign issues. The debt stood at nearly $2,400,000, and almost a third of that the city had incurred during the preceding two years. Whites, including a large number of Republicans, blamed Bowen and the blacks on the city council for the increase. Bowen, considered by many whites to have been a chief initiator of the "social revolution," received the mayoral nomination on May 5 from the Republican General Committee, but his nomination caused a split in the city's Republican Party. On May 13 the "Regular Republican Convention" nominated as opposition candidate Matthew G. Emery, a former alderman. Both Bowen and Emery campaigned as the true Republican candidate. The Democrats of-

---

[71] *The Chronicle, Evening Star*, June 4, 1869.
[72] *The Republican, Evening Star*, June 4, 5, 1869.

A Blueprint for Change 385

TABLE II
Washington, D.C, Municipal Election Returns, June 6, 1870
Evening Star, Daily Morning Chronicle, June 7, 1870

	\multicolumn{8}{c}{Wards}
	I	II	III	IV	V	VI	VII	Total
Mayor								
M. G. Emery*	1,312	1,300	1,498	1,953	1,033	1,155	1,845	
S. J. Bowen	1,245	1,292	865	993	743	621	1,118	
Aldermen								
D. M. Davis (B)*	1,293							
A. P. Fardon (E)	1,262							
Council								
E. E. Brooks (E)*	1,290							
W. A. Freeman (A) (E)*	1,293							
A. S. Taylor (E)	1,230							
W. H. A. Wormley (A) (B)	1,239							
J. Johnson (A) (B)	1,227							
J. T. Murray (B)*	1,293							
Aldermen								
J. S. Crocker (B)*		1,308						
G. A. Hall (E)		1,267						
Council								
G. Burgess (B)*		1,305						
H. Piper (A) (B)*		1,303						
A. F. Mouldin (B)*		1,289						
J. A. Bayloy (E)		1,275						
H. Kilbourn (E)		1,274						
D. Fisher (A) (E)		1,219						
Aldermen								
A. B. Shepherd (E)*			1,497					
B. J. Beall (B)			851					
Council								
W. H. Pope (E)*			1,502					
R. C. Lewis (E)*			1,465					
G. Willner (E)*			1,474					
J. T. Johnson (A) (B)			861					
M. Duffy (B)			856					
W. A. Walter (B)			846					
Aldermen								
W. W. Moore (E)*				1,936				
J. H. Crossman (E)*				1,931				
J. M. Dalton (B)				976				
A. K. Browne (B)				988				
Council								
S. Robertson (E)*				1,922				
J. O. Donnoghue (E)*				1,921				
B. McCoy (A) (E)*				1,880				
Allen Coffin (B)				962				
James Ryan (B)				980				
J. M. Talley (A) (B)				960				
Aldermen								
G. F. Gulick (E)*						967		
A. P. Clark (B)						762		

TABLE II—Continued

	Wards							Total
	I	II	III	IV	V	VI	VII	
Council								
C. H. Holden (E)*					1,010			
G. T. Barrett (E)*					978			
F. A. Gant (A) (E)*					937			
A. B. Tinney (A) (B)					752			
R. Oulahan (B)					752			
E. L. Schmedt (B)					736			
Aldermen								
D. McCathran (E)*						1,051		
J. L. Venable (B)						729		
Council								
C. M. Barton (E)*						937		
B. F. Palmer (E)*						1,057		
F. D. Gaines (A) (E)*						883		
M. Davis (B)						797		
J. E. Herrell (B)						641		
Isaac Shiner (A) (B)						693		
Aldermen								
L. G. Hine (E)*							1,358	
H. M. Knight (E)							485	
Joseph Williams (B)							1,084	
Council								
W. R. Hunt (E)*							1,568	
J. C. McConnell (E)							1,046	
J. Reisinger (E)							944	
W. Taliaferro (E)							608	
T. Thompson (E)							687	
J. W. Green (E)							313	
Anthony Bowen (A) (B)*							1,100	
T. Carrahor (B)*							1,157	
S. A. Douglas (A) (B)							1,093	

*Winner.
(A)—Black candidate, (B)—Bowen ticket, (E)—Emery ticket.

fered no candidate for mayor, instead they formed a coalition with Emery's faction.[73]

There was a host of candidates for the board of alderman and the common council. Seventeen whites ran to fill the eight available aldermanic seats; no blacks sought membership on that board. Forty-four candidates, thirty whites and fourteen blacks, ran for the twenty-

---

[73] Green, *Washington: Village and Capital*, 327; Many whites called the emancipation of slaves, the establishment of black public schools, the enfranchisement of blacks, the election of blacks to office, and the passage of an ordinance prohibiting discrimination in public facilities (never enforced) a "social revolution". Green sees the "revolution" occurring between 1868 and 1871 (See especially Chapter XIII in *Washington: Village and Capital*).

TABLE III
Black Candidates for Board of Common Council, Washington, D.C., 1870
Daily Morning Chronicle, National Republican, Evening Star, May 31–June 6, 1870

Name	Ticket	No. Votes	Results	Rank among Candidates
Ward I				
William A. Freeman*	Emery	1,293	Won	Tied for 1st of 6
W. H. A. Wormley	Bowen	1,239	Lost	4th of 6
Jerome Johnson	Bowen	1,227	Lost	5th of 6
Ward II				
Henry Piper* †	Bowen	1,303	Won	2nd of 6
David Fisher	Emery	1,219	Lost	Last among 6
Ward III				
John T. Johnson†	Bowen	861	Lost	4th of 6
Ward IV				
Benjamin McCoy*	Emery	1,880	Won	3rd of 6
James Talley	Bowen	960	Lost	Last among 6
Ward V				
Thomas A. Grant*	Emery	937	Won	3rd of 6
Andrew B. Tinney†	Bowen	752	Lost	Tied for 5th of 6
Ward VI				
Frank D. Gaines†	Emery	883	Won	3rd of 6
Isaac Shiner	Bowen	693	Lost	5th of 6
Ward VII				
Anthony Bowen*	Bowen	1,100	Won	3rd of 9
S. A. Douglas	Bowen	1,093	Lost	4th of 9

* Winners.
† Incumbents.

one seats on the common council. In these races the basic issue was the candidate's alliance with the Bowen or Emery group. In fact, newspapers did not refer to candidates as "Republicans" or "Democrats" but as Bowen or Emery candidates.[74]

In the mayoral race Emery soundly defeated Bowen by carrying every ward. His total vote count was 10,096 to Bowen's 6,877. In the races for city council Emery candidates scored complete victories in four wards. Overall the Emery group elected six of the eight aldermen and sixteen of the twenty-one councilmen. Four Emery-allied blacks won membership on the council compared with two blacks endorsed by Bowen.[75]

On June 2, 1870 city newspapers printed official figures for each ward released by the Board of Registration; there were 17,989 registered voters in the city. These figures are in Table IV.

Registration judges did not keep official records of the number

---

[74] *Evening Star, Chronicle, Republican.* I gathered information from the May 13 to June 6, 1870 issues. Only the *Chronicle* supported Bowen.
[75] *Ibid.*, June 7, 1870. See Tables II and III.

TABLE IV
The Official Number of Washington D.C. Registered Voters Released by Board of Registration, June 2, 1870

Wards	Total
I	2,798
II	2,855
III	2,597
IV	2,977
V	1,790
VI	1,805
VII	3,167
	17,989

Source: The *Evening Star*, Washington, D.C., June 2, 1870. *Daily Morning Chronicle*, June 3, 1870.

of black and white registrants, but interested persons in the Bowen and Emery groups made the distinction. The unofficial numbers in Table V appeared in several newspapers on June 1.

Since the official number of registrants in each ward exceeded the number listed for each ward in Table V, it is reasonable to assume that the actual number of black and white registrants in each ward at least equalled the unofficial totals in Table V.

Political tickets in wards one and seven had similar characteristics: there was more than one black candidate on the Bowen ticket in those wards, and neither ticket won complete victories. In ward one there were six candidates for the three council seats: three Bowen supporters and three Emery backers. Three of the six candidates were black, two allied with Bowen, one with Emery. William A

TABLE V
Unofficial Number of Black and White Registered Voters in Washington, D.C.'s Seven Wards, 1870

Wards	White	Black	Total
I	932	1,322	2,254
II	1,191	1,119	2,310
III	1,539	702	2,241
IV	1,950	669	2,619
V	1,028	606	1,634
VI	1,252	523	1,775
VII	1,581	1,354	2,722
			15,555

Source: The *Evening Star*, June 1, 1870. *National Republican*, June 1, 1870.

A Blueprint for Change 389

Freeman, a black Emery-supported candidate, and J. T. Murray, the white candidate aided by Bowen, led the race by polling 1,293 votes each. The two black candidates endorsed by the Bowen camp lost by small margins. Possibly black voters outnumbered white voters in the ward, but since the votes were somewhat evenly distributed among all candidates, it is not possible to say all-black votes elected Freeman. Nor can it be said that a combination of black and white votes elected him, although that is a strong possibility. Since, however, Freeman and Murray received an identical number of votes, it is clear that blacks in ward one did not solely and consistently vote for black candidates.[76]

In ward seven the Bowen group won two of the three council seats because a split occurred within the Emery faction. Emeryites fielded two slates of candidates while the Bowen group had one. Even with the split, the Emery faction won the aldermanic seat and one of its candidates finished first in the council race. Bowen supporters, T. Carraher, white, and Anthony Bowen, black, won the other two council seats. Since Carraher and Bowen had quite similar vote totals, their victories probably resulted from a combination of black and white votes. Also, Sampson Netter, a retiring black councilman, had received 1,897 votes in 1869 to lead all candidates in ward seven and it is almost certain that Netter had received white votes.[77]

Ward two was the only one in which Bowen supporters won the aldermanic race and the three council seats. Henry A. Piper, a black incumbent, polled 1,303 votes and finished second behind his white-ticket mate, G. Burgess, who received 1,305 votes. A. F. Mouldin, a white candidate, won the third seat with 1,289, while David Fisher, the black candidate supported by the Emery group, finished last with 1,219 votes. In ward three, black incumbent Councilman John T. Johnson received only 861 votes as he and the entire Bowen slate suffered a crushing defeat. A year earlier Johnson had polled 1,225 votes. Andrew Tinney lost heavily when he got only 752 votes in the fifth ward. Like Johnson, Tinney had won handily in 1869 with 1,124 votes. It appears that the common element in Johnson's and Tinney's defeats was the alliance with the Bowen camp, an unpopular one in wards three and five. In the third ward there was not a black candidate on the winning Emery ticket, but Thomas A. Gant won with the Emery ticket in the fifth ward.[78]

Voting results in wards four and six give the strongest evidence

---
[76] *Ibid.*
[77] See Tables I and II.
[78] *Ibid.*

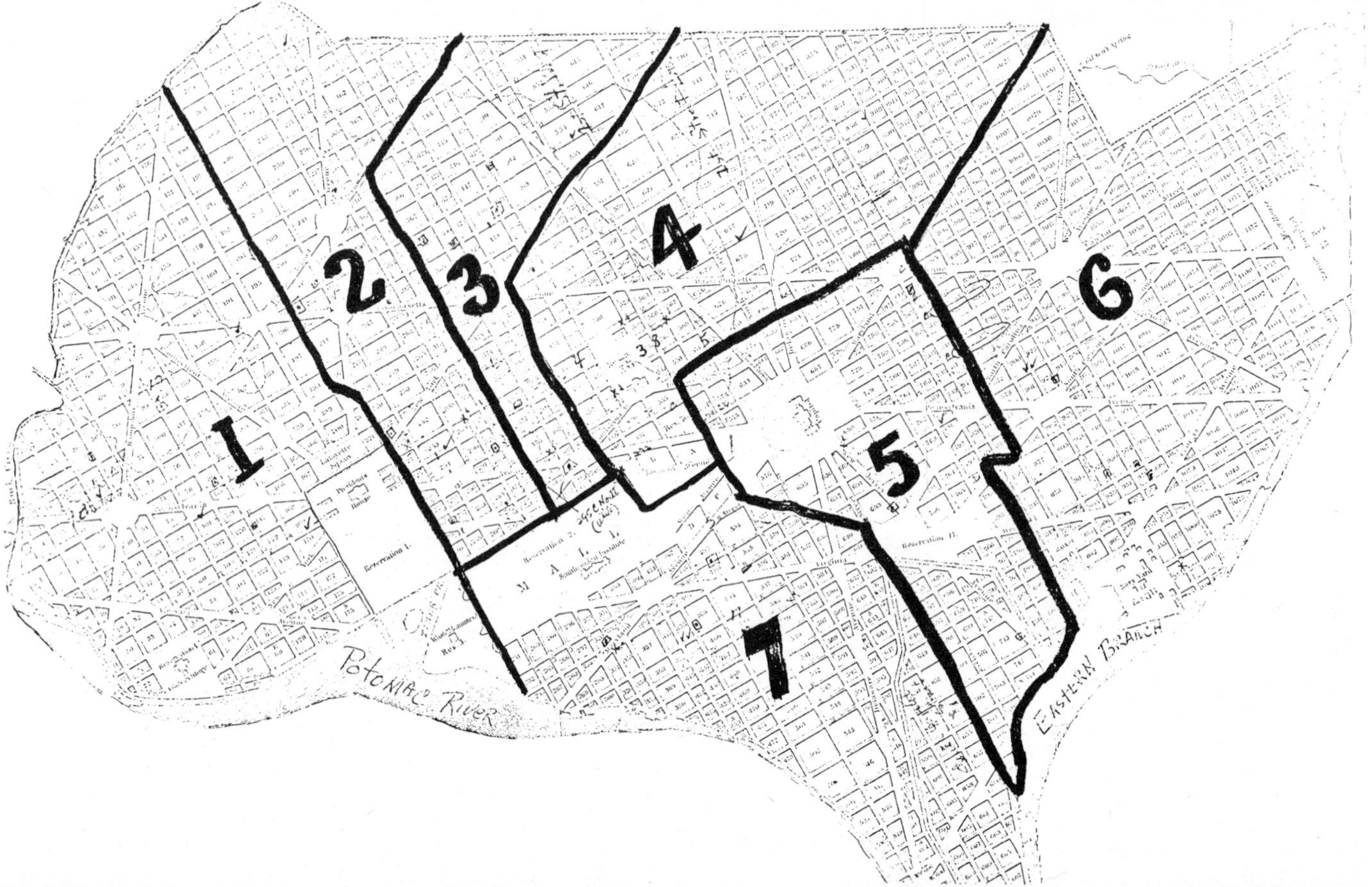

Map from the author

A Blueprint for Change 391

that whites voted for black candidates. Frank Gaines, a black incumbent councilman from the sixth ward won the third seat on the successful Emery ticket with 883 votes, ten more than he received when he made his first successful bid for the council in 1869. Since unofficial registration figures showed only 523 black voters in the ward, a good part of Gaines strength must have come from whites.[79] In ward four it is also clear that a large number of whites voted for Benjamin McCoy, the black candidate endorsed by Emery, who won the ward's third council race. If one uses unofficial registration figures, only 669 of McCoy's 1,880 supporters could have been black; and if one divides officially registered voters in the same proportion as the earlier unofficial tally indicated, McCoy's maximum number of black supporters could not have exceeded 848. In all probability he received at least 1,032 white votes.[80]

With the exception of the maverick seventh ward, amazing consistency existed among voters of the wards. Usually mayoral candidates received vote totals similar to those their groups' candidates for the two boards got. For example, the widest margin of difference in votes received by Bowen and all Bowen candidates in ward two was sixteen. In ward three the widest margin between Emery and his slate was thirty-seven. This consistency indicates that if voters considered the race of a candidate, they also considered the candidate's political alliance.[81]

One other idea warrants consideration. Except in the first and second wards, black candidates consistently received fewer votes than did white candidates on the same tickets. Blacks usually ranked from third place through sixth, or last place. Such ranking suggests that some whites deliberately split their tickets to avoid voting for black candidates, or they simply scratched off the names of black candidates.[82] Whites, when they cast their ballots for black office

---

[79] See Tables II, IV and V. Unofficial registration figures listed 523 black voters and 1,252 white voters among a total of 1,775 registrants. The official registration figures showed that the ward had 1,805 registered voters, 30 more than the unofficial figures showed. If half or 15 of the registrants were black, the total number of blacks eligible to vote was 538. Since Gaines won with 883 votes, it is highly possible that whites provided 245 votes.

[80] *Ibid*. Unofficial records listed 669 black voters and 1,950 white voters—a total of 2,619. The official registration for the ward was 2,977—358 more than the unofficial total. If 50 per cent or 179 were added to the number of black registrants (669), the total black registration was 848. It was unlikely, however, that black registration increased equally with white registration since the black population of the ward was only slightly more than 23 per cent of the white population. If one assumes, however, that the increase was the same for both races, the maximum number of blacks voters was 848.

[81] See Table II.

[82] See Table III.

seekers, frequently voted for blacks on the Emery ticket. For example, white voters probably outnumbered black voters by two to one and three to one margins in wards three, four, and six; all Emery candidates in those wards won, including three blacks. Many whites probably voted for Emery candidates to stop the "social revolution." Blacks who ran on the Emery ticket and those who supported it probably took that political stance because they believed endorsement of that ticket was the surest way of electing black candidates. No doubt whites supporting the Bowen slate did so, not to continue social and political progress, but to assure the dominance of the city's Republican Party.

Washington had undergone some basic social and political changes during the eight preceding years and many whites not only felt that the city's "social revolution" had gone too far, too fast, but that it should not have been initiated in the first place. The *Intelligencer,* reflecting the sentiments of a number of whites, had bitterly attacked three measures passed by Congress: the act emancipating slaves in the city, the law establishing public education for blacks, and the legislation providing black suffrage. Congress, then, was the real initiator of the "social revolution." Possibly Congress was also the agency chiefly responsible for the retrogression of that revolution. On February 21, 1871, Congress passed the District territorial act which took the city's government out of the hands of local citizens and made it the full responsibility of Congress.[83] A newspaper article, in speaking about the act, said "thereupon the territorial government of the District of Columbia passed away, unwept, unhonored, and unsung. And with it passed the right of suffrage which its whites had enjoyed for three-quarters of a century." The article said that during the debates over the act, both Democrats and Republicans concealed the paramount reason for the wholesale disfranchisement of Washington citizens. The Republicans could not admit that their favorite prescription for the ex-Confederacy was bad medicine for the District; the Democrats could not object to the act, to do that would drag their own election methods into the limelight. "Everyone knew and nobody denied, however, that the menace of the Negro's presence constituted the sole reason for the abolition of suffrage in the District. The nation, through its Congress, set the example for disfranchising the Negro."[84] If these conclusions are

---

[83] Green, *Washington: Village and Capital,* 355, 356.

[84] This newspaper clipping was in the file on Black History in the Washingtoniana Room of the Washington Public Library (now the Martin Luther King Memorial Library). The article did not have the name of the newspaper in which it appeared or the date of publication.

correct, Congress and white citizens of Washington never accepted the gains granted to blacks or, if they did, in 1871 they simply agreed to turn back the progress of the preceding years. In either case, they demonstrated the inability of the nation's capital to lead in reconstructing the country, and they illustrated that revolutions can and sometimes do go backward.

Alexander R. Shepherd and the Board of Public Works

WILLIAM M. MAURY

Alexander R. Shepherd is thought of by some as the father of modern Washington, by others as a villain who was almost single-handedly responsible for the failure of this city's first real attempt at self government and for the continuing lack of that precious commodity to this day. Whichever evaluation one makes must be tempered by the fact that Shepherd was, above all, an archetypal man of the Gilded Age, neither far seeing nor short sighted but, instead, wrapped up entirely in the problems of his own place and time.

Except for the fact that he was a native Washingtonian, Shepherd's early life was hardly exceptional. Born in 1835, the eldest son of a reasonably well-to-do lumberman, Shepherd lived a comfortable upper-middle-class existence until his early adolescence. His father's death in 1845, and the rather sudden diminution of the family fortunes meant that Shepherd, by age 13; was forced into the business world to help support his mother and the six younger Shepherds.[1]

For the next four years, Shepherd worked at a variety of menial jobs. Finally, in 1852, at the age of 17, he took what turned out to be a very important professional step by apprenticing himself to the largest plumbing and gas fitting company in the city, J. W. Thompson's.[2] In the next eight years, Shepherd, as have innumerable ambitious American youths, began to work himself to the top of a limited hierarchy.

By the time of the Civil War, he had gained a bit of prominence in Washington. He had even joined a local militia unit known as the National Rifles, a somewhat suspect group of Washingtonians known both for their general Southern tendencies as well as for the fact that they were supposedly the first Federal troops to set foot in the Con-

---

Delivered before the Columbia Historical Society on March 21, 1972.

[1] *The Evening Star* (Washington), September 24, 1887.

[2] Mrs. Elden E. Billings, "Alexander Robey Shepherd and His Unpublished Diaries and Correspondence," *Records of the Columbia Historical Society, 1960–1962*, 1963, p. 150.

National Archives
Alexander R. Shepherd as he appeared during the territorial period.

federacy after the outbreak of hostilities. Shepherd's military career was short and unexceptional. Three months after being sworn into the army by Major Irwin McDowell, his enlistment ran out and he found himself again a civilian in the employ of J. W. Thompson.[3]

---
[3] *Ibid.*; Margaret Leech, *Reveille in Washington 1860-65* (New York, 1941), p. 28.

Despite, perhaps even because of, the garrison aspect that Washington took on during the war, Alexander Shepherd and the J. W. Thompson Company did quite well during these years. Shepherd's name and signature appear on many of the bills that the company sent to the government for services rendered during the Civil War years.[4]

By two years after the close of hostilities, Shepherd had proved to all that he was a man of no mean business ability. His work at J. W. Thompson enabled him to salt away enough savings to buy a pleasant house in the rural area of the District of Columbia known as the "county," where he moved with his wife of five years. Nor were Shepherd's talents directed entirely toward business for, in 1867, shortly after purchasing his new house, he was named to the "county's" local governing body, the Levy Court, and in the succeeding two or three years found himself serving on the board of directors of such diverse groups as the SPCA and a local baseball team.[5] But as Shepherd's star was rising, the star of the city of his birth was sinking. Washington became less and less a city of magnificent distances and more and more one of magnificent intentions.

The Civil War acted as a force to bring to a head many long-festering sores in the capital city. The increase in number and type of citizen put an extreme load on the District's antiquated, three-sided governmental structure.[6] Further, the large number of heavy-wheeled vehicles called for by the army made Washington's already miserable road system nearly impassable.[7] And finally, the great influx of blacks into the city, already possessed of a large Negro population, made many of the old, Southern oriented residents fear that the District was to be the testing ground for radical reconstruction politics.[8]

---

[4] Bills and orders with the Thompson Company and Shepherd's signature appear in R. G. 92, Office of the Quarter Master General, Consolidated Correspondence File 1794–1895 at the National Archives.

[5] *The Evening Star*, June 27, 1867; Shepherd's scrapbook Box 4, Library of Congress, Shepherd Papers.

[6] The District of Columbia at this time was divided into three autonomous local governments: Washington City, Georgetown, and "The County" or that portion of the District which lay outside both Washington City and Georgetown but within the District's boundaries. Although each unit had its own governmental structure Congress acted as an overseer for all.

[7] *The New York Times*, December 26, 1870, commenting on the condition of Pennsylvania Avenue wrote that the avenue which connected the White House with the Capitol was little better than a dirt road "undrained, unpaved and unswept."

[8] The depth of the anti-radical reconstruction feeling in the District may be seen by a vote taken among the white residents of Washington City and Georgetown in 1865. Of 6,556 Washingtonians voting, 35 favored black enfranchisement. In Georgetown the count was 813 to 1. Edward Ingle, *The Negro in the District of Columbia*, ed. by Herbert

A. R. Shepherd and the Board of Public Works 397

Misgivings about Washington's future led a sizeable group of people, some residents of the city but most visiting solons from the provinces, to suggest that the capital of the nation might well be located in some more salubrious neighborhood. To born and bred Washingtonians, and to businessmen with a stake in the Potomac capital, such suggestions seemed heresy. Leading the fight against the heretics was Alexander Shepherd, a born and bred Washingtonian and one with a great stake in the future of the town.

In seeking to retain the capital, Shepherd and his cohorts needed to satisfactorily quash the three major objections of the removers. The piebald governmental system had to be replaced with something more effective. The city had to be made more palatable physically. And an effective and legal way of allaying fears of a black takeover had to be found.

Aware of their three-sided goal, Shepherd and his friends warmed up for their great adventure by launching an attack against Mayor Sayles Bowen.[9] Bowen, elected mayor of Washington City in 1868, was denounced equally as a radical in racial matters and as a philanderer who would tax the city into oblivion. By attacking the mayor, Shepherd's group effectively demonstrated which side of the racial fence it was on. By the judicious placement of ideas and concepts in such papers as *The Evening Star* (a paper Shepherd had part ownership of) and the *Daily National Republican* (a paper on which Shepherd's brother Arthur served), the group was able to suggest alternatives to the old tri-partite governmental system.

Washington City's charter, amended many times since its origin, finally expired in 1868. Although the charter was twice extended, with alterations each time, in the succeeding two years, the end of the mayoral system of government in Washington City was obviously in the offing. Suggestions as to the type of government that would most effectively rule the city varied, but the most often heard suggestion, and the one most heavily supported by Shepherd in the *Star,* was that the entire District of Columbia be consolidated as a territory.[10]

The territorial consolidation plan, although very much within the urban trends of the time,[11] did not go unopposed. A second group,

---

B. Adams, Johns Hopkins University Studies in History and Political Science (Baltimore, 1893), p. 65.

[9] John Crane, *The Washington Ring!!!* (Washington, 1872), p. 6. Bowen was known as a champion of the blacks in Washington. His political strength lay among them and he was generally disapproved of by the city's moderate and conservative elite.

[10] *The Evening Star,* January 18, 1868; Helen Nicolay, *Our Capital on the Potomac* (New York, 1924), p. 390.

[11] At or around this time such cities as Boston, New York, and Philadelphia were also in the process of consolidation.

composed primarily of old-line Democrats, sought to return the Federal City to antiquity by returning the old three-man governing commission.[12] While the two plans are quite different, there are some similarities worthy of note. Both plans moved in the direction of less, rather than more, self-government. This is significant in that it meant that the newly enfranchised black man was enough of a threat to make white Washingtonians forego their own right to vote in order to disenfranchise him. And by giving Congress or the President the right to appoint their governing officers, both Shepherd's group and the group seeking a commission form of government were making a bid to become wards of the state, thus easing the way for a Federal subsidy to perform needed repairs.

For the next two years, 1868–1869, the debate as to the style of government to seek from Congress continued on the street corners and in the press and Congress continued to toy with the idea of picking up and leaving. Finally, in mid-1870, Shepherd's group sent to Congress a petition signed by 150 prominent Washingtonians calling for a territorial form of government. A bill which would give the territorial government a great deal of political freedom, and its black citizens a great deal of political strength, passed the Senate. But the House of Representatives argued heatedly about the racial aspects of the bill. The anti-black block, led by Fernando Wood, was able to table the bill.[13]

When Congress reconvened, a heavily altered territorial bill was taken under consideration. The Shepherd group lobbied Congress effectively, even taking some members on a cruise down the Potomac entertaining them with food and drink all the while.[14] This time the bill passed. The District of Columbia became a single governmental unit. The President was to appoint the Governor and Council as well as members of the major departments. The citizens would elect a twenty-two member House of Delegates and a non-voting delegate to the House of Representatives. Although this governmental set-up was radically different from the plan favored by Senate liberals, and was, in fact, a step backward for Washington voters, it did have the sanction of tradition.

Once the bill was passed, Washingtonians began to wonder who would be appointed Governor. Most of the speculation centered on Alexander Shepherd. Shepherd had shown his organizational ability

---

[12] *National Intelligencer,* January 18, 1868.

[13] See U. S. Congress, House, *Congressional Globe* (41st Cong., 3d sess.), pt. 1, p. 643, for examples of Wood's logic.

[14] Henry M. Hyde, "The Man Who Made Washington," *The American Mercury,* November 1931, p. 314.

in the fight to oust Mayor Bowen and to get territorial government for the District. Both campaigns showed that he handled himself well in dealing with established Washington families and that he was familiar with the political ropes. With Shepherd's star in its ascendency, it might be well to stop for a minute and further examine his background.

Like many other urban leaders in the Gilded Age, Shepherd held little allegiance to political parties. His early leanings had been pro-Southern (his father was a slave-holder) and, even as late as the 1868 nominating convention, his enemies said that he worked to defeat Ulysses Grant's bid for the presidency.[15] But by the time Grant arrived back in Washington as President-elect, Shepherd was gaining the General's support by encouraging him to buy into paving and stone companies that were sure to make a profit if Washington were to undertake a sizable improvement campaign.[16]

But business, not politics, was Shepherd's forte. Unlike the robber barons of the Gilded Age, Shepherd did not seek to "control the narrows" of a particular industry and thereby gain a fortune from all those who needed to pass through. Instead, he was involved in almost every facet of the city's business life. In addition to the paving and stone companies already mentioned, Shepherd was the president or a member of the board of directors of at least four of the city's trunk and street rail companies. While hardly placing Shepherd in the same league as Thomas Fortune Ryan, the New York traction magnate, it did show that Shepherd was aware of the trend of the times and did not want to miss getting his fair share. With his great interest in modes of transportation, it is not surprising that Shepherd also had a significant interest in the land around and at the end of the train lines. His ability to see the direction of growth the city was taking enabled him to buy sizable tracts of land at quite low prices for profitable later sale. Those who needed to borrow money to pay for lots they bought from Shepherd could go to one of the banks of which he was a member of the board of directors to obtain their loan. If these people needed insurance for the houses they were going to build, again the man to see was Shepherd. And given his interest in the growth of the city, what could be more natural than his desire

---

[15] Letter from Albert Grant, a resident of Washington, to Governor Cooke, August 18, 1871, Washingtoniana Room, Public Library, District of Columbia, Territorial Section.

[16] Of particular note in this area was Grant's holdings in the Maryland Freestone Mining and Manufacturing Company, known as the Senecca Sandstone Company. At one time the President held $25,000 in this company. Walter L. Fleming, *The Freedman's Savings Bank* (Chapel Hill, 1927), pp. 78–9.

National Archives

Pennsylvania Avenue looking east. Wood block paving seen here was done just before the territorial government began and is typical of the period.

to provide a place for Washington's growing population to buy its food? Shepherd was deeply involved in the directorship and building of Washington's markets. When one adds to this Shepherd's ownership of the largest plumbing and gas fitting establishment "south of New York," and his part ownership of the city's largest newspaper, one's sympathy that Shepherd did not "control the narrows" of a particular industry should be at least partially allayed.[17]

As were many young businessmen in America, Shepherd was very much a joiner and a clubman. Among his more notable activities in this realm were serving as president of the Union Club and cofounder of the Washington Club.[18]

---

[17] The railroads were the Union Railroad, the Metropolitan Railroad, the Columbia Railroad, and the National Junction Railroad. Shepherd's brother William was one of the original incorporators of the Piedmont Railroad. *The Evening Star,* June 22, 1871, March 18, 1872, *The Daily Patriot* (Washington), July 26, 1872, U. S. Congress, *Report of the Joint Select Committee of Congress Appointed to Inquire into the Affairs of the Government of the District of Columbia* (43 Cong., 1 sess., S. Rept. 453), pt. 3, vol. IV, p. 875, 1874. Hereafter *Report of the Joint Select Committee.* Hyde, "The Man Who Made Washington," p. 317. William Boyd, *Boyd's Directory of Washington, Georgetown and Alexandria 1871* (Washington, 1871), pp. xxxix, xl, xli, and iii. *The Evening Star,* July 22, 25, 1871.

[18] Shepherd to O. O. Howard, April 7, 1871, Bowdoin Library, Bowdoin University, O. O. Howard Collection. *Daily National Republican* (Washington), February 27, 1872.

This, then, was the man many thought most likely to become the first Governor of the territorial government. Tall and well proportioned, the handsome Shepherd was obviously deeply concerned about the future of the city to which he owed his fortune. Though still in his salad days, he was well known and generally respected by all in the city. The only sizeable group opposed to his appointment as Governor, outside of those who were totally opposed to the territorial government from the beginning, were blacks. Many felt that Shepherd's early leanings, the fact that his father had owned slaves, his attacks against Bowen, the treatment he gave his black employees, and his misuse of Freedman's Savings and Trust moneys, were enough to deny Shepherd the appointment.[19] So indignant were some black leaders that when their self-avowed friend, General O. O. Howard, announced his support of Shepherd, he was visited by a delegation of blacks who stated that Shepherd had "uniformly acted against their interest." [20]

On the other hand, in addition to the occasional donation to the scholarship fund of Howard University, Shepherd noted, in replying to General Howard about the distaste that blacks had for him, that not only had he always been and always would be a friend of the blacks, but that he favored a single school system for the new territory and was opposed to discrimination in it or any other place.[21] Shepherd was fairly safe in saying this because the organic act left control of the black schools in the hands of the Federal government.

Racist or humanist, Shepherd was not to be Governor, at least not at first, because President Grant favored another man. The President, while pleased by Shepherd's willingness to advise him and impressed (as he always was with such men) by Shepherd's business acumen and drive, was more or less bound to choose Henry D. Cooke, the brother of millionaire Jay Cooke, one of Grant's best friends. Jay wanted his brother to have the job. It would add luster to his firm's already shining reputation to have as its Washington manager the territory's Governor. He firmly suggested his views to the President.[22]

---

[19] Shepherd's dealings with Freedman's Savings and Trust were large and varied. He himself borrowed heavily from the organization, taking advantage of its low interest rate, and helped others do the same. See R. G. 101, The Records of the Comptroller of Currency, Freedman's Savings and Trust minutes of Board and Committee meetings, National Archives, and Fleming, *The Freedman's Savings Bank*, p. 73.
[20] Shepherd to Howard, February 23, 1871, Howard Collection.
[21] *Ibid.*
[22] Letter from Jay to Henry Cooke, quoted in Paxon Oberholtzer, *Jay Cooke: Financier of the Civil War*, reprint (New York, 1968), vol. 2 of 2 vols, p. 417.

Though he missed the honor of being appointed the district's first Governor, Shepherd was appointed a member of the Board of Public Works. In this position, Shepherd exercised considerably more power than did the Governor. Henry Cooke was the ex-officio president of the board, but unofficial leadership quickly came to rest with Shepherd. At an early meeting of the Board of Public Works, months before the territorial government was to go into effect, Shepherd made his leadership of the board official by having it provide for a vice-president and then having it name him to fill the extra-legal position. This decisive movement into a position of command was typical of Shepherd in all his activities.[23]

In order to understand Shepherd the man, it is necessary to understand his style while serving on—or perhaps better said, serving as— the Board of Public Works. Shortly after the board went into effect, Shepherd called for the organization of a planning panel to determine the form improvements should take and the areas of the city to be first improved. Included on this panel were some of the country's most notable architects and experts on city development, among them General Montgomery C. Meigs and Frederick Law Olmsted. The panel made some recommendations that were later followed, for example the arching of much of the canal, the improvement of access routes between Washington City and Georgetown, and the use of parked center strips as a way of decreasing the amount of pavement needed for Washington's wide streets. In addition, it was the advisory board that made the general estimate that the improvements would cost approximately $6 million. Shepherd listened to the words of the advisory panel, took what he wanted, and discarded the rest.[24]

For the good of the city it was fortunate that Shepherd had an advisory panel for, as his later career showed, he was much more of a doer than a planner. He felt that what was needed was immediate and drastic action. It was this type of thinking that led him to suggest to Mayor Emory that the filling and grading of F Street west of the White House be begun prior to the legal start of the territorial government on June 1, 1871. Shepherd's good friend, A. B. Mullet, testified that this work was not prompted by Shepherd's sizeable holdings on this portion of F Street. As a matter of fact, throughout the territorial period Shepherd seldom seemed upset that the improvements he ordered might improve the value of his own property or

---

[23] *The Evening Star*, December 11, 1871.

[24] Speech in Congress by Norton P. Chipman, June 3, 1872, privately printed, p. 4, Washingtoniana Room of Washington Public Library. See also plan of improvements quoted in *The Evening Star*, August 19, 1871.

National Archives, Brady Collection

Pennsylvania Avenue at the site of Columbia Hospital. The street has been graded and paved with cobblestone.

that of his particular friends.[25] At any rate, with the running start that he had gotten on filling, grading, and paving prior to the date established as the time contracts for general improvement could be awarded, September 1, 1871, Shepherd was able to spend a very busy summer.

While directing the work on the city's roads, Shepherd kept a high profile in the new government's financial affairs. He arranged to have the territorial legislature grant him $4 million to carry out planned improvements and when this was blocked by a court injunction he got an interim sum of more than $500,000 to pay bills. He then started a campaign to have the people of Washington vote on a proposed $4 million bond issue. As a prod to those who might have thought twice about voting a $4 million city debt, Shepherd ordered selected portions of the work already begun to cease. When complaints came in about piles of dirt and ditches in strategic places throughout the city, Shepherd was quick to blame those who had pushed for the injunction. To further insure passage of the bond issue, Shepherd sought to rid the House of Delegates of enemies by pressing Governor Cooke to call a second election. Registration and voting figure ratios, among other things, suggest very strongly that fraud and corruption played a large part in this election.[26]

---

[25] *Report of The Joint Select Committee*, pt. 3, vol. IV, p. 576.

[26] Governor Cooke called for a November plebicite on the issue of the loan on August 20, 1871. This election would also serve to elect a new House of Delegates, despite the

The local pundits had a field day describing Shepherd and his actions, saying such things as "Why is the new Governor (Henry Cooke) like a sheep? Because he is led by A. Shepherd." Or later, "That Shepherd who tends his flock by night/For he needeth no light of day/To change the grade of a street or a walk/Or to move a market away." This last reference was to Shepherd's nighttime destruction of the old Northern Liberties Market, which had long stood on Mt. Vernon Square and which, in addition to being a haven for rats and other vermin, was in competition with the new Central Market, an institution in which Shepherd had financial interests.[27]

Shepherd showed the extent of his strength on September 1, 1871, the official day of receipt for contracts on Washington's proposed improvements. He announced that the bids received on construction were not to his liking and that the board would no longer rely on low bids as the sole criterion for letting contracts but instead would consider many factors in making their decisions. His call for rebidding noted that he would establish a general price range and would select bidders from within that range. By this technique, and by the fact that he generally conducted board meetings in a summary fashion, Shepherd gained almost complete control of contract letting for the territory.[28] Shepherd announced that he would not always take the low bid because the low bid would likely be unrealistic and might mean that the bidder would simply do as little as possible to get the lion's share of the money alloted and then leave. This point might have been well taken. However, there are indications that there may have been more than just a desire to get the best possible job at the lowest price involved in Shepherd's decision. A very large number of Shepherd's friends and relatives were awarded contract. This, in itself, is hardly surprising, since Shepherd was a contractor and therefore knew personally many Washingtonians engaged in the business. An examination of the occupations of some of the supposed contractors, however, shows them listed as bankers, printers or newspapermen. These bogus con-

---

fact that the original delegates would have been in office less than one-half a year. In this election most of those delegates who were opposed to the administration of Shepherd, Cooke, et al, were defeated by those in favor of them and the loan. The second election was rife with charges of corruption. Undoubtedly some did occur. *The Evening Star,* which supported the Cooke, Shepherd group, reported with complete accuracy the vote count in a paper published the afternoon the voting was taking place. Governor's Proclamation, R. G. 351, Records of The District of Columbia, Letters Sent from the Executive Secretary's Office, 1871, 1872, 1874, 3 vols., vol. I, pp. 358–9, 1871. *The Evening Star,* November 22, 1871.

[27] *The Daily Patriot,* May 9, 1871; stanza from the poem "Our City People" by J. A. Wimbaugh (Washington, 1874).

[28] William Tindall, *The Standard History of Washington* (Washington, 1914), p. 251.

tractors sold the contracts. This was the icing on the cake of corruption.[29]

A case in point is Shepherd's continued good faith in and consequent contract letting to J. V. W. Vandenburg. Vandenburg got his start in contracting while serving as a functionary in the Freedman's Bureau. Like many others, including Shepherd himself, he borrowed heavily from the Freedman's Savings and Trust, taking advantage of the low interest rate. But unlike Shepherd, Vandenburg generally avoided repayment. Shepherd's early connections with Vandenburg are shown by the fact that Vandenburg was able to get a loan of $30,000 from Freedman's Savings and Trust simply by having Shepherd testify to chief cashier William Stickney that Vandenburg was a "good man." Vandenburg reneged on the debt and Shepherd, although he told Stickney that he must be a "damn fool" to lend money without proper collateral, paid the balance of the debt.[30] Shepherd was aware of Vandenburg's risk and was interested in seeing that Vandenburg attained at least a modicum of business success. Both are important when one sees that Shepherd continued to favor Vandenburg with enormous contracts for the improvement of Washington's streets.[31]

If Vandenburg were the only contractor so favored, it might be thought that affection shielded Shepherd's eyes from the truth. But as noted there were numerous similar cases. The stone companies, *The Evening Star,* the market companies and street railways with which Shepherd was associated got the major contracts while he was in office. Shepherd and his good friend A. A. Mullet (known in his day as a great architect for his work on the many pillared State-War-Navy Building), while both were on the Board of Public Works and, as such, officials of the Federal government gained contracts for roofing many Federal buildings about the country.[32]

---

[29] *Report of the Joint Select Committee,* pt. 3, vol. IV, p. 1808.

[30] *Ibid.,* passim.

[31] Vandenburg ended up owing Freedman's Savings and Trust in excess of $100,000. It was in large measure because of people like this that the savings institution failed. For lists of friends of the Territorial Government who borrowed from the institution see R. G. 101, Records of the Office of the Comptroller of the Currency, Signature Books of the Freedman's Savings and Trust, Rolls 4 and 5; Minutes of the Board and Committee Meetings of Freedman's Savings and Trust; R. G. 105, Records of the Bureau of Refugees, Freedmen and Abandoned Lands, Letters received, Freedman's Bureau, District of Columbia.

[32] The two investigations of the Territorial Government demonstrated that many of the same people, people who had earlier worked with Shepherd, belonged to the various organizations. A few of the more notable companies in each category were the Maryland Freestone and Mining Company, the Artificial Stone Company, the Portland Stone Company, the National Junction Railroad, the Columbia Railroad, the Piedmont Rail-

As a result of these and other activities, Washington's debt grew to what was then the astronomical figure of $20 million. Shepherd drew on many sources to continue payments for improvements. He divided the city into sewer districts and charged each district a rate, regardless of whether it got sewage, and assessed an improvement and contingency tax on areas improved. He called on Congress to help out and held back payments to those contractors not favored by him.[33]

Two Congressional investigations exonerated Shepherd of any actual fraud. The first, in 1872, concluded, with a strong dissent from minority members, that the territorial government was performing generally as it should and that those who protested had little reason for their protests. The second, in 1874, found that although the territorial government had allowed enormous amounts of mismanagement, had used bad judgment, and should be terminated, Shepherd himself could not be held guilty of fraud.[34]

The findings of the Congressional investigations might be explained in three ways. First, the books of the territorial government were in such a chaotic condition that it was impossible to determine what payments had been made, to whom, or for what purpose those that had been made were made. Second, Shepherd was allied with the Grant faction of the Republican party and the General's supporters in Congress did not want yet another blot on the party's record. Many Democrats hoped that by exposing Shepherd they would gain support for their 1876 presidential candidate. Finally, Shepherd had a persuasive and likeable personality. He had helped many members of Congress to buy real estate in Washington. These may have felt that it was better simply to let Shepherd off with a reprimand and close the books on the territorial form of government than to pursue the matter.[35]

---

road, *The Evening Star, The Daily Republican,* Central and Eastern Markets, and the Vaux Roofing Company. Member and friends of the Shepherd family served as directors and stockholders of all of these companies and various other banks, insurance companies and real estate concerns.

[33] By law the special taxes had to be voted by the territorial legislature, but the use of carefully planned elections by the leaders made the legislature merely an appendage to the Board of Public Works. For the story of the development of the sewer tax see *Washington Past and Present: A History,* ed. by John C. Proctor (New York, 1930), 4 vols., vol II, p. 141; Walter F. Dodd, *The Government of the District of Columbia: A Study in Federal and Municipal Administration* (Washington, 1909); *Report of The Joint Select Committee,* pt. 3, vol. III, p. 1375: *ibid.,* pt. 3, vol. II, pp. 488–503.

[34] U. S. Congress, *House of Representatives Reports for the Second Session of the 42nd Congress* (42 Cong., 2 sess., House Misc. Doc. 72), vol VIII, passim. *House of Representatives Reports for the Third Session of the 43rd Congress* (43 Cong., 3 sess., Rep. 647).

[35] R. G. 351, Records of the Government of the District of Columbia, Appropriations

In Shepherd's behalf, it must be noted that he was a man of great energy and drive, concerned with the immediate attainment of results, and was not a man who worried about how those results were reached. Nor was Shepherd alone. The "Washington Ring," as it became known, included nearly all those who held prominent positions in the territorial government. Also included were many national political figures and local businessmen. In evaluating Shepherd, it must be remembered, too, that Washington seemed little more than a quagmire when he came to office. The streets, which were wider and occupied porportionately more area than in any other major city, were in a state of complete disrepair, the sewer system was almost non-existant, and a brackish canal divided the city. Through the efforts of Shepherd and his associates, the city bordered on being pleasant by June 1874. That much of the work had to be redone in a matter of two or three years is, to a degree, as much a reflection on the state of the arts of paving and tunneling as on the shoddy workmanship of the people Shepherd hired.[36] Even if one does not subscribe to the Vernon L. Parrington view of the Gilded Age as one enormous barbeque, one cannot deny that it was a time when the most lauded men were those whose drive and ambition produced results. Shepherd was very much a man of his times. Finally, it was an open secret among those who worked to set Washington aright that all sought the eventual payment of the city's debts by the Federal government. With the government picking up the tab, then why not just spend, spend, spend? [37]

In September 1873, Grant rewarded Shepherd by appointing him Governor of the territory. But by this time it was obvious that the life of the territory was limited. The panic of 1873, which all but obliterated the financial empire of Shepherd's predecessor, Henry D. Cooke, and of Cooke's brother, put all finances on shaky footing and the demands to rid the city of the territorial incubus increased.

Journal, June 30, 1871 to June 30, 1874; Fiscal Ledgers, Washington City, 1871–1874. Grant consistently praised Shepherd's work. He even selected him to coordinate his second Inaugural program. Shepherd miserably flubbed this job when he failed to provide heat in the temporary building built for the occasion. Senate, *Report of the Joint Select Committee*, pt. 3, vol. IV, p. 1849; *The Evening Star*, December 14, 1924.

[36] *The New York Times*, December 4, 1874. From February 21, 1871 to November 1, 1873, the Board of Public Works laid 123 miles of sewers, 208 miles of sidewalk, 157 miles of improved roads, 30 miles of water mains, 39 miles of gas mains, planted 6,000 trees, graded 3,340,000 cubic yards of dirt, and filled in much of the ugliest part of the canal. *Report of the Joint Select Committee*, pt. 3, vol. IV, p. 1603. George W. Tillson, *Street Pavements and Paving Materials of America* (New York, 1900), p. 307.

[37] In his testimony before Congress Shepherd admitted that his hope was to get the Federal government to pay a substantial portion of the territorial debt. *Report of the Joint Select Committee*, pt. 3, vol. IV, p. 466.

Within nine months Shepherd was out of office. As the territorial government ended, Grant attempted to appoint the ex-governor as one of the commissioners of the temporary commission form of government that followed. The Senate at first appeared ready to follow the President's suggestion but upon rethinking the matter felt it best to exclude Shepherd from any governmental post.[38]

Shortly after returning to private life, Shepherd stated that his services in the territorial government cost him about $200,000. Such a claim is difficult to substantiate. Shepherd had about $350,000 in real and personal property when the territory began and he stated that by mid-1876, two years after the end of the territory, his assets were in excess of $600,000. He spent large sums on parties to which the elite of Republicanism were invited and even dabbled in the art market. Considering that this was at a time when the panic was taking a dreadful toll of American fortunes, Shepherd was doing quite well indeed.[39]

In November 1876, Shepherd declared bankruptcy and galvanized the Washington financial community. Newspapers mentioned several meetings of local leaders with Shepherd concerning his precarious state. In a lead article, the *Baltimore Sun* noted that much of Shepherd's difficulties seemed to stem from his close alliance with the Republican party. At the time of his misfortune, it appeared that the Democrat Samuel J. Tilden would be the next president. *The Sun* speculated that Shepherd would have been able to weather the storms if Rutherford B. Hayes had been the expected victor. Whatever the reason for his trouble, it is evidence of the degree to which Shepherd still had his fingers in the Washington financial pie that local bankers and financiers made arrangements for a moratorium on the collection of debts from him. They noted that Shepherd had $500,000 more in assets than in liabilities. As a result, Washington financiers agreed to float bonds in multiples of $100 to help Shepherd pay off the debts. Shepherd agreed to this and all of his holdings, except for the plumbing concern, were turned over to the control of a triumverate of Washington businessmen.[40]

Despite this support, demands for Congressional investigations of Shepherd and the territorial government continued. On May 1,

---

[38] Wilhelmus Bogart Bryan, *History of the National Capital* (New York, 1916), 2 vols., vol. 2, p. 622.

[39] Ninth Census, vol. 3 (Section for West of 7th Street Road in the County), p. 49, National Archives. *The Evening Star*, November 10, 1876, February 23, 1876. Shepherd papers, General Correspondence Box 4.

[40] *The Daily National Republican*, November 16, 1876. *The Baltimore Sun*, November 14, 1876. *The Daily National Republican*, November 16, 1876.

"DON'T LET US HAVE ANY MORE OF THIS NONSENSE. IT IS A GOOD TRAIT TO STAND BY ONE'S FRIENDS; BUT—"

Library of Congress

Thomas Nast cartoon in Harper's Weekly, July 18, 1874. "Don't let us have any more of this nonsense. It is a good trait to stand by one's friends; but—"

1880, after making arrangements with a New York mining firm, Shepherd left Washington to take control of the Batopilas Mining Company in Chihuahua, Mexico. In Mexico Shepherd more than recouped his fortune. Seven years after leaving Washington, he returned to a hero's welcome to view the city upon which he had left such a mark. Though he continued to have ties with Washington, Shepherd remained a permanent resident of Mexico until his death in 1902. He was buried with great honors in Washington in Rock Creek cemetery.

On balance, one's evaluation of Shepherd must be as one's evaluation of many of the better known men of the Gilded Age. If one accepts modernization as an absolute good, and agrees that almost any means are justified in attaining that good, then the evaluation of Shepherd must be favorable.

If, on the other hand, one feels that corrupt means inevitably corrupt the end to which they are used, then Shepherd must be condemned. I hold to the latter view.

While I do not blame Shepherd for the failure of the city to obtain home rule—whether he wanted it or not, Shepherd was forced to settle for a form of government in 1871 that diminished the amount of home rule—I feel that he was to blame for the vast expenses the city incurred and for much of the shoddy workmanship. His obvious conflict of interest, while less than that of some others of the time, is nonetheless unpardonable and his part in rigging elections in the city added another blot on an already dark record.

A man of undoubted drive, ambition, and talent, Shepherd, as have other public officials, allowed his lesser instincts too much sway over his direction.

The Black Militia in the District of Columbia, 1867-1898

MARTIN K. GORDON

The District of Columbia militia, indeed the entire American militia system as it developed after the Revolution, is not an easy subject for study. It is truly a "many splendored thing." These volunteer groups are occasionally as important as a volunteer fire department, as status-conscious as the Masons, as party-loving as any American Legion convention, somewhat expensive to maintain and, above all, a traditional part of American public life anchored on the myth of the minute man. They are also armed and, hopefully, trained bands of soldiers.

Congress first acknowledged the ability of the black man to contribute to the militia in the July, 1862 militia call-up which in section 1 omitted the customary qualifying word "white" and then in section 12 went on expressly to authorize the President to use "persons of African descent" in whatever military capacity he deemed best. After the Civil War Congress expanded on this new development with a rider to an 1867 army pay act which deleted "white" from all Federal militia legislation then in force. As Constance McLaughlin Green points out in *Secret City,* the District of Columbia, by act of Congress, had adopted universal manhood suffrage 12 months before ratificaion of the Fifteenth Amendment extended this right to the nation as a whole. These two acts of Congress, deleting racial restrictions from the militia law and extending full civil rights to the black community of D.C., paved the way for the formation of black militia organizations in Washington.[1]

If Otis Singletary is correct in his book, *Negro Militia and Recon-*

Delivered before the Columbia Historical Society on December 14, 1971.

The author wishes to express his gratitude to Prof. Letitia Brown of The George Washington University for criticizing this manuscript and to Brig. Gen. C. C. Bryant for authorizing the use of the District of Columbia National Guard Archives and to Col. Tom Simon and CWO Ralph Becraft for their assistance with them. These officers are with the D. C. National Guard.

[1] 12 *Stat* 599; 14 *Stat* 423; 16 *Stat* 3; Princeton, Princeton Univ. Press, 1967, p. 94.

struction, and I think that to some extent he is, that the Negro militia in the reconstruction states is a political phenomenon growing out of the need of the unpopular Radical administrations in these states to defend themselves, then I can state with some assurance that the black units organized in the District between the late 1860's and the 1890's are "Northern" by nature and not at all related to Singletary's reconstruction troops. These units began to form about the same time as comparable white companies in the late 1860's after the nation had begun to recover from the exhaustion and horror of the Civil War. The first of these units to organize themselves probably were the Butler Zouaves, named after Gen. Benjamin F. Butler, and the Stanton Guards, named after the Secretary of War. Illustrations of their uniforms are preserved in the painting now hanging in the D.C. Armory titled "The Uniformed Militia of the District of Columbia, 1873" which includes these two units along with an unidentified but obviously black officer labeled simply "officer of colored troops." They were joined after the formation of the District's territorial government in 1871 by the Territorial Guards Company.[2]

One of the early concerns of this new territorial government was the passage of a militia act giving the new governor, Henry D. Cooke, all of the authority of any other state governor over his militia with the exception that the Secretary of War had to commission his officers for him. This short-lived territorial militia law carried out the anti-segregationist intent of Congress when, in section 1, it specified that "every able-bodied male citizen, between the ages of 18 and 45 years, residing in the District" and not otherwise exempt shall be subject to military duty.[3]

The Butler Zouaves became the most important of these early units when it survived the decline of the militia in the late 1870's and went on to enter the new National Guard of the District of Columbia as its Fifth Battalion upon its organization in 1887. The first unit destined to become a permanent part of the D.C. Guard, however, was the Washington Cadet Corps, organized as a single company June 12, 1880, expanded to become a three company battalion in October, 1884, and reaching its full four-company strength a year later in 1885. Assuming that each company met its minimum strength requirement of 40 men, this black battalion would have had 160 enlisted men plus company and battalion officers. We do know

---

[2] Austin, Univ. of Texas Press, 1957; National Guard of the District of Columbia, *Historical and Pictorial Review.* Baton Rouge, Army and Navy Pub. Co., 1940, p. xxv and 101. This source must be used with caution.

[3] First Legislative Assembly, Sess. I, Ch. 55, 1871.

that by the time of the 1887 National Drill competitions held in Washington, it had a total of 450 officers, men, and bandsmen. This unit's annual drill was one of the highlights of black Washington's social season. Its arch-competitors for the affections of this social set was the Capital City Guards, organized in 1882 and also destined to become a permanent part of the D.C. National Guard. The Cadet Corps remained under the leadership of Captain, later Major, Christian A. Fleetwood, a Civil War Medal of Honor winner, from its beginning to its consolidation with the Capital City Guards eleven years later in 1891. The Guards likewise operated under only one commander, Major Frederick C. Revells, up to the forced consolidation.[4]

The Washington Cadet Corps proved its pre-eminence when, in October, 1883, its original Company A won a competition held at Athletic Park in D.C., for all the black units. The other competing units were Company A from the Butler Zouaves, Company A from the Capital City Guards, and the Lincoln Light Infantry.

The Cadet Corps was also the only black D. C. unit to participate in the 1887 National Drill competitions held in Washington. This meeting reflected the public interest in National Guard affairs which was growing throughout the nation. Indeed, the citizens of Washington, D. C. contributed $50,000 to support this country-wide gathering of Guardsmen. Black militia units from Virginia and perhaps other states also competed in this Drill. Although the Washington Cadet Corps did not camp with the white D. C. units, as the black Virginia militiamen did with theirs, it did march with them in the Grand Review. This activity caused the white units from Vicksburg and Memphis to drop out of the parade and march around on their own as a protest against having to march past the White House behind this black unit. The Cadet Corps placed 25th out of the 30 militia companies which lasted through the entire meet. This rating was the highest of any black company and prompted the *Evening Star* to comment that Company A, the original company of the Cadet Corps, was the best colored unit to appear and one of the better units in the over-all competition.[5]

In July of 1887, Albert Ordway, a Civil War brevet Brigadier

---

[4] The history of the Washington Cadet Corps is from an undated May, 1887 clipping from the *Evening Star* filed in a scrapbook labeled "1887 encampment" in the archives of the D. C. National Guard. The social significance of these companies is discussed in *Secret City*, p. 208–209. Their officers are listed in *Historical and Pictorial Review*, p. 101.

[5] Frederick P. Todd, "Our National Guard: An Introduction to its History." *Military Affairs*. Vol. V (1941) 162; the National Drill is reported and commented on in the Washington *Evening Star*, May 1–31, 1887.

Washingtoniana Division
Martin Luther King Memorial Library

Company A, Captain A. Brooks, Washington Cadet Corps, National Drill and Encampment, May 1887.

General whom President Grover Cleveland had commissioned a Brigadier General and commanding officer of the District's militia brigade in 1885, achieved the first of his goals for the D. C. militia when he succeeded in bringing most of the independent companies of the militia together in battalion organizations, with the whole of these battalions denominated the District of Columbia National Guard. The first four of these battalions were white and second three of them were black. Thus the blacks who, according to the 1880 census, composed 33.6 per cent of the D.C. population made up approximately 42 per cent of the strength of its active militia. (Ten out of 24 companies were black.) These units were all infantry. There were no artillery or cavalry groups in the D. C. National Guard at this time.[6]

This happy situation did not last long. General Ordway, on March

---

[6] *Vide:* the obituaries of General Ordway appearing in the *Washington Post* and the *Evening Star,* November 22, 1897; General Orders No. 4, July 18, 1887, Headquarters, Dist. of Columbia Militia.

Library of Congress

Christian A. Fleetwood, Civil War Medal of Honor winner, who as Captain and later as Major commanded the Washington Cadet Corps from its organization in 1880 until its consolidation with the Capital City Guards in 1891.

10, 1888, disbanded the oldest continuous black militia group, the Butler Zouaves (Fifth Battalion) because, when only 39 of its 128 members were present at an inspection and they scored an average of 1.76 out of six, he decided that the Brigade could no longer afford the equipment and expenses of the battalion. No loud protest was raised and the other two black organizations continued to participate in all Brigade activities including the sharing of a common rifle range. The Sixth Battalion, or Washington Cadet Corps, participated in the annual Brigade inspection in June of 1888 and with 170 of its 259 man enrollment present had a satisfactory attendance of 66 per cent. Its Company A scored above average in the overall inspection ratings and its worst unit, C Company, still ranked 18th out of the 21 units competing or fourth from the bottom.[7]

Although these black units trained and marched with their white counterparts, they were still not "out of uniform" friends of the white guardsmen. When General Ordway paid out of his personal funds for the reception which marked the opening of Brigade headquarters in the Pennsylvania Avenue market building, he invited all of the white and none of the black officers in the Guard, justifying himself on the grounds that this was a social and not a military function and that besides Guard funds were not used to pay for it.[8]

The April, 1889 reorganization of the entire D.C. National Guard struck a more serious blow at the morale of the two historic groups, the Washington Cadet Corps and the Capital City Guards, when it reduced their battalions from four to two companies each. General Ordway justified this because of the declining enrollment in the companies and the repeated refusal of Congress to appropriate sufficient funds to enable the National Guard to maintain so many companies. He had just pushed a new D.C. National Guard Act through Congress which replaced the 1803 law which had governed the militia from that date to 1889, except for the years when territorial legislation governed this subject. This new law provided for a maximum of 28 infantry companies and Ordway also cited this law as the reason why he had reduced the number of Negro militia companies. He did offer, though, to organize the black battalions as a regiment, which would be the Third Regiment of D.C. Militia, but the two historic competitors refused, each group apparently feeling that its autonomy was more important than the promotion of a black to the rank of Lieutenant Colonel.[9]

Two years later, in March, 1891, General Ordway, as a result of a $2,200 reduction by Congress in his budget, announced that he would have to disband all the remaining colored units in order to reduce his budget by that amount. As soon as this news was made public, a furor arose which lasted until the order was rescinded. As one anonymous black officer commented, "We are not permitted to join the white companies and now are not to be allowed separate companies. Even our white citizens, I am sure, will not approve this action." He blamed the order on Ordway's need to appease Southern Congressmen. George W. Evans, an officer in the white National Rifles, an independent company which had not joined the Brigade and had

---

[7] General Orders No. 10, March 31, 1888; General Orders No. 24, June 14, 1888, both issued by Headquarters, Dist. of Columbia Militia.

[8] *Evening Star,* March 20, 1891.

[9] *Washington Post,* March 12, 1891; *Evening Star* April 4, 1891.

been forced to turn its Federal equipment over to the colored troops, wrote a series of letters to the editor accusing Ordway of being an incompetent, extravagant bigot, and arguing that if Ordway had wanted to retain these two battalions he could find a way to do so. A committee composed of some of the leading citizens of Washington's black community, men such as ex-Senator Blanche K. Bruce, former minister to Liberia John H. Smyth, Lewis H. Douglass, the son of Frederick Douglass, Robert H. Terrill, and others carried the protests of their community to President Benjamin Harrison who said that he did not know that the order had already been issued to disband the black units. He suggested a possible compromise to them which would consist of the consolidation of the two battalions. After the committee left, he called in General Ordway, with whom he had already conferred on the subject, and asked him to cancel the disbandment order. The battalions accepted this compromise and brought their two half strength organizations into one full strength unit. The General then undertook to finance it out of the regular militia appropriation. Arsonists had twice attempted to burn down the center market armory during this controversy. They were not caught but the newspapers blamed the fires on the "somewhat strained military situation." Since neither unit would serve under the officers of the other one, Ordway granted the commissioned officers of the two units the unusual privilege of meeting jointly to elect their new battalion commander, a post usually filled by an appointee of the Commanding General. The officers elected Capt. James A. Perry of the Capital City Guards, Eighth Battalion, and a life-time resident of the District. But after a delegation of black citizens protested his selection to the Secretary of War because of some possibly illegal dealings of his in the past, Major Frederick C. Revells, commander of the Eighth Battalion, was made the new commander of the consolidated unit which now carried the designation of First Separate Battalion.

Major Fleetwood, the Civil War veteran who had commanded the Seventh Battalion until the consolidation, and, while being praised by many citizens for his work, had mildly criticized Ordway as being prejudiced, retired.[10] He soon had charges placed against him by the National Guard under the direction of the Secretary of War for not being able to account for $700 worth of the federal property that

---

[10] *Vide:* the *Washington Post* and the *Evening Star* March 7 to April 4, 1891 for the reportage, editorials, and letters to the editor on this disbandment controversy. George W. Evans who wrote the letters to the editor discussed above read a paper "The Militia of the District of Columbia" before the Columbia Historical Society which did not mention this controversy at all. *CHS Records,* Vol. XXVIII (1926) 95–105.

had been entrusted to him during his eleven year career in the militia.[11]

Ordway was at various times called prejudiced, incompetent, a tool of Southern Congressmen—or a victim of Republican Congressmen who wanted to use this episode to get rid of him, a Cleveland appointee.[12] It is my opinion, in view of his earlier offers and attempts to merge these units, that, although he may have been prejudiced, his primary reason for making the black units bear the brunt of the budget cut was to force their consolidation, a goal towards which he had been working for two years. These units had been rivals for some time and antagonisms between them were such that they had turned down an earlier offer by Ordway to let them continue as one consolidated unit. Although I doubt that he would have been saddened by their leaving the organized militia, he did treat them fairly in a military way, as exemplified by their scores on the annual inspections, and, once, under pressure from the black citizens committee, they had agreed to the consolidation, he cancelled the public appeal for funds which they were just starting and gave them full support from the militia budget.

The new organization soon began to work together and its high morale and fair treatment between this episode in 1891 and the beginning of the Spanish American War in 1898 is demonstrated by its repeated high standings in both percentage present and average score attained at the annual musters and inspections. No unit from this battalion fell into the bottom 25 per cent of the units being inspected during these years as can be demonstrated from a reading of the Brigade General Orders for 1892–1897. In 1891, the Brigade split into its component groups for the annual summer camp and the new First Separate Battalion, composed of the old Washington Cadet Corps and Capital City Guards, was carefully watched at its Camp Federick Douglass since this was the first time the unit had encamped as an independent command. In spite of heavy rains, this camp at Collingwood Beach, Virginia, was a tremendous success. Some 1,200 visitors including Frederick Douglass himself watched its grand review, begun with hymns and a sermon. This indicates the social importance of this battalion because its 1,200 visitors compare quite favorably with the 1,500 which the socially elite Washington Light Infantry Battalion attracted to its encampment.[13]

---

[11] *Evening Star,* June 22, 1891.

[12] That last possible explanation is from the *New York Post,* March 18, 1891.

[13] *Evening Star,* August 25, 31, 1891; *Washington Post,* August 31, 1891.

The first Separate Battalion was also involved in the peace-keeping functions of the National Guard. In the spring of 1891, General Ordway became worried about the possibilities of riots in Washington. He budgeted for and developed a series of street riot drills for that summer.[14] In April he devoted a special lecture to "Street Riots" at the end of a course of lectures on the duties of National Guard officers while on active duty. In that lecture he discussed the relations of military to civil authority, how to handle troops in the streets, attacking and dispersing mobs in streets, the attack of barricades, and the attack and defense of buildings. He did not mention any problems peculiar to the District of Columbia but did criticize the California and New York riot control plans as being too complicated for ordinary militiamen. He laid stress on the dangers from anarchist labor riots in the United States and merely mentioned race prejudices as one of a number of other possible causes of American riots.[15] Several of the organized labor and political groups in the District reacted angrily to his riot control lecture and argued that other groups also rioted and that Ordway should not have singled out labor as a cause of disorder. District Assembly No. 1 of the Knights of Labor listed other types of riots such as the lynch mobs in New Orleans, but did not mention racial violence as such in its list.[16] The riot control plans published by the D. C. National Guard further support the impression that massive interracial violence was not a major concern of Washington's Guard between the Civil War and the Twentieth Century. The plans centered mainly around three possible contingencies: to guard the Treasury Department against mob attack; to retake the Treasury building from any mob which had seized it; and, to secure the Baltimore and Potomac railroad so that reinforcements could quickly be brought into the District.[17] The black First Separate Battalion had a significant role to play in these riot control plans. The Battalion's specific mission, along with the cavalry and engineer units, was to either guard or retake the State, War, and Navy build-

---

[14] *Evening Star,* March 7, 1891.

[15] Albert Ordway, *The National Guard in Service. A Course of Lectures.* . . . Washington, J. J. Chapman, 1891. This book became the standard D. C. National Guard textbook for officers. His lecture no. 13 on street riots was reprinted separately with his street combat formation drill as *Drill Regulations for Street Riot Duty.* . . . Washington, J. J. Chapman, 1891.

[16] *Evening Star,* May 25, 1891; *Washington Post,* May 28, 1891.

[17] These plans are described under "Mobilization" in the annual review of National Guard activities for the years 1894 and 1895. U. S. Adjutant General's Office, *The Organized Militia of the U. S. in the Year.* . . . Washington, G.P.O., 1895 and 1896. By 1896 the mobilization plans were considered classified information and were no longer included in these annual reports.

ing, on the other side of the White House from the Treasury building.[18]

At the Brigade summer camp mock battle in 1897 this unit led the attack and the umpires declared the attacking force, which also included white battalions, victorious when they stopped the battle because some of the men were becoming too excited.[19]

When war with Spain finally came in 1898 the entire District of Columbia National Guard was called into active service. The War Department mustered it out of service almost immediately and allotted one volunteer regiment to the D. C. militia and local volunteers. After the War Department rejected many of the Guard companies for active duty, their members practically disbanded them when they resigned from them to go into immune companies and thus to get into the war. The same thing happened to the First Separate Battalion, only it was rejected because it was black, not because its members were physically unfit. Brigadier General George H. Harries who had succeeded Ordway in 1897 made the decision not to accept any of the volunteers from the First Separate Battalion. He had written in 1891 during the disbandment controversy of that year the "proposition to mix white and colored troops in the two regimental organizations is not possible of application, and the only reason for suggesting such a combination is a desire to cause trouble and foment disturbances." And in 1898, when he had to reduce his Brigade to a Regiment, he held to and enforced this statement of his, much to the bitter disappointment of the District of Columbia black militia.[20]

The brilliant performance of this battalion as the First Battalion, 372d Infantry, assigned to the French Army, in World War I, proves, however, that this unit was more than a focus of the social life of black Washington, more than just another expression of the club or fraternal spirit which motivated so many militiamen: it was also a first rate combat unit.[21]

---

[18] "Memorandum Relative to Parade on May 30, 1894." Headquarters, Dist. of Columbia Militia, May 22, 1894, on file with the General Orders and circulars series in the D. C. National Guard archives. General Ordway kept a small scrapbook of clippings about labor riots in the 1890's and this was probably his main source of information. The scrapbook is now in the D. C. National Guard archives.

[19] U. S. Adjutant General's Office, *The Organized Militia of the U. S. in the Year 1897*. Washington, G.P.O., 1898. P. 418.

[20] General Orders No. 7, April 23, 1898; General Orders No. 8, April 25, 1898; General Orders No. 9, May 10, 1898, all issued by Headquarters, Dist. of Columbia Militia; *Secret City*, p. 130–131; *Evening Star*, March 18, 1891.

[21] For its performance in World War I, see Emmett J. Scott, *Scott's Official History of the American Negro in the World War*. Chicago, Homewood Press, 1919. *Passim.*

John Mercer Langston and the Rise of Howard Law School

MAXWELL BLOOMFIELD

In the fall of 1871 the prominent Republican columnist John W. Forney informed his readers in the Philadelphia *Press* that he had recently attended the first commencement exercises at the Howard Law School in Washington, D.C., where Professor John M. Langston had presided over a class of young Negroes who were just completing their legal studies. "Some of them," Forney wrote,

> had only a year before been unable to read and write, and one bright, black fellow was especially patronized by the Professor, because six months before he did not know his alphabet. Nearly all had been slaves. There were oral and written arguments. The manner in which they spoke or read their productions displayed extraordinary talent. I thought I could detect in their flowing cadences and graceful gestures close copies of the old Southern statesmen, who in past years lorded it over both parties. There was scarcely an error of grammar or pronunciation. The logic and the appreciation of the subjects treated, which included landlord and tenant, titles to real estate, divorce, borrowing and lending, promissory notes, etc., proved not only careful study, but intense determination to succeed.... I doubt whether the older and more extensive Law School connected with Columbia College, where the offspring of the other, and what is called the superior race, are educated, could show, all things considered, an equal number of graduates as well grounded and as completely armed for the battle of the future. There are colored lawyers in most of our courts, even in the highest judiciary. They are the pioneers of an interesting and exciting destiny. With them, unlike their more fortunate white brethren, the bitterest struggle begins when they receive their sheepskins. They go forth to war against a tempest of bigotry and prejudice. They will have to fight their way into society, and to contend with jealousy and hate in the jury-box and in the court-room, but they will win, as

---

The author wishes to acknowledge that research for this paper was made possible through a grant from the American Bar Foundation in 1968.

Library of Congress

John Mercer Langston. A Brady Studio photograph.

surely as ambition, genius, and courage are gifts, not of race or condition, but of God alone.[1]

After making due allowance for Forney's partisanship and characteristic exuberance, one must acknowledge that his rose-colored picture did point up several undeniable truths. One was the importance of Howard Law School as a national center for the training of black lawyers; another was the immense gap that separated such training from professional success in a legal environment shaped by white practitioners, most of whom accepted the racial implications of Darwinian biology. The early law professors at Howard fully appreciated the magnitude of their task, and brought to their teaching chores something of the same crusading zeal they had formerly displayed as antislavery activists. For them the creation of a well trained Negro bar represented a potential breakthrough in the long struggle for equal rights that began with the black convention movement of the 1840's and 1850's. No man had served that movement more faithfully than John Langston, the first dean of Howard Law School; and no man understood better than he the peculiar difficulties that awaited the aspiring Negro attorney.

Born in 1829 on a Virginia plantation, Langston was the son of a white planter and his part-Indian, part-Negro freedwoman. His father, Captain Ralph Quarles, belonged to that generation of Revolutionary War veterans who took seriously the libertarian guarantees of the Declaration of Independence. Quarles believed in educating his slaves and then freeing them, as he had freed his favorite, Lucy Langston, almost a quarter of a century before the birth of their third son, John Mercer. Young John thus came into the world legally free, and never experienced at firsthand the brutalizing effects of the slave system. Indeed, in the autobiography he wrote some sixty years later, he described life on the old plantation in almost idyllic terms, recalling that Captain Ralph was the only white man on the place and that he treated his slaves with fairness and compassion.[2]

---

[1] John W. Forney, *Anecdotes of Public Men* (N.Y., 1873), 180–181.
[2] John Mercer Langston, *From the Virginia Plantation to the National Capitol* (Hartford, Conn., 1894), 11–12. For the factual background of Langston's career, I have also relied upon William F. Cheek's careful studies: "Forgotten Prophet: The Life of John Mercer Langston," (unpublished Ph.D. dissertation, Dept. of History, Univ. of Virginia, 1961); and "John Mercer Langston: Black Protest Leader and Abolitionist," *Civil War History* XVI (June, 1970), 101–120.

Few manuscript sources exist. According to Langston's granddaughter, Mrs. Nettie L. Mathews, almost all of his papers were destroyed after his death by his son-in-law James Carroll Napier. What remains is a meager collection of miscellaneous tax receipts, bills, a few early letters and drafts of speeches at the Amistad Research Center of Fisk University, Nashville, Tennessee; and some scrapbooks and other materials relating to his later career in the Moorland Room of Howard University, Washington, D.C.

But Langston's boyhood memories of Virginia could not have been very extensive, since both his parents died when he was four years old, at which time he was taken to the free state of Ohio, pursuant to the terms of his father's will. During the next ten years he lived with five different families, two white and three black, shuttling back and forth between Chillicothe and Cincinnati as educational opportunities or other considerations suggested themselves to his guardians. The emotional insecurity of his position perhaps encouraged him to cultivate a strain of arrogance—his trademark in later years—as a protective veneer for what seems to have been a sensitive and vulnerable nature. In any event his elitist pretensions were not without some foundation in fact: He did enjoy a substantial income as the heir to one-third of his father's estate; he was waited upon by a white domestic at one point; and he did have access to the best available private schooling, culminating in a college education at Oberlin, from which he graduated with honors in 1849, at the age of eighteen.

His college experience was crucial to his later professional development. Oberlin, which was one of only four schools in the nation to admit Negro students at the time, was a bastion of the western antislavery movement, where undergraduates were treated to a classical education strongly laced with ethics and evangelism. Under the tutelage of men like Asa Mahan and the lawyer-turned-evangelist Charles Grandison Finney, Langston encountered fervently held beliefs about the vast improvability of man and the personal duty of every individual to work for social betterment. By the end of his senior year he had decided that he had a racial mission to fulfill and—given his predilection for literature and debate—that the law offered the best means of advancing his own interests along with those of the Negro masses.

But he soon found that no law school would accept him, despite his excellent academic record. When he applied to the Cincinnati Law School, the great training ground for practitioners throughout the Mississippi Valley, Timothy Walker promptly turned him down, noting that the "students would not feel at home with him, and he would not feel at home with them." The same results obtained at the more obscure establishment conducted by James W. Fowler at Ballston Spa, New York. Fowler, however, was more sympathetic to Langston's plight, and in a personal interview with him suggested an unusual alternative. "I will let you edge your way into my school," he said; then, in answer to Langston's query, "What, Mr. Fowler, do you mean by your words 'Edge your way into the school?'" he explained: "Come into the recitation-room; take your seat off and apart from the class; ask no questions; behave yourself quietly; and if after a time no one says anything against, but all seem well inclined toward you, you may move up nearer the class; and so continue to do till you are taken and considered in due time as in full and regular membership." [3] Langston understandably found this proposition somewhat less than appealing, and tried clerking for a Cleveland attorney instead, only to find at the end of a year that he knew little more law than before.

In desperation he sought advice from some of his old professors, who suggested that a few postgraduate courses in theology might be good for his soul and also provide some useful pre-law training. Three years later he obtained a degree in theology from Oberlin, becoming the first Negro theological graduate in the United States. But whatever carryover value the preparation and delivery of sermons and the demands of scriptural exegesis may have had for him as a prospective lawyer, he recognized that holy writ was no substitute for Blackstone when it came to bar examinations, and accordingly resolved to give the apprenticeship system one last chance.

This time he entered the law office of Philemon Bliss, a white newspaper editor and antislavery advocate from the neighboring town of Elyria, who taught him all the law he knew in about a year and then pronounced him fit to enter the legal profession. In September, 1854, Langston passed his qualifying examination and was admitted to the Ohio bar. The five-man District Court that issued his license avoided any possible difficulties from the state's "Black Laws" by ruling, on the basis of visual examination, that the applicant was properly a "white man," within the loose meaning attached to that term by several previous judicial decisions.[4] And with that appeal to creative jurisprudence Langston's legal career was formally launched.

The good luck that had played so large a part in his life until now did not desert him in his early practice. There were only a handful of Negro lawyers in the nation on the eve of the Civil War, and almost all of them were clustered in the great metropolitan centers of the Northeast, especially the Boston area, where such figures as Macon B. Allen, Robert Morris, and Aaron Bradley enjoyed the active patronage of Ellis Gray Loring and other antislavery practitioners and judges.[5] Langston, the first and only black lawyer in Ohio, tapped

---
[3] Langston, *Virginia Plantation*, 108.
[4] *Ibid.*, 121–125. Relevant cases establishing the criteria for "white" citizenship in Ohio include: Jeffries v. Ankeny, 11 Ohio 372 (1842); Lane v. Baker, 12 Ohio 237 (1843); and Anderson v. Millikin, 9 Ohio (n.s.) 568 (1859). See also: Charles Thomas Hickok, *The Negro in Ohio, 1802–1870* (Cleveland, 1896), 45–46.
[5] Charles Sumner Brown, "The Genesis of the Negro Lawyer in New England," 22

similar sources of support in the backwoods. He settled initially at Brownhelm, a small farming community close by Lake Erie that prided itself on its progressive outlook and catered to a local elite of reform-minded Yankees. Grandison Fairchild, the town's leading citizen, was a strong antislavery man who was quite prepared to welcome a black college graduate of independent means and courtly manner (particularly since he was the sole Negro in the area and therefore something of a special advertisement for the abolitionist cause).

Within a month of his arrival Langston was invited by a local attorney to assist in the defense of a landowner involved in a property dispute of some notoriety. His successful courtroom pleading as co-counsel brought him his first clients the following day: several white liquor dealers who were charged with violating the state's temperance laws. A string of such liquor cases from Lorain and adjoining counties, along with an occasional murder trial, made up the most important items in his practice through the Civil War years. In addition, he handled some routine civil litigation that came to him through his involvement in municipal politics.

With the help of the Fairchilds he was nominated for the post of town clerk in 1855 and elected on the Liberty Party ticket by an all-white vote. His victory made him the first of his race ever to hold an elective office in the United States; it also made him ex officio attorney for the township. When he moved to Oberlin a year later in search of broader opportunities, he was promptly elected to the same position there. But at that point his prospects for further advancement within the legal profession stalled. Even in a uniquely favorable environment, he found it impossible to attract a large or diversified clientele. Certain white practitioners never let him forget his racial origins, insulting him in open court in ways that sometimes led to after-hours brawls on the courthouse green; while, from another direction, Negro clients shunned him, fearing the impression he might make upon all-white juries. Thwarted in his professional ambitions, he found full scope for both his legal talents and his reformist zeal in the black protest movement of the 1850's, in which he soon rose to a position of national leadership.

By the time he joined the antislavery crusade, it had already begun to fragment along racial lines. Most white abolitionists preferred to direct their total energies toward the liberation of the Southern slave, while black militants were equally concerned with securing full civil

---

Negro History Bulletin (April, 1959), 147–152; Martin Robison Delany, *The Condition, Elevation, Emigration, and Destiny of the Colored People of the United States* (Philadelphia, 1852), 117–119.

rights for the "half-free" Negro population of the North.[6] Langston did much to weld the black reformers of Ohio into an aggressive lobbying group that agitated for Negro suffrage and an end to every other kind of legal discrimination against Negroes within the state. "If we are deprived of education, of equal political privileges, still subjected to the same depressing influences under which we now suffer, the natural consequences will follow," he warned Ohio legislators in 1856; "and the State, for her planting of injustice, will reap her harvest of sorrow and crime. She will contain within her limits a discontented population—dissatisfied, estranged—ready to welcome any revolution or invasion as a relief, for they can lose nothing and gain much." [7]

The implied threat of a black uprising in the North was not a characteristic tactic, however; for the most part Langston kept his speeches low-keyed and appealed for peaceful reform within the existing legal system. He owed his fame as an orator not to passion or charisma, but to the meticulousness with which he prepared his speeches and the wealth of supporting detail that went into them. His best efforts resembled carefully constructed legal briefs that relied upon a mass of factual data to overcome the prejudices of his listeners. Contemporaries habitually described him as a "gentleman," and this was the public image that he cultivated, affecting an ostentatiously expensive wardrobe for his lecture tours that included: a blue or brown frock coat, black doeskin pants, a fancy silk or satin vest and a black cravat. In that get-up there was no mistaking him for a fugitive slave, nor did he attempt to identify himself in any personal way with the slave system. He rather held himself out as a product of white middle-class culture, one who fully understood the ways of the Establishment and was prepared to fight it on its own ground and with its own weapons.

Only in the case of the Fugitive Slave Law, which he believed to be both unconstitutional and immoral, did he advocate higher law principles and urge his followers to acts of civil disobedience and violent resistance. "Let us swear eternal enmity to this law," he told a mass rally convened in 1859 to protest the conviction of two Oberlin residents for their part in the rescue of fugitive John Price. "Exhaust the law first for these men, but if this fail, for God's sake let us fall back upon our own natural rights and say to the prison walls 'come

---

[6] On the tensions between white and black abolitionists, see: Leon F. Litwack, "The Abolitionist Dilemma: The Antislavery Movement and the Northern Negro," *New England Quarterly* XXXIV (March, 1961), 50–73; and William H. and Jane H. Pease, "Antislavery Ambivalence: Immediatism, Expedience, Race," *American Quarterly* XVII (Winter, 1965), 682–695.

[7] *Proceedings of the State Convention of Colored Men ... 1856* (Cleveland, 1856).

down,' and set these men at liberty." [8] No violence in fact grew out of this situation, for both prisoners were shortly released through the intervention of Governor Salmon P. Chase; but Langston practiced what he preached in the matter of civil disobedience by providing food and shelter to runaway slaves in the Oberlin area.

During the Civil War he helped to recruit three black infantry regiments for the Union Army, and kept the issue of Negro rights before the Northern public by lecturing widely on behalf of the recently formed National Equal Rights League. Republican party strategists, impressed by his wartime services, sent him on a speaking tour of several border states in the fall of 1865, to build up the morale of the freedmen and to indoctrinate them in sound Republican principles. He succeeded so well in the role of party organizer that his assignment eventually stretched out to four years, during the last half of which he visited Negro educational establishments throughout the South as General Inspector of Schools for the Freedmen's Bureau.

"Above all other things, get education! Get money! Get character!" he told attentive audiences from North Carolina to Louisiana. "Don't ape the vices of the white men, but their virtues." [9] Translated politically, this meant: vote the Republican ticket; in cultural terms it meant an unqualified endorsement of white middle-class mores. Langston himself was something of a black Babbitt on questions of personal morality, forever exhorting ex-slaves to "put away their filthy and expensive practices" of tobacco-chewing and whiskey drinking, and start saving their greenbacks. His cultural conservatism, no less than his active campaigning for Grant in 1868, contributed to his selection by the Trustees of Howard University to head their newly created Law Department. The position promised to utilize all of his varied talents—as scholar, lawyer, orator, reformer, and administrator—and he lost no time in accepting the offer.

Howard University was one of eight institutions of higher learning founded in the immediate postwar years to serve the educational needs of the freedmen. Sponsored by a group of Congregational ministers and radical Republican politicians, the school was originally envisaged as a training center for black ministers and teachers. By the time of its incorporation by Act of Congress in March, 1867, however, the design had been broadened to encompass all of the departments proper to a major university, including a prospective law school. General Oliver Otis Howard of the Freedmen's Bureau shortly succeeded to the presidency of the institution, and personally selected a

---

[8] Quoted in Fitzhugh Lee Styles, *Negroes and the Law* (Boston, 1937), 119.
[9] Cheek, "Forgotten Prophet," 84; Langston Papers, Box 5, Fisk University.

permanent site for the campus on a tract of one hundred fifty acres in northwest Washington. Undergraduate classes began on May 1, 1867, under an admissions policy that prohibited the exclusion of any student for reasons of race or sex. A year later school administrators, encouraged by favorable publicity and rising enrollment figures, embarked upon an ambitious expansion program that looked to the immediate development of law and medical faculties.

The Howard Law School officially opened its doors on January 6, 1869, when Langston was informed by the Trustees that "a respectable number" of students had applied for admission. The number in fact turned out to be six, although an additional fifteen persons showed up for classes by the end of the term in June. At the time (and throughout Langston's seven-year tenure as dean) there were no entrance requirements for potential lawyers beyond "suitable age and good moral character." As a result, many individuals turned up from year to year who were seriously handicapped by a lack of adequate prior education. To meet this problem, which became all too apparent with the very first batch of applicants, Langston and his colleagues found it necessary to offer an introductory cram course in remedial English, arithmetic, and other basic subjects, before moving into the regular law school curriculum. The first genuine law classes did not, therefore, begin until September 1869; and this pattern of a compulsory pre-law period continued for some three years, until the Board of Trustees ordered Langston to stop duplicating the work of the College and to confine himself to a strict two-year law program.

All classes at Howard Law School met in the evening, from five to nine p.m. This arrangement enabled students to hold down full-time government jobs during the day, and so to pay for their living expenses, their textbooks, and their annual tuition of forty dollars. The Grant administration, which owed a great deal to the Negro vote in the South, went out of its way to provide employment opportunities for Langston's pupils in the Freedmen's Bureau and other executive agencies. Langston later boasted that at one point he had been able to place one hundred law students in various government positions; but the figure seems somewhat inflated, since at no time during his years at Howard did the total enrollment at the law school exceed eighty-four persons.

Like the students, the faculty spent their daylight hours working at non-academic occupations that supplied the lion's share of their income. Langston, who received $3,000 a year from the University in his dual capacity of law professor and department head, also served on the Board of Health of the District of Columbia from 1871 to

1877; and his two white subordinates relied even more strongly on outside sources of support. Assistant Professor Albert Gallatin Riddle, a zealous abolitionist and wartime Congressman from Ohio, was a successful practicing attorney with a reputation as the "official advocate of the Negroes of the Capital;" while Instructor Henry D. Beam was the chief clerk of the Freedmen's Bureau. Together with Judge Charles C. Nott of the United States Court of Claims, who taught during the 1870–1871 term, these men comprised the full faculty of Howard Law School in its formative period, meeting their first classes in a rambling red frame building on Georgia Avenue that, tradition asserts, had previously housed a German saloon and dance hall.

Their teaching methods, like those in vogue at other institutions, emphasized the importance of memorization and formal classroom drills on assigned subjects. Students were expected to master the basic legal principles set out in standard texts and to recite them by rote when called upon; while their teachers provided supplemental lectures to fill in the gaps. Members of the first year class at Howard ploughed their way through such old favorites as Walker's *Introduction to American Law,* Blackstone's *Commentaries,* Kent's *Commentaries,* and Smith on *Contracts.* Seniors read Greenleaf on *Evidence,* Hilliard on *Torts,* Washburn on *Real Property,* Williams on *Real Property,* Parsons on *Bills and Notes,* Stephen on *Pleading,* Adams on *Equity,* and Bishop on *Criminal Law.* The combination lecture-text approach made it possible for the Law Department to advertise that it offered its students "thorough instruction" in some twenty-eight different subjects, ranging from international and constitutional law to equity and admiralty jurisprudence.[10]

One can gain some insight into the quality of early law lectures at Howard by turning to a small book titled *Law Students and Lawyers,* that Riddle had privately printed in 1873. It contains eight of the lectures that he delivered before the first graduating class, in which he expounded an instrumentalist view of the law as an equalizing force in American society. Written in a plain, straightforward style with no pretensions to erudition, his remarks centered on the practical difficulties that lay ahead for black practitioners, and sought to bolster their confidence by offering detailed advice concerning

---

[10] *Howard University Law Department* (pamphlet), *1870–71* (Washington, 1871), 3–4. A more circumstantial picture of conditions at Howard University in its formative years may be found in Rayford W. Logan, *Howard University: The First Hundred Years, 1867–1967* (N.Y., 1969); and Walter Dyson, *Howard University, The Capstone of Negro Education* (Washington, 1941). See also: A. Mercer Daniel, "The Law Library of Howard University, 1867–1956," 51 *Law Library Journal* 203 (1958).

courtroom pleading, public speaking, the location of their first practice, and related problems. In "The Philosophy of Political Parties" he presented a strong argument for continued Republican dominance; his "Observations on the Constitution" were predictably nationalistic; and his essay on "Government" defended the positive state, arguing that "government should do for a people whatever is necessary for their advancement and welfare, and which as individuals they cannot do for themselves." [11]

The emphasis on pragmatism and morale-building that characterized Riddle's lectures found further expression in certain extracurricular student activities sponsored by the department. Every Thursday evening the Junior Class met with Dean Langston for "forensic exercises," which included instruction and practice in debating, extemporaneous public speaking, and the composition and delivery of formal essays on legal topics. Seniors drafted legal papers and argued moot court cases once a week under the direction of Henry Beam. And all law students were expected to attend "Bible exercises" between nine and ten o'clock each Sunday morning, at which time Langston usually gave a short lecture on professional ethics.

If a student survived two years of course work and related forms of group therapy, he was then ready for graduation—provided he first passed a stiff written examination of one hundred questions covering, in Langston's phrase, "the whole body of law, in theory and practice," and also prepared an acceptable dissertation on some legal topic, to be read or recited at Commencement. The reason for these rigorous procedures lay in the fact that a diploma from Howard Law School until 1878 automatically entitled its possessor to practice before the D. C. courts, on the motion of Langston, Riddle, or any other lawyer in good standing.

Ten students made up the first graduating class in February, 1871, and heard a stirring commencement address from Charles Sumner, who urged them to give top priority in their practice to civil rights litigation. "You are all free, God be praised!" Sumner told them;

> but you are still shut out from rights which are justly yours. Yourselves must strike the blow, not by violence, but in every mode known to the Constitution and law. I do not doubt that every denial of equal rights, whether in the school-room, the jury-box, the public hotel, the steamboat, or the public conveyance, by land or water, is contrary to the fundamental principles of republican government, and therefore to the Constitution itself, which should be corrected by the courts if not by Congress. See to it that this is done.... Insist upon equal rights

[11] A. G. Riddle, *Law Students and Lawyers* (Washington, 1873), 195–196.

everywhere; make others insist upon them. ... I hold you to this allegiance; first, by the race from which you are sprung; and secondly, by the profession which you now espouse.[12]

Three more students received degrees in a special ceremony the following July; and for the next two years the number of graduates remained constant at fourteen. The Law Department was "prosperous," Langston reported to President Howard in 1873, and had begun to attract students from Northern states and the West Indies, as well as every portion of the South. In general they were an "obedient, teachable, and faithful" lot, with only one of their number expelled for misconduct during the previous twelve months. This optimistic prognosis, filed on the eve of the Panic of 1873, took no account of certain external pressures and circumstances that already threatened the future prospects of every department within the University.

The school's "time of troubles" really began with the closing of the Freedmen's Bureau in 1872, amid charges of widespread corruption and misuse of funds. General Howard, under whose regime more than half a million dollars of Bureau money had been transferred to the University, was twice called before Congressional investigating committees to explain various irregularities in the management of the organization. Although he was ultimately acquitted of any personal wrongdoing, the hint of scandal clung to his name and perhaps had much to do with his decision to return to active military duty late in 1873. At that time he tendered his resignation as President of the University; but the faction-ridden Board of Trustees, unable to agree upon a suitable replacement, prevailed upon him to take an indefinite leave of absence instead. A new office—that of "vice president and acting president"—was created to oversee the administrative program of the University; and on Howard's personal recommendation, the Trustees elected Langston to the post by a vote of seven to two. So began a chain of events that led inexorably to one of the most bitter racial episodes of the decade.

By the time that Langston entered upon his executive duties, the nation was in the grip of a major economic depression. The University's rapid expansion and unwise investment policies had already resulted in a deficit of more than $100,000. Now, in a period of frequent bank failures and the drying up of private philanthropic sources of revenue, there was little that an administrator could do except to cut back on expenses and wait for the storm to blow over. Under Langston's direction a vigorous economy drive was launched that sub-

---
[12] "Address of Hon. Charles Sumner," in *Howard University Law Department, 1870–71*, 14–15.

stantially reduced salary levels throughout the academic community and looked to the elimination of all nonessential teaching and administrative personnel. In the law school (where he continued to serve as Professor and Dean) he and his colleagues relied exclusively upon student tuition fees for their pay—a form of remuneration that was uncertain at best and amounted to a virtual donation of their services as government job opportunities decreased and student enrollment fell off. (The graduating class from the law school in 1874 consisted of only seven students, or one-half the number of those graduating in previous years.)

Probably no college executive could have pushed through such a stringent retrenchment program without generating considerable opposition from some associates; but in Langston's case the predictable tensions were aggravated by personality factors. No sooner was he installed as vice-president than his customary imperiousness—or what Rayford Logan more charitably terms a "punctiliousness, probably stemming in part from his legal training" [13]—asserted itself. He demanded a written statement defining the full scope of his authority, to give binding force to Howard's informal assurance that he should be President "in all but name." The Board of Trustees passed a resolution that satisfied his legalistic scruples, but the incident—which seemed to impugn the Board's good faith—did not sit well with some members. Those who questioned Langston's administrative pretensions, moreover, soon found added grounds for mistrust in the circumstances surrounding the collapse of the Freedman's Savings and Trust Company.

This well publicized firm, of which Langston was a director, had been founded in 1865 to serve as a showcase for black economic achievement, just as Howard University was designed to demonstrate black intellectual advancement. There were still closer links between the two institutions: the University deposited some of its funds in the Freedmen's Bank, whose thirty-four branches in turn helped to recruit students for the school. When, therefore, the bank was forced to suspend operations in June, 1874, as a result of incompetent management and occasional outright fraud by some officials, the repercussions of the scandal were felt within the University as well. White critics blamed the debacle upon the Negro's ineptitude in money matters (ignoring the fact that most of the plundering had been done by a dominant group of white trustees); and any black man who, like

---

[13] Logan, *Howard University*, 72. I have generally followed Logan's revisionist interpretation of campus politics, which is less favorable to Langston than earlier accounts.

Langston, had played even a nominal role in the bank's affairs, became an object of public interest and scrutiny.[14]

Against this background of community-wide interrogation and scandalmongering the fight for the control of Howard University moved toward a climax. In December, 1874, General Howard again announced his resignation, and this time it was accepted. The Board of Trustees, at a meeting on Christmas Day, drew up a slate of five presidential candidates that included Langston, Frederick Douglass (who was also a Howard trustee), Erastus M. Cravath of Fisk University, and two white men. The election itself was postponed until the end of the academic year in June, with Langston agreeing to continue as acting president in the meantime.

Seventeen of the twenty-one trustees upon whose votes the presidential issue depended were white sectarians, affiliated in greater or less degree with the Congregational church; the remaining four board members were Negroes. Not surprisingly, racial feeling ran high on campus as the spring term progressed. At one point a group of twenty law students drafted a petition to the Board in support of Langston's candidacy, and pleaded that his "color (might) not operate as an invidious bar to his election." In the minds of many other observers, too, the election shaped up as a choice between black self-direction and white paternalism.

All four Negro trustees, along with eleven whites, attended the crucial Board meeting of June 16, 1875, and cast a secret ballot for one of the presidential nominees. Rev. George Whipple, secretary of the American Missionary Association and one of Langston's former professors at Oberlin, received a clear majority of ten votes; Langston came in second with four votes, while Douglass received one. The outcome, although not unexpected, was a bitter blow to Langston's aspirations, and he did not accept his defeat with equanimity.

In a scathing post-mortem of the election results that he published in the New York *Evening Post* some ten days later, he denounced the Congregationalist trustees for allegedly using their power to subvert the original goals of the University and make it conform to narrow sectarian purposes. These white liberals, he charged, had lost faith in the Negro's capacity for higher education. They no longer believed it desirable to train him beyond the normal school level, and so took little interest in the problems of the law, medical, or theological departments. Nor did they pay much greater attention to the

---

[14] The standard treatment of the Freedmen's Bank is Walter L. Fleming, *The Freedmen's Savings Bank* (Chapel Hill, 1927). See also: Constance McLaughlin Green, *The Secret City: A History of Race Relations in the Nation's Capital* (Princeton, 1967), 84, 94, 99, 113; and Langston, *Virginia Plantation,* 343.

legitimate grievances of individual black faculty members or trustees, whom they regarded as valuable chiefly for the symbolic effect they might have in attracting the attention of private philanthropists. On the other hand, while many worthy educational programs were being curtailed for lack of funds, the First Congregational Church of the District of Columbia continued to pay only 8 per cent interest on its indebtedness to the University—a figure well below the current interest rate that the University was being charged on its own outstanding debts. Such sectarian exploitation of academic resources fully explained the outcome of the recent presidential contest, Langston concluded, implying that his four votes came exclusively from the bloc of independent Negro trustees. (This interpretation of his voting strength, which he reiterated more dogmatically in his autobiography, remains uncorroborated by any positive evidence, however. The Minutes of the Board do not indicate who voted for whom; and Langston himself was not even present at the election.)

With charges of bad faith and duplicity being leveled at them in the press, Howard's white trustees retorted in kind. Besides denying Langston's general allegations, several University spokesmen accused him of trying to destroy the school to gratify his own frustrated ambitions. In an acrimonious debate that lasted for several weeks, the only significant new material was provided by Charles B. Purvis, the well-known black reformer, who reported on July 10th that Langston owed his defeat to the action of the Negro trustees, one of whom in particular had been working against him for months. Purvis did not name names; but his published statement suggests the interesting possibility that Douglass may have had a hand in deflating the ego of a rival race leader.

In view of the unsavory publicity generated by the entire episode, Rev. Whipple announced in mid-July that he would not accept the presidential post. His action left the University without an executive head for the next five months, until Edward P. Smith—a white Trustee—agreed to take on the job in December. By that time morale within the academic community had sunk to an all-time low; and nowhere was the lack of leadership and direction more apparent than in the Law Department, where Langston's resignation as dean prompted the immediate withdrawal of the two remaining faculty members, Riddle and Beam.

Thereafter law classes continued on an ad hoc basis, with students meeting from time to time in the downtown offices of several white practitioners. As the range of available courses fluctuated erratically to suit the skills of a constantly changing staff, student patronage all but ceased to exist. Not a single person was graduated by the Law Department between 1877 and 1881, when a new era began with the appointment of Dean Benjamin Leighton. Under Leighton's guidance the law curriculum was thoroughly remodeled, a more competent and dedicated faculty assembled, and permanent off-campus quarters established at 420 Fifth Street, N.W. Rapid progress resulted from these improvements; and, especially after the civil rights activist William H. H. Hart joined the faculty in 1890, the Howard Law School took up with renewed vigor the libertarian mission prescribed by its founders.

How well did the fifty-eight graduates trained by Langston and his associates between 1869 and 1875 carry out *their* part of that mission? Did they measure up to the expectations of their teachers, and of such well-wishers as Sumner and Forney? How many of them even practiced law?

The record, unfortunately, is too fragmentary to permit anything like a systematic survey, but we can pin down some relevant statistics. Langston himself kept tabs on the first group of graduates, and reported at the end of June, 1871, that nine out of ten were already engaged in active legal practice. Most of these had settled in various Southern states: one in Louisiana, two in North Carolina, one in South Carolina, one in Arkansas, one in Mississippi, and one in Missouri; while two remained in the D.C. area.[15]

A somewhat different pattern emerges if we attempt to trace the immediate postgraduate occupations of all those who continued to live for a year or more in Washington. Of the thirty-two Howard law graduates listed in Boyd's annual *Directory of the District of Columbia,* only eight were practicing lawyers. A majority of the rest held clerical jobs in some government agency: six worked for the Treasury Department; three for the Postoffice; two for the Land Office; one for the War Department; one for the Engineers; one for the Board of Public Works; one for the Freedmen's Bureau; and five simply styled themselves "clerks." There was also one messenger, one doctor, one teacher, and one printer in the group. This breakdown, of course, reflects only a temporary situation; fifty per cent of the individuals in question left Washington after a few years and may have established themselves in legal practice elsewhere.

Among those who did become practitioners, several made notable contributions to the cause of civil rights. D. Augustus Straker successfully defended the constitutionality of Michigan's public accommodations law before the state supreme court in the landmark case

---

[15] *Howard University Law Department,* 1870–71, 8.

John M. Langston and the Rise of Howard Law School 437

of Ferguson v. Gies (1890);[16] John Wesley Cromwell appeared before the Interstate Commerce Commission to protest segregation on interstate carriers; James M. Adams, one of Langston's few white students, built up a strong civil rights practice before his untimely death in 1892; Nathaniel G. Wynn was murdered in Lake Village, Arkansas, while defending a Negro client. These are isolated instances, to be sure; but they do point to the possibility that a lost generation of black civil rights lawyers, largely Howard-trained, may have flourished in the last decades of the Nineteenth Century.

Straker suggested as much in 1891, when he published an admirable essay on "The Negro in the Profession of Law." In every state, he noted, the Negro lawyer was barred by "arbitrary custom" from representing the interests of white clients. Viewed exclusively as the advocate of his race, he occupied within the black community a special position of trust that entailed an obligation on his part to work untiringly for Negro civil rights.[17] And there is good reason to think that many besides Straker took that obligation seriously, at least during the rather tolerant decade of the 1880's, when a Howard graduate like Josiah T. Settle (B.A., '72; LL.B., '75) could still be elected to the state legislature even in Mississippi. The subsequent enactment of repressive "Jim Crow" laws in the South and a general hardening of white racial attitudes across the nation by the turn of the century may well have cut short a promising experiment in peaceable social reform.

Certainly few black lawyers of the Gilded Age—or their exploits—are remembered today. Even Langston, who did so much to shape the sweeping provisions of the Civil Rights Act of 1875, has been largely ignored by posterity. So it is not surprising that, when a new generation of civil rights activists arose in the South after World War II, they found little evidence of any prior tradition of black legal reform. In Louisiana, reported a survey conducted by the Howard Law School in 1951, thirteen of the state's fourteen black lawyers had been in practice for only five years; and a substantial proportion of all Negro attorneys in Alabama, Florida, Georgia, and Virginia had been practicing less than ten years.[18] The lack of any strong connecting links with the past should not, however, be permitted to obscure

---
[16] 82 Mich. 358 (1890).

[17] D. Augustus Straker, "The Negro in the Profession of Law," *A.M.E. Church Review* VIII (Oct., 1891), 180–182.

[18] George M. Johnson, "The Integration of the Negro Lawyer into the Legal Profession in the United States," a paper delivered at the Annual Conference of the Division of Social Sciences, Howard University, May 4, 1951. (Johnson was Dean of the Howard Law School at the time.) A mimeographed copy of his informative address is available at the Moorland Room of the University Library.

the genuine, if limited, achievements of those Nineteenth-Century advocates whose collective experience forms an honorable and important chapter in the history of the American bar.

Despite discrimination and a continuing lack of professional opportunity, Straker remarked in 1891, the black lawyer could look back upon two decades of slow but steady progress, for which Langston and his Howard-trained disciples deserved much credit: "Today hundreds of colored and white lawyers bear the insignia [of the Howard Law School] through the energy of Mr. Langston's devotion to the Negro's advancement. We owe him gratitude for this, and he must be regarded as the pioneer of the colored lawyers in America, it may be he is the *pater familias* of the Negro lawyers in America. It is said he has not had any extensive practice, and cannot be rated as a great pleader, save in criminal cases; but he has otherwise done a great work, of which no just criticism can rob him." [19]

---

[19] Straker, "Negro in the Profession of Law," 179–180. Very few cases involving Negro rights ever reached the United States Supreme Court, Straker also pointed out: "Many other cases would have been carried to our Supreme Court but for the great expense consequent upon doing so. Our court costs are hinderances to many suitors seeking justice but not getting it." (p. 182). His analysis of the practical limitations imposed upon black lawyers in their professional efforts is further corroborated by the experience of another Negro civil rights activist, Mifflin W. Gibbs (LL.B., Oberlin, 1869), who became a municipal judge in Little Rock, Arkansas, during the 1870's. See: Mifflin W. Gibbs, *Shadow and Light* (reprint ed., N.Y., 1968). And, for a fictional treatment of the more systematic forms of repression employed against black professionals by the end of the century, read Charles W. Chesnutt, *The Marrow of Tradition* (Boston and N.Y., 1901). Chesnutt, who was himself a Negro lawyer, made a firsthand study of the facts surrounding the Wilmington, North Carolina race riot of 1898, upon which his novel is based.

Gallaudet College:
A High Victorian Campus

FRANCIS R. KOWSKY

"The architect, the mechanic, the laborer, have one by one withdrawn to other fields of toil, but what change they have wrought." [1] Spoken on a cold February day in 1878, these words of a deaf student commemorated the accelerated evolution of Gallaudet College from a humble orphanage housed in a farm cottage into an institution possessed of impressive buildings and grounds. Coincidental with its maturation as the nation's first college for the deaf grew a distinguished Victorian campus. The purpose of this article is to trace the Nineteenth Century history of that campus, a chronicle which mirrors important anti-classical tendencies in American design and includes the names of men notable in our artistic and political past.

Founded in 1856 by Amos Kendall (1780–1869) who was then living in semi-retirement on his northeast Washington farm, romantically referred to as "Kendall Green," the Columbia Institution for the Deaf, Dumb, and Blind (the name was later changed to Gallaudet College) opened with a student body of five orphan children of whom Kendall wrote: "They all answer to their name, but it is not certain that they are all correct." [2] The fledgling institution occupied a dilapidated house which, along with two acres of ground, had been donated by Kendall from his farm. A smaller dwelling,[3] rented from William Stickney, Kendall's brother-in-law and a member of the Board of Directors of the institution, served as combined living quarters for the staff, their families, and the pupils.[4]

During the first year of its existence the nature of Kendall's project

[1] Columbia Institution, Twenty-First Annual Report (1878), p. 9.
[2] Letter from Amos Kendall to Jacob Thompson, Secretary of the Interior, May 3, 1857. National Archives, Gallaudet College file box.
[3] Known as Rose Cottage, it stood where the present Chapel Hall now stands.
[4] Valuable information on the formative years of Gallaudet College can be found in Edward M. Gallaudet, "A History of the Columbia Institution for the Deaf and Dumb," *Records of the Columbia Historical Society*, 15 (1912), pp. 1–22.

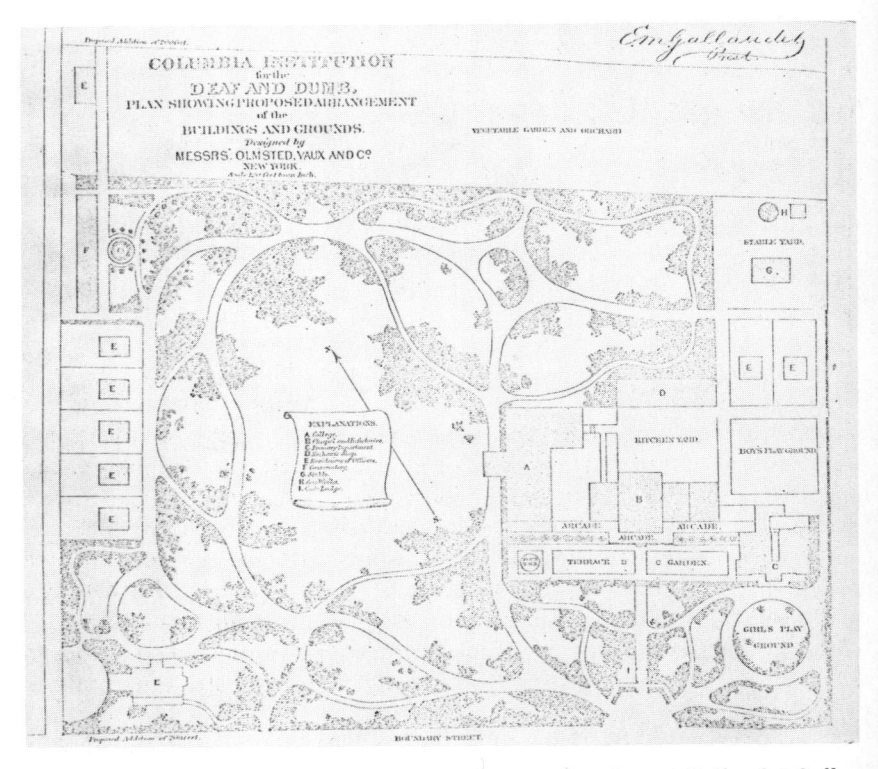

Courtesy of Gallaudet College

Figure 1. Olmsted and Vaux. Master plan for the buildings and grounds of Gallaudet College (formerly the Columbia Institution). 1866. From the Ninth Annual Report (1866).

was changed profoundly. Endowed with keen political acumen from his days in Andrew Jackson's "kitchen cabinet," Kendall successfully petitioned Congress to incorporate the institution under its jurisdiction and to provide a tuition allowance for indigent pupils from the District of Columbia. One of the earliest instances of federal assistance to the physically handicapped, the action was, after West Point and Annapolis, only the third case of direct Congressional support of education.

Kendall immediately took steps to improve the new school. The state of education for the deaf in America in the 1850's was poorly advanced, and there was only one place to which he could turn for help in setting up a serious program of instruction. The American School for the Deaf in Hartford, Connecticut, founded in 1817 by

Thomas Hopkins Gallaudet, received warmly Kendall's application for aid. From Hartford came Edward Miner Gallaudet (1837–1917), the son of the renowned director of the American School. A compassionate young man of twenty, Gallaudet arrived in 1857 with his mother, a deaf-mute herself, to begin what would be a lifetime of work in Washington devoted to raising the quality of teaching of the deaf to a level commensurate with that of hearing students.[5]

With Gallaudet in charge the school grew steadily in the number of pupils and in the size and quality of its accommodations. Already in 1858, an additional building was needed. This, the first new campus structure, was designed by Gallaudet himself and built by a friend of Kendall's at the latter's expense.[6] The unpretentious brick edifice, adjoining the original house Kendall had donated, was completed by 1859; its nineteen rooms furnished living and classroom space for forty students. Graced by a dignified classic porch and an Italianate cupola the building appeared decidedly more domestic than institutional. Reflected in its simplicity was the filial closeness then existing between faculty and students.

Notice of the next important improvement appeared in 1862, in the institution's Fifth Annual Report. In spite of the overriding concern with the rebellion, Congress had set aside $3,000 for alterations to the brick building of 1858.[7] The money was spent on two projects. The first was a two story wooden rear extension that provided a dormitory above and a large chapel room below. The latter was the first campus space designated for religious purposes. Here each Sunday Gallaudet personally conducted services, for his deep religious convictions and eventual ordination to the ministry put him in that large category of Nineteenth Century college administrators, headed by such men as Noah Porter of Yale, who were also churchmen.

The major portion of the 1862 appropriation was spent on a much larger addition to the front of the building. Higher and wider than the original structure, it brought forward the facade twenty eight feet and changed the building into one of much greater pretense (at

---

[5] For the biography of Gallaudet see Maxine Tull Boatner, *The Voice of the Deaf* (Washington: Public Affairs Press, 1959). The history of Gallaudet College is recorded in Albert W. Atwood, *Gallaudet College, Its First One Hundred Years.* (Washington: By the College, 1964.)

[6] Gallaudet said of this structure, which was demolished in the twentieth century to make way for the present Fowler Hall: "I prepared plans... and without calling in any architect these plans were submitted to an old friend of Mr. Kendall's, an experienced builder of Washington, Mr. Charles F. Wood.... 'Go ahead and put up the building' said Mr. Kendall, no contract being signed nor specifications submitted." Gallaudet, *loc. cit.*, p. 4.

[7] Fifth Annual Report (1862), p. 5.

Courtesy of Gallaudet College

Figure 2. View of Gallaudet College c. 1870. In the center is Chapel Hall; at the left is the college building by Friedrich which was destined to become the rear wing of the present College Hall; between the college building and Chapel Hall can be seen a portion of the Shop Building; and at the right appears the Primary Department building, the rear of which was designed by Gallaudet.

the right in Figure 2). Built of smooth pressed brick with brownstone trim, the Primary Department building, as it later came to be called, was a homely approximation of elegance reminiscent of the fashionable Tuscan style that had become popular during the 1840's. A curved mansard roof[8] and stone quoins on the central tower contributed a faint French flavor that may have been suggested by the handsome new building belonging to a member of the Board of Directors, W. W. Corcoran. His elegant art museum (1859) on Pennsylvania Avenue at Seventeenth Street by James Renwick (1818–1895) was the first example in the city of the Second Empire style.

These works were designed by Emil S. Friedrich (dates unknown), the first professional architect associated with the institution.[9] Friedrich, an obscure man apparently employed as an engineer at the Navy

---

[8] The roof was never executed. For a drawing of the proposed building, see the Ninth Annual Report (1866).

[9] Fifth Annual Report (1862), p. 5.

Yard,[10] must have come to Gallaudet's attention through one of those chains of acquaintanceship so commonly responsible for government commissions. Saying the enlarged building reflected "great credit upon him for its beauty . . . it will be an ornament to the city." [11] Gallaudet expressed unequivocal confidence in Friedrich. In the next several years he would call upon him to draw up plans for four new buildings.

In addition to mention of the expanded physical facilities, the Fifth Annual Report (1862) contained Gallaudet's proposal for a national college for the deaf. From the very beginning of his appointment as head of the school, Gallaudet had emphasized the need for upper level training and had pressed for the establishment of a college curriculum. Nowhere, he argued, could graduates from the various state schools, which then existed through the secondary level, complete their education. While the number of perspective applicants was too small in any single state to justify the existence of separate state colleges, the total number of qualified students throughout the country could easily sustain a national college. That the Columbia Institution was eminently suited to this mission Gallaudet cleary saw, not only because of its location in the nation's capital, but also by reason of its charter which, theoretically at least, already provided for advanced instruction by not setting any limit on the length of time that a pupil could remain enrolled as long as he progressed in his studies.

In 1864 Gallaudet was in a position to implement a college program. He composed a bill which Senator Grimes of Iowa, a member of the District Committee and the Board of Directors, introduced into Congress.[12] Opposition was slight and the motion passed both the Senate and House unanimously. The act thus creating the National Deaf Mute College was signed by President Lincoln on April 8, 1864, a year and a day before Lee's surrender at Appomatox.

The college was officially inaugurated on June 28, 1864, only two weeks before Early's troops threw the city into its greatest panic of the war. Ceremonies were held at the First Presbyterian Church whose rector, the controversial Byron Sunderland, was a member of the Board of Directors. The college department opened the following September with an enrollment of eight students. This marked the beginning of the institution as it is known today and paved the way for its growth into the most important center for the education of the deaf in the country.

---
[10] Several letters from Friedrich to Gallaudet were written on Navy Yard stationery.
[11] Fifth Annual Report, p. 6.
[12] Twelfth Annual Report (1869), pp. 27-28.

Building activity was immediately stimulated by a new sense of pride and urgency. In 1865, $39,000 was appropriated and work began on a gas works, a carriage house, a shop building (Figure 1: H, G, and D), and a college building, all erected from designs by Friedrich.[13]

Despite its eighteen "lofty windows of the Byzantine style," [14] as Friedrich described them, the brick and brownstone Collegiate Department building (at the left in Figure 2) looked for all the world like an uninspired institutional building in the Second Empire style. Built as only a portion of a much larger structure projected for the future, the college building, as envisioned by its designer, was to have contained a grand room on the third floor "the whole size of the building ... to be used besides regular religious services, for public examinations and exhibitions." [15] Perhaps Friedrich's patronizing tone (one might wonder what he had meant by "public examinations" at a school for the deaf) or simply practical considerations prompted Gallaudet to reduce the chapel room to half the size proposed by Friedrich. The new building was in use by the end of 1866.[16]

The shop building was the other important structure undertaken in 1865. A simple rectangular building with pedimented windows and a curved mansard roof, its interior held two open floors supported by iron columns. A maximum of space for mechanical equipment, such as the printing presses which formed the nucleus of the vocational program, was thus provided. Of all the buildings designed by Friedrich this was perhaps the best from the functional as well as esthetic point of view. It had added historical interest in being one of the earliest collegiate buildings in the nation specifically designed for vocational training.[17]

By the close of the Civil War, eight years after its founding, the Columbia Institution had grown from a tiny home for half-a-dozen deaf and blind children into a unique educational center. It occupied sixteen acres and had three substantial buildings in various stages of construction. Its young president felt both satisfaction with its achievements and excitement for its future. On the crest of this spirit, Gallaudet, late in 1865, requested Frederick Law Olmsted (1822–

---

[13] Minutes of the Board of Directors, March 15, 1865, pp. 90–91 and Tenth Annual Report (1867), p. 6. With the exception of the college building, all of these structures have been torn down.

[14] Letter from Friedrich to Gallaudet, June 15, 1863. In the collection of the Edward Miner Gallaudet Memorial Library, Gallaudet College. All correspondence referred to in this article, unless otherwise noted, is in the Gallaudet Library.

[15] *Ibid.*

[16] It was demolished early in the twentieth century to make way for Fowler Hall.

[17] The building has been demolished.

1903), who had known the Gallaudet family in Hartford, to prepare a master plan for the grounds and future buildings of the institution. Olmsted, man of letters turned horticulturist, had recently returned to New York from Washington where during the war he had been the Secretary of the Sanitary Commission. In New York he resumed his career as the nation's most renowned landscape architect. With his partner Calvert Vaux (1824–1895), who in Olmsted's absence had supervised the development of Central Park, the work that had made them famous, Olmsted operated the firm of Olmsted, Vaux and Co., Landscape Architects. It was under this name that the proposed improvements for the college were drawn up.[18] The design, published in the Ninth Annual Report (1866) (Figure 1), was worked out during the first six months of 1866.[19]

The sort of landscape scheme mapped out for the college was epitomized by Central Park in New York, the most important example in America of the natural or informal arrangement of mixed plantings, open spaces, and winding roadways. Initially developed in England, this style of landscaping had been popularized here during the 1840's by Andrew Jackson Downing (1814–1852). Through his extensive writings and due to the prestigious commission President Fillmore had given him in 1851 to lay out a romantic pleasure ground between the Capitol and the White House,[20] Downing, before his untimely death in a steamboat explosion, had formulated the principles of landscape design in America. Central Park, which ultimately owes its existence to Downing's labors, was created four years after his death by men deeply affected by his ideas.

Downing had preached that landscaped areas within cities should be a relief from the surrounding urban environment and, indeed, should be antithetical to it. It had been Downing's intention (emulated by Olmsted and Vaux in Central Park) to preserve and enshrine nature in an autonomous tract for the health, enjoyment, and education of city dwellers. This conception of a separate enclave not communicating with the urbanscape outside was basic to the landscape design for Gallaudet College, for, like Central Park, it took little account of the street patterns or probable development which would someday engulf it.

In several particulars the Washington plan bore a close relationship

---

[18] The first indication of a formal contact with the landscape firm in New York appeared in a letter from Vaux to Gallaudet dated December 26, 1865.

[19] Letter from Vaux to Gallaudet, June 13, 1866.

[20] See Wilcomb E. Washburn, "Vision of Life for the Mall," *Journal* of the American Institute of Architects, vol. XIX (March, 1967).

to Central Park. The distinguishing feature of that design was, in the words of the critic Clarence Cook (1828–1900):

> ... that the boundary line must be avoided ... this made them [Olmsted and Vaux] lead their drive at once toward the center, and ... where it assumes more the character of a circuit drive ... the curves continually lead in ... the road, in its whole length approaches very near the boundary, but once or twice.[21]

The same may also be said of the Gallaudet College plan. The primary roadways were kept well within the boundaries of the site and were made to continually turn inward. Where lanes approached the outer limits, such as on the north side, they were screened from the outside by foliage. On the western side houses for the staff walled in the space.

Another similarity between the Washington and New York plans was the division of the land into two major areas. In Central Park the dichotomy was between a northern and a southern section; in Washington the separation was into eastern and western portions. In both cases this was a response to topographic conditions. Whereas the New York site contained two distinctly different terrains, the Washington property presented two small rises which were developed to their best advantage. They became the nodular points in the distribution of buildings; a small hill on the eastern half of the tract was where Chapel Hall, the main campus building, and the other buildings of the institution were clustered, and a low knoll at the southwest corner afforded a secluded spot for the President's House north from which ran a row of professor's dwellings.

Also analogous to the Central Park scheme was the distinction made between the functions of the two areas. The Washington plan followed the precedent established in the New York park of having one section include the majority of the buildings or man-made objects (the eastern portion at Gallaudet College, the southern half in Central Park) and the other be given over almost entirely to nature. At the college, the more pastoral western zone, containing only the staff homes along the boundary, was seen by the planners as a "healthful resort" for the students and faculty.

Estrangement of vehicular from pedestrian traffic, a foremost consideration in the planning of Central Park, was also part of the Washington design; the broad lines on the map represented traffic

---

[21] Clarence Cook, *A Description of the New York Central Park* (New York: Huntington, 1869), p. 19.

roadways, the narrow lines foot paths. However, due to the fact that there was to be little carriage traffic within the confines of the campus, the disengagement was more casual than in Central Park with its ingenious sunken transverse roads.

Finally, as in Central Park, there was a general avoidance of straight lines in the college plan. Access to the buildings was indirect (except in the case of the main building) and over roadways intended to follow the gentle contours of the site and to articulate its dimensions. Reminiscent of how Downing had recommended to lay out approaches to great houses, the lanes and paths passed alternately through open and planted areas thereby affording, as one traversed them, a variety of impressions of the grounds and buildings.[22]

Acceptance of the Olmsted and Vaux plan marked the end of Emil Friedrich's role as chief architect of the college. He was replaced by Frederick Clarke Withers (1828–1901), an associate of Olmsted's and the partner of Vaux in the firm of Vaux, Withers, and Co., Architects. Born in England, Withers had received his architectural training in London where he had become a disciple of the Gothic Revival. In 1852, as the result of an employment notice placed in a London newspaper by Downing, Withers came to America to work with Downing (and Vaux who had come from England in 1850 to be Downing's assistant) in Newburgh, New York. Withers remained in Newburgh until 1863 when, after a short military career as an engineer in the Union army, he moved to New York once again joining Vaux. Through Vaux and Olmsted he became acquainted in 1866 with Gallaudet who employed him for the next twenty years. By the spring of 1867 construction had begun on his designs for a main building, known as Chapel Hall, the President's House, and House No. 1 for a professor.

Facing south toward the Capitol one mile away, Chapel Hall is the architectural showpiece of the Gallaudet campus (Figure 2, center). The initial notice of the building was the floor plan that appeared on the Olmsted and Vaux master scheme (Figure 1, B). A large rectangular chapel room is the heart of the building (Figure 3). On the west it was flanked by a dining hall for the college students and on the east by two rooms, a lecture hall, which by means of movable panels could be thrown open to form a deep stage area for the chapel room, and a dining hall for the primary school students. Across the front

---

[22] Unfortunately, it was never carried out completely as Olmsted and Vaux proposed and many of the original plantings have died without being replaced. A major modification of the plan was the decision to shift the main entrance to the grounds on Florida Avenue to the west of its original position directly in front of Chapel Hall.

of the long eastern extension runs a corridor leading to the chapel and off of which opened the lecture hall and primary dining room.

The decision to erect a building of grand proportions but limited usefulness must have been inspired by the recent examples of Harvard and Yale, for, by 1866, those schools had approved plans for similar structures. These were the first important models of a new type of collegiate building devised to commemorate students and graduates who had died defending the Union. Harvard's Memorial Hall by William R. Ware (1832–1915) and Henry Van Brunt (1832–1903) and Yale's Memorial Chapel by Withers (never constructed) contained only large congregational spaces rather than numerous rooms for various purposes. Conceived as inspirational, not practical, architecture, they were, in the words of Charles Elliot Norton, "to stand permanently as memorials of our respect and honor for our dead brethren; we are bound not only to build worthily of their dear memory and of our own grateful and tender reverence for them, but also with reference to the effect of the edifice upon the hearts and imaginations of the future generations of youth who will gather within them." [23]

Although the Columbia Institution had sent no soldiers to the front, the fact that its well-being was intimately allied with that of the national government, which had treated it generously even during perilous times, was reason enough for the creation of an edifice that would honor the triumphant Union, the true hope and benevolent patron of the deaf. That Chapel Hall was intended to celebrate the Union was made explicit by the prominent eagle and shield emblem in the central tympanum of the porch.

Harvard's Memorial Hall, like Chapel Hall, served as the main assembly and dining facility of its campus. But the similarity between the two buildings was more than conceptual. The compositions of both employed the intersection of a long horizontal mass by an asymmetrical placed vertical section; each was divided into three basic parts (in Memorial Hall these were the dining hall, hall, and theatre; in Chapel Hall, the college dining room, chapel, and eastern extension); and the entrances were placed on one of the long sides rather than at the end of the major axis of the building. Ecclesiastical overtones were also pronounced in the two structures with their stained glass, bell towers,[24] and clear implication of nave, crossing and polygonal chancel.

---

[23] Charles Elliot Norton, "The Harvard and Yale Memorial Buildings," *The Nation*, vol. V (July 11, 1867), p. 34.
[24] The tower of Chapel Hall closely resembles that of writer-minister E. P. Roe's First Presbyterian Church, Highland Falls, New York, which Withers designed in 1865.

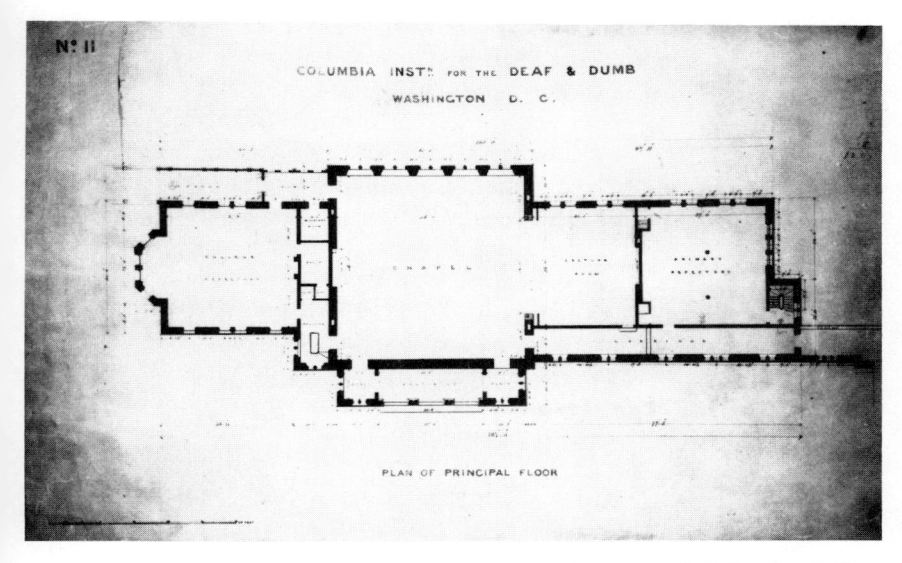

Courtesy of Gallaudet College

Figure 3. F. C. Withers. Plan of Chapel Hall. 1868.

More than its Harvard counterpart, however, Chapel Hall responded to the routine of daily life at its campus. The plan of Chapel Hall (Figure 3) was a methodical adaptation to the requirements of the Gallaudet community. The primary school dining hall was on the east end of the plan near the Primary Department building. The college dining room was placed on the western end close to the college building. Hence, both groups of students could reach their dining room without entering any other part of the building. In addition, from the primary school side the long corridor provided direct access to the central assembly room, as did a small porch on the rear of the western section from the college side. By this arrangement, the two departments were also linked to each other, since, by going through the chapel room, the symbolic focal point of the institution, the students of each department could reach the opposite division. Thus, the ground plan of Chapel Hall coordinated the institution's dual requirements of separation and communication.

When construction began in the spring of 1867,[25] the building had been worked out only in its general outlines. The conclusive form of the elevations was not decided until the following year. Early

---
[25] Minutes of the Board of Directors, March 27, 1867, and the Tenth Annual Report (1867), p. 6.

in January, 1868, Withers wrote to Gallaudet that a tentative final solution had been committed to paper and was being sent to Washington.[26] Gallaudet inspected the drawings soon after and showed them to the Board of Directors, winning their approval except for a few minor points. Withers came to Washington for a last consultation in March, 1868.[27] In April, in reply to Gallaudet's prodding for the finished products, he wrote: "We have not hurried about the drawings for the chapel building as you did not seem in a hurry for them. The general drawings will, however, be completed and forwarded to you this week, whilst the details will be ready to follow in a few days."[28] That they were overdue because of more than the leisurely attitude attributed to Gallaudet was hinted at in the conclusion of the same letter: "If you could manage somehow to let us have $1,000 by the first of May you would oblige."

At last, on May 1, 1868, Withers wrote to Washington that the "general drawings and specifications...have been sent off by the after-ns Express, the details are in hand and will be furnished whenever you require them."[29] The working drawings were sent to the institution before the end of the following December.

Well pleased with the design and the reception it had received in New York, Withers told Gallaudet that the "elevation, as completed, is liked by everyone who has seen it, and many say it is the best thing I have ever done. I do wish I could feel that you agreed with them."[30] Gallaudet did agree. He ordered a large number of photolithographic reproductions of the architect's perspective drawing for publication in the Annual Report for 1870 and for general circulation. The design, proudly exhibited by Withers at the National Academy of Design in 1869,[31] was published in Charles Lakey's *American Builder*,[32] one of the two architectural journals in the country at the time, and was later included in Withers' own book *Church Architecture* (1873).[33] A writer in the *Old and New Magazine* commented that the "main central building is one of the most beautiful specimens of architectural taste around the city." [34]

[26] Letter from Withers to Gallaudet, January 9, 1868.
[27] Letter from Withers to Gallaudet, March 3, 1868.
[28] Letter from Withers to Gallaudet, April 20, 1868.
[29] The elevation drawings are in the Gallaudet Library.
[30] Letter from Withers to Gallaudet, May 1, 1868.
[31] National Academy of Design Exhibition Catalogue, 1869, No. 60.
[32] *The American Builder*, vol. II (April, 1870), p. 91.
[33] F. C. Withers, *Church Architecture* (New York: Bicknell, 1873), vignette to Design IV.
[34] "National Deaf Mute College," *Old and New Magazine*, (October, 1872), p. 495.

Construction of Chapel Hall lagged due to delays in Congressional appropriations. In the Eleventh Annual Report (1868) Gallaudet stated that because his request for funds was not approved until July 27, "the season for building operations [summer, 1868] was too far advanced to admit of the completion of any portion of the building in time for the opening of our fall term in September. We therefore determined to defer the resumption of the work on this building until next spring." [35] In October, the Board of Directors approved the estimate of James Naylor, the builder, of $101,600 as the amount required to conclude the job.[36] They authorized Gallaudet to sign a contract with him that stipulated the work would be done "only so far as appropriations therefore shall be made by Congress." At the opening of the building season in 1869, with funds remaining from the previous year, Naylor agreed to "furnish and complete the east wing and the entire basement story on or before the fifteenth day of September A. D. 1869, and the entire building on or before the first day of June A. D. 1870." [37] Circumstances did not permit the fulfilment of this schedule; no money at all was provided by the 1869 legislature. In the Twelve Annual Report (1869) Gallaudet proposed to ask Congress for $94,000 to complete the building which stood uselessly unfinished and in danger of deteriorating.[38]

Successful in his bid for funds, Gallaudet saw considerable progress made on Chapel Hall in 1870. He reported to the Board of Directors in mid October that the structure was nearly erected.[39] The Thirteenth Annual Report (1870) contained the statement that he foresaw the completion of the building by January, 1871.[40] Already in September the kitchen and other basement rooms, which were connected by a hand railroad, were put into service, along with the two dining halls on the main floor. On January 7, 1871, the Chapel Hall was officially dedicated in the presence of President Grant.[41]

Fashionably High Victorian Gothic, Chapel Hall was, in staunchly Neo-Classic Washington, the first important example of its stylistic genre. Evolved from the earlier Gothic Revival, Victorian Gothic,

---

[35] Eleventh Annual Report (1868), pp. 9–10.
[36] Minutes of the Board of Directors, October 26, 1868, p. 123.
[37] The contract, dated April 16, 1869, with Naylor is preserved in the Gallaudet Library.
[38] Twelfth Annual Report (1869), p. 8.
[39] Minutes of the Board of Directors, October 16, 1870, p. 150.
[40] Thirteenth Annual Report (1870), p. 16.
[41] At the time of the dedication, neither the cast iron cresting nor the clock in the tower were in place. The trim went up the following year, but the clock, costing $1,000, was not installed until 1874.

alternately called Venetian or "Ruskinian" Gothic, originated in England in the late 1840's chiefly in response to the writings of John Ruskin (1819–1909) who extolled the beauties of northern Italian Gothic buildings. All Saints, Margaret Street, London, of 1849 by William Butterfield (1814–1900) was its fountainhead, but the books of the English architects George Street (1824–1881)[42] and George Gilbert Scott (1811–1898)[43] did much to sanctify the modern marriage of English with Italian medieval architecture, a union surrounded by moral and social as well as artistic philosophizing.[44]

In America the idiom did not become popular until the Reconstruction period with which it is closely identified. Withers' Dutch Reformed Church (1859) in Fishkill Landing (modern Beacon), New York, was perhaps the earliest example in the United States[45] of the polychromatic Italianate style, but the National Academy of Design (1862) in New York, by Peter Bonnet Wight (1838–1925), and Ware and Van Brunt's Memorial Hall, as well as Withers' Yale memorial chapel project, solidified the position of Victorian Gothic in America. Chapel Hall was the first edifice erected incorporating the quasi-ecclesiastical style with the new building type, the memorial hall. (The Harvard building was not completed until 1878.) The choice was a natural one for the age; no longer could the placid Greek Revival portico satisfy the convictions of men who, as Unionists, had thought of themselves as latter-day Crusaders.

Esthetically, Chapel Hall is an eloquent essay on the Victorian Gothic theme of forthright expression of architectural reality. The Connecticut River brownstone facade (Figure 2) demonstrates in its complexity the composite character of the interior. Withers created the elevation according to an intuitive Victorian Gothic principle of exterior design that can be called differentiation or, as Professor Hersey prefers, "creatureliness." [46] This dictated that the functions of the building could be defined by emphasizing the volumes that housed them and that the character of these significant masses should be annotated by their minor elements. In Chapel Hall, legibility of the size of the central room compared to the smaller low dining halls announced the main purpose of the building as an assembly hall. Subtlely, the windows of each of the three sections of the facade suggest the nature of the spaces behind them: those of the chapel room

---

[42] George E. Street, *Brick and Marble in the Middle Ages* (London: Murray, 1855).
[43] George G. Scott, *Remarks on Architecture* (London: Murray, 1857).
[44] See George Hersey, *High Victorian Gothic* (Baltimore: Johns Hopkins, 1972).
[45] Withers, *op. cit.* Design XIII.
[46] Hersey, *op. cit.*

are the larger and more elaborate, those of the college dining room are smaller and utilitarian, and those of the eastern passageway are smaller still and repetitive. The position of the buff Ohio stone belts also was determined by this feeling for distinctness; they answer not to the overall facade but to the height of the windows in each segment of the building. Equating different exterior forms and details with different interior uses, Withers brought the methodical logic he exhibited in the creation of the ground plan to bear on the realization of the elevations.

An assimilation of the latest ideas in American collegiate architecture with the stylistic vocabulary of the late Gothic Revival, Chapel Hall was a commission that posed both abstract and pragmatic problems. The architect responded enthusiastically, creating a reverent and practical building that was admirably suited to its spirit-stirring animus and national importance. With age it has taken on the character of a venerable monument symbolic of the aspirations that surrounded its erection and subsequent existence. This fact was duly recognized by the nation, when, in 1965, Chapel Hall was placed on the National Register of Historic Places.

Contemporary with Chapel Hall is the President's House (Figure 4). Unlike the former building the house for Gallaudet was finished quickly. It was ready for occupancy late in 1868,[47] two years before the official opening of the main building.

Situated in the southwest corner of the campus, on ground purchased after the 1866 Olmsted and Vaux plan had been prepared but which had been stipulated by the landscape architects as a necessary addition to the original site, the house looks north toward Faculty Row. (The first of the staff houses, that nearest the President's House, was begun at the same time and ready for occupancy by the end of 1869.) Location and orientation assure the residents the greatest possible degree of privacy. The arrangement also provides that the parlor and library, placed on the eastern side, have pleasant prospects overlooking the grounds. The President's House literally turned its back on the city.

Gallaudet's home was a villa, a term Downing had used to describe a large country or suburban dwelling, not a city house. Withers, who in 1857 had collaborated with Vaux in the publication of *Villas and Cottages*,[48] a work that had established them as Downing's artistic heirs, was thoroughly versed in the Downing tradition of do-

---

[47] Eleventh Annual Report (1868), p. 10.
[48] Calvert Vaux, *Villas and Cottages* (New York: Harper, 1857).

Courtesy of Gallaudet College

Figure 4. F. C. Withers. Drawing of the facade of the President's House. 1867.

mestic architecture. Like Downing, who had waged the battle against the bald white American home that stood aloof from its environment, Withers sought to harmonize the house with nature. The boldly projecting roof of the President's House, the gables and dormers treated in the same way, the wide veranda, and subdued color are designed to assimilate the building to the landscape. The asymmetry of the composition, a result of the informal arrangement of the plan, the honest expression of materials and structure, and the prominence of the roof also derive from Downing's notions of what was architecturally natural and good.

Nonetheless, the President's House is High Victorian rather than Mid Victorian. The polychromatic variety of the surface (dark and light voussoirs alternate and bands of yellow stone are set into the red brick walls—wits called it the "lean bacon" style), the Florentine arches of the first floor windows, the eccentric herringbone brickwork, and the vaguely ecclesiastical portal ornamented with naturalistic

Courtesy of the Avery Architectural Library, Columbia University
Figure 5. F. C. Withers. College Hall. 1875. From *The Building News*.

foliage carving[49] recalling Ruskin's activity at the Oxford Museum, never appeared in Downing's designs.[50] Withers, so to speak, brought the ante-bellum style up to date, infusing it with the robustness of the Gilded Age.

Plans for the new college building (Figure 5) (actually the long arm of the inverted "L" shape of A in Figure 1) were discussed as early as 1869,[51] but it was not until several years later that the project was actively pursued. There was no pressing need for a new building, as the initial section designed by Friedrich in 1865 served adequately. Moreover, in 1872 additional land adjoining the campus on the north had been purchased from the Kendall estate for $80,000, an action which led the Board of Directors in October of that year to

---

[49] Many of the carved details were taken from James K. Colling, *Art Foliage* (London: By the author, 1865).

[50] The architect's elevation drawing is slightly more elaborate than the building as constructed.

[51] Letter from Withers to Gallaudet, November 29, 1869. A sketch was enclosed, but it is now lost. In 1870 another perspective drawing, a photograph of which is preserved in the Gallaudet Library, was sent to Washington. No action was taken on this building, for when interest revived in the construction of the college building in 1874 an entirely new plan was prepared.

conclude that it would be "inexpedient" to request additional building funds in the next session of Congress.[52]

Interest was once again stirred in the college building by Gallaudet's annual letter to the Secretary of the Interior in the Sixteenth Annual Report of 1873. Gallaudet proposed to ask Congress for $54,000 for two additional professor's houses and to begin the college building extension.[53]

Before any appropriation was actually granted, Gallaudet was in touch with Withers. In April, 1874, Withers wrote that he was sending "studies for the plans of the college building.... The general arrangement varies very little from your suggestions which I have endeavored to follow as closely as possible." [54] Toward the end of June, after a $29,000 appropriation had been voted, the Board of Directors charged Gallaudet and Stickney to "prepare plans and prosecute the work on the new building." [55] In October they reported to the Board that excavations for the foundations had been begun and that John Meyers had been appointed supervising architect at a salary of $1,000 a year.[56] An entry in the Minutes of the Board of Directors for January 27, 1875, mentions that the final scheme was, appropriately enough, adopted within the walls of the legislative mansion:

> A special meeting of the Board was held in the Judiciary committee room of the Senate, in the Capitol, Wednesday January 12, 1875 at two o'clock P. M. Present Messrs Gallaudet, Niblack, Sunderland, Cooke and Stickney. The President submitted a drawing of the new College Building, which on motion was approved.

Favorable action was taken by Congress on a $75,000 appropriation in March, 1875, after which Gallaudet pressed Withers for more drawings so that work could progress. Withers replied on March 11th, that he "would put in hand the drawings for the College Building at once and forward when finished. It will be necessary that the general drawings should be completed now, but for the purpose of contracting I will send a set of tracings showing how much is proposed to be done this year."

Early in April the architect wrote again, this time asking Gallaudet permission to employ Lewis W. Leeds as a consultant on the proper

---

[52] Minutes of the Board of Directors, October 26, 1872.
[53] Sixteenth Annual Report (1873), p. 15.
[54] Letter from Withers to Gallaudet, October 13, 1874.
[55] Minutes of the Board of Directors, June 24, 1874, p. 170.
[56] Minutes of the Board of Directors, October 22, 1874, p. 171.

installation of ventilation pipes.[57] Ever since the Houses of Parliament (1836), architects had, for supposed reasons of health, insisted that the air inside large buildings be changed continuously. Leeds at the time was designing the elaborate ventilation system for the new Johns Hopkins Hospital in Baltimore. His charge of fifty dollars for his services, however, caused Gallaudet to reject the request; Withers, forced to tackle the intricate problem single-handedly, designed the flèche above the entrance bay as the terminus of a network of internal flues.

On May 5, 1875, Withers forwarded the completed elevation and perspective drawings to Washington. Later in the month he presented his bill for $2,000, but intimated to Gallaudet that "if you have $500 *now* to spare, it would be very acceptable." [58]

In the Eighteenth Annual Report (1875) Gallaudet stated that the building had been advanced to a level slightly above that of the second floor. He asked for an additional $50,000 for the coming year, admitting, however, that the "works are not yet sufficiently advanced to admit of absolutely final estimates." [59]

Construction moved slowly during the building season of 1876. Naylor agreed only in August to carry the southern portion to the roof line and the northern section to the bottom of the third story windows. Neither was there any correspondence between Gallaudet and New York during this year, for aside from the slow progress, Withers was then engaged on one of the most important commissions of his career, the William Blackhouse Astor Memorial Altar and Reredos in Trinity Church in New York City. He even spent part of the year in England superintending the stone cutters, sculptors, and mosaicists who were making the altar's components.

While he was abroad Withers had brought the Washington building to the attention of his English colleagues. It appeared in July, 1876, as one of the rare illustrations of American architecture in *The Building News*[60] (Figure 5), a leading British architectural journal. A testimony to its excellence—for the English architectural press generally ignored the American scene—the publication of College Hall was actually used to bolster the prejudicial British view that the only good architecture in America was done by immigrant architects. During the same year, the remarks of William Fogerty (1829–1899),

[57] Letter from Withers to Gallaudet, April 3, 1875.
[58] Letter from Withers to Gallaudet, May 15, 1875.
[59] Eighteenth Annual Report (1875), p. 10.
[60] *The Building News*, vol. XXX (July 28, 1876). It also appeared in *The American Architect and Building News* vol. II (November 3, 1877).

a Fellow of the Royal Institute of British Architects who had spent several months in the United States, were aired in *The Building News*.[61] Fogerty presented the building situation in this country, from the esthetic standpoint, as generally dismal. America, he said, was destitute of trained architects and offered superior opportunities to any professional who would care to immigrate (as Withers had done twenty years earlier). By publishing College Hall, the editors were producing concrete evidence of Fogerty's contention.

Back in America, Withers wrote Gallaudet late in the winter of 1877, as the building season was again approaching, apologizing for a slight delay in the completion of the final set of detailed working drawings. This, he explained, was due to the long drawn-out process of having to furnish the specifications in installments as money from Congress became available rather than being able to complete the job all at once: "The making of drawings for the contract on only portions, has involved an immense amount of extra labor—I think that it is the fourth specifications." Religiously devoted to his work, Withers tempered his objection by confiding, "I do not mind the labor . . . if everything turns out well." [62]

Dedication ceremonies were held on February 16, 1878, the twenty-first anniversary of the institution. President Hayes presided and heard Gallaudet praise Withers for the "beauty and convenience" of his building and for his "readiness to give time for consultation without extra compensation." [63] Speaking for the student body, Mr. S. M. Freeman, a member of the senior class, effusively thanked Congress for its generosity and with Ruskinian eloquence assured everyone present that "the elegant and commodious structure into which we have just moved is . . . a symbol of all that is beautiful and noble in life. Durable, substantial, and elegant, it is well fitted to serve as a pattern after which to mold our character." [64]

The new administration and dormitory building set the variegated exuberance and fairyland grandeur of Withers' most famous work, the Jefferson Market Courthouse (1874) in New York City (Figure 6), down beside the sedate dignity of Chapel Hall. Yet for all its ostentation, College Hall, when seen from the grounds of the Nineteenth

---

[61] William Fogerty, "The Prospects of Architecture in America," *The Building News*, vol. XXX (February 18, 1876).

[62] Letter from Withers to Gallaudet, March 2, 1877. The finished drawings were closely followed in the actual construction of the building. The only difference occurs in the treatment of the roof of the original back wing designed by Friedrich, which was left nearly unchanged instead of being altered to bring it into closer harmony with the newer portion.

[63] Twenty-First Annual Report (1878), p. 9.

[64] *Ibid.*

Courtesy of the Historic American Buildings Survey

Figure 6. F. C. Withers. The Jefferson Market Courthouse, Sixth Avenue and West Tenth Street, New York City. 1874.

Courtesy of Gallaudet College

Figure 7. View of Gallaudet College in 1878. From the Twenty-First Annual Report.

Century campus (Figure 7), assumed an harmonius relationship with its neighbor. Withers achieved this union of opposites by employing, in his College Hall design, bands that corresponded to the belt courses in Chapel Hall, a lowered roofline on the portion of College Hall nearest the older building, and a northwest corner tower of the same height as the spire on Chapel Hall.

Internally, College Hall was a typical institutional building with rooms ranged on each side of a long corridor on each floor. Only the museum, with its bay window in the base of the tower, and the vaulted Lyceum room, with a large stained glass window on the north side of the third floor, were exceptional.

On the exterior of College Hall Withers lavished his attention. In addition to the lively black brick patterns and forceful color contrasts used on the Jefferson Market Courthouse, he invigorated College Hall with structural ornament. Saw-tooth courses of black brick, corbeled bay windows, herringbone brick gable fronts, and muscular arches on slender granite columns (in the arcade) impart stamina to the fabric of College Hall.

The inspiration for all of this came from Street's *Brick and Marble* which taught the doctrine of "constructional colour":

> ... we may so construct our buildings as that there may be portions of the face of their walls in which no strain will be felt, and in which the absence of strain will be at once apparent; obviously, to instance a particular place, the spaces enclosed within circles constructed in the

spandrels of a line of arches can have no strain of any kind. They are portions of the wall without active function, and may safely be filled in with materials the only object of which is to be ornamental. All kinds of sunken panels enclosed within arches or tracery would come under the same head, so also the spaces between stringcourses might very frequently, if, as in old examples, the stringcourses were large slabs of stone bedded into the very midst of the wall.[65]

Extracting and amplifying the essence of appropriate passages from his earlier buildings, Withers, in this, his last Victorian Gothic design (the style did not survive the economic and cultural changes produced by the 1873 Panic and the 1876 Centennial Exposition), exemplified the theories of Street. Black saw-tooth courses occur where, in Street's words, "no strain will be felt," that is, in the spandrels of the arcade connecting the building with Chapel Hall (Figure 9) and along the top of the first floor between the windows. The remainder of unorthodox brickwork is likewise confined to non-structural areas, such as gable fronts. An impression of strength and stability, highly esteemed Victorian virtues, is therefore retained despite the surface richness.

Begun in the summer of 1875, the terrace in front of Chapel Hall was built at the same time as College Hall (Figure 8). Withers' plan, however, was altered, for the terrace, a portion of which appeared in the perspective drawing of College Hall in *The Building News* (Figure 5), was originally conceived as uniting the southern front of College Hall with the facade of Chapel Hall.[66] Some time after the spring of 1875, when Withers' drawings were sent to Washington, it was decided to cut back the terrace on the western side to exclude the new college building. The modification was unfortunate. Intended to visually join the two buildings, it now separates them and contradicts the linkage implied by the arcade. If the architect's drawing had been followed, the visitor, approaching from the south or southwest, would have mounted to a gracious esplanade where, on an elevated platform, he could have comprehended equally the two imposing buildings.

"The interests of the institution," wrote Gallaudet in 1873, "make it desireable that its officers and employees should reside on the premises." [67] Toward this end he requested money from Congress to erect two more of the staff dwellings projected in the 1866 master plan.[68] An appropriation was secured in 1874 after which Gallaudet

---

[65] Street, *op. cit.*, p. 279.
[66] Withers original drawing for the terrace is in the Gallaudet Library.
[67] Sixteenth Annual Report (1873), p. 15.
[68] Two additional houses, inferior to the ones under discussion, were constructed

Figure 8. F. C. Withers. College Hall; detail showing courses of sawtooth brickwork in the arcade connecting College Hall with Chapel Hall.

contacted Withers. The architect took up the work along with the continuation of the College Hall project. Unlike the plans for that building, however, those of House A (Figure 9) and House B, immediately adjacent to House No. 1 on Faculty Row, were ready in a short time. By September 1, 1874, both sets of drawings were forwarded to Washington.[69]

In the interests of economy, the floor plans of the two dwellings, the arrangement of which recalled a vicarage illustrated in Robert Kerr's *The Gentleman's House*,[70] were made identically the same. Individuality was imparted only to the exteriors. Because of this, a question

during the summer of 1883 without the aid of an architect. Minutes of the Board of Directors, October 27, 1883.

[69] It was probably at this time that the gate house was also designed.

[70] Robert Kerr, *The Gentleman's House* (London: Murray, 1865), plate 25.

Gallaudet College: A High Victorian Campus 463

Courtesy of the Peabody Institute Library

Figure 9. F. C. Withers. House A. 1874. From A. J. Bicknell's *Wooden and Brick Buildings*.

arose as to the proper fee Withers was entitled to receive. He proposed to charge Gallaudet "the customary 3½ per cent on A and 1½ per cent on B," but conceded, "if this is not entirely satisfactory to you please say so and I will endeavor to meet your views." [71] Gallaudet did object to the formula. The difference between the designs, he insisted, was so slight as not to justify any additional payment for the second house. Withers, ever the gentleman, acquiesced in his patron's opinion, assuring Gallaudet he did not "wish to charge more than what you consider fair," and insisting he accept supplemental drawings which Gallaudet had not thought absolutely necessary.[72]

On October 22, 1874, Gallaudet reported to the Board of Directors that a contract had been signed with Naylor who had committed himself to a total amount of $22,380.60 for both dwellings, a figure that reflected the decline in construction costs after the Panic of 1873. In the Annual Report for 1875, Gallaudet indicated that "the two dwelling houses are now occupied." House A, published as a model low cost dwelling in the popular architectural anthology *Wooden and Brick Buildings*[73] (1875) (Figure 9) compiled by Amos Bicknell, was a bulky and severe version of the style of the larger President's House.

---
[71] Letter from Withers to Gallaudet, August 27, 1874.
[72] Letter from Withers to Gallaudet, September 16, 1874.
[73] A. J. Bicknell (comp.), *Wooden and Brick Buildings with Details* (New York: Bicknell, 1875), vol. 1, Design 31.

Courtesy of Gallaudet College

Figure 10. F. C. Withers. The gymnasium. 1880.

The steep roof, the broad Eastlakian veranda, and the ponderous corbeled gable which imparts a slightly top-heavy look to the facade today evoke an image of somber Victorian domesticity.

A gymnasium (Figure 10) had not been called for in the 1866 plan, but in 1878 Gallaudet saw a pressing need for one "to give proper attention to the physical development of our pupils." Particularly disturbed by the fact that "no less than four of our older pupils have met death by drowning," he urged "that in connection with a gymnasium there should be a bathing pool of sufficient size to enable us to teach all our pupils how to manage themselves in the water." [74]

Unfortunately, Congress did not immediately respond to Gallaudet's concern. The 1879 session, held amid an atmosphere of lingering recession, refused to vote any funds for the project. In the Twenty-Second Annual Report (1879) Gallaudet renewed his request pleading that the need was "even greater than in ordinary schools and colleges, for in many cases the causes which have operated to produce deafness . . . exert a depressing effect on the system generally." [75] This time his voice was heard and Congress granted the institution $5,000 toward the erection of the type of building Gallaudet wanted.

The only American gymnasium with an indoor swimming pool

[74] Twenty-First Annual Report (1878), p. 19.
[75] Twenty-Second Annual Report (1879), p. 15.

was the newly completed Hemenway Gymnasium at Harvard by Robert S. Peabody (1845–1917) and John G. Sterns (1838–1915). In February, 1880, Gallaudet requested an appointment with Darcy Allen Sargent, the Hemenway's director, to inspect the building and the special equipment Sargent had designed for it.[76] Gallaudet also contacted Withers in New York. By the middle of March preliminary sketches for the new building, which incorporated ideas Gallaudet had gotten from Sargent, were approved.

The plans for the gymnasium were finished in April, 1880. Pleased with the design, Withers wrote Gallaudet that "everything works out capitally and the building will I am sure look well." [77] Its location, near the northwest corner of College Hall, was settled upon soon after, apparently on the advice of Olmsted who visited Withers in May to discuss the subject.[78]

Immediately after the receipt of the specifications and working drawings from New York, Gallaudet awarded the contract to Henry Conradis for the unusually low figure of $11,650,[79] a sum which greatly surprised the architect who, even with the slugglish market, had anticipated a much higher cost. Construction started in the summer of 1880, but in the fall Gallaudet reported that, due to the insufficiency of funds, all work had to be suspended after the principal walls were erected. Work would resume the following spring if Congress approved an allowance for the balance of the Conradis contract. The appropriation was granted and the gymnasium was completed in July, 1881. Special equipment designed by Sargent was installed by the following October.[80]

"Old Jim," as the building came to be called, contained on the ground floor a large heated pool, the first in Washington, and in the tall second story a lofty timber framed exercise room. Undoubtedly aware of Schulz and Haver's gymnasium in Hanover, Germany, which had been published by Felix Narjoux in his *Notes and Sketches of An Architect Taken During a Journey in the Northwest of Europe* (1877), Withers covered his structure with a sturdy roof of wood (a material more difficult to work with than iron but, as Narjoux pointed out, a natural insulator) and repeated in the plan of the exercise room the arrangement of the German building. From the outside, the well-toned appearance of the exterior, with its rich com-

---

[76] Letter from Charles Eliot to Gallaudet, February 2, 1880.
[77] Letter from Withers to Gallaudet, April 16, 1880.
[78] Letter from Withers to Gallaudet, May 22, 1880.
[79] Minutes of the Board of Directors, June 23, 1880, p. 218. The structure ended up costing more than originally proposed. The final figure was $14,600.
[80] Letter from Sargent to Gallaudet, October 6, 1881. For a description of the gymnasium see the Twenty-First Annual Report (1881), p. 13.

bination of textures, its mighty roof, and its bold framing system made more virilent by accentuation, would have inspired the weakest student with a desire for physical fitness.

Stylistically, the gymnasium departed from the previous campus buildings. With the demise of Victorian Gothic after 1876, the center revivalistic gravity had migrated from the colorful Italian city to the grey northern European countryside. Stimulated by the example of the British architects Phillip Webb (1831–1915) and Norman Shaw (1831–1912), a new interest had been aroused by 1880 in the late medieval vernacular architecture of England. Withers, continuing his steadfast allegiance to architectural developments in his homeland, followed suit. Broadly designated Queen Anne, the style of the gymnasium enjoyed a brief but prolific life in America before being swept away by the Romanesque Revival fostered by H. H. Richardson (1838–1886). Barn-like "Old Jim," badly treated by later generations, was an accomplished, if not primary, example of its picturesque genre.

Another Queen Anne building designed by Withers for Gallaudet was Kendall Hall (previously called The Kendall School). Used originally by the primary department rather than the college, it, like the gymnasium, had not been anticipated in the 1866 master plan. Due to its less important character, it was assigned a relatively obscure position behind Chapel Hall where it formed the final unit of a quadrangle at the rear of the major buildings.

The history of Kendall Hall is incomplete, for no correspondence between the president and the architect exists on the subject and even the actual plans for the structure have been lost. Linking its design conclusively to Withers, however, are several entries in Gallaudet's personal diary for 1884, the first of which is dated October 27.[81] On that day he recorded a meeting with Withers in New York City where they had "arranged about the new school building plans." A short time later he saw Withers again and "looked over his plans for our new school building, which I found very nice." By November 15, 1884, the completed drawings had arrived in Washington, and Gallaudet commented that he found them "very satisfactory." Congressional funding was also provided in 1884 and notice was taken of the proposed building in *The American Architect and Building News* in the January 17, 1885, issue where it was described as "a two story and basement brick and stone school-house, 50′ × 60′." In March, 1885, Gallaudet met with the Board of Directors and presented an estimate which he and a professor Bryant had prepared of $14,000. This was $3,000 under the appropriation granted by Congress; the

---

[81] Gallaudet's diaries are in The Library of Congress, Manuscript Division.

remainder went toward the construction of a separate laboratory building designed by Bryant.[82] Kendall Hall was completed by the end of 1885.

It was Gallaudet who suggested that the building be named in honor of Amos Kendall. His idea was approved by blustery Senator Henry L. Dawes of Massachusetts, a member of the Board of Directors, who told him: "do it and if any body praises you for doing it, take the credit to yourself—if any body blames you tell them I did it." [83]

Subdued and monochromatic, Kendall Hall contrasts with College Hall and Chapel Hall. It is close in feeling to the Queen Anne style house at 1416 Rhode Island Avenue that Withers created in 1884 for Commander J. H. Upshur. Both of these brick and terra cotta buildings partake of the mellow autumnal spirit that descended on American architecture after the hot, vibrant summer of the Victorian Gothic.

With the completion of the plans for Kendall Hall, Withers' relationship with Gallaudet came to an end. By 1885 the number of major buildings on the campus had nearly reached the point at which it was to remain until the Twentieth Century. When another dormitory, Dawes House (behind Kendall Hall), was required in 1895, Gallaudet, out of understandable pride, asked a former student who had become an architect, Olof Hanson, of Farribault, Minnesota, to furnish the plans.

One of the notable examples of High Victorian landscape design and architecture in the United States, the campus of Gallaudet College stands as a tribute to the enlightened intelligence of Edward Miner Gallaudet. For him, Olmsted and Vaux created, concurrent with the grounds of the University of California at Berkeley, an early instance of the transplantation of advanced notions of urban park planning, and the Utilitarian conceptions implicit behind them, to the modern college campus.[84] Working with Olmsted and Vaux, Withers proved that the High Victorian Gothic style, imported from England, was capable of satisfying the patriotic sentiments and practical needs of Reconstruction America as well as of fulfilling Downing's desire to integrate architecture and nature.

[82] The Laboratory building, constructed in 1896, was destroyed in the 1950's. It stood on the present site of the college library.
[83] Diary of Gallaudet, March 6, 1885.
[84] Parenthetically, the work of Olmsted and Vaux has outlived (albeit in a mutilated form) Downing's historic work in Washington, for upon the recommendation of Olmsted's successor, Frederick Law Olmsted, Jr., Downing's Washington pleasure grounds were swept away in 1902 to make way for the present Mall.

A National Monument for a National Library: Ainsworth Rand Spofford and the New Library of Congress, 1871–1897

JOHN Y. COLE

The grandiose Italian Renaissance building of the Library of Congress, imposingly situated directly across the east plaza from the Capitol, is one of the most striking monuments to American cultural nationalism in a city filled with similar architectural tributes. When its doors were first opened to the public in 1897, the Library represented an unparalleled national achievement: its 23-carat gold-plated dome capped the "largest, costliest, and safest" library building in the world; its elaborately decorated facade and interior, for which more than 50 American painters and sculptors produced works of art, "proved" that the United States could surpass any European library in grandeur and devotion to classical culture. A contemporary guidebook boasted: "America is justly proud of this gorgeous and palatial monument to its National sympathy and appreciation of Literature, Science and Art. It has been designed and executed entirely by American art and American labor [and is] a fitting temple for the great thoughts of generations past, present, and to be." This new national Temple of the Arts immediately met with overwhelming approval from the American public.[1]

The most important aspect of the new building's national character, however, was not its architecture nor decorative features, but its purpose: a national library for the United States. It was built specifically to serve as the American national library and its architecture and decoration both express and enhance that purpose. Viewed thusly, the

---

[1] Of the many guidebooks published when the Library building opened, the most thorough is Herbert Small's well-illustrated *Handbook of the New Library of Congress in Washington* (Boston, 1897). This edition includes, as appendices, two important essays about the Library: "The Function of a National Library" by Ainsworth Spofford and Charles Caffin's "The Architecture, Sculpture, and Painting."

structure acquires a meaning often overlooked today, when it generally is referred to as a quaint, albeit splendid, "period piece."

The Library building and national library idea are linked in the most fundamental way: both were the dream and ultimately the achievement of Ainsworth Rand Spofford (1825–1908), the energetic Librarian of Congress from 1864 to 1897. The new building was a crucial step in Spofford's effort to develop the Library of Congress into the American national library. This essay explores the relationship between the building and its function as originally conceived by Spofford and eventually amplified by others, particularly its construction engineers, General Thomas L. Casey and Bernard R. Green.

SPOFFORD AND THE IDEA OF A NATIONAL LIBRARY

The notion of a national library in the United States had many advocates before Spofford. By the middle of the Nineteenth Century, New England intellectuals such as Rufus Choate and George P. Marsh considered a great national library to be a cultural necessity; America needed the library to prove its cultural worth *vis à vis* Europe and, at the same time, establish its "intellectual independence" from the Old World. During the Congressional debates which resulted in the establishment of the Smithsonian Institution in 1846, Choate and Marsh urged that the Smithson bequest be used to create such a national library. Charles Coffin Jewett, the Smithsonian librarian from 1847 to 1854, went further: he tried to mold the Smithsonian into not only a national library but also a national bibliographic center. But Joseph Henry, the Secretary of the Smithsonian, was adamantly opposed to its development as a national library and instead saw it as an institution which would encourage the "increase and diffusion" of scientific knowledge. Since Jewett's plan was directly opposed to the Secretary's, in 1854 Henry dismissed his librarian, ending the possibility that the Smithsonian might someday become the national library. Jewett became librarian of the Boston Public Library and lost interest in a national library. Ironically, the idea was kept alive in the 1850's by Joseph Henry himself, who favored such an institution so long as it was not the Smithsonian. Once the ambitious Ainsworth Spofford arrived at the Library of Congress, Henry lent not only his personal support but also that of the Smithsonian Institution to the cause of the Library of Congress as the national library.[2]

Spofford's personal qualifications for the national library task he set

---

[2] I have discussed early 19th century national library views and the Jewett-Henry controversy at greater length in "Of Copyright, Men & A National Library," *The Quarterly Journal of the Library of Congress*, v. 28 (April, 1971), p. 114–136 (hereafter cited as *QJ*).

Library of Congress

Ainsworth Rand Spofford (1825–1908), Librarian of Congress from 1864 to 1897.

for himself could scarcely have been better. Between 1844 and 1861 he was in Cincinnati, where he had three careers which were of direct benefit to him at the Library of Congress: bookseller and publisher at the firm of Truman & Spofford; cultural entrepreneur at the Literary Club of Cincinnati (where one of his feats was to persuade Ralph Waldo Emerson to make his first western lecture tour); and editorial writer and political correspondent for the Cincinnati *Commercial*, the city's leading newspaper. By September of 1861, when he took the job of Assistant Librarian of Congress, Spofford had acquired the book-trade skills, the knowledge of books, and the political acumen, which enabled him to expand the Library into an institution of national importance. He also had made several friends in Cincinnati who helped him in his national library effort. The most influential, Rutherford B. Hayes, served as a member of the Joint Committee on the Library from 1865 to 1867.

From the day he joined the four-man staff of the Library of Congress, then located in the west front of the Capitol, Spofford considered the Library the national library. His view notwithstanding, in 1861 its collections were meager in quantity and undistinguished in quality. They were surpassed in size by those of Harvard, New York's Astor Library, the Boston Public Library, the Boston Atheneum, and Yale. Nor had Congress demonstrated much interest in transforming its Library, which it considered a legislative library, into the national library. Whenever such an expansion was proposed or hinted at by a Congressman or journalist, as happened on occasion, the idea was quickly dismissed. Members of the Library's governing board, the Joint Committee on the Library, and the various Librarians of Congress before Spofford, had generally been content with the institution's status. Nonetheless, by virtue of its co-establishment with the national government in Washington in 1800, and the strong interest taken in it by Thomas Jefferson, whose 6,000 volume library served as its basis, the Library of Congress had substantial claim to a national role. Until Spofford arrived, however, no one had the interest, skill, or perseverance to capitalize on that claim.

Spofford saw no conflict between the functions of a legislative and a national library. He pointed out that there was no book in any subject which might not at some time "prove useful to the legislature of a great nation in their manifold and responsible duties." A comprehensive collection covering all subjects was therefore as important to Congress as it was to scholars and the general public. Once this collection was developed for the use of the national legislature, it should be made available to the rest of the American people, for the strength of the Republic itself depended upon "the popular intelligence." Liberal public access to the Library was of great importance to Spofford for, like most Nineteenth Century bookmen, he was convinced that reading had a positive moral value. A centralized accumulation of national literature thus could not be anything but beneficial to the American people.

Spofford and Charles Coffin Jewett shared many ideas relating to a national library, particularly in recognizing copyright deposit as the best method of building a collection which would reflect all aspects of American life. Yet in one way there was a major difference. Spofford never pictured the library as the center of a network of American libraries, a focal point providing those libraries with a wide range of cataloging and bibliographic services. Instead, he viewed the national library as a unique, independent institution; it was to be a single, comprehensive collection of national literature used freely both by Congressmen and the American people. This "great national collection," constituting "the only really representative library of the nation," was to be patterned after the great European national libraries, particularly the British Museum.

Spofford's relatively narrow view of the role of a national library helped him achieve his goal. Taking advantage of a favorable post-Civil War intellectual and political climate, between 1865 and 1870 he gained Congressional approval for several important expansions of the Library. With the exception of the $100,000 appropriated in 1867 for the purchase of Peter Force's library, each was accomplished at little expense to the government. Each legislative achievement was a logical extension of the previous enactment—until the copyright law of 1870 provided the national capstone. In all, there were six legislative acts which insured a national role for the Library of Congress: (1) an appropriation providing for an expansion of the Library within the Capitol building, approved in early 1865; (2) the copyright amendment of 1865, returning the flow of copyright deposits into the Library's collections after an absence of six years; (3) the transfer, in 1866, of the 40,000-volume library of the Smithsonian Institution to the Library of Congress; (4) the 1867 purchase of the nation's outstanding collection of Americana, the private library of the archivist and historian, Peter Force; (5) the international exchange resolution of 1867, which provided for the continuing development of the Library's collection of foreign public documents; and (6) the copyright law of 1870, centralizing all United States copyright registration and deposit activities at the Library and thus guaranteeing by law the future growth of the Library's collection of current American publi-

Library of Congress

Wedgwood Plate commemorating the new Library of Congress building.

Copyright, 1900, by Jones McDuffee & Stratton Co., Boston, "sole importers," the design is accompanied by the quotation: "It stands today the largest, most imposing, most sumptuous and most costly Library Building in the world."

cations. In five years Spofford had gathered his "national collection" of books and materials and provided for the continued growth of that collection. The Library of Congress suddenly became the nation's largest library and, even if Congress never appropriated another dollar for its use, the rapid growth of its collections was certain.

Since it was of great importance to Spofford's future effort to secure a separate Library building, the 1865 expansion of the Library's rooms in the Capitol bears close examination. That expansion was significant because it established a precedent for the future enlargement of the Library; because it set the pattern for Spofford's tactics and arguments in his future dealings with Congress and the Federal bureaucracy; and for an immediate, practical reason: it enabled the Librarian to acquire two collections which helped immeasurably the Library's development into a nationally-recognized institution, the Smithsonian library and Peter Force's Americana collection.

In 1851 the Library of Congress had suffered a disastrous fire which destroyed 35,000 of its 55,000 volumes. Congress appropriated $72,500 to construct a new Library, one which would occupy the entire western projection of the Capitol. However the "officers of Congress" then occupying the rooms at each end of the projection would not be budged, so Architect of the Capitol Thomas U. Walter was unable to complete the authorized plan and the Library remained restricted to the central portion. In a handwritten annual report prepared in 1862, Assistant Librarian Spofford complained about the crowded conditions in the Library and noted that the Congressional intent to extend the Library to the limits of the western projection had never been carried out. The young Assistant Librarian personally discussed the problem with Walter and Benjamin F. French, Commissioner of Public Buildings, urging not only the proposed extension but also several major modifications in the main Library room. Walter estimated the cost of the extension to be $160,000; the eager Spofford saw that this sum was included in the Library's budget request for the next year. Such a sizable request, particularly from an office which had been relatively dormant for decades, required a special explanation, and on October 22, 1864, Spofford justified the request to the newly-appointed Secretary of the Treasury, William Pitt Fessenden. His letter combined practical considerations with appeals to national pride, and included a generous dose of personal flattery. Spofford emphasized that the Library was especially deserving, since it had existed for eleven years with only one carpet and no new furniture, "exhibiting an economy of expenditure sufficiently rare, if not unequalled, in any department of government." Moreover,

> ... the appropriation asked is not unreasonably high, as may be seen by comparing the cost of similar Library accommodations elsewhere. The new Reading Room of the British Museum (constructed entirely within the old edifice) cost ... half a million dollars. ... The sum of $160,000, although large in itself, is not so in comparison with the great object of providing safe and permanent room for this rich historical collection.

The letter closed with a characteristic appeal:

> ... it is therefore with some confidence that Congress is now asked to provide permanently for the security of the invaluable literary stores which have been accumulated in the Capitol.[3]

The expansion of the Library's rooms was approved in the appropriation act of March 2, 1865. But Spofford did not rest on his success. He followed the progress of the construction work closely, never hesitating to propose changes nor to criticize the work being performed under the supervision of Architect of the Capitol Edward Clark. Effectively utilizing his friends on the Library Committee, particularly Representative Hayes and Senator Timothy O. Howe of Wisconsin, Spofford frequently forced Clark to make the modifications he desired. When the first *Annual Report of the Librarian of Congress* was published on December 3, 1866, the initial item mentioned by Librarian Spofford was the extension, which would be completed during the next month. He noted with satisfaction that this expansion would result in a tripling of the space available in the Library, and provide "for the safe-keeping of about 210,000 volumes."

A SEPARATE BUILDING

The expansion soon proved to be insufficient, for between 1866 and 1870 the Librarian acquired materials far more rapidly than he could find space for them. The situation was described in his 1871 report:

> The constant and rapid growth of the Library under my charge renders it necessary to call the attention of the committee to the emergency which will soon compel the provision of more room for books. The large additional space provided by the construction of the two wings opened in 1866 was soon nearly filled up by the almost simultaneous acquisition of the Smithsonian Library as a deposit, and the Force Historical Library, by purchase, together with the annually growing accessions of new books by copyright and by purchase.

The copyright law of 1870, which brought 19,826 books, periodicals, musical and dramatic compositions, photographs, prints, and maps into the Library during 1871, was the principal reason for the steadily increasing need for space. Assuming that "the constant and rapid growth" of the Library left Congress no alternative but to provide additional space for the collections, Spofford submitted two sug-

---

[3] Spofford to Fessenden, Oct. 22, 1864, Librarian's Letterbook No. 6, Library of Congress Archives, Library of Congress (hereafter cited as LC Archives).

Library of Congress

The Library of Congress in the Capitol, about 1895.

gestions. He preferred "a separate building, designed expressly for [the Library's] accommodation and for the copyright business of the country." As a second choice, he felt that the extension of the Capitol's west front might be acceptable. By the end of 1872 he had changed his mind on the second. In his report for that year he urged the Library Committee to recognize the "absolute necessity of erecting a separate building for the Library and the copyright departments conjoined." The expansion of the west front simply could never "make the present inadequate apartments subserve the wants of a great national library." A national library required its own building, a structure commensurate with its unique national purpose.[4]

The Librarian devoted more than half of his 1872 report to delineating the desirable features in the building he envisioned. That report is the most important document in the history of the new Library building, for it outlines the basic concept behind the structure, which itself would not be completed for a quarter of a century. That Spofford's conception of the national library building should survive after a virtually endless architectural competition, countless Congressional arguments about its design and location, and several changes during construction of architects and engineers, is a considerable tribute to his foresight, tenacity, and political skill.

Spofford felt there were "three ruling considerations" which should be kept in mind when planning the new building: "fireproof materials in every part, the highest utility and convenience in the arrangement of details, and the wants of the future." Regarding the latter, he felt the building should accommodate not less than three million volumes. He was confident that the Library of Congress would someday surpass in size both the Bibliothèque Nationale and the British Museum because of the "growing development and intellectual enterprise of the country." A better librarian than prognosticator, he predicted that by 1975 the Library of Congress would hold at least 2,500,000 volumes (in 1972 it reached 16,000,000 volumes). He looked to the British Museum as a model for a central reading room with outward radiating book alcoves and he insisted upon adequate space for five separate "apartments": copyright, maps, fine arts, periodicals, and a packing-room.

In his advocacy of the separate building, Spofford employed the same nationalistic and practical arguments he used in persuading Congress to approve the earlier laws which helped the Library towards a national status:

> ... In every country where civilization has attained a high rank, there should be at least one great library, not only universal in range, but whose plan it should be to reverse the rule of the smaller and more select libraries, which is exclusiveness, for one of inclusiveness. Unless this is done, unless the minor literature and the failures of our authors are

---
[4] *Annual Report of the Librarian of Congress for 1872*, p. 7-8 (hereafter cited as *Annual Report*).

preserved, as well as the successes, American writers will be without the means of surveying the whole field trodden by their predecessors.... In every great nation this comprehensive library should be obviously the library of the government, which enjoys the benefit of the copy tax, and has thus supplied without cost a complete representation of the intellectual product of the country in every field of science and literature.[5]

As usual the Library Committee accepted Spofford's arguments, and for a few months it seemed that a separate building might be obtained quickly and without difficulty. On March 3, 1873, Congress appointed a three-man commission consisting of Spofford, Library Committee Chairman Howe, and Justin S. Morrill of Vermont, head of the Senate Committee on Public Buildings and Grounds, to "select a plan and supervise the location and erection of a building." A competition to design the structure was authorized and $5,000 authorized for the use of the commission. In August of 1873 the competition was advertised in newspapers in Washington, Boston, and New York, and the commission issued "specifications for the guidance of those who may submit designs."

The 1873 specifications were prepared by Spofford, who relied primarily on his annual report of the previous year. He was quite specific about the dimensions of what would someday become the largest library in the world:

> The general plan of the building will embrace a circular reading room in the center, of one hundred feet diameter, with alcoves radiating from the circumference of the inner circle outward.
> The exterior walls are to be within a space of 270 by 340 feet. The elevation is not to exceed 60 to 65 feet.... No dome nor towers of greater height than 70 feet can be admitted on account of the proximity of the projected building to the Capitol.
> All parts of the building [are] to be of fire-proof materials, no wood being employed in any portion of the structure.
> The precise location of the Library building not being determined, it can only be stated ... that the reservation the building is to occupy will have a front on two streets, and probably on three; that the size of the lot will be either 300 by 520 feet, or possibly 400 by 475 feet; and that suitable approaches and decorative shrubbery will be provided for, while the front of the edifice will look out upon a park the dimensions of which are about 500 by 800 feet, lying directly east of the Capitol and having Greenough's statue of Washington in its center.

The Librarian noted that the alcove system of shelving was to be used, ranging as high as five stories, and that eight large rooms, "not

---
[5] *Ibid.*, p. 10.

less than 40 to 60 feet diameter and 20 to 25 feet high," be provided for "map-rooms, newspaper files, copyright records, works of art, catalogue-rooms, and a packing room."[6] On December 22, 1873, the commission announced its decision. A total of 27 architects had submitted a variety of designs, but the commission seemed to have little difficulty in choosing the winner: the Italian Renaissance design submitted by the firm of Smithmeyer & Pelz of Washington, D.C. The commission apparently preferred it primarily because of its "conformity" with the architecture of the Capitol.

It is obvious that Spofford never anticipated the controversies and delays which soon plagued the Library building. He assumed that the location across the east plaza from the Capitol would be approved, and with the selection of the Smithmeyer & Pelz design he was anxious for work to proceed. The design and location of the building, beyond those requirements which he had already enumerated, were not so important to him as the existence of the building. Conditioned by his earlier legislative achievements, he had every reason to expect immediate success. To his dismay, he soon found that the Library Committee itself would constitute the first obstacle. Like most of their Congressional colleagues, members of the Committee did not disagree with the need for a separate Library building. Nor were there serious Congressional objections to Spofford's intention, now more obvious than ever, to expand the Library from a legislative into a national institution. But many Congressmen did have personal preferences regarding the structure's design and location, and these were the questions which delayed the building for the next 12 years.[7]

The agony for Spofford began on June 23, 1874, when Congress voted—on the recommendation of the Library Committee—to appropriate $2,000 for "additional designs" for the proposed building, thus reopening the architectural competition. Senator Howe of the Committee had recommended such action after visiting other national libraries while on vacation in Europe and finding the Smithmeyer & Pelz design too "small and plain" compared to the libraries of Europe. At the request of the Committee, Smithmeyer & Pelz submitted new designs, not only in the Italian Renaissance style but also in French Renaissance, Modern Renaissance, Romanesque, German Renaissance, and Thirteenth-Century Gothic. Nearly a dozen other archi-

---

[6] *Specifications for the Guidance of Those Who May Submit Designs for a New Building for the Library of Congress* (Washington, 1873), p. 1–3.

[7] I have told the story of the design and construction of the Library building from the architects' point of view in "Smithmeyer & Pelz: Embattled Architects of the Library of Congress," *QJ*, v. 29 (October, 1972), p. 282–307. This special issue of *QJ* commemorates the building's 75th anniversary.

tects forwarded new designs to the Committee and to the various Congressional commissions which were concerned with the building during the next decade.

Congress was as indecisive about the projected Library's location as it was about its style. The *Library Journal* explained that in the Senate there were "two camps—one advocating the extension of the Capitol building in one or more directions... and led by Senators Conkling, Dawes, and Edmunds; the other favoring a new building separate from the Capitol and led by Senators Bayard and Morrill, the latter preferring East Capitol Park instead of Judiciary Square." Senator Conkling favored the extension of both Capitol wings "toward the west, so as to form an enclosure something like that embraced by the colonnades at St. Peter's at Rome." Another suggestion came from Senator Howe, who favored a site at the foot of Capitol Hill near the Botanic Garden until tests showed the ground there to be too spongy. Senator Daniel W. Voorhees of Indiana opposed any extension of the Capitol building because "the westward course of

Library of Congress

The Library of Congress in the Capitol, an illustration by W. Bengough in *Harper's Weekly* for February 27, 1897.

Ainsworth Rand Spofford is shown standing at the right. The caption in *Harper's Weekly* is: "Scene in the old Congressional Library, Washington, D.C., showing present congested condition.—Drawn by W. Bengough."

empire would soon render it necessary to remove the seat of government to some point in the Mississippi Valley." [8]

Spofford's arguments during the first years of the delay again combined nationalistic rhetoric, pleading, flattery, and practical logic. In his 1874 annual report, he informed those Congressmen who favored the expansion of the Capitol building to accommodate the Library that: "In no country of Europe, of the first rank, is it attempted to keep the library of the government under the same roof with the halls of legislation." He felt that when Congress passed the law requiring the deposit in the Library of two copies "of every book or other publication protected by copyright" that it "took a step which rendered the separation of this vast collection from the Capitol, sooner or later, a necessity." In 1875, when the Library ran out of shelf space and the collections began to accumulate in rapidly-growing piles upon the floor, a note of desperation appeared in his annual report:

> Congress has deliberately founded by its legislation this great depository of a nation's literature and art; and now that it has grown to a magnitude which will favorably compare with some, at least, of the most useful libraries in the world, it is impossible to believe that the legislature of a great and intelligent people will continue to neglect making some suitable provision to preserve and extend this noble collection. If left in its present condition, the neglect of Congress will soon place its Librarian in the unhappy predicament of presiding over the greatest chaos in America; but if permanently provided for, with a liberal foresight for the future, this Library will become not only one of the foremost ornaments of the national capital, but a perpetual honor to the United States.[9]

Spofford was a skilled behind-the-scenes politician, but not in a partisan sense; his cause was the Library of Congress as the national library, his immediate purpose the construction of a separate building. To this end he gladly drafted letters and even speeches for his friends in Congress. He was active among politicians, the press, and library groups. During the 1876 meeting in Philadelphia at which the American Library Association was founded, Spofford shepherded through a resolution imploring Congress to appropriate funds for the building. When his old friend from Cincinnati, Rutherford B. Hayes, became President of the United States in the disputed election of 1876, Spofford persuaded him to include a plea for a new library building in each of his State of the Union messages. In his 1878 mes-

---
[8] *Library Journal*, v. 4 (February, 1879), p. 4 (hereafter cited as *LJ*).
[9] *Annual Report, 1875*, p. 9–10.

sage, for example, President Hayes pointed out, in Spofford-like language: "As this library is national in its character and must, from the nature of the case, increase even more rapidly in the future than in the past, it cannot be doubted that the people will sanction any wise expenditure to preserve it and enlarge its usefulness." The following year Spofford again looked to the new American Library Association for support, proposing that the next national convention be held in Washington in order to give impetus to the movement for a new Library building.

Spofford's most dependable supporters were two Senators, both personal friends and frequent users of his library: Justin S. Morrill and Daniel W. Voorhees. On the last day of March, 1879, Morrill delivered a major speech in which he strongly endorsed a separate Library building and Spofford's national library concept:

> We must ... either reduce the Library to the stinted and specific wants of Congress alone, or permit it to advance to national importance, and give it room equal to the culture, wants, and resources of a great people. Any mere enlargement will be a temporary expedient, and by the time completed more room would be required. The higher education of our common country demands that this institution shall not be crippled for lack of room.[10]

Senator Voorhees, Chairman of the Joint Committee on the Library, was more grandiloquent. In a May 5, 1880 speech about the Library, he expressed his belief in the essential moral value of books and intellectual activity:

> The physical man must grow old, his hair must whiten, and his face bear the furrows of years; his step must falter and his hand grow feeble. Not necessarily so with the intellectual man. The mind fed at the crystal fountains of accumulated knowledge will continue its growth, and its expansion until it makes its final transition to a sphere of endless and unlimited development. Let us therefore give this great national library our love and our care. Nothing can surpass it in importance. Knowledge is power, the power to maintain free government and preserve constitutional liberty. Without it the world grows dark and the human race takes up its backward march to the regions of barbarism. I cannot believe that the plain and imperative duty of Congress on the subject of its Library will be longer neglected.[11]

---

[10] "The Library of Congress. The Capitol and its Grounds." *Speech of the Hon. Justin S. Morrill of Vermont in the Senate of the United States, March 31, 1879* (Washington, 1879). For a full description of Morrill's role see John McDonough's "Justin Smith Morrill and the Library of Congress," *Vermont History*, v. 35 (July, 1965), p. 141–150.

[11] "The Library of Congress." *A Speech Delivered by the Hon. D. W. Voorhees of Indiana in the Senate of the United States, May 5, 1880* (Washington, 1880).

Voorhees, Morrill, and Spofford shared the view that a national library, as a centralized accumulation of knowledge, was a necessity for an enlightened nation. Without such an institution, America always would be inferior to Europe. Voorhees' speech was followed a week later by another from Morrill, and their combined efforts brought forth a new committee which was finally to resolve the controversy: the Joint Select Committee on Additional Accommodations of the Library of Congress. Voorhees became chairman and he headed the Committee during its entire existence, which lasted nearly two decades, except for one session of Congress in which Morrill was chairman. The Committee appointed three architects, John L. Smithmeyer, winner of the first competition seven years earlier, Edward Clark, the Architect of the Capitol, and Alexander Esty, a government architect in Boston, to investigate and report on the feasibility of enlarging the Capitol for the use of the Library. If they found such an enlargement to be impractical, the architects were instructed to submit individual plans for a separate library building in accordance with specifications once again furnished by Spofford.

Not unexpectedly, in September of 1880 the architects reported that it would be "inexpedient" to extend the Capitol and each submitted plans for a separate Library structure. When the Washington convention of the American Library Association was held in February of 1881, Spofford announced that the Joint Select Committee had chosen Smithmeyer's plan for the proposed structure. Nor could that choice have come as any great surprise. Spofford had favored Smithmeyer since the first competition, finding the Washington architect receptive to the idea of a building of "national" significance and a serious student of library architecture. The 1881 Smithmeyer & Pelz plan contained several practical improvements over their 1873 prize-winning design, but the basic dimensions, layout, and Italian Renaissance design were the same. Unfortunately, Smithmeyer's explanation of his plan before the librarians assembled in Washington created yet another barrier in the path of the new building.

Many of the librarians simply found the proposed plan too old-fashioned. The most prominent librarian taking this view was William Frederick Poole of the Chicago Public Library, who called for a rejection of traditional library architecture, typified by lofty central reading rooms and centralized book storage. Smithmeyer's plan not only incorporated these features but was deliberately designed as a "showplace." In the architect's words, "the National Library of the United States" should be "more of a museum of literature, science, and art, than strictly taken as a collection of books." The building

Library of Congress

View along East Capitol Street in the late 1870's.

The First Street houses known as Carroll Row, shown in the upper right hand portion of the photograph, occupy the future site of the Library of Congress. Horace Greenough's statue of George Washington is near the center of the photograph.

would be "first class in every particular, a credit to the country, and a monument of architectural art"; each American would want to visit it once in his lifetime, making it "the mecca of the young giant Republic."

Poole found such views objectionable and favored a more functional approach in which separate library departments were divided by subject and the appropriate books were arranged accordingly within each department instead of in a central bookstack. The Chicago librarian felt that no library should be subjected to a "noisy army of sightseers" and he was particularly dismayed to learn that Smithmeyer consciously planned to attract and accommodate visitors in the spacious exhibit halls which connected the corner pavilions. Poole criticized architects in general for building impractical monuments instead of useful libraries and urged librarians to play a more active role in planning the buildings in which they were to work.[12]

Poole obviously did not understand that Smithmeyer had closely followed Spofford's ideas. The Librarian's instructions, as outlined in the 1873 specifications and adhered to since, called for a large, monumental building suitable for a unique, national institution. The idea of such a library appealed to most Congressmen and architects; Smithmeyer had merely added his own embellishments. Unfortunately, the architect's enthusiastic rhetoric at the 1881 meeting practically buried his, and Spofford's, more important argument: the Library of Congress, as the national library, was unique and rules which might apply to the construction of other libraries did not apply to it. Poole and most of the other librarians at the convention missed this point.

This difference of opinion over the architecture of the Library building did not emerge until the librarians' convention was nearly over, however, and in the meantime Spofford gained an endorsement of the idea of a separate building. The convention resolution on this question went even further, stating that the librarians shared "the conviction of the people of the United States that the Library of Congress is the one national library, the only one in the country destined to be encyclopedic and universal in its comprehensiveness." Spofford must have been well pleased.

Like many others, Senator Thomas A. Bayard of Delaware favored a new Library building in part because he wanted an American national library which would overshadow the British Museum, the Bibliothèque Nationale, and the other great libraries of Europe. In 1880 Bayard had introduced a joint resolution to appropriate $2,500 to send Spofford to Europe to inspect the libraries he was expected to surpass. Swamped by the incoming copyright receipts, the Librarian demurred, but in 1882 he persuaded Senator Voorhees, Chairman of the Joint Select Committee, to send Smithmeyer in his place. Spofford presented the architect with a list of specific features to examine (alcove and shelf arrangement, ventilation systems, provision for readers, etc.) and asked that he visit the British Museum and the "national libraries at Paris, Berlin, Munich, and Vienna, and the new library at Rome." Smithmeyer followed the Librarian's suggestions, taking care-

---

[12] John L. Smithmeyer, "The National Library Building—The Proposed Plan," *LJ*, v. 6 (April, 1881), p. 77–81. William F. Poole, "The Construction of Library Buildings," *LJ*, v. 6 (April, 1881), p. 69–77.

ful notes about each library and preparing, upon his return, a pamphlet entitled "Suggestions on Library Architecture, American and Foreign." The pamphlet served as a rebuttal to the views on library architecture expressed by Poole, who had protested directly to Congress about Smithmeyer's proposed building.

Shortly thereafter, Spofford made his personal views known on the Smithmeyer-Poole controversy. While Spofford did not disagree that efficiency in library architecture was more important than appearance, he wrote that Poole's plan was "wholly unsuited to a National Library" since a building "of national importance" should never be "dwarfed to the dimensions of a prolonged series of packing boxes." Poole was chagrined to learn that most librarians agreed with Spofford, or at least were willing to trust him. The general view was voiced in an editorial in the *Library Journal:* "Any building that is large enough will be better than the present overcrowded quarters. Whether the proposed plan is the best possible or not, it is no slight recommendation that it has satisfied the Librarian of Congress in many years brooding over it." [13] Convinced that he lost because he started his campaign against a monumental Library of Congress building too late, Poole began his next crusade—opposition to the proposed new Boston Public Library building—early and with his usual enthusiasm.

Having gained at least unofficial approval of Smithmeyer's design from both Congress and the library profession, Spofford once again turned to the problem of a site for the structure. The delay in Congress had narrowed the choice by eliminating Judiciary Square, near Fifth and G Streets, N.W., as a potential site. That location was, about 1882, reserved for the Pension Office.

At this time the most astonishing proposal of all came briefly under consideration. The Joint Select Committee, acting through Spofford, asked Montgomery Meigs, who had been Engineer in Charge of the Capitol from 1853 to 1859, if it were feasible to raise the dome of the Capitol fifty feet "in order to secure additional space in and near the rotunda for the Library." A negative reply from Meigs ended all speculation about extending the Capitol in any direction to house the Library.

Congressional attention once again focused on Senator Morrill's proposed East Capitol Street site. But the delay continued. The *New York Times* complained that "the backwardness of Congress about making an appropriation for the national library is as confusing as it

---

[13] *LJ*, v. 9 (Nov., 1884), p. 188.

is irritating. This apathy shows how much the men who give character to Congress are out of relation to the culture of the country."

On April 15, 1886, the matter was settled; Congress approved a bill to erect a new Library of Congress on the East Capitol Street site utilizing the Italian Renaissance design of Smithmeyer & Pelz. While Spofford was the driving force for a separate building, Senators Morrill and Voorhees were the legislative catalysts, and the three men held a small celebration of their own in the Senate chamber, an event described by Morrill's biographer:

> ... when he [Morrill] saw his bill triumphantly passed by both houses, he was overjoyed. Many of his fellow Senators knew how dear the measure was to his heart and the announcement of its passage gave rise to a pleasing little scene on the floor which the reporters described with evident delight. "In his excitement and joy at the realization of his hopes [Morrill] forgot the dignity that is his most conspicuous characteristic and tossed a kiss across the chamber to Senator Voorhees ... who kissed his hand in return." Senators waved their hands to the reporters' gallery. "A page was hurried off with the news to Librarian Spofford, who came ambling in and the three men [Morrill, Voorhees, Spofford] embraced each other warmly." There were general congratulations and handshakings, and then the little love feast ended.[14]

But one final exertion from the determined Librarian was required. An additional $35,000 for the purchase of the site became necessary, and on the last day of the Congressional session the appropriation still had not been approved. Spofford spent three hours on the floor of the House promoting it, "watching its chances, removing objections," and taking care of possible opponents. It finally was approved, and Spofford described the rest of his last-minute efforts in a letter to a friend:

> At once I hurried it back to the Senate to be enrolled—got the signatures of Sherman and Carlisle, and was made special messenger to carry the bill to the White House for the President's signature. This goal was reached at 3:10 p.m. and both Houses had resolved to adjourn *sine die* at 4. Mr. Cleveland was at lunch, but I sent the bill down to him by Mr. Pruden, the Secretary, and it came back in fifteen minutes with Grover Cleveland's name "approved." This saved the day—and I am again the happiest man in Washington—the last obstacle in the way of the Library Building being removed.[15]

---

[14] William B. Parker, *The Life and Public Services of Justin Smith Morrill* (Boston, 1924), p. 321–322.

[15] Quoted in Florence P. Spofford, "Reminiscences of Her Father," *Records of the Columbia Historical Society*, v. 12 (Washington, 1909), p. 179.

Library of Congress

The new Library of Congress about 1897.

The dome and Torch of Learning at its apex were gilded with 23-carat gold. Horace Greenough's statue of George Washington is in the right foreground.

To supervise the construction, the new law provided a three-man commission: Spofford, Architect of the Capitol Edward Clark, and Secretary of the Interior Lucius Q. C. Lamar. The commission also selected the exact lots on which the building was to be situated and hired Smithmeyer as architect. Unfortunately, the lines of authority between Smithmeyer and the commission were unclear and a dispute between Smithmeyer and Clark erupted almost immediately concerning the clearing of the site and the excavation. One of the controversial points was the exact placement of the structure. Smithmeyer insisted that it be situated in the center of the west portion of the site, which was directly in the path of Pennsylvania Avenue. Clark endorsed a plan submitted to him by landscape architect Frederick Law Olmsted, which showed "how the building might be placed on the reservation without shutting out the whole view of the Capitol building from Pennsylvania Avenue—the main approach from Capitol Hill." Smithmeyer's view prevailed on this point, but the architect was soon involved in another controversy, this one with the contractor who was to furnish the cement for the building's foundations. This conflict delayed all work on the Library for more than six months, and Congress and the public grew impatient. Senator Morrill complained to Secretary Lamar: "I really had hoped to see the building completed within my lifetime, but now I fear I never shall see it done." [16]

---

[16] Morrill to Lamar, Aug. 8, 1887, LC Archives.

Smithmeyer had made enemies during his long association with the Library building, and his Congressional foes sided with the cement contractor against him. It was rumored that Smithmeyer had "padded" the construction payroll and that he had deceived Congress with a low cost estimate for the construction of the building. The pressures on Smithmeyer were intense; he was caught between an inexperienced commission which did not always support him and several Congressmen who both criticized him and tried to obtain jobs for their friends on his payroll. The construction delay made matters worse, and a Congressional investigation was instigated.[17]

The inquiry showed severe conflicts within the building commission. While he defended Smithmeyer, Spofford confessed that he was too occupied with his duties as Librarian to be an effective member. William F. Vilas, who had replaced Lamar as Secretary of the Interior and as a commission member, favored turning the construction of the Library over to the U.S. Army Corps of Engineers. Clark, admitting that relations between himself and Smithmeyer were "by no means cordial," wanted to resign. Shortly after the hearings started, the House of Representatives voted to stop construction. This action was protested both in the press and in the Senate, but the House stood firm. *Nation* magazine joined the attack on the architect: Smithmeyer was "incompetent and known to be more of a lobbyist than a builder" and the deficiencies in his plan had been exposed by "Mr. Poole, the Chicago librarian." The *American Architect and Building News*, however, accurately countered the latter argument:

> ... To bring up the ideas of Mr. Poole of Chicago, as a reason for depriving Mr. Smithmeyer of his great commission is both unfair and mean. All architects know that Mr. Poole and Mr. Spofford ... differ radically in their ideas of the proper arrangement of such a building, and if Mr. Smithmeyer, as is not denied, followed the programme which Mr. Spofford, both as head of the Library itself and a member of the Commission imposed upon him, he has only done his duty.[18]

The controversy focused on Smithmeyer, not on the need for the building. That battle had been won. According to the Washington *Evening Star:* "In the Senate the sentiment in favor of carrying forward the construction of the building is unanimous, and in the House, it is said, the opposition [is] more against Mr. Smithmeyer than from any spirit of hostility to the Library enterprise."

---

[17] For details see U.S. Congress. House. *Special Committee to Investigate Contracts for the Construction of the Library Building.* Congressional Library Building (Washington, Govt. Print. Off., 1889) 144 p. (50th Cong., 2d sess. House. Report no. 3795).

[18] *American Architect and Building News*, v. 24 (Aug. 11, 1888), p. 57.

On October 2, 1888, an agreement was reached. The three-man commission was abolished, Smithmeyer was fired, and construction of the new Library of Congress building was placed under the direction of Brigadier General Thomas Lincoln Casey (1831–1896), Chief of the U.S. Army Corps of Engineers, who was asked to submit a plan for a building which would cost no more than $4,000,000. Casey was the engineer who had successfully completed the construction of the Washington Monument and, more recently, the State, War, and Navy Building adjacent to the White House. The Superintendent of Construction, in charge of day-to-day operations, would be civil engineer Bernard R. Green (1843–1914), Casey's assistant in the work on both the Washington Monument and the State, War, and Navy Building.

With a reputation as an efficient businessman who kept costs down to a reasonable level, Casey was popular with economy-minded Congressmen. There appears to have been an understanding between the General and his friends in Congress; a popular magazine noted that Casey accepted the job with the proviso that construction money would be provided as needed and that Congress would not "interfere unduly" with his management of the construction. The General decided to submit not one but two plans for a new Library: the $4,000,000 structure required by the 1888 law and one for a more spacious $6,000,000 building. Both plans were prepared by Paul J. Pelz, Smithmeyer's former partner, whom Casey shrewdly employed as the new architect. While Smithmeyer had lost his job, his monumental concept of a national library building was not altered, for Pelz retained in his drawings the general features and the Italian Renaissance design of the 1886 Smithmeyer & Pelz plan. Casey and Green would soon expand and embellish that concept.

Casey immediately turned to Spofford for help, asking the Librarian to list "the desired specifications relating to space required for various purposes" in the building. Spofford's detailed reply, published in the report containing Casey's two plans, urged the adoption of the larger plan: "as the Library will ultimately require for its proper accommodation every foot of space embraced in the original plan adopted by Congress in 1886, i.e. a building measuring 460 by 310 feet, it is greatly to be desired that the structure now authorized by the amended law should be constructed upon lines so far in harmony with the original plan as to admit of finally carrying it out in its full extent." Spofford listed a total of 15 points which needed consideration, including details such as the minimum dimensions of each room. Books were to be shelved in a combination of the alcove and stack systems. Spofford's attention focused on the central reading room,

Library of Congress

Bernard R. Green (1843–1914), Superintendent of Construction for the Library of Congress building.

Photograph by F. B. Johnston.

which he wanted arranged in the most efficient manner possible. The Librarian had his own idea as to how that room should be decorated:

> The walls of this public reading room, lighted by a glass dome, should be lined with books from floor to ceiling; and it is suggested that the aesthetic effects most in harmony with the place and its object will be better realized by surrounding the readers with tier above tier of volumes, in rich and variegated bindings, than by any attempt at crass architectural display.

This was the national library and, apart from the central reading room and the basic functional apparatus, the unique features of the Library and its collections should be displayed:

> An art gallery has always been contemplated, for the arrangement and exhibition of the many thousands of objects of the graphic arts and the arts of design now buried in immense piles in the basement of the Capitol and elsewhere in the Library. This should be a fine and imposing room, of some 300 feet in length by about 50 feet in width.[19]

There was no need for Spofford to worry about General Casey's preference between the two plans. By completing the Washington Monument and the State, War, and Navy Building, Casey had personally stimulated the development of "monumental architecture" in post-Civil War Washington, and the Library of Congress presented him with yet another opportunity. He favored the larger structure, as did most Congressmen. With Smithmeyer gone and construction safely in the hands of the U.S. Army, the Library of Congress building once again became a matter of national pride. The new American national library would surpass the libraries of Europe in every detail. The Washington *Evening Star* editorialized that only the $6,000,000 building would be "creditable to the Republic." On March 2, 1889, in the midst of preparations for the inaugural of President Benjamin Harrison, Congress overwhelmingly approved the construction of the larger edifice. It could not come soon enough for Spofford who, according to local newspapers, was being "wedged in closer and closer" in spite of the transfer of the newspaper files into eight "dark rooms" beneath the Capitol.

Construction started shortly thereafter and progress was rapid. Congress was pleased to have Casey in charge, and Bernard Green personally managed to quell any fears still remaining in the library profession. Challenged by Spofford's insistence on rapid book service

---

[19] U.S. Army. Corps of Engineers. Letter from the Chief of Engineers of the Army Transmitting a Report Relative to the Construction of the Library. (Washington, Govt. Print. Off., 1888) 11 p. (50th Cong., 2d sess. House. Miscellaneous Doc. no. 12).

from the stack area, Green designed new steel bookstacks, nine tiers high, which were serviced by the first efficient library pneumatic tube and conveyor system in America. Green's impressive achievement earned him the gratitude of librarians and he was singled out for praise in a resolution of the American Library Association in October 1891:

> The American Library Association heartily congratulates the nation on the progress made toward the final completion of a worthy and adequate building for the national library, and its members especially felicitate their associate, the librarian of Congress, on the fact that in Capt. (sic) B. R. Green . . . he has a coadjutor who, as architect and engineer, has shown both the desire and the ability, in his modifications of the previous plans, to provide for practical library requirements, both in his general plans and in his novel and ingenious treatment of detail, such as shelving and transfer arrangements.[20]

Green's bookstacks were manufactured by the Snead & Company Iron Works of Louisville, Kentucky, which won a medal for its new product at the 1893 World's Columbian Exposition in Chicago.

COMPLETION AND DECORATION

In 1896 Congressional hearings on the reorganization of the Library of Congress, necessitated by the impending move into the new building, Spofford asserted that his involvement in the construction of the building ended in 1888 when the three-man commission was abolished and the U.S. Army Corps of Engineers took over. While the Librarian's formal responsibilities ended at this point, Casey and Green consulted with him constantly and followed his suggestions regarding the arrangement of the central reading room, the allocation of space for various administrative units, and on other questions concerning the "library apparatus." Further, Spofford made a unique contribution to the elaborate decorative scheme instituted by Casey and Green, ornamentation with which the Librarian was not completely in sympathy but which undeniably enhanced the national character of the building.

The extensive interior decoration, which combined sculpture, mural painting, and architecture on a scale unsurpassed in any other American public building, was possible only because General Casey and Bernard Green admirably lived up to their reputations as efficient construction engineers, completing the building for a sum sub-

---

[20] *LJ*, v. 16 (Dec., 1891), p. 117–118. For details concerning Green and the development of the steel bookstack see Charles H. Baumann's *The Influence of Angus Snead Mac-donald and the Snead Bookstack on Library Architecture* (Metuchen, N.J., 1972), p. 65–75.

Library of Congress

Photograph of the laying of the cornerstone for the Library of Congress, August 28, 1890, at 3 p. m.

Bernard R. Green is on the left, supervising the laying of the cornerstone. Ainsworth Rand Spofford and a companion are in the right foreground.

stantially less than that appropriated by Congress. Embellishment on a grand scale had no place in the original plans. In April of 1886, Smithmeyer had explained to a reporter that the building generally would be "void of lavish ornamentation," with the use of sculpture "restricted to the spandrils of the main entrance doors and to portions of the attics, with few minor parts, such as keystones for example." Paintings were not mentioned. A fountain in front of the Library appears in plans drawn by architect Pelz in 1888 and, under the direction of Bernard Green, in 1891 thirty-three carved heads representing the races of mankind were utilized as keystones in the first story pavilion windows. When it became apparent in 1892 that funds for additional "artistic enrichment" would be available out of the original appropriation, Casey and Green seized the opportunity and turned an already remarkable building into a cultural monument.

The two engineers were infused with a nationalism which complemented Spofford's national library aspirations. Their efforts probably went further than Spofford would personally have preferred. The Librarian originally specified that the dome over the Library's reading room should not exceed 70 feet, to avoid competing with the dome of the Capitol, and all the early designs complied with his instructions. Between 1889 and 1893, however, Casey and Green raised the dome of the Library to a height of 195 feet and covered it with 23-carat gold leaf. While Spofford always wanted the national library to serve an educational purpose, providing the American people a cultural monument, Casey and Green felt the Library should also have an inspirational function.

Known primarily for his ability to keep construction costs to a minimum, General Casey also displayed a definite preference for rich interiors in his buildings. He encouraged Richard von Ezdorf's ornate baroque designs in the wings of the State, War, and Navy building. But it was Bernard Green, with architect Edward Pearce Casey, General Casey's son, who ultimately exerted the greatest influence on the Library's decorative scheme. Green viewed the interior art work as an essential part of the building's "architectural composition," a component necessary "to fully and consistently carry out the monumental design and purpose of the building." He insisted on employing only American artists and commissions were given to 20 sculptors and 23 painters, all American citizens, though a number resided in France. Green proudly pointed out that the finished building was "a product of American talent and skill in architecture and art." The *Library Journal* explained that the engineers in charge of construction had wanted to give American artists "an unprecedented opportunity to display their capacity both in ideal and portrait figures." [21]

Edward Pearce Casey (1864–1940) was hired as architect of the Library in late 1892, replacing Paul J. Pelz. The younger Casey was well-qualified to aid in the planning and design of a national showpiece, particularly one which was to reflect the taste of the period. After graduating from Columbia University in 1888 with a degree in civil engineering, he served a brief apprenticeship with McKim, Mead & White when that firm was constructing the Boston Public Library. He soon left for Paris, where he spent the next two years studying architecture at the Ecole des Beaux Arts, a school which had great influence on American architects and architecture. Casey returned to New York where he entered private practice for a short period before his father brought him to Washington. Once at the Library, he and Bernard Green became good friends and found themselves in close agreement regarding the building's interior design and decoration.

---

[21] For additional information about Green and his contributions to the construction and decoration of the Library, see Helen-Anne Hilker's "Monument to Civilization," *QJ*, v. 29 (Oct., 1972), p. 234–266.

Casey formulated most of those designs himself and actively supervised all artistic decoration. His chief assistants were sculptor Albert Weinert and Elmer E. Garnsey, an artist who had supervised the decorative work in the Boston Public Library and at the Chicago World's Columbian Exposition in 1893. Casey's assistant in charge of mosaic and glass work, Herman T. Schladermundt, had also participated in the Chicago Exposition. Charles McKim, Edward Pearce Casey's mentor, provided yet another personal link between the Boston Public Library, the World's Columbian Exposition, and the Library; instrumental in the planning and design of the first two undertakings, McKim also advised Casey on the selection of painters for the Library's interior.

The Boston Public Library and the Chicago Exposition provided the two Caseys and Bernard Green with examples of cooperative artistic endeavors combining architecture, sculpture, and painting. Their effort at the Library of Congress particularly resembled the

Library of Congress

The West Facade of the Library of Congress, May 22, 1895.

The writers selected by Ainsworth Rand Spofford for portrait busts in the portico are, left to right, Emerson, Irving, Goethe, Franklin, Maccaulay, Hawthorne, and Scott. Demosthenes and Dante are not shown.

Ainsworth Rand Spofford and the Library of Congress 497

Exposition: it was an artistic venture on the same massive scale and, for the most part, in the same Beaux-arts classical style. Most of the artists who contributed works to the Library building either helped design the imperial facades of the White City or exhibited their works within its pavilions; moreover, many of them repeated the idealistic themes and togaed likenesses they produced in Chicago.

Augustus St. Gaudens, J. A. Q. Ward, and Olin L. Warner, representing the National Sculpture Society, selected the sculptors who participated in the Columbian Exposition. Less than five months after the Exposition closed, the three met with General Casey and Bernard Green to "plan the sculpture" and select the individual sculptors for the Library. On June 18, 1894, as the building's superstructure neared completion, individual commissions for specific works were offered to twenty well-known American sculptors "on behalf of the United States." In a form letter accompanying each offer, Green succinctly explained that "the price of $5,000 for each figure or statue is governed by the limit of funds available for all of the sculpture required in the Building and it is trusted that you will find yourself able to accept the commission referred to and execute it essentially within the time stated, one and a half years, with justice to yourself and the subject." [22] George Barnard was the only sculptor in the original group of twenty who turned down the offer. Additional sculptors received commissions at a later date and the final list was so impressive that the critic Montgomery Schuyler wrote that no important American sculptor was conspicuous by his absence.[23]

General Casey, his son, and Bernard Green exercised military-like control over the work. Circulars were periodically sent to those providing figures for the Main Reading Room, informing each sculptor of changes in requirements and usually urging greater attention to the deadlines for submitting sketches and models. The artistic merit of each piece was discussed, since the administrators had the final word. For example, Paul W. Bartlett, who held commissions for three figures, learned in a letter signed by General Casey that "there is no improvement to be suggested concerning the figure of *Law*, but I want to say regarding *Columbus* that, while it is very good and has a

---

[22] Green to Paul W. Bartlett, June 18, 1894, Paul W. Bartlett MSS, Library of Congress.
[23] Montgomery Schuyler, "The New Library of Congress," *Scribner's*, v. 21 (June, 1897), p. 726. In his annual report as Superintendent of Construction for 1896 (54th Cong., 2d sess. House Doc. no. 20), Green lists the sculptors who "furnished" works for the Library building. They were: Herbert Adams, Paul W. Bartlett, Theodore Bauer, George Bissell, John J. Boyle, Charles E. Dallin, John Donoghue, Daniel C. French, John Flanagan, Augustus St. Gaudens, Louis St. Gaudens, J. Scott Hartley, Frederick MacMonnies, Philip Martiny, Charles H. Neihaus, R. Hinton Perry, Edward C. Potter, Bela L. Pratt, F. W. Ruckstuhl, J. Q. A. Ward, Olin L. Warner, and Albert Weinert.

good deal of character the figure is so broad or *large round,* and the coat so short comparatively as to seem a little droll, a tendency however that you certainly will have no difficulty in correcting." The anxious Casey, never missing an opportunity to prod, concluded his letter: "How soon may we expect to receive your sketch of *Michaelangelo?*" [24] In fact, only six of the 18 figures and statues commissioned for the Main Reading Room arrived before the January 1, 1896 deadline, but all except Bartlett's Columbus and Michaelangelo were in place a year later. Bartlett was so delinquent that he received a special admonishment from Green, who described the incident in his daily journal of operations:

> *November 21, 1897* Bronze statue of *Columbus* arrived at last... and so did the sculptor, Paul W. Bartlett, from Paris. I took him to task for his delay in fulfilling his contract of 3½ years ago and the fact this his third piece, *Michaelangelo,* is not yet even modeled. This, he said, he could not stand and precipitately left the room and finally left the building without returning to the office.[25]

The Michaelangelo was not received and placed in its designated location in the Main Reading Room until late in December of 1898, more than a year after the Library had opened its doors to the public.

Spofford was asked to select the subjects for the portrait statues executed by Bartlett and the other sculptors. The nine writers he selected for busts for the building's west facade were, quite simply, his personal favorites: Demosthenes, Emerson, Irving, Goethe, Franklin, Maccaulay, Hawthorne, Scott, and Dante. For the Main Reading Room, Spofford was asked to pick subjects for sixteen bronze portrait statues to be placed on the balustrade; the statues were to depict men considered "illustrious" in the "eight characteristic features of civilized life and thought" featured in the Room's iconographic scheme. Each of those features, in turn, was represented by a symbolic female figure. The symbolic figures and bronze portrait statues depict: Religion, Moses and St. Paul; Commerce, Columbus and Robert Fulton; History, Herodotus and Gibbon; Art, Michaelangelo and Beethoven; Philosophy, Plato and Bacon; Poetry, Homer and Shakespeare; Law, Solon and Chancellor Kent; and Science, Newton and Joseph Henry. Eight inscriptions, each appropriate to the subject represented by a symbolic figure, were chosen by President Charles Eliot of Harvard and placed above each figure. (Eliot had also

---

[24] Thomas L. Casey to Bartlett, Feb. 15, 1895, Paul W. Bartlett MSS, Library of Congress.
[25] Bernard R. Green, "Journal of Operations on the Building for the Library of Congress, October 4, 1888–August 19, 1902," LC Archives.

Library of Congress

The House of Representatives Reading Room in the Library of Congress shortly before completion.

Above the fireplace is Frederick Dielman's mosaic panel *History*.

Library of Congress

Frederick Dielman's mosaic panel *History*.

furnished inscriptions for the Water Gate and the Transportation Building at the Chicago Exposition.) Spofford selected the quotations used in the Pavilion of the Seals, the second-story pavilion in the Library's northeast corner. According to the anonymous author of an article about the Library in the February 1917 issue of *Art World,* other inscriptions and the numerous "lists of names of individuals celebrated in various fields" which cover the Library's walls and ceilings "were very frequently supplied by the artists themselves as appropriate to their decorations." The same author counted, in all, 60 "separate compositions of sculpture" and 112 "pieces of composition" by specially-commissioned painters in the Library.[26]

Selection of the painters to execute the murals desired by General Casey and Green in the Library's corridors, corner pavilions, and within the dome of the Main Reading Room, proved to be a difficult and time-consuming task. Green told a friend that James Whistler was the first artist asked to "oversee" the mural painting; Whistler was also asked to "furnish what he would" for the building, but the artist stated "that he once worked for Uncle Sam—as a draughtsman in the Coast Survey—and didn't want any more of it." Green next approached Edwin A. Abbey, "whose paintings at the Boston Public Library set a standard," and then John Sargent, but neither accepted his offer, so Green and General Casey "just went ahead and hired artists on our own." [27] Contemporary accounts mention also John LaFarge, first as head of a "commission" of painters and later as a participating artist, but his work, like that of Whistler, Abbey, and Sargent, is absent from the Library. In 1894 Edward Pearce Casey asked Charles McKim to review "a list of painters" who were under consideration for Library commissions and McKim apparently lent his advice.[28] In January of 1895 the first group of commissions was offered; the recipients were Edwin H. Blashfield, Kenyon Cox, William L. Dodge, Carl Gutherz, George W. Maynard, Edward Simmons, and Elihu Vedder, all participants at the Columbian Exposition. Commissions were offered to other artists for the next 18 months.[29]

---

[26] *Art World,* v. 1 (Feb., 1917), p. 358. See Small's *Handbook* for details regarding most of the Library's decorative features.

[27] Quoted in William Warner Bishop, "The Library of Congress, 1907–15: Fragments of Autobiography," *Library Quarterly,* v. 18 (Jan., 1948), p. 18.

[28] McKim to C. S. Reinhart, Oct. 8, 1894, Charles McKim MSS, Library of Congress.

[29] Green's complete list of painters who contributed works to the building is as follows: John W. Alexander, G. R. Barse, Frank W. Benson, Edwin H. Blashfield, Kenyon Cox, Frederick Dielman, Robert L. Dodge, William L. Dodge, Carl Gutherz, Walter McEwen, George W. Maynard, Gari Melchers, Charles Sprague Pearce, Robert Reid,

Library of Congress

Edwin H. Blashfield's painting *The Evolution of Civilization* in the collar of the Main Reading Room dome.

The twelve figures represent "the twelve countries, or epochs, which have contributed most to the development of present-day civilization in this country."

In his *Handbook of the New Library of Congress,* Herbert Small refers to Blashfield's paintings in the collar and lantern of the dome of the Main Reading Room as "the noblest and most inspiring in the Library" and as the artistic work which puts "the final touch of completion on the whole decorative scheme of the interior." Blashfield's subject was "The Evolution of Civilization," consisting of twelve figures "representing the twelve countries, or epochs, which

---

Herman Schladermundt, Walter Shirlaw, Edward Simmons, W. B. Van Ingen, Elihu Vedder, and Henry Oliver Walker (54th Cong., 2d sess. House Doc. no. 20).

have contributed most to the development of present-day civilization in this country." Chronologically arranged, the figures depict: Egypt (Written Records), Judea (Religion), Greece (Philosophy), Rome (Administration), Islam (Physics), The Middle Ages (Modern Languages), Italy (Fine Arts), Germany (Art of Printing), Spain (Discovery), England (Literature) France (Emancipation), and America (Science). The face of the figure representing Germany is modeled after the features of General Casey.

According to *Art World,* "to better insure a harmony in the result it was determined as far as possible to have all the painting in each hall or compartment executed by one individual." George W. Maynard received a commission for all the paintings in the Pavilion of the Discoverers at the Library's southeast corner. Maynard's instructions from Green were explicit: "The subjects for the four tympanums will be respectively 'Adventure,' 'Discovery,' 'Conquest,' and 'Civilization,' and for the dome a recall and incorporation of the same subjects." Other painters apparently were free to suggest their own subjects, but Green and the Caseys made the final choice. The amount of money paid each artist varied according to the number executed, their location, and their size. The highest fee ($8,000) went for the corner pavilions (in addition to Maynard, the artists were Robert L. Dodge Pavilion of the Elements; William B. Van Ingen, Pavilion of the Seals; and William de L. Dodge, Pavilion of Art and Science) and to Walter McEwen and Edward Simmons for their first-floor corridors honoring The Greek Heroes and The Muses, respectively. At least one artist, Charles Sprague Pearce, managed to negotiate an increase in his commission from Green. After signing a contract for a series of murals in the north corridor adjacent to the Great Hall (then called the Staircase Hall), Pearce proposed several subjects. On April 13 1895, Green informed the artist that the approved topics were: Labor, Rest, Study, Recreation, Religion, and, for the large tympanum at the east end, The Family. Shortly thereafter, Pearce asked for an increase in his fee from $4,000 to $6,000, since the agreed upon paintings would cover a larger area than originally planned. Green reluctantly agreed to a $500 increase, but scolded the artist in a statement which reveals much about the engineer's attitude toward the Library: "As a rule, the artists employed on the Building are believed to be sacrificing something for the opportunity afforded them." When considered as a group, the mural painters were more responsive to Green's deadlines than were the sculptors. All the paintings were finished by May 28, 1897, when Elihu Vedder's 15-foot marble mosaic of Minerva was

Library of Congress

A 1961 photograph of the Main Reading Room.

Portrait statues of men selected by Ainsworth Rand Spofford as "illustrious" in the "characteristic features of civilized life and thought" can be seen along the balustrade of the upper gallery. Photograph by Peter C. Costas.

put into place near the entrance of the Visitor's Gallery overlooking the Main Reading Room.[30]

The total cost of the mural and decorative painting, the sculpture, and the three massive bronze doors at the main entrance (representing Tradition, Writing, and Printing), was $364,000. In addition, Hinton

---

[30] Green to Maynard, Jan. 12, 1895; Pearce to Green, March 16, 1895 and April 26, 1895; Green to Pearce, April 13, 1895 and May 15, 1895, "Building of the Library of Congress," GAO Survey 12, National Archives.

Perry's 50-foot wide fountain, depicting a scene in the court of Neptune and described as "the most lavishly ornamental" fountain in the country, cost $22,000. The price of gilding the dome, including the flame of the Torch of Learning at its apex, was $3,800. Yet, as Bernard Green reported to Congress in late 1896, the building was still completed for a sum $200,000 less than the total Congressional authorization of approximately six and a half million dollars.[31]

As the building neared completion, Spofford reported a plan for the reorganization of the Library to Congress. His 16-page special report of December 3, 1895 is essentially an extension of the basic ideas he expressed in his 1872 annual report. He now advocated nine separate departments: printed books, periodicals, manuscripts, maps and charts, works of art, cataloging, binding, copyright, and that of the superintendent of the building. He urged a considerable expansion of the Library's staff in the new building, pointing out that its size (38) compared unfavorably to that of the Boston Public Library (140) which had "two-thirds as many volumes and no copyright business" and to that of the British Museum which "with no copyright business and no circulation" employed "220 attendants in its eight departments, besides 160 engineers, electricians, laborers, window cleaners, police, etc." In late 1896 the Joint Committee on the Library held hearings on the reorganization of the Library in which it took extensive testimony not only from Spofford and Green but also from nine distinguished librarians from throughout the country, including Herbert Putnam, a future Librarian of Congress, and Melvil Dewey. In the hearings it was apparent that the Library of Congress was considered to be the American national library, although one in need of many improvements. Appended to the 279-page volume of hearings, published in 1897, is a table prepared by Spofford which compares the "proposed force and expenditure in the Library of Congress in its new building . . . with similar service in the library of the British Museum, the National Library of France, the Royal Library of Prussia, and the Boston Public Library." [32] Another special report from Spofford, entitled "Use of the Congressional Library" and dated January 18, 1897, lists the collections and functions which the new building would have to accommodate. On February 19, 1897, Congress approved a reorganization plan incorporating Spofford's recommendations and increasing the Library's staff from 42 to 108.

---

[31] *Report of the Superintendent of Construction for the Building of the Library of Congress,* December 7, 1896 (54th Cong., 2d sess. House Doc. no. 20), p. 3.

[32] U.S. Congress. Joint Committee on the Library. Condition of the Library of Congress. (Washington, Govt. Print. Off., 1897) 279 p. (54th Cong., 2d sess. Senate Report no. 1573).

The new Library of Congress building opened to the public on November 1, 1897. For months popular magazines had carried articles about the structure and few visitors were disappointed. Here was an American library building to match or surpass the finest in Europe. On November 25, 1897, more than 4,700 visitors toured the library during special Thanksgiving Day hours. Some reactions were estatic: Joseph E. Robinson of Washington informed the Librarian that "not until I stand before the judgement seat of God do I ever expect to see this building transcended." On July 8, 1898, when the building was illuminated at night as an experiment, more than 13,000 persons came to view it.

Senator Morrill, who had played such a crucial role in the building's history, appreciated the "rare merit" of the artistic decorations, and was convinced that the "grandeur and the felitious finish" of the Main Reading Room and the Great Hall would "be likely to long remain unrivalled in this or any other country." Montgomery Schuyler praised the structure as "a national possession, an example of a great public building monumentally conceived, faithfully built, and worthily adorned." Fellow critic Charles Caffin hailed the building as evidence of the "brilliant period" into which the United States had moved, "not only in arts and sciences, but in material and social advancement." Caffin also saw in the building the beginning of a "distinctively American School of Mural Painting," a "pre-eminently democratic movement" through which art, sanctioned by government, could become "an idealized embodiment of the national life." Speaker of the House of Representatives Joseph G. Cannon called the library the best public building in Washington, adding: "I am proud of it. My constituents are proud of it. . . . It is a great show building. It is our building and worth the money." [33]

The enthusiastic reaction to the building from the public, critics, and Members of Congress was not only gratifying to Spofford but useful: admiration of the Library as a national showplace focused attention on the institution and helped it to attain its unique status. The most significant aspect of the new building for the aging Librarian was the 326,000 square feet of floor space available for the "national collections" which he had been accumulating for three decades. For the first time those collections could be efficiently organized and serviced. With ample space for growth, an expanded staff, and support from a well-pleased Congress, the Library of Congress could soon undertake the national services (inter-library loans,

[33] Charles Caffin, "The Architecture, Sculpture, and Painting," in Small, *Handbook*, p. 113–122. The Cannon quote is from Charles Moore, comp., *The Promise of American Architecture* (Washington, 1905), p. 62.

Library of Congress

The Grand Stair Hall of the Library of Congress.

Most of the sculpture was executed by Philip Martiny. The inscription just above the archway in the lower right of the photograph reads:

ERECTED UNDER THE ACTS OF CONGRESS OF
APRIL 15, 1886 OCTOBER 2, 1888 AND MARCH 2, 1889 BY
BRIG. GEN. THOS. LINCOLN CASEY
CHIEF OF ENGINEERS U.S.A.

BERNARD R. GREEN SUPT. AND ENGINEER
JOHN L. SMITHMEYER ARCHITECT
PAUL J. PELZ ARCHITECT
EDWARD PEARCE CASEY ARCHITECT

LIBRARY OF CONGRESS

cataloging, and classification) expected of a truly national library. Amherst librarian William I. Fletcher recognized the full impact of the new structure in "Our National Library" in the February 13, 1897 issue of *The Critic:* "With the occupancy of this magnificent building, the Library of Congress should enter on a new career. It should now become in name, as it must in fact, the National Library."

The completion of that task would be left to others. On July 1, 1897, President William McKinley appointed John Russell Young, a journalist and diplomat, as the new Librarian of Congress. The 71-year old Spofford left the post gracefully and became Chief Assistant Librarian with the knowledge that the National Library for which he had "appealed, argued, and prayed" for 26 years was now a reality.

November 24, 1873, The Precise Moment of Impressionism: Claude Monet's "The Bridge at Argenteuil" at the National Gallery of Art in Washington, D.C.

CHARLES MERRILL MOUNT

Neither the birth nor origins of any great artistic innovation can be pin-pointed so exactly as Impressionism. Displayed at the National Gallery in Washington, on loan from Mr. and Mrs. Paul Mellon, is *The Bridge at Argenteuil* which, more than any other canvas, constitutes an exact witness of that moment. The greatest alteration in artistic methods since the Renaissance is taking place on that canvas. A second version of the same work belonging to the Louvre Museum, Paris, repainted in Monet's studio, shows a full-fledged utterance of this wildly melodic art. Between the two canvases lies the greatest artistic discovery made by a single man. It broke through barriers to an art totally new, producing pictures whose unexpected reality and hallucinatory power persuaded the world it was undergoing a revelatory experience.

Claude Monet is thus among the really heroic figures in the history of painting, one of those who wrestled with his times and imposed his personality on them. That he made history, not merely manipulated events, is undeniable. How remarkable that at the moment of his enormous discovery such a man was no more than a peddler, adrift between two dowries and his own class-conscious obsessions. His motives in fact were no more profound than to scramble for crumbs to feed his wife and child.

Any prolonged study of art history demonstrates that decisive factors determining events frequently are an intermingling of personal, psychologic, and economic matters not among textbook ingredients.

Photograph from the author

The earliest known photograph of Claude Monet (1840–1926).

"The younger son of a prosperous merchant at Le Harve, all his life Monet felt his natural element to be the world of the bourgeoisie."

Charles Beard brilliantly showed in his *An Economic Interpretation of the Constitution* that persons will act for causes that are of overwhelming force, but hidden from history. Applied to the arts his penetration would discover, for example, that American painting was shaped by Gilbert Stuart who returned in 1793 for a reason so dissociated as the short three months session of the Irish Parliament, which did not allow him time each winter to ply his trade profitably.

Sir Anthony Van Dyck was forced onto his great international career, founding long portrait traditions in Italy, France, Holland, and England, through the suffocating dominance Rubens maintained in his native Antwerp. The great flowering of Rubens' own last years was owed to international politics and the diplomatic journeys he undertook to Spain and England: seeing again the great art of the past while receiving orders for the Whitehall ceiling and the Torre de la Parada, the confluence of new impulse with large commissions regenerated his art.

A most striking example is afforded by Claude Monet's personal response to bourgeois impulses and a peddler's existence. From his witches brew of psychic wounds and vaulting pride grew the artistic revolution we know as Impressionism. The younger son of a prosperous merchant at Le Havre, all his life Monet felt his natural element to be the world of the bourgeoisie. Few rag-tag members of the lower orders penetrated the circle of his friends. As a youth he shared quarters with Frederic Bazille, medical student and sometime painter, who lived on an allowance from wealthy landowner parents in France's richest province. Bazille's father was a Senator, just as Alfred Sisley's father was a wealthy merchant in the import-export trade.

Ludovic Napoleon, Viscount Lepic, son of the Emperor Napoleon III's aide-de-camp, was another in this youthful clique formed at the studio of Charles Gleyre. Renoir, impoverished son of a tailor at Limôge, was the sole representative of lower things. His presence is nonetheless explicable, for my recent delving into the prize-book at the Ecole des Beaux-Arts has demonstrated that Renoir was the only member of this circle to win prizes at the school's annual examinations.

How wounding to Monet's pride therefore that though in the difficult years of the 1860's he was a conscientious imitator of the prosperous Gustav Courbet, he sold few pictures. The figure compositions of this period represent his compulsive efforts to find fame at the Salon, that great annual art exhibition which was the most successful art salesroom ever devised. His relationship with Camille Léonie Doncieux, who at eighteen possessed a fetching choir-boy bloom, is

From the Collection of Mr. and Mrs. Paul Mellon
The Bridge at Argenteuil by Claude Monet.

"With his own quirky logic Monet formed a design by placing one black-hulled sailing craft in the foreground of his composition. Manet, a few feet to his right and closer to the bridge, copied all three craft." This picture is witness to the precise moment Impressionism was born.

inseparable from this obsession because she was the constant model essential for his Salon pictures. Indeed, it was at Easter 1865 when Monet left Paris for Chailly, near the Forest of Fountainbleau, to work on the most madly gigantesque of these dream masterpieces, that Camille left the security of her own bourgeois parental home to accompany him.

The corollaries to her decision were many, for their first years of unblessed liaison were a gothic horror sequence. Forced to abandon her shortly before the birth of their son in 1867, Monet left Camille lodged with a medical student instructed to realize his fee by disposing of the child. By their very irrelevance the beach scenes Monet then painted at his parents' summer home at St.-Adresse are harrowing documents. Equally passionate are the letters that flew to Bazille for funds, until at last, unable to bear the strain, Monet made his way to Paris where he rescued Camille and saved the child. His friends

Photograph from the author

A painting by Edouard Manet (1832–1883) at the same time and place as Monet's "The Bridge at Argenteuil."

"Though he saw Monet's finely modulated canvas grow beside him, Manet retained his own broad color washes and occasional rough scumbles.... Monet's canvas was gently observed modulations across an idyllic scene; Eduoard Manet produced a more brutal vision of industrial encroachment and belching smoke on the same riverbank."

Zacherie Astruc and Alfred Hatté undertook the delicate mission of going to the Mairie of the seventeenth arrondissement to report the birth. Parents' names were duly recorded as Oscar Claude Monet and Camille Léonie Doncieux, without the addition of that significant word *married,* which normally completes the line in every French register.

At twenty Camille had brought a son into the world, a sad treasure exhibiting his father's massively broad forehead, small ears, and pouting mouth. Retribution was prompt, for the previous May 28th, Antoine Pritelly, former *Receveur de Finance* to whom Camille's mother was sole heir (he may have been her natural father) had died at Reuil. That worthy bourgeois had been aware of Camille's defection from the path of virtue. In his will, written December 14, 1866, Pritelly eliminated all possibility that the needy Camille might profit

Photograph from the author

Inn at Chailly.
Le Cheval Blanc, the inn at Chailly where Camille accompanied Monet at Easter 1865, beginning the liaison that led to their marriage in 1870. Living on the second floor, Monet attempted in the stables across this cobbled court to paint the most madly gigantesque of his dream masterpieces. Camille was the necessary model.

from his fortune: "I give and bequeath to Madame Doncieux, née Léonie Françoise Manechalle, wife of Charles Claude Doncieux, the use during her life, and to her daughter Geneviève Françoise Doncieux ... the property that I possess" were words by which he disinherited Camille in favor of her younger sister.

That October Frederic Bazille returned to Paris from a holiday with his family at Montpellier and sold to his kinsman, the Commandant Lejosne, one of Monet's still-lifes stored in his studio. Two hundred francs immediately were realized and "M. Lejosne has [also] given me an appointment for this morning, and we have shown some works by Monet to several persons who are buying them," wrote Bazille. The artist and his little family meanwhile had settled out beyond Mantes on the river Seine, at Bonnieres. These sales arranged

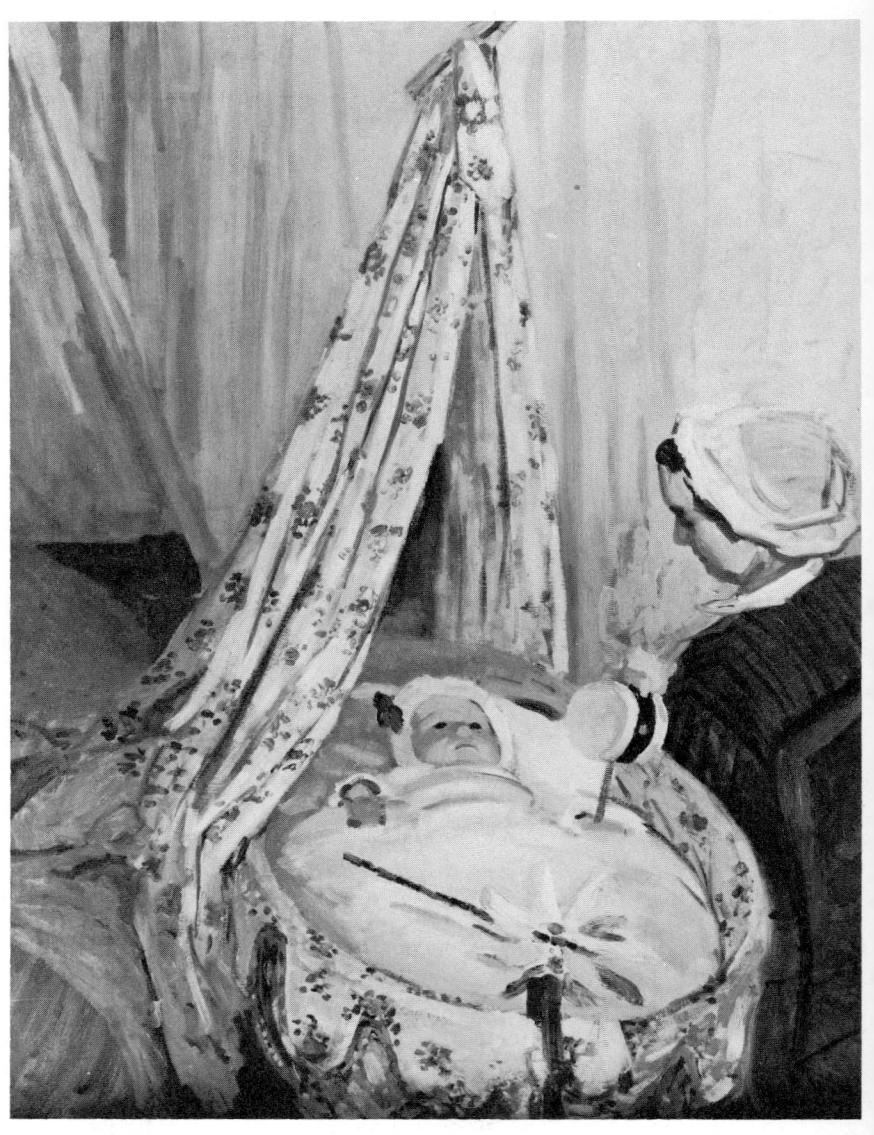

From the Collection of Mr. and Mrs. Paul Mellon

The Cradle, Camille with the Artist's Son Jean, by Claude Monet.

"...sales arranged by Bazille and Lejosne had enabled adoring parents to squander money for a lavish chintz-hung cradle. In its delightful comfort baby Jean appeared enormously pink and cozy, his pinwheel an elaborate festoon." Assuming the baby to be more than six months old, this work was painted in 1868.

The Precise Moment of Impressionism

From the Collection of Mr. and Mrs. Paul Mellon

Street scene in the town of Argenteuil by Claude Monet, 1872.

Camille and Jean walk on the sidewalk at the left. "Monet stood in the street, Sisley's position a more cautious one on the sidewalk to his right. Apart from quite tonality and fragmentary composition, it is the date '72' Sisley put on his canvas which informs us that Monet's picture was done so shortly after the house at Argenteuil was occupied in June that year."

by Bazille and Lejosne had enabled adoring parents to squander money for a lavish chintz-hung cradle. In its delightful comfort baby Jean appeared enormously pink and cozy, his pinwheel an elaborate festoon. Both parents derived a warm glow from the sight, for, in truth, another side of Monet's nature was emerging as by pity and love he moved towards a strange new nobility.

His large canvases stored, some with Bazille in Paris and others at his parents' houses in Le Havre and St.-Adresse, a few occasionally shown by the Paris dealers Cadart and Latouche, Monet and his little family found themselves moving among country inns. Their practice appears to have been to take shelter and food even when unable to pay. Put out of the inn at Fécamp Monet threw himself into the harbor. A pause full of death punctuated his anguish: then salt water sobered him for this act again was an irrelevancy. However much pain he bore he had to provide for Camille and their Jean.

Harboring sensations of guilt Bazille sent 100 francs. Pictures he shipped from Paris for Le Havre's *International Maritime Exhibition* were seen by Louis Gaudibert, at whose chateau an astonishingly

From the Collection of Mr. and Mrs. Paul Mellon

Interior by Claude Monet, 1872.

"Unaware that one of the lamplight interiors was the property of Mr. and Mrs. Paul Mellon, I illustrated it in my biography *Monet*... to convey that portion of a career which knew few such moments of peace. 'I am surrounded here by all that I love,' Monet wrote to Bazille from that same round table...' The identities of the persons have never been established. The woman with her back turned probably is Camille; the presence of only two coffee cups suggests that she may have posed both seated figures.

floreated image of Madame Gaudibert issued from Monet's brush. A large portrait of Camille exhibited at the previous Salon was parted with for the derisory sum of 800 francs, and following a rigged auction from which his creditors realized nothing Monet returned to Etretat, on the coast north of Le Havre, where he rented part of a divided summer residence on the tiny main street.

The cost of their quarters was small during winter's grim season, and here, the apparition of poverty for the first time banished, Monet and Camille played at being gentry. If their stage were a trifle compact every necessity was present for the comedy of manners into which they launched. Hung with lace curtains, lit by a glass-shaded oil lamp, their tiny dining-room by night became sitting-room too.

From the Collection of Mr. and Mrs. Paul Mellon

Camille a sa Fenetre, Argenteuil, by Claude Monet, 1873.

One of the surprises of the Mellon Collection is this sketch of Camille at a window of the Argenteuil house. Her cloche hat suggests that it was painted in 1873. Presumably it was among the Monet pictures which remained at Giverny after his death. The stamped signature at the lower left is of the type affixed by the artist's younger son Michel beginning about 1955.

Here was the fire by which they sat and if their unmarried state was reprehensible among the bourgeois people they emulated, the reticently bourgeois exterior they gave their life is clearly recognizable.

Camille no longer was a minor. With her twenty-first birthday, the previous January (1868), had come freedom to marry without consent from her parents. Yet Monet remained unwilling to bind himself to a woman without bourgeois dowry. Their unnecessary charade of a married state thus continued with meals that were modest imitative rituals served by a sour-faced servant-woman. But when dinner appeared under lamp-light, bizarre illumination crept over table and faces. Two small studies of these effects that Monet executed possess an original touch of lamplight fantasy impossible to dissociate from the sense of a stage. Perhaps unconsciously, the artist in him already probed the narrow area between the viable and the impossible, prodigies of ingenuity revealing him to be in full creative flood.

Unaware that one of the lamplight interiors was the property of Mr. and Mrs. Paul Mellon, I illustrated it in my biography *Monet* (Simon and Schuster, New York, 1966, 444 pages) to convey that portion of a career which knew few such moments of peace. "I am surrounded here by all that I love," Monet wrote to Bazille from that same round table:

> I pass my time outdoors on the flint beach when the seas are heavy, or when the boats go off to fish, or I even go into the country, which is so beautiful here that I find it perhaps more agreeable in winter than summer. And, naturally, I am working all the time, and believe that this year I will do some important things.
>
> And then the night, my dear friend, I find in my tiny house a good fire and a good little family. If you could see your Godson—how sweet he is at present. My friend, it is adorable to see his little being grow, and really, I am terribly happy to have him . . .

"I am going to paint him for the Salon, with other figures around him, as is proper. . . . And I want to do them in an astonishing way" Monet concluded. For to this class-conscious Frenchman respectability and success at the Salon still were the height of his ambition.

As the decade of the 1860's rolled to its end these happy circumstances never recurred. Claude Monet found himself beaten ever lower, with repetitions of the terrible ordeals through which he had passed. Unable to endure the continued poverty and degradation, in June 1870 he allowed his mistress to beg assistance from her haughty bourgeois parents. It was forthcoming; but its price, as was predictable, was marriage. After the necessary formality of a *contract of*

From the Collection of Mr. and Mrs. Paul Mellon

Woman with a Parasol (Camille and Jean) by Claude Monet.

... his many sketches of Camille, frequently with little Jean, painted in the environs of the house, were essays directed towards unexecuted Salon compositions." The indistinct date has been variously read but Jean's hat appears in many studies done in 1873.

marriage drawn by a notary, June 28, 1870, Monet and Camille were wed at the Mairie of the eighth arrondissement, 11 rue d'Anjou, Paris. Overtones of doubt so colored this ceremony Emile Zola employed it for his novel *Le Chef d'Oeuvre.*

After five years of courtship and one son Camille thus became a bride. An initial installment was paid on the interest of her dowry and immediately assuming the prerogatives of their class the Monets went off for a festive honeymoon at Trouville cut short by eruption of the Franco-Prussian war. Not able to produce his army discharge papers Monet was liable to re-impressment and fled to England, abandoning his new wife and their child. Among masses of French refugees in London he found the Paris art dealer Paul Durand-Ruel who began systematic purchases of Monet's work.

Camille's dowry and pictures bought by Durand-Ruel were the twin pillars that supported Monet's world after the war. They occupied another small house, this one by the banks of the river Seine at Argenteuil. Renoir and Alfred Sisley were the first to visit and together with the latter Monet undertook a sketch in the more urban quarter of Argenteuil. Monet stood in the street, Sisley's position a more cautious one on the sidewalk to his right. Apart from quiet tonality and fragmentary composition it is the date "72" Sisley put on his canvas which informs us Monet's picture was done so shortly after the house at Argenteuil was occupied in June that year. Possibly Monet had painted by the river at Argenteuil even before the leasing was completed by documents dated June 14 and July 9, for the list of Durand-Ruel purchases shows that in May he had bought *La Grande Voile,* a river subject.

Tentative figure compositions continued at Argenteuil, for the fixed idea of a success at the Salon could not be abandoned. To some degree his many sketches of Camille, frequently with little Jean, painted in the environs of the house, were essays directed towards unexecuted Salon compositions. To us, this other purpose discounted, they record delightfully the exterior of an existence that had become one of ease. Between February 1872 and March 1873 Durand-Ruel purchased fifty-six canvases for which he paid 21,900 francs. In March 1873 alone the dealer gobbled nineteen canvases for which he paid 10,700 francs, raising an average price of 300 francs, paid earlier, to 500 francs.

Monet had not yet reached the period of his most prolific and unpredictable imagination, but his relations with his son, his wife, and the town of Argenteuil, were of tenderness. Never before, nor ever after, were his charm and affability so pronounced, and in his person, as in his art, simplicity of style and clearness of thought were irresist-

Photograph from the author

Claude Monet about 1873.

This prosperous, carefully dressed man spent the whole of November 24, 1873 in lengthy legal proceedings.

able. Nevertheless the existence into which he was settled at Argenteuil remained curiously lush on the surface and ice-cold beneath, at once a fable of dedication and love and a statement of cruel bourgeois logic. For the moment this thematic conflict was lulled by his prosperity and Camille's capacities as wife and house-keeper, for at Argenteuil they had found happiness.

Origins of something more elemental can be traced to the financial panic which hit France that year 1873, forcing Durand-Ruel to suspend purchases. Monet at first was unwilling to believe the recent calm ascent of his career had ended: Durand-Ruel urged Faure, de Bellio, and Hoschedé, among his patrons those most interested in Monet's art, to buy direct from the artist. But the smoothness of life at Argenteuil was ruffled by faltering and erratic income. And when forced to interest the recommended patrons with individual canvases, to do the dealer's task in addition to the artist's, Monet showed improbable zig-zags in his artistic development. Calculated to accommodate economic circumstances, the sudden aesthetic development of that late summer and autumn sprang directly from renewed need.

Monet was not assisted by weather that remained unusually cold and wet. Despite this additional unpleasantness he worked beside the river that passed almost before his door. Hastily he produced the small salable works his clients most easily bought. Soon he found that in his rapidity and carelessness the browns and black spread on his pallette before each day's work often were left untouched. In time he ceased to force them from the tubes, improvising a kind of suspended syntax and oblique progressions of tones which brought a distinctively clear new tonality to his pictures.

The new chemically constituted colors that he employed for their greater tinting power now produced hidden resources. When viridian was taken with alizarin crimson on the brush a black more striking, clear, and forceful, was produced than any he had found in a tube. Equally macabre and glistening darks were obtainable from other pigments combined in this same dissonant manner. Though his sketches tended to be brutal and perfunctory Claude Monet in fact had stumbled on a new technique whose clarity, resonance, and harmonic resource were the overwhelming discovery of the century. *Impressionism,* an art employing chemically constituted pigments to create a synthetic coloration and more powerful accents without the use of black or brown, had been born.

Yet no one knew less than Monet concerning the new art to which he had given birth. In the years ahead he faltered many times, and the pictures produced are only Monet's scrappy and ill-assorted usages

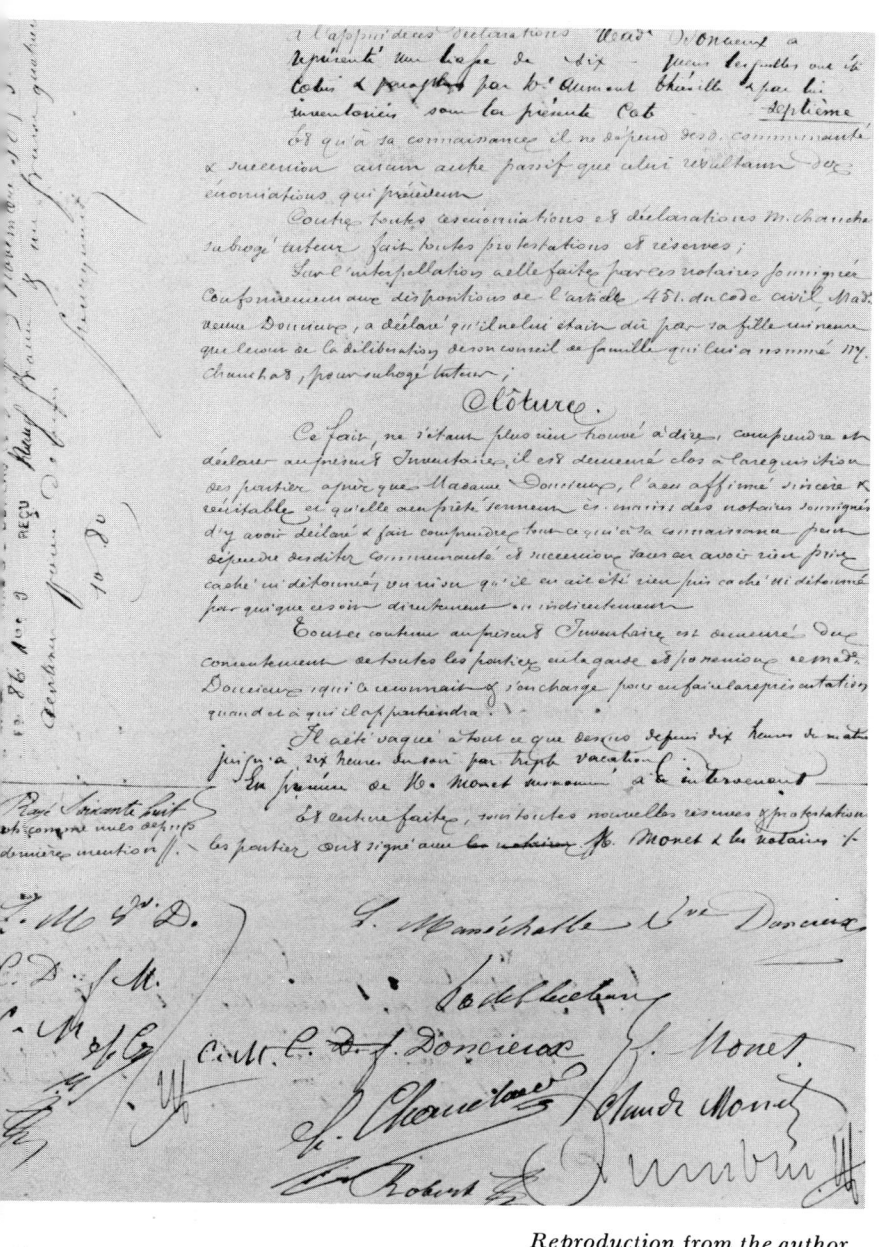

Reproduction from the author

Holograph minutes.

The last of eleven pages of minutes taken during examination. Madame Doncieux's signature is first, the second below it is Camille's, followed by Monet's. Revisions are attested by initials at left.

of a transcending discovery whose capabilities they limited rather than exploited. Among those who came from Paris to share Monet's river and the mysteries of his pallette was Edouard Manet, that elegant Parisian lightweight who like Monet sought his fame within the portals of the Salon. Possessed of the moderate wealth that supported his rarely successful professional career, Manet maintained his bourgeois standards and was treated by Monet as a man of distinction.

On a succession of days both men concentrated on depicting three sailboats moored just beyond the main Argenteuil bridge. With his own quirky logic Monet formed a design by placing only one black-hulled sailing craft in the foreground of his composition. Manet, a few feet to his right and closer to the bridge, copied all three craft. Though he saw Monet's finely modulated clear canvas grow beside him, Manet retained his own broad color washes and occasional rough scumbles. Mixed with normal components of ochre and umber, as well as black, Manet never reached the high key his friend obtained by use of synthetic accent and color. At one point only did Monet falter: confronted by an unredeemed black in the hull he surrendered sufficiently to Manet's prejudices to find a real black for his pallette and brush it onto his canvas. Through personal inclination or fear of Manet's sharp tongue, Monet had created a singing *Impressionist* canvas and then hesitated.

To Edouard Manet his friend's flexible method of orchestrating motifs and effects seemed both assured and resourceful. Distinctions are obvious: Monet's canvas was gently observed modulations across an idyllic scene; Edouard Manet produced a more brutal vision of industrial encroachment and belching smoke on the same riverbank. In Manet's work the delightfully balanced pattern of Monet is neglected in favor of a snapshot effect.

Both men began anew. Edouard Manet produced a larger oblong canvas on which to sketch the three moored sailboats. Determined to grasp the elusive brilliance of his friend, and unwilling to admit it derived from the chemistry of his pigments, Manet introduced ripples and waveletes which, with his broad stroking, riverbank structures, and cross-painted sky, never approached unity nor the heightened reality of Monet. To rescue an operation grown decidedly off-balance, Camille and little Jean were sent to stand where the tall grasses grew by the water's edge. This was a facility intended uniquely for Manet, whose foreground their figures filled. Monet required no such adornment for moving a few feet further down the river away from the bridge he had executed a study nearly identical with his first in

Reproduction from the author

Holograph agreement.

First page of agreement under which Madame Doncieux accepted responsibility for half the dowry promised her daughter.

which as his only modification all three black-hulled boats were introduced. Painted from a slightly higher perspective, his enlarged foreground of water required no embellishment such as the distant sail which decorated his first effort.

But the basic economic problem still was present to create its disturbance. Tied by sentiment and through his marriage to the monied bourgeois world of Paris, Monet knew that it lived by interminable variations on the themes of marriage and inheritance. And late that summer the lurking, nostalgic conservatism and class-consciousness so deeply a part of his nature were revitalized by news of the grave illness of Camille's father. From his second floor apartment at 17, Boulevard des Batignolles, Charles Claude Doncieux was transported to the Maison Municipal de Santé Dubois, in the Faubourg St.-Denis, where he died September 22, 1873.

The occasion was one of sadness and anxiety. Yet for the Monet family it generated also a rare excitement by the fantastic fizzing combination of notaries, authorizations, inventories, and Camille's dowry, the principle of which, named as 12,000 francs in her contract of marriage, must now be paid. Camille, fortunately, was a lady, possessed of an instinctive feeling for what was possible in social relations. To excessively farcical proceedings she brought her own grace. But she made the mistake of restraining Monet's habitual desire to cull the plots of best advantages. Following on her father's death and funeral, Camille may actually have spent a few October days in Paris, to assist her mother, her younger sister Geneviève, and Louis Edouard Baudry, a commissioner and valuer, who compiled an inventory of property in the Boulevard des Batignolles apartment. If Camille was present the whole time her attention surely was not directed to the most important considerations.

The preserved inventory faithfully records the furniture found in each of that apartment's six rooms, the thirty bottles of ordinary wine valued at five francs in the cellar, the gas oven, and twenty-two copper pots. Two iron beds had two mattresses each and a simple step beside them; in the dining-room were champagne glasses, wine glasses, ordinary glasses, and eighteen knives with ivory handles; in the Salon a Baumann piano, a taboret, music stand, four arm chairs, four other chairs, a mahogany settee covered in velvet, a fire guard in gilded copper, a mantle-piece in marble signed by Mercier, two torchiers and six lights decorated with griffons' feet, two bronze paper-weights, a terra cotta statuette of *a woman in repose,* and objects of faïence. More interesting is that scattered throughout the apartment were

Paris, Jeu de Paume

Camille Doncieux Monet by Claude Monet.

Camille was already ill, suffering from the effects of an abortion, when she moved with Monet to Paris. Here her husband has painted her in their apartment. Her death in 1879 freed Monet to bring Alice Rengold Hoschedé to live with him.

fifteen pastels (eight in the sitting-room alone) which presumably were by Camille's husband, Claude Monet.

After completion of this inventory, Maître Aumont-Thieville, who long had been notary to the Doncieux family and three years before had written Camille's marriage contract, prepared the customary attestation that it represented an accurate accounting of the property. On October 16, in a lengthy interview before his own notary at Argenteuil, Claude Monet duly executed an exhaustive authorization permitting Camille to treat for him in the matter of her father's estate. Armed with this Camille took the train to Paris, where on that same day the inventory was certified by Maître Aumont-Thieville and signed by Camille.

The result immediately created a wide-spread scepticism, and indeed, the inventory itself proved a very blackguard and entertaining document, for if it were believed the total value of *all* property left by Charles Claude Doncieux was 3,196 francs. By an elaborate plan of greed Camille's mother had secreted everything of value left by her husband. Even the 12,000 francs promised as Camille's dowry could not be found. The certification itself ended with an oath sworn by Madame Doncieux that she had "neither taken, hidden, nor turned away, directly or indirectly," any property belonging to the estate. Gravely written in compact Nineteenth Century script, these words bore a simper heightening their effect, for nowhere was any mention made of the securities on which Charles Claude Doncieux had lived the many years since his retirement from commerce in Lyon.

Occupied beside his river at Argenteuil, Claude Monet was not present at the certification of that inventory. Doubtless he considered it a mere formality, but on hearing the contents he immediately intervened. The accent Monet's tongue affected became unashamedly bourgeois, and fortunately he had the funds with which to make felt an ardent disposition. The distinguished attorney Charles Louis François Postel-Dubois was retained by Monet to act in behalf of Camille. His purpose was to discover hidden resources, and secure from the estate of Charles Claude Doncieux payment of the 12,000 francs promised Camille in her contract of marriage.

Postel-Dubois showed himself energetic and acted with dispatch. Ten o'clock on the morning of November 24, 1873, at the study of Maître Aumont-Thieville, Madame Doncieux's notary, a dramatic confrontation was brought about. Conducting his inquiry according to polite convention, Postel-Dubois obliged Madame Doncieux not only to account for all goods belonging to her husband, but to permit explorations into her own inheritance from Antoine Pritelly, the former *Receveur de Finance* following whose death, May 28, 1867, she had been named universal legatee. As they occurred these proceedings were minutely recorded:

> Monsieur & Madame Doncieux were married without contract at the city hall of Lyon (Rhône) the thirty-first December, eighteen hundred forty-five, and they found themselves therefore under a regime of a Community Property Law conforming to the dispositions of the Civil Code.
>
> At the moment of the marriage they possessed no furniture, and had neither use nor legal possession of anything of this description.
>
> M. Doncieux had not received during the marriage any inheritance, nor the benefit of any gifts nor legacies.
>
> Madame Doncieux had not received during the same time any inheritance—

Photograph from the author

Alice Rengold Hoschedé by Claude Monet.

A rare charcoal drawing by Monet shows Alice Rengold Hoschedé as she appeared about four years before she went to live with the artist. Her considerable dowry of 125,000 francs altered the basis of his career.

But she had been called to receive during this period the benefit of a universal legacy of personal property and real estate in usufruct left by M. Antoine François Pritelly, former *Receveur de Finance* living at Reuil where he died the twenty-eight May eighteen hundred sixty-seven....

Throughout this questioning Madame Doncieux gave replies carefully framed to show no disposable assets. This is most clear from the nature of her next response:

During the marriage no furniture was acquired by Monsieur or Madame Doncieux.

After thus straining the credulity of all those present in the notary's small office, Maître Léon Aumont-Thieville, representing Madame Doncieux, began pedantic examination of the estate papers. No legal formula was neglected. The notary examined minutely the dates and registration of every document, then proceeded to read the simple will of Camille's father:

I, the undersigned, Charles Claude Doncieux, aged forty-four years, merchant at Lyon and living in the Cours Morand, No. 51, at the Guillotine (Rhône) being sound of body and mind and wishing to dispose of my goods while I still have the faculty I have drawn up and written entirely by my own hand and sign in this testament my dispositions of last wish which follow. I give to Madame Françoise Léonie Manechalle, my wife, all that I possess and enjoy at my death as things which belong to her in full possession.

The present testament, drawn, written entirely, dated, and signed by my hand, in my home, Cours Morand, No. 51, June 23, eighteen hundred and fifty two.

Throughout the groaning legal formulas that next filled the air it became apparent Maître Aumont-Thieville meant to examine the inheritance Madame Doncieux had received from Antoine Pritelly. Since nothing would be ignored, the notary began by copying into his minutes the fact that he had executed the papers himself July 10, 1867, and had registered them after the death "at Bougival, commune de Reuil (Seine & Oise) rue de Paris No. 340, the twenty-eight of May, eighteen hundred and sixty-seven, of M. Antoine Pritelly former Receveur de Finance and Officer of the Legion of Honor."

The droning did not abate, for he also noted that these papers had been prepared at the request of "(1) M. Pierre Desiré Robillard, of the notary's office, living at Paris, Boulevard Bonnes Nouvelles, No. 10 bis," who in fact was his own *Principle Clerk* and in this capacity had been named an executor. "(2) M. Charles Claude Doncieux

From the Collection of Mr. and Mrs. Paul Mellon

Cliffs at Pourville by Claude Monet, 1882.

Painted at Pourville in 1882, this canvas demonstrates the new joyousness that invaded Monet's work immediately upon the arrival of Alice Rengold Hoschedé in his household. All cares were lifted and he designed pictures deliberately, as here, thinking of them as flat patterns in the Japanese way. The figures are probably Mme. Hoschedé and one of her daughters who appear in many canvases of this period.

(rentier) and Madame Léonie Françoise Manechalle, his wife, living together at Paris, rue Truffault, No. 4." After explaining that the Doncieuxs took part because Madame Doncieux had been named universal legatee, Aumont-Thieville gave this meager accounting of the Pritelly inheritance:

The objects of private property were worth 2313 francs
Other objects 326
The last account found at the death 1900

The testament of M. Pritelly next was examined, with emphasis on the fact it was drawn deliberately to exclude Camille:

I give and bequeath to Madame Doncieux, née Léonie Françoise Manechalle, wife of Charles Claude Doncieux the usufruct during her life, and to her daughter Geneviève Françoise Doncieux all the property the usufruct of which has been given to her mother which comprises all that I possess. I appoint her universal legatee at my death.... I name for my executors M. Léon Aumont-Thieville living at Boulevard Bonnes Nouvelles number 10 bis, and M. Robillard, first clerk to Maître Aumont-Thieville at Paris.

From the Collection of Mr. and Mrs. Paul Mellon

Bateaux de Peche au large de Pourville by Claude Monet, about 1882.

Presumably prepared to record these fishing boats at Pourville in 1882 so they could be inserted in the many seascapes he was painting, this is by accident or by intention a brilliant example of Monet's Japanese design. Note that as with so many Japanese prints the signature is an integral part of the balance.

In particular I leave full rights to Madame Doncieux in all my furniture, my portrait by Ary Scheffer, my bust by E. Brunet, my jewels, chains and watches; I understand that all that little outside my furniture, portrait, bust, chains, watches, jewelry and above left to Madame Doncieux will depend on my succession. The same applies to the price of the house that I possess at Reuil, Avenue de Paris, no. 340, in which case it will come to Madame Doncieux from the sale held to accumulate funds for the death duties. Also the railroad bonds will be placed in the hand of Madame Doncieux for her usufruct and for her daughter Geneviève Françoise Doncieux.

For my other property, I understand equally that the full value they have acquired will rest in the hands of my testamentary executors until the death of Madame Doncieux who will have the monthly income from

From the Collection of Mr. and Mrs. Paul Mellon

Poppies at Giverny by Claude Monet, 1885.

Monet's house at Giverny, as seen from the hillside directly above. "... onto a simple farmer's house Monet built a studio in which to re-organize his outdoor canvases." In the foreground fields, now built over, Monet began the first of his *series,* the "Haystacks."

them on her simple receipt and without requiring the authorization of her husband....

However restless Claude Monet, his wife Camille, and their attorney Postel-Dubois may have become by this point, it was certain that Maître Aumont-Thieville was finding his task equally heavy. A new person now took over the task of writing minutes, the script of which developed a bolder more legible character.

It was now stated that Monsieur Pritelly had died without leaving a direct heir. The papers of his marriage were produced, and those concerning his wife, who died in their previous Paris home at 8 Place Vintimille, November 22, 1862. The survivors were Messieurs Francois Joseph Fleury and Jules Joseph Fleury, Madame Pritelly's

From the Collection of Mr. and Mrs. Paul Mellon

Port Donnant, Belle-Île, by Claude Monet, about 1887.

Monet visited Belle-Île, in the Atlantic off the French coast, in 1886, returning to Giverny with about twenty canvases. These were then reworked in the studio over a period of months and indifferently dated "86" and "87." This one demonstrates the richer texture associated with Monet's mature work. As with many Monet masterpieces, an almost identical canvas exists.

sons by her former marriage. Their rights in their mother's estate Pritelly had satisfied by dividing between them bonds of the *Credence Colby de Saint-Paul* and thirty-six shares in the *Societé des Falieres*. M. Pritelly remained debtor to the Messieurs Fleury for the sum of two thousand thirteen francs, on account of furniture: this sum was still due.

The purchase M. Pritelly had made from Pierre Ferdinand Prevôt of a property at Reuil, Avenue de Paris, No. 340, consisting of a bourgeois residence with a small court before and garden behind, next was examined. A contract had been drawn by Maître Desforges, notary at Bougival, September 5, 1866, in which the price was stated to be 20,000 francs. A receipt was given for 4,000 francs, the balance

From the Collection of Mr. and Mrs. Paul Mellon

Iris Field by Claude Monet, about 1890.

Though in his mature works Monet was a fascinating flat-toned designer who imposed his own sense of order on nature, he remained also the same artist who had been fascinated by luminous color. Here, enjoying the hues of an Iris field about 1890, he creates a work that means nothing at all in black and white.

of 16,000 francs to be payable October 1, 1871, and until then bearing interest at five per cent.

M. Pritelly had paid another 5,000 francs against the price of the house, reducing the balance to eleven thousand francs:

> Madame Doncieux declares on this subject: "That the balance of the price of the house has been paid since the death of M. Pritelly by her monies received from the testamentary executors—that the house is rented but the rent for the present year had been borrowed [by Camille?] during the marriage."

A debt of 17,500 francs had been owed to Pritelly by Monsieur A. de Serionne, on which 1750 francs had been paid April 10, 1867:

> Madame Doncieux declares on this subject: "That this debt has been completely repaid, and that the funds have been employed by the testamentary executors of M. Pritelly in a manner conforming to the testamentary dispositions of that latter."

Abundantly clear from these examinations was that Madame Doncieux had received large sums unknown to Camille and Claude Monet, and that these were systematically invested by her notary for the purpose of producing income. Under the Pritelly testament, which granted her only usufruct and entailed everything for her daughter Geneviève, Madame Doncieux could not touch the sums themselves. But there was still the question of the sizeable personal income she was receiving monthly. The extent of this, and of the capital from which it was produced, remained mysterious. But now at last they were coming to an examination of the securities left to Madame Doncieux. M. Pritelly had been heavily invested in the *Societe Anonyme des Anciennes Salines:*

> Sixteen shares numbered 2037 to 2053
> Five other shares numbered 4491 to 4495
> Ten shares numbered 7231 to 7240
>
> All the said shares entirely free and commanding rights and interest and dividends payable April and October each year.
>
> On the back of each certificate were the stamps indicating payment for the semestre of April eighteen hundred sixty seven, before the death:
>
> Madame Doncieux declares on this subject: 'That these shares still exist; but they have not produced any interest this year. . . .'

Examination next disclosed that in addition to the house at Reuil, M. Pritelly had rented an apartment, on the second floor at 99 rue Blanche, Paris, for one thousand fifty francs a year. Retaining only a maid's room, M. Pritelly had sublet the apartment at 900 francs a year. The balance of 150 francs had been paid from funds in charge of the notary; but when questioned further concerning the arrangement Maître Aumont-Thieville ordered this portion of the papers closed.

By closing papers before the eyes of this assembled company Maître Aumont-Thieville accentuated the curious powers he retained to protect his client and her deceased benefactor. Throughout a long morning and well into the afternoon he had sought to show that Madame Doncieux was without disposable assets. Nothing was in her name; she owned no furniture nor real property; she possessed no bonds nor securities. That she lived on an income furnished to her monthly was all that had been gained, and whenever they approached the question of how large this income was they were unable to pry the information from anyone present.

They were coming at last to the crux of the problem; on what had Charles Claude Doncieux lived before his death? The question was posed for reasons that had technical ramifications in the mind of Postel-Dubois who was exerting himself to force his opponents into a corner. The success of his strategy was not immediately apparent when the answer came forth in Maître Aumont-Thieville's own

Photograph from the author

Claude Monet in the 1890's.

Monet as he came to Paris during the 1890's. "His ultimate position of extraordinary dominance had been achieved not alone by the most significant artistic discovery since the Renaissance, Impressionism, but also by a process of clever dealing. This was predicated on his own strong financial position astride the Rengold dowry and by forcing the public to take notice by a succession of shocks."

words: "That at the moment of death M. Doncieux was dependent upon the Community"—or, on property jointly owned by himself and his wife under the Community Property law that applied because they had been married without a contract. M. Aumont-Thieville opened the way to say Monsieur Doncieux had been supported by his wife, which further stressed that he had left nothing. He did not dare go so far, and in fact produced record of eight bonds that had belonged to the deceased:

> 1. Five bearer bonds of the Societé Anonyme des Ancienne Salines . . . producing interest and dividends payable in April and October of each year and bearing the numbers 4299 to 4302.
>
> 2. Three bearer bonds of a thousand francs each, freed by five hundred francs each, and stamped by subscription of the Bank de Paris & des Pays Bas, bearing numbers 9980, 17015, and 27016.

These eight bonds were small enough assets for a man who lived in retirement so comfortably as Monsieur Doncieux and promised his daughter a dowry of 12,000 francs.

That he had been invested in bearer bonds meant no record of his ownship would exist anywhere. And the worst fears were realized when it was learned that "since the death and to satisfy her needs and affairs, she [Madame Doncieux] had sold these securities, which have produced the total sum of five thousand five hundred francs. And that following on this there has been credited to the community property which existed between her and her defunct husband the said sum." The appalling discovery that previously unadmitted sums had existed, and that in the two months since Monsieur Doncieux's death they had been converted to cash, was the major event of the day. Obviously the extent of Monsieur Doncieux's holdings never would be learned.

To offset this slight gain by opponents now grown restless, Maître Aumont-Thieville attempted to becloud the issues once more by launching into an examination of two insurance policies on the house at Reuil. The property's value was dimly glimpsed when it was stated the policies were for 40,000 francs and 96,000 francs. The expenses of Madame Doncieux then were brought forward: she had spent 59 francs 55 centimes that very month, and five francs for the tax on her dogs. The burden of this was summed up: "Madame the widow Doncieux declares to complete the analysis that no more remains to her than the sum of 27 francs 55 centimes."

In the midst of so much property she thus perversely entered her plea of poverty.

And so, late that afternoon of November 24, 1873, Madame

From the Collection of Mr. and Mrs. Paul Mellon

The Artist's Garden at Giverny by Claude Monet, 1900.

About the turn of the century Monet essayed *art nouveau* ideas by employing square, round, and sometimes scalloped shapes, struggling to find appropriate subjects for them. This study of a wild section of his garden is held in place by the vertical tree stems which function like the columns in more classical landscapes.

Doncieux laboriously had established a claim that she was without funds. Against this were arrayed the explicit provisions written into Claude and Camille Monet's marriage contract, which was copied into the minutes verbatim. Camille's claim for 12,000 francs from her father's estate, in addition to her normal portion, was bonafide. To answer it a general declaration was entered that "there did not exist at the death of Monsieur Doncieux any last accounts; to her [Madame Doncieux's] knowledge no other assets existed."

Expenses of the funeral were quoted to a total of 434 francs 85 centimes; mention was made that rent on the Boulevard des Batignolles apartment was one thousand seventy francs a year, and Madame Doncieux employed one domestic servant at 35 francs a month.

At six in the evening all those present began the process of initialling each sheet of minutes, affixing full signatures to the bottom of the eleventh page. Darkness covered the Boulevard outside; for eight hours they had been together under a barrage of unscrupulous half-truth and falsehood. But all was not lost. Through those long hours Postel-Dubois had kept certain points clear in his mind. Whether or not Charles Claude Doncieux had died penniless, his assets were so well secreted they would never be found. Because he was married without contract however, his widow was legally responsible for *half* the dowry promised Camille and Claude Monet. This was an unshakeable fact of law. It had been established that Madame Doncieux had no disposable assets with which to meet this debt, for she enjoyed only usufruct of the Pritelly estate entailed for the ultimate possession of her younger daughter Geneviève. The monthly income paid her by the notary *could be attached* however, and on this basis Postel-Dubois began his renewed bargaining.

In hopes an interminable session could be brought to an end, Maître Aumont-Thieville began drafting a new document to codify their work of the day. Madame Doncieux now promised to pay over to Camille immediately, "the sum of four thousand francs, receivable as a loan against the portion of her dowry of twelve thousand francs..." In return Aumont-Thieville extracted from Camille a price: the sum of the dowry would be reduced from twelve to six thousand francs. It would be established, in other words, that Charles Claude Doncieux had died without assets and his widow was bearing responsibility for her half only: "By means of the present payment it is understood that the part of the charge of Madame Doncieux in this dowry is henceforth found reduced to the principle sum of two thousand francs."

Ferocious irony existed in the fact Madame Doncieux was contriving to cheat Camille of half her dowry. But argument was only now becoming heated. The unpaid balance of two thousand francs, small as it was, must continue to pay interest as had been stipulated in the marriage contract. Aumont-Thieville wrote:

> This sum expressly held in security will continue to produce interest on the footing of five per cent a year payable by semestres the twenty first of June and December each year.
>
> The payment of the first semester, that of December eighteen hundred and seventy three to June eighteen hundred and seventy four, will take place the twenty-first of June, eighteen hundred and seventy four.

From the Collection of Mr. and Mrs. Paul Mellon

Waterloo Bridge, London, at Sunset by Claude Monet, about 1904.

"... eventually he undertook further series of a more restrained poetic nature, *Mornings on the Seine, London,* and *Venice....*" Monet made many trips to London where his son was at school but, as usual, when the *series* was completed he was indifferent to the dates he put on them. While two Mellon canvases represent Waterloo Bridge neither is dated: other versions bear dates as far apart as 1900, 1902, 1903, and 1904.

From the Collection of Mr. and Mrs. Paul Mellon

Waterloo Bridge, London, at Dusk by Claude Monet, about 1904.

The unpainted edges of this work mark it as a canvas which escaped studio retouching. Frequently the canvases Monet brought back to Giverny were in this condition and were touched-in as a part of the larger process of re-working that took place in the studio.

The confrontation had become a brilliant structure of collective absurdities and frustrated human purposes. With the comic eccentricity proper to his role Aumont-Thieville attempted to force into this paper a provision favorable to Madame Doncieux:

> It is understood that the two thousand francs will not become tangible except three months after the death of Madame the widow Doncieux.

This proved agreeable to no one, and in renewed battle Aumont-Thieville was forced to cross it through and consider new formulas. He tried again:

> With regard to the tangibility which will be given the two thousand francs, the holding and delay of which has been consented to by Madame Monet always under the authorization of her husband, until the death of Madame the widow Doncieux. . . .

Aumont-Thieville got no further. Madame Monet did *not* agree to this sum being retained until after her mother's death, and Monet gave her no authorization. The notary again turned back on his words, crossing out the phrase *until the death of Madame the widow Doncieux*. After *two thousand francs* he inserted a mark directing the eye to the margin where he wrote "exaction of which is demanded now."

In the end no agreement was reached and a flimsy tissue of words left the question unsettled: ". . . the period at which this sum of two thousands francs must be paid to Madame Monet is as will be verified to the stipulation of principle and outside the portion contained in the contract of marriage of Monsieur and Madame Monet." Greed had become an illness so widespread as to reach the dimensions of a plague, yet callous and brutal as it had made mother towards daughter, its final action lacked decision and disciplined detail.

So agonized had the scribbled paper become, so different its crossings-out, marginal notes, and anguished script from the contract of marriage engrossed three years before, everyone was pleased to sign and initial as directed to end the interview. For the Monets the entire question of a dowry, entered into with misgivings in 1870, now again had risen to haunt them. Despite the skill of Postel-Dubois, in two neat cuts Madame Doncieux first had halved, then sliced to a third, the promised sum of Camille's dowry. Only four thousand francs had been extracted, and little hope existed they ever would see one franc more.

Blighted by a lack of funds the whole pattern of life altered at

Argenteuil. The four thousand francs must be made to last through all eventualities and forever, for so far as Monet and Camille could see there was no other prospect of money from *any* source. Working rapidly before the river, taking each group of newly completed sketches on the train to Paris, running the streets to the homes of his few patrons, Monet's working procedures visibly manifested his nervous harassment. When the second of those bridge scenes produced with Edouard Manet was sighted once more in the studio its gentle harmonies seemed dull beside more recent agitated works.

Examination of this canvas, now in the Louvre Museum, indicates how in his anxiety over the presence of a real black Monet dragged an untoned crusted white over the boat hulls. Large areas of reflection then were made white in agreement, a studio alteration that created a jarring foreground. To bring the canvas into agreement he dabbed at the distant trees, increased the strength of bridge reflections in the water, loaded new pigments onto the sky. The credibility of carefully observed scudding clouds was destroyed, and this was a general truth, for what the picture had gained in brilliance it lost in authenticity. Still, since it had been brought into line with his most sparkling works of the new year, this canvas begun before the legal torments of November 1873 was duly signed *Claude Monet 74*.

The motif was a successful one: both versions were sold, and before they left his studio Monet copied from them a hasty pastiche. On a rough version of the distant river-bank which lacked authentic tree forms and shapes, and from which in his haste he omitted the intricate bridge structures that contributed so much to the pattern, Monet brushed a violent blue river untroubled by color nuances. The three hulls, copied from his later bleached version, are an impossible white on this blue flood: a sailboat from the Mellon version is copied twice to fill gaps in the empty composition. A yawning foreground is filled by an extension of the grassy bank at the right in the Mellon version.

Not painted from nature and consequently unfelt, this wildest of the three related canvases has found its way to the Rhode Island School of Design in Providence. It is eloquent testimony to the course an over-riding economic motive had set on Monet's art. Not artistry but crude economics governed him at every level of his life. Only the extraordinary richness of his creative faculty made so much of it into sublime artistic expression. Unable even by these means to keep the house at Argenteuil, Monet and Camille took little Jean to Paris. There an effort to live in sedate frugality and paint portraits in a studio, which records show to have been paid for by Gustav Caillebotte, an amateur painter, collector, and former neighbor at

Collection of Cyril Benabo, London

Church of Santa Maria della Salute, Venice, by Claude Monet, 1908.

Painted in 1908 but not exhibited until 1912, Monet's *Venice* series was his last effort to tackle any subject outside his own garden at Giverny. This is one of seven nearly identical views of the church of Santa Maria della Salute seen through the gondola posts before the Prefectura.

Argenteuil, ended quickly in utter failure. Camille meanwhile had undergone a back street abortion, effects from which, after they moved further out on the river Seine to Vetheuil, caused her death in 1879.

Psychic imbalances associated with his sudden freedom and its causes threatened for a time to destroy Monet, who was a deeply emotional man. But this too became translated into economic terms that marked his emergence from poverty. Camille's unpaid dowry of 12,000 francs was a meager thing beside the sums of 25,000 francs and 100,000 francs given in her contract of marriage to Alice Hoschedé, the deserted wife of Monet's patron. Some degree of liaison had existed since the disappearance of her husband, and now, free of Camille, and after the observance of a decent interval, Monet brought Madame Hoschedé and her many daughters to live with him.

If her smile was engagingly crooked and her short torso un-

Claude Monet in 1920.

Monet in his sitting room at Giverny in the summer of 1920. The canvases wired to racks on the wall were mostly painted more than thirty years before. Studies done at Etretat (1882–1886), a Belle-Ile fisherman (1886) and studies done in the Creuse valley (1889) can be identified. On his desk are photographs of himself taken by Sacha Guitry and of Renoir in his wheelchair. Against two canvases leans a small plaster relief plaque by Renoir.

The room was originally the carriage house which Monet converted into his first studio. When the second studio was built, it became a sitting room and though three steps lower than the rest of the house it served in this capacity until Monet's death.

redeemedly plump, Alice Hoschedé was the highly cultivated daughter of the Rengold family, raised in the Hôtel de Ville quarter of Paris where her father owned the palatial residence built by the Duke d'Epernat. True, a front court facing the street had in its wall an elegant shop where the bronzes and ormolus manufactured by Alice's father under imperial appointment were displayed to the public. Inside all was equally gilt, but chaste as befitted a home of Parisian wealth. And since her marriage in 1864 Alice Rengold Hoschedé had been able to count on a private income from her dowry in excess of 6,000 francs a year.

Relieved from immediate financial necessity, secure on a modest scale, once more exhibiting his works in Paris, Claude Monet no longer was the haphazard magician of Argenteuil. Now he planned his canvases with the taste of a Japanese designer. After a suitable motif was discovered he repeated it until every possible utterance had been wrenched from it. Figure compositions and the fixed idea of glory at the Salon disappeared. This plump middle-aged couple with its caravan of teen-aged daughters moved to Giverny, near Vernon on the borders of Normandie, where onto a simple farmer's house Monet built a studio in which to re-organize his outdoor canvases. Simplification, refinement, repetition in the studio became an essential part of his outdoor art.

Near Giverny the first of Monet's acknowledged "series" began, the *Haystacks,* whose clamorous success when exhibited together in Paris brought immediate response in the series of *Poplars.* Single canvases still sold, but the Wagnerian spectacle of a single motif seen in fantastic permutations of color and effect were what drew the Parisian public and American collectors to Monet with mad adulation. *Belle Isle* and the *Creuse Valley* series were followed by the most sensational of all, *The Rouen Cathedral,* engulfed so extraordinarily that Monet's own self-hypnosis was transferred to the canvases, leaving stones and mortar irradiated, magnified, and rising to a truly shattering climax. Fifteen thousand francs each were demanded for these astonishing creations, and if for the moment Monet had overreached himself, when eventually he undertook further series of a more restrained poetic nature, *Mornings on the Seine, London,* and *Venice,* his movement forward was unimpeded.

His last series of all, begun at the turn of the century in the water-garden that he enlarged and continually replenished with bushes, trees, plants, benches, and a bridge that in time sported a roof, occupied him until his death in 1926. And truly it is strange to remember that this man who died nearly into our era had suffered so terribly in the sixties of the preceding century. His ultimate position of extraordinary dominance had been achieved not alone by the most significant artistic discovery since the Renaissance, Impressionism, but also by a process of clever dealing. This was predicated on his own strong financial position astride the Rengold dowry and by forcing the public to take notice by a succession of shocks. These shocks began with the canvases painted at the moment of those extraordinary interviews at which he attempted to save Camille's dowry. Together the Mellon canvas and the Louvre canvas of *The Bridge at Argenteuil* demonstrate how nature was modified for his purpose.

In a larger sense the career of Claude Monet pointed a way that others followed into a blind alley of irrelevant voguishness. Art, in Monet's youth an examined and controlled product of academies, became the bastard calling for which no credentials or examinations were required. Monet thus proved another essential corollary that has haunted the art world ever since: a genius in isolation can produce great art, even make overwhelming discoveries as can be seen bursting forth on the Mellon canvas of *The Bridge at Argenteuil*. But only secure financial backing can make an artist a success.

Daniel Chester French: His Statue of Lewis Cass in the United States Capitol

MICHAEL RICHMAN

Any survey of American sculpture of the Nineteenth and early Twentieth Century must include the works of Daniel Chester French (1850–1931). During a career that spanned six decades, French produced hundreds of portrait busts, commemorative and ideal statues, public monuments, and architectural groups. Washington, D.C. is fortunate to have a varied and comprehensive collection of his sculpture, both in museums and in public areas. French's most famous monument is the seated *Lincoln* (1915–1922), a marvelous icon in American history. Representative of his late sculptural style are the *Dupont Fountain* (1917–1921) and the *First Division Memorial* (1921–1924). In the Corcoran Gallery of Art, there are four powerful maquettes or first sketches for the decorative groups, *The Four Continents* (1900–1907), which embellish the entrance of the United States Custom House in New York City. Examples of French's early work in portraiture can be seen at Gallaudet College where the bust of *James Abram Garfield* (1882) is located and at the National Portrait Gallery where the portrait of *John Sherman* (1886) is included in the permanent collection.

The subject of this study is another early work by French, his little-known *Lewis Cass* (1886–1889) in the United States Capitol. It is both a pivotal statue in French's sculptural development and a major work in the National Statuary Hall collection. The history of the creation and execution of the *Cass* commences two decades earlier at the time when the old Hall of Representatives was "... worse than uselessly occupied as a place of storage and traffic...." [1] To correct this, Justin Smith Morrill, a Representative (and later Senator) from Vermont proposed on January 6, 1864, that a national statuary hall be created:

[1] *Legislation Creating the National Statuary Hall in the Capitol.* Compiled by H. A. Vale. (Washington: Government Printing Office, 1916), p. 5.

Office of the Architect of the Capitol

Marble statue of Lewis Cass by Daniel Chester French in Statuary Hall in the United States Capitol.

> ... where pilgrims from all parts of the Union, as well as from foreign lands, may come and behold a gallery filled with such American manhood as succeeding generations will delight to honor, and see also the actual form and mold of those who have inerasably fixed their names on the pages of history.[2]

The legislation was approved by Congress on July 2, 1864, and provided that:

> ... the President is hereby authorized to invite each and all the States to ... furnish statues in marble or bronze, not exceeding two in number for each State, of deceased persons who have been citizens thereof, and illustrious for their historic renown or from distinguished civic or military services, such as each State shall determine to be worthy of this national commemoration. ...[3]

It was not until June 17, 1885, that the state of Michigan acted to submit its first commemorative statue for the Capitol:

> Resolved by the Senate and House of Representatives of the State of Michigan, that the sum of ten thousand dollars be and the same is hereby appropriated out of any money in the treasury not otherwise appropriated, for the purpose of securing and placing in Old Representative Hall ... a statue of Gen. Lewis Cass, as one of the illustrious men of America.[4]

The Governor, Russell Alexander Alger, who approved the Joint Resolution, was empowered to appoint a three-member committee to choose a sculptor and oversee the project. He selected Hamilton E. Smith, H. R. Ledyard and Philo Parsons. The real authority seems to have been given to Parsons, who was named Chairman, to find a competent sculptor. Exactly when he began his search cannot be determined for none of the papers or related documents of the Cass Statue Commission, which had its headquarters in Detroit, have survived. Writing at a later date, Parsons explained: "My wife and two daughters were with me [in Boston] a month and in New York nearly a month before deciding on the Artist." [5] There is no mention in the Daniel Chester French family papers as to when, during the last months of 1885, Philo Parsons might have visited either French's home in Concord, Massachusetts, or French's studio in Boston. French

---
[2] *Ibid.*, p. 9.
[3] *Ibid.*, p. 13.
[4] *Public Acts and Joint and Concurrent Resolutions of the Legislature of the State of Michigan.* (Lansing: W. S. George and Co., 1885), pp. 374–375.
[5] Letter from Philo Parsons to Cyrus G. Luce, June 22, 1889. Records of the Executive Office, 1810–1910, State of Michigan, Lansing, Box 67, Folder 8.

kept a visitors book, which he started on April 19, 1881, but it was discontinued by June 30, 1885.

It must be assumed that French met Parsons in October or November of 1885. The meeting was productive for French wrote to his brother, William Merchant Richardson French, on January 10, 1886:

> I am somewhat surprised to find myself so far from home [in Detroit]. The Hon Philo Parsons summoned me to meet the Cass statue committee.... He says he is in favor of employing me and I think my chances are good as he is chairman and most influential member.... That body is to meet tomorrow to look me over and will come to a decision soon.[6]

Perhaps the most regrettable feature of the history of the *Cass* is that no record of French's instructions from the commissioners are extant, nothing as to what they expected French to accomplish, what images they thought he should examine in order to produce an acceptable likeness of Cass, or at what moment in Cass's career he should be portrayed. In light of the dearth of information, it seems logical to assume that French was provided with a copy of Matthew Brady's daguerreotype of Lewis Cass (c. 1850).[7] French must have been able to interview those residents of Detroit who were Cass's friends to gain further insight into his personality. The sculptor also could have consulted published biographies of Cass such as those written by William L. G. Smith in 1856 or William T. Young in 1852.[8]

Before concentrating his attention on the accurate representation of Cass's physiognomy, French first addressed himself to the selection of a suitable sculptural motif. The design of the statue had first to be approved by the commission before a contract could be signed. French returned from Detroit determined to conceive a powerful composi-

---

[6] Letter from Daniel Chester French to William Merchant Richardson French, January 10, 1886. Daniel Chester French family papers, Manuscript Division, Library of Congress, Box 82.

[7] This daguerreotype was brought to my attention by Karen L. Duffy, Assistant, Research Service, Office of the Architect of the Capitol. Also I wish to thank Florian H. Thayne, Head, Research Services, for her continuing help, and to acknowledge the support provided by James R. Ketchum, Curator of the United States Senate. The author is contemplating publishing an article on the busts of the Vice-Presidents in the Senate's collection.

[8] There were no copies of these books in the Chesterwood collection, but it seems plausible to suggest that French would have tried to learn something about the personality of the man he was to commemorate. William L. G. Smith, *Fifty Years of Public Life: The Life and Times of Lewis Cass* (New York: Derby and Jackson, 1856) and William T. Young, *Sketch of the Life and Public Services of Gen. Lewis Cass: With the Pamphlet on the Right of Search, and Some Speeches on the Great Political Questions of the Day* (Detroit: Markham and Elwood, 1852).

Library of Congress

Daguerreotype of Lewis Cass about 1850 by Matthew Brady.

tion which would be appropriate for his first portrait statue commission. His two previous large scale efforts had been the *Minute Man* (1873–1875) and an idealized portrait of the seated figure of *John Harvard* (1883–1884). French had waited almost fourteen months for the Cass commission and he must certainly have begun his maquette immediately on reaching Concord. On March 3, 1886, he reported to William:

> I am still at work upon Mr. Brimmer and Gen. Cass, both nearly done. Gaugengigl came in to see me Monday [March 1] and amused me by exclaiming as his eyes fell on the Cass model. "Ah, the king of America!" I have doubts still whether I can make my simple motive go. It is pretty severe.[9]

French made no other report of his progress to his brother but he must have finished the model in the early summer of 1886. Although the maquette has not survived, a photograph of it has been preserved in the archival collection at Chesterwood.[10]

The maquette is integrally significant in trying to understand French's creative methods. Available evidence strongly indicates that French made very few drawings during the initial stage of a sculptural project. He seems to have preferred to work in clay and at small scale. While the sketch of the *Cass* has not been preserved, many other maquettes, probably numbering well over fifty, can be seen at Chesterwood. French was responsible for preserving these modellos, affirming that these small objects are not only important ingredients in the artistic process but also valuable sculptural entities in their own right. Philo Parsons summarized the progress of the commission in a December letter to Governor Alger:

> The commission charged with the responsibility of having executed in marble a suitable statue of General Lewis Cass . . . , visiting the studios of the most eminent artists of Boston and New York, and holding correspondence with the distinguished artists in other sections of the country, examing the finished work of these artists, as far as possible, finally selecting Daniel C. French of Boston to present a model, which if satisfactory should ensure him the contract. Mr. French presented the Commission in this city in August last a model which met their entire approval, and a large number of our older citizens, who were personally acquainted with General Cass. They have therefore, . . . contracted with Mr. French under the date October Fourth (4th) to place in the Capitol in Washington in eighteen (18) months, a statue of General Cass, seven feet high and well proportioned, of the finest Carrara marble in accordance with the model accepted. . . . Mr. French is now engaged in Paris, France, in modelling the statue, and will they believe, in due time,

---
[9] Daniel Chester French to William Merchant Richardson French, March 3, 1886, Box 82. Ignaz Marcel Gaugengigl was a Boston painter.
[10] The author wishes to acknowledge his gratitude for the assistance given him by Paul W. Ivory, Administrator, and the sculptor's daughter Margaret Cresson. Together their help has made the research on Daniel Chester French rewarding.

Chesterwood, Stockbridge, Massachusetts
National Trust for Historic Preservation

Photograph of destroyed plaster maquette (1886) for statue of Lewis Cass by Daniel Chester French.

present a work of superior excellence, honorable to the state, and a very worthy memorial.[11]

Before the contract was signed in October, 1886, French was asked to delete the marvelous cloak which in the plaster maquette disguised Cass's portly girth. In so doing, the bulk of the figure becomes more explicit. It seems probable that the commission's criticism also necessitated altering French's more timeless effort to incorporate the specific details that show that Senator Cass is engaged in some official duty.

French had modelled two large sculptures and while enlarging the full-scale model of the *John Harvard* he expressed dissatisfaction with his ability to render the surface of the clay. This technical deficiency could be corrected, French felt, only by study in Paris. In 1874, French had chosen to journey to Florence, Italy, to study antique sculpture and to work in the ambience of the last vestiges of the American neo-classic school, instead of following the advice of his friends, Abbott Thayer and Benjamin C. Porter, to enroll in a Parisian atelier.[12] By 1878 French regretted this decision. Writing to his brother on April 3, French lamented:

> I have been thinking for some time that I needed a course of training in drawing and have really thought I should go to Paris next fall and spend the winter with those frenchmen who are masters of technical skill. If I don't do it now I never shall and shall consequently feel weak all of my life, whenever I meet a Parisian trained man.[13]

Now as October 21, 1886, approached,[14] French made his final preparation for his first trip to Paris, where he was going to enlarge the *Cass* model and seek modeling instruction. French's immediate concern on reaching Paris was to establish himself in a suitable studio and search about for an available master. Some discrepancies are apparent when one tries to determine which Parisian master French visited in Paris. Margaret Cresson wrote that "Dan signed up for Mercie's sculpture class several evenings a week." [15] Conflicting testimony is presented by William Coffin:

---

[11] Philo Parsons to Russell Alger, Decembr 27, 1886. State of Michigan, Box 231, Folder 1.
[12] Michael Richman, "The Early Public Sculptures of Daniel Chester French," *The American Art Journal*, 4 (November, 1972), pp. 108–109.
[13] Daniel Chester French to William Merchant Richardson French, April 3, 1878. Box 82.
[14] Daniel Chester French to Edward Clark, Architect of the Capitol, October 7, 1886. Files of the Office of the Architect of the Capitol. In this letter French mentioned to Clark that he was preparing to leave for Paris on October 21.
[15] Margaret Cresson, *Journey into Fame* (Cambridge, Massachusetts: Harvard University Press, 1947), p. 145.

In 1886 he again went abroad, this time settling in Paris, and remaining a year. He drew from the model in the class of M. Leon Glaize, and studied the masters in the public galleries. This sojourn in Paris had a strong influence on his work, and his full maturity as a sculptor may be said to date from that time.[16]

French himself does not mention whether he studied with Antonin Mercie (1845–1916) or with the portrait-, genre- and history-painter, Pierre-Paul Leon Glaize (1842–1932). What is important is that French was at long last in Paris and able to experience first-hand the lessons of Parisian sculpture. He remarked:

> I have enjoyed my stay here immensely and feel that I have gained very much by contact with the clever men and the great art treasures of the city. A wonderful place is Paris....[17]

French did not report to his brother during the execution of the full-scale model. He did, however, write to Charles Moore from Paris on July 2, 1887:

> I have thought of you many times in these last six months when I have been whittling away at the Cass statue.... Gen. Cass is an accomplished fact so far as the clay image is concerned. Only a finger-nail or a button or some such trifle remains.
> I wish you could see the statue in clay. In some ways it is more interesting than it will ever be again. If you like the small model I am sure you would approve of the large one.... I can't help feeling as if it had enough of the character of the American senator of his period and of Gen. Cass in particular to win the respect of his friends and others. It has been a most difficult problem to solve... I shall have it photographed next week.... Speaking of photographs, I sent Mr. Parsons long ago a photograph of the statue when it was hardly more than blocked out, thinking it would interest him to see how a statue was made.... [A]pparently the committee got hold of it... and regarded it as a finished product and were accordingly dismayed.[18]

A photograph of the completed clay model has survived in the Chesterwood archives and must presumably be a copy of the one which French sent to the commissioners. The large clay is a strongly rendered work. The cloak has been dropped to the ground, partially covering the support, and provides a necessary structural complement

---

[16] William Coffin, "The Sculptor French," *The Century Magazine*, 59 (April, 1900), p. 873.

[17] Daniel Chester French to Charles Moore, July 2, 1887. The Charles Moore Papers, Manuscript Division, Library of Congress, Box 5.

[18] *Ibid.*

Chesterwood, Stockbridge, Massachusetts
National Trust for Historic Preservation

Full-scale clay model (1886–1887) for statue of Lewis Cass by Daniel Chester French.

Detroit Historical Museum
Detroit, Michigan

Portrait of Lewis Cass (1840) by George Peter Alexander Healy. Oil on canvas.

for the slender legs. French received a favorable response from the portrait painter George Peter Alexander Healy:

> I was very much pleased the other day by the opinions of Mr. Healy. . . . He was a friend of Gen. Cass and painted his portrait . . . and his judgment is therefore of great value. He said the likeness was admirable and congratulated me on my success with the costume and predicted that it, the statue, would please artists as well as the people generally.[19]

French did not see Healy's life-portrait of Cass which was executed in 1840 and is now located in the Detroit Historical Museum. A comparison of the painted and sculpted renditions by the two artists indicate that each has presented a softened interpretation of the general's rugged physiogonomy as recorded in the Brady daguerreotype. French has replaced Healy's more general statement with an explicit interpretation which, according to Parsons, depicts Cass as he finishes a Senate speech. The right arm no longer needed to hold the cloak has been dropped slightly and clenches some papers. To further accent the solidity of pose and silhouette, the sculptor has introduced the column upon which Cass weightily rests his left hand. The factual details of clothing which the painter could neglect must be described in the full length sculpted portrait. It is to French's credit that the sartorial accessories do not predominate. French, as Healy had done in 1840, understated Cass' facial blemishes in his portrayal of a man in his late fifties.

With the clay model finished, French's creative involvement with the statue was all but over. A cast in plaster, needed by the carvers in order to execute the final marble, was made. With his mechanical task completed, French had only to wait the approval of the Detriot officials. He was eager to return home for he had been asked by Dr. Edward Miner Gallaudet to make a bronze statue for Gallaudet College in Washington.[20] Undoubtedly French hoped that the Cass commission would act promptly. Confident of approval, French secured the services of a competent firm of Parisian carvers and delivered the plaster to their workshop. Finally in early September he learned why authorization had been delayed. Some persons were dissatisfied with the portrait of Cass. On September 7, 1887, French wrote to Charles Moore:

> Many thanks for your letter which came at the same time with one from Mr. Parsons informing me of Judge Campbell's dissatisfaction with the likeness. I seem to have failed where I am probably the strongest. Mr.

---
[19] *Ibid.*
[20] For a discussion of this second important early work by French in Washington, see "The Early Public Sculptures of Daniel Chester French."

Donaldson's concise expression of approval pleases me greatly.... I shall be glad when this thing is settled.... Catch me taking another statue subject to the verdict of a committee![21]

By October 3, 1887, French was back in Concord when he again wrote to Moore:

Your letter has come today and I know not what to say in return for your loyalty to me, without which I am well aware there might, in deed, *would* have been a disaster for me and the statue, I appreciate particularly your ability to keep the matter out of the newspapers. If you had not done so the difficulty would have been published all over the country and caused me no end of annoyance. I wish you would express my thanks to Mr. Donaldson and Mr. Ives for fighting my battle for me. I am very glad if they (and you) could do so conscientiously. Poor Mr. Parsons! He has had a hard time of it all around. He apparently has had to do all the work and the other men . . . have been only stumbling blocks.[22]

French was dismayed by the criticism of the correctness of the portrait. From 1878 he had repeatedly been given portrait commissions which were well received and praised for their fidelity. In a heretofore unpublished life portrait of the Reverend John H. Morison, modeled in 1880, French's ability is demonstrated. He has captured the demeanor of the Unitarian minister by first manipulating the plaster so that the translucent surface of the marble will accurately describe his countenance. Regretably, the unavailability of the Cass Statue Commission papers makes it impossible to determine the extent of the dissatisfaction, or what were James Valentine Campbell's objections, but French had powerful allies and eventually the chairman triumphed. Philo Parsons declared that "the likeness . . . is perfect from my memory of the man." [23]

One critic, who apparently found fault with the statue not for the veracity of the portrait but for its pose, was the Frenchman Eugene Antoine Aizelin (1821–1902). Nothing, unfortunately, of the relationship between French and Aizelin can be learned. All that has survived is the account published by Lorado Taft:

The "General Cass" did not altogether please some of the Paris sculptors. Mr. French related how M. Aizelin criticised its ponderous and solid pose, with the weight carried equally on the two legs. He adds

---
[21] Daniel Chester French to Charles Moore, September 7, 1887. Moore Papers, Box 5.
[22] *Ibid.*, October 3, 1887.
[23] Philo Parsons to Cyrus G. Luce, June 22, 1889. Michigan.

Photograph by Michael Richman

Marble portrait bust (1880) by Daniel Chester French of John H. Morison in the Morison home, Upland Farm, Peterborough, New Hampshire.

with a smile that the eminent sculptor evidently thought that he "did not know any better." [24]

French had absorbed the lessons of Parisian academicism but without imitative subservience. The perceptive criticism of Lorado Taft must be mentioned:

> But like St. Gaudens, with his Farragut, Mr. French had a sturdy subject to deal with, and selected the position best suited to reveal the character of the man. With all its solidity, the artist has so well treated the surface, has made the flesh so mellow and the drapery so crisp and full of color, that the figure easily takes its place among the best portrait statues of the country. It unites admirable characterization with no less attractive technique. The first quality, the artist had already shown, the second was the result of the Parisian experience.[25]

The *Farragut* is an acknowledged masterwork in Nineteenth Century American sculpture and by comparing French's *Cass* with the work of Augustus Saint-Gaudens, Taft is dramatically praising French's achievement. It must in fairness be added that the *Farrugut*, erected in 1881 and now located in Madison Square Park, could have been seen by French who during the 1880's made several trips to New York City. But French certainly did not imitate Saint-Gaudens' design. As Taft states, each artist, faced with portraying a study subject, choose postures of coincidental strength instead of a more elegant ensemble which was prevalent among Parisian monument makers.

Washington, D.C. has several such academic monuments which are erected in Lafayette Square. The collaborative effort of the Frenchmen Jean Alexandre Joseph Falguiere and Marius Jean Antonin Mercie in the Lafayette Memorial (1887–1891) precisely illustrates the flamboyant style that portray the man as well as document his historical achievements with numerous attendants.

The next reference to the *Cass* appears in the French family papers. On June 20, 1888, French wrote to his brother and listed the various projects in which he was involved, including:

> [The] statue of Cass, being cut in Paris expected home in Sept., pedestal to design and get executed here [in New York City].[26]

---

[24] Lorado Taft, *The History of American Sculpture* (New York: The Macmillan Company, 1903), p. 319.

[25] Lorado Taft, "Daniel Chester French, *The Monumental News*, 7 (January, 1895), p. 20.

[26] Daniel Chester French to William Merchant Richardson French, June 20, 1888. Box 82. It seems plausible that French might possibly have asked the help of Arnold Brunner, a New York architect who in 1888 was remodeling French's new house at 125 West 11th Street. By the early 1900's French was collaborating almost entirely with Henry Bacon, who designed the Lincoln Memorial.

Photograph by Michael Richman

Detail of the marble statue of Lewis Cass by Daniel Chester French in Statuary Hall in the United States Capitol.

French was probably responsible for designing the pedestal, which was made from Tennessee marble, but it has been impossible to determine what company manufactured the base.

Finally on December 11, 1888, French notified Edward Clark, architect of the Capitol, that the statue had reached New York:

> The marble statue of Gen. Lewis Cass the gift of the State of Michigan to the United States has just arrived at this point together with the plaster model of the same. To avoid delay and the risk attending opening, repacking and carting to and from the Custom House, I should consider it a great favor if you would get an order from the Secretary of the Treasury to have the cases delivered to me without examination as being for Government use.[27]

---

[27] Daniel Chester French to Edward Clark. Files of the Office of the Architect of the Capitol.

Photograph courtesy of Saint-Gaudens National Historic Site

Farragut Monument, New York City, bronze (1876–1881) by Augustus Saint-Gaudens. An early photograph.

Some confusion resulted and on December 17, French corresponded with Clark:

> My original request was for an order to deliver the statue without examination, not to avoid paying duty. There is no question of duties, the statue being the work of an American artist.
>
> I have ordered sent to your care by Pa. R. R. freight the marble pedestal for the Cass statue. It will probably leave here tomorrow.[28]

Two days later French again wrote:

> Thank you for your kind letter of Dec 18 enclosing a copy of a letter from Asst Sectary Maynard. The order for the statue came the day I wrote to you—Monday—and the statue has today been made over to me and is, I hope, on its way to Washington;

---

[28] *Ibid.*

There will be something for me to do upon the marble, a matter of two or three days, and I shall go on to Washington for that purpose as soon as the statue arrives.... I think you told me you could arrange a screen so that I could work upon the figure after it had been placed in the old Hall.[29]

On Sunday, December 23, French wrote:

I am intending to go to Washington on Thursday, if the statue will be by that time so placed that I can work upon it or if I can assist at setting it up.[30]

Sometime between December 27, 1888, and mid-January, 1889, the statue was erected in Statuary Hall and French was able to execute such minor changes to the marble as he felt were needed. It must be inferred from his letter of December 19 that he was working with the statue. French was fastidiously concerned about each step in the sculptural process, anxious that his first official portrait be well received.

The required legislation was introduced on January 21, 1889,[31] permitting the statue to be formally accepted from the state of Michigan. Somewhat disturbed, French wrote to his step-mother Pamela Prentiss French on January 27:

The *Cass* is to be formally presented to the U.S. Feb. 18 and I have to wait till then for my money. It is vexatious and inconvenient but I can't help it.[32]

The Nineteenth Century American sculptor, when executing a public monument, worked under a system that dictated that his money be paid in installments, with the major portion paid only after the statue was erected. French did not receive the final payment until March 6, 1889.[33]

The dedicatory exercises on February 18, 1889, were highlighted by lengthy eulogies for Lewis Cass and intermittent commendations for the sculptor. Both Senator Justin Smith Morrill of Vermont and Representative James O'Donnell of Michigan lauded French's effort. Senator Morrill said:

Let us welcome the statue of Lewis Cass as a felicitious contribution

---

[29] *Ibid.*
[30] *Ibid.*
[31] *Proceedings in Congress Upon the Acceptance of the Statue of Lewis Cass Presented by the State of Michigan* (Washington: Government Printing Office, 1889), p. 4.
[32] Daniel Chester French to Pamela Prentiss French, January 27, 1889. Box 76.
[33] Letter from Fred Warner, Secretary of State of Michigan, to George Peabody Wetmore, January 6, 1890. Files of the Office of the Architect of the Capitol.

to our American Pantheon, where are clustered precious memories that will be for all future generations an inspiration of noble deeds.[34]

Further official praise for the *Cass* was expressed by Senator George Frisbie Hoar of Massachusetts:

> ... [W]ithout claiming for myself any experience or taste which entitles me to pronounce a judgment more than all other men, I think I am not mistaken in affirming that this statue will be regarded always as one of the very finest, if not the very finest work of its kind, which has yet been contributed to our gallery under the joint resolution passed in 1864. It is a figure, manifestly accurate in portraiture, and not only that, but it is a figure full of strength spirit, and life.
>
> The State of Michigan has been wise and fortunate in the selection of the artist . . .[35]

The *Cass* is a pivotal sculpture in French's early career and one of the preeminent monuments in the National Statuary Hall collection. As the seventeenth statue erected there, it was preceded by only a few successes, notably Erastus Dow Palmer's *Robert R. Livingston,* erected in 1875, and Henry Kirke Brown's *Nathanael Greene,* erected in 1870.

In praising French's effort, Lorado Taft criticized the unevenness of the collection in the Capitol:

> This statue is the only good thing in our "National Statuary Gallery". Among those hard, conventional figures, it stands alone. It has an individuality, an equipoise, and a technical perfection undreamed of by the earlier generation of American sculptors.[36]

One need only compare the *Cass* to the contemporary effort of a less talented sculptor, Alexander Doyle (1857–1922). Doyle executed three statues for the United States Capitol, two ordered by the state of Missouri and one by the state of West Virginia. Representative of Doyle's efforts is *Francis Preston Blair,* which was commissioned in April 1895 and delivered to the Capitol by November 1897.[37] In most respects, the various ingredients of the *Cass* and *Blair* are similar. But in the composition it is apparent that Doyle's *Blair* is more casually posed and the treatment of the trouser and frock coat seem slick and overworked.

---

[34] *The Congressional Record,* February 18, 1889 (Washington: Government Printing Office, 1889), p. 2005.

[35] *Proceedings in Congress Upon the Acceptance* ..., pp. 56–57.

[36] Lorado Taft, "Daniel Chester French, Sculptor," *Brush and Pencil,* 5 (January, 1900), p. 149.

[37] Files of the Office of the Architect of the Capitol.

Office of the Architect of the Capitol

Marble statue of Francis Preston Blair by Alexander Doyle in the Hall of Columns in the United States Capitol.

The portrait monument, whether erected in a public park or commemoratively displayed as in the United States Capitol, is an important motif in American sculpture. America's monumental sculpture has been neglected and is only slowly being reexamined.[38] It is now proper to begin a more thorough and thoughtful reappraisal rather than persist in the easy condemnation of this aspect of American art. A promising place to focus scholarly efforts is the collection of the monuments in the United States Capitol. A number of writers have imperiously dismissed the sculptures. One such caustic evaluation was that made by Thomas Nelson Page in "What Ails Art in America?" published in the *New York Times* on January 15, 1911. An accompanying photograph, with the caption "The Horrors of Statuary Hall," whether by plan or accident showed Frederick E. Triebel's *George L. Shoup,* Larkin G. Mead's *Ethan Allen,* Frederick W. Ruckstuhl's *John C. Calhoun,* Daniel Chester French's *Lewis Cass* and Charles Henry Niehaus' *James Abram Garfield.* Page wrote:

> ...Go to that round hall in the Capitol in Washington known as Statuary Hall. Significant and admirable nomenclature! And gaze if you can with unshaded eyes upon the frightful collection of marble effigies which are classed properly under the simple generic name of "statuary". Even the most patriotic sentiment of the most devoted American cannot view that collection without a shudder at the grotesqueness of that group of men, who, it may well be said, have deserved better at the hands of their countrymen. That some are good, and one or two are fine may be admitted, but jumbled together as they are in every freak of modern dress, of every size from pigmies to giants, they present together a terrifying spectacle of what the best of this country is able to achieve. The good are belittled by the mean, without being able to lift the latter from the low level of their insignificance.[39]

Specific and perceptive criticism is needed. The view that the entire collection is mediocre and all the sculptors incompetent should not go unexamined. Sweeping statements, whether disparaging or complimentary, are likely to have little merit. I hope that this examination of one of the more successful portrait statues in the Capitol may be followed by other specific studies.

The history of the *Cass* is of particular interest because the entire process of execution, from the maquette to the final marble, can be examined. Even from the partial glimpse that has survived of the

---

[38] Recently published is the survey by Wayne Craven, *Sculpture in America* (New York: Thomas Y. Crowell, 1968). The Autumn 1972 number of *The American Art Journal* contains eight articles on American sculptors.

[39] Thomas Nelson Page, "What Ails Art in America?," *New York Times,* January 15, 1911.

behind-the-scenes controversy that arose when the clay was finished, it is readily apparent that the sculptor commissioned to execute a commemorative portrait monument was at the mercy of his patron. The amount of innovation and experimentation that can be incorporated in such a project is severely limited, particularly when the progress is so closely monitored by a well-intentioned committee. French was in 1886 and 1887 still developing his sculptural style and in this respect the execution of the *Cass* in Paris was vitally important. French was able to render clay with greater sophistication and the marble transmits much of French's newly acquired modeling skill. His *Cass* is a successful statue. It is a work of lasting worth among the neglected marbles and bronzes in the United States Capitol, a major collection of Nineteenth Century American sculpture which still awaits fair and thoughtful study.

The Old Post Office Building in Washington, D.C.: Its Past, Present and Future

GAIL KARESH KASSAN

The old Post Office Building in Washington, D.C. is located on Pennsylvania Avenue between 11th and 12th Streets, N.W. It is the second major vertical element in an otherwise horizontal city, rising to a height of 330 feet from base to tower top; 45 feet taller than the dome of the Capitol, the Post Office tower is second in height only to the Washington Monument. "Integral with the tower is a rare example of what many people feel will be an extinct species—an American Romanesque Revival structure of the late 19th century." [1] This Romanesque style of architecture is considered by many to be the most American of the revival styles and the first creative contribution of American architects to the history of architecture.[2] The total Post Office Building is an example of this American Romanesque style, often characterized by its vigorous, uninhibited, and creative use of materials to form a well-integrated mass.

In architectural style the old Post Office Building followed the current fashion popularized by the work of Henry Hobson Richardson. Richardsonian Romanesque, as the American version of Romanesque architecture was called, was popular in the period 1880 through 1900. Buildings composed and designed by Richardson were built of rock-faced masonry with arches, lintels, and other structural features emphasized by being of a contrasting stone. The main characteristics of the style were round arches, towers, and steep gabled wall dormers. The arches were usually large, forming cavernous entrance ways. Towers were often square, rising far above the roof line and topped

---

Delivered before the Columbia Historical Society on October 19, 1971.

[1] Arthur Cotton Moore, Testimony before Subcommittee on Public Buildings and Grounds, Committee on Public Works, U.S. Senate, April 21, 1971, p. 1.

[2] Wolf Von Eckardt, "Why Can't We Keep the Old Post Office?" *Washington Post*, March 8, 1970; Moore, p. 1.

by roofs of pyramidal shape. Turrets usually enhanced the corners of the building with small narrow windows to let in light. Straight topped windows, divided into rectangular lights by stone mullions and transoms, were employed in the main facade along with arched windows and ribbon windows. Their arches or lintels were often supported by colonettes. A sense of massiveness and weight is reinforced by the depth of the window reveals, the breadth of the planes of the roofs, and a general largeness and simplicity of form.[3] All of these elements were employed in the Allegheny County Courthouse by Richardson and in the Washington, D.C. Post Office by W. J. Edbrooke.

During Richardson's lifetime there was little Richardsonian Romanesque that did not come from the master's own office. Montgomery Schuyler wrote in 1891:

> While he was living and practising architecture, architects who regarded themselves as in any degree his rivals were naturally loth to introduce in design dispositions or features or details, of which the suggestion plainly came from him. Since his death has "extinguished envy" and ended rivalry, the admiration his work excited has been free to express itself either in direct imitation or in the adoption and elaboration of the suggestions his work furnished.[4]

Richardson died in 1886 and the next ten years were bumper years of Richardsonian Romanesque. The successors to his practice, Shepley, Rutan, and Coolidge, designed some buildings in the style in the late 1880's. Their Lionberger Warehouse in St. Louis is a reflection of Richardson's Marshall Field Wholesale Store. In 1887 they designed some of the first buildings for Stanford University in the Richardsonian Romanesque style. In Pittsburgh Frank E. Alden, who had been sent there by Richardson to supervise construction of the Courthouse in 1885, designed a number of structures in the same style. In Chicago Burnham and Root employed Richardsonian Romanesque features in the Rookery; and Louis Sullivan took suggestions from the style for his Auditorium. The style continued to be popular in the 1890's, finding expression in Henry Ives Cobb's Newberry Library in Chicago. Richardsonian Romanesque was also used in the Los Angeles County Courthouse and the California State Bank at Sacramento.[5] In Washington, D.C. Richardson designed houses for John Hay and Henry Adams, for N. L. Anderson, and one, the Tuck-

---
[3] Marcus Whiffen, *American Architecture Since 1780: A Guide to the Styles* (Cambridge: The M.I.T. Press, 1969), p. 133.
[4] Ibid., p. 137.
[5] Ibid., p. 138–140.

erman house, which was finished after his death, all now destroyed. There are many buildings in the style designed by other architects but few of excellent quality and significance. The old Post Office Building is one of Washington's last remaining Romanesque revival structures on a monumental scale.

The reason for Richardson's popularity and the proliferation of architectural structures in his style is that he was recognized as a hero in his own lifetime. In a poll conducted by the journal *American Architect and Building News* in 1885, several of Richardson's buildings were among the top ten structures voted as the best examples of American architecture. The participants in the poll were 75 practising architects from across the country. They chose large imposing buildings, regardless of their interiors, and favored the Richardsonian style above all others. The result of this poll "goes far to prove that he (Richardson) was indeed a hero, but a hero respected in his lifetime, not a hero in revolt against a time that did not understand him." [6]

THE WASHINGTON POST OFFICE

The Washington Post Office had no structure to call its own in the late Nineteenth Century. The sentiments of the city's postal employees and indeed of the city itself were in favor of a new structure to house the operations of this large department. Madison Davis, Assistant Postmaster for the City of Washington in the late 1890's and early 1900's and postal historian, said:

> The question of providing a government building for the Washington Post Office occupied the attention of the Department and Congress for fully twenty-five years without result. Other large cities were provided from time to time with magnificent post offices; even small places were sometimes granted stately and costly structures for post office use. But the Capital of the nation during all this time was neglected.[7]

The Washington Post Office had been located in a number of sites prior to the erection of the Post Office Building on Pennsylvania Avenue between 11th and 12th Streets. There is some evidence that it was even located in the same square, 323, during the term of Thomas Munroe, between 1799 and 1829. After the War of 1812 the Post Office was moved from the Executive Building near the White House to a building in square 323 where it remained until a fire destroyed it in 1835, or 1836. The Post Office then moved to the

---

[6] John Burchard and Albert Bush-Brown, *The Architecture of America* (Boston: Little, Brown and Co., 1961), p. 185.

[7] Madison Davis, *A History of the Washington City Post Office*, (Lancaster, Pa.: New Era Publishing Co., 1903), p. 76.

Courtesy of John J. G. Blumenson

View of the Post Office shortly after its completion.

ground floor of Carusi's Saloon on 11th Street, an entertainment hall of supposedly good repute.[8] A couple of moves later the Post Office was located on the first floor of the F Street Government Post Office Building between 7th and 8th Streets. There it remained from 1857 until 1879 when it was moved to the Seaton House on Louisiana Avenue between 6th and 7th Streets. In 1892 the Post Office was removed to the Union Building on G Street between 6th and 7th Streets where it remained until November 27, 1898, when the new structure on Pennsylvania was sufficiently complete for the Washington Post Office's occupancy.[9]

The Post Office Building on Pennsylvania Avenue was located in square 323, a site previously used as a landing place for the Washington Canal. During the Nineteenth Century houses stood on the site and some of the ancestors of Washington's best families lived there. In the late Nineteenth Century it was the location of numerous shops, a Masonic Hall, the Franklin Fire Company, and saloons frequented by Congressmen and citizens. The site for the Post Office Building was reportedly chosen by Senator Leland Stanford of the Committee on Public Buildings and Grounds and a Mr. McCarthy, a local newspaper writer. As they were touring Washington, the Senator asked McCarthy, "Where would you put the Post Office?" McCarthy replied, "Right there," pointing to the site on Pennsylvania Avenue.[10]

On June 25, 1890, the President approved and signed into law an act authorizing "the acquisition of certain parcels of real estate embraced in square 323 in the city of Washington to provide an eligible site for a city post office." [11] On August 30 the act was amended to authorize the Secretary of the Treasury to:

> Acquire for the purpose, and in the manner hereinafter provided the real estate in square 323 of the city of Washington, District of Columbia, bounded by Pennsylvania Avenue in the north, C Street on the south, Eleventh Street on the east, and Twelfth Street on the west and a sum of money sufficient to pay for said square 323 in the manner hereinafter provided is hereby appropriated out of any money in the Treasury not otherwise appropriated and the said secretary is instructed to cause to be erected upon said square a commodious and substantial building with fireproof vaults, heating and ventilating appa-

---

[8] *Washington Evening Star*, November 23, 1898, p. 9.
[9] Davis, *passim*.
[10] *Washington Evening Star*, January 31, 1932.
[11] United States Post Office Department, *Post Office Site 323*, (Washington, D.C., n.d.), p. 1.

George Washington University Library

Early Twentieth Century view of the Post Office with the Southern Railway Building on the right.

Courtesy of John J. G. Blumenson

Dead Letter Sale in the Assembly Room of the Post Office about 1930.

ratus, elevators and approaches for use as a United States Post Office for said city, and for other governmental purposes, the cost of the said building not to exceed $800,000.[12]

The thirty parcels of land in the square were finally purchased by October 3, 1891, for a total cost of $655,490.77.[13]

Considerable interest had been aroused in and around Washington by the pending proposals for a new Post Office Building. In August, 1891, William A. Richardson, Chief Justice of the Court of Claims, suggested to Edbrooke, the Supervising Architect of the Treasury in charge of designing the building, that a clock be placed on a tower on the building. He wrote, "There is not now a public building in Washington with a clock upon it. In point of fact there is but one clock in the city upon any building, and that is upon the Washington Post structure, near but not on the Avenue." [14] In September, 1891, John S. Gallaher, a citizen and businessman of Washington, also suggested a clock tower. He wrote to Edbrooke:

> Now that a permanent and most eligible site for the City Post Office building has finally been decided on, and as the contemplated structure will necessarily and most appropriately be, of colossal dimensions and imposing design, under your special supervision, and as the community of our City and public in general, have *never* had the long needed convenience and advantage in a business way of a *Town Clock*, it is most respectfully suggested that in making the necessary plans and designs of the building aforesaid, that provision be made for a mammoth or suitably large *time-striking* clock, of four dial faces ... to be illuminated at night with gas or electricity. The cupola ... of octagonal shape.... The alternate four spaces or compass points to be provided with large nightly illuminated dial faces.... The cupola could be surmounted with points of compass indicators, a weather vane, or some appropriate emblematic or historical figure, all, making a useful as well as unique finish to the building.[15]

Undoubtedly the Post Office building was regarded as a significant addition to the city and the beginning of an important era in Washington. As the first large government structure on Pennsylvania Avenue, it was looked upon as unique and monumental, and as such it should have a landmark clock tower visible from as many parts of the city as possible.

The Washington Post Office was designed by Willoughby J. Ed-

---
[12] Ibid., p. 2.
[13] Davis, p. 77–78.
[14] Public Building Service, *Records and Correspondence, Record Group 121.*
[15] Ibid.

Courtesy of John J. G. Blumenson

Interior Court of the Post Office decorated for Flag Day ceremonies about 1930.

brooke, Supervising Architect of the Treasury under President Harrison. He was responsible for all post offices, custom houses, court houses, and Marine hospitals proposed and under construction during his term of office. Edbrooke was a native of Illinois, born in September, 1843, in Deerfield, Lake County, Illinois. His father, a contractor and builder, had settled there seven years before Willoughby's birth. The family was descended from colonial settlers of New England. Edbrooke was educated in public schools and then was sent to Chicago to study under professional architects. In 1868 he went into his own business and a few years later formed a partnership with his two brothers who were also influenced by their father to go into architecture. The partnership was dissolved a few years later and Edbrooke again went into business alone. His most notable works from this period were structures for Notre Dame in Indiana and the Tabor Grand Opera House at Denver. In 1891 he was appointed Supervising Architect of the Treasury. During his term, which lasted until 1893, he designed a number of post offices, court houses, and custom houses in the Richardsonian Romanesque style. He also designed several buildings in the new style of the late 1890's—the Beaux Arts style. For the Chicago World's Fair of 1893 he composed a neo-classic building to house the government's exhibits. He also designed the State Capital at Atlanta in the neo-classic Beaux Arts style shortly before his death in 1896.[16]

Edbrooke's plans for the Washington Post Office were completed by the beginning of 1892. In March the *American Architect and Building News* published plans and a description of the proposed building. It was to be "erected for the accommodation of the Washington City Post Office, which will occupy the first floor and all that part of the basement not occupied by heating, elevators, or electric light apparatus." The second story was to be used for offices for the Post Office Department, the top floor for sitting rooms, dormitories, and other accommodations for Railway Postal clerks. "An act of Congress provided for a building of eight stories but they have not been assigned yet." The building was to be 200 feet long on Pennsylvania Avenue and 300 feet in depth on the side streets. The main entrance would be on Pennsylvania Avenue and the entrances to the elevators and staircases on 11th and 12th Streets. The C Street entrance was to be reserved for the dispatch of city mail. A tower 300 feet high with clock faces 20 feet in diameter and 250 feet above the

---

[16] "Obituary: W. J. Edbrooke," *The Inland Architect*, April, 1896.

The Old Post Office Building

sidewalk "will be visible along the whole of Pennsylvania Avenue and from greater portions of the city." [17]

The exterior of the building was to be composed of Maine granite. Other features of the exterior were described:

> Over the entrance arches of the main front, a projecting balcony, over each, above the second story, will form supporting pedestals for groups of statuary emblematic of the postal service, the coat of arms of the United States, etc. The spandrels of the arches at all the entrances will be enriched with carved ornaments, but there will be but little other carved-work on the exterior of the building.[18]

The general plan of the interior revealed a series of stories for offices around an interior court. "The entire central portion above the second story will be an open light well about 100 by 200 feet in dimensions, roofed over with ornamental iron trusses and covered with a glass skylight, around which will be a clear story of moderate height furnished with movable sash." The main body of the post office working room was the first floor and it was to be protected by a curved glass ceiling supported by elliptical ornamental trusses which would be independent of the columns that support the galleries. This glass ceiling over the first floor was so designed to give direct light and ventilation to the area below it. "The corridor partitions of all the first floor offices will be of glass, and as glass is used, as before stated, for the ceiling, it is believed that this lobby will be well-lighted." [19]

CONSTRUCTION OF THE POST OFFICE

Work began on constructing a fence around the site of the building in January, 1892. General excavations began in March and trench and pit excavations began during the summer. By the end of 1892, the Postmaster general made the following report:

> The general excavation has been completed, the foundations are nearly finished and the concrete and stone footings have been put under contract. Drawings for the basement masonry have been completed and the drawings for the superstructure are so far advanced as to insure the placing of the masonry and ironwork of the entire building under contract before the basement masonry is finished. The entire building ought to be completed by the spring of 1894.[20]

---

[17] *The American Architect and Building News,* XXXV (March 12, 1892), 174–175.
[18] Ibid.
[19] Ibid.
[20] Postmaster General of the United States, *Report for 1892* (Washington, D.C., 1893), p. 42.

But delays crept in and construction fell behind. During 1893 little progress was made on the structure. Edbrooke was replaced by Jeremiah O'Rourke in April, 1893, but no significant changes were made in the plans of the building. By the end of 1893 the work had not progressed beyond the excavation, piling, and erection of part of the cellar walls.[21] This was partly due, as the Superintendent of Construction said, to "some mismanagement on the part of the contractor, or the parties furnishing him the steel and iron." [22]

More delays occurred in 1894 when some blocks of granite were found to be defective. O'Rourke was replaced by Mr. Kemper as Supervising Architect of the Treasury in September, 1894, and Kemper was replaced by William Aiken in March, 1895.[23]

Throughout this period there were debates on a House Bill of December 4, 1894, to revise the Supervising Architect of the Treasury's office to allow for open competition for the design of government buildings. An earlier bill suggesting open competitions where feasible had been passed and signed into law by President Harrison in 1893, but it had been ignored by the government architects. Both Edbrooke and O'Rourke had opposed it, saying that government buildings were equal to private work in magnitude of artistic effort, cost, and time of completion. But a study of 1894 revealed that government buildings cost 6 per cent more than private buildings and paid the Supervising Architect 9 per cent of the cost of the building, where private architects received only 6 per cent of the cost of their buildings in fees. A comparison of the times it took to complete the two types of buildings revealed that large private structures took an average of 29 months to complete, whereas public buildings took an average of 96 months for completion. As an example of the cost and time delays, the report cited the Washington Post Office Building which by the end of 1893 had been appropriated $500,000 and had reached only the cellar walls.[24] The issue of whether or not to open competition for government buildings to private architects was not settled until the early part of the Twentieth Century.

Construction continued throughout 1895, although at a much slower pace than expected. By the beginning of 1896, the fifth year of work, the erection of the structural steel and iron of the roof was underway. By summer all of the brickwork and stonework was com-

---

[21] "Government Buildings Compared to Private Buildings," *American Architect and Building News* XLIV (April 7, 1894), p. 2–4.
[22] *Record Group 121*.
[23] Ibid.
[24] "Government Buildings Compared to Private Buildings", p. 2–4.

Courtesy of John J. G. Blumenson

Interior Court of the Post Office decorated for Flag Day ceremonies about 1930.

plete except for some trim. It was expected that the building would be ready for occupancy in 1897, but this did not occur due to more delays centering around a scandal involving two major figures in the building. In June 1897, there was again a new Supervising Architect, James Knox Taylor, who immediately called for the resignation of the Superintendent of Construction, Thomas Steward, because of his alleged selling of materials from the construction site for his own benefit. It was also reported that the previous Superintendent, John Kinsey, had been negligent in reporting the deterioration of large areas of concrete in the building.[25]

In 1897 *Harpers Weekly* reported that public sentiment was very emotional over delays in building the new Post Office Building. It was supposed to be finished in 1897, but "a syndicate of well known politicians" were credited with having a hand in the delay "due to their ownership of the building then leased to the post office which pays a rental of $20,000 each year for cramped quarters." The article further commented: "The syndicate presumably will not obtain as much for the space from anyone but the government. Hence its desire to prolong the present occupancy." [26] The people of Washington and the nation looked forward with anticipation to the building's completion, for "when it is completed and occupied, Washington's Post Office will be a model which the Postmaster General can exhibit with pride to the distinguished visitors from other countries, who often come to Washington to study our postal system." [27]

By November, 1898, the interiors of the basement, first, and second floors were sufficiently complete to allow the City Post Office to move into its quarters. During 1899 numerous interior projects on the upper stories were undertaken to make it ready for occupancy by the Post Office Department, then located on F Street. On September 15, 1899, moving operations began for the Department; it was described as the largest operation undertaken in the city in some time. A team of 500 men and 400 horses and carts were employed. The move was under the supervision of former City Postmaster James Polk Willett who had been appointed to the position of Superintendent of the new building in July after his retirement. Willett had been the first postmaster to serve in the new building and was given the job to keep him on the payroll.[28] In September he was told that after the moving operations were completed, he would no longer be

---
[25] *Record Group 121.*
[26] *Harpers Weekly,* October 16, 1897, p. 1039.
[27] Ibid.
[28] *Washington Evening Star,* June 30, July 1, July 3, 1899.

needed. While inspecting the delivery of departmental material to the new building on September 30, 1899, Willett fell into an open elevator shaft from the fifth floor and was instantly killed.[29]

In the Postmaster General's Annual Report for 1899, it was reported that the Post Office Department had finally moved into its new quarters. The Postmaster General had the following comments about the new building:

> In most respects it is found to be convenient and well-adapted to the requirements. As generally happens when a public building is assigned to a use for which it was not originally designed, but which has required changes and modifications during the course of its construction, there are some defects which it is hoped may be remedied in due course of time.... [The eighth floor was reserved for outside use] But experience has already demonstrated the necessity of its use by the occupants of the remainder of the building. Serious considerations must be given to changing this law.[30]

Even at its completion the building was felt to be almost too small for all the occupants assigned to it.

LIST OF COSTS FOR POST OFFICE BUILDING

Entire purchase of site	$ 655,490.77
August 30, 1890, Appropriation	250,000.00
August 5, 1892, March 3, 1893, August 18, 1894, March 2, 1895, June 11, 1896, June 14, 1897 appropriations	2,160,000.00
January 28, 1898, final appropriation	175,000.00
Total	$3,240,490.77
Other funds	835.00
Total prior to occupancy	$3,241,325.77
Fitting building with	
machinery, furniture	112,780.00
gas and light fixtures	19,220.00
electric light and heating	64,992.00
partitions and radiators	1,847.00
Additional allotment from supervising architects office	2,000.00
Changes and repairs after occupancy	60,000.00
	$ 260,839.00

---

[29] Ibid., September 30, 1899.
[30] Postmaster General of the United States, *Report for 1899* (Washington, 1900), p. 18, p. 869.

Summary:

Cost of land	655,490.77
Cost of building	2,585,835.00
Cost of furniture and machinery	260,839.00
	$3,502,164.77

(From Madison Davis, *A History of the Washington City Post Office,* 1903.)

THE CHANGING STATUS OF THE POST OFFICE BUILDING

Within a year of the Post Office Building's completion, it was considered inadequate and stylistically obsolete. An editorial in the *New York Times* for January 21, 1900, commented on its faults. "This Post Office Building, which is large but otherwise unimpressive unless the impression made upon Senator Hawley that it is 'a cross between a cathedral and a cotton mill' may be mentioned, was believed to be ample for the accommodation of the Post Office Department." But with the City Post Office occupying the main and mezzanine floors and the General Post Office occupying the rest of the building, there was little extra room for the City's operations and "they are already cramped." The editorial also criticized the high government officials' offices. "Their rooms are fitted up with a solid magnificence that is assurance of the liberality of the government and the Superintendent of Buildings." The shoddiness of construction was also blasted. The skylights were insecure, the floors badly laid, and the window frames imperfect and a menace to health in their leakiness.[31]

However, most critics seemed to agree with Madison Davis's observations that the Post Office "is one of the most majestic in the country, and it is admirably adapted to its purposes." The only concrete faults were the unavailability of room to grow. "The City Post Office ... although not generally crowded, takes up every available foot of the space that has been allotted to it. The time is not far distant, however, when, through the increase of business, and through encroachments upon its quarters by the ... Post Office Department ... the (City) Post Office will have to seek other accommodations." [32]

The Post Office Building's style of architecture was also criticized due to a growing wave of neo-classicism, started by the World's Columbian Exposition of 1893. This prompted both government and private architects to abandon the Richardsonian Romanesque style for a newer style. Chicago architects had created a dazzling "white

---
[31] *New York Times,* January 21. 1900.
[32] Davis, p. 77.

city" for the Fair on a site which had formerly been a swamp on Lake Michigan. The grounds were laid out and the buildings designed in a neo-classic manner in the Beaux Arts tradition of architecture and city planning. The impact of the Fair was tremendous; it started a city beautiful movement which emphasized the importance of planning whole areas, not just buildings. Daniel Burnham, creator of the Fair, gave the movement a slogan, "Make no little plans. They have no power to stir men's souls." [33] City dwellers and civic leaders across the country adopted as many aspects of the new theories of planning as their budgets would allow.

The implications of the Chicago Fair and the accompanying city beautiful movement for Washington were the return to neo-classicism for the architecture of government buildings and a rediscovery of L'Enfant's plan for the city. This return to neo-classicism "pleased a public tired of the vagaries of the preceding half-century—the romantic red sandstone Norman castle of the Smithsonian, the mansard-roofed Department of Agriculture building . . . the State Department building, the heavy square-towered Post Office on Pennsylvania Avenue, and the ornate Italian Renaissance Library of Congress." [34]

The movement to beautify and monumentalize Washington, and Pennsylvania Avenue in particular, actually started in 1896 when the Supervising Architect of the Treasury William Aiken proposed the concept of a Federal Triangle. He reported that a large federal building complex be started in the area now known as the Federal Triangle. Aiken recommended Pennsylvania Avenue as the site of all future federal buildings. The Post Office, which was then under construction, was to be the first step in making "the Avenue a processional way unrivaled in grandeur among the capitals of the world." [35]

In 1900 demands by Congressmen and writers for Washington to be brought up to date and beautified resulted in the creation of the Senate Park Commission, so-called in an effort to disguise its real purpose of changing the character of central Washington. Under the supervision of Senator James McMillan, the Park Commission was headed by Burnham, Charles McKim, Augustus St. Gaudens, and Frederick Law Olmsted, Jr. The staff was coordinated by Charles Moore, McMillan's secretary. The McMillan Commission viewed the entire triangle area as a possible site for future administrative

---

[33] Constance McLaughlin Green, *Washington: Capital City* (Princeton: Princeton University Press, 1963), p. 133–140.
[34] Ibid., p. 140.
[35] National Capital Planning Commission, *The Old Post Office and Clock Tower and Its Relationship to the Development of the Federal Triangle* (Washington, D.C., 1971), p. 3.

buildings for the District government. But, even though they regarded the Post Office Building as exemplifying, as Cass Gilbert said, "what should be avoided, irrespective of its bad design," (referring to its undue height and excessive prominence) they did not recommend tearing it down.[36]

The McMillan Commission, obviously due to the ideals of its members who had served in various capacities in planning the Chicago Fair, was decidedly neo-classic in its designs for Washington. This naturally spelled the end for all earlier styles of architecture, and especially for the Richardsonian Romanesque. But there were many architects and critics who revolted against the growing wave of neo-classicism, finding merit in the older styles and the freedom for which they stood. A critic commented, "The Chicago World's Fair was a shattering blow at the only conspicuous progressive effort of the century to resolve the growing contradiction between the ideology and the mechanics of American building. Historically, this was perhaps inevitable, but the loss was nonetheless disastrous." Sigfried Gideon said, "American architecture was undermined by the most dangerous reaction since its origin." [37]

During the period 1910 through 1928 various plans were made for the Triangle area. In 1910 Congress approved plans for three new executive department buildings, Justice, Commerce and Labor, and State, but these were not built during that time. They were to be designed in the neo-classic style which the McMillan Commission had decreed for future government buildings. In 1914 the Washington Post Office moved from the Pennsylvania Avenue building to a new building in the neo-classic style next to Union Station and the Post Office Department took over the entire older structure. In 1917 the Public Buildings Commission recommended the construction of both federal and district buildings in the triangle area and the Chairman of the Commission on Fine Arts, Charles Moore, criticized the old Post Office Building in a letter to the Chairman of the Public Buildings Commission.

> It was designed at a time when American architecture was in a transitional state, before the necessity for an adequate amount of light and air was sufficiently recognized even by Government builders. The style had its brief day of novelty and popularity; then it retired because of

---

[36] Mary Cable, *Avenue of The Presidents* (Boston: Houghton Mifflin Company, 1969), p. 183; National Park Service, *Verification of Significance and Evaluation of Effect: The Old Post Office Building in Washington* (Washington, D.C., February, 1970), p. 5.

[37] James Marston Fitch, *American Building I: The Historical Forces that Shaped It* (Boston: Houghton Mifflin, 1966), p. 208.

Courtesy of John J. G. Blumenson
View of the Post Office from the north side of Pennsylvania Avenue.

its failure to fulfill modern requirements. The Government is fortunate in having but one such example among its public buildings.[38]

In 1925 President Coolidge requested from Congress a substantial appropriation to begin a major building program. Congress responded with $50,000,000 for buildings in the District of Columbia to be administered by the Secretary of the Treasury and assisted by a board of architectural consultants and the Commission of Fine Arts and Public Buildings Commission. Plans for the triangle were prepared in 1926, and in 1927 that committee submitted its designs to the Secretary of the Treasury Andrew Mellon. On January 13, 1928, Congress passed a new act authorizing the acquisition of all private lands in the triangle area at a cost not to exceed $25,000,000. "With the assurance that the entire triangle would be planned as a unit, as the Fine Arts Commission urged, the board of architectural consultants prepared a comprehensive scheme for the area."[39] Their plans and models were revealed in April, 1929, and showed a complex of monumental buildings grouped around two large courts or plazas. The buildings were designed in the neo-classic style with fixed cornice and belt lines along Constitution and Pennsylvania Avenues to tie them together and relate them to each other. Several buildings—the Old Post Office, the District Building, and the Coast Guard Building—which did not conform to the general concept of the plan, were to be demolished.[40]

The development of the triangle followed this plan very closely, although individual buildings took a somewhat different form, the proposed central court between the Commerce and New Post Office became a parking lot, and none of the buildings proposed for demolition has yet been torn down. Congress declared itself in 1934 to be opposed to the authorization of demolition funds for the Old Post Office Building, even though it was stated that, "the building was very wasteful as to space, perhaps one of the most uneconomical buildings used by the Government in the entire country, comparing the amount of total cubic space in ratio to the net square feet of space produced."[41] The building was spared demolition at the hands of the Mellon Commission due to lack of funds and the triangle remained only 85 per cent complete.

In the 1960's the problem of the "unfinished" Federal Triangle

---

[38] *Verification*, p. 5.
[39] John W. Reps, *Monumental Washington* (Princeton; Princeton University Press, 1967), p. 170.
[40] National Capital Planning Commission, p. 3.
[41] *Verification*, p. 7.

The Old Post Office Building

and of Pennsylvania Avenue in particular came to the attention of the President and leading political figures. In 1962 Daniel Patrick Moynihan expressed the view that Pennsylvania Avenue should be a great thoroughfare for the city. As it stands, it is "unsightly by day and empty by night... it should be lively, friendly, and inviting as well as dignified and impressive." [42] The Pennsylvania Avenue Commission reported in 1964 that the avenue should be designed as a monumental, ceremonial, and formal composition between the Capitol and the White House. Nathaniel Owings, head of the Commission, presented the plans: 1. the extension of the Federal Triangle to the District Building by demolishing the Old Coast Guard Building, 2. rescuing the Grand Plaza as a formal garden park by moving parking underground, 3. the demolition of the Old Post Office Building to enable completion of the Great Circle on 12th Street, but preservation of the clock tower "as a momento of the time it represents, as a vertical punctuation on the Avenue, and as a city lookout." [43]

Originally the clock tower was to be embedded into the extension of the proposed Internal Revenue Service Building, but in 1966 the plans were slightly altered by architect John Carl Warnecke to make it free-standing in a tight little semi-circular recess. The buildings he designed to complete the Triangle were in a modern style and the tower was to be a contrasting, but interesting, visitor's center with an elevator and glass enclosures around the observation deck. However, in 1969 Warnecke lost his job to Vincent Kling, and Kling altered the plans for the new building. He wanted the area completed in the Mellon tradition of neo-classicism and suggested keeping the tower only if it could be made economically feasible.[44] As it now stands, the tower is to be free-standing though engaged to the IRS Building by a passageway. The sentiments for keeping the tower are that it is a treasured landmark, a warm and vital addition to an otherwise cold and sterile composition, and a vertical element to enliven the avenue. It is to be finished with a Romanesque entrance created with elements removed from the old building.[45]

One minor detail remains to be solved before the Old Post Office can be destroyed. In 1965 all of Pennsylvania Avenue was declared a National Historic Site and both the Federal Triangle and the Old Post Office Building were recommended for inclusion in the National Register of Historic Places as Category II Landmarks. The definition

---

[42] Cable, p. 203.
[43] National Capital Planning Commission, p. 4.
[44] Eckardt; NCPC, p. 11.
[45] *Verification,* p. 12–13.

of Category II Landmarks is: "Landmarks of importance which contribute significantly to the cultural heritage or visual beauty and interest of the District of Columbia and its environs, and which should be preserved or restored, if possible." [46] The problem was choosing which should be preserved—a Nineteenth Century building or a 1930's grouping. The National Capital Planning Commission decided that the completion of the Federal Triangle as originally designed should take precedence over the retention of the Old Post Office Building.[47]

Although the "pro-tower" forces seem to have won out over the "destroy-the-whole-thing" forces, there are many people in Washington who insist on retaining the entire Post Office Building. They feel it is necessary to keep the landmark building and use it for various visitor purposes that would connect the Triangle, Mall, and downtown. John Wiebenson and Arthur Cotton Moore have made two different, though related, suggestions for the building's re-use. Their common concern is that visitors to Washington not be cut off from the downtown area by making Pennsylvania Avenue an impassable border of governmental buildings. A re-use of the building by either plan will greatly enhance the avenue, keep people on the streets at night, make the area safer, and provide a bridge between the city and the Mall.

The importance of saving the Old Post Office Building for re-use is best expressed in the ideas of Jane Jacobs, author of *The Death and Life of Great American Cities*. She felt that an area should serve more than one primary function, and preferably more than two. "These must insure the presence of people who go outdoors on different schedules and are in the place for different purposes, but who are able to use many facilities in common." [48] Districts must also mingle buildings that vary in age and this involves retaining many older buildings. Improvements must be made to generate diversity and supply needs that are missing, and this can be done by renovating old buildings, not by wiping out great areas built in an earlier age.[49] One element that destroys cities is the massive single use of an area. They form borders which are usually destructive to the whole region around. Borders form vacuums of use adjoining them and this means fewer users with fewer purposes and destinations at hand. "This is

---

[46] Charles H. Conrad, Testimony before Subcommittee on Public Buildings and Grounds, Committee on Public Works, U.S. Senate, April 21, 1971, p. 8.

[47] Ibid., p. 10.

[48] Jane Jacobs, *The Death and Life of Great American Cities* (New York: Random House, 1961), p. 152.

[49] Ibid., p. 187, 198.

Courtesy of John J. G. Blumenson

View of the Post Office from Twelfth Street.

serious because literal and continuous mingling of people, present because of different purposes, is the only device that keeps streets safe."[50] Most modern planners agree to a certain extent with her theories, even the Pennsylvania Avenue Commission in 1967 altered its plans for the avenue to try to bridge the gap between the downtown, the Triangle, and the Mall. But obviously they did not feel the need to retain old buildings for diversity and possible re-use, for they planned to demolish whole blocks of lower downtown for modern office space.[51]

John Wiebenson, a Washington architect and professor at the University of Maryland, suggested turning the Old Post Office Building into a visitor's center to preserve the dignity of the avenue by making it serve the people better, making it safer after dark, and connecting it to the downtown and the Mall. The building, in the center of a natural thoroughfare, could be an elegant setting for cultural and commercial services. "Its many floors . . . wrap around a high central court capable of being brilliantly sun-lit, hung with plants and banners, rich with people exploring its by-ways."[52] Shops, restaurants, resting places, and display areas could be provided for visitors during the day and at night. Decorated in an exciting manner, the building would attract a variety of people and help make Pennsylvania Avenue safer at night for both tourists and office workers. Its re-use would also serve as a vital link between the downtown and the visitors to the Mall's museums. In order to realize the Old Post Office's potential, it must be included into the area to be developed by the Bicentennial Corporation. It could be used to house certain exhibits, such as flags or even windmills, for the Smithsonian. "The Old Post Office would be a remarkable exhibit facility for 1976. Afterwards, large portions of the space would be emptied of exhibits and leased for shops, restaurants, services, music, etc."[53] The subway under construction is to have a station next to the building and shops are to be located underground with a decorative fountain on the surface. Wiebenson feels this would be a tragic mistake, pointing to the near failure of L'Enfant Plaza designed in this manner, and proposes that the Old Post Office Building could better serve the needs of the people in this manner by providing a larger above-ground facility.[54]

Arthur Cotton Moore, D.C. architect and planner, proposed that

---

[50] Ibid., p. 257, 259.
[51] President's Temporary Commission on Pennsylvania Avenue, *Pennsylvania Avenue* (Washington, Government Printing Office, 1969) passim.
[52] John Wiebenson, Testimony before Subcommittee on Public Buildings and Grounds, Committee on Public Works, U.S. Senate, April 21, 1971, p. 2.
[53] Ibid., p. 6.
[54] Ibid., p. 5–6.

the Old Post Office Building be maintained and turned into a new and active use as a visitors' center and 500 room hotel. It would offer both American and European tourists "generous and exciting accommodations at competitive rates with beltway motels, but within the center of Washington with direct relationship to all the major monuments they came to see." [55] Some rooms of the hotel would offer panoramic views of the city while others would open onto the large central court. He cites the Regency Hyatt House in Atlanta as an example of that type of hotel plan. Moore's plan for a visitors' center for the first two floors is similar to Wiebenson's proposal, and he, too, is concerned with revitalizing downtown and Washington's night life. "The combination of the exciting commercial levels below and the 24 hour use of the hotel . . . would be the first new infusion of continuous life in an area which now shuts up and goes home at 5:00 p.m." This re-use of the building would benefit everyone, the American and European tourists who seek low hotel rates, the businessmen of downtown, and in addition it would be "an identifiable, immediately achievable showcase project for the 1976 Bicentennial." [56] Furthermore, "the success of this preservation effort would demonstrate that we are a people mindful and sensitive to our heritage, who are sincerely interested in the future and quality of life in our cities." [57]

A closing comment by Elbert Peets will serve to illustrate the special problems Washington has in regard to its plan, the way that plan has been carried out, and the need for rethinking for the future.

> The government capital is turning away from the city; the government buildings are being concentrated together and separated from the buildings of the city. This was not L'Enfant's idea. On the contrary, he made every effort to amalgamate the two, to make them serve each other. He distributed government buildings, markets, seats of national societies, academies, and state memorials at points of architectural advantage throughout the city, as if with the definite purpose of putting the impress of the National Capital on every part. This was sound sentiment and sound architectural judgment.
>
> From the Chicago Fair of 1893 came the architectural idealogy that sees a city as a monumental court of honor sharply set off from a profane and jumbled area of concessions . . . There is no evidence, in this procedure, of feeling for the city as an organism, a matrix that is worthy of its monuments and friendly with them. . . . The loss is social, as well as esthetic.[58]

---

[55] Arthur Cotton Moore, p. 2.
[56] Ibid., p. 4.
[57] Ibid.
[58] Jacobs, p. 173.

BIBLIOGRAPHY

Books

Burchard, John, and Bush-Brown, Albert. *The Architecture of America.* Boston: Little Brown and Company, 1961.
Cable, Mary. *The Avenue of the Presidents.* Boston: Houghton Mifflin Company, 1969.
Davis, Madison. *A History of the Washington City Post Office.* Lancaster, Pennsylvania: New Era Publishing Company, 1903.
Development of the United States Capital. Washington: Government Printing Office 1930.
Fitch, James Marston. *American Building I: the Forces that Shaped It.* Boston: Houghton Mifflin Company, 1966.
Green, Constance McLaughlin. *Washington: Capital City.* Princeton: Princeton University Press, 1963.
Hitchcock, Henry-Russell. *The Architecture of Henry Hobson Richardson and His Times.* Cambridge: The M.I.T. Press, 1936.
Jacobs, Jane. *The Death and Life of Great American Cities.* New York: Random House 1961.
President's Temporary Commission on Pennsylvania Avenue. *Pennsylvania Avenue* Washington: Government Printing Office, 1969.
Reps, John W. *Monumental Washington.* Princeton: Princeton University Press, 1967.
Schuyler, Montgomery. *American Architecture.* Cambridge: Belknap Press, 1961.
United States Post Office Department. *Post Office Site 323.* Washington; n.d.
Whiffen, Marcus. *American Architecture since 1780: A Guide to the Styles.* Cambridge: The M.I.T. Press, 1969.
Works Progress Administration, Federal Writers' Program. *Washington, D.C.* New York: Hastings House, 1968.

Articles

Eckardt, Wolf Von. "Why Can't We Keep the Old Post Office?" *Washington Post,* March 8, 1970.
"Government Buildings Compared to Private Buildings." *American Architect and Building News,* XLIV (April 7, 1894), 2–4.
"Granite Defiance." *The Washington Post.* March 19, 1971.
Harpers Weekly. October 16, 1897, 1039.
Mellon, Andrew. "The Development of Washington." *American Magazine of Art,* XX (January, 1929) 3–9.
Moore, Charles. "Personalities in Washington Architecture." *Records,* Columbia Historical Society, XXXVII (1937) 1–15.
"New Post Office Building, Washington." *American Architect and Building News.* XXXV (March 12, 1892) 174.
New York Times. January 21, 1900.
"Obituary: W. J. Edbrooke." *The Inland Architect.* (April, 1896).
"Rally Seeks to Save Old D.C. Landmark". *Washington Post,* April 19, 1971.
Washington Evening Star. 1898, 1899, 1900, 1932.

Papers and Manuscripts

General Services Administration. *Report on the Completion of the Federal Triangle* Washington, 1970.
National Capital Planning Commission. *The Old Post Office and Clock Tower and its Relation to the Development of the Federal Triangle.* Washington, 1971.
National Park Service. *Verification of Significance and Evaluation of Effect: The Old Post Office Building in Washington.* 1970.
Postmaster General of the United States. *Reports for 1890–1900.* Washington, 1891–1901.

Public Buildings Service. *Records and Correspondence,* 1891–1899. Record Group 121, Federal Records Center, Suitland, Maryland.

Supervising Architect of the Treasury. *Reports for 1890–1900.* Washington, 1891–1901.

U.S. *Congressional Record.* House. "Protect our Heritage- and Profit by it." March 17, 1971.

U.S. Congress, Senate. Subcommittee on Public Buildings and Grounds, Committee on Public Works, Hearings on the Old Post Office Building, April 21, 1971. Testimony of: Arthur F. Sampson, Charles Conrad, Richard Howlans, David Yerkes, James Biddle, Arthur Cotton Moore, John W. Hill, John Wiebenson, Jerry A. Moore.

The East and West Wings of the White House

ELLEN ROBINSON EPSTEIN

When the Federal Government was moved from Philadelphia to Washington, D.C., the first building planned was the President's House. A competition was held in 1799 for its design and James Hoban, an Irish immigrant architect then residing in South Carolina, was awarded First Prize.

Hoban designed a three-story Palladian style building with a terrace and a wing extending on each side of the mansion. When the White House was built, however, neither the third story nor the wings and terraces were constructed, chiefly because of lack of funds. In the course of time the third story was constructed out of the previous attic and the intended extensions were added to both the east and the west sides.

The historian William H. Prescott has written that

> the surest test of the civilization of a people—at least, as sure as any—afforded by mechanical art is to be found in their architecture, which presents so noble a field for the display of the grand and the beautiful, and which, at the same time, is so intimately connected with the essential comforts of life.[1]

Applying Prescott's test to the President's House, which from its beginning has served both as his place of business and as his residence, it should have, but did not always exemplify "the display of the grand and the beautiful," nor was it at all times "intimately connected with the essential comforts of life."

Historians writing of the White House have made these points in

---

Delivered before the Columbia Historical Society on April 18, 1972.

I would like to thank my husband, David, for his help and guidance during the many hours spent revising, editing, and proofreading this paper. Without his patience and understanding the task would have been much more difficult.

[1] William H. Prescott, *History of The Conquest of Peru*. Introduction by Samuel Eliot Morison. (New York, The Heritage Press, 1957.) Book I, Chapter V, p. 72.

The East and West Wings of the White House

discussing various aspects of the history of the mansion but surprisingly they have largely ignored the wings of the White House, where, at various periods, the character of the mansion was determined. To understand the White House requires a comprehensive view. Others have described the mansion; this paper is a history of the wings.

THE FIRST EXTENSION

The second resident of the President's House, Thomas Jefferson, who had himself submitted a design in the competition for its plan, called the mansion, after moving into it, "large enough for two emperors, one Pope and a Grand Lama." In apparent conflict with this evaluation, Jefferson directed the architect Benjamin H. Latrobe to build two additions to the mansion to extend 150 feet on each side. The presidential instructions to Latrobe were a blend of Hoban's original design for the wings and Jefferson's own admiration for classical Roman architecture.[2]

These Jeffersonian additions were used as "offices," a word which at that time connoted household facilities such as kitchens, pantries, ice houses, coal bins, stables, saddle rooms, and hen houses, all disguised behind the new classical colonnades. Some writers have erroneously concluded that Jefferson used these "offices" in today's sense of the word, as a place for the transaction of business and clerical affairs. This was not their function.

These terraces, or colonnades, did little to alleviate overcrowding in the mansion, and subsequent presidential families frequently complained about limitations of space.

The point was made dramatically in 1860, when the Prince of Wales, later to become Edward VII, visited the United States. This, the first official visit of British royalty to the United States, unless one reckons the visit by "representatives" of the Crown in 1814, caused protocol problems for the White House. President James Buchanan, a former Ambassador to the Court of St. James, and his accomplished niece, Harriet Lane, who served her bachelor uncle as hostess both in England and in the White House, were eager to entertain the Prince in a suitable manner. The White House could not provide adequate accommodations for the Prince and his entourage because the President's office and his living quarters occupied the second floor of the mansion and the first floor was devoted entirely to ceremonial

---

[2] Hoban's original drawing has been lost but from other primary sources and from copy drawings of the plan made contemporaneously with Hoban's design we can be fairly sure that Hoban intended terraces and wings to be added to the mansion. Jefferson undoubtedly knew of Hoban's design.

rooms. The only spare bedroom in the mansion was given to the Prince. His Minister of State, the Duke of Newcastle, was given the President's private bedroom. The President was relegated to a couch in the public anteroom.

MICHLER'S SOLUTION

The Civil War intervened and left little time or money for such concerns as the President's House. Two years after the end of the war a solution was proposed by Brigadier General Nathaniel Michler. Michler, a member of the Corps of Engineers of the United States Army in charge of Public Buildings and Grounds, studied the conditions in the White House and found that the President's staff had, during the war years, encroached upon the entire eastern portion of the second floor of the mansion.[3] The Jefferson-Latrobe colonnades, originally used for storage space, were now smothered by the attached greenhouses on the west and, on the east, with the growth of the White House staff and kitchen requirements. The mansion was unbearably cramped.

In addition to the problems of overcrowding, Michler considered many complaints about the White House site. At that time, immediately to the south of the mansion, along the route of today's Constitution Avenue, flowed a branch of the Potomac River. The ill effects arising from these waters and swampy land were, in the view of some, a cause of the death in 1841 of President William Henry Harrison; yet not until 1871 was the canal filled in, only then controlling this source of malaria and miasma.[4]

Michler proposed a solution to the two-fold problem of space and health: the abandonment of the mansion as a residence and its limited use solely as a place of business. The President and his family would live elsewhere, on a site to be selected from one of eleven proposed areas which included, among others, the estate at Meridian Hill. Michler's report was presented to Congress but failed to receive legislative support, partly because of a strong outcry against moving the President's residence. Another factor which may have influenced

---

[3] For Michler's report see the *Report of the Chief of Engineers Accompanying the Annual Report of the Secretary of War, 1867*, Appendix T and T-1, pp. 519, 532–538. The report can be found also in Senate Miscellaneous Document 21, 39th Congress, 2nd Session, January 1867, and the *Congressional Globe*, 39th Congress, 2nd Session, Vol. 147, pp. 1577–1579.

[4] John B. Blake, the Commissioner of Public Buildings in 1857, wrote: "The President's House, as is well known, is in a very unhealthy location. Its inmates are subject to intermittent fever, which of late years has proved obstinate to cure." See the *Annual Report of the Commissioner of Public Buildings*, Record Group 42, National Archives.

this proposal's defeat was that Andrew Johnson was President at this time and was not liked by many members of Congress. The men who were in the process of trying to impeach the President would hardly be enthusiastic about building or buying him a new home. Con-

Washingtoniana Room, Martin Luther King Memorial Library, Washington, D.C.

Figure 1. Frederick D. Owen, architect of the 1891 and 1901 plans for an expanded White House.

sequently in the following years, despite occasional other proposals, Presidents continued to reside and work in an unchanged White House.[5]

MRS. HARRISON'S PLAN

In 1891, Caroline Scott Harrison, wife of President Benjamin Harrison (grandson of President William Henry Harrison), a talented woman with strong artistic inclinations which were evidenced by her floral designs for some of the White House china, prepared, with the professional assistance of a Washington architect, Frederick D. Owen, elaborate plans for extensions to the White House.

"Mrs. Harrison's Plan," as it became known, provided sufficient space for the President and Mrs. Harrison, for Mrs. Harrison's father, for the President's and Mrs. Harrison's two children and their respective spouses, five grandchildren, governesses, servants, and pets, all of whom were then living in the western half of the second floor of the White House.

Mrs. Harrison's plan envisioned an elaborate rectangular complex of buildings: on the east, a National Wing for a historical art gallery; on the west, an Official Wing for diplomatic receptions and staff functions, both joined to the mansion by small halls or rotundas to house statuary and painting of Americans and Americana. Also proposed was a glass greenhouse, stretching across the south lawn, parallel to, and with the same linear dimensions as, the White House. In the center of this rectangle, created by the two wings, the greenhouses and the White House, was a courtyard which would contain an allegorical grouping of statues commemorating three important events in American history: (1) the discovery of America on October 12, 1492; (2) the laying of the cornerstone of the White House on October 13, 1792; and hardly last in importance, (3) the laying of the cornerstone for Mrs. Harrison's Plan, an event scheduled to occur on October 12, 1892.

This baroque plan violated the basic simplicity of Hoban's original design and was more an expression of the Gilded Age than of that period of republican simplicity in which the White House originally was conceived. Ironically, her plan was not approved by Congress, not for reasons of aesthetics, but because of President Harrison's viola-

---

[5] For additional proposals see: Journal of the Senate, S. 1842, Serial 1984; Journal of the House, H.R. 5988, Serial 2008; Senate Miscellaneous Document No. 81, Serial 1993; Senate Report No. 451, Serial 2359; House Report No. 4042, Serial 2890, Journal of the Senate, January 28, 1890, page 97 Serial 2677, and Senate Bill 1842 in 1882 and Senate Bill 1868 in 1886.

The East and West Wings of the White House

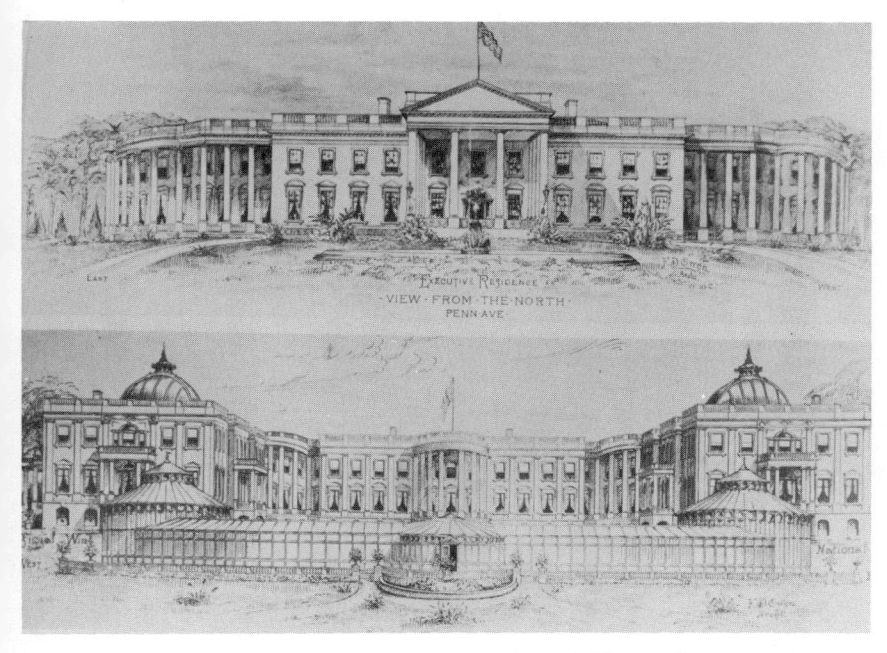

Manuscript Division, Library of Congress

Figure 2. Mrs. Harrison's Plan of 1891. Top, as seen from Pennsylvania Avenue. Bottom, as seen from the Ellipse.

tions of a well-established principle: powerful politicians must be satisfied. A year earlier the President had refused to appoint Speaker of the House Thomas B. Reed's candidate to the office of the Collector of Customs in Portland, Maine, and for this slight, "Czar" Reed, so appropriately characterized, refused to allow the Harrison legislation to come to a vote. In retrospect, this twist of fate was a fortunate one, allowing the White House to remain in its original Palladian style and preventing it from becoming something wholly different from what it was in the past. Less than a year later Caroline Scott Harrison was dead and there was no one to champion her plan.

THE BINGHAM PROPOSAL

The year 1900 was the centennial both for the city of Washington and for the White House. One of the events in the celebration of the anniversary year included the unveiling of a plan for an extended White House by Colonel Theodore A. Bingham. As the Officer in

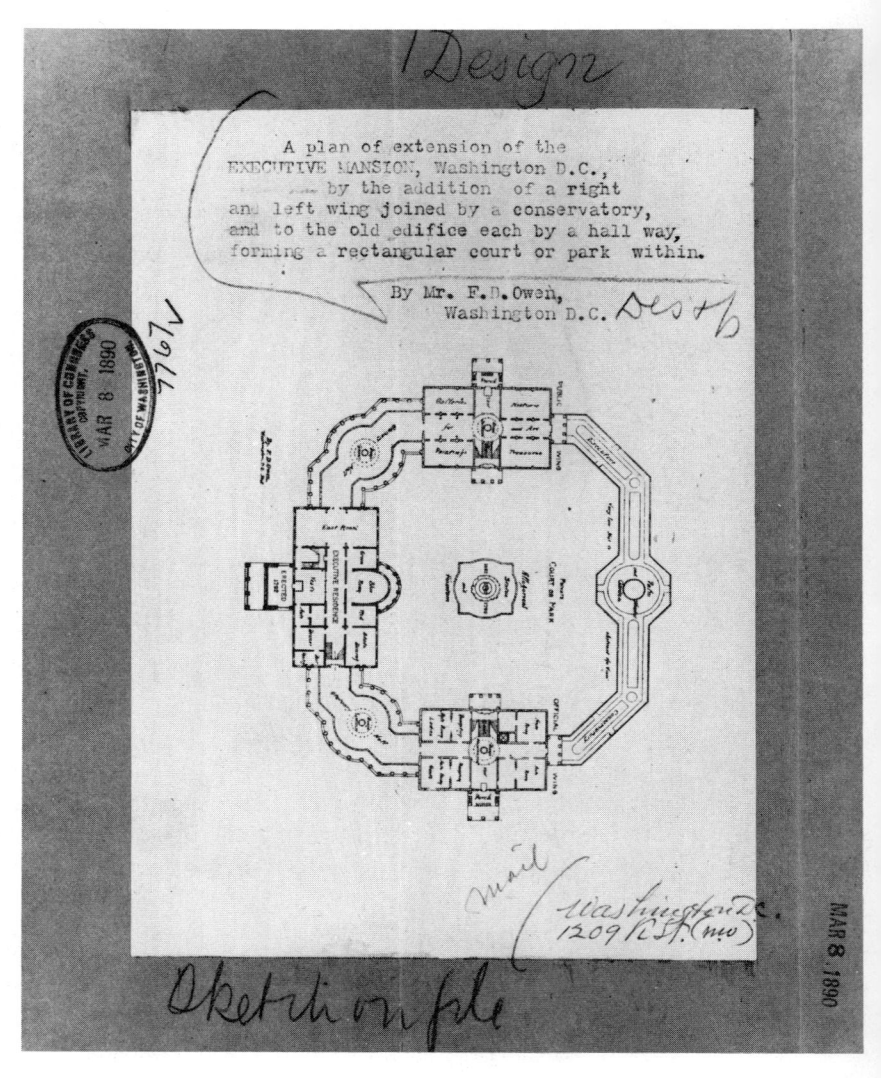

Copyright Division, Library of Congress

Figure 3. One of several sketches deposited by Frederick D. Owen with the Copyright Office of the Library of Congress. Owen had several plans, all of which were basically the same but varied slightly in the design of the Official and Public Wings.

Charge of Public Buildings and Grounds,[6] Bingham, a very self-assured and aggressive man, wanted an accomplishment to his credit while in this office. On December 12, 1900, in the East Room of the White House, in the presence of President William McKinley, Vice-President Theodore Roosevelt, Admiral George Dewey, members of the Supreme Court, and other elite government officials, Bingham dramatically unveiled his red-draped, palm-banked model. This model, although not quite so elaborate, closely adhered to the earlier plan of Mrs. Harrison, a predictable result of the fact that Frederick D. Owen was the architect of both designs.[7]

The following day, December 13, 1900, the American Institute of Architects vehemently denounced the plan, calling it "a mongrel," a "monstrosity," and "an unrecognizable contraption out of harmony with, and destroying, the individuality of the old building."[8] The Institute then voted resolutions which stated that the White House was one of the best examples of American architecture and that a committee of architects should be appointed to consider any contemplated changes in the mansion.[9] Either because of this criticism or other circumstances the Bingham plan, much to its sponsor's disappointment, was set aside.

THE FIRST MR. ROOSEVELT

In September 1901, Theodore Roosevelt became President following the assasination of William McKinley. With his wife, six somewhat untamed children, and their various pets and toys—a kangaroo rat, bicycles, skates, wooden stilts and marbles[10]—the family and per-

---

[6] This extremely prestigious position, filled by an Army colonel from the War Department, was a presidential appointment. The specific office was in existence from 1867 until 1925 when the duties of this position were assumed by an employee of the Department of the Interior. In the years following the responsibility for the White House was repeatedly transferred among a variety of positions until these basic power were given to the Chief Usher.

[7] Frederick D. Owen went into government employ in 1899, joining the Office of Public Buildings and Grounds at the request of Colonel Bingham. Among his many duties were designing the decorations for the Inaugural Parade and Ball every fourth year. Owen was also the designer of the police badges for the District of Columbia Police Department, the first War Room for President McKinley, and the first Presidential flag.

[8] Bess Furman, *White House Profile* (New York, 1951), p. 262. See also: Glenn Brown, "Roosevelt and the Fine Arts", *American Architect*, vol. 116, December 17, 1919, pp. 739-52; Glenn Brown, "Personal Reminiscences of Charles Follen McKim", *Architectural Record*, vol. 39, January 1916, pp. 84-88.

[9] Furman, *op. cit.*, p. 262.

[10] Ike Hoover, *Forty-Two Years in the White House* (Boston, 1934), p. 29. Hoover came to the White House as an electrician in the administration of President Benjamin Harrison (both the President and his wife were reluctant to turn the electric lights on or off) and was later elevated to the position of Chief Usher.

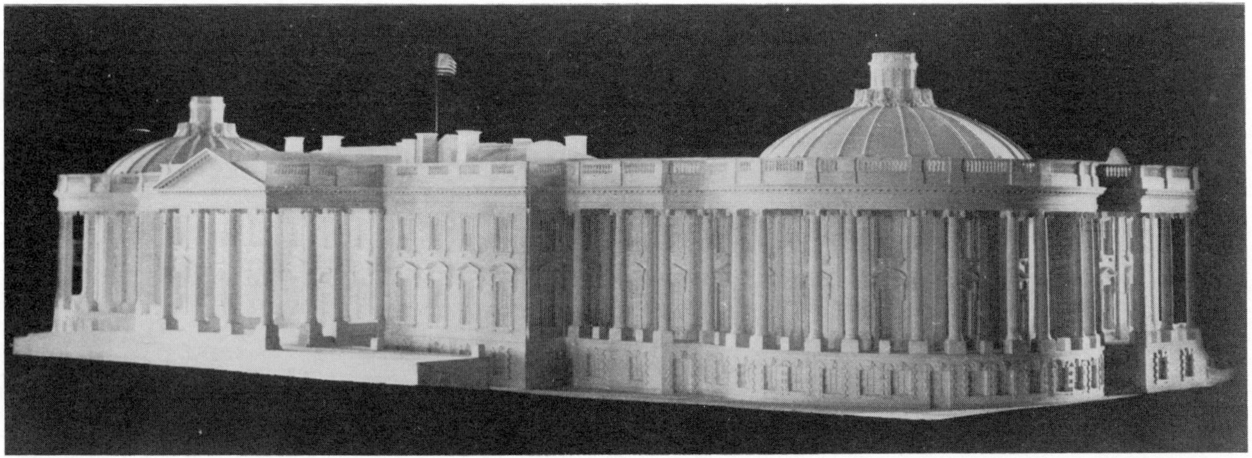

1901 Annual Report of the Officer in Charge of Public Buildings and Grounds

Figure 4. The 1900 Model promoted by Colonel Theodore A. Bingham.

sonal staff occupied the entire residential space on the second floor of the mansion, spilling into the presidential office space. The children on occasion were seen running through their father's office while he conducted affairs of state. While the White House may have been a source of pleasure for the presidential children, it was anything but this for the official staff: fifteen men were assigned to an office suitable for three. With this large family and the new large presidential staff, these conditions were no longer tolerable. Theodore Roosevelt personally selected McKim, Mead, and White, of New York, the preeminent architectural firm of the day, designers of the New York Public Library, numerous buildings at Harvard, Columbia, and New York Universities and several buildings at the Columbian Exposition in Chicago in 1893, for White House renovation. Following the designs and plans prepared by McKim, Mead, and White, construction began on the White House in 1902, and for a period of four months the presidential family moved to a temporary home at 22 (now 736) Jackson Place on Lafayette Square.

Work executed in the mansion proper included the conversion of a third story from an attic to living space and the reconstruction of the basement for use as a kitchen, laundry, and drying room. Prior to this time, the First Family hung its laundry in the outdoor drying yard near the vegetable garden, both of which were immediately to the south of the West Colonnade. Only in America can one imagine a Chief of State looking out of his dining room to see the family linen on the line and turnips in the garden.

In addition to work on the mansion, the long colonnades extending east and west were rebuilt and buildings at each wing were added. On the east, where an entire wing once existed but had been removed either in the latter part of the Andrew Johnson administration or in the early part of the Grant administration,[11] McKim, Mead, and White specified a colonnade and wing with a handsome portico and porte-cochere. When completed, the new addition became the official entrance for White House visitors.

The most needed of the additions was built on the west, a one-story "temporary" office building with an attic and structural support sufficient for an additional story. Located at the end of the West Colonnade, the latter newly visible after the greenhouses had been dismantled to provide space for the extension,[12] this West Wing was

---

[11] Research into primary source material in Record Group 42 has failed to provide a definite date for the dismantling of the East Wing.
[12] The greenhouses were moved to the foot of 15th Street, very near the spot which the Bureau of Printing and Engraving occupies today.

Library of Congress

Figure 5. The McKim, Mead, and White new East Portico of 1902. The colonnade was also rebuilt at this time.

1900 Annual Report of the Officer in Charge of Public Buildings and Grounds

Figure 6. The White House greenhouses and conservatories about 1898. In the upper left corner of the photograph can be seen the South Portico of the mansion. The West Wing is today located on this site.

to be used until a permanent office building was constructed since, at the time, Congress gave its approval for a temporary structure for this site. The office was approximately 100 feet by 50 feet and included a private office for the President, a large room for the Cabinet, and a reception area for congressional and other official visitors. Adjacent to the new presidential office was the tennis court where, in this athletic President's administration, according to legend, Cabinet "meetings" were often conducted, and on which Roosevelt was playing when he heard his secretary, William Loeb, Jr. shout from a window in the presidential office that William Howard Taft, the President's hand-picked choice as his successor, had received the 1908 Republican nomination.

When they were completed, the President was delighted with the offices, although not everyone was quite so pleased. The building was ridiculed and condemned in Congress. One member termed it "unfit to accomodate a second-class lawyer or a third-rate doctor";[13] while another called it "an abortion." [14] The Washington *Post* referred to the building as "an abomination" [15] and a national periodical wrote that it was "an example of Congressional niggardliness . . . as plain as a pipestaff within" and that it was "mostly regarded with regret." [16] Charles F. McKim was attacked as one of those "high priced architects" [17] in spite of the fact that he had returned more than $7,000 in unused funds. Dissatisfaction with the offices was expressed by those who viewed them as too simple and who felt that a more ornate building would have been more appropriate, but today this simplicity of design in the wings, which affords priority to the White House, is generally regarded as evidence of the sound architectural judgement of McKim whose buildings were usually more ornate than austere.

THE 1909 OVAL

Less than seven years later, in the Taft administration, the need for additional space once again became so acute that yet another extension was built, this time by Nathan C. Wyeth, a private Washington architect, later municipal architect of this city. Wyeth, having rejected the idea of adding an additional story to the office building for fear of dwarfing the White House, added instead an extra 50 feet

---

[13] *Congressional Record*, 58th Congress, 2nd Session, vol. 38, part 3, Senate debate of February 29, 1904; Senator Jacob H. Gallinger, Republican, of New Hampshire.
[14] *Ibid.*, Senator Benjamin R. Tillman, Democrat, of South Carolina.
[15] The Washington *Post*, March 1, 1904.
[16] A. Burnley Bibb, "The Restoration of the White House," *House and Garden*, March 1903, p. 135.
[17] *Congressional Record, op. cit.*, Senator Gallinger.

1903 Annual Report of the Officer in Charge of Public Buildings and Grounds

Figure 7. The McKim, Mead, and White 1902 West Wing. The basement story of the building was entirely below ground. The tennis court can be seen on the right.

to the south, making the new extension approximately 100 feet by 100 feet.

The most dramatic design innovation was the new oval office for the President. By adopting Hoban's concept of an oval, which was to be found in the White House, Wyeth not only helped solve the spatial problems for the time being but with this beautiful, graceful curvilinear office he joined in spirit the West Wing with the White House. The President now had both an elegant and a distinctive office.

Wyeth's technological innovations included a simple air cooling and ventilating system. The system involved using air blown across blocks of ice trays of chemical dehydrants and was designed to remove

Courtesy of Mrs. Nathan C. Wyeth

Figure 8. Nathan C. Wyeth, architect of the 1909 addition and of the President's Oval Office.

moisture from the air and cool the oval office. Unable to keep the stout Mr. Taft cool, the system was pronounced a failure and abandoned.[18]

No construction work was done for the next twenty years, until after the West Wing was destroyed by a five-alarm fire in 1929. President Herbert Hoover, leaving a staff Christmas party in the East Room, watched the raging fire from the roof of the mansion while Mrs. Hoover and the guests remained inside listening to the Marine band play.[19] Reconstruction began the next day and the Wing was restored within a few months to its former condition.

THE WHITE HOUSE SWIMMING POOL

In March of 1933, the next occupant of the White House arrived. Franklin D. Roosevelt, who had been an invalid for twelve years, required frequent physical therapy, his favorite form of exercise being swimming. To provide this facility for him, a nation-wide public subscription campaign, sponsored by more than forty newspapers, was initiated without his knowledge to raise sufficient funds for the construction of a pool in the West Colonnade. Approximately $22,316 was received in a month's time in cash, equipment, and services. To allow for the acceptance of the donations, authorization was sought from Congress, which, when assured that this campaign had begun without the previous knowledge or solicitation of the President, gave its approval. Within a few weeks construction began, and the pool, 15 feet by 50 feet and 8 feet in depth, was completed in thirty days.

ERIC GUGLER'S WORK

Extensive changes were made to the West Wing in 1934. Eric Gugler, a private architect from New York, promised the President that he could increase the interior space of the West Wing threefold without measurably affecting the exterior size of the building. This promise stemmed from Gugler's desire to persuade the President not to accept a design which can only be described as monstrous. That scheme envisioned a huge addition, one which would have dwarfed the White House. The President was persuaded and the architect proceeded to fulfill his promise. Gugler raised the West Wing roof several feet, thereby creating in a set-back, penthouse fashion, an

---

[18] "The President's Weather," *Literary Digest*, September 13, 1930, p. 27. It is also claimed that President Calvin Coolidge kept a gadget filled with chemicals on his desk to purify, or at least to deodorize, the air.

[19] "White House Fire," The Washington *Star*, December 25, 1929, p. 2.

The East and West Wings of the White House

1910 Annual Report of the Officer in Charge of Public Buildings and Grounds

Figure 9. The 1909 addition. The Oval Office may be seen in the center of the south side of the building. On the west side an entrance has been opened to the basement story. (Compare with figure 7.)

Domestic Engineering, September 1933

Figure 10. The swimming pool in the West Colonnade.

additional story; renovated the basement to create additional office space; lowered the grade of West Executive Avenue, giving the west side basement rooms, for the first time, access to the outside and thus creating new office space; added a sunken courtyard with a fountain around which additional offices were installed but which were camaflouged by three feet of soil and grass; and moved the President's Oval Office from the center of the West Wing to the southeast corner of the building. With the completion of the extension of 1934, the executive offices of the President assumed the basic design which they have since had to this day.

Gugler's design thus maintained the integrity of the White House, providentially intervening, as had "Czar" Reed almost fifty years earlier, to foil a plan which would have accomplished the contrary.

Figure 11. Eric Gugler's 1934 West Wing. (Compare with figures 7, 9, and 12.)

This photograph was taken in the early 1950's and the only visible differences are that the skylights on the roof no longer exist and the sunken court has been covered over. On the right can be seen where the court has been covered with sod in the center of the south extension. Gugler's work included moving the Oval Office from the center of the south side to the southeast corner, raising the second story roof to add a penthouse type third story, regrading West Executive Avenue to permit light to enter the basement offices, and extending the building south with offices completely underground.

The East and West Wings of the White House 613

General Services Administration
Figure 12. A 1960 view of the 1934 addition. (Compare with figure 11.)

THE EAST WING 1942

In 1942, on the east side, a total reconstruction, the first since 1902, took place. In this design, the architect, Lorenzo S. Winslow,[20] provided more office space and a motion picture theatre. Also on the east, an underground bomb shelter was constructed as a war-time precaution. This necessitated removing the fountain in front of the east entrance, which, curiously, although on White House property, had been constructed in 1867 by the Treasury Department, and was known, in fact, as the "Treasury Fountain".[21]

---

[20] Winslow was from 1934 until 1953 closely involved with the architecture of the White House. As an employee of the National Capital Parks, he worked on the 1933 swimming pool design, on the 1934 renovations with Gugler, and on various other reconstructions needed from time to time. In 1948 Winslow was designated Architect of the White House, a designation which continued until his retirement in 1953.

[21] The fountain was scheduled to be removed in 1942 but was not actually removed until 1946.

National Park Service

Figure 13. A photograph of a model of the White House and its wings in 1942. The East Wing is complete. The West Wing has been rebuilt. The sunken court is intact.

1948–1972

Because of the relatively modern construction techniques employed in the wings, from their origin in 1902 and thereafter, no need existed for their renovation in 1948–1952 when the mansion itself was completely gutted, save for the exterior walls, and then reconstructed.

In the years following, few structural changes were made to the wings. In 1970, the inadequate and unsightly awning over the north entrance of the West Wing was replaced by a neo-classical porte-cochere extending over a newly constructed circular driveway.

More recently attention has turned to the interior spaces. The offices, previously decorated in dismal colors and containing nondescript government-issue furniture, were transformed into an elegant, tasteful interior furnished in the style of colonial Williamsburg. The press room, formerly a cramped space without sufficient room for typewriters, telephones, or desks, is now located in the West Colonnade in spacious quarters created by placing a floor over the

Roosevelt swimming pool. Even the ticker tape machine has a suitable location, where once, as recently as the Eisenhower Administration, it occupied a corner of the men's lavatory.

Offices in the East Wing have been repainted and redecorated providing its occupants, the President's military aides and the First Lady's social secretaries, with more elegant working quarters. The

General Services Administration

Figure 14. The West Wing entrance in the 1960's. An awning has been replaced by a neon-lit canopy.

General Services Administration

Figure 15. The West Wing entrance in the 1970's. A small portecochere and circular driveway have been added. (Compare with figure 14.)

ground floor entrance, used for tours and official receptions, has remained unchanged since 1942 except for minor repairs.

It is unlikely that any significant alteration to the White House or its wings will occur in the future because, for any major changes, the Fine Arts Commission, the National Capital Planning Commission, and the Joint Commission on Landmarks, while not now so required by law, undoubtedly would be requested to advise and approve such proposals. As these are groups which are especially concerned with preserving the beauty of the Palladian mansion they would hardly permit any change to occur which would affect the harmony of Hoban's design. There would also undoubtedly be strong public opposition to any significant exterior change in the White House. It is ironic that a century after Michler's proposal to move the residence, and maintain the White House for business purposes only, precisely the opposite has occurred. With the completion of the new office buildings in 1966 on Lafayette Square, the offices once in the Old Executive Office Building were removed to these new buildings. As a result, the majority of the presidential staff, now grown to more than 1,500, has taken over the vacated offices in the Old Executive Office Building. Even the President and the Vice-President maintain working offices in this building, the Vice-President having relinquished his personal office in the West Wing and the President making use of his Oval Office only for ceremonial purposes.

We can thus reasonably hope that the White House will be preserved as the Eighteenth Century building that it is, symbolic of and embodying an important part of the nation's early history.

The Rabbit and the Boa Constrictor: John Singer Sargent at the White House

CHARLES MERRILL MOUNT

The President's wife was surprised.

Averting his eyes and resting his enormous frame on hands that clutched the back of a chair, her guest admitted: "You know, Mrs. Wilson, I have never been so nervous over a portrait in my life."

"This is a surprise from the great Sargent," she responded half in sarcasm, half coaxing. For with the possible exception of Gilbert Stuart, no American artist ever has had the prestige of John Singer Sargent and already he had created in his devastating image of Theodore Roosevelt the outstanding portrait of an American President. That he would do no less for Woodrow Wilson had not been doubted.

Sprung from a distinguished Massachusetts family that figured among the earliest settlers and ship-owners of Gloucester, this hulking man with red face, bristly beard, and tiny bulfinch nose, carried the stolid integrity of his stock into the world of art. For him no labor was too great, no artistic effort too complicated. Conscientious, an inscrutable bachelor, what astonished those of his time was the dazzling panache with which he conquered every difficulty to produce portraits that were trenchantly characterized and frequently pyrotechnical display-pieces.

Something lushly Italian lingered about his most chaste and puritanical works. This was only natural, for Sargent had been born, on January 12, 1856, in Florence. Trained in Paris under Carolus-Duran, dominating the artistic world of London where he lived, he carried an authority few painters since Rubens have acquired. Distinctly American in the approach to personality that distinguished his portraits, his art at the same time was cosmopolitan: French in its zest and wit and the Impressionist formula of color he pioneered in portrait painting, Italian in his sometimes sensuous opulence and the massively correct draftsmanship underlying his most bravura passages.

With the possible exception of sculpture, in every medium he founded a school whose characteristics remain visible today.

A perverse law of nature early decreed that few artists of stature have consistent association with the city of Washington. And in his case too, though the thread of Washington runs through every phase of Sargent's life, it is so lost in the fabric that even posthumously its presence is overlooked. A tidy biographic feature is that he came to the capital city almost immediately on setting foot for the first time on his "native" shore. For only in 1876, when he was twenty, did his patrician, culture-loving, and slightly impoverished parents bring together funds sufficient to permit John, his sister Emily, and their mother, to cross back over the Atlantic for a visit. The tourist circuit travelled was dictated by necessary stops with relatives in Boston and Philadelphia. The peripatetic Mrs. Sargent then eagerly shepherded her son and daughter north as far as Quebec and Montreal, west to Chicago, east to New York, and as far south as Washington.

It is only fair to state that if the youthful artist made any observations when he first saw his nation's capital they have not been found. Apart from sketches done at sea only two American works exist from that period and both feature Indians. Were we unaware of their authorship by a twenty-year-old boy they certainly would be considered the more than competent work of a mature French craftsman.

His choice of the American Indian as subject reflects the romantic and superficial allure of tourism, so much a part of his mother's nature. Conventional tastes can score too heavily this aspect of that unusual woman, possessed of a meager personal income, who scorned a stable home. Over two decades she had dragged her husband and offsprings between wintering places and summering places on the European continent. So much so that despite a depth of erudition in his maturity one expects only in scholars (again the parallel to Rubens is striking) Sargent appears to have had almost no formal schooling.

A preserved letter written when he was eight, addressed to "My dear Grandmother" bears the date "Mornex, July 11, 1864" and is eloquent of that strange boyhood:

> I have never seen you and grandpapa, but I love you very much and Papa says that you are both fond of little children, and that you love me and Emily and dear little sister Minnie. I am more than eight years old. Papa teaches us writing and arithmetic and geography and history. I am very fond of drawing, and I have got such nice books full of pictures of birds, and animals, and insects and fishes; so that I have plenty of models to copy. On Sunday, we learn hymns, just as Papa did when he was a little boy.

Pedantic punctuation and correctness of sentiment suggest parental guidance and reflect further the atmosphere of Yankee Victorians wending a slightly threadbare existence abroad. Nor was it a youth untouched by grief, as another letter from Biarritz, dated May 28, 1865, makes abundantly clear. "Dear Grandma" it begins:

> ... I suppose that Papa has written to you that our little sister Minnie is dead. She is buried at Pau. Papa and I rode in the carriage with her little coffin. She was a dear little girl and we cried very much when she died; but now we are glad that she is not sick any more now.

If perhaps his unconventional youth fostered an alienation, its standards of lonely decision and self-reliance became positive factors in Sargent's artistic development. Guided and adored by his parents, he seems never to have had ordinary doubts. Recognition of his complete and undeviating assurance in his own gifts is essential to any understanding of his art. Within ten years his altogether unusual degree of confidence made him a force to be reckoned with first in Paris and then in London.

His reputation was so great by 1887 that Sargent received an invitation to paint a portrait at Newport, Rhode Island. On this, his first professional trip to America, the discovery that such a remarkable artistic phenomenon was of distinguished American lineage had heartening effect. He was overwhelmed with orders, and from this trip, and another in 1889–1890, he brought back to England the start of a fortune. The 1890's were not without moments of relative quiet in his career. It nonetheless presents the spectacle of movement and unceasing work that produced portraits at Paris, London, Boston, New York, and even North Carolina, where in 1895 he went as the guest of George Vanderbilt. Most curious among the unexpected combinations of person and place that sparked his creative power was his portrait of Thomas B. Reed of Maine, Speaker of the House of Representatives, executed in 1891 in a studio borrowed in Paris.

Reed's portrait owed its genesis to Henry Cabot Lodge, then a member of the House of Representatives, whom Sargent had painted the previous year at Nahant. Unlike the handsome future Senator, whose splendid image hangs in the new National Portrait Gallery, Speaker Reed's grotesque bulk was not acutely pictorial. For all his fluent urbanity his was distinctly the figure of an overstuffed barnyard animal. The unhappy result was summarized in the artist's report to Charles Fairchild, who picked up the bill: "I found him awfully hard and this is the result of a second attempt different in view and character from the first, which I destroyed. His exterior does not somehow

Photograph from the author

Theodore Roosevelt by John Singer Sargent. Painted at the White House in 1903.

Begun in vexation, completed in anger, Sargent's portrait of Theodore Roosevelt, painted at the White House in 1903, has for seventy years remained a masterpiece among Presidential portraits.

correspond with his spirit and what is a painter to do? I am afraid you and your friends will be disappointed and that I could have made a better picture with a less remarkable man. He has been delightful." The last sentence anticipates others very similar when a portrait was less than expected.

Reed's own views demonstrate how great was the personal equation which permitted Sargent to glide from occasional failures to more frequent successes. "That portrait has given me a queer experience in life," wrote Reed. "All my friends are hurt, and the Democracy seem to think all my sins must be expiated by the treatment I have received therein. As for me, I like it. I am under the dreadful thrall under which I am told all Mr. Sargent's subjects are, and I am not in the least moved by the criticism of so many, except perhaps I am willing to admit the picture is not so good looking as the original...."

And though in fact this is an instance where Sargent's failure is attributable to momentary inflexibility—better lighting and shadows might have made manageable unpleasant contours and proportions— it remains to be noted how a cool, quiet, erudite artist, who wrought so furiously at his easel, already put men of authority under a "dreadful thrall". Even when unsatisfied his subjects went away fascinated by the experience. This factor of personality was decisive to each portrait. There are few routine works by Sargent, and those that exist lack the interest of his great performances because they show his spirit unaroused. Whether sitters excited him by physical distinction or produced delight, outrage, or occasional sexual phantasy, it was the force of this personal reaction that determined how successful the portrait became. At their most intense his powerful feelings created masterpieces.

Nowhere is the aura that surrounded Sargent better illustrated than in a letter forwarded to his London studio by Henry White, American Minister in London:

May 13, 1902

Dear Mr. Sargent

I must send you a line to say how greatly I am pleased at the good news that you will paint my portrait for the White House. Disregarding entirely my personal feelings, it seems to me eminently fitting that an American President should have *you* paint his picture. I cordially thank you.

Sincerely yours,
Theodore Roosevelt

Whether any Chief Executive before Roosevelt had addressed such words to an artist must remain doubtful. Such singular courtesy inaugurated a chain of events that created the most striking of all White House portraits.

From Boston later that summer of 1902 an announcement was made that Sargent would arrive in December to supervise installation of a second portion of his murals for the Public Library, and also, while in America, he would paint the President. But London sittings in that coronation year made Sargent despair of keeping the announced date. Finally, in the cold early morning of January 17, 1903, J. Carroll Beckwith, with whom twenty years before Sargent had shared a Paris studio, went to watch for the delayed liner *Lucania*. Again the following day he went to the pier where in Siberian weather the ship was edged into her berth.

Reporters had questioned Beckwith, then turned to Sargent as he made his way down the gangway puffing frost through his beard. As he responded to a barrage of questions, all noted his deliberation, an evident feeling of embarrassment, and the modesty of his tone. He spoke most readily of the murals about to be installed at Boston. Only after he had explained their several phases and ideological program was he prodded to talk of Washington.

"From Boston I shall return to New York and also visit Philadelphia and Washington," he explained. "I expect to paint the portrait of President Roosevelt in the historical series of the Presidents of the United States. It is the official portrait." Such an institution was Sargent that an editorial in the *New York Times* congratulated him on his return and his intended portrait of the President. When he proceeded to Boston and the manual labor of applying decorations to walls and ceiling, unprecedented publicity brought down on him social obligations and enormous demands for portraits. Charmed to recognize that this conspicuous lion was from one of their own families, Boston ladies crowded over each other to tease sittings from an overburdened artist.

In the midst of this spectacle Theodore Roosevelt raised the stakes:

January 29, 1903

Dear Mr. Sargent

Will you give Mrs. Roosevelt and myself the pleasure of staying at the White House during the time you are occupied in painting the portrait? Come any time after next Monday during the month of February. How long will you take?

We look forward to seeing you.

Sincerely yours,
Theodore Roosevelt

Photograph from Peter A. Juley & Sons, New York

John Hay, Secretary of State, by John Singer Sargent. Painted in Washington in 1903.

Sargent's portrait of Hay, painted two years before the death of the Secretary of State in 1905, was executed at Hay's Washington home between Roosevelt's sittings at the White House. It is in every way a reaction from the portrait of the President. Roosevelt's is a public image, this is intensely private. Because Roosevelt posed badly, Sargent studied Hay with greater diligence than had been his recent practice. The result is a sensitive psychologic document, anything but the public portrait of a Cabinet member.

Sargent's response brought another:

February 3, 1903

Dear Mr. Sargent

Good! We shall expect you on the 10th or 11th, and shall look forward to a visit of at least a week from you. Your room will be ready the evening of the 10th; then we can settle where you are going to paint.

Sincerely yours,
Theodore Roosevelt

Matters could hardly have begun on a better note. Roosevelt's invitation to the White House doubtless reflected the personal esteem of Charles F. McKim, Henry White, Joseph Hodges Choate, and John Hay, mutual friends who shared the special reverence so long accorded Sargent. Yet had they foresight these estimable people might have wondered what reaction an overbearing President would have before a dominant artist. Short, vigorous, and active, the Chief Executive was only 44, as much in the prime of life as Sargent, who at 47, and a head taller, was accustomed to cloak a very similar strength of character beneath socially acceptable restraints. Sargent's sophistication was matched by Roosevelt's ebullience, yet Roosevelt was more literate than he pretended and Sargent less even-tempered. Though initially both men were determined to be agreeable, the confrontation was doomed. Questions of the honor done him aside, it would have been far wiser had Sargent lodged at a hotel where he could rest quietly from his labors.

Nor did the White House appear propitious for his work when Sargent went exploring its available areas. Accompanied by the President he first looked in the South Portico, but objected to that. They went next to the Blue Room, and Sargent objected to that. Roosevelt exhibited signs of irritation as they made their way upstairs. "The trouble with you, Sargent," he called back over his shoulder, "is that you don't know what you want."

"No. The trouble, Mr. President, is that you don't know what a pose means."

Roosevelt had reached a landing half-way up the stairs. Stung by Sargent's unexpected rejoinder he grasped the glass-topped newel to swing about sharply. "Don't I!" he shouted.

"Don't move an inch. You've got it now," said the painter with what must have been professional imperturbability.

Roosevelt's moment of pettishness had thrown him into an inspired stance, showing all his arrogant, strutting nature. It would typify him nicely and, by giving him something to hold, anchor him to the spot.

At their first encounter the two men had struck sparks off each other. From this point on the confrontation was not unlike that of Napoleon with the Tsar of Russia, where tensions were hid for the sake of a momentary cordiality that meant nothing. Roosevelt, that advocate of the strenuous life, while innocent of such intention nonetheless made Sargent's life strenuous at the White House. The first few days, immediately after lunch, he issued from the executive wing carrying a batch of papers. The President walked quickly to the living quarters where a tense artist awaited him on the stair. Blinds had been erected over nearby windows to give what approximated studio light in its single direction. Breathless on his arrival, the President urged that work commence. His entire retinue was present. He bellowed to everyone in sight, gestured and twisted, often forgetting the purpose for which Sargent was present. Then, his interest abated, Roosevelt started off again towards the executive wing, his retinue at his heels.

To Sargent this was singularly vexing. Coupled with the unusual honor paid him was the inescapable reality that he was being treated like a lackey and without consideration for professional necessities. His reputation would ride on this much publicized portrait, which, for good or ill, would achieve a singular eminence. Failure was out of the question. In such deplorable circumstances success would be purely fortuitous. Sargent's true stature can be gauged by the way he overcame a situation so impossible.

His artistic intellect wrestled with an insuperable difficulty, deliberately sacrificing the subtleties of portrait painting to a simple direct effigy. Fortunately Roosevelt's athletic air was stamped on the position he assumed that first petulant moment on the stair. His characteristic squint, behind a pince-nez with trailing black ribbon, would contribute to a strong image. The overstressed muscularity of his hand grasping the newel post was equally significant. When the thick bull-necked body was silhouetted these several features would fuse together into an essence of the man.

Irritation generated at the short and abruptly ended sittings carried over to personal relations. Except at table Sargent was left alone in the White House. He devoted his time to painting sketches of the grounds which he presented to Mrs. Roosevelt. Such graciousness did little to ease the situation when the President took conversation into his own hands. Instead of talking with Sargent on music, books, or criminology, subjects on which he was expansive, Roosevelt made

Photograph from the Library of Congress

General Leonard Wood by John Singer Sargent. Painted in Washington in 1903.

Sargent first saw General Wood when they were both given honorary degrees at the University of Pennsylvania. After the ceremony Sargent remarked to Wood's aide: "He has a magnificent head, and I was painting his picture in my mind's eye. Do you think he would want me to paint him?" A tour-de-force of rapid notation executed in an attic in Wood's house on Connecticut Avenue, it conveys the aspect that most struck Sargent, a head that "looks as though it had been hacked out of granite with an axe."

the natural mistake of turning his talk to art. His guest was equally pleased to turn it away, for generalities did not suit his mental equipment and technical jargon was difficult with an impatient Roosevelt. Literature, or the peevishness of Henry Adams, doubtless would have filled the White House with thoughtfulness and good humor. But Roosevelt, impatient to get the best out of everyone, could not be led.

Then, too, the White House was filled with children, that brood of outrageous juveniles the President nurtured. His self-styled "White House gang" thought it sport to shine mirrors on the roof of the Senate Chamber and bring their ponies upstairs in the new White House elevator. Sargent was to be counted lucky if they did not attend their father's sittings on horseback, and as a stolid bachelor, he could not be expected to share their joys.

The President at first made no difficulty over sittings, but went hurrying off just as it seemed some progress might be made. If Sargent hoped for an amelioration of this he was disappointed. Soon the President complained of the demand on his time. Work entered a second week and there no longer were sittings every day. The portrait now more in doubt, Sargent adopted makeshift procedures he detested. In Roosevelt's presence he worked only on the head. The President's frock coat was fitted on a White House guard whose figure conveniently paunched in the same direction. The hand, a key feature in the bare design, possibly was painted before a mirror from Sargent's own broad, short-fingered left hand. These devices exhausted, he turned to the other picture expected of him in Washington.

The second week was singularly busy. In addition to the difficulties with Roosevelt, on Thursday Sargent expected to leave for Philadelphia where on Friday the University of Pennsylvania would confer on him an honorary degree. On Monday and Tuesday he appears to have had sittings with John Hay, Secretary of State, at his home on H Street. All was secret, only Henry Adams completely savoring this, for he had wormed the secret out of Mrs. Hay. On Wednesday Roosevelt decided to give a sitting. Sargent sent a note to the Secretary of State:

[Wednesday, February 19, 1903]

Dear Mr. Hay

The President has decided to sit this afternoon, so I am obliged to ask you to excuse me—I am leaving for Philadelphia tomorrow morning, with the intention of returning on Saturday night—Can you give me a sitting on Monday morning at 10 or so? Or Sunday afternoon? Or, if not Sunday, Monday? . . .

In his vexation and wrath it was a different John Singer Sargent who faced Theodore Roosevelt that fateful Wednesday afternoon. All sense of restraint was lost. Sargent let loose a fiery flood of pigment that raised the portrait far above the common run of portraits. The silhouette, intended to be treated with delicacy—as in Sargent's earlier portrait of Joseph Chamberlain—suddenly was made shockingly harsh. A loaded brush angrily chopped away every nuance, leaving the President's head and shoulders sharp and incisive, even the ribbon trailing from his pince-nez giving way to a clear edge. To compensate for the added brilliance, new lights and a new impasto was spread across the high forehead and onto projecting nasal folds. This canvas's brutal outlines, hippopotamus ears, and grasping gesture, made no mild statement about Roosevelt. Here was the trenchant indictment of an equal who felt himself ill-used and commanded the slash and dash to make himself heard.

Roosevelt, who stayed to see the result of Sargent's silent paroxysm, sensed nothing of the seething drama he had witnessed. "This afternoon I had my last sitting with Mr. Sargent," he dictated in a note to his son Kermit after returning to the executive wing. "I like his picture enormously. I am going to play single-stick with General Wood."

For Sargent the extraordinary honor of the occasion had turned to abject humiliation. He described himself as feeling "like a rabbit in the presence of a boa-constrictor", but omitted to mention that he had not hesitated to hit back. Apart from the fury evident in the portrait, he gave vent to a second avenging act. Retiring by nature, evading and avoiding every public exposure, he now allowed the press to be called into the White House where he spoke of the task just completed. His composure masked biting irony as he estimated the President's sittings were approximately half an hour in length. With morbid humor he explained that the President's characteristics were so well defined *he needed no time for study.*

The next morning, as the press reported his bizarre remarks direct, Sargent made his way through snow to catch a train for Philadelphia. An added sweetness lingered over this journey. The University of Pennsylvania was his father's school, where FitzWilliam Sargent, like his son a sepulchre of respectability, earned Bachelor's and Medical degrees. How proud he would be now to see his son granted an honorary LL.D.

During the ceremony Sargent for the first time saw General Leonard Wood, of whom he had heard much in the White House but had never met. Decidedly a good-looking man and Roosevelt's boon com-

*National Portrait Gallery
Smithsonian Institution*

Henry Cabot Lodge by John Singer Sargent.

Painted at Nahant in 1890, Sargent's portrait of the forty-year-old Lodge is an excellent example of his direct and virile manner on these early trips to the United States. The strength of the hands is a consistent feature, and the artist brilliantly accommodates himself to the unusual lighting from an ordinary window which strikes his subject from below.

panion, Wood was also receiving a degree that day. After the ceremony Sargent mentioned to Wood's aide: "He has a magnificent head, and I was painting his picture in my mind's eye. Do you think he would want me to paint him?"

Another recipient of the Doctor of Laws Degree that day passed unnoticed by Sargent. A lean Professor of Political Science at Princeton University, Woodrow Wilson was not unaware of the aura surrounding Sargent. One day he too would have him at the White House.

Returned to Washington, Sargent continued his interupted sittings on H Street with Secretary of State John Hay. A certain revulsion for what he had produced of Roosevelt made him intent on creating a more balanced portrait in depth. Hay's well-known badger look was not avoided. But penetration of gaze and clarity of mind are more marked. Here too the painter's tools were manipulated with a certain brute energy. Pigment was loaded on, the fingers used to knead a rich impasto. Bright in the unnatural light reflected from snow outside, Hay's white beard shone against a shimmer of red lip.

General Wood had been pleased to learn of Sargent's interest. At Wood's invitation Sargent called to look over the General's house on Connecticut Avenue. A small trunk room in the attic was chosen as the best place to work. "Sargent is a nervous man," Wood noted in his diary after the first sitting on February 23, 1903. "Very intense, and working rapidly... with tremendous concentration." On the second day Wood was surprised to see all the work of the previous session scraped out, and what appeared to be a new start made. For short periods the two talked casually, the painter smoking his cigarettes furiously and apparently as much concerned with the conversation as his work. Then, amid puffs even more volcanic, he strode to the easel and forced almost to turn his back on Wood because of the very tight quarters painted as furiously as he smoked.

Wood tried to interest Sargent in the Philippine Islands, which he described as containing much fine subject matter in a brilliant light. The highly decorative flora and beautifully built Igorot natives seemed perfect for an artist whose murals concentrated on the more decorative aspects of painting. Possibly because he felt tropic lands without a classic heritage were outside his art Sargent expressed little interest. Besides, the sea trip across the Pacific Ocean alone was enough to dissuade a perpetually bad sailor. "Nothing but bananas, bananas," he replied, pronouncing the prejudicial word with a broad British *a*, "and besides, Winslow Homer has already done them."

To McCoy, the General's aide, Sargent spoke again of Wood's

Office of the Architect of the Capitol

Thomas B. Reed, Speaker of the House of Representatives, by John Singer Sargent.

Though brushed with much of Sargent's youthful fluency, his portrait of Thomas B. Reed (1839–1902), painted in Paris in 1891, is one of his admitted failures. Sargent wrote that "... this is the result of a second attempt different in view and character from the first, which I destroyed. His exterior does not somehow correspond with his spirit and what is a painter to do? ... I could have made a better picture with a less remarkable man. He has been delightful." Unattractive though the result is, there is a longer view for only in Rubens' portraits of monks will its artistic equal be found. Distinguished linear draftsmen, both artists had a compelling mastery of form.

The Rabbit and the Boa Constrictor 633

magnificent head. "It looks," he said, "as though it had been hacked out of granite with an ax." A note of sincerity rings through this comment for Wood's clear broad features did have fine sculptural qualities accentuated by the light falling from above. After sittings every morning the picture was finished on February 26, 1903, and looking it over Sargent seemed pleased.

His three Washington portraits completed, and Boston beckoning to him, it seemed a necessary courtesy for Sargent to call on Henry Adams before he left the capital. Surely another commission might derive from the brief visit. The moment was perhaps ill-chosen, for Adams was put out by having been refused permission to see the completed picture of Roosevelt which was sent to a framer with instructions that it was to be seen by no one until a public viewing on March 28. Seated in Adams' upstairs library the two men eyed each other and spoke cautiously. Adams recorded his impressions:

> March 3, 1903
> At last the man I sought, the corruscating lime-light of enthusiasm, John Sargent. Holy Virgin, how useless civility is when you have an artist to handle. Still, I did my little phrase book, and he looked as irresponsive as ever, and so he soared to heaven.... Sargent is stodgy!
>
> He came in to see me before he left for Boston, and was pleased to say that Washington seemed pleasanter than New York. I can understand how an American catches English manners; and how they do catch English minds! Especially how they do keep such in these days when the English mind is no longer good form even in England. The generation of Henry James and John Sargent is already as fossil as the buffalo. The British middle class must be exterminated without remorse....

One grasps that a scene of drawing-room comedy had unfolded. Sargent, his antipathy to Adams intense, in the previous decade had described him as a "noxious humbug". In a private letter he had written in January 1894: "Henry Adams' approval tickles me although I consider him a noxious humbug—I came across a phrase in my pious reading that must apply to his book which I haven't read: 'ce livre cheri des begomiles de Thrace et des cathares de l'occident.' This, like another quotation from me, that you once investigated at a tea party may be obscene so look out."

This contempt, politely concealed in Adams' house, left Sargent in silence. Adams never penetrated the cause of his guest's glazed look. Nor did it occur to Adams that the purpose of the call was to give him an opportunity to speak if he wished to join the hallowed group painted on this Washington expedition. In fact, aware of the strength of Sargent's antipathy, it is obvious that his portrait of Adams might have been the greatest and most devastating of his Washington works. The subject unfortunately was unaware of what creative forces awaited him and missed this opportunity which never came again.

Adams was more concerned by the social phenomenon he saw unfolding about him. Within a week he had wheedled permission and called at the framer where at last he saw Sargent's Roosevelt:

March 8, 1903

The portrait is good Sargent and not very bad Roosevelt. It is not Theodore, but a young intellectual idealist with a taste for athletics, which I take to be Theodore's idea of himself. It is for once less brutal than its subject, and will only murder everything in the White House. Of course we all approve it. Indeed it offers nothing to criticize except Sargent.

That last sentence—after all, there *had* to be criticism—must have caused Adams some effort, for at best it is weak, if in fact it means anything. Had the picture actually conveyed as much as Adams saw in it Sargent would have been exceedingly pleased.

Paradoxically, this extraordinary portrait of Theodore Roosevelt remains a work without precedent in the history of art. Neither in America nor elsewhere had any Chief of State been painted in full silhouette, nor with a gesture of such vehemence. Adding to the impact was its bold execution, massed pigment laid on the pale background forcing a brilliance of ensemble. It is a picture beside which, as Henry Adams suggested, no other dare hang. Those it does not defeat by brilliant design it shouts down by sheer force. And curiously enough this consummate result is achieved with the greatest economy of means. The sumptuous accessories of marble, gold, and velvet which Gilbert Stuart required to project Washington as Chief of State are entirely absent. Only Roosevelt himself in his normal clothing is present, grasping a simple newel post that is a thing of no beauty.

No less remarkable is that so much was accomplished during Roosevelt's five extremely brief sessions of posing. This demonstrates Sargent's masterly control of his art and the degree of erudition he brought to bear. He has been accused of studying Velasquez, a rather superficial influence rarely visible in mature works. Technically the structure of his work was totally different from Velasquez' wisps of transparency over a monochrome preparation. The full frontal pose of Roosevelt and his grasping hand more likely owe their genesis to Frans Hals, in whose spirit the portrait is conceived. Significantly it

Photograph from the author

John Singer Sargent, a photograph about 1903.

Sargent as he appeared when he stayed at the White House in 1903. At forty-seven he was at the height of his career and his power: "complete and undeviating assurance in his own gifts is essential to any understanding of his art." Sargent evidently approved of this photograph for he gave it to Flora Priestley, whom earlier he had asked to marry him. She did not and he remained a bachelor.

Photograph from the author

An 1876 American painting by John Singer Sargent.

Only two works exist from the period of Sargent's first visit to the United States in 1876 and both feature Indians.

resembles no one picture by Hals, demonstrating that Sargent was able to imbibe the essential spirit of the great masters without copying them direct. Roosevelt's position can also be said to derive from Rigaud's portrait of Louis XIV, whose position would be the same were he seen from the front (instead of the side) as Roosevelt is seen. The daring originality of such full frontal treatment, heightened by harsh silhouette, is all the more striking.

Another notable feature of the portrait, its torrent of pigment charging outward from the President's head like some burst of celestial glory, derives from Sargent's knowledge of his contemporaries, the French Impressionists. Since the turn of the century he had adopted Monet's practice by using but little turpentine when beginning his portraits, then painting backgrounds, draperies, and accessories almost entirely without medium. The thick impasted quality of this facture was an essential new element in Impressionist paintings, which Sargent adopted for portraits. Comparison of his Roosevelt with the flat pigment in Sargent's earlier portrait of Joseph Chamberlain, painted in silhouette in 1896, shows radical alterations in his handling of pigment. The use of ochres, umbers, and black in the Roosevelt, colors Sargent like Monet banished in purely Impressionist works painted out of doors, demonstrates that this indoor portrait while adopting elements of Impressionism is no *Impressionist* picture. It is in fact a uniquely personal amalgam of temperament, style, and erudition, that can only be described as *Sargent*.

Had John Singer Sargent been psychologically equipped to profit from his aura, certainly he would have become the greatest of all artist-tycoons. Sir Joshua Reynolds had averaged 150 portraits a year, and Romney not less, a far cry from the ten or twelve which in his prime Sargent annually completed. His attitude and methods were wrong for volume. Notoriously he kept the banker Sir Edgar Speyer waiting two years before commencing a portrait of his wife then required over twenty sittings compared to Reynolds' standard request of three.

Limitation upon Sargent's financial rewards came from something which closely resembled a puritan conscience. Aware of his own reputation he felt obliged to make it a reality with each canvas. The strain often left him frustrated and vexed or assuming the par-boiled look which typified his appearance. His God-son, the psychiatrist Dr. John Alfred Parsons Millet, suspected that Sargent himself doubted how long such extraordinary fashionability would last. He made earnest efforts to find other aspects of art on which to concentrate.

For his Boston murals he frequently closed himself up in a second London studio in Fulham Road, accepting no portrait orders while he did so. Yearly he brought back scores of dazzling watercolors and oil landscapes from continental trips which eventually swallowed summer, autumn, and part of the winter.

Pecuniary rewards continued to flow only from portraits. The landscapes he each year brought back to London rarely were shown and almost never sold. With success and affluence he remained a thoroughly vexed soul, tied to portraits he was unwilling to exploit commercially. By 1907 he spoke openly of giving up portrait painting, in letters passing over it in the most natural way. To D. S. MacColl, who asked advice concerning Robert Brough's memorial exhibition, he suggested the Chantrey Bequest make a purchase: "I should have been tempted to buy it so as to give the Chantrey their choice of the two, and hand the money over to the children. That would be the simple thing to do, but as I am chucking portrait painting I can't be so lavish."

His genuine pleasure in painting useless and unsalable landscape studies is seen in lines written from Rome in response to an invitation to Venice: "The time is getting so short now, and I have complicated matters by beginning two or three studies that threaten to fill it up quite. For with this uncertain weather I can't polish things off and go as I would like to do. I foresee that I will hang on here until the train starts for Chelsea.... In spite of scirocco and lots of rain we have been seeing all the villas within miles thanks to Mrs. Hunter's motor. They are magnificent and I would like to spend a summer at Frascati and paint from morning till night at the Torlonia, or the Aldobrandini, or the Falconieri—Ilexes and Cypresses, fountains and statues,—ainsi soit il—amen."

Hidden behind the screen of his portraitist's career was an undiscovered landscape painter struggling to find recognition. Enjoying his idle holidays on the continent, Sargent became the master whose perfect draftsmanship and technique brought Impressionism to final fruition by imposing the necessary ultimate discipline on a disordered fabric created by Monet. By perfecting the most significant artistic discovery since the Renaissance, Sargent became greater by far than his purely professional work as a portraitist suggests.

By 1910 the dream of "chucking" portrait painting had become a reality. Freed of demands upon time and energies he launched into a new life of murals and sketching abroad which absorbed him entirely. For funds he did rapid and frequently ravishing charcoal drawings, prices for which rose as demand became insatiable. The outbreak of

Photograph from the author

Dr. FitzWilliam Sargent (1820–1889) by John Singer Sargent.

A rare image of the artist's father, Dr. FitzWilliam Sargent of Philadelphia, who taught his children arithmetic, geography, history, and, on Sunday, hymns, and was responsible for the basic education which his son received. In 1903 his school, the University of Pennsylvania, gave his son an honorary degree along with ones to Woodrow Wilson, president of Princeton, and General Leonard Wood.

Photograph from the author

John Singer Sargent (1856–1925), at the age of twenty, by **Carolus-Duran.**

Sargent as he appeared when he first visited the United States in 1876, painted in Paris in that period by his teacher Emile Auguste Carolus-Duran.

Boston Public Library

Murals by John Singer Sargent in the Boston Public Library.

Installed in 1903, the murals in the Boston Public Library were an elaborate assemblage of painting and sculpture, all by Sargent's own hand. Until his death in 1925, Sargent continued to work on this hall, never considering it completed.

the First World War found him behind enemy lines in the Austrian Alps: "Travelling in this part of the world was impossible for a long time. You have to have a passport to take a train (& I haven't got one)," he wrote October 18, 1914. "I still don't know when or how to make a move. The Stokes and I are very comfortable and happy at the home of an old Austrian friend of mine, and we are painting away while Rome is burning."

War-time fund-raising caught him up on his return to London. For the British Red Cross Society he agreed to take part in an auction at Christie's where leading artists contributed empty frames, the winning bidders to have their portraits inserted. The sale was held April 16, 1915, Sargent's two charcoal drawings surpassing in the bidding all but an oil by Laszlo. A proposal to the Red Cross followed that a donation of ten thousand pounds outright would be made for a Sargent portrait in oil. Sir Hugh Lane, an art dealer, became this donor and under pressure Sargent agreed. Lane then took ship to America, evidently with no idea whose portrait he would ask Sargent to paint.

For his return to England, Lane took passage on the ill-fated *Lusitania* which was torpedoed on May 7, 1915. Shortly before he went on board Sir Hugh had scribbled a will which did not take into account his donation to the Red Cross nor possession of an unpainted portrait. Litigation still continued the following year when Sargent himself decided that despite torpedoes he would bring a third phase of the Boston Library murals for installation. In his absence the Chancery Division upheld Lane's will as drawn, and a plebiscite was begun in Ireland to select the sitter. Two years after his gallant gesture for the Red Cross, at Boston in July 1917, Sargent therefore received horrifying news. Now that America had entered the war his portrait would be painted of President Woodrow Wilson.

The White House was not a place of happy memory. In the full powers of his prime he had overcome the problems inherent in a state portrait of a restless Chief Executive. At sixty-one, no longer an active portraitist, it was questionable whether he could make out so well, especially in the emotional conflict he felt on recollecting the White House. Dutifully, if without enthusiasm, he wrote to President Wilson. An answer came back:

July 18, 1917

Dear Mr. Sargent,
...Apparently it is in vain to hope for sittings while Congress is in session and, unfortunately, with the extraordinary dilatory practices possible in the Senate no man would be rash enough to predict how long the present session will last. I do not see how it can well continue beyond the first of September, and I had in a general way formed the expectation that I might during that month have a chance to give myself the pleasure of seeing you. I should consider it a privilege to do so. . . .

Despite the curiously hedged and convoluted style, so different from Roosevelt's pointed brevity, strange reflection of that predecessor existed in the last line: another American President would "consider it a privilege". Neither time nor age had dimmed the lustre of Sargent's name. It was essential not to dim it himself by feeble work. In October came his dreaded summons:

Dear Mr. Sargent,
   Congress has adjourned and my mind turns to the suggestion I made that probably after the adjournment it would be possible for me to sit for the portrait which the Governors of the National Gallery of Ireland so generously desire.

Photograph from the author

John Singer Sargent, photographed sketching in the Alps.

"Hidden behind the screen of his portraitist's career was an undiscovered landscape painter struggling to find recognition." This is a photograph of Sargent sketching in the Alps, where he worked every year between 1908 and 1911.

Photograph from the author

An architectural study by John Singer Sargent.

Sargent wrote: "The time is getting so short now, and I have complicated matters by beginning two or three studies that threaten to fill it up quite." The Garden Terrace, Villa Papa Giulio, painted at Rome in 1906, demonstrates the genuine pleasure he took in painting "useless and unsalable" pictures.

I would be glad to know your own engagements and whether it would be convenient for you to come down next week or the week after.

I would also like to know, if it is possible for you to answer such a question, how much time it would probably be necessary for me to set aside for the purpose.

With the pleasantest anticipations of knowing you,

Cordially and sincerely yours,
Woodrow Wilson

Possibly unaware of the invitation extended so many years before, the President did not ask Sargent to stay at the White House.

Accompanied by his valet, Sargent settled into the Willard Hotel. If he sought to maintain a low key visit, that first evening he made an extraordinary error by accepting Senator Henry Cabot Lodge's invitation. So disinterested in politics was Sargent that perhaps he can be forgiven for not being aware that there were *two* political parties. Nor was Lodge the man to show restraint. He proclaimed himself delighted about the portrait of Wilson: *a great opportunity for the artist to serve his party*. (!) Remembering the portrait of Speaker Reed, painted 26 years before, Lodge said he was certain some sinister, beastly trait must lie hidden inside Wilson. Sargent's duty would be to reveal it to the world.

Here was an unhappy thought to lay before a painter already under strain. Apart from the absurd notion that Sargent cared for any party, Lodge's suggestion was removed from any realm in which he operated. Possibly it was stimulated by Sargent's boyish habit of drawing faces distorted into Disney-like animals to pass railway trips and long evenings with friends. Such party tricks bore no relationship to his portrait work, despite an undoubtedly piggish likeness of Speaker Reed.

But until Lodge spoke it had not occurred to Sargent that the contending politicians of the United States would exploit his work for advantage in the political rough and tumble. This new burden increased his dislike of the portraitist's trade, making it unbearable. After his few years of happy retirement, through no wish of his own, he found himself with an expectant world hanging on his brush. Since the United States entered the war, six months before, the light shining on President Wilson had become more intense than on any other single figure of the time. Could Sargent have fled Washington he would have done so.

The following day, October 16, 1917, Mrs. Wilson received him at the White House. Except for changes in furniture and different

Photograph from the author

A view of Corfu by John Singer Sargent.

Sargent became a master whose draftsmanship and technique brought Impressionism to a fruition by imposing discipline on a disordered fabric created by Monet. Here, visiting in Corfu, Sargent demonstrates both the capacities of the Impressionist palette and his own personal sense of beautiful shapes.

portraits on the walls it looked much the same. Together they took a turn around the Rose Room, selected for the north light that streamed through two large windows. The housekeeper was called to drape a huge four-poster bed with dark curtains against which the tonalities of a head could be observed. Sargent requested a platform on which to raise Wilson while he sat, finding it necessary to explain why the sitter benefitted from being at the artist's eye level.

Finally, he wanted a chair that would "paint well". With Mrs. Wilson he toured the White House, discovering nothing appropriate. Weary at last he selected one from the corner of an upstairs hall. The choice was surprising for Sargent, who previously had shown considerable taste in the selection of accessories. Nonetheless this dark, leather-covered office chair was brought to the Rose Room, and then, arrangements completed, Mrs. Wilson expressed the ordinary sentiment that she hoped so much trouble would be rewarded by a fine portrait. Her remark hit Sargent peculiarly.

He was slow to reply. "You know, Mrs. Wilson, I have never been so nervous over a portrait in my life."

She looked at him in surprise. He averted his eyes, putting his hands on the back of the chair and slowly leaning his weight on them. Cabot Lodge was in his mind and there was nothing he could say.

To bridge an awkward moment into more pleasant conversation Mrs. Wilson coaxed: "This is a surprise from the great Sargent." But the artist had no humor.

A peculiar expression of suppressed pain was evident as he turned his face slowly upward. "Well, I only hope I can do it," was all he said.

His first sitting with Woodrow Wilson, the following afternoon at 2:30, came as a distinct relief. The President showed himself to be a polite, considerate man whose face bore the stamp of intellect. Excellent portraits frequently had been made from such men, and Wilson's benevolent attitude, that of a restrained but correct schoolmaster to whom honor was being done, suggested no problems. Feeling it his duty to entertain the silent painter the President even tried to make conversation through a lengthy session.

Less favorable was that the platform for which he had asked Mrs. Wilson the previous day had not materialized. Instead of postponing the sitting, as would have been reasonable, he felt obliged to begin. If this was courtesy it was deeply destructive. Wilson found the chair selected for him too deep and low for comfort, seating himself well forward on its edge, his knees raised. That an experienced artist began important work under these conditions is surprising. An imbalance of his creative forces immediately showed itself, for first indications of a head and body roughed on his canvas were over life-size, a fault for which he castigated students.

One penetrates his mind when it is remembered he asked for the chair *before* meeting Wilson. This may only have carried on a habit acquired that spring while doing two seated portraits of John D. Rockefeller, also for the Red Cross. A more likely motive was that because Roosevelt had stood he deliberately intended Wilson to appear different altogether, even though the President's slender figure might best have been shown standing. The nature of such a prejudgement, attacking the basis of portraiture as individual treatment, betrays the distressed mind he brought to the White House.

Despite Wilson's genuineness and courtesy from their first moments together, when preliminary nervousness vanished, Sargent's creative powers remained perversely frozen. Nothing came forth but wrong decisions. Doubtless he felt the picture would come together at a later stage. Instead, the elements of over-size, poor position, a bad chair, and downward perspective, forced him to work against unnecessary obstacles which lowered further his capacity to master this present challenge.

Inevitably his own sense of distress and an accompanying depression were transfered to his image of Wilson. Upward perspective as normally seen in portraits not only shows heads to best advantage, and shortens a nose too exuberantly formed, but also gives the sitter a dominance derived from his exalted position. By beginning Wilson in a downward perspective, Sargent tilted this essential psychological balance away from the President, assuring that he would appear insignificant in the large canvas. Where Theodore Roosevelt had burst forth in the emphatic nature of his personality, Wilson must retire into shadows.

Still, the artist was not unpleased, and expecting that all would go well he mused poetically: "The White House is empty, the habitation of the linx and the bittern. How different from the days of Roosevelt who posed or rather didn't pose, in a crowd. . . ." Such comparisons appeared to haunt him. The differences were striking indeed, for Wilson allowed no interruptions. Even Mrs. Wilson, though frequently present, withheld all opinion. Each day saw progress, but such quiet plodding before a serene executive left the smoldering genius of Sargent unroused. Roosevelt's rowdiness had stimulated him to supreme effort. Wilson bored him.

The following day, Thursday, Wilson sat again at 2:30 and arranged a further sitting for Saturday. Before his Monday session Sargent was asked to lunch. Away from his easel he impressed Mrs.

Photograph from the author

A view of Venice by John Singer Sargent.

The landscapes which Sargent each year brought back to London rarely were shown and almost never were sold. This ravishing view of Venice suffered exactly that fate. Still the property of Sargent's family, it has never been exhibited and is here reproduced for the first time.

Wilson as extremely courteous and well-bred but, as he had nothing to say, uninteresting. Three more sittings of an hour and a half each were given that second week. Sunday evening he began explaining to friends he would remain a third week in Washington. "It takes a man a long time to look like his portrait, as Whistler used to say—but he is doing his best, and has been very obliging.... I have met a good many old friends—Harry White, Mrs. George Vanderbilt, the Spring-Rices and others, so I have done less cursing of God and man than I might otherwise have."

His mind was playing tricks of the purely technical sort that absorbed him when the fascination of personality was absent. He accentuated the dry "hard planes" of Wilson's head, which he likened to "a head hewed out of wood". He noted the dark eyelashes and lighter eyes of the President, which he attempted to give "the look of those warriors in a Japanese print." His "principle pre-occupation was to construct the head on flat planes with very slight modelling" diminishing all half-tones for the purpose. Nothing he did made the President's jut-jawed head more interesting, and though he gave evidence of a certain fascination with the Presidential ears, like well fluted handles on fine tea-cups, he dared not give them the luxurious abandon they deserved.

Slowly through the sittings an inevitable conviction formed that what Sargent feared most, a failure, was developing on his canvas. Nothing increased his interest. Neither pigment loaded onto the forehead, nor tricky flashes of light on the pince-nez, made it a real "Sargent" head. A new high of intensity and interpretation had been reached only a few months before with Rockefeller. Instead, between himself and Wilson something had gone wrong from the start. Partly it was the White House which enervated him. But also, both men were too reserved and ill at ease. Wilson "has not a very paintable brow, & I expect people who expect a political cartoon will be disappointed," he wrote. But the other side was mentioned too: "He has a very set expression of face and his thoughts are entirely behind the scene, and masked by great suavity of manner."

"He seems serene and not oppressed by his tremendous responsibilities. Very agreeable withall": those last words his formula when the failure of a portrait must be taken on his own shoulders. "He has been delightful" were parallel words of 26 years before, also tacked to the end of a letter concerning Speaker Reed.

More significant is that whereas he had made two efforts at Speaker Reed, destroying the first, as he had done many times since, now he did not mercilessly discard this disappointing canvas. In his prime he would have done no less. In 1917, at the White House, chafing to return to Boston, the sixty-one year old master temporized and plod onward, believing in his star and hoping that at some point his sad effort would take on life. Nothing else can account for the peculiarities creeping into its execution; the nose delicately finished beside a squared and rough-hewn mouth, impasto dabbed on the forehead that is certainly a purposeless afterthought, or the ugly dry-brush execution of a fold across the chin. Even the two hands differed in execution. One is heaped in clogged pigment, the other an improvisation in rapid thin brushwork that has turned claw-like.

Wilson now left his frock coat behind after each sitting, and Nicola d'Inverno, the Italian valet who for many years had served Sargent, slipped into it. In this way the figure was advanced. On Tuesday of the third week Wilson could spare only half an hour at noon. Wednesday he gave an hour and a half, and conversation turned to camouflage. The President was about to inspect the American University Camouflage Camp near Washington. Experiences Sargent had with Abbott Thayer in London, when that American artist arrived to introduce the practice to British generals, suddenly made humorous telling. Wilson suggested Sargent accompany his party, making a sixth in the open touring car, with chauffeur, that later made its way out of Washington.

At the camp a staff demonstrating its work was delighted at the unfeigned response when a stone moved aside and a soldier emerged. To disguise shell holes in open country, where it might be necessary to place look-outs, was a greater problem. Quick response came from Sargent: "Line them with black velvet. It absorbs light and reflects nothing," a logic to which army engineers were unequal.

After a final sitting, on Saturday, November 3, Sargent packed to leave Washington and the controversy that immediately raged over his portrait. Personally and emotionally he took refuge in Boston, "working away like a nigger at the projects for my new decorations of the big rotunda in the Boston Museum—mostly modelling and architecture so far," as he wrote on December 22. And though he had escaped, the portrait began an immense tour, exhibited first at the Corcoran Gallery in Washington, then New York, Pittsburgh, Boston, Cleveland, Detroit, and Chicago. Very marked divergences of opinion developed. Those loyal to Sargent and his undoubted genius tended to believe that something great they failed to recognize must be present. *The Studio* claimed outright that it was a "masterly accomplishment [that] takes rank among the best things Sargent has done" and the Washington *Herald* was even more committed: "Sar-

Photograph from the author

John Singer Sargent, 1914 passport application photograph.

Sargent was caught behind enemy lines when World War I began. This photograph is from an application he made to the American Consulate in Le Havre to obtain documents to return to England.

Photograph from the author

John Singer Sargent, photograph from his last passport.

At this time "something of his earlier self-confidence was no longer present." Any portrait of which there was a real expectation now froze him.

gent has shown us the President's character and personality in this portrait, one of the noblest of all his works." The most acute observation of all appeared in the *Saturday Review,* whose critic considered that it "might almost be taken for a school piece . . . Does not strike one as an authentic Sargent."

A certain justice existed in raising the question of authenticity, for Wilson was painted by Sargent while his genius was absent. Even so, the question remained, what had gone wrong in Washington? No facile answer is possible. Sargent had arrived in fine form. His two recent portraits of Rockefeller showed strength and interpretation that reached a new level. Even his style and handling of pigment were broadening out. The key appears to be that he had enjoyed painting Rockefeller, whose aged asceticism he equated with St.-Francis. The second Rockefeller portrait, painted in June 1917 in the garage of the Pocantico estate, became one of the great portraits of this century. More than that of any other portraitist, Sargent's genius depended upon the sitter to arouse it. Anyone might accomplish that: a pretty woman, a devastating matron, an acute official, a handsome nobleman, someone frail with age. Rockefeller had touched Sargent, as Roosevelt had shaken him. By contrast, Woodrow Wilson's suave agreeableness, his desire to be helpful while maintaining a set expression, left Sargent deeply inhibited.

For the many errors of judgement which contributed to his final defeat, deeper causes must be found. His normal good sense was absent and this can only be because he so feared a political storm that his artistic powers had entirely ceased to function. He had painted Wilson with a seriousness, sincerity, candor, and conscenciousness worthy of the artist he was. By not insisting upon a platform to raise the President he jeopardized dominance at the start. After Wilson settled into the ugly chair that was selected, his portrait proved a fiasco, lacking the brilliant conception, the fire of execution, and the immense tenderness brought to other recent portraits. The fault was no one's. The personal equation between this artist and this subject had proved out to a negative answer. History was the loser.

As time passed and all thought of his most recent adventure faded, to Sargent came a vague loathing of all things associated with Washington and that certain house. The few portraits he did after that experience rarely were formal affairs and when they were they could be treated with alarming casualness. His taste for portraiture had so far abated he dreaded anything approaching real orders. The true interpretation is that like his Wilson any picture of which there was a real expectation now froze him. Casual sketches he continued to produce with careening brush and sparkling displays. A formal portrait like that of his close friend Sir Phillip Sassoon was less successful. Beginning on a large canvas, he felt unable to continue, cutting it down after a few sittings to an elongated bust portrait that preserves little more than a head too hard in drawing, labored, dull, and uninteresting.

His own crankiness on the subject did not escape him, as one request demonstrated: "I don't remember exactly what it was you

Photograph from the author

John D. Rockefeller by John Singer Sargent.

This portrait of John D. Rockefeller (1839–1937), painted in the garage of the Rockefeller Pocantico estate in June 1917, shows that Sargent was in excellent form in the year when he undertook to paint Woodrow Wilson in Washington four months later.

wanted..." he wrote on October 22, 1924, "beyond my getting the impression that it was one of those miraculously successful impromptus that leave no trace of a hundred preliminary failures, one of those spontaneous brilliant trifles that leaves a waste paper basket bulging with discarded experiments—In other words the sort of thing that terrifies me more than making an after dinner speech or than decorating a dome. If I am wrong, please tell me again—and I shall pull myself together."

Only one year of life was left to him when he wrote and an occasional photograph will show that something of his earlier self-confidence was no longer present. Washington was distinctly a thing of the past. He had received great honors there, and had painted one undoubted masterpiece. It was an arena he would not re-enter, despite the good Massachusetts man named Calvin Coolidge who was now President. The new President was aware of Sargent's lineage and reputation, and entertained the surprising secret ambition to be painted by this unique American master. His wish was confided to the artist's favorite cousin, Mary Potter, who determined to go about her mission with every advantage that accrued from extensive knowledge of Sargent's habits.

She selected a visit to Holm Lea, home of her father, the artist's cousin Charles Sprague Sargent, where the painter customarily relaxed and refreshed himself among Boston kin. After he finished his dinner and lit a cigar, this elderly, heavily paunched man, his red face now ringed by white hair and beard, was in genial mood. Into this ready situation Mary Potter dropped gentle mention that President Coolidge would like a portrait.

Sargent started back in his chair as though hit by a rifle bullet. His expression changed to the well-known purple apoplectic look. *"You've ruined my whole dinner!"* he bellowed.

A note written on Copley-Plaza stationary, on January 3, 1924, completes the story. "My dear Mary... You will be pleased to know that I have regretfully declined to paint Mr. Coolidge—I was pale, but firm—."

The White House saw him no more.

New Life in an Old Movement: Alice Paul and the Great Suffrage Parade of 1913 in Washington, D.C.

SIDNEY R. BLAND

The American woman suffrage movement in the early Twentieth Century was experiencing the frustration of inactivity. Between 1896, when Utah and Idaho enfranchised women to raise the total number of states in which American women could vote to four, and 1910, no new state victories were won. Only six state referendums were held and three of these were in Oregon. Interest in a federal constitutional amendment was at an all-time low. The annual hearings on the bill before Senate and House Committees had become routine; woman suffrage had not been debated on the floor of the Senate since 1887, and had never reached the floor of the House. With the decision at the 1893 convention of the National American Woman Suffrage Association (NAWSA) to hold the annual meeting in Washington, D.C. only in alternate years, the steady pressure the NAWSA had kept on Congress dissipated.

The NAWSA itself was in a state of disarray by the time of the death of suffrage pioneer Susan B. Anthony in 1906. Its president, Anna Howard Shaw, had proved ineffective as an administrator and organizer. While she was by no means the sole reason the NAWSA was floundering, she was emblematic of its problems. With her evangelical ideas and vocabulary, Miss Shaw was unable to communicate with the educated professional women and the union organizers of the cities. She remained throughout her presidency too much the rural westerner to understand the need of combining with urban progressive and labor forces to win over the eastern cities. She worked with the evangelical churches and temperance women of the small frontier towns and here woman suffrage was successful. She typified the old-fashioned, small-town, "woman in her place" orienta-

---

This paper is based upon research done in partial fulfillment of the requirements for the degree of Doctor of Philosophy at George Washington University.

National Woman's Party Papers, Manuscript Division, Library of Congress

Figure 1. A youthful Alice Paul at the time of the Washington Suffrage Parade in 1913.

tion of the NAWSA which had the women suffrage movement in limbo.

Into this vacuum came new, militant leadership and dramatic, unprecedented tactics designed to gain the widest possible publicity for the suffrage cause. The new leadership came in the person of Alice Paul, a young New Jersey Quaker, and her techniques of persuasion were borrowed from the English militant suffrage movement.

Alice Paul graduated from Swarthmore College in 1905 with a keen interest in social service. She continued her study, receiving a Master of Arts degree from the University of Pennsylvania in 1907 with a major in Sociology. In 1907–1908, she was a graduate student at the Universities of Birmingham and London, but her graduate study and her resident social work gradually was pushed into the background as she became captivated by the British suffragettes led by the fiery Emmeline Pankhurst and her daughters. Alice Paul participated in suffragette demonstrations, endured imprisonment, hunger strikes and forced feeding, and witnessed how the English militants took advantage of violence to discredit their adversaries and to evoke sympathy for themselves and their cause. She returned to the United States determined to reshape the American suffrage campaign as the militants had reshaped the movement in England.

On her return, Alice Paul attempted to inject some life into the woman suffrage movement in the state of Pennsylvania. Effective campaigning in the city of Philadelphia in the summer of 1911 resulted in progressively larger audiences. A final meeting in late September in Independence Square drew a crowd estimated at two thousand with NAWSA President Anna Howard Shaw one of a parade of speakers from several stands scattered around the historic square.[1]

Flushed with this success, Alice Paul began to apply pressure to the NAWSA to inaugurate a program that would call for a federal constitutional amendment for woman suffrage. She argued the obvious, that arranging for referendums on the question of woman's right to vote in state after state was costly and much too slow,[2] and urged the NAWSA to create a permanent woman's congressional committee rather than one that came into existence at the beginning of each new Congress and disbanded once the amendment was introduced.[3]

[1] Caroline Katzenstein, *Lifting the Curtain* (Philadelphia: Dorrance and Company, 1955), p. 52.
[2] *Suffragist*, November 15, 1913, p. 4; November 29, 1913, p. 20.
[3] The ineffectiveness of the Congressional Committee within the NAWSA is illustrated by the fact that the chairman of this committee in 1912 was given $10 for expenses connected with Congressional hearings and refunded change at the end of her term.

Though she often met a chilly reception, Alice Paul persisted in her efforts, presenting the NAWSA National Board a detailed plan for congressional work and making it clear that raising funds to finance this work would be the responsibility of the committee itself. At its annual convention in late 1912, the NAWSA relented, with Jane Addams making the motion to establish a permanent congressional committee.[4]

In her talks with the NAWSA National Board, Alice Paul had made it clear that as part of her effort to awaken enthusiasm for a federal amendment she planned to stage a large suffrage parade in Washington, D.C. NAWSA President Anna Shaw had witnessed such parades in London and was favorably inclined to such a project in the United States.[5] She gave Miss Paul the blessing of the Association to continue in this direction. With this immediate goal in mind, Alice Paul made significant strides in planning her Washington procession before ever opening congressional committee headquarters there. She lined up as lieutenant her colleague from English militant suffrage days, Lucy Burns, who had just returned from graduate study abroad. Another member of the congressional committee was added in late 1912, Crystal Eastman Benedict, a graduate of Vassar and New York Law College and sister of Max Eastman, editor of a new radical magazine, *Masses*. A letter from Miss Paul to Mrs. Benedict on the last day of the year noted that twenty committees had already been appointed and that a delegation of "influential women" were daily calling on Washington officials in an endeavor to obtain a desirable parade route.[6]

Alice Paul subsequently added two others to her select committee in Washington. One was Mary Beard, wife of a struggling but soon-to-be famous Columbia University history professor, Charles A. Beard. Mrs. Beard's close connections with the sympathy for the laboring classes made her a very valuable worker during the early years of Miss Paul's suffrage campaigning. The other addition was a socialite prominent in both Baltimore and Philadelphia, Mrs. Lawrence Lewis. A founder of the Equal Franchise Society in Pennsylvania, Mrs. Lewis' interests spilled over into settlement work, but she became a devoted friend of Alice Paul and a financial standby to her

---

[4] Katzenstein, *Lifting the Curtain*, p. 117.

[5] Ida Husted Harper, ed., *History of Woman Suffrage*, V (New York: National American Woman Suffrage Association, 1922), p. 378.

[6] Letter, Alice Paul to Crystal Eastman Benedict, December 31, 1912, Box 4, National Woman's Party Papers, Library of Congress (hereinafter cited as NWP Papers, LC).

suffrage organization.[7] With this core of four dedicated women, Alice Paul officially opened Washington operations from a basement room on F Street on January 2, 1913.

Although Miss Paul's congressional committee of the National American Woman Suffrage Association was to take the lead in staging a suffrage parade, the effort was to be a joint one with the District of Columbia Suffrage Associations, whose activities for years had been purely social. Alice Paul quickly asserted her new authority by naming herself and Lucy Burns to head the Joint Procession Committee, relegating to the District Associations, without any apparent ill-feeling, the choice of persons to be Treasurer and Pageant Secretary. A detailed letter by Alice Paul in early January to the NAWSA Secretary, Mary Ware Dennett, informed the Association of this procedure as well as other progress in the parade plans.[8]

Although there was opposition in the NAWSA to holding the parade on Inauguration Day, 1913, Alice Paul, by virtue of her observations of Pankhurst demonstrations, was too attuned to the value of the dramatic not to capitalize on the audience which would be assembled in the District of Columbia for the inauguration. She decided to hold the parade not on Inauguration Day itself but on March 3, the day before President-elect Woodrow Wilson would take office. In mid-January she wrote to Alice Stone Blackwell, daughter of Lucy Stone and long-time editor of the NAWSA newspaper, the *Woman's Journal*, of the necessity for the March 3 demonstration. Miss Paul pointed out that since the President and Congress were now partially elected by women, too great an opportunity would be lost in not protesting against woman's general disfranchisement, especially as practically every member of the House and Senate, as well as the enormous inaugural crowds, were sure to view such a protest. Miss Paul noted that Washington newspapers were already giving extensive coverage to the undertaking and hinted that the *Woman's Journal* might do well to do the same because of the need of marchers for the lines and contributions for the pageant to be presented.[9]

Alice Paul's decision to hold her Washington procession the day before Wilson's inaugural met with the complete approval of Harriot Stanton Blatch, daughter of pioneer suffragist Elizabeth Cady Stanton. Mrs. Blatch had injected the campaign technique of the English militants into New York state suffrage work; her expertise in staging

---

[7] Henrietta L. Krone, "Dauntless Women: The Story of the Woman Suffrage Movement in Pennsylvania, 1910–1920" (unpublished Ph.D. dissertation, University of Pennsylvania, 1946), p. 44.

[8] Letter, Alice Paul to Mary Ware Dennett, January 6, 1913, Box 6, NWP Papers, LC.

[9] Letter, Alice Paul to Alice Stone Blackwell, January 15, 1913, Box 299, NWP Papers, LC.

demonstrations punctuated with great pageantry had, in fact, prompted NAWSA in late 1912 to designate her "directress of parades." Harriot Blatch called Miss Paul's parade idea magnificent and wrote Miss Paul she hoped it would bear "rich fruit." In the midst of planning another big parade for New York, Mrs. Blatch saw no conflicts arising between Miss Paul's effort and her own and volunteered about seventy-five members of her New York organization to march in Washington. She journeyed to the nation's capital herself on the eve of the parade to take part in an enthusiastic rally at the Columbia Theater.[10]

The choice of a parade route proved no problem, but Alice Paul encountered some opposition in obtaining authorization to use the traditional Pennsylvania Avenue route. Consequently a delegation of prominent women, including Mrs. William Kent, whose husband was a California congressman, Mrs. Robert M. LaFollette, and Mrs. Helen Gardener, a well-known journalist, visited Police Chief Richard Sylvester, the commissioners of the District of Columbia, and several District business associations. Whether a change of attitude was brought about by the influence of the business community, the pressure of socially prominent women, two days of newspaper publicity on the proposed suffragist parade, or simply a letter from the Inaugural Committee chairman stating a March 3 parade on Pennsylvania Avenue would not interrupt inaugural preparations, is not clear. But Police Chief Sylvester relented and agreed to the demands of the suffragists, claiming to have misunderstood their earlier request. Miss Paul was skeptical of Sylvester's sincerity, however, and confided privately to NAWSA Secretary Dennett that it was merely his way of getting out of a difficult situation.[11]

From the beginning it was not the intent of Alice Paul to make the Washington demonstration simply a parade of numbers; in fact, she had her own reservations about how large a crowd could reasonably be expected to participate.[12] Instead, the major emphasis was on artistry and pageantry, to make the procession noteworthy because of its beauty. In this way Alice Paul consciously copied the English suffragettes as well as Harriot Blatch. To achieve her spectacle, however, Alice Paul went considerably beyond the somewhat amateurish showmanship of Mrs. Blatch's earlier parades. Two professional pageant producers were contacted, each subsequently agreeing to donate her services to the cause of woman suffrage.

[10] Harriot Stanton Blatch and Alma Lutz, *Challenging Years* (New York: G. P. Putnam's Sons, 1940), pp. 194 and 197; *Washington Post,* March 3, 1913, p. 2.
[11] Letter, Alice Paul to Mary Ware Dennett, January 6, 1913, Box 6, NWP Papers, LC.
[12] Letter, Alice Paul to Mary Blackwell, January 18, 1913, Box 4, NWP Papers, LC.

An integral part of the procession pageantry was an allegorical tableau to be staged on the steps of the Treasury building. Through the central figure of Columbia and her beautifully attired associates, Justice, Liberty, Charity, Peace, and Hope, the past achievements of woman were to be surveyed to orchestrated accompaniment, the climax to be a silent, motionless review of the mammoth procession as it approached the Treasury steps. The tableau was to commence simultaneously with the beginning of the parade near the foot of the Capitol steps. Carrie Chapman Catt, President of the International Woman Suffrage Alliance, was to leave the line of march at the Treasury building to join a group of parade reviewers that was to include Mrs. William Howard Taft, if not the President himself.

The Washington parade was to be divided into several sections, which included delegations from the states with and those working toward equal suffrage, women from numerous businesses and professions, groups from the International Woman Suffrage Alliance representative of countries having woman suffrage, and a section depicting the past seventy-five years of the woman's rights struggle. To dramatize suffrage demands while adding greatly to overall parade pageantry, floats were to be interspersed throughout the marching units. Many of the major displays, including a model of the Liberty Bell from Philadelphia, a float representing the First Equal Rights Congress and another representing a suffrage map, and a set of golden chariots from the city of Baltimore, were placed near the end of the parade to retain interest. There were no restrictions as to size of floats but the emphasis was on decorations of simplicity and dignity. NAWSA President Anna Howard Shaw expressed reservations that Alice Paul was amassing too much lavish display, and informed the parade organizer in early 1913 that while she could see the value of women marching as they did in England, she could not see the advisability of putting a great deal of money into floats "and other things" which had no direct bearing on suffrage itself.[13]

Alice Paul was not the least dissuaded by the reservations of the NAWSA President and authorized painstaking attention to be devoted to the task of costuming the marchers. Though each state delegation was to carry its own banner, adding color to the procession and showing its separate identity, Alice Paul felt that there should be official parade colors. White, purple and green were chosen. These were also the colors of the militant suffragists in England. NAWSA Secretary Mary Dennett was alarmed lest the use of these colors be mistaken as an endorsement by the NAWSA of the militants. She

---

[13] Letter, Anna Howard Shaw to Alice Paul, January 22, 1913, Box 3, NWP Papers, LC.

courteously informed Alice Paul that while she loved the militant colors from a purely aesthetic standpoint, yellow and white were international suffrage colors and the NAWSA had by custom always used yellow as its distinctive color. Miss Paul's letter in reply maintained that making any color predominant in the procession would entail increased expense for more banners. The controversy still continued in late February when Anna Howard Shaw personally threatened to bow out of the parade unless the colors of the militants were removed from their positions of pre-eminence.[14] Miss Paul grudgingly agreed only that purple, white, and green would not be referred to as official colors.

All of the pageantry and beauty to be portrayed through floats, costumes, banners, and the tableau, Alice Paul hoped to sum up in the person of a herald who would head the procession. Designated for this task was Inez Milholland, a young Vassar College graduate and socialite. Miss Milholland had already attracted national attention, because of her charm and loveliness and because she, too, had tried to introduce into the American suffrage scene the campaign methods of the British militants whom she had observed on a post-graduation trip to Europe. In 1912 one periodical had assessed her youthful abilities and concluded "she makes speeches, leads parades and wins many a convert to the cause."[15] Inez Milholland had indeed led several of Harriot Stanton Blatch's parades in New York, prompting Mrs. Blatch to say of Miss Milholland's beauty, "Helen of Troy was not more upsetting."[16] Alice Paul was quick to recognize the value of someone as versatile and energetic as Miss Milholland and solicited her services for the pre-inaugural procession. Miss Milholland was overjoyed with Miss Paul's invitation, and wrote Lucy Burns that she decided to abandon her traditional role of medieval herald for

> something suggesting the free woman of the future, crowned with the star of hope, armed with the cross of mercy, circled with the blue mantle of freedom, breasted with the torch of knowledge and carrying the trumpet which is to herald the dawn of a new day of heroic endeavor for womanhood.[17]

In deliberate contrast to the beauty of the herald and the parade

---

[14] Letter, Mary Ware Dennett to Alice Paul, February 3, 1913, Box 6, NWP Papers, LC; Alice Paul to Mary Ware Dennett, February 6, 1913, Box 6; Lucy Burns to Mrs. James E. Laidlaw, February 12, 1913, Box 4; Anna Howard Shaw to Alice Paul, February 24, 1913, Box 3.

[15] Mary Kinkaid, "The Feminine Charms of the Woman Militant," *Good Housekeeping*, February 1912, p. 152.

[16] Blatch and Lutz, *Challenging Years*, p. 109.

[17] Letter, Inez Milholland to Lucy Burns, February 7, 1913, Box 155, NWP Papers, LC.

pageantry were a group who in the drabbest of attire planned a march to publicize the March 3 procession. Wearing long brown cloaks with hoods and carrying staffs and knapsacks (see figure 2), some fifteen "pilgrims" left New York on Lincoln's birthday to hike to Washington, arriving in time for pre-parade banquets. Led by "General" Rosalie Jones, and including such notable feminists as Lavinia Dock, long-time worker in the Henry Street Settlement in New York and internationally known in the nursing field, this "Army of the Hudson" bore an appeal from NAWSA President Anna Shaw which they hoped to deliver to President-elect Wilson. The petition urged him to recommend equal suffrage in his inaugural address and to use his influence throughout his administration for the attainment of woman suffrage.

Despite the obvious benefit of the publicity of the pilgrim journey, some suffragists were fearful of setting a precedent which would be difficult to live up to, especially since well-known personalities were being sought to add lustre to the Washington procession. Not all suffragists are born hikers, Caroline Reilly confided to Lucy Burns. She was thinking specifically of Mrs. Oliver H. P. Belmont, a New

Bain Collection, Prints and Photographs Division, Library of Congress

Figure 2. Suffrage hikers arrive in Washington for the pre-inaugural parade of 1913.

York socialite who had married into and was divorced from the wealthy Vanderbilt family, and who for several years had contributed generously to the suffrage cause. Mrs. Belmont had participated in Harriot Blatch's May 1912 New York torch-light procession, but according to Caroline Reilly had been a failure as a walker. Miss Burns drafted a note at the bottom of Caroline Reilly's letter to one of the pageant directors asking if Mrs. Belmont could be used as a figure in the pageant, because she was a "newspaper item, and once here would probably contribute." The note was signed, "greedily." [18]

Alice Paul sought a large turn-out of marchers but was forced abruptly to modify her open-door policy with a request in mid-January for a separate Negro section in the parade. The introduction of the racial issue into parade planning posed a dilemma and carried with it a threat of severely limiting white participation. Mary Beard surveyed segments of the colored suffrage community and reported to Miss Paul some determination among Negroes to march "where they belonged, and not just where some women were willing they should march." Mrs. Beard's assessment concluded with a note of caution: "we ought to be intelligeent enough to avoid a race war. This is a perfect nightmare to me." [19]

In an attempt to head off an impending crisis, Alice Paul wrote a lengthy letter to Alice Stone Blackwell for publication in the *Woman's Journal*. Miss Paul carefully prefaced her remarks by citing her equalitarian Quaker northern background and added that so far as she was aware she was actuated by no race prejudice. But she acknowledged that strong prejudice existed, especially in the Washington area, and that this bias would drive white marchers from participating if Negroes formed a part of the parade. The additional fact that the inaugural would be Democratic, with a large southern element in the crowds, prompted Miss Paul to judge that "we must have a white procession, or a negro procession, or no procession at all." [20]

She felt that few Negroes would in fact desire to participate and that these could be scattered among some of the northern and Quaker delegations. She also believed that if the Washington parade helped to speed up the winning of woman suffrage the status of Negro women would also be raised. In this belief she appears to have differed significantly from the NAWSA leadership which in the early Twentieth

---

[18] Letter, Caroline I. Reilly to Lucy Burns, January 30, 1913, Box 8, NWP Papers, LC.

[19] Letter, Mary Beard to Alice Paul, January 1913 (no specific date), Box 155, NWP Papers, LC.

[20] Letter, Alice Paul to Alice Stone Blackwell, January 15, 1913, Box 299, NWP Papers, LC.

Century, especially in using the principle of states' rights as a basis for the relationship of state suffrage organizations to one another and to the national, all but officially sanctioned second-class citizenship for Negroes.[21]

Had it not been for the shocking treatment accorded the marching suffragists on parade day, the race issue might well have overshadowed other aspects of the Washington spectacle, for racial reverberations were still being felt weeks after the march was staged. The April issue of the Negro periodical, *The Crisis,* carried an article by W. E. B. DuBois criticizing treatment of blacks in the suffrage procession. Alice Paul not only answered the criticism but persuaded Mary Beard to write also, arguing that what she might say would probably seem more credible to the Negro leader. Absent from his office, DuBois did not respond till mid-June, but his letter was no more acceptable to Miss Paul than the article had been. She caustically charged in a return letter that he had no first-hand knowledge of the facts connected with the suffrage procession, and denied his statements that an order had been issued to segregate colored women and that telegrams and protests had been received at parade headquarters. Mary Beard again corroborated Miss Paul's story with a follow-up letter.[22]

NAWSA President Anna Howard Shaw's letter to Alice Paul the day after the inauguration, upholding her actions regarding Negroes and the parade,[23] typifies the support the association gave Alice Paul, concealing, at least for the moment, developing differences over the route to be followed in achieving woman suffrage. Especially noteworthy were the efforts of Helen H. Gardener, who subsequently became Carrie Chapman Catt's capable associate and valuable liason with President Wilson. During the early weeks of 1913 Miss Gardener was in charge of all the press work, getting out news stories twice a day

---

[21] Aileen S. Kraditor, *The Ideas of the Woman Suffrage Movement, 1890–1920* (New York: Columbia University Press, 1966), in Chapter VII, "The Southern Question," pp. 163–218, concludes that the universality of racism in America after 1890, with its emphasis on white Anglo-Saxon superiority, prompted the emergence of a suffrage movement of Southern white women in alliance with a northern movement that contained many old abolitionsits, including Henry Blackwell, who believed that the vote for women was the all-important objective, even if it meant other sectors of the population must pay part of the cost. An exception to this attitude among NAWSA membership is Mary Ware Dennett, Corresponding Secretary from 1910–1913. Writing to Alice Paul, January 14, 1913, concerning possible Negro participation in the Washington parade, Dennett made her position perfectly clear: "The suffrage movement stands for enfranchisement for every single woman in the United States, and there is no occasion when we would be justified in not living up to our principles."

[22] Letter, Alice Paul to Mary Beard, April 18, 1913, Box 155, NWP Papers, LC; Alice Paul to W. E. B. DuBois, July 12, 1913, Box 2; Mary Beard to W. E. B. DuBois, July 20, 1913, Box 2.

[23] Letter, Anna Howard Shaw to Alice Paul, March 5, 1913, Box 2, NWP Papers, LC.

for the press bureaus of Washington and each week a long feature story for country-wide distribution. Alice Paul frankly admitted "she was about our only helper in the beginning." [24] Alice Stone Blackwell also earned credit, through her editorials and coverage in *The Woman's Journal,* for arousing interest in the procession. Her job was eased in late January 1913 when Alice Paul began to send a daily news bulletin to her in Boston.

Throughout the weeks of parade organizing, Alice Paul marshalled her limited forces at the F Street headquarters with military precision. She put requests tersely, in the full expectation they would be granted. At times, when there were not enough workers to get out letters or answer the phones, shoppers were actually recruited for labor. The energetic Miss Paul, however, never demanded from others what she was not willing to do herself. She and Lucy Burns frequently stayed up late at night to handle tasks they could not concentrate on earlier. One woman remarked that she had worked with Alice Paul for three months before she saw her find time to take her hat off.[25]

Two days before the parade, marchers began arriving in Washington. Highlighting the pre-parade festivities was a huge rally on March 2 at the Columbia theater. Carrie Chapman Catt and Harriot Blatch made speeches against the anti-suffragists, a group of whom had announced their hopes of detracting from the effectiveness of the procession by displaying cartoons and mottoes on a large screen erected on the roof of a Pennsylvania Avenue business establishment. The pilgrim marchers, in their cloaks and hoods, were again recognized. Then, under the presiding genius of Mrs. Blatch, the large audience, which included a number of city and government officials, was stirred into enthusiasm and generousity which resulted in more than five thousand dollars in contributions.

The March 3, 1913 edition of the *Washington Post* predicted: "It will be an impressive sight. Nothing like it has ever been seen before. It will be a milestone in the progress of women." [26] This was accurate on all three counts. The parade was impressive; it could be considered something of a milestone; and nothing like it had ever been seen before, for the parade had hardly begun when it became a series of near-riots.

---

[24] Alice Paul, interview with author, NWP headquarters, Washington, D.C., May 8, 1969.

[25] Olivia E. Coolidge, *Women's Rights: The Suffrage Movement in America, 1848–1920* (New York: E. P. Dutton and Co., Inc., 1966), p. 115.

[26] Editorial, *Washington Post,* March 3, 1913, p. 6.

The estimated five thousand marchers had to fight their way from the start. It took more than an hour to walk the first ten blocks, and by then many were in tears from the insults of those who lined the route. At Fourth Street, progress was halted until some members of a Massachusetts National Guard regiment helped clear the way. Automobiles in wedge formation, followed by a platoon of mounted police, then forced people toward the curb, only to have them immediately surge back on the Avenue. At Sixth Street, police protection gave way entirely and solid masses of spectators on each side came so close together that the marchers could not walk three abreast. A group of Maryland College students locked arms to form a crowd-breaking vanguard. At the reviewing stand the crowd became so disorderly that Mrs. Taft and other guests left before the procession arrived there. Finally, cavalry troops from nearby Fort Myer were called upon to restore order. The rally in Continental Hall following the disbanding of the marchers became a meeting of indignation and protest.[27]

Alice Paul's efforts to make the suffrage demonstration a spectacle of spectacles succeeded. The parade presented "an irresistible appeal to the artistic and completely captivated the hundred thousand spectators," the *Washington Post* reported. The floats "far surpassed" those in the last New York suffrage parade, said the *New York Tribune*, which was impressed also with "the colors, the grouping, the whole spectacle" of the tableau and concluded "if that is woman suffrage, it is mighty good to look at." The *Chicago Tribune* called the "scheme of colors and tints and shades in rainbow rotation . . . a record parade for inventiveness." [28]

But the public only cursorily considered parade artistry in its rage against the way the suffragists had been treated. Newspapers and periodicals across the country carried columns of editorial protest. In the opinion of the *New York Tribune* in an editorial entitled "Disgrace to the Capitol," the timely arrival of the United States cavalry prevented greater brutality and insult, and it called for a "searching investigation" with "swift and severe" punishment. The *Chicago Tribune* commented under the heading "Hoodlums vs. Gentlewomen." The *New York Times* urged suffrage women to "exploit

---

[27] A youthful Helen Keller was to have joined Carrie Chapman Catt and Anna Howard Shaw in this post-parade rally, but had been so unnerved in attempting to reach a grandstand where she was to have been a guest of honor that she did not come to the hall. A letter from Alice Paul to Helen Keller, March 14, 1913, Box 5, NWP Papers, LC, apologized for the poor police protection and offered to reimburse her for the trip from Massachusetts.

[28] *Washington Post,* March 4, 1913, p. 1; *New York Tribune,* March 4, 1913, p. 3; *Chicago Tribune,* March 4, 1913, p. 1.

their grievance, since it is a real one, and of real grievances they have had few in this century." [29]

Washington Police Chief Richard Sylvester was the target of sharp criticism, especially since the March 4 inaugural crowd was contained and the inaugural parade uninterrupted. The *Chicago Tribune* speculated that if Sylvester had been recognized the night of March 3 by the indignant woman suffragists he might not the next day have been considered handsome enough to head the police escort for the inaugural parade. One periodical scored what they called Sylvester's disposition to blame individual policemen rather than to assume responsibility for his department. A handbill, signed "Justice," was circulated among the throng at Wilson's inaugural charging that the police chief held his job by blackmail and urging that letters from every Congressional district be written demanding his removal and an investigation of the Washington police force. The *Washington Post* was almost alone among newspapers in its defense of Sylvester, saying that he had long been in favor of woman suffrage and that the police department's past record for efficiency entitled it to a fair hearing.[30]

The indignation meeting at Continental Hall following the parade was the initial volley in a barrage of suffragist protest. Back in New York on inauguration day, Harriot Stanton Blatch dispatched a telegram to President Wilson, on behalf of her own state suffrage society, so he would not be unmindful as he rode "in safety and comfort" to the Capitol that

> yesterday the Government which is supposed to exist for the good of all, left women while in peaceful procession in their demand for political freedom at the mercy of a howling mob on the very streets which are being at this moment efficiently officered for the protection of men.[31]

Anna Howard Shaw issued a statement to the press charging not only the police but the "whole official government" in Washington with a determined effort to mar the success of the parade because of anger over possible interference with the inaugural ceremony.[32] Reso-

---

[29] Editorial, "Disgrace to the Capitol," *New York Tribune*, March 5, 1913, p. 8; editorial, "Hoodlums vs. Gentlewomen," *Chicago Tribune*, March 5, 1913, p. 6; editorial, "Anti-suffragism Gets a Hard Blow," *New York Times*, March 5, 1913, p. 6. In an editorial, "Spitting on the Procession," *Woman's Journal*, March 22, 1913, p. 92, Alice Stone Blackwell commented on the overwhelming newspaper condemnation of the manner in which the suffragists were treated.

[30] *Chicago Tribune*, March 4, 1913, p. 1; *LaFollette's Magazine*, March 22, 1913, p. 3; handbill from "Justice" dated March 4, 1913, in Box 3, NWP Papers, LC; editorial, *Washington Post*, March 6, 1913, p. 6.

[31] Blatch and Lutz, *Challenging Years*, p. 197.

[32] *Washington Post*, March 5, 1913, p. 1, as located in Harriot Stanton Blatch, *Scrapbooks 1908–1915*, VII, Library of Congress (hereinafter cited as Blatch, *Scrapbooks*, LC).

Alice Paul and the Great Suffrage Parade of 1913 671

lutions came from state suffrage societies, sometimes accompanied by vivid testimony of members allegedly mistreated, condemning the riot-like conditions that had prevailed.

Alice Stone Blackwell began a running box score in the pages of the *Woman's Journal* of protest meetings and resolutions, urging her readers to make their dissent effective by writing their congressmen. Her second issue after the parade said that the list was becoming so lengthy as to be impossible to enumerate. She continued her own editorial attacks on the police, anti-suffragists, and the American male. In a late March column she asked: "Is it possible that real American men stood calmly by and witnessed such an exhibition of cowardice and did nothing about it? It is possible that the men of the Eastern states have degenerated into the degraded moral condition of Asiatics?" [33]

The parade participants took advantage of the riot to discredit anti-suffragists and to solicit sympathy from the public. With the widespread criticism in the press of the treatment of the women they made significant gains in being identified by the public as victims. There was probably also an increased commitment among many marchers themselves to the cause of woman suffrage because of the hostility vented against them. This has been characteristic of patterns of martyrdom in other movements. Silvan Tomkins has written that abolitionists William Lloyd Garrison, James G. Birney, Wendell Phillips and Theodore Weld, despite some temporary doubts, became more firmly wedded to the cause of anti-slavery reform as a result of public antagonism toward their strong reform stands. Tomkins concluded that there logically follows a cycle of risk-taking and suffering which results in a reformer's commitment deepening until it reaches a point of no return.[34]

That the morale of woman suffragists, and especially of those who paraded, was boosted as a result of the angry crowds, and that there was a stronger conviction of the rightness of the movement, was reflected in one young marcher's letter to her father noting "the whole thing has created a great stir and we have hosts of sympathizers we would never have gotten otherwise." [35] In sharing the common experience of being on parade and being subjected to the actions of an un-

---

[33] Editorial, "The Fire Spreads," *Woman"s Journal,* March 15, 1913, p. 84; editorial, "Spitting on the Procession," *Woman's Journal,* March 22, 1913, p. 92.

[34] Silvan S. Tomkins, "The Psychology of Commitment," in Martin Duberman, ed., *The Anti-Slavery Vanguard: New Essays on Abolitionists* (Princeton: Princeton University Press, 1965), pp. 270–298.

[35] Letter, Florence Hedges to H. C. Hedges, March 9, 1913, National Woman's Party Collection of Documents, Division of Political History, The Smithsonian Institution, Washington, D.C. (hereinafter cited as NWP Collection, Smithsonian).

controlled crowd, the participants developed a new esprit de corps. A greater sympathy for the English militants, for their techniques and their suffering, also resulted from the March 1913 parade. As one suffragist wrote: "We know exactly how the English women feel when a drunken man spits tobacco juice on your clothes and then laughs; it is time to be a militant."[36]

The wide range of the protests probably prompted Congress to its investigation of the event. Suffragist pressure alone might well have been a key factor, though Lucy Burns for one denied it.[37] It is certain, however, that a joint resolution before the parade by both houses of Congress, directing the superintendent of police of the District of Columbia to clear the parade route and prevent any interference with the March 3 suffrage procession, had not been complied with. The Senate passed two resolutions on inauguration day demanding first to know why the joint resolution had not been enforced and secondly instructing the Senate Committee on the District of Columbia to investigate the District police and police department to ascertain if negligence were involved. On March 5 a subcommittee to take testimony was appointed, consisting of Senator William P. Dillingham of Vermont, Atlee Pomerene of Ohio, and Wesley L. Jones of Washington. The latter, at whose insistence the resolution of inquiry was adopted, was designated chairman, and on the afternoon of March 6, 1913, the subcommittee began to examine witnesses.

Testimony continued for almost two weeks in March and again for two days in mid-April. Numerous policemen on duty, spectators, procession organizers and participants, and District and federal government officials were among the nearly one hundred and fifty witnesses who were called. Countless affidavits of alleged police inefficiency and negligence were introduced; in late March, Alice Paul was still soliciting such evidence to bring before the subcommittee.[38] More than seven hundred printed pages of testimony was taken.

Alice Paul's testimony, given early in the proceedings, revealed not only her difficulties with Police Chief Sylvester in establishing the date and route desired for the procession but also her efforts to secure adequate protection for the marchers. The police chief was questioned for two days regarding the pivotal role he played in the controversial events and he attempted to extricate himself by placing blame elsewhere. He maintained there had been no neglect in assembling an adequate force for the procession, noting that over a hundred more men performed duty in connection with the suffrage parade than with

[36] *New York Tribune,* March 5, 1913; Blatch, *Scrapbooks,* VII, LC.
[37] *Washington Post,* May 30, 1913, p. 4.
[38] *Woman's Journal,* March 29, 1913, p. 100.

the inaugural parade. The real difficulty, Sylvester insisted, was in the joint resolution of Congress which ordered him to clear the parade route but granted him authority to stop traffic and travel, including street cars, only between the hours of three and five o'clock. The police chief had ordered Pennsylvania Avenue cleared from curb to curb. When he was asked if his force had not been negligent, since the route was not properly cleared by three o'clock, Sylvester answered affirmatively and said he was "surprised and shocked" by the conditions. He testified that improper communication resulted in his learning only about three hours before the procession that cavalry troops were at his disposal and he categorically denied stating he would be unable to protect the marchers.[39]

Photographs provided the most damaging evidence of the lack of crowd control and the heart of the suffragists's case. On the first day of the hearings Abby Scott Baker, with obvious delight, turned over to the Senators some snapshots which had been purchased from a commercial photographer that morning. Particularly crucial to her testimony was a print entitled "Waiting for the Parade" (see figure 3). Taken as the parade was about to begin, from a point near Fourteenth Street where the procession was to turn south around the Treasury building, looking up Pennsylvania Avenue, it showed how completely congested the parade route was at the precise moment it was supposed to be clear. Ground level photographs presented to the subcommittee (see figure 4) showed the narrow lanes through which units of the parade had to pass and the tendency of the crowd to surge together between units. With other prints in hand, the three investigating Senators questioned whether the throng might have been moved back to allow a wider lane. They looked especially long at a photograph taken from the top of the Washington *Star* newspaper building at Pennsylvania Avenue and Eleventh Street (see figure 5) which showed considerable room on each side of the Avenue in which the crowd could have been moved toward the curb.

The Senate District Committee released its findings on May 29, 1913. It exonerated Police Chief Sylvester of any hostility toward the suffragists or their parade but chided him for his lack of wisdom in not seeking the necessary authority to stop traffic sooner and to provide more adequate parade protection. While it held that some of the uniformed and special police acted with "more or less indifference" and thus did little to check the crowd, the report cautioned against discrediting the whole force and added that there was not sufficient proof

---

[39] U. S. Congress, Senate Committee on the District of Columbia, *Suffrage Parade*, S. Rept. 53, 63rd Cong., 1st Sess., 1913, pp. 136–74, 181–216.

Report, Suffrage Parade, U. S. Senate Committee on the District of Columbia, 1913

Figure 3. A packed crowd on Pennsylvania Avenue awaits the start of Alice Paul's 1913 suffrage parade.

upon which to single out any particular individual for condemnation. The report found that the War Department went to the limits of its authority, if it did not exceed it, in detailing a troop of cavalry from Fort Myer. In conclusion the Committee labeled the parade new, interesting, novel and in a broad sense political in character, with the crowd either for or against the idea represented, but anxious to see the spectacle. With the streets of the city filled with people close to the time of march, and with the police having no authority to stop cars and vehicles until the minute set for the start of the parade, it was not surprising that the crowd was not kept back and got out of control.[40]

Publication of the District Committee's findings was met with cries of whitewash from both the suffragists and the press. The Washington *Post* noted with chagrin that the heavy weight of denunciation which fell on "our old nefarious acquaintance unusual conditions" was to be expected. Under the heading "A Poor Piece of Whitewashing," the *New York World* maintained that "the plea the report makes in defense of the police force is lame and its conclusions offend common

---
[40] *Ibid.*, pp. ix–xvi.

Bain Collection, Prints and Photographs Division, Library of Congress

Figure 4. A 1913 suffrage parade entry, with Negroes leading it, moves along the narrow lane between the crowd.

sense." Speaking for the National Association, Alice Stone Blackwell termed the report a disappointment and then leveled a final blast at the Washington law enforcement structure:

> The mere statement of the facts by the committee amounts to a charge of police inefficiency. A police force that cannot handle a street parade has not been taught the first principle of its business. What Washington evidently needs is a thorough reorganization of its police department. When men and women cannot march along Pennsylvania Avenue without being insulted and mobbed under the eyes of the police, it is time to make radical change.[41]

There is little doubt that the failure of the police to maintain order, and not the procession itself, was the chief contributor to suffrage progress in March 1913. In one of her columns, Alice Stone Blackwell related the story of a man who, while tipsy, saw his reflection and labeled himself the homeliest person he had ever seen. The parallel, she said, was that in the conduct of the crowd the "ugliness and stupidity" of the opposition to equal suffrage had been shown as in a mirror and woman's cause had benefitted.[42] Shortly after the March

[41] *Washington Post,* May 30, 1913; Blatch, *Scrapbooks,* VII, LC; editorial, "A Poor Piece of Whitewashing," *New York World,* as cited in editorial, "A Coat of Whitewash," *Woman's Journal,* June 7, 1913, p. 180.
[42] Editorial, "An Object Lesson," *Woman's Journal,* March 8, 1913, p. 76.

Report, Suffrage Parade, U. S. Senate Committee on the District of Columbia, 1913

Figure 5. A photograph from the top of the Washington *Star* newspaper building, though somewhat blurred, shows the space close to the curbs where police might have moved portions of the 1913 parade throng.

3 procession Anna Howard Shaw was quoted as saying she had never felt so sanguine before, because she had captured a spirit of loyalty on the part of men to women and believed nothing could stop women in their fight for the ballot.[43] There were many who agreed that the results of the parade had given woman cause for great optimism. In the judgment of one member of the House of Representatives, Clyde H. Tavenner, "more votes were made for woman suffrage in the city of Washington on the afternoon of March 3rd than will perhaps ever be made again in the same length of time so long as the government stands." [44]

There was a definite upsurge in suffragist activity and interest in the federal suffrage amendment in the wake of the pre-inaugural parade. Pilgrimages were organized to Washington from all over the country with petitions collected at the grass-roots level. Delegations

---

[43] *Washington Post*, March 5, 1913, p. 1.
[44] Account by Clyde H. Tavenner (D., Ill.) of March 3, 1913 suffrage parade, as located in Box 6, NWP Papers, LC. Cited in Katzenstein, *Lifting the Curtain*, p. 117.

Columbia Historical Society Collection
Photograph by the Blakslee Studio, Rock Island, Illinois

Figure 6. Clyde H. Tavenner (1882–1942), who was in 1913 a young Congressman from Illinois, wrote that "more votes were made for woman suffrage in the city of Washington on the afternoon of March 3rd than will perhaps ever be made again in the same length of time so long as the government stands."

quickly began to visit the new president, whose early pronouncements on woman suffrage, especially his remarks that the matter had never been brought to his attention, were not promising. Alice Paul capitalized on this fresh momentum to establish her independence from the National American Woman Suffrage Association. An independent suffrage organization, which in time became the National Woman's Party, was established less than a month after the Washington parade.

The great suffrage parade of 1913 marked a split in approaches to a common goal. For the youthful Alice Paul it was a significant step in rejuvenating the cause of woman suffrage in America. Through it she succeeded in establishing an identity for herself and her little band of followers. She used the Washington spectacular as a starting point for other action-oriented techniques which differed dramatically from the more traditional approaches of the National American Woman Suffrage Association. Their programs would henceforth be different, too, for Alice Paul believed that a state-by-state method of achieving woman suffrage was too slow and was destined to take forever. She saw a federal suffrage amendment as a more practical goal and sought a concentrated effort to achieve it. The great suffrage parade of 1913 in Washington, D.C. was a long step toward the achievement of national equal voting rights for women in 1920.

The Relief of General Barnett

BENIS M. FRANK

In the May 24, 1947 edition of the *Washington Post,* there appeared a news story with the headline: "Gen. Barnett's Widow Sues Josephus Daniels for Libel." The story went on to say that Mrs. Lelia Montague Barnett, a socially prominent Washingtonian and widow of the one-time Commandant of the Marine Corps, had brought suit for $50,000 the previous day against President Woodrow Wilson's wartime Secretary of the Navy. The basis for this suit was that Daniels had described General Barnett as "The-Man-Afraid-of-His-Wife" in his book, *The Wilson Era: Years of War and After, 1917–1923,* published in 1946. Although the events surrounding this allegedly libelous statement had happened 30 years earlier, and General Barnett had been dead for 16 years, the bitterness against Mr. Daniels remained and the surviving protagonists seemed as implacable as ever.

To put the story of General Barnett's relief as Commandant of the Marine Corps by Secretary Daniels in perspective, we must go back to the beginning of the Spanish-American War and continue on to the first years of the Twentieth Century when an expanding Marine Corps found its roles and missions and its entire character changing dramatically. Guiding the destiny of the Marine Corps in these years before World War I were four Commandants: Charles Heywood, 1891–1903; George F. Elliott, 1903–1910; William P. Biddle, 1911–1914; and George Barnett, who was appointed in 1914.

General Biddle's tenure of office was marked by Navy and Presidential hostility to the Corps, a residue from the administrations of Presidents Theodore Roosevelt and Taft. The choice of an acceptable successor to Biddle by the Wilson administration was therefore a matter of some importance, considering the state of international tensions at the time and the portents for the future.

In late October 1913, John A. Lejeune, senior Marine Corps Lieutenant Colonel, was called to Washington from his barracks command

---
Delivered before the Columbia Historical Society on May 19, 1971.
  The author wishes to express his appreciation to another outstanding Commandant, the late General Clifton B. Cates, USMC (Retired), for permission he gave to quote from a taped interview with him in the Marine Corps Oral History Program.

Photograph from the author
George Barnett as a cadet at the Naval Academy, 1878.

at the Brooklyn Navy Yard for a conference with Secretary of the Navy Josephus Daniels. As it turned out, this interview was for the purpose of determining at first-hand Lejeune's fitness for the Commandancy. In his memoirs later, General Lejeune said that he believed he was not chosen at this time because of his relative youth and rank. Others seriously considered for this most coveted of all Marine Corps appointments were Colonels Littleton W. T. Waller, Lincoln Karmany, and George Barnett—first, third, and sixth in lineal precedence, respectively, and all men with exceptionally fine records.

Chosen to become the 12th Commandant of the Marine Corps was George Barnett, who took office on February 25, 1914. By all accounts, he was an austere, gentle, and scholarly individual, and one of the most admired and respected Marines ever to have served as Commandant of his Corps. A member of the Naval Academy Class of 1881, he was the first graduate of that institution appointed to the Commandancy and, based on the provisions of a law passed in 1913, he was also the first Commandant appointed to a four-year term.

Almost from the beginning of his incumbency, General Barnett managed to establish more effective cooperation and cordial relations with the Navy. The fact of his being a Naval Academy graduate and his early contacts with the Navy undoubtedly figured largely in this rapprochement. With his assumption of office, General Barnett was appointed an ex-officio member of the Navy General Board—the first Commandant so appointed to represent the Marine Corps on this major planning group.

In his memoirs, General Barnett said that this appointment was made:

> ... largely at the request of Admiral Dewey, the President of the Board. I was gratified by this appointment because I considered it highly proper that the Marine Corps should be represented on a board where practically all naval matters are thoroughly considered and because the Corps is an integral part of the Navy and very often had questions considered by the Board. I enjoyed my duty as a member of that very important Board, and I always felt that if Marine Corps matters presented did not at all times meet the approval of the Board, I at least had my day in court, and had been able to present the case from the marine viewpoint.

At a time when Marine Corps-Navy relations were on the mend, it seemed that the Corps was in better stead also with the Administration, and particularly with the Secretary of the Navy. In General Barnett's words:

... there never was a time during my service as Commandant of the Marine Corps when the Secretary expressed anything but satisfaction in regard to my performance of duty. In fact, his report on fitness in my case was all that any officer could wish; and to me he seemed to have gone out of his way to express satisfaction at the manner of performance of my duty. . . .

Upon taking office in 1914, and joined shortly afterwards by Colonel Lejeune as his assistant, General Barnett commanded a Corps of approximately 10,343 Marines. In 1916, when it became apparent to most that the United States would become involved in the war in Europe, Congress increased the size of the Marine Corps to 15,577 and gave the President authority to augment this number by about 2,400 more if necessary. In addition, the 1916 legislation authorized the Corps to undertake considerable internal reorganization and, for the first time in its history, it was given an adequate proportion of higher-ranking officers to permit the proper organization of larger military formations than the Corps had ever mustered before.

On April 6, 1917, the United States declared war on Germany and the Central Powers. Just 11 days earlier, the size of the Marine Corps had been increased to a force of 18,093 officers and enlisted men. In May, this number was nearly doubled and before the end of World War I, the Marine Corps had a strength of slightly more than 75,000 men in uniform. General Barnett directed the affairs of this greatly enlarged Corps with a firm hand. Not all of these Marines fought in Europe, however, for the Corps was committed during this period also to providing occupation troops for Haiti and Santo Domingo, a brigade to occupy portions of Cuba, and part of another brigade in Galveston, Texas, where it was held in reserve for service on the Mexican border.

In addition, the Commandant had to provide troops to man posts and stations and other men to maintain and conduct the training at the large training centers at Quantico, Virginia, and Parris Island, South Carolina. And, while concerned with these matters, he scored the greatest coup of his first tour as Commandant when he almost single-handedly forced the Army high command to accept Marines for service in France. This, however, is apart from our story here and may be told at another time.

Students of this period are aware of how men flocked to join the Marine Corps, spurred on by the slogan, "First to Fight," and of how the 5th and 6th Marine Regiments and the 6th Machine Gun Battalion were formed and sent to France to become the 4th Marine Brigade of the 2d Army Division, AEF. The outstanding fighting

Major General George Barnett as Commandant of the Marine Corps.

qualities and exploits of these men in combat in such famous actions as Belleau Wood, St. Mihiel, and the Meuse-Argonne, among others, overshadowed the equally important accomplishments of General Barnett in forming, equipping, training, and deploying these troops.

If for no other reason, he should be remembered for the fact that, under his Commandancy, the Marine Corps rendered to the American defense effort the greatest possible service by sending every available Marine overseas into combat. There were, as is true of every war in which Marines have fought, few rear-area or uncommitted Marines in World War I.

In recognition of General Barnett's able performance during his first tour as Commandant, he was reappointed by the President to a second four-year term which began on February 25, 1918. His reselection had been announced nearly two weeks earlier, on February 12, by Secretary of the Navy Daniels, who stated effusively:

> During the incumbency of General Barnett as head of the Marine Corps, that organization has attained its highest efficiency and this is due to in large manner to his personal efforts and to his ability as an organizer and administrator. . . .

Daniels was equally unsparing in his praise of General Barnett later in 1918, when, in his Annual Report to the President, the Secretary said:

> The splendid service of the Marines at home or abroad is the best proof of their efficient training in peace times, and the country as never before appreciates their quality and their courage. The administration of this fine Corps under the direction of Gen. George Barnett, Major General Commanding the Marine Corps, the best type of Marine whose service in the field equals his services as an executive, and his able associates, has been worthy of the unstinting commendations given by Europe and America.

A short time later, on behalf of the President, the Secretary awarded the Commandant the Distinguished Service Medal "For exceptionally meritorious service in a duty of great responsibility as Commandant of the Marine Corps in the administration of the manifold and distinguished service of the Marine Corps at home and abroad."

Mr. Daniels' award of the DSM to and praise of General Barnett appears to have hid the Secretary's real feelings towards the Commandant. Although the latter was not aware of any existing schism in his relationship with his superior, perhaps he should have been. In the first place, Barnett's reappointment was made with a limitation artificially placed on the length of his second tour as Commandant—artificial in the sense that Congress had already passed legislation which stated that the tour of office for the Commandant of the Marine Corps was four years. According to General Barnett:

> The day that my time was up [at the end of the first four years], the

The Relief of General Barnett

Photograph from the author

Left to right: Lieutenant Colonel C. S. Hill, Captain J. A. Rossell, Brigadier General J. A. Lejune, Major General George Barnett, Brigadier General C. L. McCawley, and Colonel C. G. Long, Philadelphia, 1917.

Secretary of the Navy sent for me, and because of the importance of what took place every word of his remarks is absolutely engraved on my memory. He said, "General Barnett, the President has decided to reappoint you Commandant of the Marine Corps, but desires you to sign your resignation in blank, the same as the chiefs of bureaus of the Navy Department, who have been reappointed, have done." I flushed at this and replied that I was unwilling to sign a resignation in blank and saw no reason for it because my commission read for "four years or at the discretion of the President..." I said that I would like to see the President about the matter of signing my resignation in blank, and the Secretary said, "I will see the President about it."

The next day, Daniels sent for the Commandant and told him to forget the matter they had discussed previously and to let things stand as they were.

In Mr. Daniels' memoirs, *The Wilson Era,* there is a somewhat different account of this episode. In a section of the book entitled "Marine Corps Commandant Defiant," Daniels recalled how, during World War I, it was his belief that no man should remain on duty in

Washington longer than four years, no matter how important was the position he held. The exceptions to this rule were department heads whose experience required their retention for the full period of the war. Daniels wrote that his bureau heads were "reappointed with the full understanding that upon termination of the struggle their resignation would be accepted." According to the former Secretary's account, when General Barnett was called in, informed of Mr. Daniels' policy, and asked to sign the resignation, the Commandant in turn requested permission to consider the situation and return the next day. Daniels recalled:

> Upon his return he said he would prefer not to sign the resignation, and added, "I am a gentleman, and no gentleman would remain a day after his resignation was desired. I will tender it if you desire as soon as the war is over."

Mrs. Barnett's libel suit against Mr. Daniels was based on Daniels' account in his memoirs of a conversation with an unnamed admiral about the reluctance of General Barnett to submit a signed and undated resignation. As Daniels related the story, the admiral replied: "You understand, don't you? If Barnett lived among the Indians and was given the name that best fitted him, he would be called 'The-Man-Afraid-of-His-Wife!' "

The next event leading to an eventual confrontation between the two men occurred on June 18, 1918, when the House of Representatives met to consider a Naval Personnel Bill designed to increase the strength of the Navy. A Senate amendment to this bill called for the promotion of the Major General Commandant to the rank of Lieutenant General and of his key staff officers—the Quartermaster, the Adjutant and Inspector, and the Paymaster—to Major General.

In expectation that this bill would be passed pro forma, the Commandant and Mrs. Barnett, and Brigadier General Charles H. Lauchheimer, the Adjutant and Inspector, were in the House gallery to witness the debate. When it came time for the so-called Barnett amendment to be voted upon, one of the first to speak on the measure was Representative Thomas Butler, Chairman of the House Naval Affairs Committee, and doting father of Colonel Smedley D. Butler, who was impatiently chafing at the bit in Haiti where he hopefully awaited the orders that would assign him to a combat command in France.

Rising to address the House, Mr. Butler charged that the amendment was unfair to the men who were fighting in France so brilliantly and that if any promotions were deserved they were for the Marines overseas and not "for 'swivel chair officers,' who will never get outside of Washington." Warming to the attack, he called his colleagues' attention to the presence of Marine officers in the gallery, pointed towards them, and thundered dramatically, "The place for fighting men is at the front, not here in the gallery!"

In addition to a charge that the Commandant was a "rocking chair warrior," Butler pointed out that Secretary Daniels not only had refused to endorse the promotion, but "had gone on record that no military necessity is served by this promotion." Further, in an oblique attack on Mrs. Barnett, who had long been prominent in Washington society, Butler accused the Commandant of exerting social influence to gain preferment.

Following up this performance was a demand by Representative Edward Keating of Colorado that General Barnett be court martialled for attempting to go over the head of his commanding officer, Secretary Daniels, for promotion. Like so many other ridiculous suggestions that have from time to time been made on the Floor of the House, this one quietly died. So did, by a vote of 73 to 49, the amendment to promote General Barnett.

Disregarding this affront to him, to the office of the Commandant, and to the Marine Corps, General Barnett continued on as before to guide the Marine Corps wisely. Having supervised the wartime expansion of the Corps, it was his duty, with the coming of the peace, to oversee a demobilization which reduced the size of the Corps to 17,400 men, an entirely insufficient number to perform its many and widespread duties.

At the beginning of May 1920, General Barnett left Washington for a month-long inspection trip to west coast posts and stations. Returning in early June to the heat of the nation's capital, he resumed his normal duties. This state of normalcy was disrupted at:

> ... 1:30 p.m. Friday, June 18th, [when] I received a letter from the Secretary of the Navy ... informing me that he contemplated making a change in the position of Commandant of the Marine Corps, and that the change would be made "one day next week most suitable to you."

The scene that took place in the Commandant's office upon receipt of that note remained for many years a matter of conjecture. Present at that time, and in fact the individual who took the note in to the Commandant, was his aide, Captain Clifton B. Cates, who was to become the 19th Commandant of the Marine Corps on January 1, 1948. Recalling that event in an interview many years later, General Cates said:

> ... you can imagine the tailspin it threw General Barnett in. He

yelled, "Get Charlie McCawley [Quartermaster of the Marine Corps]. Get Long [the Assistant Commandant]. Get so-and-so and so on. Get me Mrs. Barnett on the phone." So there this Negro messenger stood... and waited.... After about 15 or 20 minutes, General Barnett sent a note back and in effect it said, "I wish to remain on the active list subject to your orders."

Daniels' note and its contents came as a great surprise to General Barnett because he had conferred with the Secretary almost daily prior to this and nothing had been said about his imminent relief, nor had he any reason to believe that either the Secretary or the President were anything but pleased with his stewardship of the Corps.

Daniels demanded in his note that the Commandant report in writing, that afternoon, whether he wished to retire according to law as a Major General or to remain on the active list as a Brigadier General. If Barnett chose the latter course, then he was to inform the Secretary what duty assignment he desired. It would appear that neither Daniels nor any of the other people behind this action to remove Barnett from the Commandancy expected that he would swallow his pride and remain on active duty in reduced rank.

At this time, Headquarters Marine Corps and the Navy Department occupied the same building, so young Captain Cates was able to notice "... all kinds of conferences going on between Congressman Butler and Secretary Daniels and General Butler. For the next few days, we'd see them" hurrying in and out of the building.

General Barnett wrote later in his memoirs that he would not have been surprised at his treatment at the hands of Daniels if there had been any official reason for it, but, as has been noted, all public pronouncements and private reports on the General's fitness for and conduct of office were overwhelmingly favorable.

On the basis of Mr. Daniels' note, Barnett had exactly three hours to make up his mind concerning his future, for the Navy Department's office hours ended daily at 4:30 p.m., and the Secretary had asked for a reply that afternoon. Deciding to remain on active duty as a Brigadier General, Barnett asked to be assigned to Quantico. In addition, he requested permission to take the four months' leave he had accumulated since 1918. Back came the reply, also in writing, to the effect that Quantico had already been promised to another general officer and that he could take only two months of leave.

On the next day, 19 June 1920, General Barnett had a private interview with Mr. Daniels, who, according to the General:

> ... appeared to be very much surprised that I was anything but pleased—that I had not expected it [the request for the resignation]. He

said that under similar circumstances, if his resignation was called for by the President, he would thank the President for past courtesies and say that, of course, he acquiesced in it with pleasure. I remarked that even a servant was entitled to thirty days notice and that he gave me only three hours. I told him that I . . . felt that I had been treated unjustly, after long years of faithful service. He then remarked, "Then that very materially lessens the sorrow of our parting." I said, "Good day, Sir," and left his office.

According to Daniels' memoirs, by asking for Barnett's resignation, the Secretary was merely cashing in a post-dated check he believed General Barnett had given him in 1918 when the Commandant had been re-appointed to office. According to Daniels, he "asked Barnett if he intended to keep his word. He was defiant in spite of his pledge. 'Very well, Good Morning,' I said. . . ."

Eleven days later, on June 30, General Lejeune arrived at Headquarters to relieve General Barnett as Commandant. Present at this confrontation were only the two general officers, and Barnett's two aides, Captains Charles Murray and Clifton Cates. Cates recalled that the relief:

> . . . was a very unofficial thing. . . . General Lejeune came in. I showed him into the office and he started to sit down. General Barnett said, "John, stand up there just a minute. We've been good friends all our lives—close friends. Why didn't you let me know what was going on?" General Lejeune replied, "George, my hands were tied." General Barnett then said, "Don't you know that if I had been in your place, I would have come to you and told you exactly what was happening?" And General Lejeune repeated, "George, my hands were tied." General Barnett then said, "'Alright, I stand relieved. You're the Commandant."

Just what circumstances tied Lejeune's hands have not been determined, but what makes this confrontation between these two men all the more interesting, and at the same time difficult to understand, is the fact that both were honorable, highly respected individuals whose backgrounds show little signs of or capacity for backstairs politicking or double dealing. It is accepted that, like the soldiers of Napoleon who purportedly carried marshals' batons in their knapsacks, every Marine officer worthy of his commission aspires to the Commandancy. There is little doubt but that Lejeune felt that he would succeed Barnett at some time, but certainly not under these circumstances and not as a tool of Daniels. In *Reminiscences of a Marine,* Lejeune recalled the time in early 1917, when he asked to be relieved as Assistant Commandant in order to obtain a combat command. General Barnett at that time told him:

"I don't want you to go. If you are leaving because you feel that you want to be free to work for appointment as my successor as Commandant when my term expires next February, I am perfectly willing for you to stay here and do so." I thanked him and then said, "General, I do not want to be Commandant during the war, I now have but one desire and that is to go to France, and I am asking now for transfer to duty with troops at Quantico...." I further told him that, in my opinion, he ought to continue to serve as Commandant for the period of the war, as it would not be wise to make a change in such an important office in the midst of war.

Nothing in Barnett's memoirs suggests that he believed himself the victim of a plot, nor did he even mention his visit to the House gallery or his reaction to the nonsense he heard at that time. Following his relief as Commandant and having some time to dwell over the possible reasons for the relief, he came to the conclusion that "the Secretary had all the time resented the fact that I refused to sign the resignation in blank." Barnett found it difficult to believe that President Wilson wanted him to sign a blank resignation, especially when the Commander in Chief always had the power to relieve any officer at any time at his discretion.

An interesting facet to this affair recently came to light with the discovery in the files of the Franklin D. Roosevelt Library at Hyde Park of a letter written to the then-Assistant Secretary of the Navy by Mrs. Barnett on July 6, 1920, little more than two weeks after General Barnett had stepped down from the Commandancy. It reads:

Dear Mr. Roosevelt:

May I tell you the circumstances of the removal of my husband from office in order that if there is anything you can do to remedy such a gross injustice the facts may be in your possession. And, may I add that I am writing this without my husband's knowledge or consent and that being a good soldier he has accepted this humiliation and degradation, with out one word against those who have so treated him.

When the General was re-appointed he was told the President wished his resignation in blank as had been done by all the other bureau chiefs. The General said this was not necessary as at any time the President was dissatisfied with his services he could ask for his resignation. He requested leave to see the President but was told the next day it was not necessary and the resignation was not signed. He has always been of the opinion that the other Chiefs signed.

Of course, you realize that the position of Commandant of the Marine Corps is different from the other chiefs and is more military and less technical. And to remove an officer from his high command while the country is still "at war" according to the President's edict is an ineradicable blot on that officer's record.

General Barnett's record is and has always been a spotless one and his reports of fitness from the Secretary of the Navy are really fulsome in their praise. Certainly he needs no defense of his management of the Corps during his six years as Commandant. He only asked to be allowed to serve out his remaining eighteen months. He was given France's highest honor, decorated by the State of New Mexico, given the Distinguished Service Medal by Mr. Daniels and had no idea that he would be removed from office before the expiration of his term.

The shock has been a very serious one to him as in one moment his life work was torn from him and he stood humiliated before the world. A man sixty years old with forty three years service at least deserved some slight consideration if for any reason it was considered advisable to remove him but the brutality with which General Barnett was treated is unheard of and of course has aroused nation-wide resentment.

No warning was given him officially and though outside gossip was brought him he refused to believe in such duplicity and took no steps to ascertain if there was any truth in these rumours. At 1:30 p.m. on Friday, June 19, a messenger from the Secretary brought a brief note, asking for his resignation before the office hours were over (4:30) and an immediate decision as to his future plans. *The messenger was instructed to wait for an answer.* Three hours were given him to make his life decision.

He decided to stay in the Corps which he loves, and as a reward for his courage, devotion to duty and patriotism was refused the command he asked for at Quantico, refused his accumulated leave (having had none since the war) and his request for the permanent Major Generalcy laid over until time should be found to take it up. The Judge Advocate General rendered his opinion that it was legal. And we were given ten days to leave our home, an almost impossible task and with no provision for the future were turned out with less notice than the law requires to be given a discharged servant. So, at sixty years, his reward of merit is the loss of his command, his rank and reduction in pay and his humiliating position in the Corps to which he has given his entire life. No matter what any other man accomplished this is not the way to reward merit. And General Barnett made possible all the honor and glory of those who were fortunate enough to go overseas—a thing he would gladly have given his life to do.

If you had seen his eyes as we took his stars from his shoulders, I think you would understand, and would *never* forget it. I wouldn't like to see an animal with such a look in its eyes and not try to help it in some way. Dear Mr. Roosevelt, justice should be shown this splendid officer and the wrong done him righted so far as may be possible. There is more to this case than meets the eye at first but it is sure to be known later on. I cannot believe our country will permit this to be done without protest. You have always been a friend, Mr.

Roosevelt, and a good and just man. You are young, and strong, happy and the recipient of signal honors from your country. I ask your interest and help for the man so shamefully treated and who now has "to see his life work broken and stoop to build it up with worn out tools." I apologize for taking up your time. Please forgive me.

Thanks so much for all your kindness and goodness to me and my love and congratulations to Mrs. Roosevelt.

Yours sincerely as ever,
Lelia Montague Barnett

There is no record that Roosevelt replied to this letter.

Although his presence in this affair is shadowy, one can assume that a force in the relief was General Butler's frustrated desire for more rapid advancement. He did get orders assigning him to France and a promotion to Brigadier General, but he arrived overseas too late to take part in the fighting. Butler's frustration manifested itself in his—and his powerful father's—implacable hostility to the Commandant. If Barnett remained on active duty, even as a Brigadier General, he would still be senior to Butler and, in view of the promotion procedures in those days, he would remain so. On the other hand, if Barnett retired when Lejeune was appointed, Butler could expect to receive his second star. Butler could also assume that he would be Lejeune's logical successor as Commandant. But, as history shows, Butler did not become a Major General immediately after General Lejeune's appointment, nor did he ever become Commandant.

Neither General Butler's autobiography, *Old Gimlet Eye,* nor his personal papers mention a single word about the affair, nor did Butler ever allude to what, if any, his role had been in the sorry business. Lejeune was equally silent about the circumstances under which he was appointed Commandant, circumstances which would have caused a greater uproar in the ranks of the Corps had Lejeune not been as popular and respected as he was.

A new command was set up for General Barnett in San Francisco, far away from Washington—from Headquarters Marine Corps, from the Barnett's society friends, from friendly politicians, from all who might be inclined to speak out on the General's behalf. The Department of the Pacific, the new command, was nothing more than a paper command in the beginning. General Barnett asked Captain Cates to accompany him to California as his aide. General Cates recalled that when "the Department of the Pacific was organized, he [Barnett] had no authority whatsoever. He couldn't even transfer an enlisted man in the Department of the Pacific."

On March 5, 1921, the day after the Harding administration took office, General Barnett received word that he had been nominated to the rank of permanent Major General and had been immediately confirmed by the Senate. To General Barnett, this must have been a happy vindication.

General Barnett retired from active duty on December 9, 1923, after 42 full years of service. He died on April 27, 1930, at the age of 71.

As a footnote, the libel suit against Mr. Daniels was dropped in 1948.

Flowers to Gladden the City: The Takoma Horticultural Club, 1916–1971

ARTHUR HECHT

After fifty-five active years, one of the oldest, the most energetic and influential garden clubs of Washington, D.C. is falling victim to the ravages of time. The once large and proud Takoma Horticultural Club still maintains a skeletal organization, but its work and its ranks have dwindled due to loss of members because of old age, death, and the departure from the vicinity coupled with inability to secure an active and stable new and younger membership.

The THC was one of many such clubs throughout the country, and its activities compare favorably with the prominent agricultural societies of the Nineteenth Century. In the interest of recording an interesting phase of American living of an era and type which is fast disappearing, I have prepared a compilation and history of its successful operations and a title inventory of its extant records.[1]

Sometime in the war year of 1914 a group of Takoma Park citizens, drawn together by a common love of gardening, met to discuss the formation of a garden club. On March 1, 1916, the Takoma Horticultural Club,[2] patterned after one of the New England horticultural so-

---

[1] Until the late spring of 1963, the records of the THC were mainly in the custody of J. Wallace Talley, historian and editor of the Club newsletter. More current records have been held by the various officers. In Mr. Talley's home about three cubic feet of the records were stored in boxes and drawers in an attic closet. During May of 1963 about two and a half cubic feet of the records were transferred from several homes in Silver Spring, Maryland, to the public library of the City of Takoma Park, Maryland. They were carefully examined, identified, arranged, and placed in loose-leaf folders and these in large expanding envelopes. The envelopes were then stored in two, locked, steel cabinets in the storage area of the fire-proof library building.

There continues to be non-current and current records in the possessions of the editor of the newsletter and of each of the officers and committee chairmen. They will eventually be turned over to the archivist of the Takoma Park Historical Society at the end of the year and then deposited in the library.

[2] It was originally known as The Takoma Park Horticultural Improvement Club. This name was considered too long and cumbersome, and in 1922 the name was simplified.

Publication No. 2   April 1, 1918

The Takoma Park
Horticultural Improvement Club
Takoma Park, D. C.

OFFICERS

PRESIDENT, W. T. SIMMONS
27 MAPLE ST.

VICE-PRESIDENT, H. C. SKEELS
210 HOLLY AVE.

SECRETARY, W. J. MORSE
6809 FIFTH ST.

TREASURER, C. C. CARROLL
6801 SIXTH ST.

LANDSCAPE GARDENER, H. C. SKEELS
210 HOLLY AVE.

COMMITTEE CHAIRMEN

MEMBERSHIP, S. SCRIVENER
6908 SIXTH ST.

PURCHASING AND PLANTING, C. C. CARROLL
6801 SIXTH ST.

EXHIBITION, W. A. ORTON
600 CEDAR ST.

INSTRUCTION, D. N. SHOEMAKER
82 EASTERN AVE.

TABLES AND LANTERN, H. B. HENDRICK
9 SYCAMORE AVE.

COMMUNITY GARDEN, F. L. LEWTON
113 CHESTNUT AVE.

SPRING ANNOUNCEMENT, 1918.

OBJECTS. The Takoma Park Horticultural Improvement Club was organized a few years ago for the purpose of bringing together the citizens of Takoma Park, with a view to securing co-operation in the beautifying of lawns, grounds, and parkings, and to encourage the planting of flowers and vegetables. Under the present food conditions, it is hoped that every member of the Club will feel it his patriotic duty to plant a home garden, and, if necessary, to curtail his flower space in order to plant more vegetables.

REGULAR MEETINGS. The regular meetings of the Club are held at the Takoma library, on the first Wednesday evening of each month, beginning at eight o'clock.

BENEFITS TO MEMBERS. The services of the Landscape Gardener are free to members of the Club. By co-operative buying of seeds, plants, shrubbery, etc., wholesale rates are obtained. Instructive

From the author

Publication No. 2, April 1, 1918, of "The Takoma Park Horticultural Improvement Club."

cieties, was officially organized. Its objective was to promote horticultural improvement (or appreciation) throughout Takoma Park, Maryland, and the District of Columbia:

(1) By serving as a medium for co-operative buying of seeds, plants, and garden sundries;

(2) By encouraging through lectures and expert advice, artistic plantings about homes, public buildings, and in parkings;

(3) By advising

    (a) Regarding the varieties of flowers, trees, shrubs, fruits and vegetables best adapted for local conditions and

    (b) Regarding the best cultural methods applicable in this area;

(4) By stimulating through exhibitions, demonstrations, and lectures, the objective of the Club.[3]

The THC has a constitution and by-laws which, to date, have been revised six times.[4] Its officers consist of a president, a first vice-president who is also the program chairman, a second vice-president, a recording secretary, a corresponding secretary, a treasurer, and a landscape gardener, all of whom serve for one year beginning January 1 following their election, or until their successors are elected and qualify. There is the usual executive committee consisting of the elected officers, past presidents of the Club, together with chairmen of the standing committees.

Article VI of the 1963 Constitution describes the standing committees as follows:

1. Membership committee solicits applications for membership and receives applications for membership. It maintains a membership list and cooperates with the treasurer in securing payment of dues.

2. Purchasing committe buys cooperatively for the Club.

3. Exhibition committee arranges for and conducts exhibitions at the proper seasons.

4. Instruction committee advises as to planting and demonstrates cultural methods.

5. Publicity committee gives publicity through newspapers, radio, posters, etc., to the activities of the Club.

6. Plant sale committee arranges for the disposal of garden materials.

7. Program committee arranges for speakers and the entertainment at the meetings of the Club.

---

[3] Constitution. Revised on November 25, 1963.

[4] Revised on November 24, 1930, May 24, 1948, January 24, 1949, September 25, 1950, November 25, 1957, and November 25, 1963.

There are two special committees: a nominations committee and auditing committee, the latter gives its report at the January meeting.

MEMBERSHIP AND MEETINGS

The THC was the first garden club organized in the Washington, D.C. metropolitan area which comprises adjacent Maryland and Virginia environs. The original membership consisted of the following eleven men: C. C. Carroll, W. C. Gerdson, David Griffiths, F. L. Newton, Lisle Morrison, W. A. Orton, A. J. Pieters, H. C. Skeels, William Stuart, D. N. Shoemaker, and W. F. Wight. The membership increased to 55 in 1917. During the following year the constitution was modified to admit women[5] as individual members or to share membership with their husbands. There were 91 members in 1919, 128 in 1920, 300 in 1947, 537 for 1953, 354 for 1960, and 203 for 1963. The THC compiled the following interesting statistics about its 1960 membership:

61 had been members for 20 years or more
93 had been members for 15 years or more
159 had been members for 10 years or more
250 had been members for 5 years or more
104 had been members for less than 5 years

Location of membership

Takoma Park (20012)	102 members	30%)	
Washington, D.C. (20011)	39 members	11%}	161 members
Northeast Washington and Maryland	20 members	5%)	46%
Silver Spring, Maryland	130 members	30%)	
Bethesda-Chevy Chase, Maryland	68 members	20%}	181 members
Rockville, Maryland	11 members	3%)	51%
Virginia and others	12 members		3%

Originally, membership dues consisted of a 25-cent initiation fee and a 10-cent payment for attending each meeting. This financial arrangement was changed: in 1917 a straight dues of $1.00 per annum, $2.00 in 1951, and $3.00 in 1962. The dues were paid in January for one year in advance. Paid-up membership of one member gave the whole family the privileges of the Club. In 1932 membership cards were first issued, serving also as a receipt for dues. Not until the beginning of 1964 was it necessary to send statements to members reminding them that their annual dues were due in January. Hitherto,

---

[5] The minutes of regular meetings show that Miss Susan J. Campbell and Mrs. D. L. Spence became members on March 5, 1918, and Mrs. S. G. Clark became a member on May 1, 1918. Reports of talks about the history of THC given at annual dinners and articles in newspapers concerning the history of the THC erroneously show that in 1919 Mrs. W. W. Stoneberger was the first woman to become a member.

698   Records of the Columbia Historical Society

reminders appearing in newsletters and circulars and personal pleas by the treasurer at each meeting were sufficient.

The first public library branch in Washington, D.C. was in Takoma Park and was opened during November of 1912 at 5th and Cedar Streets, N.W. The executive and special meetings of the THC were held in the basement conference room, beginning about 1914. Regular monthly meetings (at which there were symposiums, talks, illustrated lectures and demonstrations) were held in the children's room on the first floor. The large folding doors separating the adult and children's rooms were closed and the side entrance to the building on 5th Street was used, thereby making it possible to carry on regular library work without interruption during meetings. Until 1923 the regular meetings began at 8 p.m. on the first Wednesday of each month.[6] Thereafter, the meetings were held on the fourth Monday of each month.[7] An amendment to the THC constitution on September 25, 1950, changed the annual meeting (election of officers and reading of reports) from December to November. Thereafter, no monthly meetings were held during December. Beginning in 1934 the annual banquet was held in place of the regular January meeting. In 1960 the June and August regular meetings were held in air-conditioned facilities for the first time, and an annual picnic was held for the first time in July in Sligo Creek Park, Maryland. These became annual events. The picnics were "pot luck" suppers and each member and guest was asked to bring homemade food which the picnic committee then arranged and served in buffet style.

Beginning February 25, 1950, the executive as well as regular meetings were held in the Takoma Elementary School at Piney Branch Road and Dahlia Streets, N.W., Washington, D.C. The executive meetings were held in the school library on the second floor and the

---

[6] The January 2, 1918, meeting was postponed to January 16 because of weather and other adverse conditions. The October 4, 1921, meeting was held in the Assembly Hall of the Cosmos Club with the Botanical Society of Washington and three bontanists spoke about dahlias. A tulip exhibition was held in place of a regular meeting on May 3, 1922.

[7] A special meeting during February of 1925 reported that the regular meeting of January 26, 1925, beginning at 8 p.m. and lasting until 9:45 p.m. was "of course... far too long for any meeting...." Because the floor of the branch library was being repaired, the September 1938 regular meeting was held in the "parlor" of the Takoma Park Baptist Church, Piney Branch Road and Aspen Street, N.W., Washington, D.C. The February 14, 1943, meeting was held on Wednesday instead of Monday (the reason for the change is not given). There was no meeting during February 1945 because of wartime restrictions relating to conserving fuel and light. The March 1951 meeting was held on the third Monday instead of the fourth Monday of the month (the reason for the change is not given). Nationwide mourning for the death of President John F. Kennedy postponed the November 25, 1963, annual meeting for two weeks. It was held on the first Friday on the following month.

regular meetings were held in the school auditorium. The large auditorium always left the impression that the attendance was outrageously small. The present, "permanent" location of the meetings of the THC in the air-conditioned and modern auditorium of the Perpetual Building, 8710 Georgia Avenue, Silver Spring, Maryland, was made on September 26, 1960.

Attendance figures of members at regular meetings have been reported irregularly in the minutes of the Club and in the monthly reports of the branch librarian. These fluctuated depending on whether or not a speaker was scheduled and the weather. On February 28, 1925, Dr. Wetmore of the Smithsonian Institution spoke on "Migration of Birds."[8] This was evidently a popular subject and 125 people were present at the meeting. On the whole, the average number of members attending regular meetings has been about thirty-five and has depended on the popularity of the speaker or his subject as well as his professional standing.

Speakers at Meetings

Speakers at THC programs have lectured with and without plants (seedlings, branches, or flowers), slides, or motion pictures.[9] These have included floriculturists, horticulturists, agronomists, pathologists, and entomologists of the Department of Agriculture; representatives of the Agriculture Department of the University of Maryland; horticulturists of Mount Vernon, the National Arboretum, and the Walter Reed Hospital Reservation; naturalists of the National Park Service and the Maryland Planning Commission; newspaper and radio garden columnists; tree service specialists; landscape architects; the secretary of the National Wild Flower Society; distributors of photographic equipment; representatives of nationwide transportation companies; amateur photographers of flowers and plants throughout the United States, Japan, Europe, and Africa; and hobby specialists of individual plants (hollies, lilies, dahlias, chrysanthemums, etc.).

About a dozen of the plant and insect specialists of the Department of Agriculture have been active members of the THC. There were also a few members who were professional landscape architects and writers of garden articles and pamphlets. Consequently, it was not

---

[8] Discussions relating to birds usually occurred at one of the winter meetings of the THC.

[9] During the first week of March of 1924 the THC made arrangements through Mr. Bolgiano, owner of one of the largest seed, plant, and garden supply companies in Washington, to have two motion pictures, "Starting Plants in the House" and "Management of the Hot Beds," shown at the Takoma Theatre at 4th and Butternut Streets, N.W., Washington, D.C.

uncommon for these members to give talks and hold occasional panel discussions of the regular meetings.

Announcements of Meetings and Newsletters

Supplementary to the lectures, talks, and discussions at the regular monthly meetings are the announcements of meetings (or activities) and the important and highly informative newsletters. These are more fully described in another portion of this article.

COMMUNITY PARTICIPATION

Within a year after its establishment, the THC was energetically involved with civic activities in the geographic area of Takoma Park. During March of 1917 it agreed to assist the City of Takoma Park, Maryland, in securing several small tracts of land on various streets for parks. In the fall of the same year, when the Children's Garden Club of Takoma Park held its exhibtion of flowers, vegetables, and fruits in the branch library, the THC contributed $7.00 for prizes. On October 2, 1919, the Club met jointly with the Takoma Park Citizens' Association to help promote better cooperation between the citizens of Takoma Park, Maryland, and Takoma Park, D.C.[10] A year later these two organizations joined the Civic Study Club of Takoma Park in protesting the closing of the branch library on three evenings a week because of lack of congressional appropriations. (Each of these organizations met regularly at the library.)

In 1933 the THC joined the Takoma Public School Parent-Teachers Association of Washington, D.C. in developing a 5 by 25 foot plot on the school grounds for roses and shrubs. The $25.00 the Club had authorized for participation in the project was used for purchasing fertilizer and employing labor to dig up the plot. THC members donated chrysanthemums, peonies, irises, narcissus, perennials, and barberry bushes. According to a newspaper story in 1934, the THC prepared a float for the annual Takoma Park 4th of July parade and it attracted favorable comment. During December of 1938, Clarence W. Moore, THC president, served on a committee of five judges to select the winner of the Christmas contest sponsored by the Takoma Park Chamber of Commerce for the best decorated home in the Takoma Park area. In March of 1952 members of the THC gave some of their evergreens and shrubs for landscaping the grounds of the J. Enos Ray Elementary School in Takoma Park, Maryland. Joining the other garden clubs of metropolitan Washington in 1954, the

---

[10] Awards were made in contests for better gardens and products: (1) large gardens, (2) small gardens, (3) Walter Reed Hospital soldiers' own gardens, (4) girls' and boys' gardens, (5) sweet corn gardens, (6) bean gardens, and (7) tomato gardens.

Flowers to Gladden the City 701

THC contributed $50.00 for buying azaleas and other shrubs for the grounds of the Home for Incurables at Upton and 37th Streets, N.W., Washington, D.C.

In 1958 the THC again became interested in landscaping the grounds of the Takoma Elementary School. The overgrown rose plants were clipped; iris, peonies, and evergreens were planted; fertilizer was added to the shrubbery beds; and about 200 plugs of zoysia grass were planted in the plot at the entrance to the school auditorium. Also in the same year, two magnolia trees were planted on the grounds of the library of the City of Takoma Park, Maryland. A check of $25.00 was given to the Maryland librarian for the purchase of twelve sasanqua camellias to be planted on the library grounds.

At the request of the Swartzell Home (orphanage) at Second and Sheridan Streets, N.W., Washington, D.C., nine THC members cleared the planting area in front of the home on April 18, and on May 27, 1959. Members then planted an azalea bush, camellia plants, iris, grape hyacinths, daffodils, and peonies.

The branch library received the largest amount of civic aid from the THC. The Club felt continuously indebted to the District government for allowing the use of the branch library for meetings and exhibitions. Such appreciation was first expressed by letter in 1916.[11] Irregular payments to the janitor at the branch library began in 1919 and continued until 1940.[12] He set up the chairs for meetings, the tables and equipment for floral, fruit and vegetable exhibitions, and then cleaned up the lecture hall for library use. In 1925, $100.00 was appropriated by the Club for landscaping the library grounds. A box hedge (supplied by B. Y. Morrison) was planted and surrounded the library property. Ten years later plantings on the library ground were discussed again; however, the minutes of the THC fail to show any action taken.

In the late spring of 1963, the THC agreed to assist the City of Takoma Park, Maryland, in becoming known as the Azalea City of the nation. Money was later authorized for the purchase of azalea plants and these were planted in a bed in the Upper Portal Park on Piney Branch Road at Eastern Avenue. During August of 1963, the THC, along with other local community groups, library patrons,

---

[11] The minutes of June 7, 1916, show that it was moved and carried that the "Secretary write a letter to the Librarian expressing the appreciation of the Club for the courtesies extended to it."

[12] $2 on February 5, 1919; $3 on December 3, 1919; $10 on December 29, 1924; $35 for 1926 and 1927; $1 for each hour or a fraction thereof which the meetings of the THC extended past 9 p.m. (March 28, 1932); $25 on November 28, 1932; $20 for 1933; $2 on March 27, 1939; and $2 on May 22, 1939.

From the author
Spring Flower Exhibit, 1925, in the Takoma Park Branch Library.

businessmen and friends, donated a modest sum to be added to the gifts given at a ceremony honoring the retirement of Mrs. Ruth B. Pratt, librarian for twenty-eight years at the Maryland library.

The THC has also participated in regional and national horticultural activities. In the immediate area, it has been a member of the National Capital Garden Club League and the Federation of Garden Clubs. Because of the floricultural interests of its members, it was not strange that the Club was one of the organization members of the American Horticultural Society, the American Iris Society, and the American Rose Society.

Announcements in the THC newsletters included notices concerning the National Arboretum displays; the National Flower and Garden Shows; Virginia and Maryland garden spring tours; camellia displays at Norfolk; Potomac Rose Society exhibitions; garden shows in New York, Philadelphia, and Baltimore; local radio programs relating to gardens and vegetables; flower arrangement and garden school courses at Maryland University (1938); corsage-making classes; and the 1960 tour of The Netherlands by the National Tulip Society.

LITERATURE

The earliest reference to garden literature given to the branch library by the THC pertains to 1916 catalogs of seeds, bulbs, plants, shrubs, and trees. These and other lists collected over the next twenty-four years were retained on the library shelves to guide the

THC members with their cooperative buying. A revival of catalog holdings for Takoma Park gardners began in 1959 but ended in 1962. The catalogs concerned themselves with the sales of Monmouth pottery.

Although the branch librarian in 1918 allotted space for books relating to horticulture and gardening, it was not until 1924 that the THC considered increasing the number and variety of books donated by the Club. At a December executive board meeting a committee of two was appointed to recommend the purchase of garden books. Three of the books chosen were briefly reviewed at the May 25, 1925, general meeting. Finally, the Club appropriated $15.00 for the purchase of books,[13] and there was a report of their delivery to the branch library in November of 1925. In the same year, Milton Whitney of the Bureau of Soils, Department of Agriculture, presented the branch library with a copy of his *Soil and Civilization.*

Certain members of the THC were interested in obtaining more enduring literary works on agronomy, agriculture, floriculture, entomology, landscaping, etc. The eventual acquisition of such specialized literature was aided by the following donations[14] by the THC to the branch library:

1930	Bailey's Cyclopedia of Horticulture
1932	$20.00
1934	$ 9.11 (7 books)
1939	$23.45 (9 books)
1940	$10.00 (5 books)
1947	$27.00[15]
1949	$25.00 to $30.00
1950	$25.00[16]

The THC continued its original policy of appointing a committee of two of its members to choose or to work with the branch librarian concerning the purchase of horticulture books. In 1939, for instance, Drs. Powell and Magruder selected a list of books and included one

---

[13] On October 21, 1925, (at the discount price of $9.80) the D.C. Public Library purchased from The Baker and Taylor Co. of New York City the following books: *The Complete Garden* by Albert D. Taylor, *Book of Practical Landscape Gardening* by Gridland, *Plant Propagation* by A. H. Hottes, and *Little Book of Perennials* by A. H. Hottes. Additional books were to be ordered within a short period.

[14] The THC newsletter of April 1943 erroneously states that "every year the THC presents the Takoma Park Public Library with $10.00 worth of garden books."

[15] A letter of October 13, 1947, from Miss Rosalie Manning, librarian of the Takoma Park Public Library, to Mr. J. Wallace Talley, president of the THC, states that the money is to be used "to get some up-to-date books on landscaping and to buy other desirable garden books that have not been purchased because of lack of funds."

[16] Included were subscriptions to garden periodicals.

suitable for children. From 1940 the choice of literature for the branch library was left to the librarians.

Lists of Books

At the regular meetings[17] of the Club during November 1925 and January 1933, the minutes included lists of books given by the THC to the branch library. During the 1930's there was a two-page, single spaced, mimeographed list of books issued to members.[18] The books are grouped under the following subjects: gardens, floriculture, landscape, lawns, vegetable gardens, shrubs, herbs, bulletins, and garden encyclopedias. As the donations increased for the purchases of botanical literature, lists of garden books accessioned by the branch library were included in the following issues of the THC newsletters:

1937, January and February
1943, April and November
1948, February
1951, February and April
1952, September
1958, April
1964, March

The lists in the newsletters for February 1948 and September 1952 include also books in the custody of the library in the City of Takoma Park, Maryland.

Book Reviews

For the years 1925 and 1926 there were books reviews on gardening and horticulture given by certain THC members at regular meetings. In the May 1960 newsletter, there appeared an interesting review of an Eighteenth Century book relating to gardeners.

Publications of the Department of Agriculture

In 1916 *Farmers' Bulletins* were distributed to Club members at several of the meetings. The January 1918 *Farmer's Bulletin No. 856* was mailed to each Club member. In the 1950's the newsletter began to notify its readers of the existence of certain publications issued by the Department of Agriculture. The February 1952 newsletter announced that Bulletin No. 9 of the *New Home and Garden Series* was available at the Department to those who called for it. The May 1956 newsletter listed the numbers and various Department publica-

---

[17] On March 15, 1925, a list of bird books at the branch library was given to members who attended a regular meeting.

[18] Although this list is not dated or identified as issued for the benefit of the THC members, it was located among the minutes of the regular meetings.

tions available to the public without cost. Also, during the 1950's there were references in the newsletters to the Year Books of the Department of Agriculture.

Special Publications

A few bulletins of Cornell University were ordered by the THC for distribution to its members. Four printed publications of the THC for 1916, 1918, 1919, and 1923 were distributed to each home in Takoma Park. These pamphlets, however, were mainly promotional and publicized the objectives and activities of the THC for the purpose of attracting local inhabitants to join the Club. The following mimeographed bulletins of the THC and other organizations were also given to the Club members:

Landscape Bulletin No. 1. By B. Y. Morrison (Landscape Architect of the THC). 1926.

The Easter Lily. By Dr. David Griffith. 1921.

Raising Peonies in the Washington, D.C. Area. By Leland H. Cole. (Undated).

Newer Roses. By Dr. Whitman Cross. 1935.

Garden Columnists

In the 1924 and 1925 issues of *The Takoma News,* Chester J. Hunn served as managing editor of the THC column, "Timely Hints." The various editors of the THC newsletters have always exercised the prerogative of advising, instructing, persuading, and warning gardeners about their chores and plants. For more than thirty years a THC member, William Youngman,[19] has prepared a garden column for the Washington *Star.* Mr. Youngman, garden consultant, judge of flower exhibitions, and landscape gardener, has been a member of the THC for thirty-five years or more.

EXHIBITIONS OF FLOWERS, FRUITS, AND VEGETABLES

Flower, fruit, and vegetable exhibits have always been the dominant activities of the THC because of the belief that there is no better way to stimulate the acquisition of new varieties of plants than by their actual exhibition.

The first flower show staged by the Club was held in the lecture room of the branch library on April 22, 1916, and consisted of a display of narcissus brought by Dr. David Griffiths from the grounds of the Department of Agriculture at Arlington. At that time only a few

---

[19] He and his wife were co-authors of *The Star Garden Book* which is frequently revised and concerns itself with the soils and plants of Washington metropolitan area, together with the culture of flowers, shrubs, trees, and vegetables.

cultivated flowers were grown in Takoma Park. Vases were supplied by Homer C. Skeels and were bottles discarded by the Office of Foreign Seed and Plant Introduction of the Department of Agriculture. There was no competition and no prizes were awarded, but it made the members of the newly organized THC aware of the potentialities of the unsightly narcissus bulb. Also during 1916 the THC sponsored tulip (182 attended), iris (244 attended), and chrysanthemum (125 attended) shows. The THC joined the Community Garden Club exhibition of fruit, flowers, and vegetables on October 7, 1916 (203 attended). Such joint exhibitions continued at the branch library during the next three years. During 1918 and 1919 exhibitions were not only held monthly for the period of April through November, but there were prizes awarded for the best garden record (production, crop succession, dates of planting, harvesting, etc.), and for the best gardens. After 1919 there were no further reports about the Community Garden Club exhibitions and most likely the club was absorbed by the THC.[20]

Until May 20, 1950, there were from three to nine annual flower and vegetable shows in the lecture hall of the branch library.[21] The shows were thereafter held at the Takoma Elementary School auditorium, and beginning in November of 1962 in the gymnasium of the Takoma Junior High School (Maryland). There were separate exhibitions for narcissus (and daffodils), tulips, irises, azaleas, peonies, roses, gladiolas, dahlias, chrysanthemums, fruits, vegetables, and winterplants (household). The necessary tables, vases, posters, and other equipment for the exhibitions were successively stored in the basement of the branch library, the elementary school basement, and finally in a rented garage in Silver Spring, Maryland.

Statistics gathered from minutes and announcements of the THC and from annual reports of the branch librarian show the following number of horticulture shows at the library:

1912:	1	1917:	4	1921:	8	1925:	6
1914:	1	1918:	1	1922:	7	1926:	9
1915:	2	1919:	1	1923:	6	1927:	7
1916:	4	1920:	4	1924:	7	1928:	5

[20] In a 1961, four-paragraph history of the THC, the editor of the newsletter states: "During World War I, the Takoma Club concentrated on the production of vegetables. They purchased and distributed seeds, obtained and developed garden sites, and sponsored the Boys' and Girls' Garden Club, which was the forerunner of the 4-H Clubs."

[21] The iris show on May 26 and 27, 1931, was held at the Takoma Theatre at 4th and Butternut Streets, N.W., Washington, D.C. From 1932 the iris and dahlia shows were occasionally held at the Volunteer Fire Department hall at Carroll and Denwood Avenues, Takoma Park, Maryland.

1929:	5	1935:	5	1941:	2	1947:	4
1930:	4	1936:	2	1942:	2	1948:	2
1931:	6	1937:	2	1943:	2	1949:	6
1932:	7	1938:	2	1944:	1	1950:	1
1933:	6	1939:	6	1945:	3		
1934:	10	1940:	3	1946:	3		

By the end of 1963 the following types and numbers of exhibitions had been held by the THC:

1963: 36th annual chrysanthemum show[22]
1963: 46th annual rose show
1963: 36th annual peony show
1960: 44th annual narcissus and daffodil show
1960: 43rd annual tulip show
1960: 7th annual azalea show
1960: 6th annual camellia show
1959: 39th dahlia and fall flower show
1958: 41st annual iris show
1956: 39th annual fruits and vegetable show[23]
1941: 21st annual gladiola show (thereafter grouped with fall flowers)
1935: 2nd annual house plants show

Participation of the THC in exhibitions with other organizations in Washington, D.C., occurred frequently. The iris exhibition of 1942, 1943, 1945, 1947, and 1950 were held in cooperation with the American Iris Society and were either at the branch library or at the Takoma Elementary School. The first National Capital Narcissus Show was held on April 16, 1950, at the Taft Junior High School, South Dakota Avenue and Perry Street, N.E., Washington, D.C., and was sponsored by the THC, the Silver Spring Garden Club, and the Woodridge Garden Club. On May 13 and 14, 1950, the THC and the Silver Spring Garden Club sponsored the national tulip show at the Takoma Elementary School.

In 1934 the cup of the National Capital Dahlia and Iris Society was won by a number of the THC members on behalf of the Club. The Society later disbanded and the cup remained in possession of the THC.

[22] The 28th annual chrysanthemum show was held on October 28 and 29, 1955, at the Shoreham Hotel, Washington, D.C., in connection with the 10th Annual Congress of the American Horticultural Council.
[23] For 1919, 1920, and 1921 there were also special vegetable and flower shows on Labor Day.

In 1951, for the fourth consecutive year, the THC won the Blackstone Silver Bowl. This handsome trophy was awarded each year at the Annual Fall Rose Show of the Potomac Rose Society to the garden club whose members received the highest total number of points in the show.

Mimeographed announcements were sent before each exhibition. These contained general information including schedules (or classifications of specimens). Later, these announcements included themes for artistic arrangements, notices and instructions to exhibitors, lists of officers and committee members of the Club. Rarely were the names of the judges of exhibits given.

Pruning Demonstrations

Beginning in 1918 and continuing to the present, demonstrations of rose bush pruning were held on February 22 of each year in the yards of members (exceptions as to the date occurred in 1934, 1946, 1954, 1963, and 1964 when the pruning demonstrations were held in March). In the 1920's pruning demonstrations also included fruit trees, grape vines, and berry bushes. Occasionally, there was a spraying demonstration.

COLLECTIVE BUYING

Five or six months after the THC was established, it became involved with its first cooperative buying for its members. During the summer of 1916, the Department of Agriculture decided to import some new bulbs and wrote to various foreign firms, enclosing a list of specified bulbs, and asking for bids. Bids were received from all the firms except the M. Van Waveren & Sons Company of Holland. An order was placed with the firm submitting the lowest bid. The bulbs were delivered in September, and a few days later a similar shipment was received from the M. Van Waveren & Sons Company. It had mistaken the request for a bid for an order for specified bulbs. As the Department of Agriculture had already received and accepted the bulbs ordered from another firm, and not wanting two shipments of identical bulbs, the Van Waveren shipment was refused. This left the bulbs on the hands of the Company without a buyer in this country.

Dr. David Griffiths, one of the charter members of the THC, was in charge of bulb growing for the Department of Agriculture, and the New York agent of the Van Waveren Company appealed to him for advice as to how to dispose of the refused bulbs. Dr. Griffith called the officers of the THC together, told them of the opportunity to obtain the unusually fine bulbs at wholesale rates. They decided that the

Club would buy the shipment and resell it to the members. This was done largely on faith without a vote by the general memberships and with a treasury totaling $15.31. Their faith was well founded; all the bulbs were bought by the members. The M. Van Waveren & Sons Company was so well pleased that it wrote to Dr. Griffiths as follows: "If the Takoma Park Horticultural Improvement Club is an organization which, in six days, can absorb $600.00 worth of bulbs, it is an organization with which we would like to do future business," and offered to furnish the THC bulbs at wholesale rates. As late as 1963, the Club imported bulbs from the company.

The cooperative buying of seeds, bulbs, plants, fertilizers, soil conditioners, top soil, mulches, insecticides, and garden and plant labels and markers has always been an important feature of the activities of the THC and of special appeal to its members who saved between 10 to 15 per cent in costs.

In 1919 there began the collective buying of seeds ($125), roses ($169), shrubs, and pulverized limestone. There were 144 members and friends in 1926 who paid $1,744.74 for 50,000 bulbs. Metal and wooden garden markers were purchased for the first and only time in 1932. The high point of collective buying occurred during 1933 when 75 persons bought 19 tons of fertilizer, $3\frac{1}{2}$ tons of pulverized lime, 18,000 bulbs, 9,250 pansy plants, 1,056 rose bushes, 24 bales of peat moss, and 10 seed flats. During the 1930's rose bushes were bought both in the spring and in the fall. Roses and pansies were purchased together in the fall of 1934 and 1935, chrysanthemums for the period 1935–1939, gladiolas for the years 1934–1936, day lilies and oriental poppies in 1936, and fall shrubbery and trees for 1940.

PLANT EXCHANGE SALES

For the period 1918–1925 there existed a plant exchange committee. This committee organized plant sales to assist members in disposing of their surplus plants. Sales were at first held at different times of the growing season, and notices of such sales were usually posted on the bulletin board at the branch library. Items sold included bulbs, iris, shrubbery, small fruit trees, and vegetable plants. Prices for the plants were exceptionally attractive and members received the greater part of the returns, only a small percentage finding its way into the Club treasury.

In March and November of 1925 surplus plants were sold in the front yards of specified members; $7.75 was turned over to the THC from the November sale. There were some minor activities of the plant and exchange committee between 1926 and 1935, but the sales[24] were not centralized. On May 19, 1932, a plant sale was held in the yard of Mrs. John Quill, 227 Maple Avenue, Takoma Park, Maryland. There was one during March 1935 at the home of George A. Williams, 1916 17th Street, S.E., Washington, D.C., a location many miles from Takoma Park. During June of 1936 a plant exchange sale was held at 7415 Blair Road at the home of a former THC president. There seems to be no written evidence of sales during 1937.

Between 1938 and 1943, plant sales were held annually during May at 228 Willow Avenue, Takoma Park, Maryland. They were strongly supported by the Club members and were mainly patronized by them. The net income to the Club was in the range of $80 to $120 per sale. For the rest of the 1940's the regular plant sales were held in the backyard of Mr. and Mrs. Joseph J. Sazama who resided at 9th and Tuckerman Streets, N.W., Washington, D.C.

Occasionally, the THC newsletters mentioned the availability of plants from members. The November 1948 issue mentioned that Sam Blick of 518 Aspen Street, N.W., Washington, D.C. offered canna roots free and W. T. Simons of the same address offered a two-year-old plum tree. In the October 1950 newsletter it was announced that Paul Otterbach at 311 Tulip Avenue, Takoma Park, Maryland, had 18-inch and 20-inch bushy wintergreen barberry plants available for fifty cents apiece.

Plant sales continued throughout the 1950's in the yards of several Maryland members; in 1960 for the first time the sale was held on an empty lot which was located on the corner of Piney Branch Road and Van Buren Streets, N.W., Washington, D.C. Sales for 1961–1964 were held on the corner of Colesville Road and Spring Street, Silver Spring, Maryland.[25]

Until 1960, week-end plant exchange sales were held in May for two days. Thereafter it was limited to one day, a Saturday in May. Members retained 75 per cent of their sales and contributed the remaining 25 per cent to the Club. From the 1950's the sales included

---

[24] 1926, June 5: Perennials. July 22: Iris.
  1932, March 28: Mimeosa trees, butterfly bushes, and raspberry bushes.
  1933, April 24: Garden tools of Mrs. Orton.
  1931, May 25 and 28: Boxwood plants of Edwin C. Powell and choice gladiolas of Mrs. Orton. September 28: Pansies of Mr. Fred Harris.
  1934: $1.50 earned for the THC.
  1935: $12.37 earned for the THC.
  1935, February 22: Surplus canna roots of Mr. William Youngman. October 23: Narcissus bulbs.

[25] At plant exchange sales during the mornings of May 13, 1961, and of May 9, 1964, William Youngman, editor of the garden column of *The Sunday Star*, was available to advise and answer questions about gardens and plants.

Flowers to Gladden the City

vases, clay pots, jardinieres, used garden books and tools, and bird houses. Starting with the 1958 sale and ending in 1961, sandwiches, cookies, cakes, coffee, and cola, which were donated by the THC members, were sold. There were also raffles for large azalea plants and bags of fertilizers donated by nurseries. The sales of May 16 and 17, 1959, brought in a gross of $733.54, netting the Club $210.45.

Monmouth pottery was ordered for members during 1936, 1939, and 1950. In 1949, $2,200 was spent to purchase 22,000 pansy plants. The purchase of these plants increased to 37,000 in 1954. In October of 1948 the THC received from M. Van Waveren & Sons Company of Holland, 2,500 pounds of bulbs for 116 persons. (These were 12,460 tulips, 51,110 narcissus, 2,360 crocuses, 930 hyacinths, and 980 miscellaneous bulbs.) Members ordered camellia plants for 1951–1953, 1955, and for 1960 when azaleas were also included. For the years 1959–1961, Meyer Z-52 zoysia plugs with accompanying plugging tools were ordered.

As late as 1964 (and starting in the 1920's) THC members who displayed their paid-up membership cards were granted from 10 to 20-per-cent discount on purchases of seeds, bulbs, plants, fertilizers, and garden supplies from the following Washington and Maryland suppliers:

Balderson Company, Inc.
F. W. Bolgiano & Company
American Plant Food
Pendleton's Hardware
Strosniders Hardware

Woodmoor Paint and Hardware
Youngblood Paint and Hardware
Hunter Brothers
Takoma Feed Store
Takoma Paint and Hardware

J. H. Small and Sons

Until the end of 1963 the THC continued with three main collective buying orders: (1) fertilizers, insecticides, and grass seed for early spring; (2) imported Holland bulbs for early fall; and (3) pansy plants for late fall. Beginning with the 1960's these purchases no longer earned a satisfactory income for the THC, but they have been continued as a service to the members.

A Portfolio of Washington Drawings

PAUL BOSWELL

Neptune Fountain, Library of Congress
14¼" x 17¼"

    One morning a winter or two before World War II, when I worked at the Central Desk of the Library of Congress, it snowed and the figures in the *Neptune Fountain*—Neptune himself, his Tritons, Nymphs, Sea Horses, Tortoises, Frogs and Serpent—were drifted with snow and wearing white hats. When I remarked to a colleague on the Congressional Unit that somebody ought to take a picture of it all while the snow was still fresh, I was told that Mr. dePorry in the Manuscript Division always kept a camera with him and that maybe he would let me borrow it. I did, and in due time the photograph was pasted on the cover of a scrapbook of my poems. That seemed to be the end of the story of the snowed-in Neptune.
    Ten years and a World War later, having been impressed by the homemade Christmas cards of two or three of my acquaintances, I worked up a pen-and-ink version of the Neptune photograph and prevailed upon Mr. Truman Ward, printer for the Democrats in the Cannon House Office Building, to photo-offset print a batch of them as Christmas cards. Several people flattered me and I have now been drawing my own pen-and-ink Christmas cards, and occasionally larger pen-and-ink drawings for peoples' walls, for more than twenty years.
    My second drawing of Neptune, the one reproduced here, was made in 1971 as a cover for a Library of Congress Cooking Club invitation and simultaneously on 18" x 24" sheets for framing.
    Of course the real artist of the Neptune Fountain was Roland Hinton Perry, born in 1870. The Fountain, scaled much larger than life—its bullfrogs must be larger than bulldogs, and Neptune, if standing, would tower to twelve feet—is surely the prime sample of healthy pagan sculpture in Washington and a great embellishment to the Library of Congress. However, you may look in vain in the Public Card Catalog of the Library of Congress, and in several of its biographical encyclopedias and dictionaries, for any reference to

Detail, Neptune Fountain, Library of Congress

Paul Boswell

Neptune Fountain, Library of Congress.

him. The *Dictionary of American Artists, Sculptors and Engravers* and the *National Cyclopedia of American Biography* report that he was proud of the roles of his ancestors in colonial Massachusetts, in the England of Charles I, and in the Norman conquest. He studied art in Paris in the 1880's, has paintings in the Detroit Museum of Art, spent his final years as a portrait painter, and, in addition to the

Neptune Fountain, sculptured the *Lions* on the Connecticut Avenue bridge in Washington, D.C.

Frog, detail of Neptune Fountain
12″ x 9″

 The Federal Times, October 6, 1971, reviewed the second Library of Congress Employees' Art Show. In discussing my six entries, the reviewer, Don Mace, Jr., wrote that my copper plate of a frog in the Neptune Fountain was "especially noteworthy".

Detail, Neptune Fountain, Library of Congress

Paul Boswell

Frog, detail of Neptune Fountain.

The Great Hall of the Library of Congress
14½″ x 19¼″

 The early guide books to the Library of Congress pronounced the Great Hall "the finest marble interior in America". This drawing shows the northern member of the pair of Martiny staircases and a glimpse of the mosaicked vault of the Exhibits Gallery above.

Paul Boswell

The Great Hall of the Library of Congress.

Philip Martiny, born in France in 1858, came to the United States in 1878, at a time when the American-born artists Frederick Macmonnies, who made the Library's central pair of bronze doors, and Elihu Vedder, who did its *Minerva* mosaic, were sojourning in France and Italy to learn their crafts. Martiny was the prolific father of eight children and a prolific sculptor of decorative works at three World's Fairs—Chicago, Buffalo and St. Louis—and at the Library of Congress, the District of Columbia Public Library, and in numerous public buildings in the New York, New Jersey and Massachusetts areas.

The putti on the ascending sections of the balustrade are infants representing the occupations, with figures of the continents and the arts on the first and second landings respectively. The bust in the niche below the stairs is a replica of Jean Antoine Houdon's *Thomas Jefferson*.

The pen-and-ink drawing of the Great Hall was done in 1962, requiring an hour or two a day for about nine months, the hours being mostly between three and five o'clock in the morning in the attic at home. The infant figures along the stair each occupy in the original 14½" x 19¼" drawing an area smaller than a postage stamp; and the inclusion of the figures—with all their paraphernalia of rakes, telephones, butterfly nets, printing presses and the like—in spaces so small took a bit of doing.

The Main Reading Room of the Library of Congress
14½" x 15½"

The Main Reading Room of the Library of Congress is surely one of the world's architectural wonders; viewed from the Visitors' Gallery it is breath-taking. Unfortunately no camera in the last seventy-five years has been able to see a quarter of what the eye sees; there is no way to place a camera far enough back from the room to see it as a whole. Color photographs currently available at the Library's sales desk, for example, show four of the sixteen portrait statues; the visitor in the Visitors' Gallery, without benefit of camera, and standing in a fixed location, sees twelve of the sixteen statues.

Six or seven years ago I set up a pane of glass in the Gallery and tried to make a crayon tracing of what I saw when I looked at the Room through it; I must have failed to lock my eye in a fixed position, for after several attempts, over a period of eighteen months, I had to give up.

In 1972 I built a wooden frame three feet by four feet in size

A Portfolio of Washington Drawings

Paul Boswell

The Main Reading Room of the Library of Congress.

(twice the dimensions of the proposed drawing) and wove about 150 feet of venetian-blind cord through it to form a cord grid of 432 units, each two inches square. To assure that my viewing point remained consistent I anchored a nose-tall bamboo pole (with a nose ring at the top) in a block of cement. With my back against the mid-point of the Visitors' Gallery wall, I sighted through the cord grid and recorded what I saw on an 18 x 24 inch paper grid on a nearby card table.

I worked with these contraptions for thirteen Sunday mornings when the Library was closed to visitors. It soon became evident that this method was producing tremendous vertical and horizontal exaggerations the further I got away from the center of the picture. (The ellipse of figures at the top of the dome, for example, was vertical, rather than horizontal as it should have been.) I had to devise a graduated grid for the picture, rather than the uniformly-spaced grid I had started with—so each unit of the grid above or below eye-level, or to right or left of the viewing point, was narrower than the next one nearer the center. This method (combining a uniformly-spaced cord grid with a graduated grid on paper) has produced a picture which manages to include twelve of the sixteen portrait statues.

The Flanagan Clock
8½" x 11 1/16"

Neptune dominates the approaches to the Library; Minerva, in multiple forms, is to be found everywhere in the entrance halls; and Father Time, in a frozen progress, is monarch in the Reading Room. John F. Flanagan, in arranging figures atop the reading room clock, was confronted with a how-many-angels-can-dance-on-the-head-of-a-pin type problem. Father Time should be accompanied by attractive ladies representing the four seasons, but five adults trying to get their ten feet on top of one clock would have been a little bit much; so the four seasons were represented by two women and two infants floating in mid-air clutching the women's waists. The figures are not obviously particularized as to which represents what season. The six signs of the zodiac that grace the mosaic wall behind the sculpture I omitted, believing that they would confuse the composition of the drawing.

The seated figures on either side of the clock represent students. When I was drawing the student figure on the right, its face, without my intending it, began to look like my son's, so, to complete the resemblance, I gave the head a crew cut.

By no torturing of the fancy could Father Time and his gracefully draped escorts be construed as appropriate Christmas subjects, so when we used them as a card we added a jingle announcing that it was not a Christmas card but a New Year's card and sent it out a few days late.

John F. Flanagan, 1865–1952 (not to be confused with another American sculptor, John B. Flannagan) was born in Newark, New Jersey, and studied art in France. Some of his works are held by the Luxembourg Museum, Paris; the Museum of Ghent, Belgium; the Metropolitan Museum, New York; the Carnegie Institute, Pittsburgh; and the Chicago Art Institute. In Washington he is repre-

Paul Boswell

The Flanagan Clock.

sented also at the Smithsonian Institution by his bronze memorial portrait of Samuel Pierpont Langley.

The April 1, 1965 issue of *Library Journal,* which carried the article "The Answerers: a Fog-laden Panorama of LC's Collections" by David C. Mearns, used for its front cover this drawing of the *Flanagan Clock* printed in red ink.

The Minerva Mosaic
3¾" x 6½"

Elihu Vedder, an American of Dutch descent who spent much of his adult life in Italy, was a stout *bon vivant* with a red walrus moustache, a painter, illustrator, sculptor, poet and the author of an autobiography, *The Digressions of V*. In 1970, Fairleigh Dickinson University Press published a well-written, well-documented and well-illustrated biography by Regina Soria, *Elihu Vedder, American Visionary Artist in Rome, 1836–1923*, based on the correspondence preserved by Vedder's descendants.

Vedder was probably the best of the illustrators of *The Rubaiyat of Omar Khayyam*, and his paintings of *The Roc's Egg* and *The Lair of the Sea Serpent*, melodramatic as they are, are hard to forget.

Readers at the Library of Congress can scarcely avoid seeing Vedder's five tympanum murals on *Government* immediately outside the first-floor entrance to the Main Reading Room.

His *Minerva*, a vertical fifteen-by-nine foot mosaic, on the second floor between the doors opening on the Visitors' Gallery of the Reading Room, is the artistic centerpiece of the whole Library of Congress, occupying an inner sanctum at the head of the stairs connecting the Great Hall with the great Reading Room. The Latin inscription at the base of the mosaic reads:

> Nil invita Minerva quae monumentum
> aere perennius exegit.

The inscription, in a different sense, is a mosaic itself—a splicing-together of two quotations from two different books of Quintus Horatius Flaccus, (Horace), the Roman poet of the age of Caesar Augustus.

The "Nil invita Minera"—sometimes translated, "It was a not-unwilling Minerva"—comes from the *Ars Poetica (The Art of Poetry)*, in which Horace, giving literary advice to a young poet, says that the poet will achieve nothing if Minerva is unwilling. The "quae monumentum aere perennius exegit" appears in the final ode of Book III of his *Carmina* in which Horace (loosely translated) boasts, "I, who brought Greek form to Latin verse, shall not altogether die, for in my poetry I have built myself a monument more enduring than brass."

The whole hybrid quotation thus works out to mean approximately this, "It was no unwilling Minerva (Goddess of Wisdom) who built herself this monument more enduring than brass (the Library of Congress)."

NIL INVITA MINERVA QUAE MONUMENTUM
ÆRE PERENNIUS EXEGIT

Paul Boswell

The Minerva Mosaic.

I have been unable to find out whether Vedder, not collegetrained but steeped in mythology, living in Italy and perhaps knowing Latin, spliced Horace's passages together himself, or found a Latin scholar to do it for him.

The pen-and-ink reproduction of Vedder's *Minerva* mosaic was done as a cover for the *Library of Congress Professional Association Newsletter* of September 1970, and includes my presumptuous monogram below the little figure of winged Victory. The drawing was later reproduced numerous times on framed copper plates.

The Continents
3 3/8" x 4 7/8"

On the landings halfway up each of the Martiny staircases the chain of child laborers along the balustrade is interrupted by pairs of children on each staircase representing the continents. Each group consists of a globe and two small boys—the North group showing the western hemisphere and part of Africa with an American Indian and a Negro; the South group, the eastern hemisphere with a Mongolian and a European.

The drawing, used as a "peace on earth, good will toward men" Christmas card, suffered considerable darkening in the process of being reduced to card size.

Cherub Lamp Post
4 1/2" x 5 7/8"

The problem of how to transform one of the Library's elaborate outdoor candelabra into a drawing suggestive of Christmas was twofold—to change the winged, but mute, heads of the children to "herald angels", and to give the small base, with its four heads, a greater prominence than the much larger cluster of lamp globes above. The first objective was achieved by taking the liberty of opening the mouths of the three visible heads so they might be interpreted as singing; the second was to draw the picture from a viewing point about ten feet directly below the lamp post so that, in perspective, the globe cluster appeared narrower than the cherub-headed base.

Paul Boswell

The Continents.

Cherub Lamp Post.

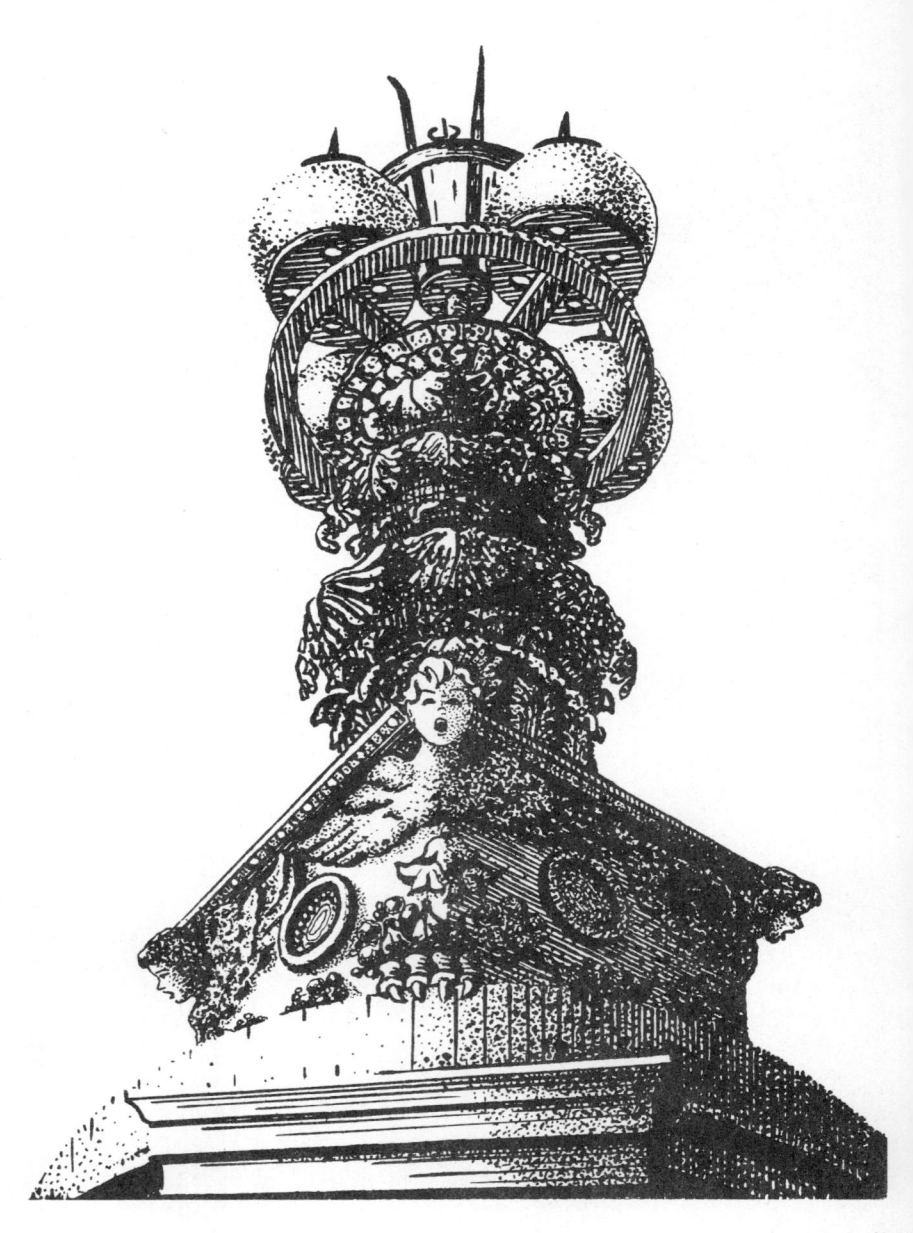

Paul Boswell

Pine and Lamp
3¼" x 4½"

    This is a view that my wife selected for me to draw, and we both like it, although we sometimes wonder whether people unfamiliar with the scene can figure out just what it is. The runty Austrian pine and horned bronze lamp post are about midway the little-frequented north side of the Library of Congress—the side toward the Supreme Court. The bronze lamp, after three-quarters of a century of exposure, has acquired the greenish-white patina appropriate to weathered bronze, except that in spots the patina is brown and looks suspiciously like plain old iron rust.

    The Austrian pine is only one of many fine trees on the Library grounds—in fact, these grounds constitute a rather respectable arboretum. Yew and holly are ubiquitous. Japanese maples abound on the south side; there is practically an orchard of Japanese crab-apple trees on the north side; a pair of large Amur cork trees shelter the entrances on the east side of the building; and three pairs of tall golden ginkgos flank the sidewalks as they enter the grounds from

Paul Boswell

Pine and Lamp.

the north, east and south. Walk around the building and you can find metal tags on the trees identifying about twenty different species.

The Whittall Pavilion Courtyard
14⅝" x 11¾"

The ivied wall on the right is the Coolidge Auditorium; the wall with the musicians' names, the Whittall Pavilion; and the white-tiled arcade above them both is an interior wall of the northwest courtyard of the Library of Congress.

In the Auditorium, the gift of Mrs. Elizabeth Sprague Coolidge, the Library's celebrated chamber-music concerts are performed and the larger assemblies of the Library's staff are held. The Pavilion, given by Gertrude (Clarke) Whittall, houses her gift collection of Stradivarius stringed instruments and provides a handsome setting for formal receptions.

The bronze figure on the pedestal in the niche, fashioned in 1892 by Frederick Macmonnies, and later given to the Library by Mrs. Whittall, has the words, "to Pan of Rohallion" incised on its base. Rohallion is the name of a castle in Perthshire, Scotland, the region in which the Macmonnies clan had its origins. There is nothing Pan-like about this image except the two Pan pipes it is blowing. It doesn't have the traditional goat's legs of Pan, but does have a pair of wings on its head like Pan's father, Mercury. The figure stands on a sphere supported by eight small fish standing vertically on their tails and clasping it with their out-spread fins. The mouths of the fish are designed to jet parabolas of water in all directions in a circular fountain, but here, in the semi-enclosed niche, the fish are not allowed to spout at all.

Other sculptures by Frederick Macmonnies at the Library of Congress are the relief figures on and above the central pair of bronze doors at the west entrance, and the statue of Shakespeare which stands, with fifteen other portrait statues, on the balustrade overlooking the Main Reading Room.

Macmonnies's most ambitious sculptures are in Prospect Park, Brooklyn, the borough of his birth, and on the Marne battlefield in France. He first achieved international renown with his "Triumph of Columbia" at the World's Columbian Exposition at Chicago in 1893, a grandiose statuary confection of twenty-seven figures on a barge, including Columbia riding high at the top, Father Time managing the tiller at the rear, and a platoon of lady oars-women functioning as the prime movers.

The Whittall Pavilion Courtyard.

Paul Boswell

To get back to the pen-and-ink drawing of the Courtyard, the pool, which does not reflect the buildings in fact because it is too shallow, was used as an exercise in drawing reflections, which, I think, made a more dramatic picture than the cement pots of water lilies would have made.

The Porte Cochere, Library of Congress
8½" x 11½"

The January 5, 1967 issue of *Library of Congress Information Bulletin* carried this notice of its new masthead:

> *New Heading for Staff Bulletin.* The pen-and-ink drawing which is used in the new heading on the front page of the 1967 *Information Bulletin* is the work of Paul Boswell, Reference Librarian in the Periodical and Government Publication Reading Room. The view of a tiny corner of the Main Building is a familiar one to staff members who make their nightly exits from the west doors through the archway into the dark of winter at 5:15 or—when working late—into the darkness in other seasons.

The drawing continued to be used, often in a rather disintegrated and blacked-out form, for five years, through December 1971.

What the public does not know is that the irregular dark area on the wall at the right side of the picture was not an intentional representation of the scaling granite. The night before I turned in the picture to the Information Office, being unsatisfied with the appearance of the right wall, I glued a strip of paper over it and redrew the lines on the patch. Apparently I left a smear of Elmer's glue unnoticed on the patch and the inked lines spread microscopically wherever they hit the glue. I assumed that it would be all right when it dried. It wasn't. With several thousand copies of the *Information Bulletin* printed each week for five years, there may have been a million memorials to my glue smear.

Paul Boswell

The Porte Cochere, Library of Congress.

730   *Records of the Columbia Historical Society*

The Puck Fountain, Folger Shakespeare Library
8⅞" x 12"

    The drawing of the snow-covered *Puck Fountain* was originally done as a Christmas card, and later, in larger form, reproduced as

Paul Boswell

The Puck Fountain, Folger Shakespeare Library.

one of eight framed copper plates exhibited in the First Library of Congress Employees' Art Show in the fall of 1970. Although I had seen Puck clothed in snow many times, I did not have a photograph of him in that condition when I made the drawing in October and November.

Puck (alias Hobgoblin, alias Robin Goodfellow), the prankster of the acorn-cup set, has in this marble incarnation been the victim of pranksters himself. At least twice that I have noticed, vandals have snapped off one of his vulnerable thumbs. At present, I believe, both thumbs are intact.

Brenda Putnam, born in 1890, the daughter of Herbert Putnam, for forty years the Librarian of Congress, was the sculptor (she says she dislikes the word "sculptress") of the *Puck Fountain*. Miss Putnam is notable for her fountain and sundial sculptures of children, her portrait busts of Pablo Casals and Amelia Earhart, her sumptuous figure of a young woman entitled *Midsummer,* her handsome textbook on the art of sculpting, *The Sculptor's Way,* and, of course, for *Puck.*

The Bethlehem Chapel, National Cathedral
11" x 14"

The Bethlehem Chapel is one of three chapels in the sub-structure of the Washington (Episcopal) Cathedral, the other two being the Chapel of St. Joseph of Arimathea and the Resurrection Chapel. The Nativity scene on the reredos is flanked by images of Matthew, Mark, Luke and John. The marble slab in the center of the main aisle covers the entrance to one of the church's burial vaults. Admiral George Dewey, of Spanish-American War fame, and a charter member of the Cathedral Chapter, is one of the personages buried here.

The year that we used *The Bethlehem Chapel* as a Christmas card I had planned to use the religion group (Religion, St. Paul and Moses) in the Gallery of the Reading Room at the Library of Congress, but the developer of my snapshots returned to me someone else's pictures. The pressure of time accounts for the necessity for using the abrupt "zip-a-tone" shading on the pillars and for the moiré shading on the left and right sides of the picture.

Paul Boswell

The Bethlehem Chapel, National Cathedral.

A Portfolio of Washington Drawings

The Supreme Court
18¾" x 8¾"

Several versions of the *Court* were done—the first was piled high with cumulus clouds and was backgrounded with a "zip-a-tone" sky in attempt to make the building and the clouds appear whiter. Somewhat embarrassed by the artificiality of the "zip-a-tone" (an adhesive cellophane sheet with ready-made, store-bought dots) I did a second sky in graduated horizontal lines, without clouds—a version I have never liked very much. A third version with a totally black sky, the one reproduced here, was used for a Christmas card on the theory that any nighttime scene comes a little closer to being appropriate for a Christmas card than a daytime one. When I had the *Supreme Court* reproduced a number of times on copper plates by Mr. Eldon Dick I returned to a cropped version of the cumulus-cloud sky. This is my favorite.

My favorite recollection of the *Supreme Court* is of the bird man. I still don't know his name or what his position is, or was, at the Court. On a cold, windy day I was standing at my center spot atop the steps that now form the base of the picture, sighting with yardstick and thumb to get the dimensions of the building, when a gentleman near the balustrade that semicircles the plaza waved his arm over his head, apparently beckoning me, and called out, "Come on." I looked behind me to see who else was around. There was no one in sight. I had just about decided that I was being summoned inside to give an account of myself, when two mockingbirds flew overhead and alighted on the balustrade and were given bread crumbs by the man who had hailed them. The performance was re-enacted several times in the next few days.

The White House
18¾" x 8¾"

We made two trips to take photographs of the White House—the first through the center of the tall iron fence on Pennsylvania Avenue, and later from Lafayette Park in order to include the Treasury and Executive Office Buildings on either end. The drawing was a composite of these two views.

It has been variously reproduced—framing size (18" x 24"), on cards with black sky, and on copper plates.

Paul Boswell

The Supreme Court.

Paul Boswell

The White House.

The Capitol
18¾" x 8¾"

This drawing of the Capitol was done in 1964 and 1965 shortly after the construction of the Rayburn House Office Building had been completed and it must have been one of the first full-length drawings to include a glimpse of the RHOB at the left of the House wing. This picture is as near to being one-hundred percent stipple as I can make it; I believe that the only inked lines in it are in the eight lamp posts.

I took photographs of the center and of the wings of the building from a central point fairly close up, but when I fitted the photographs together the Capitol curved up at the ends like a chair rocker— so I was unable to use the photographs as a means of locating the main outlines and proportions. Since photographs wouldn't work, I resorted to Albrecht Dürer's device of drawing directly on a pane of glass what I could see through the glass mounted directly in front of the Capitol.

I remember that one very cold morning before daylight my wife and I tied the mounted glass contraption to the top of our white 1958 Ford and she drove me over to the Capitol building and left me and my window pane to be sized-up by the Capitol guards. They eventually decided that I probably wasn't dangerous, and let me go ahead with my drawing. The "magic marker" crayon, cold as it was "by the dawn's early light", wouldn't make the slightest impression on the glass. I knew that the crayon had worked at home so I waited an hour or so for the sun to warm things up. Then sighting half of the building, from the center of the dome to the end of the Senate wing, through my window pane, I was finally able to trace on the glass an approximation of the main parts of half of the building. Half was all I needed, since the other half was a mirror image. Eighteen months later, with my "magic-marked" window pane and my photographs and my "umpteen" million pen-and-ink dots, I had my picture.

Paul Boswell

The Capitol.

Senate Nocturne
14⅝″ x 9⁵⁄₁₆″

This view extends along the wooded northern edge of the Mall from the west front of the Capitol to Prospect House, an apartment building on the horizon across the Potomac in Virginia. The domed buildings are the National Gallery of Art and the Natural History Museum. The dark, towered structure on the left is the Smithsonian Institution. Nestled almost invisibly at the right of the Washington Monument are the Netherlands Carillon and the Lincoln Memorial.

The picture was drawn against a time dead-line with the result that the sky and clouds received only two nights' work compared to two months spent leafing-out the rest of the picture. The viewpoint is from the center of the second arch near the north end of the west front of the Capitol.

Senate Nocturne.

Paul Boswell

Revisiting Washington's Forty Boundary Stones, 1972

EDWIN DARBY NYE

The approach of the 200th anniversary in 1976 of our nation's birth suggests that we give some thought to the original boundary stones of our national capital.

These stones, forty in all, are the oldest Federal activity in Washington, having been set in place in 1791–1792, and are today 180 years old. While many visitors are expected here for the 1976 celebration, and while our boundary stones because of their significance could become a part of the displays and festivities, a tourist unfamiliar with the area would find it difficult indeed to locate them unless he were specifically motivated. However, there is much that we Washingtonians can learn about our famous stones. It is certainly proper that some attention and publicity be given them, if only for the benefit of those of us who live here. The 1976 birthday is an appropriate time to do this.

With this in mind, a trip around the "Ten Mile Square" was made in the summer of 1972 and the location and present condition of each stone was noted and recorded as follows.

But first a brief history of the boundary stones would be helpful. When George Washington selected this area as the site for the capital of the United States he first had it surveyed. For this he selected Andrew Ellicott, son of one of the founders of Ellicott City, Maryland, who brought with him Benjamin Banneker, a free Negro who had an excellent knowledge of mathematics and astronomy. With others, they laid out a square, ten miles on a side, placing stones at one mile intervals. The stones were numbered clockwise, one to nine, from corner to corner.

In order to include then existing Alexandria and Georgetown, Jones Point was chosen as the starting point. On April 15, 1791, with proper Masonic toasts and ceremony, the South Stone was set in place. Subsequently the Jones Point Lighthouse was built and the stone was

---

Delivered before the Columbia Historical Society on December 19, 1972.

encased in a seawall but forty years later this condition was corrected and the stone exposed.[1]

Ten miles due northwest from this point, one finds the West Stone in Falls Church; the North Stone is near 16th Street and East-West Highway; and the East Stone is in Seat Pleasant.

Later surveys show the square to be tipped slightly to the west with the North Stone 116 feet west of its proper location. The southwest line is 230 feet more than 10 miles long, the northwest line is 63 feet too long, the northeast line is 263 feet over, and the southeast line is 10 miles and 63 feet in length.[2]

From a cartographer's point of view it is interesting to note that when Ellicott and Banneker finished placing the stones around the perimeter of the square they joined Pierre L'Enfant in the center of the city. Here they assisted in the laying out of the streets and early Federal buildings. Basic to the symmetry of Pierre L'Enfant's plan of the city of Washington is the location of the Capitol half-way between the north and south boundaries, and the White House half-way between the east and west boundaries.

Today we find 16th Street running due north from the White House passing east of the north corner stone by 600 feet. East Capitol Street misses the east cornerstone by 200 yards. It is more logical to think that the proper locations for the Capitol, President's House, the Mall, etc., were selected on the basis of appropriate terrain rather than where the streets would eventually meet the city's boundaries.

The boundary markers are of Aquia Creek Sandstone from a quarry in Stafford County, Virginia. They were brought up the Potomac probably to Jones Point for finishing as this is where the surveyors had their main camp.

The carving on the stones was of fine quality and with the exception of SW1 was all done by the same artisan. The stones are about one foot square and protrude about 18 inches above grade. On the side facing the District is carved: JURISDICTION OF THE UNITED STATES. This is in a bold style fitting the importance of its message. Below is given the miles number of its location. The rear sides gives the name of the state, Maryland or Virginia. A third face gives the date of the placing of the stone: 1791 for the Virginia stones and 1792 for the Maryland stones. The fourth face gives the variation between magnetic north and true north for its location at the time of the survey. The carving on these last three faces is in a lighter, more delicate and subordinate style.

[1] Fred E. Woodward, "The Recovery of the Southern Corner Stone of the District," *Records,* Columbia Historical Society, Vol. 18, 1915.

[2] U. S. Geodetic Survey, 1889.

The sandstone markers have stood up to the weather much better than to the vandalism they have been subjected to. The stones have been chopped at and shot at for many years and we should be very grateful to the Society of the Daughters of the American Revolution which instigated the protective iron grills that most of the boundary stones still have around them. The procedure of the DAR has been to assign to one of its chapters the responsibility of one boundary stone. While some stones appear to have been neglected we must appreciate the overall effort. The DAR is the only active protection our stones have.

Tribute should also be paid to Fred E. Woodward, who visited all the stones in 1906. Using a map and a pocket compass, traveling by the "electric cars" and on foot, he located the forty stones and produced a delightful hand-lettered monograph with his photographs which is in the Washingtoniana Division of the Martin Luther King Library.

Mr. Woodward read a paper on the stones to the Columbia Historical Society on May 14, 1906,[3] and was instrumental in getting the DAR interested in placing iron fencing around each stone in 1916 and the DAR's subsequent concern for their preservation.

If you follow in the steps of Fred Woodward, you will find that of the forty stones, thirty-seven appear to be those originals set in place in 1791–1792. Thirty-six still have the DAR protective enclosures. As to their legibility, 22 could be described as excellent or good considering their age and apparent rough treatment and 19 bear no readable inscription at all.

Twenty-three of them may be seen from your automobile; and with a short walk of less than fifty yards each, 11 more can be visited. The remaining six do offer a real challenge but with it a real satisfaction to the successful searcher.

Eleven stones stand on the lawns of private dwellings and 27 are on park or public land. Of these latter at least 16 need raising or resetting and better protection than the DAR has been able to provide.

South Stone: The Jones Point area has sunk over the years so that today with a spring tide the South Stone is partially under water. Its protection is a concrete cave-like enclosure built into a seawall. The slab roof of the enclosure has a six-inch hole located directly over the stone to accommodate a surveyor's plumb line. Because of its dank home, the South Stone is covered with moss. It can be seen better at low tide or at any time by boat.

---

[3] Fred E. Woodward, "A Ramble along the Boundary Stones of the District of Columbia with a Camera," *Records*, Columbia Historical Society, Vol. 10, 1907.

The seawall which at one time completely enclosed this stone is part of the construction of the Jones Point Lighthouse. There has been some effort to make Jones Point into a recreation area and a few years ago the lighthouse building was restored but it is now boarded up and the entire area is thick with bushes and vines.

SW1, located at Wilkes and Wolfe Streets in Alexandria, appears to have been moved from its original location when Alexandria grew in size and the streets were extended to reach the boundary line. The stone sits square with the corners of the sidewalks at this NS-EW intersection and has an excellent location but it has been rotated 45° in relocation as the JURISDICTION face does not squarely face the District of Columbia.

Also noteworthy, the stonecutter who carved this stone did not carve the rest of them. The inscription is smaller, shallower and less artistic than on the remaining stones and, as this is the first stone placed after the South Stone, one surmises that the surveyors did not like their stonecutter's work and hired another man.

SW2 is not an original stone. On Russell Road, 100 feet north of King Street, it is a large block of sandstone bearing no inscription.

SW3 is on the end of the parking lot of the First Baptist Church of Alexandria at 2932 King Street. It is well-protected and reasonably legible.

SW4 is found at the edge of King Street (Route 7) at Wakefield Street. In the regrading of this dual highway, this stone was nearly covered and appears to be completely neglected. It should, of course, be raised and reset in concrete.

SW5 is on Walter Reed Parkway, 200 feet east of Route 7. Again the regrading of the roadway obliterated the stone. There is a rock of some sort showing at ground level in the center of the protective fencing but one can not be sure that it is an original boundary stone.

SW6 had to be relocated a few years ago because of apartment construction. Its present location could not be better; it is situated in the median strip of Jefferson Street, 300 feet south of Columbia Pike in Arlington. Cracks in the stone have been sealed and, while there is little of the inscription than can still be read, SW6 has a prominent and yet safe location.

SW7 is the only stone on this quadrant that can not be seen from an automobile. About 100 feet from Carlyn Spring Road and Olds Street a path leading to an athletic field brings one near this stone at the edge of a woods. One or two words can still be made out as the stone looks as though it has been shot at, which is not unlikely as Confederate soldiers roamed this woods on many occasions.

SW8 is on the edge of an apartment parking lot just past the water tower at John Marshall and Wilson Boulevard. This stone must have been moved too when civilization came to the area as it has been rotated in being relocated.

SW9 is found in a lovely park at Van Buren and 18th Street. It is well-preserved and protected, enjoying a pleasant public location.

West Stone: The Falls Church Chapter of the DAR deserves the historian's congratulations for the way in which it has protected the West Stone at West Street and Arizona in Falls Church. Several building lots are devoted to a very attractive display. The area is cleared and fenced and a large six-foot square iron enclosure surrounds the stone and the stump of a large oak tree that once stood beside it. Two rows of white stones have been laid across the area; emanating from the corner stone, they indicate the actual boundary line.

The stone itself is badly battered. It bears vertical grooves, indicating that the center of the monument is the corner of the District of Columbia. It is noteworthy that this West Stone has a horizontal inscription and is the same height as the other stones, while the North corner stone and the East corner stone stand nearly 30 inches above ground and bear vertical inscriptions.

NW1 stands behind 3607 Powatan Street in Arlington. Badly chipped, it is now well-protected in rather deep woods.

NW2 is in the side yard of 5298 Old Dominion Drive. Its edges are chopped and is legible only on the center of its faces.

NW3 stands in the rear yard of 4013 Tazwell Street, Arlington. Its legend reads: "Mile 3 & 3 Poles," indicating that it was placed 3 poles (49½ feet) beyond its mile distance from NW2. This was done to give the stone higher and firmer ground for a more permanent location. The stone is erect, in good condition, and squarely in the middle of a proud owner's back yard. It is the focal point of her garden, for, as she told the author, "George Washington put it there."

NW4 is in the fenced-in Dalecarlia Reservation about 100 feet from the Baltimore and Ohio Railroad Georgetown Spur. It is well-protected, trimmed with ivy, in the rear yard of the home of one of the directors. Its legend reads: "Miles 4 and 100 Poles," as its proper location would be in the Potomac gorge. NW4 is the first stone to bear the year date "1792."

NW5 is in the Dalecarlia compound, too, about one-eighth mile from Westmoreland Circle at Massachusetts Avenue. Permission to visit this location must be obtained from the guard and his help in finding it is just as necessary as it stands in the midst of many acres of very deep woods.

NW6 at River Road and Fessenden Street has a fine grassy lawn setting. It stands upright but is badly damaged and is hardly legible.

NW7, at 5600 Western Avenue, is hidden by a high hedge but is in perfect condition. Buried for several decades, it was raised into view in 1964. Representative (now Senator) Charles Mathias of Maryland spoke at the DAR rededication ceremony on the occasion.

NW7 and its neighbor NW8 are the only stones without protective grills. Also, subsequent surveys have shown them to be the only stones that are exactly one mile apart.

NW8 is located at 6422 Western Avenue at Pinehurst Circle. It is in excellent condition for its age. It wears a benchmark on its top.

NW9 is found 50 yards down a path into Rock Creek Park from the end of Western Avenue at Oregon Avenue, N.W. It is in good condition, legible on all four faces, and enjoys a protected location.

North Stone: The North Corner Stone is 20 feet south of East-West Highway, one-eighth mile west of 16th Street, and has a round iron enclosure. It is a tall stone and was originally nearly three feet above ground. It is now nearly buried in leaves. It is known to have clear, vertical inscriptions, stating its purpose.

NE1's original position is marked by a DAR plaque in the sidewalk at 7847 Eastern Avenue. This is the only location not marked by a stone.

NE2 stands on Maple Avenue in Takoma Park, 100 feet north of Carroll Avenue, on the corner of a well-kept lawn at the edge of the sidewalk. It is in good condition.

NE3 stands neglected at New Hampshire Avenue and Eastern Avenue. It does not go unnoticed, however, as it seems to collect beer cans. Like its next neighbor NE4, the stone has sunk or been buried so that there is barely enough of it visible to ascertain if it is one of the originals.

NE4 at Sargent Road and Eastern Avenue also exhibits neglect. It appears to be another case where during road construction the fencing was raised but the stone was not and was nearly covered. The few inches of the top of the stone that are visible are completely unmarked and suggest a perfect stone below ground.

NE5 is found at 4609 Eastern Avenue. It stands prominently on a wide green lawn and is in very good condition.

NE6, at 3601 Eastern Avenue, stands behind two fences. It is in very good condition and is very well protected.

NE7 is along a fence between Fort Lincoln Cemetery and what will be Lincoln New Town. Reached through the cemetery, it is 100 feet south of an equipment storage building near the far end of the area. Nearly covered with leaves and mulch, NE7 is wrapped in a

Photograph by Edwin Darby Nye

North West Boundary Stone Number 7, face.

Located at Western Avenue and 41st Street, N.W., the stone has carved on its face "Jurisdiction of the United States Miles 7." The "Miles 7" indicates that its placement was 7 miles from the west corner of the survey (in what is now the town of Falls Church, Virginia).

Photograph by Edwin Darby Nye

North West Boundary Stone Number 7, side.

Carved on its side is Var. 0° 59′E″ which indicates that in the survey the variation of magnetic north and true north was zero degrees and 59 minutes east.

Photograph by Edwin Darby Nye

North West Boundary Stone Number 8.

NW 8 is on the front lawn of the residence at 6422 Western Avenue, N.W. Eleven of the boundary stones are on private property. The owners of the property all express pride in the stones.

rusting two-inch iron strap holding it together. What carving that can be seen is quite legible.

NE8 is behind a boarded-up low-cost apartment development 200 yards northwest of the intersection of Eastern Avenue and Kenilworth Avenue in the vicinity of the Aquatic Gardens. It is well-preserved.

NE9 is down a ten-foot bank at the property line of 919 Eastern Avenue. In the summer, its fence is completely obscured by tangled vines.

East Stone: Situated close to the old Chesapeake Beach Junction, a transfer point for the Washington, Baltimore and Annapolis Railroad and other local lines, the East Stone stood in a once very active area. Now obscured by vines and bushes in a low ravine, it can be found about 50 yards southeast of the intersection of Eastern Avenue

Photograph by *Edwin Darby Nye*

North West Boundary Stone Number 9.

In 1916 the Society of the Daughters of the American Revolution had protective iron grilles placed around each of the boundary stones. Thirty-eight of these grilles are still in place as is this one around NW 9 in Rock Creek Park.

and Southern Avenue. Its location seems to suggest a variation between the original survey and subsequent street layouts.

The stone itself, a cornerstone taller than the others, bears vertical inscriptions which are quite legible.

SE1 is in an unpopulated area where D Street, S.E. ends at the District line. It is in very good condition.

SE2 is at 4345 Southern Avenue. A flagpole stands beside this well-preserved stone and the grill is painted with bright aluminum paint.

SE3 is at 3908 Southern Avenue on high ground south of where Suitland Road leaves the District. It appears more weathered than bruised and no inscriptions on it can be read.

SE4 is situated at the very edge of a downhill curve of Naylor Road. Years of bombardment by gravel and road trash have worn this stone down to an indistinguishable nubbin.

SE5 stands undisturbed about 400 yards into the woods southwest of the intersection of Southern Avenue and Mississippi Avenue. Southern Avenue is to be extended to pass by this location which will make SE5 readily accessible.

SE6. The Henry Gilpin Company at 901 Southern Avenue has taken advantage of the presence of SE6 which stands before its building. Attractive landscaping and the addition of an old gas street lamp present this stone in excellent good taste. Well-preserved, SE6 is the best example of the beauty of the carving the boundary stones once had.

SE7 stands by the bridge which carries Maryland Route 210 over Oxon Hill Run. If this stone has any special claim to fame, it is that it stands closer to more automobile traffic than any of the others.

SE8, at the far end of the D.C. Village Area, has become a victim of a large land-fill operation, involving the D.C. auto impounding area, the new sewage treatment plant, and an eighteen-hole golf course being constructed by the National Park Service. SE8 is covered with some eight feet of landfill. A sixty-inch concrete pipe has been placed over the stone, iron fencing and all, and a cover placed over it to protect it. The stone has been uncovered and after the excavation has been completed it will be reset in a proper location. SE8 is not an original. It is a marble replacement installed only a few years ago by the Monticello Chapter of the DAR. It bears no inscription.

SE9 lies between Interstate 295 and the Potomac River and defies one to find it. Its original position became engulfed in the river's changing shoreline. The stone was moved to higher ground where it later became nearly covered by an earthen dike. The eight-foot fence that parallels the interstate highway only adds to the difficulty and the mass of thick vegetation makes locating this stone virtually impossible. It still marks the line, however, and its carving is still legible.

Our boundary stones have great historic value and should certainly be protected. They are probably unique as city boundaries go; their placement was directed by George Washington and their relationship to the over-all plan of the Capital City makes them of even more interest.

While a few of the stones are difficult to locate, many of them are quite easy to find today. The more of them you visit, the more you appreciate their historical importance. In 1909, Ernest Shuster went in search of them and wrote:

> There was an indescribable pleasure in finding the stones by means of the maps, and in only two or three cases did we ask assistance from the people living in the vicinity. Twenty-three Sunday afternoons were spent in the search from the latter part of March to the end of August, six stones being our largest afternoon's work. On two evenings, however, we returned home without adding to our score.[4]

The extension of Western, Eastern, and Southern Avenues around the perimeter of the District of Columbia increases the traffic flow and population density around the locations of the stones and adds to the threat to their welfare. They now require constant care and watchfulness.

Congress should place responsibility for the maintenance of the stones, which belong to the United States Government, in the hands of the National Park Service. This is a suggestion the DAR and the Columbia Historical Society should support.

---

[4] Ernest A. Shuster, "The Original Boundary Stones of the District of Columbia," *National Geographic*, April 1909.

Baseball Reminiscences of Washington's Jesse "Nip" Winters: "How I Struck Out Babe Ruth and Beat Lefty Grove"

JESSE "NIP" WINTERS WITH JOHN HOLWAY

Grove was great, really great. I pitched against him twice, when we barnstormed against Babe Ruth's all stars. We'd play 10 to 15 games a year in the New York-New Jersey-Philadelphia area after the regular season. At that time Judge Landis wouldn't let us play a big league team intact; we had to play all star teams. And what a club Ruth had! Gehrig was on first, Jimmy Dykes on third; Ruth, Al Simmons and Bing Miller in the outfield; Mickey Cochrane catching; and Howard Ehmke, Rube Walberg and Lefty Grove pitching.

Grove beat me the first game we pitched, 3–1. Miller and Cochrane doubled for one run, another came in on a sacrifice fly, and the third scored on an infield out. In the second game, in Philadelphia, I struck Ruth out on a curve away from him, and he grounded out twice, but Gehrig tripled and scored on a fly for one run. We tied it when George Johnson doubled and Biz Mackey singled him home. Then Judy Johnson singled, and Otto Briggs our center fielder drove him home to win it, 2–1.

Ruth was a fine man to get along with, very friendly. He got a homer off me before the series was over. He hit it over the center field fence in Darby [South Philadelphia]. When he hit one, it was gone!

Actually, though, I had a tougher time with Gehrig. I thought he was the tougher man to get out. I always tried to keep the ball on top

---

Some old-time players call Nip Winters the greatest left-hander in the history of the Negro leagues, just as Lefty Grove is usually considered the best white lefty. The two hooked up in two memorable duels when each was at the height of his powers. Winters died in Hokessin, Delaware in December 1971.

of him, on his wrists, so he couldn't get his full power on me, but he was still a rough man and could really hit it.

We had a pretty good long ball hitter in our own league, Josh Gibson. I remember one long one he hit over the fence in Forbes Field, Pittsburgh, but I think Ruth would hit more homers than Josh did.

I was born in 1899, so that makes me older than Satchel Paige. At least I'm older than Satchel *says* he is. Actually, he's older than me, I know it.

I was born in Washington and started playing ball about 1920 with the Norfolk Stars. Then I moved to the Bacharach Giants in Atlantic City for three or four years and finally joined the Philadelphia Hilldale Daisies, the greatest team I've ever seen. We played in two Negro world series, 1924 and '25, and I believe we could have beaten today's ball players easy.

Pop Lloyd was captain of the Daisies, a great base runner and a wonderful hitter. George Johnson of the Daisies I'd have to put on my all-time all-star outfield, right along with Babe Ruth and Oscar Charleston. He was a great right-handed hitter, a great thrower, and he could run the bases. Our third baseman, Judy Johnson, was one of the best third basemen I've ever seen, and Dick Warfield was the best second baseman I've ever seen in any league. I never saw Rogers Hornsby, but Warfield was a great fielder and base runner. If he got on base he was almost sure to score because he could really run. Biz Mackey was our catcher. Mickey Cochrane of the Athletics was voted the best catcher of all time, but I don't know which was better, Mackey or Cochrane. Mackey could throw harder. A man better not get too far off base, because he had a wonderful arm; he could throw, and he was a lot of help to the pitcher.

But what really made the Daisies so good was our pitching staff. We had everything on it. Red Ryan threw a fork ball, Phil Cockrell had a spitter, I threw a left-handed curve, and Scrip Lee was an underhander. In fact, I got Scrip for the Daisies. He came from my home town, Washington, and I'd heard a lot about him, so I went back and got him for us.

We used to draw some big crowds in our park in Darby, but the biggest crowd I ever played before was in Shibe Park against the Athletics around 1932—about 25,000 people. They won, 4–2, when Ed Rommel beat Cockrell.

Bullet Joe Rogan of Kansas City was a good pitcher, awfully fast—as fast as Bob Feller or Satchel Paige. I pitched against him in the

Photograph courtesy of Holsey "Scrip" Lee

Champions of Black Baseball, 1926.

The Hilldale Daisies of Philadelphia pose with their owner Ed Bolden (center rear). "Nip" Winters, the team's ace left-hander, is third from the left in the rear row. Fellow Washingtonian Holsey "Scrip" Lee stands at the extreme left. Four of these men may some day enter baseball's Hall of Fame: all are in the back row, Raleigh "Biz" Mackey, third from the left; Winters; William "Judy" Johnson, third from the right; and Louis Santop, extreme right.

Photograph courtesy of Holsey "Scrip" Lee

Washington submarine ball hurler Hosley "Scrip" Lee.

Lee poses before the old scoreboard in the Hilldale's park at Darby, outside Philadelphia. Lee came off the Washington sandlots along with "Nip" Winters to give Hilldale one of the strongest pitching staffs in black baseball in the 1920's. Lee now lives at 415 K Street, N. E., Washington, D. C.

first Negro world series game ever played, in 1924, and beat him, 5–2. I won three games in that series, but the Monarchs finally won the series, five games to four. My biggest thrill was the day I almost pitched a no-hitter against Rogan. I had a no-hitter until one out in the ninth, then the third baseman singled, the next man got a double, and Dobey Moore, a great short stop, hit a double and scored both runners and beat me, 3–1.

The guy I think should be the first to go into the Hall of Fame was Oscar Charleston. He was a center fielder, and it's tough to try to compare him and Joe DiMaggio. Both of them were great. Charleston and Willie Mays both played a shallow center field and they could both go back and get that ball, but I think Charleston was a better hitter than Mays. We had another great center fielder in our day, Cool Papa Bell. Could he run! If he hit the ball to your left or right, you might just as well toss it back to the pitcher, because you couldn't catch him at first.

I played against Charleston in Cuba. I was with Havana. The manager was Dolph Luque, who used to pitch with the Reds and Giants. But there was this little town, Santa Clara, an overnight train ride out of Havana, and what a team they had! They were all Americans—no Cubans—Charleston and Warfield and Jud Wilson, and pitching Bill Holland. They ran away with the league.

The second guy I'd put in the Hall of Fame would be a Cuban, Martin Dihigo.[1] He was a right-handed long-ball hitter who could do everything: pitch today, catch tomorrow, play first base the next day.

My third choice may surprise you: George Shively of Indianapolis, a great lead-off man and a good outfielder.

I believe we could have beaten today's players easy. Today they make a business out of it, but in the old days we played ball because we loved it.

I stayed with the Daisies for 12 or 13 years, then went up to Canada and played in Montreal until I quit in 1940. You know, I never did keep track of the games I won. I never even counted up how many I won against the big leaguers. I just wouldn't know how many it would be altogether.

---

[1] Martin Dihigo died in Havana in May 1971.

Baseball Reminiscences of Jesse "Nip" Winters

Hilldales vs. Macks, Philadelphia, October 2, 1926

Macks		h	r		Hilldales	h	r
3b	Dykes	0	0	rf	Briggs	3	1
ss	Padgett	1	0	2b	Warfield	1	0
cf	Manush	1	0	c	Mackey	1	0
1b	Burns	1	0	ss	Beckwith	1	0
rf	Miller	1	0	cf	Charleston	1	1
c	Schang	1	0	3b	Johnson	0	1
lf	Heimach	1	0	lf	Thomas	0	0
2b	McCann	1	1	1b	Carr	1	2
p	Grove	0	0	p	Winters	2	1
ph	Perkins	0	0				
		7	1			10	6

Macks   001 000 000—1 7
Hilldale   120 210 000—6 10

2b: Briggs, Winters, Beckwith, Carr
hr: Charleston
w: Winters 2, Grove 1
so: Winters 3, Grove 3

Baltimore Black Sox vs. Major League All Stars, Baltimore, October 1928

All Stars		h	r		Black Sox	h	r
lf	Bishop	1	0	lf	Holloway	0	1
1b	Neun	0	0	2b	Warfield	0	0
rf	Porter	0	0	3b	Beckwith	1	1
lf	Foxx	2	1	cf	Charleston	0	0
cf	Moore	0	0	1b	Cannady	1	0
ss	Thomas	0	0	ss	Lundy	0	0
3b	Movers	0	0	rf	Hubbard	0	0
c	Lerian	1	0	c	Clark	2	0
p	Ogden	0	0	p	Yokely	0	0
		4	1			4	2

All Stars   010 000 000—1 4
Baltimore   200 000 00x—2 4

2b: Lerian, Clark (2)
3b: Foxx
hr: Beckwith, Foxx
w: Yokely 3, Ogden 3
so: Yokely 4, Ogden 4

Washington's Jim Berryman, 1902–1971: Cartoons of Senator Dirksen

FRANCIS COLEMAN ROSENBERGER

Political cartooning has flowered—it is, to be sure, often a prickly cactus flower—in Washington, D.C.

This is one of those many instances in which Washington as a community and Washington as a national capital become inseparably mixed. Herblock (Herbert Lawrence Block) in the Washington *Post,* Gib Crockett (Gibson Milton Crockett) in the Washington *Star,* and —until the *Star* absorbed the Washington *Daily News* in July 1972— Basset (Gene Basset) in the *News,* are local residents who have both a local and a national audience. Their most frequent subjects are Washington events which have both a local and a national interest and Washington personalities, however transitorily they may be Washington personalities, who have a part in those events.

Long prominent among Washington political cartoonists was Jim Berryman (James Thomas Berryman) who died on August 12, 1971. He was a distinguished and Pulitzer Prize winning cartoonist of the *Star* and the son of a distinguished and Pulitzer Prize winning cartoonist of the *Star.*

In the delightful volume, *The Ungentlemanly Art: A History of American Political Cartoons,* Stephen Hess and Milton Kaplan wrote in 1968:

> Some cartoonists, like other mortals, have chosen their profession because it was their fathers'.... Clifford K. Berryman, the Washington *Star's* cartoonist from 1908 until he died in 1949, was the son of a crossroads merchant who spent his spare time caricaturing his customers on wrapping paper. When Cliff Berryman collapsed on May 29, 1935, while drawing a Memorial Day cartoon, his son James was called from the *Star's* art department (where he was "drawing pots and pans and stuff like that") to finish his father's work. He continued to draw for the

editorial page until his own retirement on January 1, 1965. The Berrymans, *pere et fils,* were awarded Pulitzer Prizes. . . . In all cases—Berrymans, McCutcheons, and Alleys—the styles of the sons have not been radically different from their fathers'.[1]

The Berryman family had an association with the Columbia Historical Society of Washington, D. C. over a number of years. Mrs. Clifford K. Berryman was first listed as a member of the Society in 1923. Clifford K. Berryman was elected an honorary member of the Society on October 15, 1946. Their son and daughter, James T. Berryman and Florence Berryman, were listed as members of the Society in the late 1940's and early 1950's. Florence Berryman read a valuable paper "Artists of Washington" before the Society on May 17, 1949.[2]

James T. Berryman was born in Washington, D. C. on June 8, 1902, the year that his father, then a cartoonist for the Washington *Post,* first drew the "Teddy Bear" and made it famous. He was educated at George Washington University and the Corcoran School of Art, married Louise Marble Rhees, also of Washington, and began a newspaper career as a reporter for Scripps-Howard papers in New Mexico. He joined the art department of the Washington *Star* in the mid-1920's. From May 1935, when he was called upon to finish the Memorial Day cartoon of the elder Berryman, he and his father drew cartoons for the *Star,* alternating daily, until Clifford K. Berryman died on December 11, 1949, at the age of 80. Jim Berryman, who won

---

[1] Stephen Hess and Milton Kaplan. *The Ungentlemanly Art: A History of American Political Cartoons* (New York, The Macmillan Co., 1968), p. 18.

Florence S. Berryman, who generously checked galley proof on this paper, has commented: "There is only one correction I have to request you to make, and it is the quotation from Stephen Hess and Milton Kaplan. The erroneous remark is that 'Clifford K. Berryman, the Washington *Star's* cartoonist from 1908 (actually from 1907) until he died in 1949, was the son of a crossroads merchant who spent his spare time caricaturing his customers on wrapping paper.' I *never* heard that my grandfather (Clifford's father) drew anything, and certainly a crossroads store could not have supported his wife and 11 children, his farm on the Kentucky River, and a number of slaves. He was a commission merchant who rode horseback all over Woodford County in the Lexington area and bought entire crops (tabacco, etc.) from farmers and shipped them north." Miss Berryman suggests that the story may involve a confusion of her grandfather with her father as a child. "My grandfather died when Clifford was 10 years old. My father (Clifford) as a child loved to draw, and often drew portraits on cigar box tops or bottoms and cut them out with a jigsaw. My father's little jigsaw portraits had small blocks of wood nailed to the back so they stood up, and they were shown *not* in a crossroads store but in the office of his Uncle Ed Berryman, who was involved in Woodford County politics. Senator Joseph Clay Stiles Blackburn (1838–1918) saw one of them which pleased him so much that he brought my father at the age of 17 to Washington and got him a job in the U. S. Patent Office."

[2] Florence S. Berryman, "Artists of Washington," *Records of the Columbia Historical Society of Washington, D. C., 1948–1950* (Washington, 1952), pp. 215–233.

his Pulitzer Prize the next year, continued as a cartoonist for the *Star* for another decade and a half and retired at the end of 1964.[3]

To represent Jim Berryman's work here I have chosen fifteen of his cartoons from 1958 to 1963 all dealing with Senator Everett McKinley Dirksen (1896–1969). I have made this selection because I believe that a group of cartoons dealing with a single personality provide a certain unity and because of my own interest in cartoons of Senator Dirksen. During the Senator's lifetime, I collected more or less systematically some 150 cartoons of him by a score of cartoonists with a view to the possible publication of a volume, a project which had the Senator's tolerant approval.

Senator Dirksen appreciated Berryman's work and the framed originals of five of the cartoons reproduced here, those of December 18, 1958, August 18, 1960, February 25, 1961, March 16, 1961, and July 29, 1961, hung on the wall of Room S-230 in the Capitol, Senator Dirksen's office as Senate Republican leader (Senate Minority Floor Leader).

Beneath each of the fifteen cartoons which follow here is the date on which it was published in the Washington *Star,* together with a brief word on the events or circumstances which prompted the cartoon.

[3] John Chase, *Today's Cartoon* (New Orleans, The Hauser Press, 1962), "Jim Berryman"; obituaries, Washington *Star,* Aug. 12, 1971, Washington *Post,* Aug. 13, 1971, *New York Times,* Aug. 13, 1971.

Letter to St. Nick

*Reproduced with the permission of
Mrs. James T. Berryman and the Washington Star*

December 18, 1958. The election of a new Senate Republican Floor Leader was scheduled for the Senate Republican party caucus to be held on January 7, 1959. The candidacy of Senator Dirksen was opposed by a liberal Republican faction.

Senatorial Iron Curtain

*Reproduced with the permission of
Mrs. James T. Berryman and the Washington Star*

August 18, 1960. In the last months of the administration of President Dwight D. Eisenhower in the election year of 1960, Congress returned for a short session after the two national political party conventions.

'I Always Like to Lend a Helping Hand'

*Reproduced with the permission of
Mrs. James T. Berryman and the Washington Star*

February 25, 1961. Early in the new administration of President John F. Kennedy, in a move the timing of which was widely interpreted as designed to embarrass Democrats, Senator Dirksen offered a civil rights bill as an addition to the President's "high priority" legislative program.

'We'll Show Up Jack Kennedy—and Caroline, Too!'

*Reproduced with the permission of
Mrs. James T. Berryman and the Washington Star*

March 16, 1961. With the inauguration of a Democrat, John F. Kennedy, as President in January 1961, Senator Dirksen, as Senate Republican leader, and Representative Charles A. Halleck of Indiana, the House Republican leader, became principal Republican party spokesmen and conducted a joint weekly television news conference which became known as the "Ev and Charlie Show."

'The Ev and Charlie Show' Goes High Hat

*Reproduced with the permission of
Mrs. James T. Berryman and the Washington Star*

July 15, 1961. The "Ev and Charlie Show" was frequently caricatured by cartoonists as a vaudeville act, a characterization which was sometimes encouraged by Senator Dirken's own deliberate burlesquing of his grandiloquent style.

'But Now, Mike—About the Domestic Program . . .

*Reproduced with the permission of
Mrs. James T. Berryman and the Washington Star*

July 29, 1961. Senator Dirksen, as Senate Republican leader, frequently supported Senator Michael J. (Mike) Mansfield of Montana, who had succeeded Senator Lyndon B. Johnson (now Vice President) as the Senate Democratic leader, on administration recommendations for military appropriations but was more critical of administration recommendations for domestic appropriations.

'New Year Resolutions You'll Never Hear About'

*Reproduced with the permission of
Mrs. James T. Berryman and the Washington Star*

January 1, 1962. Senator Dirksen, as Senate Republican leader, was not known for urging Democratic Senators from the South to vote with Democratic Senators from the North.

'I Hope Indiana Likes 'The Ev and Charlie Show'!'

*Reproduced with the permission of
Mrs. James T. Berryman and the Washington Star*

April 13, 1962. Senator Dirksen, enjoying a steadily increasing national reputation, easily won the Illinois Republican party's renomination for the Senate in 1962.

'He's Trying to Break Up Our Show!'

*Reproduced with the permission of
Mrs. James T. Berryman and the Washington Star*

October 22, 1962. President Kennedy appeared in Illinois with Representative Sidney R. Yates, the Illinois Democratic party's nominee for the Senate, to quiet rumors that the national Democratic administration did not want Dirksen defeated. (Three days later the President called Dirksen to come to the White House with other Congressional leaders on what later became known as the Cuban missile crisis.)

The Latest in Sidewalk Santas!

*Reproduced with the permission of
Mrs. James T. Berryman and the Washington Star*

December 20, 1962. This Christmas week cartoon was prompted by a suggestion that the "Ev and Charlie Show" might be continued as a television program paid for by public contributions.

'I Think I'm All Set for the President's Program'

*Reproduced with the permission of
Mrs. James T. Berryman and the Washington Star*

January 7, 1963. In the new session of Congress which began in January 1963, Senator Dirksen made it clear that he intended to oppose much of President Kennedy's domestic legislative program.

'I Call It Unfair Competition!'

*Reproduced with the permission of
Mrs. James T. Berryman and the Washington Star*

March 14, 1963. The announcement of the continuation of the "Ev and Charlie Show" coincided with the spring tour of the combined Ringling Brothers and Barnum and Bailey Circus.

'Spring Planting? . . . No . . . Ploughing Under!'

*Reproduced with the permission of
Mrs. James T. Berryman and the Washington Star*

March 21, 1963. In the spring of 1963, Senator Dirksen opposed legislative proposals by President Kennedy on agriculture, transportation, unemployment, a domestic Peace Corps, and other subjects.

Leadership

*Reproduced with the permission of
Mrs. James T. Berryman and the Washington Star*

November 12, 1963. Toward the end of 1963 there was criticism in the Senate of the leadership of both Senator Mansfield, as Democratic leader, and of Senator Dirksen, as Republican leader.

'Are We Class B Citizens . . . or Cabinet Officers?!?'

*Reproduced with the permission of
Mrs. James T. Berryman and the Washington Star*

November 21, 1963. Senator Dirksen is pictured as imperially and imperiously dismissing proposals to investigate the private incomes of Senators. Senate rules later required the reporting of such income.

A Member Reminisces: Problems of a Professional Writer

ALBERT W. ATWOOD

If there is anything I detest it is the habit of so many people of not defining their terms. No kind of conversation, or writing, or argument amounts to anything unless the participants, the antagonists, are talking about the same thing. But, if they define their terms the issue may clear up; there may be no dispute at all.

What do I mean by a professional writer when I talk about his problems? Of course he or she is one who makes writing their principal occupation and source of income. It is not easy however to draw the line in every case.

How about the Harvard professors who probably write more books and more articles for magazines than any of us who call ourselves professionals? These professors are professional all right, but not professional writers. Perhaps any definition means more if I give examples.

A full time newspaper reporter is in every sense a professional writer. So are members of the large literary staffs of magazines like the *Readers' Digest* and the *National Geographic*. The publicity departments of every business corporation of any size, of every government agency, of every college, university and welfare organization, has members whose chief duty is writing. They are professionals.

The line is hard to draw in some cases. A recent issue of the *New York Times Sunday Magazine* had an article by a man whom they described in a footnote as a free lance writer. But only a few weeks before he had been assistant managing editor of *Look Magazine,* which made him a free lance by going out of business.

But this does not matter to us; I am writing not primarily about how people became professional writers but what happens when they do.

Of course, my treatment cannot be complete because we do not know who does the vast amount of writing in this country, that is,

The Mind of the Millionaire

By
ALBERT W. ATWOOD, M.A.

Editorial and staff writer, *Saturday Evening Post;* former associate faculty Columbia University School of Journalism; author *Speculation and the Exchanges, Putnam's Investment Handbook, How to Get Ahead, An Elusive Panacea*

HARPER & BROTHERS PUBLISHERS
NEW YORK AND LONDON
1926

Library of Congress

Title page of 1926 book by Albert W. Atwood.

how it is allocated among the many different kinds of people. If any such breakdown exists, I have not seen it.

My guess is that the bulk of the more serious books are written by college and university professors. Anyone of any occupation or profession is likely to write one book in his lifetime, on some subject or other.

With our universal free education nearly everyone can read and also write, to a certain extent at least. And almost everyone who is educated more than the average thinks he can write for publication, whether he can or not.

And nearly all prominent and important people are expected to write, whether they have the natural ability or not.

Just because I was fortunate enough to make Phi Beta Kappa in college doesn't mean I can play the violin, but anyone who stood well in his studies in college is expected to be able to write.

Of course, both writing and playing the violin can be taught to some degree, but I submit that writing as well as violin playing needs not only some natural ability but also a decided inclination.

Of course you and I may really have in mind a free lance writer when we talk about professionals. I am one myself and naturally the problems I will speak of in this article will be those that the free lance knows exceedingly well.

This does not necessarily mean that the professional is a better writer than the great mass of millions of amateurs all around him. But it does mean that he must have more inclination to do it, more determination to do it and much courage, much guts in facing disappointments, rejections, and misunderstanding.

Your genial friend, with some other occupation, with other means of livelihood, tells you he has a wonderful idea for a book. But he doesn't get around to it. If the professional writer took that attitude he would starve.

There are always some people who feel that writing must be their way of life, even though the living be poor, just as a few others feel that playing the violin is all they want to do.

The first and perhaps greatest problem of the free lance writer is to master, in some considerable degree, the innumerable complexities of the market he is dealing with; he must adjust to it cooperatively and sympathetically.

What do I mean by the market? I mean, of course, the editors and publishers he must cope with if he is to get any of his writings "accepted", paid for and published.

This "establishment" of publishers and their editors is an incredibly vast kaleidescope; editors retire and die, and new ones of a new kind come on the scene. No individual writer can know all this or know all the units involved. But an energetic, persistent, determined person can know enough of it to make a go at free lancing. I can make my point best by a personal example.

Years ago I was slightly acquainted with another young reporter on the old *Sun* of New York. He left the paper before I did for what other occupation I did not know. We met one day years later and I discovered that he was successfully free lancing for a type of magazines I did not even know, smaller ones that paid less than the well known ones, but he turned out more copy with less work per item, with a good total result.

Whatever type of publication one writes for it seems to me as a general rule if the writer and editor meet and discuss, pro and con, the result is good. In this way ideas may evolve of advantage to both parties.

It would indicate either cowardice or the personality of Mr. Milquetoast on my part to suggest that the writer be completely subservient to the editor. In any occupation or position the individual must preserve his self-respect and dignity. But there is always the danger that if a writer becomes successful and well known he will also develop a swelled head. Modesty is a virtue even when trying to sell an editor an idea.

When anything like cordial business relations exist between editor and writer it is always a question whether the writer should persist in pressing his ideas for a story or article or seek the editor's ideas. The ideal situation is where the editor has enough confidence in a free lance to give him assignment after assignment. It is only natural that an editor favors his own ideas.

Everything depends on what kind of a reputation a writer has, of what kind the editor knows. By reputation I mean many different things. First of all, does the editor think the writer knows how to write, particularly for the editor's type of publication. Second, how reliable is the writer. Third, what good material, what new material does the writer have or can get.

In the famous Hughes-Irving case the editors and publishers were so entranced with the beat, the supposed exclusive, that they thought they were getting, that they didn't emphasize other aspects enough.

Of course, the editor learns to know about writers in many different ways. The senior vice president of a great life insurance company asked a book publisher in New York to recommend someone who could write a history of the company for its centennial celebration.

The head of the business book department of the publishers knew a free lancer who had been a college roommate of his older brother, and the insurance executive was pleased because he had read articles written by the same person.

A young man taught a course in a state university school of business administration but later in life gave up teaching for full time writing. But he had downs as well as ups, and one period was not very lush. He recalled that one of his students had become editor of a specialized magazine and asked the editor for a chance to write for it. For nearly every month for several years his articles appeared regularly. This may not be an ideal or scientific way of choosing contributors to a trade journal but personal relationships play a part in every industry and publishing is no exception.

Once the writer has a specific piece of work to do, a novel, a short story, a play, a serious book or an article, he must get his detailed ideas and material and then put it together. I know nothing about writing fiction or plays, but I have written many books and articles and while getting ideas and material is work, and often hard work, I would not describe it as a problem. It is fascinating to do.

When the editor of the *National Geographic Magazine* told me I could do an article for him on Pittsburgh, I found it no problem. Obviously one can approach Pittsburgh from many different viewpoints.

But here a real problem does arise. How complete can one be in 6,000 to 7,000 words and still appeal to general readers? Won't something be left out? Of course there will. Every publication has its limits in size, and the writer must keep within those limits. But can he be more complete and at the same time accurate within those limits? Here we have a real problem.

Not long ago I wrote a biography of a distinguished Senator, who died in 1917. A great mass of first-hand data was supplied by his family, and his work in Congress had already been put into two books. I felt I had all the material I could use. But I will always regret that I did not consult one library that might have had some data on him.

In other words the writer is never completely satisfied with what he does. He never quite reaches perfection. If he thinks he has, perhaps his real home is St. Elizabeth's.

There is much careless, sloppy writing, full of inaccuracies, but much painstaking carefulness. Once in a great while carefulness goes too far, almost to the point of disaster.

A chief villian in this respect was the charming late Miss Inez Ryan, who for years was a sort of conscience for the *National Geographic Magazine*. She found and corrected errors in article proofs that had escaped the most vigilant of editors.

Discussing in detail the origin and early history of the Lincoln Memorial with a historian of the National Park Service, he told me the panels in the ceiling had been soaked in melted wax before they had been put in place to make them more translucent, and an official book, written by the architect, bore this out.

But Miss Ryan demanded to know what kind of wax was used, paraffin perhaps. No one in Washington seemed to know and she phoned to dozens of authorities in vain. A search in the National Archives did no good, and the impatient managing editor said the issue had to go to press. An associate director of the Park Service suggested I use the phrase, "a wax like substance," and there it stands, but Miss Ryan was never pleased.

There is no union to protect the free lance writer, as there is for newspaper reporters. Editors, publishers and sponsors can be fair, just, considerate and generous, or they sometimes can, and are, prejudiced, unfair, utterly inconsiderate and unjust. There is no appeal if a book is paid for but never published for some quirk in the sponsor's mind. Stories and articles are often rejected. There is no appeal. Like the oil well producer, the free lancer strikes oil or a dry hole. No one is going to hold his hand in sympathy if the hole is dry.

Owen Penney is getting on toward 94, and the oldest member of the Washington, D. C. Rotary Club. I am not quite a year behind him, the second oldest in over 300 members.

Owen stood high as a podiatrist before he retired. But he also contributed many small articles to magazines, a part-time free lance.

We often sit together at Rotary luncheons. Last week he suddenly turned to me and said, "Writing is hard business." All I could think to say was, "Yes, writing is hard business."

But neither of us would have given up our experience as writers for anything.

BOOKS BY ALBERT W. ATWOOD

The History of the E. I. Du Pont de Nemours Powder Company: A Century of Progress. Joint author with Charles F. Rideal. 224 pages. New York, Business America. 1912.

Investment and Speculation: A description of the modern money market and analysis of factors determining the value of securities. Joint author with Thomas Conway, Jr. 443 pages. New York, Alexander Hamilton Institute. 1912.

McClure Financial Booklet. 41 pages. New York, McClure's Magazine. 1915.

The Exchanges and Speculation. 334 pages. New York, Alexander Hamilton Institute. 1917.

How to Get Ahead: Saving Money and Making It Work. 277 pages. Indianapolis, The Bobbs-Merrill Co. 1917.

Putnam's Investment Handbook: A Stimulus and a Guide to Financial Independence. 375 pages. New York, G. P. Putnam's Sons. 1919.

The Stock and Produce Exchange. 323 pages. New York, Alexander Hamilton Institute. 1921.

An Elusive Panacea: or, A Quagmire of Inheritance Taxation—And A Way Out. 132 pages. Princeton, Princeton University Press. 1924.

The Mind of the Millionaire. 263 pages. New York, Harper and Brothers. 1926.

The Great Stewardship: A Story of Life Insurance. 201 pages. New York, Harper and Brothers. 1945.

Editor. Washington Gas Light Company: Growing with Washington: The Story of Our First 100 Years, 1848–1948. By Robert R. Hershman and Edward T. Stafford. 91 pages. Washington, D. C. 1948.

These Eighty Years. 291 pages. Washington, D. C. 1961.

Gallaudet College: Its First One Hundred Years. 183 pages. Washington, D. C. 1964.

Francis G. Newlands: A Builder of the Nation. 64 pages. Washington, D. C. 1969.

Georgetown: The Twentieth Century, A Continuing Battle

MATHILDE D. WILLIAMS

A bit of popular folklore, repeated by many contemporary writers on Georgetown, is that the old port city had degenerated into a slum in the latter half of the Nineteenth Century and was rescued by the political and social elite who moved in and restored the old houses during the second World War. Like much other folklore, this has an element of truth but omits basic facts.

When reviewing the mid-Twentieth Century development of Georgetown it should be observed that the citizens had an unusually favorable situation to work with. Without minimizing the enormous efforts which have had to be put forth to preserve the town, certain factors should be kept in mind. By 1800, when the Federal City had been laid out, and was beginning to rise across Rock Creek, Georgetown was a well organized incorporated town of nearly 4,000 inhabitants with an area practically the same as it is today. The 1809 Act of Congress defining the boundaries of Georgetown placed the northern boundary east of Wisconsin Avenue at Road Street (R Street), but included a strip of land, in what was known as Beatty and Hawkins Addition to Georgetown, running up High Street (Wisconsin Avenue) as far as Mount Alto, which, lost to Georgetown today, is compensated for by the area included in Oak Hill Cemetery, Montrose Park, and Dumbarton Oaks and the adjacent parkland. Today the boundary is Rock Creek on the east, the Potomac River on the south, Foundry Branch on the west, to Reservoir Road, along Reservoir Road to Thirty-fifth Street, and along Thirty-fifth to Whitehaven Street on the north to Dumbarton Oaks. The two main commercial streets were then, as now, Bridge Street (M Street) and High Street (Wisconsin Avenue), the arteries leading east to Maryland, west to Virginia, north to Frederick, and south to a busy waterfront which connected the town with ocean traffic.

Although by the middle of the Nineteenth Century the port had declined in importance, and the confused legislative experiments of the 1870's in the District of Columbia had resulted in the loss of Georgetown's Charter and its merger with Washington City, most of its fine old houses survived through the years, carefully maintained by the descendants of the original owners, or by those who later acquired them, while many lesser dwellings belonging to small businessmen and artisans were built of sturdy stuff to last for centuries. There was some decadence during the last years of the Nineteenth Century, and in the first decade or so of the Twentieth Century, but no more, and probably less, than there was in some of the older sections of Washington.

In fact there was considerable building during this period. Its evidence may be found in the bay-window brick houses of the 1880's with their extruded brick decorations under the eaves; the big three or four-story heavily ornamented stone and brick structures of the 1890's, which mingled with the candle-extinguisher towers of the turn of the century; followed in the first decade of the Twentieth Century by the "Colonial" row house, its flat chest concealed by a pillared porch which, removed, converts it into the "typical Georgetown row house" today widely copied in some of the suburban "town house" developments.

Much of this building was carried on by speculators who would buy up several vacant lots, sometimes no more than one or two, as the original Georgetown lots averaged around 70 by 150 feet, more or less, then lay out a small so-called subdivision on which could be put a number of 20-foot-front houses. In some cases these were as little as twelve feet wide. It was this type of building that worried Miss Loulie Rittenhouse, who in 1904 circulated a petition to have the Montrose estate on R Street, then on the market, purchased by the Federal Government to be made a public park and playground. It took seven years but in 1911 Miss Loulie had her park, which with Oak Hill Cemetery and Dumbarton Oaks forms a wooded barrier between Georgetown and the City. Miss Loulie was also fighting to save Rock Creek from a scheme to convert it into a sewer, and pave it over. Happily this was dropped when, in 1915, Q Street was cut through and connected with the City via the "Buffalo Bridge" over the Creek, thus opening a fifth east-west artery through the town.

Georgetown had accepted during the *laissez faire* period some multiple dwellings, like Dumbarton Courts and The Stoddert, which had settled in comfortably among her three and four-story houses. But the threat of higher apartment houses and the encroachment of businesses on the streets off M Street and Wisconsin Avenue began to cause alarm in the 1920's. However, a new defensive tool was at hand.

In *Experiences with Zoning in Washington, D.C.*, Svante G. Lindholm remarks that: "Long before 1920 even real estate organizations tried to devise methods by which the character and value of a developed section could be protected against incongruous uses. Real estate values are to a large measure due to the uniformity and homogeneity of the improvements. The value is created by cooperative efforts, and is lessened when an incongruous use appears." New York City adopted a zoning ordinance in 1915; and the Washington Zoning Commission was established March 1, 1920.

Georgetown has one of the oldest Citizens Associations in the District of Columbia, organized in the late 1870's or early 1880's (a firm date has never been established), which by 1924 had a group of public spirited members who banded themselves together into a Home Owners Committee. In May 1924 they published an attractive pamphlet *The Future of Georgetown* which announced that: "The people of Georgetown today have the opportunity to determine its future. We can make it a constantly more and more desirable residence section, or we may let it degenerate into a crowded apartment district." To do this new zoning regulations were to be sought. "Georgetown is on the way up. During the past four or five years it has had a rebirth as a community of homes." The Home Owners, therefore, sought to have the area made a B Restricted district, and the appearance of Georgetown today attests to their success.

Although, presumably, the membership of the Georgetown Citizens Association was "men only," it may be noted that the Home Owners Committee included many wives of members; but it was not until two years later (1926) that the *Ladies' Home Journal* slogan: "Never underestimate the power of a woman" came into full flower in Georgetown when the Progressive Citizens Association was organized by and for women (although men were not excluded). For nearly forty years these organizations worked side by side, most of the time supporting identical programs, but not until December 1963 were they able to get together and adopt a Constitution acceptable to both groups although efforts toward that end had been made over a period of years.

Eternal vigilance in the matter of zoning has been essential to preserve the beauty and homogeneity of the community. By 1950 the citizens were strong enough successfully to urge Congress to pass two important pieces of legislation affecting the town: 1. An Act creating a district within the District of Columbia known as "Old Georgetown"; and 2. A Bill to purchase and preserve the Old Stone House at 3051 M Street; the second measure setting a precedent for Federal intervention to preserve a threatened site. Although the "Old Georgetown" Act gives the Commission of Fine Arts jurisdiction over new construction and remodeling within the area, some buildings worthy of preservation have been destroyed since the Act was passed.

The so-called "restoration" moved along at a steady pace during the 1930's, and was well under way in 1937, when you could buy a "beautiful modern home" newly built facing Montrose Park for around $15,000 or $16,000. But with the coming of World War II, the movement accelerated and ten years later, in 1947, an early 1900's "Colonial" with its porch removed, in the same block, was bringing $29,500. There were, however, still problems. Old buildings of great architectural merit, such as the Mountz House and the Union Hotel on M Street, were sacrificed for gas stations. Even after the Act of 1950, the Lanman-Dodge-Loomis houses on P Street were torn down by a developer in 1958, in spite of heroic efforts to save them, and in 1960 the old Academy building where students had been trained in the early 1800's for the Annapolis Naval Academy made way for a parking lot. Although property values have continued to rise, with assessments and taxes doubling and tripling, a new building is worth more to the city in taxes than an old one which would be costly to a builder to restore. Consequently a number of entrepreneurs have bought up old properties, and the city government, anxious to obtain revenue from real estate in the fashionable neighborhoods west of Rock Creek Park, has favored the new over the old.

An outstanding example of this is the demolition in 1972 of the Eighteenth Century building at 1220 Wisconsin Avenue. The "Old Georgetown" Act, Section V, says: "Nothing contained in this act shall be construed as superceding or affecting any earlier enactments relating to alteration, repair, or demolition of unsanitary or unsafe dwellings or other structures." As Colonel Robert F. Evans (Retired) of the Georgetown Citizens Association, testifying before the Commission of Fine Arts in January 1972, pointed out: "Thus an Eighteenth Century building can be permitted to run down until it is 'unsanitary' and then raised without any prior notice to the Commission."

Some notable rescues have been made in addition to that of the Old Stone House. Historic Georgetown, Inc. was organized in 1951 to save the Thomas Sim Lee House, now two buildings, at the northwest corner of 30th and M Streets. In 1959, Mr. and Mrs. Gordon Gray bought the Nathan Loughborough-Patterson Houses, east of the old Stone House, and in 1960 gave them to the Junior League. Carefully restored by Macomber and Peter, they now house the Junior

League Shop. The Old City Tavern, built in 1795, for many years O'Donnell's Drug Store, at 3206 M Street, was acquired in 1960 by the City Tavern Association for restoration as a private club. A similar happy fate has rescued an old residence at 1530 Wisconsin Avenue which has been remodeled for the Georgetown Club.

The 1960's brought three major and one minor new threats to that "future of Georgetown" so hopefully projected by the "Home Owners." Why the Whitehurst Freeway was not challenged effectively in the 1940's is not clear, but it was opened in all its unsightly length in 1949. Plans to double it *have* met bitter opposition. The whole question of the waterfront, a disgrace to all of the nation's capital, as well as to Georgetown, is very complex. All of the planning for the improvement of this important area has something of the aspect of a continual exercise in futility.

During the 1940's and 1950's, attracted by the fact that Georgetown was becoming what the late Duncan Emrich termed "Washington's best address," a number of young home owners bought property in the blocks between M Street and the River where the houses were generally small and could be bought more reasonably than those on the way to the "heights." Some quite remarkable remodeling took place in this area. A new Citizens Association, the Canal and Riverside Council, was formed in 1961, and in May 1962 presented to the National Capital Planning Commission a well-thought-out plan for the redevelopment of the waterfront. At about the same time, however, the D.C. Commissioners authorized the Highway Department to design the new Potomac River Freeway, an eight-lane divided elevated roadway to swing inland over the area from 31st and K Streets to Georgetown University, eventually linking up with the proposed George Washington Parkway. Urban renewal for the waterfront was also suggested—and opposed—and the Committee of 100 urged the National Capital Planning Commission to produce and develop a plan for the waterfront for single family and park use. Cloethiel W. Smith, who has her office in the area, came up with a plan for depressing the Freeway.

The succeeding three years produced much discussion but little action until early in 1965 when President Lyndon Johnson sent to Congress on March 3, "a far-reaching message on Cities calling for action to improve and upgrade our urban environment 'for the enrichment of the life of man.'" On March 22, 1965, the Georgetown Waterfront Symposium Committee held a Symposium on "The

Photograph by Mary Mitchell

Wheatley Row, 1018 Twenty-ninth Street, N. W., looking toward the Whitehurst Freeway and the Georgetown waterfront.

Photograph by Mary Mitchell

View from the south terminus of Wisconsin Avenue at K Street, N. W., looking toward the Whitehurst Freeway and the Georgetown waterfront.

Georgetown Waterfront Problems and Possibilities" in the State Department Auditorium, moderated by Wolf Von Eckardt and with such speakers as Secretary of the Interior Stewart Udall; Constantine Doxiadis, the Greek city planner; Hugh Newell Jacobsen, a distinguished local architect; Francis D. Lethbridge, active in rebuilding the Southwest Urban Renewal Area; Walter Posen, Assistant to the Secretary of the Interior; and John Carl Warnecke, architect of the Lafayette Square preservation project. Beyond its stimulating discussions there was no immediate impact on the problem. In June 1965 the Georgetown Planning Council was formed with a membership of some thirty-five architects and planners who proposed to seek Congressional designation of the waterfront as a National Historic Site and the replacement of the Whitehurst Elevated Freeway with an eight lane tunnel under the Potomac. Then Highway Director Thomas F. Airis unveiled a plan which "would combine the natural beauty of the Potomac River shoreline with the city's first attempt to utilize the empty space beneath the freeways for commercial or possibly a residential purpose," this to be achieved by doubling the present freeway to connect with the proposed Three Sisters Bridge, "constructing a park and promenade along the river and using the space under the freeway for shops and houses."

A group of private developers in the fall of 1965 proposed a highrise development for the area below the Canal from Key Bridge to Rock Creek, contending that the land is too costly to provide a commensurate return on town houses alone and pointing out that present zoning would permit a "wall of office buildings nine stories tall."

On December 30, 1965, the press announced that the Highway Department had chosen Constantine Doxiadis "to try to bring a little Greek glory to Georgetown's seedy waterfront," and in early 1966 Wolf Von Eckardt told his readers that Doxiadis was dazzling everyone with thirteen carefully worked-out alternatives, of which tunneling was the best solution: "tunneling four lanes first, and then putting the present elevated underground."

During the summer of 1967 the Commission of Fine Arts assigned a team of college professors and students to make a survey of the waterfront, particularly to discover buildings worthy of preservation, date them, and find something concerning their history through the years, to be made part of the on-going Historic American Buildings Survey. The two volumes which resulted are: *Georgetown Architecture: The Waterfront*, 1968; and *Georgetown Historic Waterfront, Washington, D.C.: A Review of Canal and Riverside Architecture* by Constance Werner. Both are handsomely illustrated.

The Philip Stern Family Fund gave the money for two young Yale architects to survey the waterfront and make recommendations. As reported in the press: "They're convinced the waterfront could be transformed into a valuable urban amenity by leaving it pretty much the way it is." They found that the "silos of the flour plant, the diagonal conveyor belts of the sand and gravel company and the storage bins of the waterfront's cement factory are terrific pieces of urban sculpture. We're lucky to have them. The rendering plant stinks and should go, but the others not only pay taxes, they provide beautiful and simple forms of a sufficiently monumental scale to stand against the sweep of the River and the elevated Expressway."

In May 1968, Kenneth Hudson, Professor at the University of Technology in Bath, England, who termed himself an "industrial archeologist," examined the waterfront in company with the Yale architects and found himself largely in agreement with them. The waterfront, he declared, should be a place for the people who live there. "The industrial buildings, smoke stacks and all," he suggested, "might be put to all kinds of temporary, experimental uses, such as dance and sport halls and lots of restaurants and art studios to see how people respond . . . That way you won't have to agree on any firm definitive and irrevocable plan on what to do with the waterfront. It would be a good antidote to decision making." This proposal to extend the M Street Strip to the waterfront was not taken very seriously, although elements of it may have been reflected in an almost immediate development.

In the meantime, in a ceremony accompanied by a Fife and Drum Corps and considerable pomp and circumstance, Secretary of the Interior Udall presented to Commissioner John B. Duncan the documents declaring Georgetown a National Historical Landmark under the Historic Sites Act, before a group of interested citizens who had fought long and hard to preserve the town, on a gray 7th of October 1967, alongside the Canal at the landingplace park, where a plaque was subsequently mounted to commemorate the event.

In the autumn of 1968 the first proposal to utilize an old building, a mide-Nineteenth Century warehouse on the Canal at 31st Street, in combination with new construction, was successfully projected by architect Arthur Cotton Moore in his design for Canal Square. His statement that the builders, Charles B. Coyer, of Washington, and William B. Gray, Jr., of Baltimore, agreed with him that: "We respect the area and we want to minimize any effect on it" may be noted in connection with subsequent developments.

The Citizens Association of Georgetown published in 1969 *Georgetown 1980: A Program for the Coming Decade*. This fifty-four page document, compiled by a committee of members chaired by John M. Patterson, sets forth the "Assumptions, Objectives, and Recommendations" for Georgetown's immediate future: "As things go in this imperfect world, Georgetown can be made to sound idyllic... On the other hand, Georgetown has its... detractors who call it uninvolved... Georgetown also has its problems. The major ones are speculative builders, the roads lobby, and the liquor lobby. None of the three would admit to being called detractors of Georgetown. Instead builders talk in terms of 'progress' by which too many may mean the maximum buck for the minimum space; the road people of the importance of 'movement of people,' by which is meant more roads and more automobiles; and the 'importance of free enterprise' in the eyes of the liquor lobby too often means that, if the citizens of a community rise up in wrath against 13 bars and liquor stores on one block next to a residence area, they are somehow guilty of a sin against the Republic." For the waterfront they proposed: "To use all legal means, informed public opinion, zoning regulations and other steps to assure that buildings from K to M Street do not violate the character of Georgetown."

This resolve was challenged when, on July 30, 1970, the Inland Steel Corporation of Chicago announced a $100 million redevelopment on the waterfront, on slightly more than eight acres of land between 30th and 31st Streets from the Georgetown Channel of the River to the Chesapeake and Ohio Canal, "quietly" assembled by the developers of Canal Square and employing the same architect.

A new study of the waterfront appeared in December 1970, a *Georgetown Feasibility Study for Joint Public/Private Development*, prepared by the Urban Design and Development Corporation, established by the American Institute of Architects, over the signature of Ralph G. Schwarz. In a critical review of this in the Washington *Post*, Wolf Von Eckardt wrote: "This latest and worst proposal, I am afraid, would transform the Georgetown Waterfront into a Left Bank Rosslyn." The involvements of four plans for the controversial Potomac River Freeway, including the disposal of the Whitehurst elevated Freeway, delayed any action during 1971.

In April 1971, President Richard Nixon requested a new "overall" plan for the waterfront: "New roads and commercial development threaten to change the waterfront forever piecemeal... The purpose of the plan will be to insure the preservation of historic buildings, to increase park lands, to save the open vistas of Roosevelt Island, and to provide for the harmonious development of public, commercial, and residential facilities."

At the end of January 1972, a coordinating committee under the direction of Charles Conrad, Executive Director of the National Capital Planning Commission, awarded a $250,000 contract to Wallace, McHarg, Roberts and Todd, of Philadelphia, an architectural and planning firm, to make a comprehensive study of the waterfront "concentrating on such problems as the size of allowable buildings, traffic systems, and the relationship between residential, recreational and commercial uses;" followed by a "comprehensive development plan prepared under Section 7501 of the District's Zoning regulations."

There was an intensification of Georgetown's problems when the Commission of Fine Arts approved the design for Dodge Center, another 90-foot building for office and retail use, between Cecil Place and Wisconsin Avenue adjoining the old Dodge Warehouses, and "Georgetown Inland," as it was now designated, threatened to go ahead with its part of the "Chinese Wall." Although Mayor Walter E. Washington at first yielded to the appeal of the Georgetown Citizens Association, which had requested a two-year moritorium on large scale development, and issued on June 29, 1972, a one-hundred-and-twenty day emergency order, downzoning the area between M Street and the Potomac River from its 90-foot light and heavy industrial height limit to a 40-foot residential height, the D.C. Zoning Commission on September 28, 1972, lifted the temporary ban and cleared the way for initial construction of the massive development proposed by Georgetown Inland.

The Georgetown Citizens Association carried an appeal to the U.S. District Court, only to be turned down by Judge George L. Hart, Jr. on October 13, 1972. A second appeal was denied on November 17.

Meanwhile a one hundred page study, the first phase of the three phase *Georgetown Waterfront Area Study* by the Georgetown Planning Group, was given to the National Capital Planning Commission on November 2, 1972. Fortified by this, the Georgetown Citizens Association carried its suit to the U.S. Court of Appeals, which, on November 24, 1972, "enjoined high-rise development of the Georgetown waterfront" until February 1, 1973, "by which time it expects to rule on [the] citizens group's challenge seeking to limit and control growth there."

On the eastern periphery of the town a small cloud arose in the

Photograph by Mary Mitchell
Pedestrians passing the entrance of the Farmers and Mechanics Branch of the Riggs National Bank at Wisconsin Avenue and M Street, N. W.

early 1960's when developers sought a zoning change from residential to high-rise apartment on a strip of land along Rock Creek on Mill Road entered from 27th and Q Streets. This is the old Methodist Burying Ground, owned by the Dumbarton Methodist Church and the descendants of the Ladies Female Union Band, who in 1854 bought an acre and a half of the three acre tract, adjoining the Methodist Burying Ground, for the burial of free Negroes. The Dumbarton Methodist Church acquired the land for its burial ground in 1809, but after the laying out of Oak Hill Cemetery in 1850 removals to Oak Hill caused a virtual abandonment of the small plot by the Methodists; and in the 1870's it was turned over on a ninety-nine year lease to Mount Zion, an all-Negro Methodist Church which had broken away from the Dumbarton Avenue Church in 1816. Both cemeteries have been neglected for many years, although the last burial in the Mount Zion portion was in 1954, and use was not forbidden by the Health Department until 1967 when the agitation for rezoning was well under way.

At its inception the high-rise scheme was opposed by the Secretary of the Interior, the Commission of Fine Arts, and the National Capital Planning Commission. The present R-B1 zoning was deemed "essential to achieving the highly desirable historic objective of Old Georgetown, and preservation of the scenic value of Rock Creek" as it is "one of the most narrow buffer zones between Rock Creek and private property throughout the entire length of the park."

Over the years seven attempts have been made to have the land rezoned, including a hearing before the Zoning Commission on March 3, 1971. In the latest development the Afro-American Bicentennial Corporation, in co-operation with the National Park Service, has proposed to develop the site, presumably without removal of those interred there, into a national black memorial park with a small museum and amphitheater.

Far more serious to the "future of Georgetown" is the cloud darkening the west end where the long shadows of Georgetown University are encroaching on the town. As early as 1961, when it filed plans for the high-rise library at 37th and Prospect Streets, the University published plans for 1970, and the year 2000, which would permit erecting University buildings outside the present grounds on property already owned by the institution. In August 1964, the University gained a "new paragraph 3101.46" in the regulations of the Zoning Commission which would allow: 1. The erection of high-rise institutional buildings on 35th and 36th Streets; and 2. Turning into non-residential use any property owned by the University within a "reasonable distance" of their campus—which would be moved to 35th Street. They would close to traffic 37th Street, N, O, and P Streets west of 36th, leaving Prospect Street the only open street. "They will then build a wall along the west side of 35th Street and absorb all the area into their campus." The Foundation for Historic Georgetown, organized in 1966, has set up the Georgetown Corporation to handle the business of raising funds to buy property not yet owned by the University in the threatened blocks. Ironically enough, the University had 90 acres of vacant land west of Georgetown as of April 1967.

The past six years have witnessed another development which may be more serious to the maintenance of Georgetown as one of the most desirable places to live in the District of Columbia. It began with the rise of night-life on M Street, with the consequent development of "The Strip," the hassles over liquor licenses, and the invasion of teen-agers from Virginia and Maryland in response to the District's then more liberal drinking laws. Summer nights were made difficult for those living on the streets off the west end of M, with crowds rapidly spreading up Wisconsin Avenue. The nation-wide "hippie" movement among young people which crossed the country from California and at first concentrated in Washington around Dupont Circle soon rolled into Georgetown. "Hippie" shops replaced a number of antique and specialty shops on both M Street and Wisconsin Avenue, one of the latter opening up just below Reservoir Road. Drug peddling among these groups served to intensify the problem.

Walking on Wisconsin Avenue or M Street in late 1972 the "square" pedestrian or shopper cannot but feel as though he were in the midst of some sort of carnival, surrounded by costumed revelers, street venders, and beggars. This view is upheld by the numbers of area visitors who pour into Georgetown on week ends to watch the "hippie parade." That this spectacle is part of a nation-wide counter-culture does not lessen its impact on Georgetown.

During the half-dozen years or so of this new development, various efforts have been made to ameliorate the social evils attendant on such a concentration of youth and "street people" in so small an area. *Georgetown 1980* expressed the view: "Unless loitering and public nuisance laws are strengthened and enforced, crime on the M Street Strip, on Wisconsin Avenue and on nearby side streets will increase, and the influx of homosexuals and street drug pushers will rise."

Grace Church, Episcopal, established in 1855 as a mission to workers on the Canal and waterfront on land given by Henry D. Cooke, appropriately embraced its mission to a modern group in need of help. In 1971 an "Order of Amazing Grace" was founded to carry on an experimental program with the "street people," which had the sanction of the Washington Episcopal Diocese. It embraced a coffee house where they could come together and rap, a mail and messenger center, and in cases of extreme emergency a "pad."

The *Georgetown Spectator* of August 5, 1971, observed: "Grace Church is known for its work with the drug scene in Washington and with youngsters who have run away from homes in the suburbs and cities near Washington." However, the *Washington Diocese* for December 1972 says only: "The Amazing Grace Survival Center at Grace Church, Georgetown, which is now funded by the Office of Economic Opportunity, operates a job referral service."

The Lutheran Church at Wisconsin Avenue and Volta Place houses the Washington Free Clinic in its basement. This was "set up in 1968 to provide free care to the Washington Free Community— the youth as well as the adults who for diversified reasons left the mainstream of society in search of alternative life styles." Doctors, nurses, psychiatrists and social workers from the National Institutes of Health, St. Elizabeth's Hospital, and other medical centers work as volunteers at the Free Clinic. "As well as psychiatric, gynecological, pediatric, and general medical care, the clinic offers birth control classes, draft and pregnancy counseling, rap sessions, free food and used clothing. Started with a $5,000 grant from the Stearn Foundation it now depends (1971) on donations." In March 1971 it was said to have a line of sixty to seventy people during the hours of 7 to 11 p.m.

Some murmurs are heard of "getting out of Georgetown" when only yesterday the dearest wish was to get in. One aspect of this is the conversion of single-family dwellings into rooming houses, which in Georgetown take the form of dormitories for college students, fraternity houses, and apartments for younger government employees. According to Georgetown Planning Group statistics there was a four and five-tenths per cent increase in in renter-occupied dwellings in the decade 1960–1970, with a third of the houses owner-occupied. Of the two-thirds renter-occupied, a great many are high-rental properties occupied by government officials. However, these, like the students and younger government employees, are often transients with only a temporary interest in the community.

A somewhat ambivalent attitude appears to prevail among some of those working hardest for preservation. This was expressed as early as 1969 by a writer in *Georgetown 1980:* "Georgetown's success in preserving its historic buildings and visual charm paradoxically poses a threat. As other American landmarks disappear Georgetown will attract more and more tourists ... who aggravate traffic, invade privacy, and promote the increased proliferation of shops, restaurants, bars, and joints. Tourism can be a curse rather than a blessing."

The Job of Editor

Comments in acknowledging the award of a Certificate of Commendation by the American Association for State and Local History "for the scholarly editing of the Records of the Columbia Historical Society"

FRANCIS COLEMAN ROSENBERGER

I can say little more than an embarrassed "Thank You."

Whatever there is of merit in the *Records* is to the credit of the authors whose interest and scholarship make the volumes possible.

I like to believe that I am probably more aware than is anyone else of all the editorial shortcomings of the volumes. The finished book is never quite the volume which the editor hopes at the outset that it will be.

I think of the comments, which Carroll Coleman once called to my attention, by the great American printer D. B. Updike on praise which Updike received on the Book of Common Prayer which he and Bertram Goodhue designed. After Updike had mentioned some of the shortcomings which he saw in the book, he said: "We were congratulated, we blushed, and our confusion was mistaken for modesty, so we were further congratulated."

But, however blushingly, I do value your congratulations and your good opinion.

Let me add a word on the job of editor as I see it.

It is self-evident that the quality of the *Records* can never be higher than the quality of the manuscripts which we receive. But we cannot relax and wait, as the editor of a magazine once suggested, for manuscripts to come over the transom.

Delivered before the Columbia Historical Society on December 14, 1971.

Columbia Historical Society Collection

Francis Coleman Rosenberger at the grave of Robert Louis Stevenson, Samoa, November 5, 1960, four months after his confirmation as Editor of the Columbia Historical Society by the Board of Managers on June 30, 1960.

There are scholars who are doing excellent work in dozens of subjects related to the intellectual and cultural history of this area. It is our job imaginatively to seek them out. There are many others who could be doing excellent work. It is our job to encourage them to undertake it.

And for both, we can provide a hospitable environment in the *Records* for the publication of their work.

We have never been able to pay for manuscripts. But we can provide something which is also important for scholars: publication in good company, with care in copyreading and in proofreading and in indexing and in the selection and reproduction of illustrations, and with concern, in William Targ's phrase, for "those elements which help to maintain the book's intrinsic dignity: good paper and type . . . appropriate and durable bindings"—in short a format which shows respect for the contents.

If we do this, I believe that we will find an increasing willingness by scholars, old and young, established and beginning, to submit their work for consideration for the *Records*.

Photograph by Sandra Collum

A portion of an exhibit assembled by Robert A. Truax, Librarian of the Columbia Historical Society, December 1971, honoring Francis Coleman Rosenberger.

And if this is so, the next forty-odd volumes of the *Records* will be far better than the first.

Thank you.

BIOGRAPHICAL MATERIAL ON FRANCIS COLEMAN ROSENBERGER

Francis Coleman Rosenberger: A List of Published Writings, 1938–1958. With an Introduction by Millicent Barton Rex, Ph.D. (Washington, D.C., 1959.) 48 pages.

"Virginia Writers: Francis Coleman Rosenberger," with portrait sketch by Carl Nyquist, *Richmond Times-Dispatch,* June 12, 1949.

Reviews with portrait sketch or photograph: *Washington Post,* August 1, 1943; *Richmond Times-Dispatch,* July 2, 1944; *Richmond Times-Dispatch,* November 14, 1948; *Washington Post,* November 14, 1948; *Washington Star,* November 28, 1948; *New York Star,* December 20, 1948; Fort Worth, Texas, *Star,* January 9, 1949; Lynchburg, Virginia, *News,* September 7, 1952; *University of Virginia Alumni News,* October 1952; *Richmond Times-Dispatch,* January 25, 1953; Norfolk *Virginian-Pilot,* February 1, 1953; *The Commonwealth,* Richmond, February 1953.

Other significant reviews of his work: *Nashville Tennessean,* August 22, 1943; *Saturday Review of Literature,* March 22, 1947; *Washington Times-Herald,* November 14, 1948; *New York Herald Tribune Book Review,* November 21, 1948; *New York Times Book Review,* November 28, 1948; *Chicago Tribune,* November 28, 1948; *New Orleans Times-Picayune,* December 5, 1948; *San Francisco Chronicle,* December 26, 1948; *Virginia Magazine of History and Biography,* April 1949; *San Francisco Chronicle,* February 3, 1952; *New York Times Book Review,* March 16, 1952; *New York Herald Tribune Book Review,* June 8, 1952; *Washington Post,* January 25, 1953; *New York Herald Tribune,* January 31, 1953; *New York Herald Tribune Book Review,* February 1, 1953; *Philadelphia Inquirer,* February 1, 1953; *Atlanta Constitution,* February 1, 1953; *Boston Herald,* February 2, 1953; *Los Angeles Times,* February 8, 1953; *Chicago Tribune,* February 8, 1953; *Houston Chronicle,* February 8, 1953; *Washington Star,* February 8, 1953; *New York Times Book Review,* February 15, 1953; *Pittsburgh Press,* February 15, 1953; *The Nation,* February 21, 1953; *Los Angeles News,* February 22, 1953; *Christian Science Monitor,* April 4, 1953; *The New Republic,* April 13, 1953; *Virginia Quarterly Review,* Spring 1953.

Biographical Directories:

The Monthly Supplement, Who's Who, July 1953.
Directory of the American Political Science Association, 1953.
Who's Who in the South and Southwest, 1954, 1956, 1959, 1961, 1963, 1965.
Virginia Authors' Yearbook, 1956, 1957, 1958.
American Men of Science: The Social and Behavioral Sciences, 1956, 1962, 1968.
Congressional Staff Directory, 1959 and subsequent annual volumes.
Virginia Lives, 1964.
Dictionary of International Biography, 1967.
Class Book of the Law Class of 1940 University of Virginia, 1970.
Virginia Authors: Past and Present, 1972.
International Who's Who in Poetry, 1972.
Personalities of the South, 1972.
Who's Who in Government, 1972.
Who's Who in American Politics, scheduled for 1973 publication.
Contemporary Authors, scheduled for 1973 publication.

Members of the Society, 1972

COMPILED BY R. J. McCARTHY

LIFE MEMBERS

Allen, John E.
5520 S. W. 78th Street
Apartment D
Miami, Florida 33143

Barlow, Joel
888-16th Street, N. W.
Washington, D. C. 20006

Bernstein, Leo M.
1801 K Street, N. W.
Washington, D. C. 20006

Birely, William C.
P. O. Box 965
Silver Spring, Maryland 20910

Bittinger, Donald S.
3910 Livingston Street, N. W.
Washington, D. C. 20015

Chatelaine, Leon, Jr.
1632 K Street, N. W.
Washington, D. C. 20006

Cocke, Mrs. Edmund Randolph
Hotel Weyamoke
Farmville, Virginia 23901

Cromelin, Paul
4201 Massachusetts Avenue, N. W.
Washington, D. C. 20016

Dawson, Mrs. William
Blue Hill, Maine 04614

Delaplaine, Edward S.
Frederick, Maryland 21701

Eckles, Miss Amelia Alice
2424 California Street, N. W.
Washington, D. C. 20008

Eckles, Mrs. Anita Heurich
2424 California Street, N. W.
Washington, D. C. 20008

Eckles, Charles E.
2424 California Street, N. W.
Washington, D. C. 20008

Eckles, Geoffrey Alan
2 Wildwood Drive
Dover, Massachusetts 02030

Eckles, Stanley Heurich
5201 White Flint Drive
Kensington, Maryland 20795

Evans, Mrs. Benjamin C., Jr.
3033 Woodland Drive, N. W.
Washington, D. C. 20008

Evans, Miss Karla Harrison
3033 Woodland Drive, N. W.
Washington, D. C. 20008

Evans, Miss Louise Bowler
3033 Woodland Drive, N. W.
Washington, D. C. 20008

Gibson, John T.
4830 Glenbrook Road, N. W.
Washington, D. C. 20016

Glover, Charles Carroll, Jr.
3201 New Mexico Avenue, N. W.
Washington, D. C. 20016

Glover, Charles C., IV
5235 Duvall Drive, N. W.
Westmoreland Hills
Washington, D. C. 20016

Gordon, Spencer, Jr.
7416 Ridgewood Avenue
Chevy Chase, Maryland 20015

Harrison, General and Mrs. Eugene L.
Mandalay Point
Clearwater Beach, Florida 33515

Hartson, Nelson T.
815 Connecticut Avenue, N. W.
Washington, D. C. 20006

Heurich, Christian, Jr.
1111-34th Street, N. W.
Washington, D. C. 20007

Heurich, Mrs. Christian, Jr.
6405 Elmwood Road
Chevy Chase, Maryland 20015

Heurich, Christian, III
6405 Elmwood Road
Chevy Chase, Maryland 20015

Heurich, Gary
6405 Elmwood Road
Chevy Chase, Maryland 20015

Howland, Richard H.
1516-33rd Street, N. W.
Washington, D. C. 20007

Kennedy, Mrs. John Thomas
3820 Reno Road, N. W.
Washington, D. C. 20008

Kennedy, Miss Marthajane
3820 Reno Road, N. W.
Washington, D. C. 20008

Keyser, Mrs. Carl S.
4700 Connecticut Avenue, N. W.
Apartment 401
Washington, D. C. 20008

Knox, Mrs. Katharine McCook
3259 N Street, N. W.
Washington, D. C. 20007

Kulberg, Raoul
3916 McKinley Street, N. W.
Washington, D. C. 20015

Lippitt, T. Perry
6004 Corbin Road
Washington, D. C. 20016

Martin, Mrs. Corinne Heurich
5837 Marbury Road
Bethesda, Maryland 20014

May, Paul
May's Landing
00 Beach Drive
Sherwood Forest, Maryland 21405

McCarron, Miss Catherine H.
1312-21st Street, N. W.
Washington, D. C. 20036

Mooers, Edwin A., Jr.
5005 Belt Road, N. W.
Washington, D. C. 20016

Norton, Miss Susan
1227-31st Street, N. W.
Washington, D. C. 20007

Phillips, Reverend Hugh
Mt. St. Mary's College
Emmittsburg, Maryland 21727

Plotner, Mrs. Charles H.
4808-46th Street, N. W.
Washington, D. C. 20016

Pomeroy, Miss Winifred
4550 Connecticut Avenue, N. W.
Apartment 708
Washington, D. C. 20008

Saul, Miss Edith Ray
3632 Prospect Avenue, N. W.
Washington, D. C. 20007

Members of the Society

Sinclair, A. Leftwich, Jr.
Alexander House
Moorefield, West Virginia 26836

Symington, Donald L.
3030 Chain Bridge Road, N. W.
Washington, D. C. 20016

Symington, Lloyd, Jr.
3030 Chain Bridge Road, N. W.
Washington, D. C. 20016

West, L. Perry
1805-15th Street, N. W.
Washington, D. C. 20007

Wiggins, J. Russell
Carlton Cove
Brooklin, Maine 04616

Winchcole, Mrs. Dorothy Clark
2401 Calvert Street, N. W.
Apartment 911
Washington, D. C. 20008

Zalles, Mrs. Rose Saul
3133 Connecticut Avenue, N. W.
Washington, D. C. 20008

HONORARY MEMBER

Colket, Meredith B., Jr.
Western Reserve Historical Society
10825 East Boulevard
Cleveland, Ohio 44106

COMPLIMENTARY MEMBERS

Truett, Colonel Randall B.
1622 N. Harrison Street
Arlington, Virginia 22205

Wall, C. C.
Curator
Mount Vernon, Virginia 22121

Wensinger, Mrs. Walter
4000 Massachusetts Avenue, N. W.
Washington, D. C. 20016

ANNUAL MEMBERS

LIBRARIES AND INSTITUTIONAL MEMBERS ARE NOT LISTED

A

Alexander, Mrs. Vida Ord
2033 Rosemont Avenue, N. W.
Washington, D. C. 20010

Anderson, David R.
2271 North Quincy Street
Arlington, Virginia 22207

Archbold, Mr. and Mrs. John D.
3905 Reservoir Road, N. W.
Washington, D. C. 20007

Atwood, Albert W.
Sheraton Park Hotel
Apartment I-648

2660 Woodley Road, N. W.
Washington, D. C. 20008

Avery, Rev. William G.
St. Columbas Church
White Earth, Minnesota 56591

Ayers, Mr. and Mrs. Robert R.
1100 Orchard Way
Silver Spring, Maryland 20904

B

Bacon, Mrs. Robert Low
1801 F Street, N. W.
Washington, D. C. 20006

Baker, Mr. and Mrs. George E.
223 St. Ives Drive
Severna Park, Maryland 21146

Baker, O. Kenneth
2405 South Dinwiddie Street
Arlington, Virginia 22206

Barber, Mrs. Grace H.
4600 Connecticut Avenue, N. W.
Apartment 729
Washington, D. C. 20008

Barry, Rexford G.
3636-16th Street, N. W.
Apartment B-1057
Washington, D. C. 20010

Beckman, Miss Ellen J.
7204 Adelphi Road
Hyattsville, Maryland 20792

Bernhardt, Mr. and Mrs. C. M.
1727 Massachusetts Avenue, N. W.
Apartment 507
Washington, D. C. 20036

Beers, Henry P.
2372 North Quincy Street
Arlington, Virginia 22207

Belin, Captain and Mrs. Peter
1623-28th Street, N. W.
Washington, D. C. 20007

Benington, Edward W.
7907 Kent Road
Alexandria, Virginia 22308

Billings, Mr. and Mrs. E. E.
3313 Que Street, N. W.
Washington, D. C. 20007

Birely, Mr. and Mrs. Victor M.
3315 Wisconsin Avenue, N. W.
Washington, D. C. 20016

Bishop, Miss Purnie
1910 Kalorama Road, N. W.
Washington, D. C. 20009

Blue, Mrs. William L.
3316 N Street, N. W.
Washington, D. C. 20007

Blum, Mr. and Mrs. Robert
3707 Williams Lane
Chevy Chase, Maryland 20015

Boarman, Marshall
1 Washington Circle, N. W.
Washington, D. C. 20037

Bonsal, Philip W.
3142 P Street, N. W.
Washington, D. C. 20007

Borchert, James
7034 Carroll Avenue
Takoma Park, Maryland 20012

Bornet, David
4201 Cathedral Avenue, N. W.
Washington, D. C. 20016

Brabner-Smith, John W.
University Club
1135-16th Street, N. W.
Washington, D. C. 20036

Bradley, Frederick M.
815 Connecticut Avenue, N. W.
Washington, D. C. 20006

Brearley, Mr. and Mrs. J. Meigs
5406 Goldsboro Road
Bethesda, Maryland 20034

Breen, James
560 N Street, S. W.
Apartment N-714
Washington, D. C. 20024

Briggs, Mrs. Crenshaw
2613 Dumbarton Avenue, N. W.
Washington, D. C. 20007

Briggs, Mrs. Uhler
1421 Massachusetts Avenue, N. W.
Washington, D. C. 20005

Members of the Society

Brooks, Mrs. Thomas R.
3927 Oliver Street
Chevy Chase, Maryland 20015

Brown, Miss Flora
3244-38th Street, N. W.
Washington, D. C. 20016

Brown, Mr. and Mrs. Theodore E.
4311-18th Street, N. W.
Washington, D. C. 20011

Budesheim, Norman E.
8408-11th Avenue
Silver Spring, Maryland 20903

Burgess, Howard B.
U. S. Soldiers' Home
P. O. Box 573
Washington, D. C. 20315

Burke, Thomas F.
1625 I Street, N. W.
Washington, D. C. 20006

Burns, Mrs. Charles E., Jr.
P. O. Box 7
Great Falls, Virginia 22066

Burson, Miss Freda F.
2222 I Street, N. W.
Apartment 708
Washington, D. C. 20007

C

Cantacuzene, Madame
2126 Connecticut Avenue, N. W.
Washington, D. C. 20008

Carmichael, Dr. and Mrs. Leonard
4520 Hoban Road, N. W.
Washington, D. C. 20007

Casanges, Alexander
103 West Montgomery Avenue
Rockville, Maryland 20850

Chandler, Douglas R.
2220-20th Street, N. W.
Washington, D. C. 20009

Charlick, Carl
1734 P Street, N. W.
Washington, D. C. 20036

Chase, Miss Emily T.
6200 Oregon Avenue, N. W.
Washington, D. C. 20015

Chatel, Mrs. Millicent
1210-30th Street, N. W.
Washington, D. C. 20007

Childs, Mr. and Mrs. James B.
1221 Newton Street, N. E.
Washington, D. C. 20017

Church, Lloyd E.
8218 Wisconsin Avenue
Bethesda, Maryland 20014

Clampitt, J. Wesley, Jr.
3901 Connecticut Avenue, N. W.
Washington, D. C. 20008

Clapp, Mrs. Verner W.
4 West Irving Street
Chevy Chase, Maryland 20015

Clark, Mr. and Mrs. Charles C., Jr.
11683 North Shore Drive
Reston, Virginia 22070

Clark, David Sanders
3631 Tilden Street, N. W.
Washington, D. C. 20008

Cobb, Miss Josephine
Hunt's Point Road
Box 300-B
Rural Route 1
Cape Elizabeth, Maine 04107

Colbert, Mrs. Lewis F.
2910 Dartmouth Avenue, North
St. Petersburg, Florida 33713

Cole, David J. H.
816 Massachusetts Avenue, N. E.
Washington, D. C. 20002

Cole, John Y.
122 Sixth Street, N. E.
Washington, D. C. 20002

Coleman, Mrs. Clark E.
Box 137
Mayetta, Kansas 66509

Coleman, Mrs. Dorothy S.
4315 Van Ness Street, N. W.
Washington, D. C. 20016

Coll, Mrs. Helen F.
National Savings and Trust Co.
15th and New York Avenue, N. W.
Washington, D. C. 20005

Collier, Theodore M.
1660 Lanier Place, N. W.
Washington, D. C. 20009

Corliss, Carlton J.
2218 Thomasville Road
Tallahassee, Florida 32303

Cowden, Mrs. Mignon S.
4415 Bradley Lane
Chevy Chase, D. C. 20015

Cox, H. Bartholomew
11305 Riverview Road
Oxon Hill, Maryland 20022

Craig, Peter S.
3406 Macomb Street, N. W.
Washington, D. C. 20016

Criswell, Howard D.
5711 Nebraska Avenue, N. W.
Washington, D. C. 20015

Croghan, Mr. and Mrs. John A.
208 Virginia Avenue
Alexandria, Virginia 22302

Crouch, Richard E.
2624 North 18th Street
Arlington, Virginia 22201

Cumming, Mr. and Mrs. Hugh S., Jr.
2811 O Street, N. W.
Washington, D. C. 20007

Curl, Miss Lottie M.
4550 Connecticut Avenue, N. W.
Apartment 312
Washington, D. C. 20008

Curry, Miss Mary F.
2031 Huidekoper Place
Washington, D. C. 20007

D

Daiker, Miss Virginia
9112 Volunteer Drive
Alexandria, Virginia 22309

Davison, Mrs. Donald A.
4889 MacArthur Boulevard, N. W.
Washington, D. C. 20007

Dawson, Mrs. Alva
2017 O Street, N. W.
Washington, D. C. 20036

Day, Mr. and Mrs. Henry B.
3252 O Street, N. W.
Washington, D. C. 20007

Day, Dr. Robert
2000 Massachusetts Avenue, N. W.
Washington, D. C. 20036

Deeble, Miss Elizabeth
Norwood
Sandy Springs, Maryland 20860

de Laittre, John
516 San Ysidro Road
Santa Barbara, California 93108

de Schweinitz, Miss Dorothea
1208-30th Street, N. W.
Washington, D. C. 20007

Dewey, Charles S.
3539 Williamsburg Lane, N. W.
Washington, D. C. 20008

Dickey, James W.
  Dickey Farm
  Sykesville, Maryland 21784

Diedel, Miss C. Virginia
  2900 Connecticut Avenue, N. W.
  Washington, D. C. 20008

Dixon, James L.
  1312-19th Street, N. W.
  Washington, D. C. 20036

Dodge, Mrs. Charles H.
  3310 N Street, N. W.
  Washington, D. C. 20007

Dorman, John Frederick
  2022 Columbia Road, N. W.
  Washington, D. C. 20009

Douglas, Mr. and Mrs. H. H.
  626 South Washington Street
  Falls Church, Virginia 22046

Doyle, Miss Mary Joan
  5410 Connecticut Avenue, N. W.
  Washington, D. C. 20015

Draper, Mrs. Henry White
  1521-35th Street, N. W.
  Washington, D. C. 20007

Drefs, Mrs. Arthur
  39 Glen Eagle Drive
  Clayton, Missouri 63105

Drury, F. Eugene
  3133 Connecticut Avenue, N. W.
  Washington, D. C. 20008

Dunn, Mr. and Mrs. Raymond H.
  914 Somerset Place
  Hyattsville, Maryland 20783

Dwyer, Mrs. Vernon James
  1972 Virginia Avenue
  McLean, Virginia 22101

E

Eagan, Mrs. Thomas L.
  7000 Maple Avenue
  Chevy Chase, Maryland 20015

Edwald, Henry P., Jr.
  4007 Connecticut Avenue, N. W.
  Washington, D. C. 20008

Ehrenberg, Ralph E.
  9219 Bells Mill Road
  Potomac, Maryland 20854

Eller, Rear Admiral Ernest M.
  2 Kent Road, Wardour
  Annapolis, Maryland 21401

Ellis, William L.
  1307 New Hampshire Avenue, N. W.
  Washington, D. C. 20036

Endicott, Mr. and Mrs. Benjamin Earl
  107 West Howell Avenue
  Alexandria, Virginia 22301

Epstein, Mrs. Ellen Robinson
  2218 Observatory Place, N. W.
  Washington, D. C. 20007

Evans, Frank Wesley S.
  5602 Midwood Road
  Bethesda, Maryland 20014

F

Farr, Mrs. William Sharon
  7606 Curtis Street
  Chevy Chase, Maryland 20015

Fendall, Col. Bill Gray
  2690 S. W. DeArmond Drive
  Corvallis, Oregon 97330

Fenton, John N.
  2301 Jefferson Davis Highway
  Arlington, Virginia 22202

Finley, David E.
  3318 O Street, N. W.
  Washington, D. C. 20007

Fischer, Judge John C. Calhoun

4000 Cathedral Avenue, N. W.
Washington, D. C. 20016

Fisher, Kenneth F., Jr.
525 Albany Avenue
Takoma Park, Maryland 20012

Flowers, Miss Genevieve
Box 7021
Washington, D. C. 20032

Fondersmith, John
1761 R Street, N. W.
Apartment 4
Washington, D. C. 20009

Fowle, Miss Marguerite E.
9405 Locust Hill Road
Bethesda, Maryland 20014

Fowler, Mrs. Nellie Holmead
8201 Cedar Street
Silver Spring, Maryland 20910

Fox, Mrs. Gretchen
1735 Q Street, N. W.
Washington, D. C. 20009

Frank, Dr. and Mrs. Randolph A.
2520 L Street, N. W.
Washington, D. C. 20037

Freeman, Mr. and Mrs. W. N.
3350 Runnymeade Place, N. W.
Washington, D. C. 2005

French, William C.
1727 Massachusetts Avenue, N. W.
Washington, D. C. 20036

Friis, Herman R.
8412 Conover Place
Alexandria, Virginia 22308

G

Gable, Paul
1908 Hanover Street
Silver Spring, Maryland 20910

Gallman, W. J.

3312 Woodley Road, N. W.
Washington, D. C. 20008

Gardiner, Mrs. W. Gwynn, Jr.
1316-33rd Street, N. W.
Washington, D. C. 20007

Garrett, Clyde D.
3300 Rittenhouse Street, N. W.
Washington, D. C. 20015

Gasch, Hon. and Mrs. Oliver
3673 Upton Street, N. W.
Washington, D. C. 20008

Gaskins, John W.
10 River Lane
North River Forest
Stuart, Florida 33494

Gerber, Edward F.
1233-30th Street, N. W.
Washington, D. C. 20007

Gibbs, Mr. and Mrs. Frederick R.
4450 Volta Place, N. W.
Washington, D. C. 20007

Gibbs, Mrs. Virginia
1841 Columbia Road, N. W.
Washington, D. C. 20009

Giller, Miss Sadye
1421 Massachusetts Avenue, N. W.
Washington, D. C. 20005

Gipple, J. W.
1320-19th Street, N. W.
Washington, D. C. 20036

Glassie, Henry H.
2883 Audubon Terrace, N. W.
Washington, D. C. 20008

Glenn, Rev. and Mrs. Chirles Lester
16 Kalorama Circle, N. W.
Washington, D. C. 20008

Glenum, Arthus R.
1385 Nicholson Street, N. W.
Washington, D. C. 20011

Members of the Society

Glover, Charles C., III
5235 Duvall Drive
Westmoreland Hills
Washington, D. C. 20016

Gondos, Col. Victor, Jr.
4201 Massachusetts Avenue, N. W.
Washington, D. C. 20016

Gorr, Louis F.
8326 Imperial Drive
Laurel, Maryland 20810

Graling, Col. Francis J.
The Westchester, Apartment 339-B
4000 Cathedral Avenue, N. W.
Washington, D. C. 20016

Grant, Mr. and Mrs. William Eskew
4312 Van Ness Street, N. W.
Washington, D. C. 20016

Green, Donald H.
1320-19th Street, N. W.
Washington, D. C. 20036

Green, Miss Elsie E.
3151 Tennyson Street, N. W.
Washington, D. C. 20015

Greever, Mr. and Mrs. William R.
5101 Althea Drive
Annandale, Virginia 22003

Griffin, Mark G.
127 South Glebe Road
Arlington, Virginia 22204

Griffiths, Mrs. D. W.
3016 North Pollard Street
Arlington, Virginia 22207

Grillo, Mrs. John S.
611 Whittier Street, N. W.
Washington, D. C. 20012

Groover, Mrs. Gordon L.
2809 Blaine Drive
Chevy Chase, Maryland 20015

Grubar, Dr. Francis S.
6625-31st Place, N. W.
Washington, D. C. 20015

Gutheim, Frederick
1750 Pennsylvania Avenue, N. W.
Washington, D. C. 20006

H

Haglund, Conrad R.
882 North Lexington Street
Arlington, Virginia 22205

Hall, Dom Michael, O.S.B.
St. Anslem's Abbey
14th and South Dakota Avenue, N. E.
Washington, D. C. 20017

Halsey, Miss Marion S.
4000 Cathedral Avenue
Washington, D. C. 20016

Hamilton, George E., Jr.
2330 Wyoming Avenue, N. W.
Washington, D. C. 20008

Hanback, Mr. and Mrs. William B.
2152 F Street, N. W.
Washington, D. C. 20037

Hanson, Richard G.
3015 Carvel Drive
Santa Rosa, California 95405

Harriman, W. Averell
3038 N Street, N. W.
Washington, D. C. 20007

Healy, Miss Mary U.
2022 Columbia Road, N. W.
Washington, D. C. 20009

Hecht, Arthur
704 Fern Place, N. W.
Washington, D. C. 20012

Hedberg, Mr. and Mrs. Lloyd
8830 Piney Branch Road
Silver Spring, Maryland 20903

Heilprin, William A.

W-230 Van Ness Apartments South
3003 Van Ness Street, N. W.
Washington, D. C. 20008

Heine, Cornelius W.
709 North Belgrade Road
Silver Spring, Maryland 20902

Heller, Mrs. Meta
4702-22nd Street North
Arlington, Virginia 22207

Hicks, Norton W.
P. O. Box 358
North Windham, Maine 04062

Hinkel, Col. John V.
5341-29th Street, N. W.
Washington, D. C. 20015

Hoes, Laurence G.
908 Charles Street
Fredericksburg, Virginia 22401

Hoffheins, Mr. and Mrs. Francis M.
3517 Rodman Street, N. W.
Washington, D. C. 20008

Holbrook, Miss Catherine T.
1558-33rd Street, N. W.
Washington, D. C. 20007

Holland, Samuel H.
1314 Massachusetts Avenue, N. W.
Washington, D. C. 20005

Holle, Maj. Gen. and Mrs. Charles G.
2540 Massachusetts Avenue, N. W.
Washington, D. C. 20008

Hollowell, Mrs. John J.
9860 Singleton Drive
Bethesda, Maryland 20034

Holmes, Oliver W.
3422 Fulton Street, N. W.
Washington, D. C. 20007

Howard, Edward G.
1308 Bolton Street
Baltimore, Maryland 21217

Howe, Bruce
Hammersmith Road
Newport, Rhode Island 02840

Hummer, Miss Marcellina
2006 Columbia Road, N. W.
Washington, D. C. 20009

Hunt, Frederick Drum
5309 Carvel Road
Washington, D. C. 20016

I

Imes, Mrs. McCall Henderson
3000 Tilden Street, N. W.
Washington, D. C. 20008

Ireland, Dr. and Mrs. C. T.
500-23rd Street, N. W.
Washington, D. C. 20037

Isbell, Mr. and Mrs. Charles W.
1701 Woodman Drive
McLean, Virginia 22101

J

Jachowski, Mrs. Elsie Schmidt
522 Butternut Street, N. W.
Washington, D. C. 20012

Jackson, Mrs. Sara D.
1629 Columbia Road, N. W.
Washington, D. C. 20009

Jacobs, Mrs. Ephraim
16 West Kirke Street
Chevy Chase, Maryland 20015

Jennings, James L. S., Jr.
3701 Massachusetts Avenue
Apartment 404
Washington, D. C. 20016

Jex, Mr. and Mrs. Garnet W.
6010 North 20th Street
Arlington, Virginia 22205

Johnson, Peter H.
3100 Connecticut Avenue, N. W.

Apartment 410
Washington, D. C. 20008

Jones, Mrs. Gladys L.
2248 Cathedral Avenue, N. W.
Washington, D. C. 20008

Jordan, Robert Thayer
4520 McArthur Boulevard
Apartment 2
Washington, D. C. 20007

K

Kayser, Elmer Louis
Room 500
George Washington University Library
2023 G Street, N. W.
Washington, D. C. 20006

Keller, Mr. and Mrs. Philip J.
2719 Woodley Place, N. W.
Washington, D. C. 20008

Kenney, Miss Helen M.
142 Hesketh Street
Chevy Chase, Maryland 20015

Kern, Charles E.
3812 Garrison Street, N. W.
Washington, D. C. 20016

Kessel, Mrs. Lillian Reilly
5410 Connecticut Avenue, N. W.
Washington, D. C. 20015

Keyes, Mr. and Mrs. Arthus H., Jr.
2605-31st Street, N. W.
Washington, D. C. 20008

King, W. L.
2240-47th Street, N. W.
Washington, D. C. 20007

Kiplinger Washington Editors, Inc.
c/o Mr. John W. Hazard
1729 H Street, N. W.
Washington, D. C. 20006

Kirk, Miss Helen E.

1841 Columbia Road, N. W.
Washington, D. C. 20009

Kreinheder, Mrs. Robert F.
113 Kentucky Avenue, S. E.
Washington, D. C. 20003

L

Langley, Harold D.
2515 Utah Street
Arlington, Virginia 22207

Latino, Miss Jeannie
4815-41st Street, N. W.
Washington, D. C. 20016

Lawrence, David
1241-24th Street, N. W.
Washington, D. C. 20007

Layton, Mr. and Mrs. William W.
1311 Delaware Avenue, S. W.
Washington, D. C. 20024

Lazard, James M.
3382 Stephanson Place, N. W.
Washington, D. C. 20015

Leach, Miss Gertrude
4000 Massachusetts Avenue, N. W.
Washington, D. C. 20016

Lear, Mr. and Mrs. George E.
5111 Nahant Street, N. W.
Washington, D. C. 20016

LeBreton, Edmond J.
5302 Wakefield Road
Washington, D. C. 20016

Leede, Miss Minette
1515-32nd Street, N. W.
Washington, D. C. 20007

LeGear, Mrs. Clara Egli
322 North Carolina Avenue, S. E.
Washington, D. C. 20003

Leon, Col. James

3803 Maryland Street
Alexandria, Virginia 22309

Leonard, Charles
Box 67
Sparta, Tennessee 38583

Lethbridge, Mr. and Mrs. Francis D.
4605 Drummond Avenue
Chevy Chase, Maryland 20015

Levenberg, Mrs. Kay Wood
2844-28th Street, N. W.
Washington, D. C. 20007

Liggett, Alexander C.
2339 Massachusetts Avenue, N. W.
Washington, D. C. 20008

Livesey, Mrs. Frederick
3900 Cathedral Avenue, N. W.
Washington, D. C. 20016

Lucas, Mrs. Anthony
5316 Oakland Road
Chevy Chase, Maryland 20015

Lumovich, Mrs. Victor
1203 Banton Circle
McLean, Virginia 22101

Lutton, Mrs. Louise Sturgis
7411 Hancock Avenue
Apartment 103
Takoma Park, Maryland 20012

Lyle, Robert W.
3211 Cherry Hill Lane, N. W.
Washington, D. C. 20007

Lynn, Mr. and Mrs. Wallace P.
7120 Ninth Street, N. W.
Washington, D. C. 20012

M

Machen, Thomas
907 Poplar Hill Road
Baltimore, Maryland 21210

Mahoney, Maurice Pat
391 N Street, S. W.
Washington, D. C. 20024

Mascioli, Frederick P.
1940 Biltmore Street, N. W.
Washington, D. C. 20009

Masson, Miss Helen B.
4907 Jamestown Court
Washington, D. C. 20016

Maury, William M.
7422 Hancock Avenue
Takoma Park, Maryland 20012

May, Mr. and Mrs. Ernest N., Jr.
4060-52nd Street, N. W.
Washington, D. C. 20016

McCarthy, R. J.
3539 Leisure World Boulevard
Silver Spring, Maryland 20906

McGarraghy, Hon. Joseph
U. S. Court House
Washington, D. C. 20001

McGraw, Mrs. Oliphant
2022 Columbia Road, N. W.
Washington, D. C. 20009

McKee, Mrs. Oliver, Jr.
2500 Q Street, N. W.
Washington, D. C. 20007

McKinney, Mrs. Warner H.
4910 N. 15th Street
Arlington, Virginia 22205

McLellan, Mrs. M. A.
1685 Freemont Court
Crofton, Maryland 21113

McNeil, Mrs. Doris M.
3727 T Street, N. W.
Washington, D. C. 20007

McNulty, Miss Elizabeth
416 North Lincoln Street
Arlington, Virginia 22201

Members of the Society

Meigs, Mr. and Mrs. Arthur
3224 Cathedral Avenue, N. W.
Washington, D. C. 20008

Menke, Eric F.
2153 California Street, N. W.
Washington, D. C. 20008

Merrill, Mr. and Mrs. Edward D.
3111 Hawthorne Street, N. W.
Washington, D. C. 20008

Mikules, T. Leonard
11 Cathedral Street
Annapolis, Maryland 21401

Miles, Wyndham D.
24 Walker Avenue
Gaithersburg, Maryland 20760

Mitchell, Mrs. William
1718 Hoban Road, N. W.
Washington, D. C. 20007

Montgomery, Miss Helen Louise
3302 N Street, N. W.
Washington, D. C. 20007

Morgan, LeRoy Tuttle
1311-35th Street, N. W.
Washington, D. C. 20007

Morrison, Mrs. Hamilton F.
1745 N Street, N. W.
Washington, D. C. 20036

Morton, Miss Alice Rachael
Box 462
1500 Massachusetts Avenue, N. W.
Washington, D. C. 20005

Murphy, Paul W.
1909 Glenallan Avenue
Silver Spring, Maryland 20902

Musick, Michael P.
6½ Seventh Street, S. E.
Washington, D. C. 20003

Muth, George E.

Stone Haven
Woodville, Virginia

Myrth, Miss Isabel Edna
1908 Second Street, N. E.
Washington, D. C. 20002

N

Neilson, George D.
University Club
1135-16th Street, N. W.
Washington, D. C. 20036

Nevius, Mr. and Mrs. John A.
4715 Fulton Street, N. W.
Washington, D. C. 20007

Nolen, John, Jr.
1916 S Street, N. W.
Washington, D. C. 20009

Nordlinger, Mr. and Mrs. Bernard L.
3539 Chesapeake Street, N. W.
Washington, D. C. 20008

O

O'Brian, John Lord
Metropolitan Club
1730 H Street, N. W.
Washington, D. C. 20006

Oehser, Paul H.
9012 Old Dominion Drive
McLean, Virginia 22101

Oliphant, Mrs. A. Chambers
2430 Wyoming Avenue, N. W.
Washington, D. C. 20008

Oliphant, Mr. and Mrs. Robert C.
3901 Fordham Road, N. W.
Washington, D. C. 20016

Ordway, Col. Frederick Ira, Jr.
4201 Cathedral Avenue, N. W.
Washington, D. C. 20016

Osterhus, Mrs. Hugh

2929 N Street, N. W.
Washington, D. C. 20007

Owen, Thornton W.
111 E Street, N. W.
Washington, D. C. 20004

P

Pablo, Mrs. M. T.
4640 Verplanck Place, N. W.
Washington, D. C. 20016

Parent, Mrs. Louise K.
P. O. Box 175
Oakton, Virginia 22124

Parker, Andrew
Colonnade, Apartment 1108
2801 New Mexico Avenue, N. W.
Washington, D. C. 20007

Parker, Mrs. Tompkins
4308 Van Ness Street, N. W.
Washington, D. C. 20016

Patterson, Charles
2853 Ontario Road, N. W.
Apartment 406
Washington, D. C. 20009

Pearce, John N.
6707 Loring Court
Bethesda, Maryland 20034

Philibert, Miss Helene M.
3402 North 3rd Street
Arlington, Virginia 22201

Phillips, Charles Emory
9010 Burning Tree Road
Bethesda, Maryland 20034

Pogue, Mrs. L. Welch
5204 Kenwood Avenue
Chevy Chase, Maryland 20015

Potter, W. Sutton
2003 Bedford Lane
Alexandria, Virginia 22307

Powers, Peter G.
325 A Street, S. E.
Washington, D. C. 20003

Press, Emil A.
1423-34 Street, N. W.
Washington, D. C. 20007

Press, William H.
1646-32nd Street, N. W.
Washington, D. C. 20007

Primm, Paul H.
3383 Stuyvesant Place, N. W.
Washington, D. C. 20015

Pyles, Mr. and Mrs. John C., Jr.
The Riggs National Bank
1503 Pennsylvania Avenue, N. W.
Washington, D. C. 20005

R

Rader, W. H.
6219 Third Street, N. W.
Washington, D. C. 20011

Ramsey, Dr. and Mrs. Herbert P.
3000 Tilden Street, N. W.
Washington, D. C. 20008

Reckmeyer, Miss Margaret
2029 Huidekoper Place, N. W.
Washington, D. C. 20007

Reed, Mrs. Helena D.
1515-32nd Street, N. W.
Washington, D. C. 20007

Regan, Stephen D.
N. S. C. A. Box 142
Fort George Meade, Maryland 20755

Reich, Mr. and Mrs. Robert E.
3012 O Street, N. W.
Washington, D. C. 20007

Remmey, Miss Louise Austin
3806 T Street, N. W.
Washington, D. C. 20007

Renshaw, Mrs. Mary H.
3419 Q Street, N. W.
Washington, D. C. 20007

Rich, Mr. and Mrs. Frank H.
1321 F Street, N. W.
Washington, D. C. 20004

Richards, Joseph, Jr.
6200 Kennedy Drive
Chevy Chase, Maryland 20015

Richmond, Miss Charlotte
3022 Porter Street, N. W.
Washington, D. C. 20008

Rigdon, Mr. and Mrs. Carl Allen
1207 South 20th Street
Arlington, Virginia 22202

Robb, Judge Roger
5836 U. S. Court House
Washington, D. C. 20001

Rodbell, Stanley
939-26th Street, N. W.
Washington, D. C. 20037

Rogers, Mrs. James W., Jr.
4210-49th Street
Bladensburg, Maryland

Rogers, Joseph Shepperd
Beall's Pleasure
Landover, Maryland 20785

Roloff, Ronald W.
101 G Street, S. W.
Apartment A 104
Washington, D. C. 20024

Rosenberger, Francis Coleman
6809 Melrose Drive
McLean, Virginia 22101

Rosenberger, Homer Tope
Rose Hill
Rural Route 4
Waynesboro, Pennsylvania 17268

Roth, Miss Rodris
1217-30th Street, N. W.
Washington, D. C. 20007

Rowe-Craig, Mrs. Isabel
2129 Florida Avenue, N. W.
Washington, D. C. 20008

Rubicam, Milton
6303-20th Avenue
Green Meadows
Hyattsville, Maryland 20782

S

Sameth, Nathan
130 Prince Street
Alexandria, Virginia 22314

Saul, Mr. and Mrs. Andrew
17 West Kirke Street
Chevy Chase, Maryland 20015

Schrider, Charles Thomas, Jr.
The Oaks
Cabin John, Maryland 20731

Scott, Mrs. Stuart
5735 Bradley Boulevard
Bethesda, Maryland 20014

Seabourne, Col. J. Gay
116 Lee Avenue
Apartment 305
Takoma Park, Maryland 20012

Shands, Richard E.
Shoreham Building, Room 940
806-15th Street, N. W.
Washington, D. C. 20005

Shea, Miss Zoe M.
4626-47th Street, N. W.
Washington, D. C. 20016

Sheftel, Mrs. Alice N.
2023 G Street, N. W.
Washington, D. C. 20006

Sheldon, Lt. Bert

3315 Wisconsin Avenue, N. W.
Washington, D. C. 20016

Shelton, Miss Jan
National Archives
Washington, D. C. 20408

Shivers, Miss Sue
1868 Columbia Road, N. W.
Washington, D. C. 20009

Skramstad, Harold K.
3525 Bradley Lane
Chevy Chase, Maryland 20015

Slocum, Mr. and Mrs. John J.
3230 N Street, N. W.
Washington, D. C. 20007

Small, Albert H.
7116 Glenbrook Road
Bethesda, Maryland 20014

Smith, Arthur Clarendon, Jr.
Smith's Moving and Storage Co.
611 South Pickett Street
Alexandria, Virginia 22304

Smith, Mrs. Chloethiel W.
1056 Thomas Jefferson Street, N. W.
Washington, D. C. 20007

Smith, Douglas R.
National Savings and Trust Co.
Washington, D. C. 20005

Snell, Mrs. E. M.
232 Second Street, S. E.
Washington, D. C. 20003

Spratt, Zack
1016-22nd Street, N. W.
Washington, D. C. 20007

Spriggs, Kahl K.
6325 Meadow Lane
Chevy Chase, Maryland 20015

Sprunt, Dr. and Mrs. Charles Worth
12 Primrose Street
Chevy Chase, Maryland 20015

Stanley, Samuel
3701 Connecticut Avenue, N. W.
Washington, D. C. 20008

Stead, Edward
5825 Lawyers Hill Road
Elkridge, Maryland 21227

Stehle, Raymond L.
3701 Massachusettes Avenue, N. W.
Washington, D. C. 20016

Stenhouse, Mr. and Mrs. John
3900 Watson Place, N. W.
Washington, D. C. 20016

Stephenson, Miss Jean
1111 H Street, N.W.
Apartment 1023
Washington, D. C. 20005

Stevens, Miss Marion
2100 Massachusetts Avenue, N. W.
Washington, D. C. 20008

Stevenson, Mrs. Victoria Faber
3230-19th Street, N. W.
Washington, D. C. 20010

Stone, Philip J.
3023 Macomb Street, N. W.
Washington, D. C. 20008

Studdiford, Walter S.
2039 New Hampshire Avenue, N. W.
Washington, D. C. 20009

Swearingen, Miss Anne P.
30 Lee Avenue
Takoma Park, Maryland 20012

T

Tansill, Frederick G.
1520 Newton Street, N. E.
Washington, D. C. 20017

Taylor, Miss Elizabeth A.
510 N Street, S. W.
Apartment N-430
Washington, D. C. 20024

Thayn, Mrs. Florian
2708 Cheverly Avenue
Cheverly, Maryland 20785

Thompson, Miss Mildred A.
12 East Myrtle Street
Alexandria, Virginia 22301

Thurtle, Robert G.
2000 South Eads Street
Arlington, Virginia 22202

Tobriner, Walter N.
6100-33rd Street, N. W.
Washington, D. C. 20015

Truax, Robert A.
3629 Legation Street, N. W.
Washington, D. C. 20015

Turton, Mrs. Anne G.
26108 Cornor Drive
Damascus, Maryland 20750

U

Uchida, Mrs. Nori
730-24th Street, N. W.
Washington, D. C. 20037

V

Vass, George O., Jr.
6617 Tulip Hill Terrace
Washington, D. C. 20016

W

Waggaman, Thomas E.
Route 2, Box 31
Beachcomber Drive
Vero Beach, Florida 32960

Wagner, Miss Carol Ann
1255 New Hampshire Avenue, N. W.
Washington, D. C.

Wahlberg, Mrs. Erik
10 Kalorama Circle
Washington, D. C. 20008

Waldrop, Frank C.
4900 Loughbore Road, N. W.
Washington, D. C. 20016

Wales, Mrs. Leonard A.
1701 Massachusetts Avenue, N. W.
Washington, D. C. 20036

Walitschek, Col. and Mrs. Kurt L.
6414 Princeton Drive
Alexandria, Virginia 22307

Walk, Mrs. S. D.
Washington Gaslight Library
1100 H Street, N. W.
Washington, D. C. 20005

Walker, Oliver M.
1156-15th Street, N. W.
Washington, D. C. 20005

Warren, Miss Virginia
432 South Catoline Street
Los Angeles, California 90020

Washburn, Wilcomb E.
2338 Massachusetts Avenue, N. W.
Washington, D. C. 20008

Waters, Miss Elizabeth R.
3446 Connecticut Avenue, N. W.
Washington, D. C. 20008

Weimer, Dr. and Mrs. John R.
1028 Connecticut Avenue, N. W.
Washington, D. C. 20036

Weiss, Paul H.
1903 Woodreeve Road
Avondale, Maryland 20018

Wender, Harry S.
6432-31st Place, N. W.
Washington, D. C. 20015

West, Vernon E.
23 Hesketh Street
Chevy Chase, Maryland 20015

Weston, Judge Robert M.
2401 Calvert Street, N. W.
Washington, D. C. 20008

Wilcox, Mr. and Mrs. Edward C.
2725-39th Street, N. W.
Washington, D. C. 20007

Wilcox, Mrs. Halstead
3014 O Street, N. W.
Washington, D. C. 20007

Wilfong, James C., Jr.
930 H Street, N. W.
Washington, D. C. 20001

Williams, Ames W.
6034 Fort Hunt Road
Alexandria, Virginia 22307

Williams, Miss Mathilde
4629-30th Street, N. W.
Washington, D. C. 20008

Williamson, Mrs. Nancy W. S.
2122 California Street, N. W.
Washington, D. C. 20008

Wilmer, Col. Richard H.
2600-31st Street, N. W.
Washington, D. C. 20008

Wilner, Mr. and Mrs. Morton H.

2701 Chesapeake Street, N. W.
Washington, D. C. 20008

Wiprud, Theodore
3722 Manor Road
Chevy Chase, Maryland 20015

Wohl, Stanley S.
P. O. Box 923
Annapolis, Maryland 21404

Wolf, Mr. and Mrs. Justin R.
2500 Calvert Street, N. W.
Washington, D. C. 20008

Wood, Mr. and Mrs. James T.
2401 North Dickerson Street
Arlington, Virginia 22207

Woodward, Rupert C.
2023 G Street, N. W.
Washington, D. C. 20006

Z

Zseleczky, Mrs. Emil J.
35 Champlin Street
Newport, Rhode Island

In Memoriam: Deaths of Members

Aiello, Caesar L.
July 1971

Ayre, Miss Katie May
March 1972

Clapp, Verner W.
June 1972

Cullen, Miss Mary O.
January 1971

Huntington, Mrs. Frances Carpenter
November 1972

Guy, David J.
April 1972

Hausman, Mrs. Anna V.
August 1971

Hodgkins, George W.
June 1971

Lefevre, Robert Lee
March 1971

Mutersbaugh, Mrs. Jean A.
December 1971

Norris, Charles L., Sr.
June 1971

Pumfrey, Mrs. Isabel
March 1971

Stanton, Mrs. Alice P.
May 1971

Strobel, Miss Louise E.
December 1972

Presidents of the Society, 1894–1972

Joseph M. Toner (1825–1896)	1894–1896
John A. Kasson (1822–1910)	1897–1906
Alexander B. Hagner (1826–1915)	1906–1909
James Dudley Morgan (1862–1919)	1909–1916
Allen C. Clark (1858–1943)	1916–1943
F. Regis Noel (1891–1952)	1944–1946, 1948–1950, 1952
H. Paul Caemmerer (1884–1962)	1947–1948
Frederick S. Tyler (1882–1951)	1951 (President Elect)
Laurence F. Schmeckebier (1877–1959)	1951–1952
U. S. Grant, 3rd (1881–1968)	1952–1968
Homer T. Rosenberger (b. 1908)	1968–

Officers and Managers of the Society, 1971, 1972

1971 OFFICERS

President	HOMER T. ROSENBERGER
First Vice President	WILCOMB E. WASHBURN
Second Vice President	CORNELIUS HEINE
Secretary	WILLIAM L. ELLIS
Treasurer	DOUGLAS R. SMITH
Curator	ELDEN E. BILLINGS
Chronicler	MAURICE P. MAHONEY
Librarian	ROBERT A. TRUAX
Editor	FRANCIS C. ROSENBERGER
Executive Director	R. J. MCCARTHY

1972 OFFICERS

President	HOMER T. ROSENBERGER
First Vice President	WILCOMB E. WASHBURN
Second Vice President	CORNELIUS HEINE
Secretary	WILLIAM L. ELLIS
Treasurer	DOUGLAS R. SMITH
Curator	ELDEN E. BILLINGS
Chronicler	MAURICE P. MAHONEY
Librarian	ROBERT A. TRUAX
Editor	FRANCIS C. ROSENBERGER
Executive Director	R. J. MCCARTHY

MANAGERS

Term Expires January 1972

O. Kenneth Baker
John V. Hinkel
William H. Press
Wilcomb E. Washburn

Term Expires January 1973

R. R. Ayers
Mrs. Benjamin C. Evans, Jr.
Miss Mathilde Williams
Mrs. Dorothy C. Winchcole

Term Expires January 1974

Mrs. Anita Heurich Eckles
Herman R. Friis
Christian Heurich, Jr.
Francis D. Lethbridge

Term Expires January 1975

Leo Bernstein
Herbert P. Ramsey
Miss Edith Ray Saul
Robert A. Traux

Term Expires January 1976

O. Kenneth Baker
John V. Hinkel
Elmer L. Kayser
William H. Press

Index To Subjects

Actors' Equity Association, 240
Adams, Henry, 571, 628, 633
Adams, James M., 437
Adams, John, 117
Adams, William, 258
Aiken, William, 580, 585
Airis, Thomas F., 789
Aizelin, Eugene Antoine, 560
Alden, Frank E., 571
Alexander, Colonel B. S., 332
Alger, Cyrus, 58
Alger Foundry of Boston, 34, 58
Alger, Russell Alexander, 550
Alexandria shipyard, number of vessels built, 1763–1774, 6
Allen, Ethan, statue by Larkin G. Mead, 568
Alley Dwelling Authority of 1934, 286
Ambush, Enoch, 369
American Association for State and Local History, 797
American Library Association, 481, 483, 493
American Theatre, 191
Analostan Boat Club, 26
Analostan Island, 19
Anderson, N. L., 571
Andrei, Giovanni, 138
Andrews, Ethan, 256
Anthony, Joseph, 85
Anthony, Susan B., 657
Apthorp, Sarah Wentworth (Mrs. Perez Morton), 85
Army Medical Museum and Library, 351
Army of the Potomac, 324, 325
Asbury African Methodist Episcopal Church, 366–368
Ashford, Snowden, 354
Asmodeus, 211
Association of Impartial Progress, 368
Atwood, Albert W., career as a professional writer, 776–782
   editor's function in professional writing, 779
   publications of, 781
Augur, General Christopher, 328

Bacon, George S., 153
Bacon, Joel Smith, 152
Bailey, Theodorus, 61
Baker, Gardiner, 119
Baker, O. S., 380
Baldwin, Abraham, 61
Baldwin, Henry, 173
Baldwin, Ruth (Mrs. Joel Barlow), 167
Baltimore Repository, 360
Banneker, Benjamin, 740
Baptist Church, 19th Street, 366, 367, 381
Barclay, T. B., 119
Barlow, Aaron, 164
Barlow, Joel, 164
   architectural commission to Latrobe, 133
   death in Zarnoviec, 173
   honorary Citizen of France, 167
   negotiations to prevent pirating in Mediterranean, 169
   purchase of Belair Estate (Kalorama), 167
Barnard, George, 497
Barnard, John Gross, 320, 324, 334
Barnes, James, 363
Barnett, George, 679–693
   appointment to Marine Corps Commandant, 681
   awarded Distinguished Service Medal, 684
   Congressional debate on promotion, 686
   demobilization of Marine Corps after World War I, 687
   duty in San Francisco, 692
   expansion of Marine Corps, World War I, 682
   nomination to rank of permanent Major General, 693
   notification of relief of command, 687
   second term as Marine Corps Commandant, 685
   transfer of command to General Lejeune, 689
Barnett, Lelia Montague (Mrs. George Barnett), 679, 690
Barney, Albert Clifford, 184

Barney, Mrs. Alice, 183, 184
Barrett, James G., 362
Barron, James, 173
Barry, General W. F., 324
Bartlett, Paul W., 497
Basset, Gene, 758
Batteman, Mary, 248
Battery, Civil War defenses of Washington, 332
   Decatur, 333
   Jameson, 336
   Kemble, 336
   Many, 333
   Ricketts, 336
   Rodgers, 325, 332
   Martin Scott, 336
   Vermont, 336
   White, 333
Battleground National Cemetery, 328
Bayard, Thomas A., 485
Beam, Henry D., 430
Beard, Charles, 510
Beard, Mary (Mrs. Charles A. Beard), 660
Beckwith, J. Carroll, 623
Belair estate, 166
Belen, Baron de, 175
Belen, Caroline de, 175
Bell, Sarah, 362
Bellon Foundry of Powhatan County, Virginia, 34
Bellona Foundry, Richmond, 48
Belmont, Mrs. Oliver H. P., 665
Benedict, Crystal Eastman, 660
Bentley, Reverend William, 74
Bernhardt, Sarah, 227
Bernini, Gian Lorenzo, 295
Bernsdorff, Count von, 187
Berryman, Clifford K., 758, 759
Berryman, Florence, 759
Berryman, James Thomas (Jim), Pulitzer prize, 758
   Senator Dirksen cartoons, 758–775
Bicknell, Amos, 463
Biddle, William P., 679
Bingham, Colonel Theodore A., 601
Birth of a Nation, 237
Blackwell, Alice Stone, 661, 671, 675
Blaine, James, 266
Blair, Francis Preston, 328
   statue by Alexander Doyle, 566

Blashfield, Edwin H., 500
Blatch, Harriot Stanton, 661, 668, 670
Blick, Sam, 710
Bliss, Philemon, 425
Block, Herbert Lawrence (Herblock), 758
Blodget, Samuel, 131
Boggs, Emmeline, 177
Bomford, Clara, 173
Bomford, George, 50, 173
Bonaparte, Prince Jerome, 111
Bonniniere, Gustave Beaumont de la, 256
Booth, Edwin 212
Booth, John Wilkes, 228
Booth, Junius Brutus, 212
Borglum, Gutzon, 179, 309
Boschke, Albert, 269
Bostwick, Charlotte Lovett, 174, 179
Bowdoin, James, 120
Bowen, Anthony, 389
Bowen, Sayles J., 380, 383, 384, 397
Bowman, A., 366
Boyd, William, 276
Bradley, William A., 25
Brady, Matthew, 551
Brandt, Captain Randolph, 19
Brandt, Margaret, 19
Breckenridge, John, 328
Breese, Emma, 179
Breese, Samuel Livingston, 175
Brent, William, 192
"Bridge of Argenteuil," as birth of Impressionism, 508
Bridgely, John, 363
British Embassy, 184
Brown, Austin P., 176
Brown, Emma, 369
Brown, Gleen, 354
Brown, Henry Kirke, sculptor of Nathanel Greene, 566
Brown, John, 61
Brown, William, 362
Bruce, Blanche K., 417
Buchanan, James, 597
Bulfinch, Charles, 244
Bullett, John C., 179
Burgess, G., 389
Burmese Embassy, 183
Burnham, Daniel, 585
Burns, Lucy, 660, 665
Butler, Benjamin F., 412

Subjects

Butler, Smedley D., 686
Butler, Thomas, 686
Butler Zouaves militia, 412

Caffin, Charles, 505
Cain, R. H., 368
Calhoun, John C., 40, 50
   statue by Frederick W. Ruckstuhl, 568
Calvary Baptist Church, 345
Cameron, James D., 179
Campbell, James Valentine, 560
Cannon, Joseph G., 505
Capital City Guards, 416
Capitol, Paul Boswell sketch, 736
Carraher, T., 389
Carroll, C. C., 697
Carter, John, 24, 25
Carusi's Saloon, National Theatre location, 197
   Washington post office location, 574
Casey, Edward Pearce, 495
Casey, Thomas Lincoln, 469, 490
Cass, Lewis, statue of, by Daniel Chester French, 548–560
   base of Tennessee marble, 563
   commissioned by state of Michigan, 550
   presentation ceremonies, 565
Casson, Margaret, 555
Cates, Clifton B., 687, 689, 692
Catholic University, 351
Catt, Carrie Chapman, 663, 668
Charles City Co. shipyard, number of vessels built, 1763–1774, 6
Charleston, Oscar, 756
Chase, Samuel, 367
Chesapeake, U. S. Frigate attacked by British, 73
Choate, Joseph Hodges, 625
Choate, Rufus, 469
Clark, A. P., 349
Clark, Edward, 475, 483, 488, 563
Clarke, Isaac, 248, 255
Clarke, John, 36, 48
Clermont, Fulton's steamboat, 171
Cluss, Adolph, 338–358
   architect for, churches, 344
      Department of Agriculture, 347
      public markets, 348
      public schools, 344
      Smithsonian Institution, 345
      U. S. Patent Office, 351
   awarded "Medal for Progress" at World's Exposition, Vienna, 343
   birth in Heilbronn, Würtemburg, Germany, 340
   designer of Washington sewage disposal system, 339
   dissertations on architecture, 347
   early employment in Washington, D. C., 341
   education, 340
   emigration to the United States, 341
   Fellow of American Institute of Architects, 347
   private architectural practice, 341
   retirement years, 351
   style of architecture, 356
Cluss, Heinrich, 340
Coehorn assault mortars, 38
Coffin, William, 555
Columbia Foundary, 35
Columbia Historical Society, deaths of members, 1971 and 1972, 819
   members in 1972, 801–818
   officers and managers of, 1971 and 1972, 821, 822
   presidents, 1894–1972, 820
Columbia Institution for Deaf, Dumb, and Blind, 439
Columbiad, The, 167, 169
Columbiad cannon, 39, 173
Columbian Academy, 150–163
   competition with public school system, 159
   discontinuance of, 159
   enrollment during Civil War, 154
   removal to city of Washington, 155
   required curriculum, 157
   student grade books, 158
Columbian Athletic Club, 26
Columbian Agricultural Society, 20–22
Columbian College Preparatory Department, 150
Committee for Racial Democracy, 238
Concordia Opera House, Baltimore, 345
Conrad and McMunn's boarding house, 61
Conradis, Henry, 465

"Continents", sculpture by Daniel Chester French, 548
Cook, Clarence, 446
Cook, George F. T., 369
Cook, John F., 369, 378, 383
Cooke, Henry D., 401, 407, 412
Cooke, Jay, 401
Coolidge, Mrs. Elizabeth Sprague, 726
Corcoran, William Wilson, 24, 159, 192, 362, 442
Costin, John T., 368
Council for Civil Rights, 240
Courbet, Gustav, 510
Cox, Kenyon, 500
Coyer, Charles B., 790
Cranch School, 344
Cranch, William, 70
Cravath, Erastus M., 434
Crawford, William, 256
Crockett, Gibson Milton (Gib), 758
Cromwell, John Wesley, 437
Crummell, Reverend Alexander, 368
Cullman, Howard S., 240
Cullum, General G. W., 324
Curtis School, 344
Cutts, Richard, 90

Dahlgren, John A., 58, 317, 341
Daily National Republican, 366
Daniel, Frederick, 350
Daniels, Josephus, 681, 684, 686
Daughters of the American Revolution, donation of protective grills for Washington, D. C., boundary stones, 742
Davenport, Fanny, 212
David, Jacques Louis, 300
Davis, John, 23
Davis, Madison, 572, 584
Daw, Lillian Cluss, 354
Dawes, Henry L., 467
Death and Life of Great American Cities, 590
Decatur, Commodore Stephen, 173
Decatur, Mrs. Susan, 173
Deery, John, 229
Dennett, Mary Ware, 661
Dewey, Melvil, 504
Didden, C. A., 354
Dihigo, Martin, 756

Dillingham, William P., 672
Dirksen, Everett McKinley, Jim Berryman cartoons of, 758–775
District of Columbia Militia, 317, 368
District of Columbia Suffrage Association, 661
Dix, Dorothea, 247, 256
Dodge, Robert L., 502
Dodge, William de L., 500, 502
Doncieux, Charles Claude, 526
Donn, W. E., 354
Douglas, Stephen A., 290
Douglass, Frederick, 367, 434
Douglass, Lewis H., 417
Downing, Andrew Jackson, 445
Doxiadis, Constantine, 789
Doyle, Alexander, 566
Drexel, Anthony J., 179
Drimmer, Melvin, 359
Duane, William, 76
Dubois, W. E. B., 667
Duncanson, William Mayne, 131
Dunlap, William, 78
Dupont Fountain, 548
Durant-Ruel, Paul, art dealer for Claude Monet in England, 520
D'Yrugo, Marquis, 94, 111

Early, General Jubal, 326
Eastman, Max, 660
Ebenezer Methodist Church, 366
Edbrooke, Willoughby J., 571, 576, 578
Eliot, Charles, 498
Elizabeth River Shipyard, number of vessels built, 1763–1774, 6
Ellicott, Andrew, 740
Elliott, George F., 679
Ellis, John B., 199
Ellis, Jonas, 254
Ellsworth, Colonel Elmer, 319
Elssler, Fanny, 212
Emery, Matthew G., 384
Equal Franchise Society, 660
Erlanger, A. L., 204
Esty, Alexander, 483
Evans, George W., 416
Evans, Robert F., 786
Evans, W. B., 366
Everett, Edward, 183

Executive Building, Washington post office, 1812–1836, 572

Fairbanks, Henry Parker, 186
Fairchild, Charles, 620
Fairchild, Grandison, 426
Falconet, Etienne, 295
Federal Triangle, 585, 588
Fessenden, William Pitt, 474
Fillmore, Millard, 289
Finney, Charles Grandison, 424
First Division Memorial, 548
Fisher, David, 389
Fisher, Thomas J., 183
Fitnam, Thomas, 248, 254
Flanagan, John F., 718
Fleetwood, Christian A., 413, 417
Fletcher, Charles, 175
Fletcher, Mrs. Charles, 174
Fletcher, William I., 507
Fogerty, William, 457
Folger Shakespeare Library, Puck Fountain, 730
Force, Peter, 472
Ford, John, 236
Ford's Theatre, 229, 237
Forney, John W., 421
Forrest, Edwin, 212, 218
Fort Pitt Foundry of Pittsburgh, 34, 58
Fort, Civil War defense of Washington, D. C., 319
  Albany, 319
  Ethan Allen, 332, 337
  Baker, 332
  Bayard, 336
  Bennett, 319
  Bunker Hill, 336
  Carroll, 332, 336
  Chapin, 336
  Corcoran, 319
  Davis, 336
  DeRussy, 336
  Donelson, 324
  DuPont, 336
  Ellsworth, 319, 320, 332
  Farnsworth, 332
  Foote, 325, 332, 336
  Gaines, 336
  Greble, 336
  Haggerty, 319
  Henry, 324
  Hunt, 333
  Lincoln, 320, 332
  Lyon, 332
  Mahan, 332, 336
  Marcy, 337
  Massachusetts, 320
  McPherson, 332, 337
  Morton, 332
  O'Rorke, 332
  Pennsylvania, 320
  Reno, 320, 332, 336
  Richardson, 332, 337
  Runyon, 319
  Scott, 320, 337
  Slocum, 320, 332, 336
  C. F. Smith, 332, 337
  Stanton, 332, 336
  Stevens, 320, 328, 332, 336
  Strong, 337
  Sumner, 325, 332
  Totten, 320, 332, 336
  Ward, 337
  Washington, 315, 333, 336
  Whipple, 332, 337
  Willard, 337
  Worth, 332
Fox, Ida, 238, 240
Foxall, Henry, 35, 36
Foxall-Columbia Foundry, 34–59
  arms supply during War of 1812, 46
  cannon manufacture during revolution, 36
  decline in production, 1835, 51
  description of, 1836, 42–46
  during British assault on the District of Columbia, 1814, 46
  effect of competitive bidding regulation, 48
  growth during establishment of military outposts, 1807–1812, 50
  location of, 34
  negotiations for federal purchase of, 52
  Ordnance Department contracts to, 49, 50
  ordnance manufacture, 1800–1815, 36
  purchase by, John Mason, 1815, 20
    Spencer B. Root, 1854, 59
  suspension of operations, 1842, 57
  U. S. Government contracts with, 47

Franklin School, 343, 357
Franzoni, Giuseppe, 138
Freedmen's Aid societies, 374
Freedmen's Bureau, 374, 428, 432
Freedmen's Saving and Trust Company, 433
Freedmen's School, 367
Freeman, William A., 388
French, Benjamin F., 474
French, Daniel Chester, 548–569
   creation of Lewis Cass statue, 553
      commission, 551
         delay in approval of model, 560
         payment arrangement, 565
         request for customs movement of statue to Washington, 563
   European studies, 555
French Embassy, 188
French, William Merchant Richardson, 551
Friedrich, Emil S., 442
Fulton, Robert, 169

Gaines, Frank B., 384, 391
Gale, Thomas S., 186
Gallaher, John S., 576
Gallatin, Albert, 60–80
   arrival in Washington, January 12, 1801, 60
   avoidance of formal entertainment, 76
   children of, 69, 71
   description of Washington, 1801, 61
   New Geneva Glass Works investment, 79
   nomination as Secretary of Treasury, 66
   official and personal frugality, 76
   opinion of military proximity in Washington, 75
   peace commission to St. Petersburg, Russia, 80
   property investments, 79
   remaining in Washington during summer months, 71
   residence on Capitol hill, 69
   Stuart portrait, 90
Gallatin, Hannah Nicholson, 65, 77
Gallaudet College, 439–467
   campus, 442
   Chapel Hall as memorial, 448
      construction of, 451
         Victorian Gothic architectural style, 452
   College Hall, 1876, 457
   Congressional provision for national college for the deaf, 1864, 443
   faculty housing, 463
   federal support for, 440
   growth of campus to 16 acres, 444
   gymnasium, 464
   Kendall Hall, 466
   landscaping plans, 446
   president's house, 453
Gallaudet, Edward Miner, 441, 559
Gallaudet, Thomas Hopkins, 441
Galligher, Judge Nadine, 239
Gant, Thomas A., 389
Garden, Alexander, 25
Gardener, Mrs. Helen, 662
Garfield, James Abram, portrait by Daniel Chester French, 548
   statue by Charles Henry Niehaus, 568
Garnet, Reverend Henry Highland, 370
Garnsey, Elmer E., 496
Georgetown, 783–796
   Buffalo Bridge, 784
   Canal and Riverside Council, 787
   Citizens Association, 785, 791
   City Tavern Association, 787
   Commission of Fine Arts authority in restorations, 786
   court order delaying high-rise development of waterfront, 792
   declared as National Historical Landmark, 1967, 790
   development of Georgetown University property, 794
   geographic boundaries of, 783
   Grace Church "Order of Amazing Grace," 795
   Home Owners Committee, 785
   Inland Steel Corporation water front property purchase, 791
   invasion by "street people," 795
   loss of charter, 1870, 784
   Lutheran Church, Washington Free Clinic, 795
   Mount Zion Methodist Church cemetery, 793
   National Capital Planning Commission survey of waterfront, 792
   Old Stone House, restoration, 786
   Planning Council, 789

Subjects

population, 1800, 783
river front restoration, 787
row house construction, 784
survey of waterfront architecture, 1967, 789
tourism in, 796
Waterfront Symposium Committee, 787
Gericault, Theodore, 303
Gerdson, W. C., 697
Gibbs, Harriet, 362
Gibson, J. George, 192
Gilmore, Quincy, 328
Given, John T., 383
Gloucester County shipyard, number of vessels built, 1763–1774, 6
Gordon, John B., 328
Gordon, John M., 200
Graffenried, Baron Christoph de, 18
Grant, Ulysses S., 326, 350, 399, 401
Gray, William B., Jr., 790
Greek Embassy, 182
Green, Bernard R., 469, 490, 493, 495, 497, 502
Green, Constance McLaughlin, 359, 366, 411
Green Pastures, The, 237
Greene, Nathanael, statue, 566
Greenfield, E. T., 367
Greenleaf, James, 131
Greuhn, Baron von, 173
Gribeauval cannon carriage system, 51
Griffiths, David, 697, 705, 708
Grimes, James, 375
Grover, Leonard, 227, 229
Gugler, Eric, 17, 610
Gutherz, Carl, 500

Hackett, James, 212
Hadfield, George, 131
Halleck, General Henry, 328
Hamlin, Talbot, 128, 137
Hammersley, Francis, 19
Hammerstein, Oscar, II, 238
Hammond, John Hays, 188
Hampton shipyards, number of vessels built, 1763–1774, 6
Handy, J. A., 366
Hanson, Olof, 467
Hardin, Martin, 328
Harding, Warren, 307

Hermesian Literary Society, 157
Harries, General George H., 420
Harrison, Benjamin, Virginia shipbuilder, 1763–1774, 8
Harrison, Caroline Scott (Mrs. Benjamin Harrison), 600
Harrison, Richard B., 237
Hart, William H. H., 436
Harvard, John, sculpture by Daniel Chester French, 552
Hatton, George W., 380, 382, 384
Hay, John, 228, 571, 625, 628
Hayes, Helen, 238
Hayes, Rutherford B., 408, 471, 481
Hazlehurst, Isaac, 141
Healy, George Peter Alexander, 559
Heiman, Marcus, 240
Heintzelman, Major Samuel P., 319
Henderson, Edward B., 239
Henry, Joseph, 469
Henry School, 344
Hepburn, David, 22
Herbert, John, Virginia shipbuilder, 1763–1774, 8
Herblock (Herbert Lawrence Block), 758
Hess, Stephen, 758
Heydenreich, Ludwig, 293
Heywood, Charles, 679
Hill, Henry, 362
Hill, James G., 354
Hilldale Daisies, Philadelphia black baseball team, 756
Hinton, Thomas H. C., 368
Hoar, George Frisbie, 566
Hoban, James, 596
Holmead, Anthony, 166
Holmes, Oliver Wendell, 329
Holton-Arms School, 188
Hoover, Herbert, 189
Hoschedé, Alice, marriage to Claude Monet, 544
Howard, Oliver Otis, 401, 428, 432
Howard Law School, 421–438
  curriculum, 431
  faculty, 430
  qualifications for entrance to, 429
Howard University, dedication of, 370
Howe, Dr. Frank T., 202
Howe, Timothy O., 478–480
Hubbard, Gardiner Greene, 177

Hudson, Kenneth, 790
Hughes, Charles Evans, 183
Humboldt, Alexander von, 78
Hunn, Chester J., 705
Hyson, Lewis, 363

Impressionism, precise moment of, "The Bridge at Argenteuil," by Claude Monet, 508–547
International Woman Suffrage Alliance, 663
Irving, Washington, 77
Island Baptist Church, 366
Israel Bethel Methodist Church, 366, 367

Jackson, Andrew, 254
  equestrian statue of, 289–313
    compared with other works of art, 293, 295, 300, 303, 309
    criticism of, 292
    dedication ceremonies, 290
    efforts at removal of, 307
    explanation of motif, 303
    product of Romantic movement, 300
    protective fence added to, 306
    vandalism of, 306
Jackson, James T., 319
Jacobs, Jane, 590
Jacobsen, Hugh Newell, 789
Jamison, B. A., 218
Jefferson School, 344
Jefferson, Thomas, 61, 120, 164, 167, 471, 597
  statue of, 309
Jennings, Henning, 183
Jewel, William, 24
Jewett, Charles Coffin, 469
Johnson, Adeline, 362
Johnson, Andrew, 252, 378, 599
Johnson, John D., 368
Johnson, John T., 384, 389
Johnson, Lyndon, 787
Johnson, Thomas,, 362
Johnson, William ("Judy"), 753
Jones, Alfred, 363
Jones, Matilda, 369
Jones, Wesley L., 672

Kall, Sophia Speake, 187

Kalorama, 164–189
  census value in 1860, 175
  Latrobe commission for Barlow estate, 133
  occupation by Union Army, 175
  stone quarry, 176
Kaplan, Milton, 758
Karmany, Lincoln, 681
Kassan, Mrs. Gail, 31
Kauffman, Samuel, 188
Keating, Edward, 687
Kelly, John, 248
Kendall, Amos, 345, 439
Kennedy, John F., Center for the Performing Arts, 241
Kent, Mrs. William, 662
Kilburn, Hallet, 348
King, H. I., 251
King, Martin Luther, Memorial Library, 164
King's Amphitheatre, 198
Kinsey, John, 582
Kling, Vincent, 589
Korean Embassy, 183
Kurtz, John, 24

LaFollette, Mrs. Robert M., 662
Lamar, Lucius Q. C., 488
Lambert, John W., 366
Lane, Harriet, 597
Lane, Samuel, 142
Langdon, John, 61
Lansing, Captain Arthur, 174
Lansing, Louise Lovett, 174
Langston, John Mercer, 421–438
  acting president of Howard University, 432
  antislavery movement, 426
  appointment as trustee of Howard University, 428
  apprenticeship in law, 425
  bar examination, 425
  childhood, 423
  education, 424
  efforts to enter law school, 424
  first black public official elected, 426
  law practice in Ohio, 426
  member of Washington Board of Health, 429

Subjects

political activity, 428
resignation from Howard Law School, 435
Lanston, Lucy, 423
Langworth, James, 166
Langworth, John, 166
Latrobe, Benjamin Henry, 128–149
  appointment as Architect of the U. S. Capitol, 141
  communications system design for Washington, 143
  construction of Washington Canal, 139
  description of construction and workmen in Washington, 1806, 129–132
  design and location of national university, 145
  development of Lafayette Square, 148
  engineer-architect tradition, 356
  expansion of Washington Navy Yard, 144
  housing of congressmen, 147
  interest in urban design, 134
  Jefferson expansion of White House, 597
  plan for university in Washington, 136
  principles of location and design of urban areas, 136
  provision of living quarters for Gilbert Stuart in Washington, 87
  reconstruction of Capitol building, 142
  survey of Newcastle, 135
Law, Thomas, 131, 140, 147
Lawrence, Thomas, 87
Ledyard, H. R., 550
Lee, Holsey "Scrip," 753
Lee, Robert E., 324, 336
Leeds, Lewis W., 456
Leighton, Benjamin, 436
Lejeune, John A., 679, 689
L'Enfant, Pierre Charles, 131, 149, 315
Lenox, Walter, 376
Lenthall, John, 128, 132, 137
Leonard, C., 369
Lethbridge, Francis D., 789
Lewis, Mrs. Lawrence, 660
Library of Congress, 468–507
  American artists commissioned for interior decorations, 495
  architectural competition for design, 479
  cost of construction, 504
  effect of copyright law of 1870, 475
  enlargement in 1866, 475
  Flanagan Clock in Reading Room, 718
  Great Hall, Martiny staircase, 714
  growth of, 472
  Information Bulletin, 728
  interior decoration, 493
  Main Reading Room, 716
  Martiny staircases, four continents sculpture, 722
  Minerva mosaic, 720
  inscription meaning, 720
  Neptune Fountain, 712
  frog detail of, 714
  outdoor candelabra, 722
  Porte Cochere, 728
  scheme for artwork in, 501
  selection of statuary design, 498
  tree identification on grounds of, 725
  Whittall Pavilion Courtyard, 726
    Pan of Rohallion sculpture, 726
Lincoln, Abraham, 227, 229, 262, 316, 320, 328
  statue, by Daniel Chester French, 548
Lincoln, Tad, 228
Lind, Jenny, 196, 217
Lindholm, Svante G., 785
Liverpool (England) Plantation Register of Ships, list of Virginia built ships, 1763–1774, 12
Livingston Robert R., statue, 566
Lodge, Henry Cabot, 645
Loeb, William, Jr., 607
Logan, Rayford, 433
Looker, H. B., 179
Lovett, Annie, 179
Lovett, George S., 176
Lovett Memorial Library, 176
Lovett, Mrs. Emmeline, 179
Lovett, Thomas R., 174
Lowndes, James, 187
Luchs, Frank B., 241
Luque, Dolph, 756
Lyons, Evan, 166

Macmonnies, Frederick, 716, 726
Madison, Dolley, 87
  aid in securing commissions for portraits for Gilbert Stuart, 90

Madison, James, 172
Mahan, Asa, 424
Man of the World, The, 194
Manet, Edouard, visit with Claude Monet at Argenteuil, 524
Mann, Horace, 252
Mansfield, Colonel J. F. K., 319
Manship, Paul, designer of statute, Theodore Roosevelt Island, 17
March, Frederic, 238
Marlborough, Archibald, 190
Marsh, George P., 469
Martin, James, 140
Martin, John, 258
Martiny, Philip, 716
Mason, Anna, 106
Mason, George, 19
Mason, James Maynadier, 35
Mason, James Murray, 20
Mason, John, 192
  breeder of Merino sheep, 21
  development of Columbian Agricultural Society, 20, 21
  owner of Theodore Roosevelt Island, 1792, 16
  purchase of Foxall Foundry, 1815, 20
Mason, Jonathan, 106
Mason, Miriam, 106
Mason, Otis Tufton, 155
Mason's Island, 19
Maulsby, Anna, 179
Maulsby, George, 175
Maynadier, Henry, 21
Maynard, George W., 500
Mazzei, Philip, 138
McClellan, General George B., 320
McCook, Alexander, 328
McCoy, Benjamin, 391
McDowell, General Irwin, 320
McElfatrick, J. B., 202
McEwen, Walter, 502
McGrath's Company of Comedians, 190
McKim, Charles, 496, 585, 625
McLean, Cornelius, 192
McMillan, James, 585
Mead, Larkin G., 568
Mead, Walter, 24
Mearns, William A., 186
Meigs, General Montgomery C., 324, 402·
Mellon, Andrew, 588

Merrill, Justin 505
Merry, Mrs. Anthony, 123
Metz, Frederick de, 256
Meyers, Judge Frank H., 239
Meyers, John, 456
Michler, General Nathaniel, 598
Middleton, Henry, 173
Milholland, Inez, 664
Millet, Dr. John Alfred Parsons, 637
Mills, Clark, 289-313
Mills, Robert, 128
Minute Man, sculpture by Daniel Chester French, 552
Mitchell, E. N., 187
Monday Evening Club, 278
Monet, Charles, 508
Monet, Claude, 508-547
  birth of son, Jean, 511
  contesting of wife's inheritance, 528-542
  death of wife, Camille, 544
  financial success of later life, 546
  friendship with Edouard Manet, 524
  home in, Argenteuil, 520
    Bonnieres, 513
    Etretat, 516
  Impressionism, 522
  life with Camille Léonie Doncieux, 510
  marriages, 520, 524
  move to Paris from Argenteuil, 543
  portrait of Madame Gaudibert, 516
  purchase of early work by Frederic Bazille, 513
  studio at Giverny, 546
  study at Ecole des Beaux-Arts, 510
  successful use of art dealer, 520
Monroe, James, 50, 315
Montague, Andrew P., 155
Montgomery, John, 68
Moody, Richard, 218
Moore, Arthur Cotton, 590, 592, 790
Moore, Charles, 556, 585, 586
Moore, Clarence W., 700
Moore, Joseph West, 338
Moore, Dobey, 756
Morey, Charles Rufus, 292
Morgan, Mrs. Francois Berger, 183
Morier, John, 140
Morrill, Justin S., 478, 482, 488, 548, 565
Morris, Robert, 64
Morrison, John H., 560

Subjects

Morrison, Lisle, 697
Mouldin, A. F., 389
Moynihan, Daniel Patrick, 589
Mudd, A. I., 191, 192
Mullet, Alfred B., 202, 350, 402, 405
Munroe, Thomas, 572
Murray, Anna Maria, marriage to John Mason, 20
Murray, Charles, 689
Murray, J. T., 389
Myers, George Hewitt, 186

Nansemond Co. shipyard, number of vessels built, 1763–1774, 6
National American Woman Suffrage Association, 657
National Association for the Advancement of Colored People, 237
National Cathedral, Bethlehem Chapel, 731
National Guard riot control training, 1891, 419
National League of Black Soldiers and Sailors, 368
National Museum, 351
National Rifles militia, 317, 394, 416
National Statuary Hall, 548
National Theatre, 190–242
  actor and playwright boycott, 238
  appeals for support through attendance, 205, 211, 212
  audience behavior in 1835, 204
  construction of, 192
    fourth building, 1873,
  conversion to motion picture theatre, 240
  creation of "orchestra" seats, 197
  destruction by fire, 1845, 196
    1873, 200
  fifth building, 1885–1922, 201
  fourth building, 1873–1885, 201
  "management rules for audience behavior," 217
  opening night, 193
  pit and parquet seating changes, 194
  productions during 1861–1872, 199
  rebuilding after 1857 fire, 198
  segregationist policies, 236
  sixth building, 1922–1972, 203
  use as circus arena, 195
Neighborhood House, 185

Nelligan, Murray H., record of ownership of Theodore Roosevelt Island, 19
Netter, Sampson, 384, 389
New Kent Co. shipyards, number of vessels built, 1763–1774, 6
New National Theatre, 201
Newton, A. E., 369
Newton, F. L., 697
Nicholas, John, 61
Nicholas, Wilson Cary, 61
Nicholls, William S., 24
Nicholson, John, 64
Nicholson, Maria, 68
Niehaus, Charles Henry, 568
Nixon, Richard M., 791
Norfolk shipyard, number of vessels built in 1763–1774, 6, 7
Northampton Co. shipyards, number of vessels built in 1763–1774, 6
Northumberland Co. shipyard, number of vessels built in 1763–1774, 6
Norton, Charles Elliott, 448
Nott, Charles C., 430

Oates Opera Company, 200
O'Donnell, James, 565
Olmsted, Frederick Law, 402, 444
Olmsted, Frederick Law, Jr., 585
Ord, E. O. C., 328
Ordway, Albert, 413, 418
O'Rourke, Jeremiah, 580
Orton, W. A., 697
Otterbach, Paul, 710
Owen, Frederick D., 600
Owings, Nathaniel, 589

Page, Thomas Nelson, 568
Paine, Thomas, 78
Painter, Winnie, 362
Pakistan Embassy, 183
Palmer, Erastus Dow, 566
Pankhurst, Emmeline, 659
Paper-Mill Bridge, 167
Parrington, Vernon L., 407
Parrott, R. P., 58
Parsons, Philo, 550, 553, 560
Patterson, Edgar, 166
Patterson, Elizabeth, 111
Patterson, John M., 791

Paul, Alice, 657–678
  activity in British suffrage movement, 659
  education, 659
  initiation of congressional committee for women's suffrage, 659
  Philadelphia suffrage demonstration, 659
  Washington suffrage parade, 1913, 664–678
Payne, Anna, 90
Payne, Daniel, 367, 368
Peale, Charles Willson, 81, 94, 119, 121, 169
Peale, Rembrandt, 121
Pearce, Charles Sprague, 502
Peets, Elbert, 593
Peltz, Paul J., 490
Penitentiary, Washington, D. C., *see under* Washington, D. C.
Perry, Captain James A., 417
Perry, Matthew C., 289
Peterson, F. H., 355
Philadelphia Christian Recorder, 360
Philippines Embassy, 183
Pierson, H. W., 374
Pieters, A. J., 697
Pinckney, General Charles Cotesworth, 118
Piper, Henry H., 384, 389
Playgoer's Series, 241
Plohn, Edward, 239
Plummer, William, 76
Poindexter, W. M., 354
Poinsett, Joel, 57
Pomerene, Atlee, 672
Poole, William Frederick, 483, 489
Porter, Benjamin C., 555
Portland, apartment house designed by Albert Cluss, 1883, 351
Posen, Walter, 789
Post Office, Washington, D. C., *see under* Washington, D. C.
Potomac Light Infantry, 317
Powers, Jacob W., 25
Presbyterian Church, 15th Street, 366, 367
Prescott, William H., 596
Price, John, 427
Priestly, Joseph, 119
Princess Anne Co. shipyards, number of vessels built, 1763–1774, 6
Prisoner's Friend, 367
Purvis, Charles B., 435

Putnam, Brenda, 731
Putnam, Herbert, 504, 731

Quaker Alley, 275
Quarles, Captain Ralph, 423
Quill, Mrs. John, 710

Ramseur, Stephen, 328
Randall, Henry, 192
Randolph, John, 74
Rapley, William W., 198, 200, 204
Rappahannock River shipyard, number of vessels built, 1763–1774, 6
Ratton, George W., 384
Redoubts Weed, 332
Reed, Thomas B., 601, 622
Reilly, Caroline, 665
Remond, Charles Lenox, 367
Reps, John, 145
Revells, Frederick C., 413, 417
Rhees, Louise Marble, 759
Rhodes, Robert, 328
Richards, Zalmon, 151
Richardson, Henry Hobson, 466, 570
  architecture style, 570
  abandonment for neo-classic, 586
  popularity among contemporary architects, 572
Richardson, William A., 576
Richmond Foundry, 34
Riddle, Albert Gallatin, 430
Riggs, Elisha, 24
Riis, Jacob, 280, 288
Rittenhouse, Loulie, 784
Roberts, Jonathan, 76
Robertson, Walter, 83
Robinson, Joseph E., 505
Rock, Dr. John S., 367
Rock Hill, 166
Rodman, Thomas, 58
Roosevelt, Eleanor, 267
Roosevelt, Franklin D., 188, 610, 690
Roosevelt, Theodore, 280, 603, 622
Roosevelt, Theodore, Island, 14–33
  archeological project, 1970, 31
  artifacts recovered at John Mason homesite in 1936, 29
  in 1970, 32
  Civilian Conservation Corps work on, 1935, 27
  description of, 1711, 18

Subjects

Georgetown City trading center, 18
memorial statue, 17, 31
nature preserve, 16
ownership to the Bank of the United States, 1933, 24
purchase by John Carter, 1842, 25
U. S. Army occupation of, 1861–1863, 25
value of Mason property on, 1800–1818, 20
Roosevelt, Theodore, Memorial association, 17
Root, Spencer B., 59
Rose, Willie Lee, 359
Rosenberger, Francis Coleman, 797–800
Rowan, Louisa, 259
Royall, Anne, 22
Ruckstuhl, Frederick W., 568
Russell, Mrs. C. Peyton, 183
Ryan, Inez, 781

Sargent, Darcy Allen, 465
Sargent, FitzWilliam, 629
Sargent, John Singer, at the White House, 618–656
  Boston Public Library muralist, 623
  childhood, 619
  fund-raising agreement with British Red Cross to paint a portrait, 641
  honorary degree from the University of Pennsylvania, 629
  invitation to live in White House while painting Roosevelt portrait, 623
  landscape paintings, 638
  portrait of, John Hay, 631
    Henry Cabot Lodge, 620
    Thomas B. Reed, 620
    John D. Rockefeller, 648
    Theodore Roosevelt, 628
    Woodrow Wilson, 642
    General Leonard Wood, 631
  refusal to paint portrait of Calvin Coolidge, 656
  visit to United States, 1876, 619
Sazama, Joseph J., 710
Schladermundt, Herman T., 496
Schmidt, Rosa (Mrs. Adolph Cluss), 353
Schulze, Paul, 350
Schuyler, Montgomery, 497, 571
Schwartz, Ralph G., 791
Scott, Gustavus, 166
Scott, Winfield, 317

Seaton House, location of Washington post office, 574
Seaton School, 344
Seaton, Mrs. William W., 77
Second Baptist Church, 366
Seldon, Dudley, 24
Senate Park Commission, 585
Sengstack, Charles, 254
Settle, Josiah T., 437
Shanklin, George, 380
Sharer, George L., 374
Shaw, Anna Howard, 657, 659, 660, 670
Shepherd, Alexander Robey, appointment as Governor of Washington territory, 407
  Board of Public Works membership, 394–410
  building commission to Albert Cluss, 348
  club memberships, 400
  control of contract letting for city improvements, 404
  controller of Batopilas Mining Company in Mexico, 409
  declaration of bankruptcy, 408
  directorship of Washington markets, 400
  early life, 394
  exoneration from charges of fraud, 406
  initiation of street improvements, 402
  member of Levy Court, 396
  opposition from black community, 401
  petition to Congress to make Washington, D. C., territory, 398
  real estate speculation, 399
  request for bond issue for Washington city improvements, 403
Shepherd's Row, 348
Sheridan Monument, 179
Sheridan, Philip H., Jr., 179
Sherman, John, portrait by Daniel Chester French, 548
Sherwood, Robert E., 239
Shipbuilding in Virginia, 1763–1774, 1–13
  advertisements in *Virginia Gazette,* 7
  brig ships, 4, 5, 9, 10
  crew size of, 9
  Naval Office lists of vessels, 11
  number built, 4
  schooners, 4, 5, 8–10
  shipyard locations, 6
  sloops, 4, 5, 9, 10
  snow ships, 4, 5, 8–10

tonnage of, 3, 5
Virginia-registered ships compared with foreign port registration, 10
Shively, George, 756
Shoemaker, D. N., 697
Shorter, James, 258
Shoup, George L., statue by Frederick E. Triebel, 568
Shuster, Ernest A., 751
Simmons, Edward, 500, 502
Simons, W. T., 710
Singletary, Otis, 411
Skeels, Homer C., 697, 706
Skinner, Cornelia Otis, 238
Skramstad, Harold K., 31
Small, Herbert, 501
Smith, Caleb, 262
Smith, Clement, 24
Smith, Cloethiel W., 787
Smith, Dr. J. B., 367
Smith, Edward P., 435
Smith, Hamilton E., 550
Smith, Mrs. Robert, 96
Smith, Richard, 24, 192, 195
Smith, Robert, 144
Smith, Samuel, 61, 118
Smith, Willliam L. G., 551
Smithfield shipyards, number of vessels built, 1763-1774, 6
Smithmeyer, John L., 483, 488
Smyth, John H., 417
Snow, C. A., 271
Snow's Alley, 272
Southern Annual Conference of the African Methodist Episcopal Zion Connection, 368
Spaulding, W. E., 198
Spear, Charles, 367
Spectator, Columbian Academy student paper, 157
Speyer, Sir Edgar, 637
Spofford, Ainsworth Rand, 468-507
  Librarian of Congress, 469
    qualifications for, 469
  recommendations for national library, 490
  request for removal of Library of Congress to separate quarters, 477
  reorganization of new Library of Congress, 504
  specifications for national library, 478
St. Gaudens, Augustus, 497, 585
Stanford, Leland, 574
Stanton, Edwin, 323
Stanton Guards, black militia, 412
Starbuck, Charles, 53
Sterling, Hamilton, 190
Stevens, Thaddeus, 367
Steward, Thomas, 582
Stewart, Carter A., 383
Stewart, William, 349
"Stewart's Castle," 349
Stickney, William, 405, 439
Stoddert, Benjamin, 47, 131
Stone, Colonel Charles P., 316
Stow, Edward, 99
Straker, D. Agustus, 436
Stuart, Charles, 121
Stuart, Gilbert, 81-127
  aid in securing commissions from Dolley Madison, 90
  art study in London, 83
  catalogue of portraits painted in Washington, 124-127
  Dublin portrait painter, 83
  financial difficulties, 99
  indebtedness to Benjamin Latrobe, 109
  Jefferson portrait, 118
  loss of investment in farm, 85
  move to Washington from Philadelphia, 87
  New York portrait painter, 83
  Philadelphia portrait painter, 83
  portraits of George Washington, 102
  Priestley portrait, 119
  return from Europe in 1793, 83, 510
Stuart, Mrs. Gilbert, 99
Stuart, William, 697
Suffolk shipyard, number of vessels built, 1763-1774, 6
Sullivan, Eugene, 188
Sullivan, Jeremiah, 188
Summer School, 344
Sumner, Charles, 379, 431
Sunderland, Byron, 443
Supreme Court Building, Paul Boswell sketch of, 733
Swartwont, Samuel, 24
Sweden Embassy, 183
Sylvan Theatre, 185
Sylvester, Richard, 662, 670

Subjects

Tacca, Picetro, 293
Taft, Lorado, 292, 562, 566
Taft, William Howard, 188
Takoma Horticultural Club, 694
  collective buying, 708
  discounts to membership from local dealers, 711
  dues, 697
  exhibitions of flowers, fruits, and vegetables, 705–708
  lectures, 699
  membership, 697
  newsletters, 702
  objectives, 696
  officers, 696
  plant exchange sales, 709
  pruning demonstrations, 708
  purchase of horticultural books, 703
  securing public park tracts, 700
  standing committees, 696
  utilization of Department of Agriculture publications, 704
Talcott, George, 56
Tanners Creek shipyards, number of vessels built, 1763–1774, 6
Tavenner, Clyde H., 676
Tayloe, Colonel John, 137
Taylor, Benjamin Ogle, 195
Taylor, James Knox, 582
Temple of Wisdom, Peale museum in Philadelphia, 169
Terrill, Robert H., 417
Territorial Guards Company, 412
Textile Museum, 186
Thayer, Abbott, 555
Theatre Guild Subscription Series, 241
Thomas, Elizabeth, 320
Thomas, J. W., 23
Thompson, J. W., 394
Thompson, Robert, 384
Thornley, Thomas, 248
Thornton, Dr. William, 128, 137, 149, 356
Tilden, Samuel J., 408
Tilson, Jonathan, 151
Tinney, Andrew B., 384, 389
Tocqueville, Alexis de, 256
Tone, Mrs. Theobald Wolfe, 173
Totten, George Oakley, 183
Toucey, Isaac, 317
Triebel, Frederick E., 568
Trollope, Frances, 204

Turkish Embassy, 183
Turner, Benjamin T., 366
Turner, Henry McNeal, 366
Turner, Letha, 362

Udall, Stewart, 789
Union Bethel Church, 366
Union Building, location of Washington post office, 574
Union Printing Joint Stock Association, 369
United States Patent Office, 351
United States Theatre, 191
Upshur, J. H., 467
Uz, Augustus, 141

Van Ingen, William B., 502
Van Ness, John Peter, 195
Vandelyn, John, 102
Vandenburg, J. V. W., 405
Vanderhoff, John, 212
Varnum, Joseph B., 61
Vaux, Calvert, 445
Vedder, Elihu, 500, 502, 716, 720
Viele, Herman, 177
Viet Nam Embassy, 183
Vilas, William F., 489
Virginia C.S.S., (Merrimac), 323
Virginia Gazette, shipbuilding advertisements 1763–1774, 13
Virginia Naval Office list of vessels built, 1763–1774, 11
Von Eckardt, Wolf, 789, 791
von Kammerhueber, Joseph Wildrich, 341
Voorhees, Daniel W., 480, 482

Wade, Benjamin, 367
Wade, William, 57
Wadsworth, Decius, 50
Wadsworth, James, 323
Walker, William, 277
Wallace, General Lew, 326
Wallach, Richard, 339, 342, 345, 369, 378
Wallach School, 342
Walter, Thomas U., 289, 341, 474
Ward, Henry, 205
Ward, John Quincy Adams, 179, 497
Warden, David Ballie, 23
Wardman, Harry, 183
Warnecke, John Carl, 589, 789
Warner, Olin L., 497

Washburn, Wilcomb E., 31
Washington Cadet Corps, 412, 413, 416
Washington, D. C., alley housing in, 1852–1972, 267–288
   Board of Health condemnation of, 278
   business use of, 281
   Congressional ban of, 277
   conversion to garages, 282
   development from slave quarters, 271
   "Foggy Bottom," 271, 273, 277, 288
   Friends' Society contribution to, 274
   health hazards of, 276
   Homes Commission report of, 280
   increase of, post-Civil War, 273
   Monday Evening Club Directory of, 278
   occupation of residents in, 272, 275, 276, 288
   police department census of 1897, 277
   pre-Civil War, 270
   Quaker's Buildings, 274
   segregation in, 272, 275, 277
   subdivision of housing plots, 268
   trolley transportation effect on number of, 284
   use as property investments, 275
black baseball players, 752–757
black community, 1860–1870, 359–393
   chapter of Odd Fellows, 369
   church affiliation, 366
   churches of, 371
      charitable agencies, 367
      cultural and intellectual centers, 367
      hosts of religious conferences, 368
   clergymen, 366
   distribution of residences of, 360
   elected councilmen, 384
   election to city offices, 383
   emancipation of slaves, 370, 371
   enfranchisement, 377
   family size, 363
   loss of suffrage, 1871, 392
   municipal election candidates, 385
   occupations, 364
   petition to Congress for right to vote, 378
   political activity, 380
   population of, 1860, 360
   private education, 369, 370
   property ownership, 365
   public education, 374
   tax money for education, 375, 376
   teachers' association, 369
   voter registration, 381
black militia, 1867–1898, 411–420
   Capital City Guards, 413
   consolidation of, 418
   First Battalion, 372d Infantry, service in World War I, 420
   National Drill competitions, 413
   order to disband, 416
Board of Public Works, 350, 394–410
boundary stones, current locations of, 742
   deviations from intended 10 square mile area, 741
   dimensions of, 741
   East corner, 748
   inscriptions on, 741
   North corner, 745
   placement of, 740
   protective grills, 742
   South corner, 742
   West corner, 744
Center Market, 1870, 348
city government, 1847, 382
Commission of Fine Arts, 588
construction, halted during War of 1812, 141
   post-Civil War, 338
   public building costs, compared with private, 1894, 580
criminal codes established, 243
defense of, during Civil War, 314–337
   Army of the Potomac, 316
   arrival of regiments from New York, Massachusetts, and Rhode Island, 318
   "Battle of Fort Stevens," 328
   "Battle of the Suburbs," 328
   completion of fortifications, 322
   effect of Bull Run disaster on, 320
   formation of militia, 317
   "Potomac Flotilla," 319, 325
   Virginia forts built, 319
drawings by Paul Boswell, 712–739
Eastern Market, 1873, 348
Logan Court alley dwellings, 269
loss of suffrage, 1871, 392
Masonic Temple, 345

Subjects

municipal election returns, 1870, 385
National Drill competitions, 413
National Guard, 412
Old Post Office Building, 570–595
   acquisition of land for, 574
   architectural plans for, 578
   clock tower, 576
   construction of, 579, 580
   cost of construction, 583
   early occupancy defects, 584
   plans for renovation, 592
penitentiary, 1831–1862, 243–266
   appointment of inspectors and wardens to, 254
   code for rehabilitation of prisoners, 246
   community interest in, 255
   conversion to army arsenal, 262
   convict incentive programs, 249
   corporal punishment in, 249
   cost of operation, 250
   discipline of convicts, 247
   foreign study of, 256
   industry of, opposition of free labor groups to, 251
   overcrowding in, 261
   prisoner regimen, 258–260
   recidivism of convicts, 248, 250
   religious training of convicts, 247
   single cell confinement of convicts, 247
   soldier prisoners in, 262
   wardens of, 254
post offices, early locations of, 572
Public Buildings Commission, 588
suffrage parade, 1913, 657–678
   "Army of the Hudson," 665
   Congressional investigation of disorders of, 672–674
   lack of police protection, 669
   Negro marchers, 666
   publicity generated by, 676
territorial form of government, 398, 408
Washington Gas Light Company, 17, 26
Washington, George, University, 150
Washington Light Infantry, 317
Washington Theatre, 191, 197
Washington, William Augustine, 167
Watkins, W. J., 367
Weinert, Albert, 496
Weller, Charles, 278

Welles, Gideon, 328
Wesley Methodist Church, 366
Wesley, John, Church, 366, 368
West Point Foundry of Cold Spring, New York, 34, 48, 58
Wheelright, John, 24
Whipple, Reverend George, 434
Whistler, James, 500
White, Henry, 625
White House, Bingham proposal for extension of, 601
   Boswell sketch, 733
   East wing construction, 1942, 613
   Jeffersonian additions to, 597
   Michler proposal to remove President's living quarters from, 598
   Mrs. Harrison's plans for extension of, 600
   press room expansion, 614
   Prince of Wales visit to, 597
   renovations, 1948–1972, 614
      Theodore Roosevelt family, 603
   swimming pool, provided by subscription campaign for Franklin D. Roosevelt, 1933, 610
   West wing, destruction by fire, 1929, 610
      enlargement, 1934, 610
      renovation and oval office addition, 1909, 607
   wings of, 596–617
Whitman, Walt, 310
Whitney, Milton, 703
Whittall, Gertrude Clarke, 726
Widow's Mite, The, 166
Wiebenson, John, 590, 592
Wight, W. F., 697
Wilbur, William Allen, 159
Willett, James Polk, 582
Willey, Waitman, 368
Williams, Benjamin, 254
Williams, George A., 710
Williams, Thomas, 243
Willow Tree Alley, 281
Wilson, Ellen Axson (Mrs. Woodrow Wilson), 267, 281
Wilson, Henry, 265, 367, 371
Wilson, General J. M., 353
Wilson, J. O., 343
Wilson, Woodrow, 186, 631, 642, 661
"Winchester," Sherman's horse, 179

Winslow, Lorenzo S., 613
Winters, Jesse "Nip," 752–757
   Bacharach Giants, 753
   Havana pitcher, 756
   Hilldale Daisies, 753
   Montreal pitcher, 756
   Negro world series, 756
   strikes out Babe Ruth, 752
   winning pitcher against Lefty Grove, 752
Withers, F. C., 450, 456, 458
Withers, John, 151
Woman's Journal, National American Woman Suffrage Association, 661
Wood, Fernando, 398
Wood, General Leonard, 629
Wood, Major W. H., 319
Wood, Waddy, 183
Woodward, C. Vann, 359

Woodward, Fred E., 742
Woodyard, Caleb, 366
Wormley, James, 362, 363
Wright, General Horatio, 328
Wyeth, Nathan, 183, 607
Wynn, Nathaniel G., 437

York River shipyards, number of vessels built, 1763–1774, 6
Yorktown shipyards, number of vessels built, 1763–1774, 6
Young, Ammi B., 341
Young, John Russell, 507
Young, William T., 551
Youngman, William, 705

Zion Methodist Church, 367
Zion Wesley on the Island Church, 366

Index To Illustrations

Allston, Anne, 86
Atwood, Albert W., *Mind of the Millionaire* title page, 1926, 777

Baldwin, Ruth (Mrs. Joel Barlow), 170
Barlow, Joel, 168
Barnard, Major General John Gross, 321
Barnett, Major General George, Commandant of Marine Corps, 683, 685
　Naval Academy cadet, 1878, 680
Barry, Mary, 97
Bartlett, Mrs. Thomas, 112
Berryman, Jim, cartoons of Senator Dirksen, 1958–1963, 761–775
Blair, Francis Preston, statue by Alexander Doyle, 567
Bonaparte, Jerome, 115
Booth, Edwin, 208
Bulfinch, Charles, 245

Calvary Baptist Church, 1866, 346
Cannon, ammunition, 1813, 38, 42
　irons for gun carriages, 1813, 43
　boring machines, 1772, 37
　chassis for 32-pounder carriage, 41
　Howitzer, 40
　plans for boring mill, 1836, 54
　sea coast 42-pounder, 1813, 39
Capitol building, Paul Boswell sketch, 737
Carroll, Archbishop John, 95
Cass, Lewis, Brady daguerreotype, 1850, 552
　Healy portrait, 1840, 558
　statue by Daniel Chester French, 549
　　detail of, 563
　　full-scale model of, 557
　　plaster marquette of, 1886, 554
Cluss, Adolph, 339
Columbian Academy, Preparatory School, 161
Cushman, Charlotte, 207

Department of Agriculture Building, 1869, 348

Dirksen, Everett McKinley, Berryman political cartoons of, 1958–1963, 761–775
Dix, Dorothea Lynde, 257

Farragut Monument, New York City, 564
Fenwick, General John R., 114
Fiske, Minnie Maddern, 209
Fleetwood, Christian A., 415
Folger Shakespeare Library, Puck fountain, 730
Forrest, Edwin, 206
Fort Stevens, winter quarters of 36th New York Volunteers at Brightwood, 330
Foundry, plans for, 1836, 54, 55
Franklin School, 344
French, Daniel Chester, Lewis Cass statue, 549, 563

Gallatin, Albert, 62
　declaration of war June 18, 1812, notification, 78
　holograph letter from Washington, D. C., 1805, 72
Gallaudet College, Chapel Hall, 1870, 442
　plan of, 1868, 449
　College Hall, 1875, 455
　　detail of sawtooth brickwork in arcade, 462
　faculty house, 1874, 463
　gymnasium, 1880, 464
　master plan for buildings and grounds, 1866, 440
　President's House facade, 454
　view of, 1878, 460
Georgetown, street scene, 793
　Wheatley Row, 788
　Whitehurst Freeway, 788
Gericault, Theodore, Officer of the Imperial Guard painting, 304, 305
Green, Bernard R., 491

841

Hay, John, John Singer Sargent portrait, 624
Hill, Colonel C. S., 1917, 685
Hilldale Daisies Negro league championship team, 1926, 754
Hoschedé, Alice Rengold, 529
Hubbard, Gardiner Greene, 178

Jackson, Andrew, equestrian statue by Clark Mills, 291, 299, 306, 308, 312
Jefferson Market Courthouse, New York City, 1874, 459
Jefferson, Thomas, d'Angers statue, Rotunda of Capitol, 311
  portrait by Gilbert Stuart, 108, 110
Johnson, William "Judy," 754

Kalorama, Barlow mansion, 165, 171
  pond for Robert Fulton steamboat trial, 172

Langston, John Mercer, 422
Latrobe, Benjamin, 129
Lee, Holsey "Scrip," 755
Lejeune, General J. A., 1917, 685
Lewis, Mrs. Lawrence, 100
Library of Congress, building site, 484
  Capitol building, 476, 480, 488
  cherub lamp post, 724
  cornerstone laying ceremony, 1890, 494
  "Evolution of Civilization" painting by Edwin H. Blashfield in Main Reading Room dome, 501
  Flanagan Clock, 719
  Grand Stair Hall, 506, 715
  grounds of, 725
  "History" mosaic panel by Frederick Dielman, 499
  House of Representatives Reading Room, 499
  Main Reading Room, 503, 717
  "Minerva" mosaic, 721
  Neptune Fountain, 713
    frog detail of, 714
  Porte Cochere, 729
  stairway "Continents" sculpture, 723
  Wedgewood commemorative plate, 1900, 473
  west facade, 1895, 496
  Whittall Pavilion courtyard, 727

Lodge, Henry Cabot, John Singer Sargent portrait, 630
Long, Colonel C. G., 1917, 685
Louis XIV, equestrian statue model, 296
Lowndes, Mrs. Thomas, 89
Lowndes, Thomas, 88

Mackey, Raleigh "Biz," 754
Madison, Dolley, 82
Madison, James, 105, 107
Manet, Edouard, scene of Argenteuil, 512
Mann, Horace, 253
Mansfield, Richard, 210
Map, Analostan Island, 27
  Fort Stevens, 1871, 329
  Foxall Foundry, 44
  Gallatin Washington residence, 1801, 63
  Kalorama, 1887, 180
    Barlow mansion site, 186
  Kalorama Heights, 181
  Mason's Island, 17
  Roosevelt Island, 1932, 30
  Washington, D. C., alley dwellings, 1858, 270
  1871, 274
  1897, 279
  1912, 280
  1927, 282
  1970, 287
    Blagdon Alley dwellings, 283, 284
    Civil War defense positions, 322, 327
    wards of election, 1870, 390
  Washington Mall, 1816, 146
Mason, John, homesite, 24
  1890, 28
  1906, 28
  1936, 29
  artifacts found, 1936, 31
  1970, 32
Mason, Mrs. John Thomson, 98
Mason, Otis Tufton, 156
McCawley, Brigadier General C. L., 1917, 685
Mediator, H.M.S., 2
Monet, Camille Doncieux, 527
Monet, Claude, 509, 521, 537, 545
  art of, 511, 513–517, 519, 527, 531–535, 539, 541, 544
  holograph of proceedings of inheritance claim of Madame Monet, 523, 525

Morison, John H., portrait bust by Daniel Chester French, 561

Napoleon, equestrian portrait by David, 301
Nast, Thomas, cartoon, "Georgetown Election—Negro at Ballot Box," 379
A. R. Shepherd, 409
National Cathedral, Bethlehem Chapel, 732
National Museum, main entrance, 1895, 352
National Theatre, 1868, 199
  advertisement for Lawrence Barrett performance, 1879, 213–216, 219–226
  souvenir program, *Paul Kauvar* with Steele Mackaye, 1888, 230, 231
  Opera Bouffe Company with De Wolf Hopper, 1890, 235
    The Rivals with Joseph Jefferson, 1889, 232–234

Owen, Frederick D., 599

Patterson, Elizabeth (Madame Jerome Bonaparte), 116
Paul, Alice, 1913, 658
Peter the Great, equestrian statue of, 298
Philip IV, equestrian statue of, 294
Portland Apartments, Thomas Circle, 354
Priestley, Joseph, 103

Randolph, John, 101
Reed, Thomas B., John Singer Sargent portrait, 632
Rockefeller, John D., John Singer Sargent portrait of, 655
Roosevelt, Theodore, Bridge, 16
Roosevelt, Theodore, Island, 1972, 15
Roosevelt, Theodore, John Singer Sargent portrait, 621
Rosenberger, Francis Coleman, 1960, 798
  award exhibit, 799
Rossell, Captain J. A., 1917, 685

Santop, Louis, 754
Sargent, Dr. FitzWilliam, 639
Sargent, John Singer, 635, 640, 643, 652, 653
  art of, 636, 641, 644, 646, 649

Shepherd, Alexander R., 395
Sheridan, General Philip Henry, equestrian statue, 309
Smith, Mrs. Robert, 84
Spofford, Ainsworth Rand, 470
Stewart's Castle, 349
Stuart, Gilbert, 122
  holograph receipt for portrait, 118
Supreme Court, Paul Boswell sketch, 734

Takoma Park Branch Library, spring flower exhibit, 1925, 702
Takoma Park Horticultural Improvement Club publication No. 2, April 1, 1918, 695
Tavenner, Clyde H., 677
Thornton, Mrs. William, 93
Thornton, William, 92

U. S. Patent Office interior plan, 353

Wallach School, 342
Washington Cadet Corps, 1887, 414
Washington, D. C., alley dwellings, 1942, 285
  Logan Court, 1935, 269
  Terrace Court, 1972, 286
  boundary stones, north west stone No. 7, 746, 747
    No. 8, 748
    No. 9, 749
  Civil War defenses, Battery Rodgers, 331
    Fort Carroll, 331
    Fort Gains, 335
    Fort Lincoln, 333
    Fort Slemmer, 334
    Fort Totten, 335
  Masonic Temple, 1895, 347
  penitentiary, 246, 265
    converted to arsenal, 263
    Lincoln assassination conspirators imprisonment in, 264
    plans for, 1834, 244
  Pennsylvania Avenue, cobblestone pavement, 403
    wood block paving, 400
  Post Office, 573, 575, 587, 591
    dead letter sale, 1930, 575
    interior court, 1930, 577, 581
  Purdy's Court, 1908, 272

riot scene, 1857
shipping activity, 1794, 5
  1800, 11
suffrage parade, 1913, 674–676
  hikers, 665
view of, 1882, 340
  Paul Boswell sketch from west mall, 739
Washington, George, equestrian statue by Clark Mills, 302
White House, Paul Boswell sketch, 735
  East wing portico, 1902, 606
  expansion of, 1942, 614
    West wing, 1902, 608
      1909, 611
      1934, 612
      1960, 613
greenhouses and conservatories, 1898, 606
plan for expansion, Colonel Theodore A. Bingham, 1900, 604
  Frederick D. Owen, 602
  Mrs. William Henry Harrison, 1891, 601
swimming pool, 1933, 611
West wing entrance, 1960, 615
  1970, 616
Wilbur, William Allen, 160
Wilson, Woodrow, John Singer Sargent portrait, *frontispiece*, p. iv
Winters, Jesse "Nip," 754
Withers, John, 152
Wood, General Leonard, John Singer Sargent portrait, 627
Wright, Major General Horatio G., 332
Wyeth, Nathan C., 609

Index To Authors

Atwood, Albert W., A Member Reminisces: Problems of a Professional Writer, 776–782

Beauchamp, Tanya Edwards, Adolph Cluss: An Architect in Washington during Civil War and Reconstruction, 338–358

Bland, Sidney R., New Life in an Old Movement: Alice Paul and the Great Suffrage Parade of 1913 in Washington, D. C., 657–678

Bloomfield, Maxwell, John Mercer Langston and the Rise of Howard Law School, 421–438

Borchert, James, The Rise and Fall of Washington's Inhabited Alleys, 1852–1972, 267–288

Boswell, Paul, A Portfolio of Washington Drawings, 712–739

Boyer, Robert, The National Theatre in Washington: Buildings and Audiences, 1835–1972, 190–242

Carter, Edward C., II, Benjamin Henry Latrobe and the Growth and Development of Washington, 1798–1818, 128–149

Cole, John Y., A National Monument for a National Library: Ainsworth Rand Spofford and the New Library of Congress, 1871–1897, 468–507

Cooling, Benjamin Franklin, Defending Washington during the Civil War, 314–337

Curry, Mary E., Theodore Roosevelt Island: A Broken Link to Early Washington, D. C., History, 14–33

Epstein, Ellen Robinson, The East and West Wings of the White House, 596–617

Frank, Benis M., The Relief of General Barnett, 679–693

Gordon, Martin K., The Black Militia in the District of Columbia, 1867–1898, 411–420

Gorr, Louis F., The Foxall-Columbia Foundry: An Early Defense Contractor in Georgetown, 34–59

Hecht, Arthur, Flowers to Gladden the City: The Takoma Horticultural Club, 1916–1971, 694–711

Holway, John, Baseball Reminiscences of Washington's Jesse "Nip" Winters: "How I Struck Out Babe Ruth and Beat Lefty Grove," 752–757

Kassan, Gail Karesh, The Old Post Office Building in Washington, D. C.: Its Past, Present and Future, 570–595

Kayser, Elmer Louis, Columbian Academy, 1821–1897: The Preparatory Department of Columbian College in the District of Columbia, 150–163

Keck, Andrew S., A Toast to the Union: Clark Mills' Equestrian Statue of Andrew Jackson in Lafayette Square, 289–313

Kelso, William M., Shipbuilding in Virginia, 1763–1774, 1–13

Kowsky, Francis R., Gallaudet College: A High Victorian Campus, 439–467

Mannix, Richard, Albert Gallatin in Washington, 1801–1813, 60–80

Maury, William M., Andrew R. Shepherd and the Board of Public Works, 394–410

Meersman, Roger, The National Theatre in Washington: Buildings and Audiences, 1835–1972, 190–242

Mitchell, Mary, Kalorama: Country Estate to Washington Mayfair, 164–189

Mount, Charles Merrill, Gilbert Stuart in Washington: with a Catalogue of His Portraits Painted between December 1803 and July 1805, 81–127; November 24, 1873, The Precise Moment of Impressionism: Claude Monet's "The Bridge at Argenteuil" at the National Gallery of Art in Washington, D. C., 508–547; The Rabbit and the Boa Constrictor: John Singer Sargent at the White House, 618–656

Nye, Edwin Darby, Revisiting Washington's Forty Boundary Stones, 1972, 740–751

Richman, Michael, Daniel Chester French: His Statue of Lewis Cass in the United States Capitol, 548–569

Rosenberger, Francis Coleman, Washington's Jim Berryman, 1902–1971: Cartoons of Senator Dirksen, 758–775; The Job of Editor, 797–800

Sullivan, David K., Behind Prison Walls: The Operation of the District Penitentiary, 1831–1862, 243–266

Williams, Mathilde D., Georgetown: The Twentieth Century, A Continuing Battle, 783–796

Williams, Melvin R., A Blueprint for Change: The Black Community in Washington, D. C., 1860–1870, 359–393

Winters, Jesse "Nip," Baseball Reminiscences of Washington's Jesse "Nip" Winters: "How I Struck Out Babe Ruth and Beat Lefty Grove," 752–757

ADVERTISEMENT

Comments on the 45th volume, *Records of the Columbia Historical Society of Washington, D. C., 1963–1965,* illustrated, xx, 513 pages

JOHN BEVERLEY RIGGS in *The Pennsylvania Magazine of History and Biography:* "This volume has an excellent balance, and its well-researched papers are a valuable addition to any bibliography on the City of Washington."

ALBERT W. ATWOOD: "It is not only admirable, it is superb. Well printed, good type, good paper, good pictures and contents of inestimable value to anyone interested in D. C. history."

LEONARD CARMICHAEL: "Splendid work as editor."

DOROTHY CLARK WINCHCOLE: "The new volume of the Columbia Historical Society Records is one of the best—if not the best—we have ever had."

Virginia Quarterly Review: "Contains much information difficult to find in other sources."

P. W. FILBY in the *Maryland Historical Magazine:* "A wealth of information on the Washington area."

The Journal of Southern History: "There are many interesting illustrations."

MATTIE RUSSELL in *The North Carolina Historical Review:* "Illustrations greatly enhance the articles."

Cosmos Club Bulletin: "Altogether an impressive and fascinating book for those attracted by the never-ending ramifications of local history."

ADVERTISEMENT

Comments on the 46th volume, *Records of the Columbia Historical Society of Washington, D. C., 1966–1968*, illustrated, xviii, 467 pages

Virginia Quarterly Review: "This 46th separate volume (numbered Volume 66–68) maintains the Society's high level of interest and information in its papers. Its range of topics is wide—transportation, society, economics, music, journalism, and the presidential wives. All are treated exhaustively, while many have been illustrated with enough rare material to enhance not only the record but the research value of the individual article. It is remarkable, but encouraging, that a local historical society, especially in a city with as shifting a population as Washington's, can produce such distinguished work."

ELMER LOUIS KAYSER: "A distinguished volume."

DOROTHY CLARK WINCHCOLE: "Each new volume of the Records seems to surpass the former success."

OLIVER W. HOLMES: "This volume seems better than the last and I hardly thought that the last could be made better."

HERMAN R. FRIIS: "The best of any the Society has ever had."

MARJORIE RISK DAVISON: "The best yet published."

MELVILLE J. BOYER in *Pennsylvania History:* "Valuable local and national historical contributions."

P. W. FILBY in the *Maryland Historical Magazine:* "The whole volume is heartily recommended."

THOMAS C. PARRAMORE in *The North Carolina Historical Review:* "Distinguished and useful series."

HERMAN SCHADEN in the *Washington Star:* "The book is a credit to the Society's recently celebrated 75th anniversary."

ADVERTISEMENT

Comments on the 47th volume, *Records of the Columbia Historical Society of Washington, D. C., 1969–1970,* illustrated, xxxv, 570 pages

CARL BERNSTEIN in *The Washington Post:* "The current 47th volume is the best in decades. It contains many fine scholarly contributions and some intriguing reading. Almost all the 26 contributors are historians, anthropologists or curators. Their writing is excellent at best and serviceable at worst. Their topics, with a few exceptions, should be of interest to anyone more than remotely concerned about this city's past and future."

Virginia Quarterly Review: "How is one to choose from the riches of this volume, riches which turn from a study of personalities to the institutions those personalities developed or managed. This splendidly produced volume shows no slackening in the scholarship being produced in the nation's capital and, indeed, serves to astonish the reader with the variety and depth of the capital's cultural life. We are now promised a biennial compilation of the papers instead of a triennial one as in the past. It is a welcome change."

HENRY H. DOUGLAS in *Echoes of History:* "One is equally amazed at the energy and ability of Francis Coleman Rosenberger, the editor of this and four preceding volumes."

CAROLYN ANDREWS WALLACE in *The North Carolina Historical Review:* "If the volume has a concentration other than the District of Columbia, it is the field of cultural history. More than half the essays deal in some way with art, architecture, libraries, publishing, and literature. Most were written by specialists, and a number display mastery of style as well as subject matter."

Military Affairs: "Another of the society's superb anthologies of articles devoted to the history of the nation's capital. Essays relevant to military history include two on the role of military officers in non-combat endeavors . . ."

ADVERTISEMENT

HARRY M. MEACHAM in the *Richmond News Leader:* "Of enormous importance, not only to historians, archivists, and Virginians whose forefathers played such an important role in establishing and developing Washington, but also to all Americans who want to know the history of the nation's capital."

WELFORD D. TAYLOR in the *Richmond Times-Dispatch:* "Francis Coleman Rosenberger, perhaps better known to Virginia readers as editor of the *Virginia Reader,* has edited and introduced each of the five collections with his usual degree of insight and precision."

Cosmos Club Bulletin: "Much in association with the Cosmos Club . . . six Club members have contributed essays."

PAUL R. BAKER in *The Journal of American History:* "The book is handsomely designed with over 200 illustrations."

The Journal of Southern History: "Well-illustrated volume."

MELVILLE J. BOYER in *Pennsylvania History:* "It is a privilege to review a publication of the cultural and historical magnitude of this latest edition."

P. W. FILBY in the *Maryland Historical Magazine:* "The volume will greatly interest its members—not always the case with society publications—and the range of subjects, represented will attract many other readers. The editor and the Society are to be congratulated on continuing the series so ably and efficiently."

FREDERICK GUTHEIM in *Capitol Studies:* "By comparison with the publications of other state and local historical societies, most of which receive a considerable measure of assistance from tax-supported sources, the high historical and editorial standards maintained by Dr. Rosenberger in this more distinctly private endeavor are worthy of special commendation. . . . Here are eminently readable essays, well-illustrated and presented in a balanced, skillfully edited collection. Through its pages one is introduced to Washington the national capital city, as well as Washington the distinctively local community."